Second edition

The scope and reach of commercial law are quite wide, and it has utility in many other areas of law. Fully revised and updated, *Australian Commercial Law* offers a comprehensive and accessible introduction to key aspects of commercial law in Australia. Part 1 introduces the fundamentals of contract law and business structures before examining the sale of goods, agency, bailment and personal property. Part 2 covers the Australian Consumer Law, focusing on areas important to commercial entities that interact with consumers, such as product liability, consumer guarantees and misleading and deceptive conduct. Part 3 examines international commercial law, providing a detailed introduction to the World Trade Organization and to agreements central to trade between countries.

The second edition includes:

- detailed and thorough discussion of key concepts in commercial law
- four new chapters on contract law basics, business structures, bankruptcy and international commercial law
- thorough integration of digital and e-commerce transactions throughout the text
- end-of-chapter discussion questions designed to test reader knowledge of key points and themes.

Written in a clear and concise style by an expert author team, *Australian Commercial Law* remains an indispensable resource for students who are seeking a comprehensive understanding of commercial law.

Dilan Thampapillai is a Senior Lecturer at the ANU College of Law at the Australian National University.

Claudio Bozzi is a Lecturer in the Faculty of Business and Law at Deakin University.

Mark Giancaspro is a Lecturer in the Adelaide Law School at the University of Adelaide.

George Yijun Tian is a Senior Lecturer in the Faculty of Law at the University of Technology, Sydney.

Cambridge University Press acknowledges the Aboriginal and Torres Strait Islander peoples as the traditional owners of Country throughout Australia.

Cambridge University Press acknowledges the Māori people as *tangata whenua* of *Aotearoa* New Zealand.

We pay our respects to the First Nation Elders of Australia and New Zealand, past, present and emerging.

AUSTRALIAN COMMERCIAL LAW

SECOND EDITION

Dilan Thampapillai

Claudio Bozzi

Mark Giancaspro

George Yijun Tian

CAMBRIDGE
UNIVERSITY PRESS

CAMBRIDGE
UNIVERSITY PRESS

University Printing House, Cambridge CB2 8BS, United Kingdom

One Liberty Plaza, 20th Floor, New York, NY 10006, USA

477 Williamstown Road, Port Melbourne, VIC 3207, Australia

314–321, 3rd Floor, Plot 3, Splendor Forum, Jasola District Centre, New Delhi – 110025, India

79 Anson Road, #06–04/06, Singapore 079906

Cambridge University Press is part of the University of Cambridge.

It furthers the University's mission by disseminating knowledge in the pursuit of education, learning and research at the highest international levels of excellence.

www.cambridge.org
Information on this title: www.cambridge.org/9781108728492

First published 2015
Second edition 2020

Cover designed by Marianna Berek-Lewis
Typeset by SPI Global

A catalogue record for this publication is available from the British Library

A catalogue record for this book is available from the National Library of Australia

ISBN 978-1-108-72849-2 Paperback

Additional resources for this publication at www.cambridge.edu.au/academic/commerciallaw.

CONTENTS

PREFACE

As a body of law, commercial law lacks the central defining idea that other areas of law such as contracts and intellectual property enjoy. However, what binds the wide variety of topics that arise within commercial law is their application and value to commercial life.

This textbook seeks to cover a number of the topics that are now germane to commercial activity in Australia. It covers the core commercial topics of agency law, personal property, bailment, the sale of goods and the transfer of property. However, it also takes into account areas of law that are presently quite pertinent to commercial practice. In this regard, the most crucial development in recent years has been the introduction of the Australian Consumer Law (ACL). The ACL has brought consumer law issues to the forefront in commercial law. In our view, it would be unthinkable to address commercial law as a subject within a modern law school without also addressing a number of key consumer law topics such as unconscionable conduct, unfair contract terms, and misleading or deceptive conduct. To omit such topics from a commercial law subject would be to offer only a partial and incomplete account of those matters that now are important within commercial law.

From a pedagogic perspective, commercial law can be a challenging subject to teach. We hope that this text is readable enough to suit the challenges of a 12–14 week semester, but also thorough enough to provide a substantial grounding in the key concepts and principles of commercial law.

We would like to thank Lucy Russell and Siobhan Privitera of Cambridge University Press for their editing and guidance during the writing of this text.

TABLE OF CASES

General Motors Acceptance Corporation Australia v Southbank Traders Pty Ltd (2007) 227 CLR 305, **127**
General Surety & Guarantee Co Ltd v Francis Parker Ltd (1977) 6 Build LR 18, **281**
German v Norton (1887) 8 LR (NSW) 479, **270**
Ghirardi v Allregal Corporation Pty Ltd [2001] WASCA 366, **112**
Gilbert J McCaul (Australia) Pty Ltd v Pitt Club Ltd (1954) 76 WN (NSW) 72, **8**
Gilchrist Watt & Sanderson Pty Ltd v York Products Pty Ltd [1970] 1 WLR 1262, **202**
Gilchrist Watt & Sanderson Pty Ltd v York Products Pty Ltd [1970] 3 All ER 825, **199**
Gilford Motor Co Ltd v Horne [1933] Ch 935, **46**
Gillette Australia Pty Ltd v Energizer Australia Pty Ltd (2002) 193 ALR 629, **484**
Ginnane v Diners Club Ltd (1993) 42 FCR 90, **370**
GIO Australia Ltd v P Ward Civil Engineering Pty Ltd [2000] NSWSC 371, **309, 334**
GIO General Ltd v Wallace [2001] NSWCA 299, **324, 326**
GIO Insurance Ltd v Nader (unreported, Victorian Supreme Court, Nathan J, 7 April 1994), **325**
Giorgi v European Asian Bank AG (unreported, NSW Supreme Court, Young J, 21 February 1989), **286**
Glebe Island Terminals v Continental Seagram (1993) 40 NSWLR 206, **209**
Gliderol International Pty Ltd v Skerbic & McCormack & Sheridan (2009) 170 ACTR 1, **422**
Global Sportsman Pty Ltd v Mirror Newspapers Ltd (1984) 2 FCR 82, **484**
Godley v Perry [1960] 1 WLR 9, **99**
Golden Acres Ltd v Queensland Estates Pty Ltd [1969] Qd R 378, **514–15**
Goldsborough v Ford Credit Australia Ltd (1989) ASC ¶55-946, **284**
Gollan v Nugent (1988) 166 CLR 18, **57**
Goodwin v National Bank of Australasia Ltd (1968) 117 CLR 173, **289**
Goodwin v State Government Insurance Office (Qld) [1994] 2 Qd R 15, **308**
Google Inc v Australian Competition and Consumer Commission (2013) 249 CLR 435, **470 477–8, 481**
Goss v Nugent (1833) 110 ER 713, **270**
Goudberg v Herniman Associates Pty Ltd [2007] VSCA 12, **31**
Goulston Discount Ltd v Clark [1967] 2 QB 493, **280**
GPG (Australia Trading) Pty Ltd v GIO Australia Holdings Ltd (2001) 117 FCR 23, **493**
Graanhandel T Vink BV v European Grain & Shipping Ltd [1989] 2 Lloyd's Rep 531, **147, 189**
Graham v Portacom New Zealand Ltd [2004] 2 NZLR 528, **229**
Graham v Voight (1989) 95 FLR 146, **209**
Graham Barclay Oysters Pty Ltd v Ryan (2002) 211 CLR 540, **426**
Grant v Australian Knitting Mills Ltd [1936] AC 85, **83, 93**
Grant v YYH Holdings Pty Ltd [2012] NSWCA 360, **59, 63**
Green v CGU Insurance Ltd (2008) 67 ACSR 398, **339**
Greentree v FAI General Insurance Co Ltd (1998) 44 NSWLR 706, **344**
Greer v Downs Supply Co [1927] 2 KB 28, **187**
Griffin v Pantzer (2004) 137 FCR 209, **380**
Griffiths v Peter Conway Ltd [1939] 1 All ER 685, **90–1**
Groundhog Sales & Rentals Pty Ltd v Eastern Pearl Corporation [2012] FCAFC 113, **87, 95**
Guardian Assurance Co Ltd v Underwood Constructions Pty Ltd (1974) 48 ALJR 307, **311**
Guenard v Coe (1914) 17 DLR 47, **278**
Gugliotti v Commercial Union Assurance Co of Australia (1992) 15 MVR 463, **316, 347**
Guthrie v ANZ Banking Group Ltd (1989) ANZ ConvR ¶221, **286**
Gwinnett v Day [2012] SASC 43, **59**

TABLE OF STATUTES

Australia

South Australia

Queensland

Tasmania

Western Australia

Canada

New Zealand

United Kingdom

United States

International instruments

ABBREVIATIONS

AAT	Australian Trade Commission
ABN	Australian Business Number
ACCC	Australian Competition and Consumer Commission
ACL	Australian Consumer Law
ACLFTA	*Australian Consumer Law and Fair Trading Act 2012* (Vic)
ACN	Australian Company Number
AfCFTA	African Continental Free Trade Area
AFSA	Australian Financial Security Authority
AGM	annual general meeting
ALRC	Australian Law Reform Commission
APRA	Australian Prudential Regulation Authority
ASIC	Australian Securities and Investments Commission
ASX	Australian Securities Exchange Ltd
ATO	Australian Taxation Office
AUSFTA	Australia–United States Free Trade Agreement
BL	bill of lading
CAANZ	Consumer Affairs Australia and New Zealand
CCA	*Competition and Consumer Act 2010* (Cth)
CCLAA	*Competition and Consumer Legislation Amendment Act 2011* (Cth)
ChAFTA	China–Australia Free Trade Agreement
CIF	cost, insurance and freight contract
CISG	Convention on Contracts for the International Sale of Goods
COAG	Council of Australian Governments
CPTPP	Comprehensive and Progressive Agreement for Trans-Pacific Partnership
Cth	Commonwealth
DFAT	Department of Foreign Affairs and Trade
DNS	Domain Name System
EGM	extraordinary general meeting
EU	European Union
FATA	*Foreign Acquisitions and Takeovers Act 1975* (Cth)
FIP	foreign investment policy
FIRB	Foreign Investment Review Board
FOB	free on board contract
FTA	free trade agreement
GATS	General Agreement on Trade in Services
GATT	General Agreement on Tariffs and Trade

GSA	general security agreement
GST	goods and services tax
ICANN	Internet Corporation for Assigned Names and Numbers
ICC	International Chamber of Commerce
IGAACL	Intergovernmental Agreement for the Australian Consumer Law
IP	intellectual property
IPRB	Insolvency Practice Rules (Bankruptcy)
IPSB	Insolvency Practice Schedule (Bankruptcy)
ISDS	investor–state dispute settlememt
MFN	most favoured nation
NFP	not for profit
NPII	National Personal Insolvency Index
PMSI	purchase money security interest
PPSA	*Personal Property Securities Act 2009* (Cth)
PPSR	Personal Property Securities Register
RBA	Reserve Bank of Australia
RCEP	Regional Comprehensive Economic Partnership
ROT	retention of title
SI	security interest
SME	small and medium-sized enterprise
SP	secured party
TFN	tax file number
TPA	*Trade Practices Act 1974* (Cth)
TPP	*Trans-Pacific Partnership Agreement*
TRIPS	Trade-Related Aspects of Intellectual Property Rights
UCC	Uniform Commercial Code (United States)
UK	United Kingdom
US	United States
USTR	United States Trade Representative
WTO	World Trade Organization

ABOUT THE AUTHORS

Dilan Thampapillai is a Senior Lecturer with the ANU College of Law at the Australian National University. Dilan has significant expertise in artificial intelligence, copyright and contract law. Prior to becoming an academic, Dilan was a government lawyer with the Attorney-General's Department and the Australian Government Solicitor. He has advised on treaties, copyright law and commercial matters. He convenes and lectures Commercial Law, Contract Law and Advanced Contracts. Dilan has published widely on contracts, commercial law and copyright law. His academic work has been published in a number of important journals including the *University of Queensland Law Journal*, *Law in Context*, the *University of Tasmania Law Review* and the *Australian Intellectual Property Journal*. He has recently participated in the WIPO–WTO Colloquium for IP Academics and his paper on artificial intelligence will shortly be released as part of the Colloquium Series.

Claudio Bozzi is a Lecturer at Deakin University, where he teaches the rules of proceedings, equity, and trusts. He is the supervisor of the New Ventures Clinic, which operates as a professional law firm providing legal assistance to start-ups and entrepreneurs who need help navigating areas of law that are rapidly changing, or are entirely new. Claudio is a barrister practising in commercial matters with a special interest in shipping and maritime law, and the legal implications of technical innovation.

Mark Giancaspro is a Lecturer and practising commercial lawyer at the University of Adelaide Law School. He holds an honours degree in Laws and Legal Practice from Flinders University and a PhD from the University of Adelaide. His legal employment background and research interests are primarily commercial, with issues in contract law and its applications being his principal theme. Mark teaches in contract law, commercial law, operational commercial law and sports law, and has published widely on matters including issues with the formation and renegotiation of contracts, the doctrine of consideration, and smart contracts. He currently practices through the Law School's Legal Advice Service in the Adelaide Magistrates Court and is a member of the Australian Commercial Law Association, the Adelaide Law School's Commercial Law Research Group, and the Adelaide University Research Unit on Military Law & Ethics' (RUMLAE) commercial law division.

George Yijun Tian is a Senior Lecturer and HDR Supervisor in the Faculty of Law at the University of Technology Sydney (UTS). He is also a UDRP Neutral appointed by the World Intellectual Property Organization (WIPO), and an HDR Supervisor Affiliate with the University of Sydney. George has been a Visiting Scholar of Berkman Centre for the Internet and Society at the Harvard Law School, and a Visiting Research Fellow of the Oxford IP Research Center in the Faculty of Law at the University of Oxford. His teaching and research interests include: intellectual property commercialisation, commercial law, privacy and antitrust law and cyberspace law, with a particular focus on regulatory governance issues arising from cross-border transactions. George has published extensively in international intellectual property, competition law and cyber security.

ACKNOWLEDGMENTS

We are grateful to the following individuals and organisations for permission to use their material in *Australian Commercial Law*.

Extracts from Australian Commonwealth legislation: Sourced from the Federal Register of Legislation. Reproduced under Creative Commons Attribution 4.0 International (CC BY 4.0). For the latest information on Australian Government law please go to https://www.legislation.gov.au.

Extracts from Commonwealth Law Reports: Reproduced with permission of Thomson Reuters (Professional) Australia Limited, legal.thomsonreuters.com.au.

Extracts from Victorian legislation and parliamentary documents: © State of Victoria, Australia Copyright in all legislation of the Parliament of the State of Victoria, Australia, is owned by the Crown in right of the State of Victoria, Australia.

Extracts from ICLR reports: Reproduced with permission of Incorporated Council of Law Reporting.

Extracts from New South Wales Court of Appeal: Reproduced under Creative Commons Attribution 4.0 International (CC BY 4.0).

Extracts from New South Wales Supreme Court: Reproduced under Creative Commons Attribution 4.0 International (CC BY 4.0).

Extracts from Federal Court of Australia: Reproduced under Creative Commons Attribution 4.0 International (CC BY 4.0).

Extracts from Federal Circuit Court of Australia: Reproduced under Creative Commons Attribution 4.0 International (CC BY 4.0).

Extracts from Lloyd's Law Reports: Reproduced with permission of Informa Law, London.

The extracts from *Skandinaviska Enskilda Banken AB (Publ), Singapore Branch v Asia Pacific Breweries (Singapore) Pty Ltd* [2011] 3 SLR 540 and *Cavenagh Investment Pte Ltd v Kaushik Rajiv* [2013] 2 SLR 543 are reproduced with permission from the Singapore Academy of Law. All rights reserved. No portion of the judgment may be used or reproduced without the prior written consent of the Singapore Academy of Law.

Extracts from Productivity Commission reports: sourced from Productivity Commission, https://www.pc.gov.au/, reproduced under Creative Commons Attribution 3.0 Australia (CC BY 3.0 AU) licence.

Extracts from ACCC *A Guide to Unfair Contract Terms Law*: © Commonwealth of Australia.

Extract from Bankruptcy Amendment Bill: © Commonwealth of Australia 2004

Extracts from *United Nations Convention on Contracts for the International Sale of Goods* (CISG): From Contracts for the International Sale of Goods, by The Secretary-General of the United Nations, ©1980 United Nations. Reprinted with the permission of the United Nations.

Extract from 'Introduction to the Incoterms® 2010': © International Chamber of Commerce (ICC), https://iccwbo.org/content/uploads/sites/3/2010/01/ICC-Introduction-to-the-Incoterms-2010.pdf.

Extracts from Australian Law Reports originally published by LexisNexis.

Every effort has been made to trace and acknowledge copyright. The publisher apologises for any accidental infringement and welcomes information that would rectify the situation.

AUSTRALIAN COMMERCIAL LAW

1

CONTRACT LAW AND COMMERCIAL REGULATORS

1.0 Introduction

This chapter addresses the fundamental rules of contract law and introduces nine of the significant regulators operating within the Australian commercial landscape. Contracts are of enormous importance in most established economies as they provide a means by which promises made as part of a commercial bargain can be legally enforced. Contracts also underlie a large number of transactions entered into by the principal commercial regulators in this country, and so this chapter provides a useful backdrop against which we can explore more specific concepts in Australian commercial law.

1.1 Contracts in commerce

The law of contract is fundamental to the notion of voluntary exchange, which forms the basis of any market for goods and services in such countries as Australia. The legal enforcement, in a certain and predictable manner, of agreements to exchange resources fosters confidence among market participants and increases economic growth and overall commercial prosperity. As such, contract law quite literally 'underpins our economy'.[1] While specific courses within law curricula will educate you as to the more specific and complex principles pertaining to contract law, it is essential in any examination of Australian commercial law to have at least a general understanding of the basics so as to appreciate the role and importance of contracts in commerce.

There is no general agreement among scholars as to what a 'contract' actually is. This difficulty in part stems from the fact that the term refers not only to the *bargain* manifested between the parties, but often also to the physical *form* of that agreement. That is, 'contract' describes not just the substance of the agreement but, where a written agreement is used, the document itself. Most people in business assume a 'contract' to be simply a written agreement. However, a contract does not need to be written down, and so it is probably more accurate to define a contract as an agreement or set of promises made between parties that the law will enforce.[2] In whatever form, for an agreement to be a 'contract' it need only satisfy four key requirements, which will be discussed later in the chapter.

Importantly, gifts and social agreements are not 'contracts' and so are not legally enforceable. These do not carry the force of law because they either lack *consideration* (in the case of gifts, as we will discuss in detail shortly) or were objectively not *intended* to attract legal consequences if breached. If the law regarded all such agreements as contracts, then legal liability would be unintentionally assumed in a countless number of situations and the courts would be inundated with (largely trivial) lawsuits. As such, the law of contract is careful to identify whether an agreement bears all the hallmarks of a legal contract or whether it is simply an unenforceable arrangement.

---

1 *Biotechnology Australia Pty Ltd v Pace* (1988) 15 NSWLR 130, 132.

2 See M Giancaspro and C Langos, *Understanding Contract Law: A Practical Guide* (LexisNexis Butterworths Australia, Sydney, 2016), 24 and the authorities there cited.

1.1.1 Common types of contract

Contracts can be classified in a number of ways and so there can be said to be numerous 'types'. One basic classification relates to the form of the agreement. There are two basic forms: *formal* and *simple*. A formal contract, otherwise known as a *contract under seal*, is one recorded in a deed. A deed is a special written document that transfers or affirms the transfer of property or some other interest.[3] The common law rules concerning deeds have been largely modified by statute. A simple contract, on the other hand, can be made orally and/or in writing and requires consideration (which we will hear about shortly). Formal contracts do not require consideration, and so an agreement lacking consideration can be incorporated into a deed to avoid any potential issues with enforceability.

Another classification of contracts is by nature of the obligations they impose upon the parties. Contracts can be either *bilateral* or *unilateral*. A bilateral contract is one in which both parties exchange promises to do or not to do something; the legal obligation on each party to fulfil their respective promises arises at the point of exchange. For example, Frank offers to mow Bill's lawns for $20 on a specific date, and Bill accepts this offer. Both parties are now obligated to perform: Frank to mow Bill's lawns on the agreed date, and Bill to pay Frank $20 for this service. A unilateral contract is one in which one party has made a promise to do or not to do something upon the performance of a *specified act*. The legal obligation to perform arises at the point a second party performs the act specified by the first party. For example, Melissa posts an advertisement offering $200 to anyone who finds and returns her missing dog. There is no legal obligation on anyone who sees the advertisement to go and find the dog, and so there is no contract at this point. If, however, another person finds Melissa's dog and returns it to her, then that person is entitled to the $200 offered by Melissa. The finder has performed the specified act (found and returned the dog) and so the legal obligation on Melissa to perform (pay the reward) arises at this point; there is now a contract. A useful way to summarise is that with bilateral contracts *both* parties exchange promises, whereas with unilateral contracts only *one* party makes a promise (offer).

A third classification of contracts concerns the manner of their creation. Contracts can be created *expressly* or *by implication*. When most people hear the word 'contract', they normally envisage a written document.[4] However, contracts can arise in situations where no documentation is involved at all, or where a combination of spoken and written words (in whatever form) is used to construct the agreement. An express contract is one in which the parties have explicitly stated the terms of their agreement, either orally or in writing. This is overwhelmingly the more common type of contract, as most people tend to employ effort and comprehensively outline terms when forging contractual arrangements with others. Alternatively, an implied contract is one which is inferred from the conduct of the parties within the context of the surrounding circumstances. By way of example, when boarding a bus you are impliedly agreeing to abide by the terms of carriage, even though you have not signed anything or even said a word.[5]

3 *R v Morton* (1873) LR 2 CCR 22, 27.

4 This has been verified by empirical studies. See, for example, T Wilkinson-Ryan and D A Hoffman, 'The Common Sense of Contract Formation' (2015) 67 *Stanford Law Review* 1269.

5 This is assuming that the terms of carriage have been appropriately brought to the attention of the passenger. The concept of notice is discussed briefly later in the chapter when terms and performance are addressed.

1.1.2 General principles and 'fragmentation' of contract law

The Australian legal framework, and therefore a large number of its legal rules and principles, derive from England and can be traced back centuries. Throughout the 19th century, scholars endeavoured to make sense of the complicated and disordered body of contract principles that abounded and thankfully were successful in discerning what is now generally agreed to be the basic set of rules underlying the formation, performance and termination of contracts.

Of course, over time, as industries have matured and specific requirements surrounding contractual agreements have developed for each, the principles of contract have been refashioned by parliament and the courts to suit. McKendrick has referred to this process of gradual specialisation as 'fragmentation'.[6] While the basic principles may in particular instances have undergone customisation – such as in the case of insurance and real estate contracts, which have their own sets of legislative rules – they retain significance to *all* contracts and underlie the more particular rules that have developed for particular contexts. We will now briefly examine the key principles relevant to all stages of a contract's life from birth (formation) through to death (termination).

1.1.3 Formation

For a contract to exist, four essential elements must be present: (1) offer and acceptance (agreement); (2) consideration; (3) intention to create legal relations; and (4) certainty and completeness of terms. There are also two peripheral requirements in capacity and legality.[7] We will consider each of these elements in turn.

1.1.3.1 Element 1: Offer and acceptance (agreement)

An offer is an indication by one party of a willingness to be bound to the terms of a promise they make to another party, with the latter having the option of accepting or rejecting the proposal.[8] The offer can be made orally, in writing, by conduct, or through a combination of these means. An offer must be distinguished from other forms of communication such as the supply of information or an invitation to treat. A supply of information is not an offer. For example, merely stating the lowest price you would sell property for when asked is not offering the property at that price; it is responding to the request for information.[9] Similarly, invitations to treat are not offers. An invitation to treat is an invitation to enter into negotiations. Typical instances of invitations to treat that you will encounter in the commercial world include the display of goods in a shop, advertised goods in catalogues/newspapers, auctions and tenders. In each case, parties are invited to make offers by way of proffering the price stipulated or making bids through the auction or tender processes. A common error made by laypeople is to mistake all of these scenarios as offers that they are accepting, rather than as

6 E McKendrick, *Contract Law* (Palgrave Macmillan, London, 11th edn, 2015), 2.
7 These concepts are not considered in this chapter, save to say that a party must have legal capacity to contract (eg be of sound mind, and an appropriate age in most circumstances) and cannot enter into contracts that involve or facilitate illegal conduct.
8 *Brambles Holdings Ltd v Bathurst City Council* (2001) 53 NSWLR 153, 171.
9 *Harvey v Facey* [1893] AC 552.

invitations in response to which they are making offers. In other words, they think they are the ones who have to accept, rather than make, the offer.

An offer can be revoked at any point prior to its being accepted, so long as the revocation is communicated to potential offerees.[10] The revocation can be verbal, in writing, or occur via conduct. It will be more difficult to revoke an offer in the case of unilateral contracts. Recall that a unilateral contract arises when A performs the act specified by B. To use our earlier example, could Melissa revoke her offer to pay $200 to whoever finds and returns her missing dog if someone had already found the dog and was in the process of returning it (e.g. driving to her house)? The courts typically decide whether revocation is possible in such circumstances by considering a number of factors such as the relative benefit or detriment suffered by the offeree in performance, the offeror's appreciation of the risk assumed, and the intentions of the parties.[11]

Once an offer is rejected, whether expressly or by conduct indicating that the offer has been turned down, it is terminated and cannot be accepted. Again, it is a common misconception that a vendor can simply go back to an offeror (potential purchaser) and say they have 'changed their mind' and will accept the price offered; the offer has died and cannot be revived. Rather, the offeror must make another offer to start the process again. There also seems to be general misunderstanding in commerce as to the effect of a counteroffer. A counteroffer terminates the offer on foot and supplants it; the other party can then choose to accept or reject the counteroffer.[12]

In other words, the roles reverse when a counteroffer is made. If Rachael advertises her car for $5000 (invitation to treat) and Mason contacts her and offers $4500, Mason is making an offer. If Rachael responds with 'How about $4800?', she has proposed a counteroffer – this terminates Mason's original offer of $4500 and converts Rachael to offeror. Rachael is now making an offer to Mason, which Mason can either accept or reject.

It is also critically important to note that a mere request for information or further particulars *does not* amount to a rejection of an offer.[13]

To use the example above, if Rachael made a counteroffer of $4800 for her car, and Mason said 'Would you be willing to come down a bit more on price?' or 'Does that include the alloy rims on the tyres?', Mason has not rejected the offer. Instead, he simply seeks further information upon which to make his decision whether to accept Rachael's counteroffer or not.

10 *Byrne & Co v Leon Van Tienhoven & Co* (188) LR CPD 344; *Dickinson v Dodds* (1876) 2 Ch D 463.

11 *Mobil Oil Australia v Wellcome International* (1998) 81 FCR 475.

12 *Hyde v Wrench* (1840) 3 Beav 334.

13 *Stevenson Jacques & Co v McLean* (1880) 5 QBD 346.

It is essential to examine the precise words used when determining if a party is requesting further information or actually making a counteroffer that rejects the original offer. The courts consider the parties' language to try and elucidate the meaning and effect of their dialogue.

A final observation relevant to the cessation of offers is that an offer will lapse if it is not accepted within a reasonable time, as determined in the circumstances of the particular case.[14]

Acceptance is the reciprocal stage of agreement and signals the 'meeting of the minds' (*consensus ad idem*) between the parties. To effect a valid acceptance, the offeree must be aware of the offer presented to them. This may sound odd, though it is possible for a contract to be formed inadvertently and so it must be determined if the offeree was aware of what they were agreeing to. In *R v Clarke*,[15] for example, the Western Australian Police offered a £1000 reward to anyone who provided information leading to the arrest and conviction of the person(s) who murdered two police officers. The plaintiff provided this information not knowing, however, that there was a reward at stake. As he was implicated in the murders himself, he offered this information to clear his name and not to claim the reward. The High Court held that the plaintiff was not entitled to the reward, as a unilateral contract can only be formed where the act required for acceptance is performed on the faith of the offer.

Acceptance must also be communicated to the offeror.[16] Where a mode or manner of acceptance is prescribed by the offeror, the offeree's communication must occur in this way.[17] Generally speaking, acceptance should occur via the same means in which the offer was conveyed; however, in practice, it is rare for commercial offers to stipulate an exclusive method of acceptance. Importantly, silence does not constitute acceptance.[18] As such, one cannot say, 'If I don't hear from you by Friday, I'll assume you agree.' This undermines the notion of voluntarily assumed obligation. A rare exception is where, in the absence of an express acceptance, an offeree's conduct demonstrates that they are accepting the offer. In such cases, this may suffice as valid acceptance.[19]

For example, if Rachael offered Mason the chance to buy her yacht at a discounted price provided a $1000 deposit was paid by Mason before the end of the day, and Mason, without saying anything at all, simply paid the $1000 into Rachael's bank account, this naturally implies that he has accepted Rachael's offer.

An important exception to the rule that acceptance must be communicated is the postal acceptance rule. Where acceptance is expected to be sent by post, the acceptance becomes effective as soon as it is posted (as opposed to when it is actually received by the offeror).[20] The rule emerged in the 19th century at a time when commercial parties either contracted in

14 *Ramsgate Victoria Hotel Co v Montefiore* (1866) LR 1 Ex 109.
15 (1927) 40 CLR 227.
16 *Tinn v Hoffman* (1873) 29 LT 271.
17 *Gilbert J McCaul (Australia) Pty Ltd v Pitt Club Ltd* (1954) 76 WN (NSW) 72.
18 *Felthouse v Bindley* (1862) 11 CB (NS) 869.
19 *Empirnall Holdings Pty Ltd v Machon Paull Partners Pty Ltd* (1988) 14 NSWLR 523.
20 *Adams v Lindsell* (1818) 106 ER 250.

person or via letters mailed to one another when distance proved too much. As such, the rule reflects a concern that parties might revoke an offer prior to physically receiving an acceptance, despite the offeree having done all they can to inform the offeror of their acquiescence. The advent of electronic communication technologies has somewhat complicated matters. It has been judicially stated that instantaneous forms of communication (such as telephone, telex, facsimile etc.) are not subject to the postal acceptance rule.[21] Emails have been recognised as analogous to telex[22] and so acceptance would be deemed to have been communicated when the email was *received*, rather than when it was sent.

Interestingly, s 14(1) of the *Electronic Transactions Act 1999* (Cth) provides that, unless otherwise agreed by the parties, the time of dispatch of an electronic communication (such as an email) is the time it leaves the information system under the control of the sender. If the system is not under the control of the sender, which would typically be the case between commercial parties utilising external servers to transmit their emails, dispatch instead occurs when the addressee receives the electronic communication.

1.1.3.2 Element 2: Consideration

The second element of contract formation is consideration. The doctrine of consideration requires that something be given in return for a promise in order for that promise to be legally binding. As such, it distinguishes gratuitous promises from legally enforceable promises. There are two basic elements to consideration: benefit/detriment and bargain. This can be a difficult concept to comprehend as the term 'consideration' encompasses both whatever is exchanged and the process for this exchange. Looking at the first element, Lush J in *Currie v Misa* defined consideration as 'some right, interest, profit, or benefit accruing to the one party, or some forbearance, detriment, loss, or responsibility, given, suffered, or undertaken by the other'.[23] Consideration can therefore be anything of sufficient legal value.[24] Not only must consideration be in the nature of one or more of the things listed by Lush J (above), it must also have been given *in return* for a promise. That is, it must have been bargained for. As Lord Dunedin explained in *Dunlop Pneumatic Tyre Co Ltd v Selfridge & Co Ltd*: 'An act or forbearance of one party, or the promise thereof, is the price for which the promise of the other is bought, and the promise thus given for value is enforceable.'[25]

There are many rules attending the doctrine of consideration, though we will only briefly summarise these here. First, consideration must be legally sufficient but need not be adequate.[26] The law of contract is not concerned with whether parties have received a 'fair' price; if they have willingly accepted that price, then the law will enforce the arrangement. Second, promising to perform (or actually performing) an existing legal duty will not suffice as consideration.[27] In other words, you cannot receive more in return for the same; this is a gratuitous promise, as there is no *quid pro quo* given that nothing extra is being exchanged.

21 *Entores v Miles Far Eastern Corporation* [1955] QB 327; *Olivaylle Pty Ltd v Flottweg GMBH & Co KGAA [No 4]* (2009) 255 ALR 632.

22 *Olivaylle Pty Ltd v Flottweg GMBH & Co KGAA [No 4]* (2009) 255 ALR 632.

23 (1875) LR 10 Ex 153, 162. See also *Beaton v McDivitt* (1987) 13 NSWLR 162, 181.

24 *Thomas v Thomas* (1842) 2 QB 851.

25 [1915] AC 847, 855.

26 *Westlake v Adams* (1858) 5 CB (NS) 248; *Chappell & Co Ltd v Nestlé Co Ltd* [1960] AC 87.

27 *Stilk v Myrick* (1809) 2 Camp 317; *Wigan v Edwards* (1973) 1 ALR 497.

So, if Rachael engages Mason to build her house for $400 000, and Mason asks for additional money midway through the job (which Rachael promises to pay), Rachael is not obliged to pay the additional money. Mason has given nothing extra in addition to what he was already obligated to do.

This rule can easily be avoided by, for example, tendering fresh consideration in return for the additional consideration from the other party, or putting the agreement into a deed (which we heard about earlier).

Controversially, in *Williams v Roffey Brothers & Nicholls (Contractors) Ltd*,[28] it was held that where one party promises additional consideration to the other party in return for what they were already due to receive, consideration may be found in the 'practical benefit' the promisor derives from the modification. In that case, Mr Williams was hired by Roffey Bros to complete some carpentry work under a subcontract. He started to run out of money and was not sure he could continue, so Roffey Bros promised an additional £10 300 – to be paid in instalments – to finish the work. When instalments that had fallen due were not paid, Williams sued to recover them. The English Court of Appeal held that, while Williams had merely promised to perform an existing legal duty in return for the additional money (violating the existing legal duty rule), he *had* provided practical consideration to Roffey Bros. They did not, for example, have to employ other subcontractors, the haphazard payment scheme was replaced with a new streamlined scheme, and the penalty clause under the head contract was avoided. The practical benefit principle has been accepted, though slightly modified, in Australia.[29]

An intriguing extension of the existing legal duty rule is the part-payment of debt rule, which basically states that a debtor's promise to pay part of a debt is not good consideration for the creditor's reciprocal promise to discharge the debt.[30] The rationale underlying the rule is that the offer of a lesser sum can never satisfy the greater sum due, such that the creditor is giving more than they are receiving. There are numerous exceptions to the rule, such as where the debtor repays in something other than money[31] or where a third party promises to make the part-payment.[32]

A third and final rule concerning consideration relates to when it is given. Consideration will not be found in something done or given *prior to* the making of a promise. This is because bargain theory requires that consideration be reciprocal.[33] One exception to this rule is where a party is requested to perform a service, performs that service, and the requesting party subsequently promises to pay for the service. In such cases, there is an implied understanding that the payment is in satisfaction of the service performed.[34]

28 [1991] 1 QB 1.
29 *Musumeci v Winadell Pty Ltd* (1994) 34 NSWLR 723.
30 *Pinnel's* case (1601) 5 Co Rep 117a; *Foakes v Beer* (1884) 9 App Cas 605.
31 *Pinnel's* case (1601) 5 Co Rep 117a.
32 *Hirachand Punamchand v Temple* [1911] 2 KB 330.
33 *Roscorla v Thomas* (1842) 3 QB 234.
34 *Lampleigh v Brathwait* (1615) Hob 105; *Ipex Software Services Pty Ltd v Hosking* [2000] VSCA 239.

1.1.3.3 Element 3: Intention to create legal relations

The third element of contract formation is intention to create legal relations. Once parties have reached agreement and exchanged valid consideration, it must then be proven that they intended for the agreement to carry the force of law. The courts assess this intention objectively based on what a reasonable person would have understood from the parties' dealings.[35] Domestic, family and social agreements are presumed to lack legal intent, short of evidence to the contrary.[36] Such evidence might include the manner in which the parties made their agreement. For example, friends and relatives seldom reduce the various arrangements they make with one another to writing. Putting an agreement in writing would therefore imply that it was something more than purely domestic or social. The overall context in which the agreement was made will clearly be relevant. In contrast to domestic, family and social agreements, commercial or business transactions are presumed to be legally binding.[37]

Determining legal intent can be very difficult when a business transaction occurs between close friends or family members. In *Roufos v Brewster*,[38] for example, Mr Roufos entered into an agreement with his wife's parents, Mr and Mrs Brewster, whereby he would transport his in-laws' truck from Coober Pedy to Adelaide to have it repaired and hire another driver to return the truck to Coober Pedy. This arrangement also benefited Mr Roufos, as he was able to transport liquor for his business in the truck. The truck was damaged on the return trip and the Brewsters sought damages from their son-in-law for the repair costs. The court held that the presumption against legal intent was displaced on the evidence. Notwithstanding that the parties were related, it was objectively intended that the agreement would give rise to legal consequences. They were conducting separate businesses and there was no indication of affection or gratuity underlying the agreement.

This case can be contrasted with the old English case of *Balfour v Balfour*.[39] The parties in that case were a married couple living in Sri Lanka. During a holiday to England, Mrs Balfour fell ill and remained in England to recover on the advice of her doctor. Mr Balfour made a promise to pay his wife a monthly sum of £30 until she was well enough to return. The parties subsequently separated and divorced, and Mr Balfour withheld any further payments to his wife in England. Mrs Balfour sued her ex-husband to enforce his promise to pay her. The court held that there was no objective intention on the part of the parties to create legal relations through their agreement. This was purely a private or domestic arrangement between a married couple and it could not, without more, be said that the couple were intending to form a legally binding agreement in the circumstances. As such, there was no contract.

1.1.3.4 Element 4: Certainty and completeness

The fourth element of contract formation is certainty and completeness of terms. These are technically two separate requirements, though they are typically considered concurrently.

35 *Merritt v Merritt* [1970] 1 WLR 1211.
36 *Balfour v Balfour* [1919] 2 KB 571; *Cohen v Cohen* (1929) 42 CLR 91; *Jones v Padavatton* [1969] 1 WLR 328; *Coward v Motor Insurers' Bureau* [1963] 1 QB 259.
37 *Edwards v Skywards* [1964] 1 WLR 349; *Helmos Enterprises Pty Ltd v Jaylor Pty Ltd* [2005] NSWCA 235.
38 (1971) 2 SASR 218.
39 [1919] 2 KB 571. See also *Cohen v Cohen* (1929) 42 CLR 91.

Given how crucial contracts are to most commercial activity, it is imperative that they be sufficiently certain and complete.

A contract must contain all essential or critical terms, as agreed by the parties.[40] By 'essential' is meant terms the absence of which would threaten the enforcement of the agreement.[41] Typically, these are in the more significant, operative clauses upon which the contract ultimately depends. The parties are responsible for determining which terms are critical to their agreement. Terms such as the commencement date of a lease[42] or the price and subject matter of a real estate contract[43] are clearly essential. Without all essential terms in place, a contract cannot be said to be sufficiently complete. For contracts that are entirely oral, partly written and partly oral, or comprised of numerous documents (such as emails, meeting notes, draft agreements, etc.) the contents of which jointly constitute the written agreement, the task of determining if all essential terms are present is made far more difficult. Where there is a conventional written contract, the task is somewhat easier. In any case, minor gaps or omissions within the agreement can be filled by the courts provided the essential terms are in place.

Assume, for example, that the parties to a contract for the sale of a good fail to specify the price for the good in the contract. In such cases, legislation will require the buyer to pay a reasonable price, as determined by the courts.[44] Alternatively, the parties may have forgotten to include some other detail in their contract. In such cases, provided all essential terms are in place and it is appropriate to do so, the courts may fill the gaps.[45] Where parties include a mechanism for determining terms at a later date, such as a term requiring the parties to agree to rent payable under a lease or submit to arbitration where they cannot reach agreement, the contract will not be deemed incomplete.[46]

A contract must not only be sufficiently complete but also certain in its terms. Certainty is naturally critical in the context of commercial dealings, as otherwise contracts may fail. The courts endorse a liberal approach when construing contracts and will do everything possible to give meaning to the words used by the parties unless it is impossible to do so.[47] Importantly, ambiguity does *not* automatically amount to legal *uncertainty*: a contract will not fail for want of certainty merely because its content is difficult to comprehend.[48] Where, however, those parts of the contract that are uncertain cannot be clarified or otherwise cut out of the contract, the entire agreement will be deemed legally uncertain.

In *Whitlock v Brew*,[49] the plaintiff sold a piece of land containing a petrol station to the defendant. One of the terms of the contract required the defendant to immediately lease the

40 *Thorby v Goldberg* (1964) 112 CLR 597.

41 *Anaconda Nickel Ltd v Tarmoola Australia Pty Ltd* (2000) 22 WAR 101.

42 *Harvey v Pratt* [1965] 1 WLR 1025.

43 *Hall v Busst* (1960) 104 CLR 206.

44 The Sale of Goods Acts in each jurisdiction provide for this: *Sale of Goods Act 1954* (ACT), s 13(2); *Sale of Goods Act 1923* (NSW), s 13(2); *Sale of Goods Act 1972* (NT), s 13(2); *Sale of Goods Act 1896* (Qld), s 11(2); *Sale of Goods Act 1895* (SA), s 8(2); *Sale of Goods Act 1896* (Tas), s 13(2); *Goods Act 1958* (Vic), s 13(2); *Sale of Goods Act 1895* (WA), s 8(2). On the sale of goods, see further Chapter 4.

45 See, further, Sections 1.1.4.5 to 1.1.4.7 of this chapter on implied terms.

46 *Booker Industries Pty Ltd v Wilson Parking (Qld) Ltd* (1982) 149 CLR 600; *Hawthorn Football Club Ltd v Harding* [1988] VR 49.

47 *Upper Hunter County District Council v Australian Chilling & Freezing Co Ltd* (1968) 118 CLR 429.

48 *Mineralogy Pty Ltd v Sino Iron Pty Ltd* [2016] WASCA 105 [23].

49 (1968) 118 CLR 445.

portion of the land containing the petrol station back to the plaintiff 'upon such reasonable terms as commonly govern such a lease'. The defendant then changed his mind and refused to proceed with the sale. His argument was that the clause referring to the common terms governing such leases was uncertain and that the contract was therefore invalid. The court agreed, holding that no such common reasonable terms existed and so the contract as a whole was uncertain and therefore invalid.

1.1.4 Terms

A contract is composed of terms that reflect how the parties have assigned their risks, rights and obligations. There are two general types of term: *express* and *implied*. Express terms are those specifically included by the parties. Implied terms are those implied into the contract by the courts or by statute. We will consider each type in turn.

1.1.4.1 Express terms incorporated by signature

The most common way for parties to incorporate express terms into their written contracts is through *signature*. One of the foundational rules of contract law is that a party is bound by the terms contained in a contractual document they have signed, even if they have not read or understood the terms.[50] There are two principal exceptions to the signature rule. First, the rule will not apply where the contents of the signed document have been misrepresented to the signatory.[51] As such, Maria cannot say to Jenny that a document contains or has the effect of doing X – prompting Jenny to sign the document without reading or properly comprehending it – when it in fact contains or has the effect of doing Y. Second, the rule will not apply where the document signed could not reasonably be regarded as contractual in nature.[52] If the signed document that is supposedly a contract containing terms objectively appears to be more akin to a receipt, brochure or the like, the courts may find that the document could not have been perceived by a reasonable person to be contractual and therefore it does not bind the signatory.

1.1.4.2 Express terms incorporated by notice

Another way for parties to incorporate express terms into their agreements, where they do not intend to use a signed written contract, is by *notice*. This is actually very common in the commercial world and often occurs by way of signage at the point of entry for facilities such as car parks, or on tickets for services such as public transport. In all of these situations, it would be impractical and near impossible to have every party read and sign a written contract, and so terms may be efficiently incorporated by bringing them to the notice of the party to be bound.

There are three basic requirements to validly incorporate terms by notice: (1) notice must be provided before or at the time of contracting;[53] (2) the document or form in which the terms

50 *L'Estrange v Graucob* [1934] 2 KB 394; *Toll (FGCT) Pty Ltd v Alphapharm Pty Ltd* (2004) 219 CLR 165.

51 *Curtis v Chemical Cleaning & Dyeing Co* [1951] 1 KB 805.

52 *D J Hill & Co Pty Ltd v Walter H Wright Pty Ltd* [1971] VR 749; *Curtis v Chemical Cleaning & Dyeing Co* [1951] 1 KB 805.

53 *Olley v Marlborough Court* [1949] 1 KB 532.

are contained must be contractual in nature;[54] and (3) the terms must be reasonably brought to the other party's attention.[55] If these conditions are not met, the term in question will not be enforceable and will not bind the plaintiff.

Importantly, where a term to be incorporated is particularly unusual or onerous, the party seeking to enforce that term must provide *special notice*; that is, it must make it more conspicuous or noticeable. In *Interfoto Picture Library Ltd v Stiletto Visual Programmes Ltd*,[56] an onerous lending fee contained in a contract for the hire of photographic transparencies, which was significantly higher compared to other lending fees in the industry, was held to require special notice. Given that the term was very hard to spot in the contract and was not emphasised to the plaintiff in any way, it was found not to be enforceable. The High Court has confirmed that the special notice rule does not apply to signed written contracts given that this would effectively subvert the very policy underlying the signature rule and disregard the fact the signatory has had ample opportunity to absorb the terms.[57] The concept of notice in the context of signed written contracts only arises in situations where, as explained earlier, the contents of the document have been misrepresented, or it cannot reasonably be regarded as contractual in nature.

1.1.4.3 Express terms incorporated by course of dealings

It is also possible for terms to be incorporated into a contract by prior course of dealings. This can occur when parties transact with one another on numerous occasions, even where reasonable notice of the terms has not been provided. In *Balmain New Ferry Co Ltd v Robertson*,[58] a sign placed above the defendant's private ferry wharf stipulated that a fare of one penny was payable when entering or leaving the wharf through the turnstiles. The plaintiff paid his entry fare to the wharf but missed his ferry and so attempted to leave the wharf without paying another penny. He argued he was not aware of the contractual requirement (as stated on the wharf sign) to pay an exit fee, as reasonable notice of this requirement had not been provided. The High Court held that this was immaterial as the plaintiff had travelled on the defendant's ferries many times before and was well aware of the existence and purpose of the turnstiles and the terms upon which he had obtained admittance. The terms were therefore automatically implied into the contract between the parties.

1.1.4.4 Incorporation of terms in online contracts

Again, the advent of technology has challenged the traditional methods for incorporating terms into contracts. There are now three basic types of 'online contract', which are used countless times every day. The first type is *shrinkwrap contracts*, which are contracts formed by a party opening a package containing a product. The terms are generally stipulated on the packaging and indicate that the user's agreement is effected by opening the package. Controversially, there is a known practice among some commercial parties to place the terms of shrinkwrap

54 *Causer v Browne* [1952] VLR 1.

55 *Mendelssohn v Normand Ltd* [1970] 1 QB 177.

56 [1989] QB 433.

57 *Toll Pty Ltd v Alphapharm Pty Ltd* (2004) 219 CLR 165, 184. The High Court also noted that this would place third parties, into whose hands the signed document had come, in some difficulty.

58 (1906) 4 CLR 379.

contracts *inside* the packaging. This clearly conflicts with the notion of reasonable notice (discussed earlier). Some US cases have deemed that these contracts are still valid provided the purchaser nonetheless has the option of avoiding *using* the product and returning it.[59]

The second type is *clickwrap contracts*, which are contracts formed by clicking a button on a website (normally along the lines of 'I agree/accept') or typing a statement of acceptance before clicking another button to process. The Electronic Transactions Acts in each Australian jurisdiction appear to equate clicking such buttons with a traditional signature for the purpose of incorporating contractual terms.[60] Rares J in *eBay International AG v Creative Festival Entertainment Pty Ltd*[61] similarly regarded them as being synonymous. What is important is that such buttons are placed at the *end* of any lists of terms so that no issues as to timing or reasonable notice of terms arise.

The third type is *browsewrap contracts*. These, too, are formed by users clicking a consent button; however, these contracts typically provide hyperlinks to external documents or websites containing the terms of the agreement (rather than having the terms listed in full above the consent button). Again, placement is crucial and so these links must appear prior to the consent button. It is also important that users be made to signify perusal and acceptance of these terms before proceeding.[62]

As mentioned earlier, while express terms are expressly included by the parties, implied terms are implied into contracts by the courts or by operation of statute. There are three main types of implied term: (1) terms implied in fact; (2) terms implied in law; and (3) terms implied by custom.

1.1.4.5 Terms implied in fact

Terms implied *in fact* are those implied into specific contracts in a given case and formulated upon the presumed intentions of the parties. This is often described as ad hoc implication as it affects only the contract before the courts. To imply a term in fact into a formal written contract, one must satisfy each of the five limbs of the test established in *BP Refinery (Westernport) Pty Ltd v Shire of Hastings*, as Lord Simon explained:[63]

> [F]or a term to be implied, the following conditions (which may overlap) must be satisfied: (1) it must be reasonable and equitable; (2) it must be necessary to give business efficacy to the contract, so that no term will be implied if the contract is effective without it; (3) it must be so obvious that 'it goes without saying'; (4) it must be capable of clear expression; (5) it must not contradict any express term of the contract.

The test for implying terms in fact where there is no formal written contract (eg where it is oral or only partly written) is different. In that situation, it must be shown in the circumstances

59 See *ProCD Inc v Zeidenberg & Silken Mountain Web Services Ind*, 86 F 3d 1447 (1996).

60 To use one example, s 10 of the *Electronic Transactions Act 1999* (Cth) states that, where a law requires a person's signature, electronic signature will suffice provided an appropriately reliable method (in the circumstances) has been used both to identify the person and to indicate their intentions regarding the information communicated.

61 (2006) 170 FCR 450.

62 See *Specht v Netscape Communications Corporation*, 306 F 3d 17 (2d Cir 2002).

63 (1977) 180 CLR 266, 283.

that the implication of the particular term is necessary for the reasonable or effective operation of a contract of that nature.[64]

1.1.4.6 Terms implied in law

Terms implied *in law* are those implied into all contracts of a particular class or description. This can occur at common law or through the operation of statute. Many statutes imply terms automatically into certain types of contract, such as those for the sale and supply of goods and services.[65] In other cases, the courts may deem it appropriate to imply terms into particular categories of contract. They do so by first identifying the category (eg residential lease) and then evaluating whether there are good policy reasons for necessarily implying a particular term into all contracts falling within that category. The general view is that the term must be functionally justifiable and ensure that the rights conferred under the contract are not rendered nugatory.[66] Common examples include an implied warranty of seaworthiness (in the case of the sale of marine vessels) and an implied promise that a house constructed for a client will be reasonably fit for habitation. Even though such contracts may not expressly state the same, public policy would insist upon the inclusion of such terms and will therefore be implied *in law*.

1.1.4.7 Terms implied by custom

Terms implied *by custom* are those implied into contracts on the basis of specific industry or trade customs. Typically, these are terms that develop within particular industries and become so well known that they are effectively implied on this basis alone, even where these are not expressly mentioned in the contract.[67] In *Hutton v Warren*,[68] for example, the plaintiff was the tenant of an English farm and was required under his lease arrangement to manage, till, sow and cultivate the land. The lease was one year in duration and the landlord issued a notice to quit at its expiration. The plaintiff subsequently claimed a reasonable sum for seeds and labour expended in planting the field a short time prior to his departure. It was the custom in the English agriculture industry of the time for the landlord to make such a payment, but he refused. This custom was not reflected in the terms of the lease. The plaintiff nonetheless sued to recover damages. The court held that the term requiring the landlord to pay the reasonable sum on the plaintiff's departure was implied by virtue of the custom of the land. The custom was well known and widely practised in commercial farming arrangements, such that it applied.

1.1.5 Performance and termination

The term 'performance' in contract law refers to the process of the parties undertaking and (hopefully) fulfilling their obligations. When both parties do what they were required to do and

64 *Hawkins v Clayton* (1988) 164 CLR 539; *Byrne v Australian Airlines Ltd* (1995) 185 CLR 410.

65 See Chapters 4 and 15.

66 See, for example, *Byrne v Australian Airlines Ltd* (1995) 185 CLR 410; *Commonwealth Bank of Australia v Barker* (2014) 253 CLR 169.

67 *Con-Stan Industries of Australia Pty Ltd v Norwich Winterthur Insurance (Australia) Pty Ltd* (1986) 160 CLR 226.

68 (1836) 1 M & W 466.

the bargain is fulfilled, the contract naturally comes to an end. Performance, however, is one of several ways in which a contract may end. There are six other key methods: (1) agreement; (2) operation of a contract term; (3) operation of law; (4) frustration; (5) breach; and (6) repudiation.

1.1.5.1 Termination by agreement

A contract may be terminated through the agreement of the parties. The contract may allow for this to happen, or a right to terminate may be implied. The parties are also at liberty to terminate their contract by creating another to replace it. It is even possible for a contract to be regarded as abandoned where the circumstances imply that neither party intends to carry forward with the agreement.[69]

1.1.5.2 Termination by operation of contract term

Another way for a contract to be terminated is through the operation of a term within it. A contract may, for example, be conditional on the occurrence of a specified event, the non-occurrence of which will release the parties from any obligations. A common instance of this is a clause in a real estate contract requiring the prospective purchaser to obtain sufficient funds to meet the sale price. Failure to do so means the vendor is not obligated to sell. Alternatively, a contract may contain a condition subsequent, which releases the parties from their obligations on the occurrence of a specified event. For example, Hannah may engage Austin to clean her house once per week for as long as the house is owned by her. If Hannah were to then sell the property, the parties would no longer be able to continue with their contractual arrangement and it would therefore end.

1.1.5.3 Termination by operation of law

Contracts may be terminated by operation of law. The contract may be barred by statute (ie be illegal), for example, because it contravenes the law. A party may die or become permanently incapacitated or bankrupt, in which case their contract may, subject to some limited exceptions, end automatically.

1.1.5.4 Termination by frustration

The doctrine of frustration may also bring a contract to an end. This doctrine operates whenever a supervening event (which is not caused by either party) occurs and radically affects the parties' performance of their contractual obligations to the extent it cannot be capably performed as originally envisaged.[70] One of the most common situations of frustration is where the subject matter of the contract is destroyed, as in *Taylor v Caldwell* where the accidental incineration of a musical hall was said to frustrate a contract for its hire.[71]

69 *DTR Nominees Pty Ltd v Mona Homes Pty Ltd* (1978) 138 CLR 423.
70 *Codelfa Construction Pty Ltd v State Rail Authority of New South Wales* (1982) 149 CLR 337.
71 (1863) 3 B & S 826.

1.1.5.5 Termination for breach of contract

Perhaps one of the more common reasons for a contract being terminated is because it has been breached. Depending on the severity of the breach and the type of term that has been violated, the aggrieved party may then have the right to end the agreement. Any breach entitles the innocent party to claim damages from the breaching party. However, the right to terminate only arises in particular circumstances and requires the term that has been dishonoured to first be classified as either a condition, intermediate term or warranty. Commercial parties often describe *all* of the terms of a contract as 'conditions' or 'terms and conditions', particularly when standard form contracts (contracts that are pre-prepared, non-negotiable and offered on a 'take it or leave it' basis) are used. As such, while influential, stipulation by the parties will not necessarily be conclusive.

Breach of a *condition* entitles the aggrieved party to terminate the contract. A condition is an essential term that is vital to the agreement and is of objectively critical importance. The test for an essential term is known commonly as the 'essentiality test' and derives from *Tramways Advertising Pty Ltd v Luna Park (NSW) Ltd*:[72]

> The test of essentiality is whether it appears from the general nature of the contract considered as a whole, or from some particular term or terms, that the promise is of such importance to the promisee that he would not have entered into the contract unless he had been assured of a strict or substantial performance of the promise . . . and this ought to have been apparent to the promisor.

The courts will also examine the language used, the nature and consequences of the breach, and the adequacy of damages when applying the essentiality test. An aggrieved party is entitled to terminate the contract and claim damages if a condition is breached.

A term may also be a *warranty*, which lies at the other end of the scale of contractual importance. A warranty is a minor or inessential term, the breach of which has minimal (if any) tangible consequences and still largely allows the contract to be performed as originally contemplated by the parties. Again, the courts will examine all the facts and circumstances to determine if a term is insignificant enough to be classified as a warranty. Breach of a warranty entitles the aggrieved party to seek damages only; no right to terminate arises.[73] As such, parties should be wary of prematurely seeking to terminate an agreement where they may not actually be entitled to do so!

Finally, a term may be less significant than a condition but more significant than a warranty, in which case it is an *intermediate term*. A major or fundamental breach of an intermediate term allows the aggrieved party to terminate the contract and claim damages, as with conditions. Conversely, a minor breach of an intermediate term only entitles the aggrieved party to claim damages, as with warranties. A major breach has been judicially described as one that is serious, grave and goes to the heart of the contract, and which substantially deprives the innocent party of the benefits of the agreement.[74]

---

72 (1938) 38 SR (NSW) 632, 641–2. See also *Associated Newspapers Ltd v Bancks* (1951) 83 CLR 322; *DTR Nominees Pty Ltd v Mona Homes Pty Ltd* (1978) 138 CLR 423.

73 *Bettini v Gye* (1876) 1 QBD 183.

74 *Hong Kong Fir Shipping Co Ltd v Kawasaki Kisen Kaisha Ltd* [1962] 2 QB 26; *Koompahtoo Local Aboriginal Land Council v Sanpine Pty Ltd* (2007) 241 ALR 88.

1.1.5.6 Termination by repudiation

One final manner in which contracts may be terminated is via *repudiation*. Repudiation essentially describes a party's unwillingness or inability to perform contractual obligations.[75] If, for example, a party makes clear by word or conduct that they do not wish to continue the contract, or that they will be unable to do so, this may amount to repudiation and allow the aggrieved party to terminate.

1.1.6 Remedies

There are a number of remedies available to contract parties in the event of a contract coming to an end (or being likely to do so). Generally speaking, there are two main categories of remedy: common law and equitable remedies.

1.1.6.1 Damages

The most basic common law remedy is *damages* (monetary compensation). The purpose of common law damages is to place the innocent party, as close as possible, into the position they would have been in had the contract been correctly performed. This is known as the principle in *Robinson v Harman*.[76] Damages are not designed to allow plaintiffs to profit, but rather to ensure that their losses are offset. The plaintiff must prove that the defendant's conduct caused their loss; that is, they must establish that the loss would not have occurred 'but for' the defendant's conduct, having due regard to notions of practical common sense.[77]

Any damages claimed must satisfy the test of remoteness; that is, the loss suffered must not have been too remote or so far beyond the realm of practical foresight that it would be unfair to attribute fault to the defendant. Losses must be reasonably foreseeable; they must either arise naturally in the ordinary course of events following the breach, or have been in the contemplation of the parties at the time the contract was made. These are the two 'limbs' of *Hadley v Baxendale*.[78] Baron Alderman in that case stated:

> Where two parties have made a contract which one of them has broken, the damages which the other party ought to receive in respect of such breach of contract should be such as may fairly and reasonably be considered either arising naturally, that is, according to the usual course of things, from such breach of contract itself, or such as may reasonably be supposed to have been in the contemplation of both parties, at the time they made the contract, as the probable result of the breach.[79]

Where the innocent party suffers no actual loss from their counterpart's breach, they will be entitled only to nominal damages: a token sum awarded in recognition of a breach occurring.[80] The innocent party need only establish that a breach has occurred. In all other cases, the

75 *Shevill v Builders Licensing Board* (1982) 149 CLR 620.
76 (1848) 1 Exch 850; *Addis v Gramophone Co Ltd* [1909] AC 488.
77 *Alexander v Cambridge Credit Corporation Ltd* (1987) 9 NSWLR 310.
78 (1854) 9 Exch 341.
79 (1854) 9 Exch 341, 354–5.
80 *Commonwealth v Amann Aviation Pty Ltd* (1991) 174 CLR 64, 118.

normal rules as to causation and remoteness apply to any damages claimed by the innocent party.

Other common law remedies include the action for debt, which is an action against a defendant to recover a specific sum of money (a debt) owed; and rescission, which is a right to set aside a contract.

1.1.6.2 Equitable remedies

There are also many *equitable remedies* that might be available to an aggrieved party. For example, *rectification* allows the courts to amend an error in an agreement where the parties have made a mistake. Alternatively, a *specific performance* order compels a party to execute a contractual obligation. These orders are rare and are only given at the court's discretion upon considering various factors such as the adequacy of damages and the utility of enforcement. An *injunction* is essentially the opposite of a specific performance order and prohibits a party from performing a specified action. Injunctions are normally granted to prevent the breach of a contract term.

Restitution is another remedy that is designed to prevent a defendant being unjustly enriched by their defaults. That is, restitution seeks to reverse any gains the defendant has made where it would be unfair for them to retain such gains. As an example, where a party pays another party for a product that turns out to be defective, the law of restitution recognises the unfairness in the vendor being allowed to retain the money paid for the product. Similarly, where a deposit is paid and the product or service is not delivered as promised, the deposit can generally be recovered.

1.2 Commercial regulators

This part of the chapter introduces nine of the key regulators in the Australian commercial landscape. Each of these institutions plays an important role in regulating various aspects of commercial transactions, from the establishment and governance of companies through to the use of the internet and intellectual property, regulation of financial dealings, regulation of competition, consumer protection and more. It is an absolute certainty that you will encounter one or more of these institutions in your working life and so we turn now to briefly discussing each of them.

1.2.1 Australian Competition and Consumer Commission

The Australian Competition and Consumer Commission (ACCC) is the principal statutory regulator of the Australian Consumer Law (ACL). The Commission emerged in 1995 following the merger between the former Trade Practices Commission and the Prices Surveillance Authority and is an independent Commonwealth statutory authority. It promotes competition and fair trade in markets for the benefit of consumers, businesses and the wider community. The Commission bears responsibility for regulating national infrastructure services. Its primary responsibility is 'to ensure that individuals and businesses comply with Australian competition, fair trading, and consumer protection laws – in particular the *Competition and Consumer Act 2010*'.[81]

81 See https://www.accc.gov.au/about-us.

Given the breadth of the ACL and its application across all manner of commercial practices, the ACCC is one of the most significant regulators that you will encounter in any examination of Australian commercial law. The Commission polices various illegitimate business behaviours under the ACL, including misleading or deceptive conduct, unconscionable conduct (including unfairly coercing parties into entering a contract through exploitation), and enforcement of unfair contract terms in standard form consumer and small business contracts. It further enforces provisions pertaining to such things as product safety and liability, consumer guarantees, and pricing and selling practices. The Commission also seeks to prevent anti-competitive mergers and acquisitions, and regulates mandatory industry codes prescribed under the *Competition and Consumer Act 2010* (Cth).

1.2.2 Australian Securities and Investments Commission

The Australian Securities and Investments Commission (ASIC) is 'Australia's integrated corporate, markets, financial services and consumer credit regulator'.[82] It is an independent Commonwealth statutory authority established under, and responsible for administering, the *Australian Securities and Investments Commission Act 2001* (Cth). The Commission performs the majority of its functions under the *Corporations Act 2001* (Cth), regulating 'Australian companies, financial markets, financial services organisations and professionals who deal and advise in investments, superannuation, insurance, deposit taking and credit'.[83] ASIC strives to ensure that companies and financial markets operate fairly and with integrity and, through its regulation of the financial system, fosters consumer and investor confidence.

ASIC is vested with a number of important and far-reaching powers. It can, for example, register companies and managed investment schemes, grant financial service and credit licences, issue infringement notices, register auditors and liquidators, prohibit persons from providing financial services or engaging in credit activities, maintain publicly accessible registers of information regarding companies and licensees, and even commence some prosecutions. Given that the ACL does not apply to the actual or possible supply of financial services or products,[84] and that a number of provisions within the *Australian Securities and Investments Commission Act 2001* (Cth) do, ASIC plays a central role in regulating the countless number of financial transactions that occur every day in the commercial marketplace. As such, by way of example, complaints of unconscionable conduct relating to a contract of insurance, being a contract for a financial service, would fall within the purview of ASIC,[85] whereas the same complaint relating instead to a contract for a non-financial service (such as motor vehicle repair) would be investigated by the ACCC.[86]

82 See http://asic.gov.au/about-asic/what-we-do/our-role/.
83 See http://asic.gov.au/about-asic/what-we-do/our-role/.
84 *Competition and Consumer Act 2010* (Cth), s 131A.
85 See ss 12CA–12CC of the *Australian Securities and Investments Commission Act 2001* (Cth).
86 See ss 20–21 of the ACL.

1.2.3 Australian Prudential Regulation Authority

Established in 1998 under the *Australian Prudential Regulation Authority Act 1998* (Cth), the Australian Prudential Regulation Authority (APRA) is the principal regulator of the Australian financial services industry. The Authority 'oversees banks, credit unions, building societies, general insurance and reinsurance companies, life insurance, private health insurance, friendly societies, and most of the superannuation industry'.[87] Interestingly, APRA is largely funded by levies paid by the many industries that it supervises and holds several trillion dollars worth of assets on behalf of Australian depositors, policyholders and superannuation fund members.

APRA is concerned with promoting the stability, efficiency and competitiveness of the national financial system by ensuring that institutions such as banks, credit unions, superannuation funds and others are capable of fulfilling their various financial commitments. It performs its regulatory functions in conjunction with ASIC and the Reserve Bank of Australia.[88] APRA simultaneously acts as the national statistical agency for Australia's financial sector.

Along with the *Australian Prudential Regulation Authority Act 1998* (Cth), APRA draws its supervisory powers from various statutes, including the *Banking Act 1959* (Cth), the *Insurance Act 1973* (Cth), the *Life Insurance Act 1995* (Cth) and the *Superannuation Industry (Supervision) Act 1993* (Cth).

1.2.4 Australian Taxation Office

The Australian Taxation Office (ATO) is the Australian government's principal revenue collection agency. Its role is to 'manage and shape the tax, excise and superannuation systems that fund services for Australians'.[89] It accomplishes this role by collecting revenue, conducting random audits to verify individual and company assessments, administering the goods and services tax (GST) on behalf of all Australian states and territories, administering key aspects of the national superannuation system, and more. The ATO is led by the Commissioner for Taxation and operates within the Federal Treasury portfolio under the *Public Governance, Performance and Accountability Act 2013* (Cth). It is accountable under the *Public Service Act 1999* (Cth). Although there are many statutes at Commonwealth level imposing and regulating one area of tax,[90] the two principal forms of tax with which the ATO is concerned are income tax (payable by individuals and companies) and the GST. Acts relevant to the former include the *Income Tax Assessment Act 1936* (Cth), the *Income Tax Assessment Act 1997* (Cth) and the *Fringe Benefits Tax Assessment Act 1986* (Cth), whereas the GST is administered through the *A New Tax System (Goods and Services Tax) Act 1999* (Cth).

The ATO performs a number of important ancillary functions. It administers the Higher Education Loan Program (HELP), as well as the private health insurance rebate contributed by the government towards the cost of private hospital health insurance premiums. The Office also collects excises on tobacco, alcohol and fuel.

87 See https://www.apra.gov.au/about-apra.
88 Together, the Treasury, APRA, ASIC and the RBA comprise the Council of Financial Regulators.
89 https://www.ato.gov.au/about-ato/who-we-are.
90 There are also many statutes that operate at state and territory level which concern different types of tax and reflect the power-sharing arrangement within the Commonwealth Constitution. Taxes collected at state and territory level include payroll tax, land tax and stamp duty.

1.2.5 Foreign Investment Review Board

The Foreign Investment Review Board (FIRB) was established in 1976. It is a non-statutory body created exclusively to advise the Treasurer and federal government on Australia's foreign investment policy (FIP). While ultimate decision-making responsibility vests with the Treasurer, the FIRB provides critical advice as to the administration of the FIP and related issues. The Board of the FIRB performs a number of functions as part of its advisory role, such as examining and making recommendations with respect to proposed investments in Australia subject to the FIP and the *Foreign Acquisitions and Takeovers Act 1975* (Cth) (FATA), providing support and information to prospective foreign investors as to the FIP and the FATA, and monitoring and ensuring effective operation of and compliance with the FIP and the FATA.

1.2.6 Australian Securities Exchange Ltd

Australian Securities Exchange Ltd is actually the name of the public company that owns the Australian Securities Exchange (ASX), Australia's primary securities exchange.[91] The ASX was founded on 1 April 1987 following the passage of federal legislation facilitating the amalgamation of six independent state-based stock exchanges. The ASX is one of the world's leading financial market exchanges, boasting a total market capitalisation[92] of around $1.5 trillion and offering a range of services from listings and trading to clearing and settlement.

The ASX is essentially self-regulated, enforcing internal 'ASX Listing Rules' which apply to listed entities and their associates under the *Corporations Act 2001* (Cth). This enforcement occurs through ASX's subsidiary company, ASX Compliance. ASIC also plays a role in supervising real-time trading on the nation's licensed financial markets, while the Reserve Bank of Australia oversees ASX's clearing and settlement facilities. In August 2002, the ASX convened the ASX Corporate Governance Council, which draws together a range of industry, business and shareholder groups to obtain advice and recommendations as to governance issues and practices.

1.2.7 Reserve Bank of Australia

Following the passage of the *Reserve Bank Act 1959* (Cth), the Reserve Bank of Australia (RBA) became Australia's independent central bank, assuming the role from the Commonwealth Bank of Australia. The RBA derives its powers and central functions from the *Reserve Bank Act 1959* (Cth) and describes its duty as being 'to contribute to the stability of the currency, full employment, and the economic prosperity and welfare of the Australian people'.[93] The RBA issues Australia's banknotes, sets the cash rate to meet agreed economic inflation targets (over the medium term), and works to maintain a strong financial system and an efficient payments system. It also manages Australia's gold and foreign exchange reserves and provides a variety

91 An exchange, of course, being an organised market where tradable commodities, futures, securities, options contracts and foreign exchange currencies are bought and sold.

92 The term 'market capitalisation' refers to the market value of a company's outstanding shares. It is typically a highly influential factor in stock valuation.

93 See https://www.rba.gov.au/about-rba/.

of banking and registry services to the federal government, its agencies, and certain overseas central banks and institutions.

The RBA consists of two boards: the Reserve Bank Board, responsible for monetary policy and financial stability, and the Payments System Board, responsible for matters relating to payments system policy. The bank is managed by the Governor, who is vested with numerous responsibilities pertaining to the RBA's management pursuant to the *Public Governance, Performance and Accountability Act 2013* (Cth). The RBA is an integral cog in the nation's commercial machinery.

1.2.8 IP Australia

IP Australia is the Commonwealth government agency responsible for administering Australia's intellectual property (IP) rights and legislation relating to patents, trademarks, designs and plant breeder's rights. IP Australia falls within the Department of Industry, Innovation and Science, though it operates independently of the Department on some financial and other matters. It is a listed entity under the *Public Governance, Performance and Accountability Act 2013* (Cth). Originally known as the Australian Industrial Property Office, IP Australia was established in 1992 and amalgamated the previously separate Patents, Designs and Trade Marks offices.[94]

IP Australia administers a number of statutes relevant to IP, including the *Designs Act 2003* (Cth), the *Patents Act 1990* (Cth), the *Trade Marks Act 1995* (Cth), the *Plant Breeder's Rights Act 1994* (Cth), and the *Olympic Insignia Protection Act 1987* (Cth). Together with granting exclusive rights under these Acts, the agency is also responsible for advising the federal government on IP policy, regulating the IP profession, providing advice and educational services to the business community as to IP laws and regulations, and working with the World Intellectual Property Organization to develop multilateral treaties and to strengthen global IP rights systems.

You are going to encounter IP Australia whenever you need to protect a form of IP. The agency not only administers the system for registration of interests in intellectual property, but also maintains the registers of existing designs, patents and trademarks against which new applications are assessed. Australian copyright law operates a little differently and primarily governs rights as to reproduction of subject matter such as literary, dramatic, musical and artistic works. Generally speaking, copyright protection arises automatically upon the reduction of information to 'material form'; there is no formal registration process and so no registers of copyrighted material are kept. User rights are determined by the provisions of the *Copyright Act 1968* (Cth).

1.2.9 .au Domain Administration

.au Domain Administration Ltd (auDA) is an independent, not-for-profit industry body responsible for administering Australia's top-level domain (.au)[95] on behalf of Australian internet users. Since receiving Australian government endorsement in 2000, it has remained the nation's

94 IP Australia's historical precursor was the Australian Patent Office, established in 1904. In the years that followed, the Office also assumed responsibility for trademark and design registrations.

95 '.au' is the suffix representing Australia's country code domain on the internet. It appears at the end of Australian websites when typed into an address bar.

key administrator and regulator, developing and implementing various policies pertaining to domain names and performing other critical functions such as managing and maintaining a secure and stable Domain Name System (DNS), licensing Second-Level Domain (2LD)[96] registry operators, implementing consumer protections, and representing Australia at Internet Corporation for Assigned Names and Numbers (ICANN) conventions.

Another of auDA's roles is to resolve disputes concerning .au domain names and .au registrars and resellers. Complaints about domain names will typically centre upon ineligible registrations or holdings, whereas complaints about industry registrars and resellers normally relate to breaches of the *.au Domain Name Supplier Code of Practice*. Complaints can be raised via the auDA website at https://www.auda.org.au/.

The auDA has a vital role in Australian commerce. Given the volume of commercial activity that now occurs via the internet, it is essential for Australian websites to be properly registered and administered to ensure that transactions occur safely and via authorised channels. It is also important that domain names remain unique to individual businesses so that there is no confusion or illegitimate competition within the digital landscape. Particularly when starting up a business, and developing its online presence, you are very likely to encounter the auDA.

1.3 Key points

- There are four principal elements to a contract: (1) offer and acceptance (agreement); (2) consideration; (3) intention to create legal relations; and (4) certainty and completeness of terms. The contract must also be for a legal purpose, and the parties must have legal capacity.
- Express terms are those included in a contract by the parties. Implied terms are those implied into the contract by the courts.
- There are three basic types of term: conditions (which are critically essential); warranties (which are non-essential); and intermediate terms (which are less significant than conditions but more significant than warranties). A party's remedial rights depend upon the type of term breached and the severity of the breach.
- Contracts can be terminated in a number of ways, including through performance or operation of a contract term, by agreement or operation of law, by frustration, by breach, or through repudiation.
- An aggrieved party may seek common law and equitable remedies depending upon the type of wrong they have suffered.
- A variety of regulators play different roles in Australian commerce, from the establishment and governance of companies through to the use of the internet and intellectual property, regulation of financial dealings, regulation of competition, consumer protection and more.

96 2LDs are domains that sit above (left of) the Top-Level Domain (TLD) in a domain name. To provide some examples, the available Australian 2LDs are asn.au, com.au, id.au, net.au and org.au. The type of 2LD selected typically indicates the nature of the individual or organisation that owns them. To demonstrate, com.au domains are common to commercial entities registered and trading in Australia, whereas org.au domains are common to non-commercial organisations incorporated under state and territory legislation, such as charities and sporting clubs.

- Each of the commercial regulators in Australia has, whether directly or indirectly, some involvement with contracts. For example, the ACCC can *directly* enforce the Unfair Contract Terms provisions contained within the Australian Consumer Law and bring an action against any party seeking to enforce unfair terms in standard form consumer or small business contracts. In contrast, while the ATO does not directly concern itself with contracts between commercial parties, when such contracts involve the exchange or accumulation of monetary consideration, the ATO will ensure that the taxes applicable to the same (and to the transaction generally) are paid by the parties. It therefore has an *indirect* involvement in commercial contracts.

1.4 DISCUSSION QUESTIONS

1. What is the legal difference between a gift or social arrangement and a contract, and why does the law of contract draw this distinction?
2. When will the courts imply a term 'in fact' into a contract? Does this legal test impose a difficult threshold for commercial parties to satisfy?
3. In what circumstances will a party be entitled to terminate a contract for the other party's breach?
4. What is the fundamental purpose underlying the award of damages in contract law?
5. What is the role and function of: (1) the ACCC; (2) ASIC; and (3) APRA?

1.5 FURTHER READING

Miles, C and Dowler, W, *A Guide to Business Law* (Thomson Reuters Australia, 21st edn, 2015), Chapter 8.

2

BUSINESS STRUCTURES

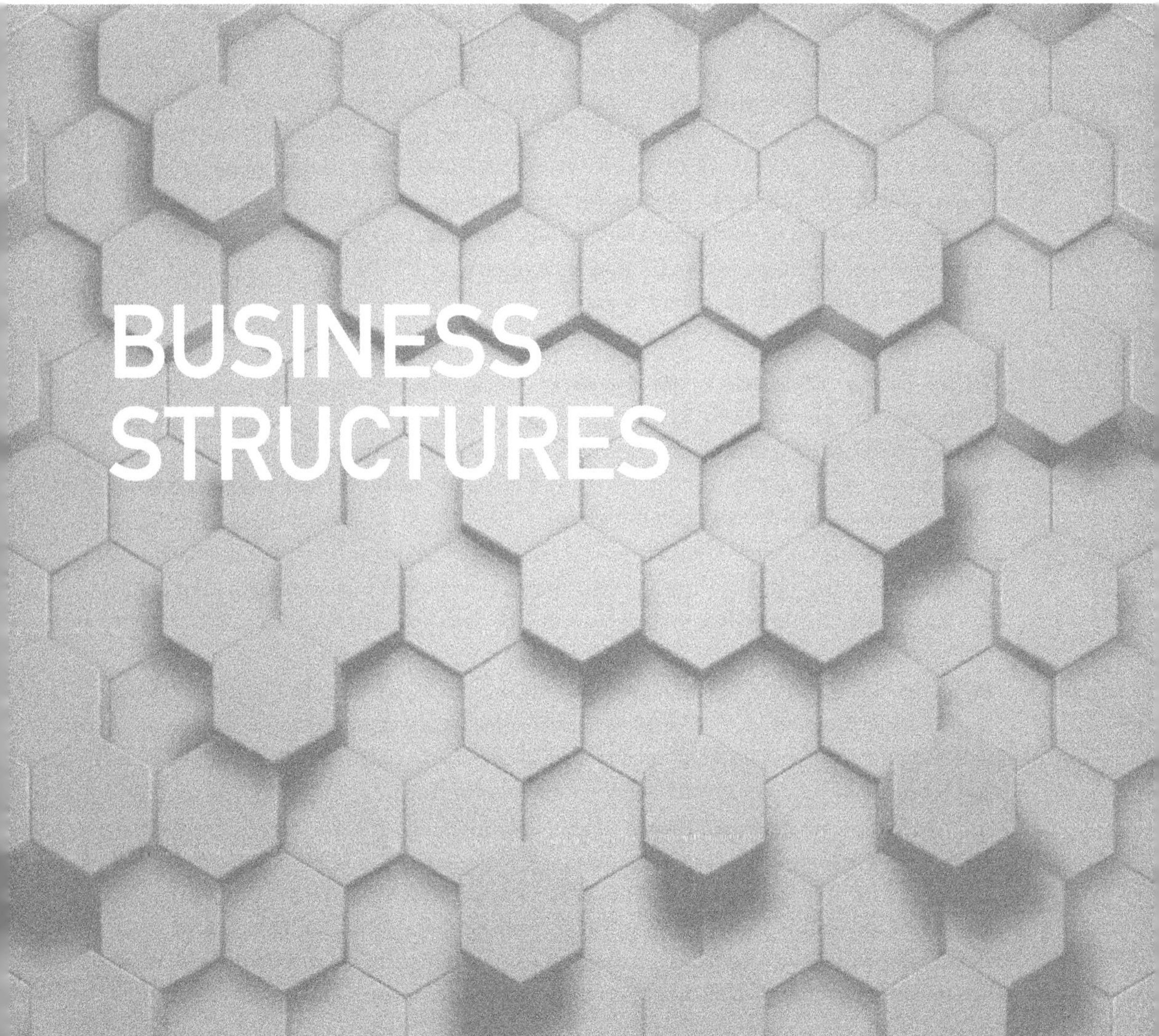

2.0 Introduction

This chapter identifies and discusses the wide variety of business structures commonly found in the commercial landscape. All organisations that supply or acquire goods or services, whether for profit or not, must choose an appropriate business structure to ensure their longevity and successful operation. That choice will be influenced by a number of factors, such as the scope and nature of the organisation's operations, its size, the risks and costs associated with its enterprises, and tax implications. The choice may even change in time as the organisation grows and its needs and challenges alter. The principal forms of business structure are discussed in turn to provide a basis for understanding how each operates in practice.

2.1 Determining an appropriate structure

The choice of structure for a new business is critical. An incorrect choice could result in unintended and potentially damaging financial and logistical consequences. In some cases, the choice will be obvious, as in the case of a sole trader working entirely for themselves. In other cases, where multiple parties are involved, it will be necessary to work out the best way to structure a legal and commercial relationship between them – for example, as a partnership, joint venture, corporation or something else. Broadly speaking, the various structures differ on four fronts: (1) how they are formed; (2) how they operate or can be dissolved; (3) how they are taxed; and (4) the liability attaching to each.

Some of the main factors that will affect choice of business structure include the following:

- ***The purpose or objectives of the business***. Organisations founded for benevolent or community purposes will likely have low start-up capital (also known as 'seed money') and invariably will not be operating for profit. As such, an (un)incorporated association structure might be more suitable compared to, say, a company structure, which generally suits larger commercial entities operating for profit.
- ***Size***. Smaller-scale businesses involving either an individual or a small group of individuals will likely attract less risk than larger-scale commercial ventures. Businesses involved in the latter might elect a partnership, joint ventureship or corporate structure to provide greater legal protection.
- ***Duration***. Some commercial arrangements might involve parties or businesses working together for a common goal. Where such arrangements are designed to be long-term, a partnership or corporate structure might be ideal. Alternatively, where the arrangement is short-term, a joint venture scheme may be more appropriate.
- ***Asset holdings and acquisitions***. Choice of business structure may impact upon existing asset holdings or planned acquisitions. For example, a sole trader's assets are unprotected from claims against that trader's business, whereas a company is a separate legal entity and attains and holds assets in its own right, insulating the assets of workers in the company. Joint ventures often involve the combining of resources, but each co-venturer retains full ownership of and responsibility for its own assets.

- ***Liability***. Some business structures differ vastly in terms of the liability that each attracts. Sole traders and partners, for example, have unlimited liability. (In the case of partnerships, the liability is joint and several.) Trustees, on the other hand, can normally be indemnified out of trust assets, while corporations are separate legal entities and the shareholders enjoy the benefit of limited liability.
- ***Taxation***. Different business structures attract different types and rates of tax. For example, where companies pay their own tax on their earnings at the flat corporate tax rate, sole traders pay tax on their individual income at the respective marginal tax rate.

The laws that apply to each type of business structure also differ, significantly in some instances. These laws are found in a number of sources, including the common law and in general and specific pieces of legislation. Each of these will be considered in greater detail shortly when each business structure is considered in isolation.

2.2 Types of business structure

The principal forms of business structure are discussed individually in this section, with consideration given to the advantages and disadvantages of each.

2.2.1 Sole trader

A sole trader (or 'sole proprietor') is a natural person who owns and operates their own business. It is the simplest and most common form of business structure. Given that a sole trader operates entirely in their individual capacity, they have unlimited personal liability and all personal assets are subject to claims made by creditors. Such liability might be mitigated through taking out appropriate insurance and exercising due care. Importantly, any profits made also belong directly to the sole trader. Of course, sole traders may, and often do, employ people to assist them or engage independent contractors to do the same. Where a sole trader employs staff, they must be sure to make appropriate tax, superannuation and workers compensation arrangements.

There are minimal legal formalities associated with establishing an individual business. Generally speaking, if a sole trader wishes to trade under a name different from their own (first and last name), they will have to apply to register a business name on the Business Name Register with the Australian Securities and Investments Commission (ASIC). Registration attracts a small fee and must be renewed every one to three years depending on how long the sole trader has registered the name for. A sole trader will also likely have to apply for an Australian Business Number (ABN) and register for goods and services tax (GST).[1] For particular professions such as the law, additional requirements, including appropriate qualifications and mandatory insurance, may also need to be satisfied.

1 It is mandatory to register for GST if: (1) you run a business or other enterprise and your annual GST turnover is $75 000 or more (the threshold is $150 000 for non-profit organisations); or (2) you are a taxi or limousine driver, irrespective of turnover. If you run a business or other enterprise with an annual turnover of less than $75 000, GST registration is optional.

The taxation implications for sole traders are unique. As the business is operated entirely by the sole trader, the business takings are the trader's own income. Consequently, the sole trader will pay income tax on these takings at the relevant individual marginal tax rate,[2] rather than the company rate for 'base rate entities' of 27.5 per cent.[3] It is most likely, therefore, that this business structure will be more beneficial for those sole traders operating on lower incomes as they will pay less tax.

A sole trader can operate for as long as they wish. As such, upon retirement or death, and provided all debts have been settled, the business comes to an end. If, however, a successor or subsequent purchaser wishes to carry the business on, they will likely need to apply to ASIC to transfer the business name and ABN to themselves.

The main advantages of carrying on business as a sole trader are that it is relatively simple and inexpensive to establish this structure, and the sole trader has total control and autonomy over the business. They also retain all profits and will typically pay less tax. The main disadvantages of a sole proprietorship are that the trader has unlimited personal liability for the business's debts and this structure normally involves an isolated working environment. Sole traders also have far greater difficulty accessing finance and, particularly when working individually, may suffer losses if they are injured or sick and incapable of working at any given time.

2.2.2 Partnership

'Partnership' describes the relationship subsisting between persons carrying on a business in common with a view to profit. Give or take some minor nuances in language, this is the definition found in each of the Partnership Acts of the states and territories.[4] Although there are similarities with companies incorporated under the *Corporations Act 2001* (Cth), and despite the limited liability company structure often being utilised in lieu of a partnership, partnerships are unique and are still commonly used in many different commercial settings and professions. Unlike companies, partnerships are not separate legal entities; they represent instead a legal relationship between the partners themselves. In partnerships, the partners own and manage the business concurrently. As such, liability is both *joint* and *several*: joint in that the parties are jointly responsible for the debts and obligations of the partnership, and several in that each partner is also individually liable for the same. If, for example, a partnership's assets are insufficient to meet a claim from a creditor, the personal assets of the individual partners are at risk.

2 The individual income tax rates for 2019/20 can be found at https://www.ato.gov.au/Rates/Individual-income-tax-rates/.

3 The company tax rates for 2019/20 can be found at https://www.ato.gov.au/Rates/Company-tax/. A base rate entity is a company that meets both of these conditions: (1) it has an aggregated turnover less than the aggregated turnover threshold ($50 million from the 2018/19 income year to 2021/22); and (2) 80 per cent or less of its assessable income is 'base rate entity passive income'. Base rate entity passive income includes sources such as corporate distributions, royalties, net capital gains and most interest income. See Australian Taxation Office, *Law Companion Ruling* 2018/D7. The company tax rate for base rate entities will reduce to 26 per cent from the 2020/21 financial year and to 25 per cent from 2021/22.

4 *Partnership Act 1963* (ACT), s 6; *Partnership Act 1892* (NSW), s 1; *Partnership Act 1997* (NT), s 5; *Partnership Act 1891* (Qld), s 5; *Partnership Act 1891* (SA), s 1; *Partnership Act 1891* (Tas), s 6; *Partnership Act 1958* (Vic), s 5; *Partnership Act 1895* (WA), s 7.

Strictly speaking, there are no formalities required to establish a partnership. Instead, one will arise and exist automatically where the requisite elements (drawn from the respective Partnership Acts in each jurisdiction) are present: (1) two or more people are carrying on a business; (2) the business is being carried on 'in common'; and (3) the business is being carried on with a view to making a profit. As such, partnerships can be formed orally or even without the express knowledge of the parties where they happen to be conducting business as a partnership. In this regard, the Partnership Acts provide rules for determining whether a partnership exists.[5] That being said, partnerships are typically brought about or at least formalised through a written partnership agreement,[6] which stipulates how the partnership will operate and outlines the rights and obligations of the partners. In the absence of such an agreement or relevant provisions, the Partnership Acts provide default rules that apply between the partners.[7]

Although most businesses structured as partnerships will be involved in numerous transactions, it is conceivable for a partnership to be formulated in order to execute a single transaction.[8] The requirement that business be 'carried on' is therefore easily satisfied in most situations. Difficulties may arise, however, where supposed 'partners' perform only peripheral or preparatory work, rather than actual business as partners.[9] A business is carried on 'in common' where the partners act together in the business enterprise, rather than as individuals. There must be mutuality between the rights and obligations of the partners. Factors that might be relevant to this assessment include whether the alleged 'partner' has contributed to establishment and ongoing administration costs, actively involved themselves in the business, or factored the venture into taxation assessment.[10] Again, as mentioned earlier, the Partnership Acts provide detailed criteria for determining whether there is a mutual partnership arrangement. The requirement that a partnership be carried on 'with a view to profit' serves to exclude common religious, community or sporting enterprises, which generally do not operate for profit but rather reinvest any profits in their principal venture(s). Partners will typically share profits equally or otherwise in proportions stipulated within the partnership agreement.

Given that partnerships are not separate legal entities, but rather unions of partners working in business together for profit, tax is payable by each partner upon the proportion of the partnership's profits they have received. While the partnership itself will not be liable to pay tax, it must still lodge an annual income tax return indicating annual turnover and how the

5 *Partnership Act 1963* (ACT), s 7; *Partnership Act 1892* (NSW), s 2; *Partnership Act 1997* (NT), s 6; *Partnership Act 1891* (Qld), s 6; *Partnership Act 1891* (SA), s 2; *Partnership Act 1891* (Tas), s 7; *Partnership Act 1958* (Vic), s 6; *Partnership Act 1895* (WA), s 8.

6 Also commonly referred to as a 'partnership contract' or 'partnership deed'.

7 *Partnership Act 1963* (ACT), s 29; *Partnership Act 1892* (NSW), s 24; *Partnership Act 1997* (NT), s 28; *Partnership Act 1891* (Qld), s 27; *Partnership Act 1891* (SA), s 24; *Partnership Act 1891* (Tas), s 29; *Partnership Act 1958* (Vic), s 28; *Partnership Act 1895* (WA), s 34.

8 As in *United Dominions Corporation Ltd v Brian Pty Ltd* (1985) 157 CLR 1, where the parties contracted to construct a shopping centre and were found to be in partnership despite the project constituting a single transaction and involving no elements of continuity or repetition. Indeed, the Partnership Acts now make provision for this possibility (see, eg, s 32(b) of the *Partnership Act 1891* (SA), which foreshadows a partnership being entered into 'for a single adventure or undertaking').

9 See *Goudberg v Herniman Associates Pty Ltd* [2007] VSCA 12; *Matthews v Australian Securities and Investments Commission* [2009] NSWCA 155.

10 See *Degiorgio v Dunn* [2004] NSWSC 767.

income is to be shared between the partners. Each partner must then file an individual tax return and pay tax at the relevant individual marginal tax rate.

Broadly speaking, ordinary partnerships may consist of a maximum of 20 partners. This restriction is imposed by s 115(1) of the *Corporations Act 2001* (Cth). However, s 115(2) provides that the regulations may specify a higher number in the case of particular kinds of partnership or organisation. Those kinds, and the respective numbers of partners that may be permitted, are stipulated in reg 2A.1.01(1) of the *Corporations Regulations 2001* (Cth) as listed in Table 2.1.

Table 2.1 Partner numbers for different kinds of partnership or association

Kind of partnership or association	Maximum number of partners
Actuaries, medical practitioners, patent attorneys, sharebrokers, stockbrokers or trademark attorneys; Partnerships or associations of the kind specified in sub-reg (2)	50
Architects, pharmaceutical chemists or veterinary surgeons	100
Legal practitioners	400
Accountants	1000

The partnerships or associations mentioned in sub-reg (2) are those whose primary purpose is collaborative scientific research and including at least one university and one private-sector participant.

Partnerships are often called 'firms' and operate under a business name. As in the case of sole traders, where the partnership is not operating under the names of the partners, a business name must be registered with ASIC. The partnership may bring in or purchase property in its own name. That property must be used exclusively for the purposes of the partnership and in accordance with the terms of the partnership agreement.[11]

The legal relationship between partners is both contractual and *fiduciary* in nature, meaning that partners must act honestly, reasonably, and with the utmost good faith towards one another.[12] They must place the firm's interests ahead of their own personal and business interests. This obligation arises in equity and at common law, but is reflected in many of the provisions of the Partnership Acts, particularly those requiring partners to account for all benefits or profits derived from transactions without the partnership's consent, and to avoid competing with the partnership.

Each partner is an agent of the firm and can enter into commercial dealings on the firm's behalf. As mentioned, liability is joint and several, and so it is imperative that partners are chosen with care to ensure that they act diligently and prudently without exposing their fellow partners to risk.

11 *Partnership Act 1963* (ACT), s 24; *Partnership Act 1892* (NSW), s 20; *Partnership Act 1997* (NT), s 24; *Partnership Act 1891* (Qld), s 23; *Partnership Act 1891* (SA), s 20; *Partnership Act 1891* (Tas), s 25; *Partnership Act 1958* (Vic), s 24; *Partnership Act 1895* (WA), s 30.

12 *Hospital Products Ltd v United States Surgical Corporation* (1984) 156 CLR 41; *Birtchnell v Equity Trustees Executors & Agency Co Ltd* (1929) 42 CLR 384.

Partners can naturally *retire* and leave a partnership. This is usually accomplished through the provision of written notice to the other partners. The retiring partner will still be liable for obligations and debts incurred while they were an active partner, subject to discharge by the remaining (and any new) partners and creditors. Normally, these obligations and debts are settled out of the entitlements due to the retiring partner under the partnership deed. Conversely, new partners will only be liable for obligations and debts arising from the time that they entered into the partnership. These rules are outlined in the Partnership Acts of each state and territory.[13] Partners can also be *expelled* from a partnership, provided there is ample authority to do so under the partnership deed and a majority of partners agree upon the expulsion.[14] The normal bases upon which a partner might be expelled include gross insubordination, criminal wrongdoing or the like.

Partnerships can normally be dissolved informally and with minimal expense. The Partnership Acts in all states and territories stipulate situations in which a partnership will dissolve (short of any agreement to the contrary existing between the partners), including:[15]

- where the partnership is entered into for a fixed term, the expiration of that term;
- where the partnership is entered into for a single adventure or undertaking, the termination of that adventure or undertaking;
- where the partnership is entered into for an undefined time, by a partner giving notice to the other partners of their intention to dissolve; or
- the death or insolvency of a partner.

A partnership dissolves automatically where the business in which the partnership is involved becomes unlawful. On application, the court may also order the dissolution of a partnership. Situations where a court might order dissolution include where the partner becomes permanently mentally incapacitated or otherwise incapable of performing their obligations, or wilfully or persistently commits a breach of the partnership agreement (or otherwise acts in a manner that may prejudice the partnership). The court might also dissolve a partnership where it can only be carried on at a loss, or where it is just and equitable in the particular circumstances that have arisen to do so.

The Australian states also make provision in their respective Partnership Acts for a distinct form of partnership known as a *limited partnership*.[16] Limited partnerships are distinct from

13 *Partnership Act 1963* (ACT), s 21; *Partnership Act 1892* (NSW), s 17; *Partnership Act 1997* (NT), s 21; *Partnership Act 1891* (Qld), s 20; *Partnership Act 1891* (SA), s 17; *Partnership Act 1891* (Tas), s 22; *Partnership Act 1958* (Vic), s 21; *Partnership Act 1895* (WA), s 24.

14 *Partnership Act 1963* (ACT), s 30; *Partnership Act 1892* (NSW), s 25; *Partnership Act 1997* (NT), s 29; *Partnership Act 1891* (Qld), s 28; *Partnership Act 1891* (SA), s 25; *Partnership Act 1891* (Tas), s 30; *Partnership Act 1958* (Vic), s 29; *Partnership Act 1895* (WA), s 35.

15 *Partnership Act 1963* (ACT), ss 37–40; *Partnership Act 1892* (NSW), ss 32–35; *Partnership Act 1997* (NT), ss 36–39; *Partnership Act 1891* (Qld), ss 35–38; *Partnership Act 1891* (SA), ss 32–35; *Partnership Act 1891* (Tas), ss 37–40; *Partnership Act 1958* (Vic), ss 36–39; *Partnership Act 1895* (WA), ss 43–46.

16 *Partnership Act 1892* (NSW), Part 3; *Partnership Act 1891* (Qld), Chapter 3; *Partnership Act 1891* (SA), Part 3; *Partnership Act 1891* (Tas), Part 3; *Partnership Act 1958* (Vic), Part 3. Western Australia has specific legislation pertaining to limited partnerships: *Limited Partnerships Act 2016* (WA). The territories do not have equivalent provisions in their Partnership Acts.

general partnerships, which have been discussed to this point. A limited partnership is one in which there is:

- at least one *general* partner (ie one with unlimited liability); and
- one or more *limited* partners whose liability for the partnership's debts and obligations is limited.

Limited partners are effectively investors who provide capital for the partnership and whose liability is limited to their contribution as well as any share in firm property or assets. Limited partners are therefore not involved in the administration or management of the partnership but rather play a more passive role. Limited partnerships must be registered with the relevant state authority (in the case of South Australia, for example, it is Consumer and Business Services). Notable advantages of limited partnerships are that they are attractive to potential partners who seek only to make capital contributions, they are very simple to set up, and they offer limited liability without the need for the establishment of a limited liability company. A further variation of the limited partnership is the *incorporated limited partnership*, essentially providing the limited partnership with separate corporate status. Most of the states and territories make provision for incorporated limited partnerships in their Partnership Acts.[17]

The main advantages of carrying on business as a partnership are that they are generally inexpensive to set up and dissolve, and allow two or more individuals to combine assets and skills in a formal commercial structure designed ideally to generate profit. Partnerships also do not attract the same compliance and regulatory costs as other business structures. Perhaps the biggest disadvantage of partnerships, however, is that partners are much like sole traders in that they are exposed to unlimited liability. Moreover, friction or disagreement may arise between partners, who are each agents of the firm and therefore capable of binding one another to particular commercial arrangements that the other partners may deem, or which may actually be, unfavourable.

2.2.3 Joint venture

Put simply, a joint venture is a contractual arrangement where two or more commercial actors (individuals or businesses) agree to a specific commercial or financial undertaking or project for a finite period of time and for individual gain. It is essentially a cooperative arrangement where knowledge, personnel, skills, finances and assets can be pooled so as to achieve a common end. The resulting profits or losses are shared according to the stipulations in the joint venture agreement. Unlike with partnerships, however, co-venturers are not mutually liable for one another's losses, debts or obligations (although this default position may be varied by appropriate contractual arrangements). They act individually and not as agents for one another; their liability is several. The joint ventureship agreement will generally restrict each co-venturer's liability and expressly stipulate their rights and obligations. Commonly, the agreement will hold each co-venturer responsible for a particular aspect of the relevant project.

17 *Partnership Act 1963* (ACT), Part 6; *Partnership Act 1892* (NSW), Part 3; *Partnership Act 1997* (NT), Part 3; *Partnership Act 1891* (Qld), Chapter 4; *Partnership Act 1891* (SA), Part 3; *Partnership Act 1891* (Tas), Part 3; *Partnership Act 1958* (Vic), Part 5. The Western Australian equivalent is Part 4 of the *Limited Partnerships Act 2016* (WA).

For example, several businesses might come together to stage a music festival with numerous national and international performers. One business might be responsible for staging and lighting, one for security, one for booking the acts, one for marketing and promotion, etc.

Joint ventures arise through contract. Unlike partnerships, which are often for longer-term commercial ventures, joint ventures are typically arranged for specific, 'one-off' projects for acute periods of time. Joint ventures are common in the mining, property development, research, farming, manufacturing and entertainment (eg film or music production) sectors, all of which are resource-intensive and frequently require various sets of skills to accomplish the project aims.

Occasionally, a joint ventureship can closely resemble a partnership, to the point it satisfies the statutory criteria for a partnership and is deemed instead to be one. This famously occurred in *Canny Gabriel Castle Jackson Advertising Pty Ltd v Volume Sales (Finance) Pty Ltd*.[18] In that case, Fourth Media Management Pty Ltd contracted to bring singers Cilla Black and Elton John to Australia for a series of concerts. Volume Sales agreed to finance the singers' contracts and so Fourth Media assigned a 50 per cent interest in the same, and to divide all profits as 'joint venturers'. A short time later, Fourth Media granted an equitable charge over its interest in the box office proceeds from the concerts to Canny Gabriel. The concerts were ultimately unsuccessful. Canny Gabriel commenced proceedings to obtain its share of the box office takings. The High Court held that the arrangement between Fourth Media and Volume Sales was actually a partnership and that, as a result, Volume Sales had a beneficial interest that prevailed over the charge in favour of Canny Gabriel. Had it actually been a joint venture, as the parties intended and understood the arrangement to be, then Volume Sales would actually have suffered unexpected financial losses. As this case demonstrates, the implications of a judicial finding that a joint venture is in fact a partnership may be highly significant and affect not only liabilities but entitlements as well.[19]

Joint ventures are not separate legal entities. Rather, as discussed above, they are contractually formed collaborations between individual persons or businesses and so each co-venturer is liable for their own taxation upon any revenue earned. By extension, joint ventures need not lodge tax returns, as they are not an entity in their own right.

In most circumstances, a joint venture comes to an end once the particular project or undertaking for which it was established is completed or achieved. Given that a joint venture comprises individual commercial actors with their own assets, separate finances and the like, it is relatively easy to dissolve. The joint ventureship agreement will often stipulate any residual obligations or responsibilities, and otherwise allow any of the co-venturers to leave at any stage.

Joint ventures are a very flexible commercial arrangement: they are easy to establish and co-venturers can come and go easily (unlike partners seeking to enter or leave a partnership). They also offer the benefits of greater privacy and autonomy for participants, and are a useful way to combine skills and assets to accomplish a goal for the individual gain of each co-venturer. The most difficult aspect of joint ventures is that the transaction costs may be high. Involving many parties charged with different responsibilities, and who may come and

18 (1974) 131 CLR 321.

19 See also *United Dominions Corporation Ltd v Brian Pty Ltd* (1985) 157 CLR 1.

go at any time, will likely involve drafting and constantly amending complex legal contracts and incur costs. It can also be difficult dealing with numerous parties to joint ventureship agreements, and so these may more readily give rise to disputes.

2.2.4 Franchise

A franchise is essentially a contractual arrangement under which the owner of a business (the *franchisor*) grants another party (the *franchisee*) the right to sell or distribute the products or services it has created, marketed or registered for a specified period of time. Common examples of franchises are *fast food chains* such as McDonald's or Subway, some *supermarkets* such as IGA, *retailers* such as Harvey Norman and Mitre 10, and *service providers* such as Bridgestone and Jim's Mowing. Technically speaking, a franchise is not in itself a business structure but, rather, a method by which to do business by trading off of the name and reputation of an established business. Franchisees are entitled to access and utilise all of the franchise's knowledge, equipment, methods and intellectual property (such as trademarked business names and registered designs or logos). Buying into a franchise is therefore a useful way of commencing a commercial business venture without the need to start entirely from scratch. Similarly, for budding franchisors, it offers a unique opportunity for expansion and entry into new markets.

Franchises are established through the creation of a franchise agreement, which is fundamentally a contract between the franchisor and franchisee. The agreement may be written, oral or implied. Like ordinary commercial contracts, franchise agreements are also subject to the normal laws and regulations that apply, such as the Australian Consumer Law. However, franchise agreements also typically impose a requirement upon franchisees to run the business according to specified rules, standards and specifications defined by the franchisor. In addition, every franchise will have an *operating manual* that outlines these requirements in far greater and more specific detail. Common examples of the sorts of matters that a franchising agreement and franchising operating manual will address, and which a franchisee must dutifully deal with, include:

- payment of franchising fees to the franchisor (normally proportionate to turnover);
- operating methods, standards and procedures;
- geographical location of franchise and its market;
- franchise inspections;
- accounting and record-keeping procedures;
- use of intellectual property such as trademarks, product names, signs, logos, etc;
- uniform or dress standards;
- staff employment, training, evaluation and remuneration;
- opening and closing procedures, including hours of operation;
- legal, licensing and insurance requirements;
- stock requirements and ordering procedures;
- workplace health and safety requirements;
- cleaning and hygiene requirements; and
- emergency procedures.

The agreement and/or operating manual will also generally include procedures for dealing with any issues that arise within the specific franchise outlet, and procedures for dealing with disputes with staff, the franchisor or a third party. Consequences for breach and rights to termination are, like all commercial contracts, a standard feature in franchise agreements.

Franchises are also bound by the *Franchising Code of Conduct*, a mandatory industry code that is enforced through s 51AE of the *Competition and Consumer Act 2010* (Cth) and administered by the Australian Competition and Consumer Commission (ACCC). The purpose of the Code is to regulate the franchising sector and the conduct of its participants towards one another.[20] Subject to some exceptions outlined in s 3 of the Code, it applies to all franchise agreements entered into on or after 1 October 1998.[21]

The principal features of the Code are its stipulation of requirements with respect to a franchisor's disclosures, franchise agreements generally (including mandatory and proscribed terms), record-keeping obligations, the provision of documents, and dispute resolution.[22] There is also express provision mandating good faith relations, as understood at common law, between the parties.[23] Some key examples of these requirements include the franchisor's obligation to maintain a 'disclosure document', which is designed to provide franchisees with information material to the running of the franchised business and essential for making reasonably informed decisions.[24] Franchisors must also provide franchisees with a copy of the Code, disclosure document and franchise agreement at least 14 days prior to entry into, renewal or extension of the franchise agreement.[25] In addition, all prospective franchisees must be provided with a basic information statement set out in Annexure 2 to the Code.[26] A franchisor may not enter into a franchise agreement unless they have received a signed statement that the prospective franchisee has received legal, business or accounting advice about the proposed transaction.[27]

The Code prohibits clauses from being included in franchise agreements that have the effect of releasing the franchisor from liability towards the franchisee,[28] requiring the franchisee to pay the franchisor's costs in relation to dispute settlement,[29] or restraining the franchisee's trade in cases where the franchisor has opted not to extend the term of the franchise agreement.[30] Importantly, the Code also allows for the transfer of franchise

20 *Franchising Code of Conduct*, s 2. The Code is actually Schedule 1 to the *Competition and Consumer (Industry Codes – Franchising) Regulations 2014* (Cth).

21 A small number of provisions also do not apply to agreements entered into prior to 1 January 2015. See Explanatory Statement, *Competition and Consumer (Industry Codes – Franchising) Regulations 2014*, Select Legislative Instrument No 168 (2014), issued by the Minister for Small Business. Importantly, a franchise agreement entered into prior to 1 January 2015 will be covered by the entire Code if the agreement is renewed, transferred or varied in any way on or after that date.

22 *Franchising Code of Conduct*, Parts 2–3.

23 *Franchising Code of Conduct*, s 6.

24 *Franchising Code of Conduct*, s 8. The disclosure document must be in the format of Annexure 1 to the Code.

25 *Franchising Code of Conduct*, s 9.

26 *Franchising Code of Conduct*, s 11.

27 *Franchising Code of Conduct*, s 10(2).

28 *Franchising Code of Conduct*, s 20.

29 *Franchising Code of Conduct*, s 22.

30 *Franchising Code of Conduct*, s 23.

agreements to third parties[31] and contains detailed provisions determining when a franchise agreement can be terminated.[32]

Taxation of franchises differs depending on whether one is a franchisor or franchisee. A franchisee's tax liability will depend upon its takings. Ongoing franchise fees may be deductible for the financial year in which they are paid. Other payments, such as staff training fees and any applicable loan interest, might also be claimed as a tax deduction. There may be other applicable taxes wherever a franchise is bought, sold or transferred, such as GST and capital gains tax (CGT). A franchisor's tax liability will similarly depend upon income derived from their business, which will include payments received from franchisees. They will also likely have to pay additional taxes that apply to businesses of certain types and sizes. Moreover, if a franchise is incorporated as a company, it will be subject to company tax.

Whereas the business that has franchised does not in itself typically dissolve (except, perhaps, in situations of insolvency and subsequent liquidation), a franchised outlet run by a franchisee may either be closed and the respective franchise agreement terminated (if, for example, it is underperforming or running at a loss), or the franchise agreement for that particular outlet may be transferred to another party. Most commercial contracts contain provisions stipulating the circumstances in which either party may terminate the agreement. Requests to transfer a franchise agreement must be made to the franchisor in writing accompanied by all contextual information surrounding the request.[33] The franchisor must not unreasonably withhold consent to a transfer, and may only do so in limited circumstances.[34] The transfer may also be conditional.[35] Consent is taken to be given where the franchisor remains silent for 42 days or more[36] and, where consent *is* expressly given, it can be revoked within 14 days.[37]

A franchise agreement may also be terminated in a variety of ways. The franchisee may terminate during the seven-day cooling-off period after signing the franchising agreement.[38] Alternatively, the franchisor may terminate for the franchisee's breach of the franchise agreement, but only where the franchisee has been allowed a reasonable time to remedy the breach.[39] Where there has been no breach by the franchisee, the franchisor may terminate the franchise agreement before it has expired and without the franchisee's consent where the agreement so allows; however, the franchisor must give both reasonable notice of this intention and reasons for the same.[40] In special circumstances, a franchisor is even entitled to terminate without providing notice or a reasonable time to remedy a breach. Where the agreement allows for either party to terminate and both parties agree, the franchisor may do so.[41] Otherwise, a franchisor may terminate if the franchisee:

31 *Franchising Code of Conduct*, ss 24–25.
32 *Franchising Code of Conduct*, ss 26–29.
33 *Franchising Code of Conduct*, s 24.
34 *Franchising Code of Conduct*, s 25.
35 *Franchising Code of Conduct*, s 25(1)(b).
36 *Franchising Code of Conduct*, s 25(4).
37 *Franchising Code of Conduct*, s 25(5). The franchisor must not revoke consent unreasonably: s 25(6).
38 *Franchising Code of Conduct*, s 26.
39 *Franchising Code of Conduct*, s 27. The franchisor is not required to allow the franchisee more than 30 days to remedy their breach: s 27(3).
40 *Franchising Code of Conduct*, s 28.
41 *Franchising Code of Conduct*, s 29(2).

- no longer holds a relevant licence to carry on the franchised business;
- becomes bankrupt or enters into administration;
- is deregistered by ASIC (where the franchisee is a company);
- voluntarily abandons the business or franchise relationship;
- is convicted of a serious offence;
- operates the business in a way that endangers public health or safety; or
- acts fraudulently in connection with the franchise's operation.

As mentioned earlier, the prime advantage of operating as a franchise is that the franchisee need not have to expend money and resources marketing the business as it will already be an established brand and most supplies, etc, will be provided by the franchisor. As such, franchises arguably carry less risk. The set-up costs may also be minimal compared to other business structures, and the franchise relationship provides a useful and mutually supportive framework for business administration. One notable disadvantage – for franchisees, in particular – is the lack of autonomy they have over their business due to the restrictions imposed by the franchising agreement and operating manual. The power imbalance may be abused, and the relationship between the parties may become strained and threaten the franchise itself. Franchises can also be expensive to operate, due to common fee structures imposed by franchisors, so a healthy turnover is critical.

2.2.5 Trust

Trusts are one of the more complicated business structures. Indeed, they were not originally conceived for use as a mechanism for business. However, they can and sometimes are used for commercial purposes. There are few situations in which trusts are used in this manner, although in some cases they offer the advantage of taxation benefits or convenient distribution of property within a network of people (particularly families).

A trust is created when one person (the *settlor*) transfers legal ownership over specified property to another person (the *trustee*) with instructions that the property is to be administered for the benefit of another person or entity (the *beneficiary*), or for a particular purpose. There may well be more than one beneficiary. The trustee has *legal* title over the trust property, while the beneficiary has an *equitable* or beneficial interest in the trust property. The trustee holds and controls the trust property for the benefit of the beneficiary. There are no precise formalities necessary to create an ordinary trust, and one may arise through implication from the conduct of the parties and the relevant circumstances. However, when used as a business structure, a trust can be highly complex to create and administer. In this context, a trust is normally created through a formal written 'deed' or 'instrument' of trust. The deed will stipulate how the trust is to operate, how the trust property is to be held (and for whom), and the rights and obligations of the trustee. In this regard, the deed will also be supplemented by the general law of equity governing trusts and legislation concerning trusts and certain forms of property in each jurisdiction.[42] The trusts legislation, in particular, broadly outlines the powers and duties of trustees. Some of the more significant duties include those to:

42 See, for example, *Trustee Act 1925* (ACT); *Trustee Act 1925* (NSW); *Trustee Act* (NT); *Trusts Act 1973* (Qld); *Trustee Act 1936* (SA); *Trustee Act 1898* (Tas); *Trustee Act 1958* (Vic); *Trustees Act 1962* (WA).

- act in the best interests of, and take advice from, the beneficiaries;
- keep and maintain proper accounts regarding the administration of trust property;
- exercise care, diligence and skill when investing trust funds;
- act impartially towards the beneficiaries; and
- avoid conflicts of interest, or attainment of profit,[43] arising from the position of trustee.

A trustee also has broad powers, including those to mortgage, lease, repair, improve and, under certain conditions, sell trust property. They can also invest trust funds, carry on a business, and exercise any other powers granted under the trust deed or by law. The trust may be *discretionary* and vest discretion in the trustee to determine which beneficiaries receive a benefit and in what amount. Alternatively, as is often the case in business settings, the trust may be *fixed* and set the amount of benefit to which each beneficiary is entitled through the terms of the trust deed.

A business structured as a trust will require the settlor to vest particular property (ie the business or its assets) in the trustee, who will then be authorised to run the business and distribute any profits made in accordance with the instructions stipulated in the trust deed. The trustee would be entitled to claim compensation – that is, a salary or wage – for their administration of the trust (business). A prospective business owner, as settlor, could even establish the business as a trust and appoint *themselves* as a trustee. They may even be a beneficiary as well, provided there is at least *one other* beneficiary. In the commercial setting, trusts are normally used as the structure for family businesses as they are flexible, easily facilitate the distribution of wealth to a pre-determined selection of people (the family members, as beneficiaries), and attract a number of tax concessions and benefits.

The most common form of trust used to operate a business is the *trading trust*, which is essentially an alternative to the more conventional company structure. A trust does not create a separate legal entity. As such, the trustee is personally liable for all debts and obligations of the trust. The trustee of a trading trust is therefore typically a company with limited liability and is referred to as a 'corporate trustee'. Ordinarily, the trustee will be entitled to indemnification from the trust assets for any liabilities or expenses arising.

Where an *express trust* is created to run a business – that is, one that does not arise through *implication* from the surrounding circumstances, or through *construction*, where the courts consider that justice or conscience require that a trust be imposed – it must satisfy three elements:

1. ***Certainty of intention.*** There must be a clear intention on the part of the settlor to create a trust.
2. ***Certainty of subject matter.*** There must be clarity as to what property is to be the subject of the trust, whether it be real/personal or tangible/intangible.

43 This duty may, of course, be modified by the trust deed, the courts, the beneficiaries (when they are of full legal capacity), or by operation of law. Indeed, the duty to draw profit from one's position as trustee will invariably be modified where a business structured as a trust is being administered by the trustee. Where the trustee is also one of the beneficiaries of the trust, they will be entitled to their share of the business profits as stipulated within the trust deed.

3. ***Certainty of object.*** There must, at the least, be a method by which to identify the beneficiaries of the trust. For fixed trusts, *list certainty* is required (ie it must be possible to conjure a complete list of all beneficiaries). For discretionary trusts, *criterion certainty* is required (ie it must be possible to determine whether a particular person or entity falls within the class of potential beneficiaries).

The absence or fault of any of these elements will result in the failure of the trust.

The taxation of trusts generally is governed by Part III of the *Income Tax Assessment Act 1936* (Cth). Businesses structured as a trust must have a tax file number (TFN) and submit a tax return. It is the trustee's responsibility to do this and to demonstrate the income earned by the trust, any deductions made for expenses, and how the trust income was distributed to the beneficiaries. The beneficiaries will pay tax on their trust income at the relevant individual marginal tax rate (unless they are minors or non-residents, in which case the trustee will pay the tax on their behalf based on their share of the trust's net income). The trustee will themselves pay tax on any undistributed trust income that has accumulated.

Trusts can be dissolved in a number of ways. The trustee can relinquish, or retire from, their position as trustee where the trust deed or beneficiaries of sufficient capacity allow, or where the courts or some other law so permit.[44] Trustees can also be removed in certain circumstances, such as where they are deemed unfit to act in that capacity. The trust may also be terminated where the trust concludes, where the beneficiaries of full legal capacity all agree to terminate the trust, or where the trustee passes away. The trust deed normally specifies the lifespan of the trust. In the event that trust assets must also be sold, as opposed to where money need only be distributed, the dissolution of a trust can take some time.

As was discussed earlier, trusts enable businesses to trade with limited liability short of having to incorporate. They are also flexible and offer tax benefits, and – given their nature – are particularly useful for family businesses. The trustee can normally be indemnified out of trust assets, and the beneficiaries themselves are immunised from liability. The main disadvantages of using trusts as a vehicle for business are the costs and complex ongoing requirements that come with doing so. Where profits are not correctly distributed in a timely manner, trusts may actually lead to adverse tax consequences.

2.2.6 Unincorporated association

Organisations that are founded in pursuit of some public purpose other than to make a profit, and which are not incorporated in any capacity, are known as unincorporated associations. Such associations are normally the structure of choice for amateur sporting clubs, community groups, societies and the like, which are composed of people with common interests but not operating with a view to profit, as with partnerships. While it is possible for not-for-profit (NFP) unincorporated associations to still generate a profit in pursuit of their objectives, those profits are reinvested into the cause rather than distributed to members. As such, unincorporated associations are not a suitable structure for businesses seeking to turn a profit.

Unincorporated associations can be created with close to no formality. Theoretically, it requires only two or more individuals with similar political, sporting, cultural, religious, social

44 The trustees legislation in each jurisdiction generally allows for the retirement or removal of trustees.

or other interests to come together and pursue their cause. Such associations will, however, typically generate and enforce their own sets of rules (normally in the form of a constitution), with a 'committee' of selected members managing the association itself. Importantly, the association is not a separate legal entity from the members; it has no legal capacity to sue or be sued, to enter into contractual arrangements, or to own assets. Instead, the members themselves do these things on behalf of their peers within the association (provided this authority is vested in them by the association rules). They are therefore individually liable for the association's debts and liabilities.

Generally speaking, the majority of unincorporated associations do not pay tax, or at least pay minimal tax. Liability to pay tax chiefly depends upon the nature of the association, the amount of taxable income it has generated, and whether or not the organisation's constituent documents prohibit any distributions of money or other assets to members.[45] Some forms of NFP association – such as registered charities;[46] gaming, sporting and animal racing clubs; scientific institutions; cultural (art, literature, music) organisations; public hospitals or NFP-operated hospitals; community service organisations; and churches and religious organisations registered as charitable institutions – are exempt from paying income tax altogether.

The lack of legal formalities involved in the creation of unincorporated associations translates to ease of dissolution. The association rules may stipulate certain procedures for the dismantling of an association. In practice, however, it is normally as simple as the members agreeing to abandon their cause and allowing the association to end naturally through inactivity.

One of the chief advantages of operating as an unincorporated association is that it is unnecessary to pay any costs associated with incorporation under state or territory legislation (for incorporated associations) or under the federal legislation (for corporations). There are also several legal, regulatory and financial requirements that an unincorporated association need not comply with. On the other hand, the lack of corporate status means that individual members of an unincorporated association are exposed to significant personal liability, particularly where the association lacks insurance. An additional disadvantage is that unincorporated associations often experience difficulty in accessing grants given that most funding programs require applicant organisations to be incorporated. Indeed, in some jurisdictions, falsely representing a body as an incorporated association is an offence.[47]

2.2.7 Incorporated association

Legislation in all states and territories permits an unincorporated association to incorporate without becoming a company.[48] Registration with the relevant authority in the respective

45 See https://www.ato.gov.au/Non-profit/Your-organisation/Do-you-have-to-pay-income-tax-/Taxable-organisations/.

46 Although registration is optional, charities *must* register with the Australian Charities and Not-for-profits Commission (ACNC) in order to take advantage of certain charity tax concessions from the Australian Taxation Office (ATO).

47 See, for example, *Associations Incorporation Act 1991* (ACT), s 112; *Associations Incorporation Act 1985* (SA), s 60.

48 *Associations Incorporation Act 1991* (ACT); *Associations Incorporation Act 2009* (NSW); *Associations Act* (NT); *Associations Incorporation Act 1981* (Qld); *Associations Incorporation Act 1985* (SA); *Associations Incorporation Act 1964* (Tas); *Associations Incorporation Reform Act 2012* (Vic); *Associations Incorporation Act 2015* (WA).

jurisdiction gives the association status as a separate legal entity. In turn, this confers the advantage of limited liability for the association's members and the management committee charged with running it. Unlike unincorporated associations, which have no separate legal status, incorporated associations have legal standing to sue and be sued, enter into contracts, and own assets in their own right.

Associations can incorporate by application to the relevant authority in the jurisdiction of choice.[49] The procedures are many and varied and so a full discussion is beyond the scope of this chapter. However, the general process is the same in that associations must normally consist of a minimum number of members[50] who must first establish a set of rules (ie a constitution) for the association, register a name, and obtain appropriate licences, etc, prior to lodging the appropriate documentation to complete the incorporation process. The various Associations Incorporation Acts require incorporated associations to comply with a number of conditions, particularly with respect to appointing a public officer,[51] keeping records, and holding annual general meetings. If the incorporated association plans to conduct business outside their 'home' state or territory, it must become a *registered Australian body* with ASIC.

The discussion in Section 2.2.6 above with respect to the taxation of unincorporated associations applies equally to incorporated associations. The ATO imposes tax liability based upon the type of association, the income it generates, and whether or not it makes any kind of monetary or proprietary distributions to its members. Whether or not the association is incorporated merely affects the association's legal status and the liability of its members.

Incorporated associations can be dissolved by following the processes outlined in the respective jurisdiction's Associations Incorporation Act[52] and the association's own constitution. In some cases, where the value of the association's assets surpasses certain thresholds, the association may be required to wind up in accordance with the *Corporations Act 2001* (Cth). Generally speaking, once the committee and members of the association have resolved to dissolve the association, the relevant state or territory authority is notified and any formalities are completed, before any surplus monies or other assets are appropriately distributed to benevolent organisations (not to the members). Where those monies or assets are of too great a value, the federal legislation may apply and a liquidator may be appointed.

Incorporation offers numerous advantages when compared to remaining as an unincorporated association. By incorporating under the state or territory legislation, an association becomes a separate legal entity and confers legal and financial protection upon its members. This also allows it to open bank accounts, enter into contracts and own assets in its own name.

---

49 ACT: Access Canberra; NSW: Fair Trading NSW; NT: Territory Business Centres; Qld: Office of Fair Trading; SA: Consumer and Business Services; Tas: Consumer, Building and Occupational Services; Vic: Consumer Affairs Victoria; WA: Department of Mines, Industry Regulation and Safety.

50 The minimum number of members is five in the Australian Capital Territory, New South Wales, the Northern Territory and Victoria; six in Western Australia; and seven in Queensland. There is no minimum number in South Australia or Tasmania.

51 The public officer is effectively the association's chief liaison and is normally tasked with corresponding with the respective regulatory body facilitating the association's incorporation.

52 *Associations Incorporation Act 1991* (ACT), Part 7; *Associations Incorporation Act 2009* (NSW), Part 7; *Associations Act 2003* (NT), Part 8; *Associations Incorporation Act 1981* (Qld), Part 10; *Associations Incorporation Act 1985* (SA), Part 5; *Associations Incorporation Act 1964* (Tas), ss 34–34A; *Associations Incorporation Reform Act 2012* (Vic), Part 10; *Associations Incorporation Act 2015* (WA), Parts 9–10.

The process formalises what is otherwise a very informal structure for doing business of any kind. Given that most private and public (especially government) funding is available only to incorporated associations, incorporation offers a greater number of options for raising capital. The fact that incorporated associations are subject to far more stringent statutory controls might be seen as a disadvantage, as might the costs and formalities involved in both the incorporation process itself and in functioning as an incorporated body.

2.2.8 Corporation

The last business structure to be discussed in this chapter is one of the most significant and has arguably had the greatest influence upon global commercial and economic activity. A corporation, also known as a 'company' or a 'body corporate', is created through incorporation under the *Corporations Act 2001* (Cth).[53] It is, as will be explained in more detail shortly, a separate legal entity into which members can invest without personal risk; they incur no individual liability for the company's debts and obligations if it fails. In the case of a company limited by shares, they are liable only for the price of the shares they own. Moreover, they need not personally manage the venture(s) undertaken by the corporation. The corporation is the only business structure that is an entirely independent and separate legal 'person' from its directors and members. To December 2019, there were a little over 2.7 million registered companies operating throughout Australia.[54]

A company can be created by following the registration process outlined in the Act. An application must be completed and lodged with ASIC,[55] along with payment of the prescribed fees. The fees vary depending upon whether or not the company will have share capital, and who is lodging the application. At December 2019, registration of an Australian company having share capital attracts a fee of $495. Other fees apply for such things as reservation of a company name. The application must specify details such as:[56]

- the type of company proposed for registration;
- the company's proposed name;
- the capital structure of the company;
- the names and addresses of consenting members (shareholders);[57]
- the full names, addresses, dates of birth, and places of birth for all proposed directors; and
- the address of the company's proposed registered office and place of business (if different from registered office).

53 For the purposes of this part of the chapter, discussing corporations, the *Corporations Act 2001* (Cth) will be referred to simply as 'the Act'.

54 Australian Securities and Investments Commission, *2019 Company Registration Statistics* (December 2019): https://asic.gov.au.

55 *Corporations Act 2001* (Cth), s 117(1). The ASIC website has a user-friendly, step-by-step process to assist with company registration: https://asic.gov.au/for-business/registering-a-company/steps-to-register-a-company/#registering-company.

56 *Corporations Act 2001* (Cth), s 117(2).

57 There must be a minimum of one member (shareholder) pursuant to s 114 of the *Corporations Act 2001* (Cth).

Once entered upon the register of companies, an Australian Company Number (ACN) and share certificate are issued.[58] The ACN is a unique nine-digit company identification number issued by ASIC, normally printed in three groups of three digits.

Incorporation is a very significant process in commercial law because it creates a separate, artificial legal entity. The word 'corporation' derives from the Latin word *corpus*, meaning body or body of people, later anglicised as 'corporation'. Given that a corporation is a legal 'person', its acts are not regarded as being those of the members, who enjoy limited liability (restricted only to any amounts unpaid on their shares if they are called upon to make payment). As such, the members are said to be protected by the *veil of incorporation*. This was established in the famous case of *Salomon v A Salomon & Co Ltd*.[59]

Mr Salomon, a cobbler and leather merchant operating his business as a sole trader, opted to incorporate and form a company so that his sons could become part of the business. He registered a company limited by shares and then sold his business to the company at an inflated price, with a nominal capital of £40 000 divided into 40 000 shares of £1 each. As the new company had insufficient funds for the purchase price, Mr Salomon loaned the money under security by debentures totalling £10 000. (The debentures operated as a floating charge over the company's assets.) Once secured, Edmund Broderip made an advance of £5000 as a loan to the company. Mr Salomon and his two eldest sons were nominated as the three directors of the new company. Only 20 007 shares were eventually issued; Mr Salomon held 20 001 shares and each of the six other shareholders, being his wife and five eldest children, held one of the remaining shares each.

The business subsequently failed and went into liquidation. Mr Broderip successfully sued to enforce his security under the debentures, and Mr Salomon retained the balance as beneficial owner of the debentures. As such, there were no funds remaining to pay the unsecured creditors, whose debts amounted to £7733. The company's appointed liquidator argued that Mr Salomon was responsible for the company's debts and that the floating charge he held under the debentures should not be honoured. The liquidator was successful in both the High Court and Court of Appeal. Mr Salomon appealed to the House of Lords in hope of enforcing his security.

On appeal to the House of Lords, it was held that the company – duly formed and registered – was a separate legal entity and that Mr Salomon was not individually liable to indemnify the company for its inability to pay the outstanding debts. The security Mr Salomon held was valid and enforceable; he had not acted fraudulently in any way and so could not be deemed personally liable.[60] Lord Macnaghten stated (at p 51):

> The company is at law a different person altogether from the subscribers to the memorandum; and, though it may be that after incorporation the business is precisely the same as it was before, and the same persons are managers, and the same hands receive the profits, the company is not in law the agent of the subscribers or trustee for them. Nor are the subscribers as members liable, in any shape or form, except to the extent and in the manner provided by the Act.

58 *Corporations Act 2001* (Cth), s 118.
59 [1897] AC 22.
60 The potential for company directors to be held personally liable for a company's debts or obligations will be discussed later in the chapter.

In limited instances, the corporate veil will be 'pierced' and the courts will disregard the otherwise indisputable separation of the company from its members and regard the acts of the company as those of the shareholder. Sadly, there is 'no common, unifying principle, which underlies the occasional decision of courts to pierce the corporate veil'.[61] However, the case law identifies a number of instances where the veil will be pierced. For example, where an individual uses the company to perpetrate fraud,[62] where the company is merely a façade or sham being used to avoid obligations (eg to circumvent a contractual restraint of trade),[63] or where an agency relationship can be said to exist between a subsidiary company and its parent.[64] The veil may also be pierced by operation of statute, such as where the Act imposes personal liability upon directors who: allow their company to trade while insolvent;[65] sanction transactions that affect their company's ability to pay employee entitlements (such as wages);[66] or provide financial assistance to a third party enabling the acquisition of shares in their company where this arrangement contravenes s 260A of the Act.[67]

Section 112 of the Act provides that the types of company shown in Table 2.2 can be registered.

Table 2.2 Types of companies that can be registered

Proprietary companies	Limited by shares Unlimited with share capital
Public companies	Limited by shares Limited by guarantee Unlimited with share capital No liability company

The liability of members of each of the various types of company listed in the second column of the table is outlined below:

- ***Companies limited by shares***. A company limited by shares has a nominal share capital and limits the liability of shareholders to any unpaid amounts on the shares they hold.[68] The majority of registered companies fall into this category. Under the Act, such companies must have the word 'Ltd' or 'Limited' as part of their name.[69]

61 *Briggs v James Hardie & Co Pty Ltd* (1989) 16 NSWLR 549, 567.
62 See, for example, *Re Darby; Ex parte Brougham* [1911] 1 KB 95.
63 See, for example, *Gilford Motor Co Ltd v Horne* [1933] Ch 935.
64 See, for example, *Smith, Stone & Knight Ltd v Lord Mayor, Alderman & Citizens of the City of Birmingham* [1939] 4 All ER 116.
65 *Corporations Act 2001* (Cth), s 588G.
66 *Corporations Act 2001* (Cth), s 596AC.
67 *Corporations Act 2001* (Cth), s 260D.
68 *Corporations Act 2001* (Cth), s 9.
69 *Corporations Act 2001* (Cth), s 148(2).

- ***Companies limited by guarantee***. A company limited by guarantee has no share capital and limits the liability of its members to the respective amounts that the members undertake to contribute to the company's property if it is wound up.[70]
- ***Companies with unlimited liability.*** An unlimited liability company is one whose members (shareholders) have no limit placed on their liability.[71] This type of company is the oldest, although it is now very rare and is typically limited to mutual funds.
- ***Companies with no liability.*** A no liability company is one registered as or converting to a no liability company under the Act.[72] It is restricted to mining companies.[73] No liability companies are not permitted to recover from shareholders any amounts unpaid on their shares. This serves to incentivise capital investment for the mining of natural resources.

Companies can also be classified according to their public status:

- ***Proprietary company***. A proprietary company is one registered as or converting to a proprietary company under the Act.[74] These are generally smaller businesses, particularly family enterprises, that do not seek capital investment from the public. They are limited to 50 non-employee shareholders.[75] Proprietary companies must have the word 'Proprietary' or 'Pty' in their name.[76] There is a distinction between *small* and *large* proprietary companies. Generally speaking, the distinction falls upon the company's consolidated annual gross operating revenue, consolidated gross assets value, and number of full-time employees.[77]
- ***Public company***. A public company is one other than a proprietary company.[78] These are generally larger businesses with many shareholders and actively seek capital investment from the public. They may have any number of shareholders, although they must have a minimum of one.[79] Public companies can be *listed* or *unlisted*. The simple distinction is that a *listed* public company is one that is listed on the Australian Securities Exchange (ASX).

There are other important steps that come with the formation of a company. For example, companies must have in place a set of internal rules to regulate and govern themselves. Prior to 1 July 1998, companies were legally required to have both a memorandum of association and articles of association (cumulatively referred to as the 'constitution'). For companies formed after this date, a choice must be made between: (1) creating and enforcing a company constitution; (2) relying on the *replaceable rules* contained in the Act and outlined in s 141; or (3) relying on a combination of both.[80]

70 *Corporations Act 2001* (Cth), s 9.
71 *Corporations Act 2001* (Cth), s 9.
72 *Corporations Act 2001* (Cth), s 9.
73 *Corporations Act 2001* (Cth), s 112(2)(b).
74 *Corporations Act 2001* (Cth), ss 9, 45A(1).
75 *Corporations Act 2001* (Cth), s 113(1).
76 *Corporations Act 2001* (Cth), s 148(2).
77 See *Corporations Act 2001* (Cth), s 45A(2)–(3).
78 *Corporations Act 2001* (Cth), s 9.
79 *Corporations Act 2001* (Cth), s 114.
80 *Corporations Act 2001* (Cth), s 134.

A heavy framework of regulation also affects corporations once established. In particular, the Act imposes a number of requirements with respect to the holding of meetings,[81] record-keeping and financial reporting,[82] and entry into contracts.[83] A full discussion of these requirements is beyond the scope of this chapter.

Being separate legal entities, companies are taxed on their earnings at the applicable corporate tax rate. For 'base rate entities' – being companies that meet two criteria: (1) they have an aggregated turnover less than the aggregated turnover threshold ($50 million from the 2018/19 financial year to 2021/22); and (2) 80 per cent or less of their assessable income is 'base rate entity passive income' – the current tax rate is 27.5 per cent (although this will reduce to 26 per cent from the 2020/21 financial year). In other cases, the tax rate is 30 per cent.[84] Dividends paid to shareholders by Australian resident companies are taxed under the *imputation system*. This system allows tax paid by a corporation to be attributed (imputed) to shareholders in certain circumstances. In such cases, 'franking credits' attach to the dividends and eligible shareholders can claim a credit to avoid being taxed twice on the same profits.[85]

Corporations can be dissolved or 'wound up' in a variety of ways. Given they are artificial entities, they have no natural lifespan and will consequently continue indefinitely until the point they are wound up. The process of winding up is also commonly referred to as 'liquidation'. This may come about through one of the following means:

- ***Members' voluntary winding-up.*** Where the company is *solvent*, the members may pass a special resolution that the company be wound up. A liquidator is appointed by the members and sets about helping the company to pay out its debts, after which any proceeds from the sale of the company's assets are distributed to the shareholders. If the company cannot pay its debts, a creditors' voluntary winding-up will be appropriate.
- ***Creditors' voluntary winding-up***. Where the company is *insolvent*, the members may similarly pass a special resolution that the company be wound up. A meeting of all creditors is called and a liquidator appointed to set about helping the company to pay out its debts. The proceeds of the company's sale of its assets are returned to the creditors.
- ***Winding up in insolvency***. On application from one of the persons listed in s 459P of the Act, the court may, under s 459A, order a company that is insolvent to be wound up. Such applications are normally made by creditors seeking to recover debts owed to them. A company is insolvent where it is not able to pay all of its debts as and when they become due and payable.[86]

81 Including board meetings, shareholder meetings (annual general meetings [AGM] and extraordinary general meetings [EGM]), and court-ordered meetings. With respect to shareholder meetings, public companies must have an AGM once per calendar year under s 250N(3), whereas proprietary companies need only do so if required under their constitution.

82 *Corporations Act 2001* (Cth), ss 286, 292, 298.

83 *Corporations Act 2001* (Cth), ss 126–127.

84 The tax rates will also vary for particular types of corporation, such as life insurance companies. See https://www.ato.gov.au/Rates/Company-tax/ for a full breakdown of the current (2019/20) rates.

85 For more information on the taxation of dividends, see: https://www.ato.gov.au/Individuals/Tax-Return/2019/Tax-return/Income-questions-1-12/11-Dividends-2019/ and https://www.ato.gov.au/individuals/tax-return/2019/in-detail/publications/you-and-your-shares-2019/.

86 *Corporations Act 2001* (Cth), s 95A.

- ***Winding up by the court on other grounds.*** For any of the other reasons stated in s 461 of the Act, a court may order a company to be wound up. Some reasons include where the company has failed to commence business within a year of incorporation (or suspended business for a year), where the company has no members, where the company is acting in a manner that is oppressive or unfairly prejudicial to the members, or where the court considers it just and equitable that the company be wound up.

One of the most significant advantages of structuring one's business as a corporation is the limited liability that its members enjoy. This benefit stems from the company's status upon incorporation as a separate legal entity. Another considerable advantage is that shareholders may be able to avoid paying some or all tax on dividends. Corporations, particularly public companies, are also generally able to raise capital more easily than other types of business. The most notable disadvantage of corporations is that they are heavily regulated under a somewhat complex statutory framework. The costs associated with creating and administering a company are also quite high compared to other business structures. Members other than directors (perhaps except in the case of small proprietary companies) also tend to have far less control over the affairs of the company.

2.2.8.1 Directors' duties

Owing to the unique and significant nature of the corporation as a business structure, directors have a number of important common law and statutory duties. At common law, directors are fiduciaries and are therefore duty-bound to act loyally and honestly in the best interests of the company.[87] They are in a special position of power, responsibility and trust and must therefore act in good faith, avoid conflicts of interest, make full and proper disclosure, and avoid taking secret benefits or profits. Directors must also exercise reasonable care and diligence when making decisions on behalf of the company.[88] The Act also imposes a number of statutory duties upon directors, many of which overlap with the various common law duties:

- exercise care and diligence (s 180);
- act in good faith and for a proper purpose (s 181);
- not make improper use of position (s 182); and
- not make improper use of information (s 183).

2.3 Key points

- There is a wide variety of business structures that one might use, with this choice being influenced by such factors as the purpose or objectives of the business, its size, its assets, the applicable taxation, the liability that attaches, and how long the business is intended to last.
- Business structures vary in complexity from the relatively simple and minimally regulated sole trader and unincorporated association through to the more heavily regulated partnership, incorporated association and corporation.

87 *Elders Trustee & Executor Co Ltd v E G Reeves Pty Ltd* (1987) 78 ALR 193.
88 *Re Smith & Fawcett Ltd* [1942] Ch 304; *Spies v The Queen* (2000) 201 CLR 603.

- Whereas sole traders and members of unincorporated associations expose themselves to significant and unlimited personal liability, members of incorporated associations and corporations enjoy limited liability.

2.4 DISCUSSION QUESTIONS

1. What are the principal differences between a joint venture and a partnership? How is one distinguished from the other?
2. What are the primary advantages of an unincorporated association choosing to incorporate under state or territory associations incorporation legislation?
3. What is ASIC's role with respect to the formation of businesses?
4. What are the main factors that influence one's choice of business structure? What basic advice would you provide to a party seeking to establish a business of any kind?
5. Do particular forms of business structure offer tax advantages when compared to others?

2.5 FURTHER READING

Ciro, T, Goldwasser, V and Verma, R, *Law and Business* (Oxford University Press, Melbourne, 4th edn, 2014), Chapters 14–15.

Lambiris, M and Griffin, L, *First Principles of Business Law* (Oxford University Press, Melbourne, 9th revised edn, 2016), Chapter 14.

Miles, C and Dowler, W, *A Guide to Business Law* (Thomson Reuters Australia, Sydney, 21st edn, 2015), Chapter 5.

Overland, J, 'Alternative Business Structures' in A Terry and D Giugni (eds), *Business and the Law* (Thomson Reuters Australia, Sydney, 7th edn, 2019), Chapter 11.

3

PERSONAL PROPERTY

3.0 Introduction

This chapter addresses the topic of personal property. It first addresses the fundamental notion of property. It then explores how the scope of personal property has become more expansive as novel challenges to existing notions of property have arisen over time. The chapter considers the important distinction between real property and personal property. Sub-classifications of personal property are considered, including the distinction between chattels real and personal, choses in action and choses in possession. The chapter explores various types of possession, and interference with possession giving rise to actions for trespass, conversion and detinue. It concludes with a discussion of how the nature of personal property rights can be lost through intermixture or accession, or by becoming a fixture.

3.1 Defining personal property

The definition of personal property is informed by the broader concept of property itself. In *Moore v Regents of the University of California*,[1] Mosk J defined property as being 'sufficiently comprehensive to include every species of estate, real and personal, and everything which one person can own and transfer to another'.[2] The concept of property refers not simply to the idea that an object or thing may become the subject of ownership but also to the rights that stem from that ownership. In *Commonwealth v Western Australia*,[3] Kirby J stated:

> The concept of 'property' has been applied most broadly. It extends beyond conventional estates and interests recognised at law and in equity whether in realty or in personality. It includes 'innominate and anomalous interests'.[4]

Property is thus not just an object but also a relationship and the source of rights. This may include such vital rights as the right to exclude others from the property.[5] Most importantly, property ownership provides the basis for the owner's 'bundle of rights'. In *Moore*, Mosk J stated:

> Being broad, the concept of property is also abstract: rather than referring directly to a material object such as a parcel of land or the tractor that cultivates it, the concept of property is often said to refer to a 'bundle of rights' that may be exercised with respect to that object – principally the right to possess the property, to use the property, to exclude others from that property, and to dispose of the property by sale or gift ... But the same bundle of rights does not attach to all forms of property.[6]

Recognition of property rights is relevant in a wide range of areas of law, including succession, crime, insolvency, trusts, taxation, marriage, and the right to compensation or other relief. For example, determining whether something is property for the purposes of taxation may involve different considerations than when determining whether property is capable of being stolen. The breadth of the concept of property may vary in each of these contexts.

1 (1990) 51 Ca 3d 120.
2 *Yuba River Power Co v Nevada Irrigation District* (1929) 207 Cal 521, 523.
3 (1999) 196 CLR 392.
4 (1999) 196 CLR 392, 455.
5 See T Merrill, 'Property and the Right to Exclude' (1998) 77 *Nebraska Law Review* 730.
6 (1990) 51 Ca 3d 120, 165.

3.1.1 Real and personal property

In the immediate context of commercial law, the word 'property' is used both to refer to the thing that is capable of being owned and to describe the nature of the rights of ownership in relation to the thing. There are two types of property: personal property and real property. Within the category of personal property there are two further categories: choses in action and choses in possession. In *Barton v Australian Consolidated Press Ltd*,[7] Isaac J set out these basic categories of property:

> The description real and personal property describes and embraces every type and class of property known to law. There is no 'property' of any sort which does not fall under one or other of the words 'real' and 'personal'. True enough each has categories: real property comprises corporeal and incorporeal hereditaments, and 'chattels real' and 'chattels personal' may be convenient subdivisions of 'personal property'; but once you exclude from that phrase real estate and interests therein and chattels real, then every other kind of property of whatever description falls within the classification of 'personal property' especially that which is visible or tangible.[8]

Real property includes land and buildings on the soil.[9] Land is defined at common law as 'any ground, soil or earth whatsoever'.[10] In *Wade v New South Wales Rutile Mining Co Pty Ltd*,[11] Windeyer J noted that land includes the soil and 'everything naturally contained within the land',[12] aside from deposits reserved to the Crown, such as minerals or petroleum. Real property also includes things attached to the land in such a way that they have become fixtures,[13] and intangible rights that attach to the land including, for example, easements.[14]

Personal property is often identified or defined by reference to what it is not; personal property is not real property.[15] Personal property is classified as chattels real or chattels personal.[16] Chattels real are confined to interests closely concerned with real property, and traditionally included leasehold interests.[17] Chattels personal may be choses in action or choses in possession. Distinguishing 'choses in possession' from 'choses in action' is apropos of personal property;[18] both are personal property, yet the distinction is a significant one.

'Choses in action' are rights enforceable by legal action.[19] In *Loxton v Moir*, Rich J explained:

7 [1970] 3 NSWR 141.
8 [1970] 3 NSWR 141, 143.
9 *Re Leber and the Real Property Act 1900–1956* [1960] NSWR 570.
10 *Re Leber and the Real Property Act 1900–1956* [1960] NSWR 570, 575.
11 (1969) 121 CLR 177.
12 (1969) 121 CLR 177, 185.
13 *Holland v Hodgson* (1872) LR 7 CP 328.
14 *Municipal District of Concord v Coles* (1905) 3 CLR 96, *Re Leber and the Real Property Act 1900–1956* [1960] NSWR 570, 575. Leasehold interests have traditionally been considered to be chattels real, a form of personal property discussed below. See *AMP Society v Gregory* (1908) 5 CLR 615, 629.
15 *North Shore Gas Co Ltd v Commissioner of Stamp Duties (NSW)* (1940) 63 CLR 52.
16 *Barton v Australian Consolidated Press Ltd* [1970] 3 NSWLR 141; *North Shore Gas Co Ltd v Commissioner of Stamp Duties (NSW)* (1940) 63 CLR 52.
17 *AMP Society v Gregory* (1908) 5 CLR 615.
18 *Colonial Bank v Whinney* (1886) 11 App Cas 426, applied in *Sydney Futures Exchange Ltd v Australian Stock Exchange Ltd* (1995) 56 FCR 236; *Your Response Ltd v Datastream Business Media Ltd* [2014] EWCA Civ 281.
19 *Torkington v Magee* [1902] 2 KB 427, 430.

> The phrase 'chose in action' is used in different senses but its primary sense is that of a right enforceable by an action. It may also be used to describe the right of action itself when considered as part of the property of the person entitled to sue. A right to sue for a sum of money is a chose in action and it is a proprietary right.[20]

A chose in action can have significant economic value and include, for example, shares in a company[21] and debts.[22] The right of action itself covers a spectrum of possibilities, including the right to bring the action directly or by counter-claim.[23] A right to sue for performance of a contractual obligation is a chose in action.[24] So, too, is a cause of action in tort.[25]

A chose in possession must have a physical existence. If you are reading a hard copy of this book, the physical book itself is a chose in possession, while the intellectual property rights of the copyright owner are a chose in action. The distinction between a chose in action and a chose in possession is not always so sharp. Money is personal property.[26] Money in the form of notes or coins is a chose in possession.[27] If those coins or notes are deposited to a bank account, the money deposited with the bank becomes a chose in action.[28] Indeed, in *Henderson v Queensland*,[29] White JA noted that a chose in action is 'the right to recover from the bank the balance standing to the depositor's credit in an account with the bank at the date of demand'.[30]

Chattels and goods are personal property. The term 'chattels' was described in *Robinson v Jenkins*[31] by Fry J as 'one of the widest words known to the law in its relation to personal property'.[32] In *The Noordam [No 2]*, the Privy Council determined that bearer securities found in mail constituted goods, noting that the word is 'of very general and quite indefinite import, and primarily derives its meaning from the context in which it is used'.[33] In that case the bearer securities were being carried by steamship diverted pursuant to a wartime reprisals order designed to prevent enemy misconduct and the free transport of property of the enemy. The underlying policy objective of the reprisals order was to prevent any kind of commodity reaching or leaving Germany.[34] The Privy Council considered that the critical consideration was the context in which the word 'goods' was used. In this case, that context included the policy objective of the reprisals order.[35] If the bearer bonds had been characterised as mail,

20 *Loxton v Moir* (1914) 18 CLR 360, 379.
21 *Pilmer v The Duke Group* (2001) 207 CLR 165; *Sydney Futures Exchange Ltd v Australian Stock Exchange Ltd* (1995) 56 FCR 236.
22 *Loxton v Moir* (1914) 18 CLR 360, 379; *Norman v Federal Commissioner of Taxation* (1963) 109 CLR 9.
23 *Commonwealth Bank of Australia v Horvath*, McDonald J; *Commonwealth Bank of Australia v Horvath*, (Senior) McDonald J, Supreme Court of Victoria Practice Court 9168/1994.
24 *Minister for Health v Brambles Australia Ltd* [2009] WADC 111.
25 *Minister for Health v Brambles Australia Ltd* [2009] WADC 111.
26 *Mutual Pools & Staff Pty Ltd v Commonwealth* (1994) 179 CLR 155, 184.
27 *Croton v The Queen* (1967) 117 CLR 326, 330.
28 *Croton v The Queen* (1967) 117 CLR 326, 330–3; *Travelex v Commissioner of Taxation* (2010) 241 CLR 510, 532, per Crennan and Bell JJ.
29 [2013] 1 Qd R 1.
30 *Henderson v Queensland* [2013] 1 Qd R 1, 15.
31 (1890) 24 QBD 275.
32 (1890) 24 QBD 275, 279.
33 [1920] AC 904, 909.
34 [1920] AC 904, 910.
35 [1920] AC 904, 909.

then they were more likely to constitute neutral trade unaffected by the reprisals order. Lord Sumner drew a distinction between the nature and value of postal correspondence and that of the bearer securities: postal correspondence typically communicated information and, as such, its value rested in the information conveyed between author and reader. This was in stark contrast to the nature of bearer securities, which represented an incorporeal property right transferable by delivery and nothing more. The paper securities were described by Lord Sumner as a 'convenient form in which to transfer wealth from one country to another'.[36]

In *Szanto v Aston*, a winning lottery ticket was located in the testator's home at the time of death.[37] The testator's will bequeathed 'all furniture and chattels that are in the house' as at the date of his death to his daughter and son-in-law. The residue of the estate was to be shared between the testator's three other children. The issue before the court was whether the winning lottery ticket was a chattel 'in the house'. The court acknowledged that while 'chattels' extends to both choses in action and choses in possession, there was a longstanding line of authority that a bequest of 'chattels in a house' did not extend to choses in action, since choses in action are incorporeal property incapable of having a location. The ticket passed into residue.

Property rights can be created by statute. The statute may explicitly state that property right is being created and identify the nature of the right. Copyright is an example of a personal property right created by statute. Section 196(1) of the *Copyright Act 1968* (Cth) provides that 'copyright is personal property, and subject to this section, is transmissible by assignment, by will and by devolution of operation of law'.

3.2 Possession

Possession is an essential concept in personal property. A right to possess is 'a normal incident of ownership; and the name of "property" is often given to it'.[38] Possession confers possessory title and can be evidence of ownership or entitlement to personal property.[39] Possessory title is good against every person other than the true owner.[40] Interference with possession of personal property is the basis standing to sue for remedies in detinue, conversion and trespass.[41] There are at least five different types of possession. These are: (1) custody; (2) actual possession or de facto possession; (3) constructive possession; (4) legal possession; and (5) a right to possess.

A person who holds a chattel is in possession of it.[42] Custody will occur where a party is holding the goods, but they do not have ownership or possession at law.[43] A clear example of custody exists where an employee uses their employer's goods in the course of their

36 [1920] AC 904, 908.

37 [2011] Qd R 484.

38 F Pollock and R Wright, *An Essay on Possession in the Common Law* (Clarendon Press, Oxford, UK, 1888), 27.

39 *Russell v Wilson* (1923) 33 CLR 538; *Field v Sullivan* [1923] VLR 70; *Anderson Group Pty Ltd v Tynan Motors Pty Ltd* (2006) 65 NSWLR 400; *Specialised Transport v Dominiak* (1989) 16 NSWLR 657.

40 *Russell v Wilson* (1923) 33 CLR 538, 546–7, per Isaacs and Rich JJ.

41 See W Holdsworth, *A History of English Law* (Methuen & Co Ltd, London, 3rd edn, 1923), vol III.

42 *Anderson Group Pty Ltd v Tynan Motors Pty Ltd* (2006) 65 NSWLR 400, 43; *Federal Commissioner of Taxation v Australia and New Zealand Banking Group Ltd* (1979) 143 CLR 499.

43 *Federal Commissioner of Taxation v Australia and New Zealand Banking Group Ltd* (1979) 143 CLR 499.

employment. The goods are in the custody of the employee, but they are also within the effective possession of the employer.

The terms 'de facto possession' and 'actual possession' are co-extensive.[44] De facto possession or actual possession involves 'the complete present personal physical control of the property to the exclusion of others'.[45] In *Williams v Douglas*,[46] the High Court held that de facto possession is an extensive concept and was not limited to physical custody.[47] In *Williams*, Latham CJ, Dixon and McTiernan JJ stated that possession is:

> wide enough to include any case where the person alleged to be in possession has hidden the thing effectively so that he can take it into his physical custody when he wishes and where others are unlikely to discover it except by accident.[48]

The High Court has subsequently interpreted this statement as implicitly requiring knowledge of the existence of the thing possessed.[49]

Legal possession is defined by Pollock and Wright as possession in 'the eye of the law'.[50] A person in de facto or actual possession is in legal possession.[51] In a revokable bailment that has not been revoked, the bailee has a present right to possession; the bailor does not.[52] While legal possession typically arises where a person has rightful physical control, a possessor may obtain legal possession wrongfully.[53] Pollock and Wright assert that a person who has been wrongfully dispossessed may remain the rightful possessor.

> A right to possession or to have legal possession includes the right to physical possession. It can exist apart from both physical and legal possession; it is, for example, that which remains to a rightful possessor immediately after he has been wrongfully disposed ... Unlike possession itself, [the right to possess] is not necessarily exclusive. A may have the right to possess a thing as against B and everyone else, while B has at the same time a right to possess it as against everyone except A ... When a person having a right to possess a thing acquires the physical control of it, he necessarily acquires legal possession also.[54]

Rights to possession can coexist. This is contemplated by the notion of constructive possession.[55] Constructive possession is the right to possession without legal possession.[56] In *Ward v*

---

44 See *Williams v Douglas* (1949) 78 CLR 521.
45 *Moors v Burke* (1919) 26 CLR 256, 274.
46 (1949) 78 CLR 521.
47 (1949) 78 CLR 521, 527. See also *Moors v Burke* (1919) 26 CLR 256.
48 (1949) 78 CLR 521, 527.
49 *He Kaw Teh v The Queen* (1984) 157 CLR 523, 538.
50 F Pollock and R Wright, *An Essay on Possession in the Common Law* (Clarendon Press, Oxford, UK, 1888), 26.
51 F Pollock and R Wright, *An Essay on Possession in the Common Law* (Clarendon Press, Oxford, UK, 1888), 17. See *Gray v Official Trustee in Bankruptcy* (1991) 29 FCR 166.
52 *Penfolds Wines Pty Ltd v Elliott* (1946) 74 CLR 204, 216.
53 F Pollock and R Wright, *An Essay on Possession in the Common Law* (Clarendon Press, Oxford, UK, 1888), 20.
54 F Pollock and R Wright, *An Essay on Possession in the Common Law* (Clarendon Press, Oxford, UK, 1888), 27.
55 See *P&O Nedlloyd BV v Utaniko Ltd* [2003] EWCA Civ 83, [16].
56 F Pollock and R Wright, *An Essay on Possession in the Common Law* (Clarendon Press, Oxford, UK, 1888), 27.

Macauley, it was argued that a landlord had constructive possession sufficient to found an action for trespass in circumstances where furniture from a house he had let fully furnished to a tenant was seized in the execution of a writ against the tenant.[57] The landlord had no actual or de facto possession and no immediate right to possession. Constructive possession can arise in trusts[58] and bailment,[59] and in the performance of sales contracts. For example, in *Gamer's Motor Centre (Newcastle) Pty Ltd v Natwest Wholesale Australia Pty Ltd*,[60] the question before the court was whether the nature of possession had changed so as to effect constructive or symbolic delivery. The High Court held that a buyer in possession could pass good title via constructive delivery.[61] Gamer sold motor vehicles to a dealer on terms that property was not to pass until payment had been made in full. The dealer took possession of the vehicles and almost immediately entered into a floor plan agreement with Natwest. It was agreed that when Natwest paid 90 per cent of the price, the dealer would then hold the vehicles as bailee for Natwest. At all times the vehicles were to remain in the physical custody of the dealer and be displayed on its showroom floor. Natwest paid 90 per cent of the agreed price. Payment was acknowledged via a delivery receipt. Subsequently, Gamer seized the vehicles as the dealer had failed to pay. Natwest, disputing Gamer's title to the vehicles, claimed it had better title as it had taken constructive delivery from a buyer in possession.[62] By majority, the High Court found in favour of Natwest, holding that a change in possession had occurred by virtue of the constructive delivery acknowledged by the delivery receipt.[63] Natwest had constructive possession of the vehicles at the time Gamer had seized them.

3.3 Interference with possession

Where there has been an interference with possession, there are three actions that the rightful owner, or their agent, might institute in order to claim damages. These are the torts of trespass, conversion or detinue.[64]

3.3.1 Trespass

Unauthorised use or handling of goods can form the basis of a personal action for trespass.[65] The tort of trespass is an action for the direct interference with actual or constructive possession.[66] An action in trespass is not available if the action is unintentional or without

57 (1791) 4 TR 489, 490.
58 *White v Morris* (1852) 138 ER 778.
59 See *Ashby v Tolhurst* [1937] 2 KB 242.
60 (1987) 163 CLR 236.
61 (1987) 163 CLR 236.
62 Natwest relied upon s 28 of the *Sale of Goods Act 1923* (NSW).
63 (1987) 163 CLR 236, per Mason CJ, Brennan and Dawson JJ, Toohey and Gaudron dissenting.
64 *Gollan v Nugent* (1988) 166 CLR 18, 24–5.
65 *Penfolds Wines Pty Ltd v Elliott* (1946) 74 CLR 204.
66 *Smith v Milles* (1786) 1 TR 475; *Penfolds Wines Pty Ltd v Elliott* (1946) 74 CLR 204; *Gollan v Nugent* (1988) 166 CLR 18, 25. *Wilson v Lombank Ltd* [1963] 1 WLR 1294 suggests that an immediate right to possession is also sufficient to sustain an action in trespass, but see *Penfolds Wines Pty Ltd v Elliott* (1946) 74 CLR 204, 216; *Slaveski v Victoria* [2010] VSC 441, [295].

negligence.[67] Actionable per se, the interference need not cause damage.[68] In *Penfolds Wines Pty Ltd v Elliott*,[69] Latham CJ stated:

> A mere taking or asportation of a chattel may be a trespass without the infliction of any material damage. The handling of a chattel without authority is a trespass . . . Unauthorized use of goods is a trespass; unauthorized acts of riding a horse, driving a motor car, using a bottle, are all equally trespasses, even though the horse may be returned unharmed or the motor car unwrecked or the bottle unbroken.[70]

Halsbury's Laws of Australia explains that trespass can be constituted by using, seizing, destroying, wilfully damaging, or removing goods, beating or killing animals, or chasing cattle.[71] In *Penfolds*, the appellant was a wine merchant who claimed ownership of wine bottles. The appellant claimed that the defendant had been taking the wine bottles and using them in his business instead of returning them to the plaintiff. The High Court found by a majority that trespass and conversion had not taken place. In *Penfolds*, Dixon J stated:

> In English law what amounts to an infringement upon the possessory and proprietary rights of the owner of a chattel personal is a question still governed by categories of specific wrong. Trespass was the wrong upon which reliance appeared to be placed in support of the appeal when it was opened, but, in the end, it seemed to be conceded that this cause of action was untenable. I think that it is quite clear that trespass would not lie for anything which the foregoing facts disclose. Trespass is a wrong to possession. But, on the part of the respondent, there was never any invasion of possession. At the time he filled the two bottles his brother left with him, he himself was in possession of them. If the bottles had been out of his own possession and in the possession of some other person, then to lift the bottles up against the will of that person and to fill them with wine would have amounted to trespasses. The reason is that the movement of the bottles and the use of them as receptacles are invasions of the possession of the second person. But they are things which the man possessed of the bottles may do without committing trespass.[72]

3.3.2 Conversion

In *Penfolds*, Dixon J noted that conversion is the intentional 'dealing with a chattel in a manner repugnant to the immediate right of possession of the person who has the property or special property in the chattel'.[73] Conversion is premised upon an interference with possession where the plaintiff has an immediate right to possession.[74] Unauthorised possession alone is not

67 *Fowler v Lanning* [1959] 1 QB 426.
68 *Penfolds Wines Pty Ltd v Elliott* (1946) 74 CLR 204, 214–15; *William Leitch & Co Ltd v Leydon* [1931] AC 90, 106.
69 (1946) 74 CLR 204.
70 (1946) 74 CLR 204, 214–15.
71 LexisNexis, *Halsbury's Laws of Australia* (at 15 December 2014), 315 *Personal Property*, [315–530].
72 (1946) 74 CLR 204, 227.
73 *Penfolds Wines Pty Ltd v Elliott* (1946) 74 CLR 204, 229; *Kuwait Airways Corporation v Iraqi Airways Co [Nos 4 & 5]* [2002] 2 AC 883, 1084, 1104, 1106; *Bunnings Group Ltd v CHEP Australia Ltd* (2011) 82 NSWLR 420, [124].
74 *Penfolds Wines Pty Ltd v Elliott* (1946) 74 CLR 204, 229.

conversion.[75] Acts of conversion include sale, pledge, transfer or destruction.[76] Acts that change the nature of a thing,[77] and acts of 'dominion',[78] are also acts of conversion. In *Penfolds*, Dixon J stated:

> The essence of conversion is a dealing with a chattel in a manner repugnant to the immediate right of possession of the person who has the property or special property in the chattel. It may take the form of a disposal of the goods by way of sale, or pledge or other intended transfer of an interest followed by delivery, of the destruction or change of the nature or character of the thing, as for example, pouring water into wine or cutting the seals from a deed, or of an appropriation evidenced by refusal to deliver or other denial of title. But damage to the chattel is not conversion, nor is use, nor is a transfer of possession otherwise than for the purpose of affecting the immediate right to possession, nor is it always conversion to lose the goods beyond hope of recovery. An intent to do that which would deprive 'the true owner' of his immediate right to possession or impair it may be said to form the essential ground of the tort. There is nothing in the course followed by the respondent in supplying wine to his customers who brought bottles to receive it involving any deprival or impairment of property in the bottles, that is of the immediate right to possession.[79]

The focus of the enquiry is upon the character of the use of the property: Is it an act of 'dominion over property inconsistent with the true owner's rights'?[80] Removal of horses from a ferry to a riverbank did not amount to conversion in *Fouldes v Willoughby*,[81] as it was not inconsistent with the owner's right to possession. The horses had been removed only to get them off the ferry after the plaintiff refused to do it himself.[82] Damage, use or loss 'beyond hope of recovery' are unlikely to amount to conversion.[83] A refusal to return cattle removed during the termination of a share-farming arrangement did not amount to conversion in circumstances where the defendant acknowledged the plaintiff's rights to possession and access for inspection as well as the right to share in any resulting proceeds of sale.[84]

3.3.3 Detinue

Detinue is the wrongful retention of goods.[85] An action in detinue can be brought where demand is made for the return of goods to the person with legal possession of them, by a person with an immediate right to possession, and that demand is unreasonably[86] refused.[87]

---

75 *Clayton v Le Roy* [1911] 2 KB 1031, 1048–50.
76 *Penfolds Wines Pty Ltd v Elliott* (1946) 74 CLR 204, 229.
77 In *Penfolds Wines Pty Ltd v Elliott* (1946) 74 CLR 204, 229 Dixon J explained that adding water to wine would be an act that changes the nature of a thing sufficient to form the basis of an action in conversion.
78 *Penfolds Wines Pty Ltd v Elliott* (1946) 74 CLR 204, 218–19; *Bunnings Group Ltd v CHEP Australia Ltd* (2011) 82 NSWLR 420, [124].
79 (1946) 74 CLR 204, 229.
80 *Bunnings Group Ltd v CHEP Australia Ltd* (2011) 82 NSWLR 420, [139]; *Gwinnett v Day* [2012] SASC 43, [51].
81 (1841) 151 ER 1153.
82 (1841) 151 ER 1153.
83 *Penfolds Wines Pty Ltd v Elliott* (1946) 74 CLR 204, 229.
84 *Gwinnett v Day* [2012] SASC 43.
85 *Bellinger v Autoland Pty Ltd* [1962] VR 514.
86 *E E McCurdy Ltd (in liq) v Postmaster-General* [1959] NZLR 553.
87 *Nelson v Nelson* [1923] St R Qd 37; *Grant v YYH Holdings Pty Ltd* [2012] NSWCA 360.

The remedies for trespass, detinue and conversion include injunctions, declarations and damages. In *Bunnings Group Ltd v CHEP Australia Ltd*,[88] Allsop J explained the basis of the assessment of damages for conversion and detinue by reference to principles of compensation.

> The damage or loss caused to the plaintiff with rights of ownership and possession who is in the business of hiring goods of the kind converted or detained is not limited to the consequences of stock depletion or to cost of replacement, but includes the denial and infringement of its rights. Those rights have been denied to the plaintiff by the commission of a tort involving the use of the goods by the tortfeasor. It is entirely logical and in accordance with justice and common sense that a wrongdoer should pay a price for using the goods of another as a matter of compensation for the denial of the right concerned. I do not see this as contrary to, or undermining of, the principle of compensation.[89]

Damages for detinue are measured by reference to the value of the goods that are the subject of the action at the date of their return or at the date of judgment. Loss of the use of the goods may be measured by reference to the costs of hire[90] or depreciation.[91] Damages for conversion are measured by reference to the value of the goods converted as at the date[92] and place of their conversion.[93] The value of the goods is taken to be the market value of the cost of replacement goods or where, no market exists, the costs of the manufacture and supply of replacement goods.[94] In *J & E Hall Ltd v Barclay*,[95] Greer LJ stated:

> Where you are dealing with goods that can be readily bought in the market, a man whose rights have been interfered with is never entitled to more than what he would have to pay to buy a similar article in the market. That rule has been acted upon over and over again, and that, I think, means that, where there is a market, the man whose rights have been interfered with is bound to diminish the damage by going into the market and buying the goods in the market so as to put himself in the position in which he is entitled to be put, namely the position which he would have been in if he had not suffered any wrong at all.[96]

In the absence of proof of damage in trespass to goods, any award is likely to be nominal.[97] Where trespass or conversion has amounted to a contumelious or cavalier disregard of the plaintiff's right, exemplary damages may be awarded.[98] A right to recover goods by recapture may exist at common law for trespass and conversion where the owner has an immediate right to possession and exercising the right to recover the goods would not involve trespass

88 *Bunnings Group Ltd v CHEP Australia Ltd* (2011) 82 NSWLR 420.
89 *Bunnings Group Ltd v CHEP Australia Ltd* (2011) 82 NSWLR 420, 467.
90 *Bunnings Group Ltd v CHEP Australia Ltd* (2011) 82 NSWLR 420.
91 *Roder Zelt-Und Hallenkonstruktionen GMBH v Rosedown Park Pty Ltd* (unreported, Federal Court of Australia, von Doussa J, 30 November 1995).
92 *Associated Midland Corporation Ltd v Bank of New South Wales* [1983] 1 NSWLR 533, 550.
93 *Sadcas Pty Ltd v Business & Professional Finance Pty Ltd* [2011] NSWCA 267, [1].
94 *J & E Hall Ltd v Barclay* [1937] 3 All ER 620, applied in *Sadcas Pty Ltd v Business & Professional Finance Pty Ltd* [2011] NSWCA 267.
95 [1937] 3 All ER 620.
96 [1937] 3 All ER 620, 623.
97 See *Cressy v Johnson [No 3]* [2009] VSC 52, [217].
98 *Healing (Sales) Pty Ltd v Inglis Electrix Pty Ltd* (1968) 121 CLR 584, 591, 622–3; *New South Wales v Ibbett* (2006) 229 CLR 638; *Randwick City Council v Burnett* [2005] NSWSC 508.

upon private land.[99] Common law recapture has drawn criticism for encouraging 'forcible redress for no satisfactory reason'.[100]

3.4 Loss of personal property rights

Property in chattels may be lost, altered or transformed through the operation of doctrines relating to intermixture, accession and fixtures. The nature of the transformation or recognition of continuing property rights may impact upon the right to bring an action for trespass, detinue or conversion.

3.4.1 Intermixture

Intermixture is the indistinguishable, inseparable mixing of goods. The doctrine of intermixture can apply to deprive an owner of their personal property rights in the goods. The doctrine was explained by Lord Moulton in the House of Lords in *Sandeman & Sons v Tyzack & Branfoot Steamship Co Ltd*.

> I do not think it a matter of difficulty to define the legal consequences of the goods of A becoming indistinguishably and inseparably mixed with the goods of B. If the mixing has arisen from the fault of B, A can claim the goods. He is guilty of no wrongful act, and therefore the possession by him of his own goods cannot be interfered with, and if by the wrongful act of B that possession necessarily implies the possession of the intruding goods of B, he is entitled to it. But if the mixing has taken place by accident or other cause, for which neither of the owners is responsible, a different state of things arises. Neither owner has done anything to forfeit his right to the possession of his own property, and if neither party is willing to abandon that right the only equitable solution of the difficulty, and the one accepted by the law, is that A and B become owners in common of the mixed property.[101]

Where there has been no wrongful act, ownership of mixed property is held as tenants in common in shares proportionate to contribution.[102] Where the intermixture is wrongful, the innocent party is entitled to receive from the whole a quantity equal to their contribution.[103] Any doubt is resolved in favour of the innocent party.[104] For example, in *Hill v Reglon Pty Ltd*,[105] scaffolding belonging to two commercial parties had been wrongfully commingled, painted red and distributed across building sites and a storage yard. Each party was found to

99 *Blade v Higgs* (1861) 142 ER 634.

100 *Toyota Finance Australia Ltd v Dennis* [2002] NSWCA 369, [141]. See also *Blade v Higgs* (1861) 142 ER 634; *Zimmler v Manning* (1863) 2 SCR (NSW) 235; *Abbott v New South Wales Mont de Piete Company* (1904) 4 SR (NSW) 336.

101 [1913] AC 680, 694–5.

102 *Spence v Union Marine Insurance Ltd* (1868) LR 3CP 427; *Hill v Reglon Pty Ltd* [2007] NSWCA 295. At first instance, in *Reglon Pty Ltd v Hill* [2006] NSWSC 1360, [22]–[23], affirmed on appeal, Windeyer J provided an instructive analysis of the law of intermixture.

103 *Indian Oil Corporation Ltd v Greenstone Shipping* [1988] QB 345, 370–1.

104 *Indian Oil Corporation Ltd v Greenstone Shipping* [1988] QB 345, 370–1.

105 [2007] NSWCA 295.

own the scaffolding in common in the proportions they had contributed, and Reglon was entitled to recover from the painted scaffolding the amount contributed.[106]

The doctrine applies to goods 'such as corn, wine, oil and the like of which there can be commingling of substance'.[107] It has been applied to cattle,[108] logs of wood,[109] chocolate and confectionery,[110] and silver coins.[111]

3.4.2 Accession

Accession arises when a chattel is incorporated into another.[112] The chattel being incorporated is often described as the accessory, and the chattel to which it is being attached is the principal. Accession deals with the difficult question of what happens to the rights of ownership in the accessory.[113] It is not axiomatic that ownership is transferred to the owner of the principal thing.[114] The doctrine of accession recognises the continued rights of the owner of the accessory.[115] The doctrine of accession was clearly stated in *Rendell v Associated Finance Pty Ltd* where the court was considering a dispute regarding ownership of spare parts that had been attached to a vehicle.

> Prima face the property in the accessory does not pass to the owner of the vehicle if the owner of the accessory did not intend it to pass. It is for the defendant by proper evidence to show that the necessity of the case requires the application of principles whereby the property is deemed to pass by operation of law. The accessories continue to belong to their original owner unless it is shown that as a matter of practicability they cannot be identified, or if identified, they have been incorporated to such an extent that they cannot be detached from the vehicle.[116]

Where separation is practically impossible the doctrine of accession will resolve issues as to ownership of the accessory, but 'if the chattels can be severed without damage to either chattel there would appear to be no necessity to invoke any doctrine of accession of title'.[117] This was the case in *Sims v SPM Business Consultants Pty Ltd*, where the court determined that it was unnecessary to apply the doctrine of accession where the accessory thing was documents that had been added to a file; these could be easily removed.[118] The doctrine has been applied to

106 [2007] NSWCA 295, [101].
107 *Indian Oil Corporation Ltd v Greenstone Shipping* [1988] QB 345.
108 *Big Top Hereford Pty Ltd v Thomas* (2006) 12 BPR 23,843 .
109 *McDonald v Lane* (1882) 7 SCR 462.
110 *Hunter Wholesale Confectioners Pty Ltd (in liq) v Sweeties Confectionery Pty Ltd* [2010] NSWSC 1257.
111 *Coleman v Harvey* [1989] 1 NZLR 723.
112 *Rendell v Associated Finance Pty Ltd* [1957] VR 604, 607.
113 *Rendell v Associated Finance Pty Ltd* [1957] VR 604, 607.
114 Although that will be the case where it is the intention of the parties. See *National Bus Co Pty Ltd v Commissioner of Taxation* (1998) 38 ATR 211, 217.
115 *McKeown v Cavalier Yachts Pty Ltd* (1988) 13 NSWLR 303.
116 *Rendell v Associated Finance Pty Ltd* [1957] VR 604, 610.
117 *Rendell v Associated Finance Pty Ltd* [1957] VR 604, 607; see also *Lewis v Andrews & Rowley Pty Ltd* (1956) 73 WN (NSW) 670, 672, per Ferguson J; *McKeown v Cavalier Yachts Pty Ltd* (1988) 13 NSWLR 303; *Sims v SPM Business Consultants Pty Ltd* [2002] FCA 1588.
118 *Sims v SPM Business Consultants Pty Ltd* [2002] FCA 1588, [67]–[68].

skins incorporated into a fur coat,[119] and engines incorporated into generators.[120] In *Grant v YYH Holdings Pty Ltd*, it was held that the doctrine of accession does not apply to living things.[121] Grant was in possession of exotic sheep owned by YYH Holdings. The company had secured exclusive rights to breed the sheep in Australia and owned all genetic material associated with the breed. A dispute arose; YYH Holdings demanded the return of the sheep and associated genetic material including their progeny, embryos and straws of semen. Grant refused. The company brought an action in detinue, conversion and trespass. At first instance, the claim succeeded in relation to the genetic material, but the claim in respect of the sheep failed as it was time barred by the *Limitation Act 1969* (NSW).[122] On appeal, Grant argued that the entire claim was time barred since the sheep and their genetic material ought to be considered as one and the same goods, on the basis either of intermingling or of the doctrine of accession.[123] The Court of Appeal rejected both arguments,[124] finding that the doctrines of intermingling and accession had developed in relation to inanimate objects. Basten J stated that the law did not allow for people or animals to be treated as chattels 'equivalent to inanimate objects'.[125]

3.4.3 Fixtures

Fixtures are real property. A chattel will not retain its nature as personal property where it becomes a fixture. The question of whether a chattel has become a fixture is determined by a consideration of the purposes, nature, degree and mode of annexation in all the circumstances of the case.[126] Fundamentally, courts will have regard to the degree and the purpose of annexation.[127] In *Holland v Hodgson*,[128] Lord Blackburn stated:

> [It] is a question which must depend on the circumstances of each case, and mainly on two circumstances, as indicating the intention, viz, the degree of annexation and the object of the annexation. When the article in question is no further attached to the land than by its own weight it is generally considered a mere chattel. But even in such a case, if the intention is apparent to make the articles part of the land, they do become part of the land ... On the other hand, an article may be very firmly fixed to the land and yet the circumstances may be such as to show that it was never intended to be part of the land, and then it does not become part of the land.[129]

119 *Jones v De Marchant* (1916) 28 DLR 561.
120 *Hendy Lennox (Industrial Engines) Ltd v Grahame Puttick Ltd* [1984] 1 WLR 485.
121 *Grant v YYH Holdings Pty Ltd* [2012] NSWCA 360.
122 *YYH Holdings Pty Ltd v Grant* (unreported, District Court of New South Wales, Rolfe DCJ, 23 March 2012).
123 [2012] NSWCA 360, [46]–[58].
124 [2012] NSWCA 360, [57].
125 [2012] NSWCA 360, [72].
126 *Holland v Hodgson* (1872) LR 7 CP 328; *Lee v Taylor* [1902] AC 157. See also *Agripower v Blomfield* [2015] NSWCA 30, [74]–[81]; *Power Rental Op Co Australia, LLC v Forge Group Power Pty Ltd (in liq) (recs and mgrs apptd)* (2017) 93 NSWLR 765.
127 *Elitestone Ltd v Morris* [1997] 1 WLR 687. See also *Australian Provincial Assurance Co Ltd v Coroneo* (1938) 38 SR (NSW) 700.
128 [1872] LR 7 CP 328.
129 *Holland v Hodgson* (1872) LR 7 CP 328, 334–5.

In *Palumberi v Palumberi*,[130] Kearney J has observed:

> [T]here has been a perceptible decline in the comparative importance of the degree or mode of annexation, with a tendency to greater emphasis being placed upon the purpose or object of annexation, or, putting it another way, the intention with which the item is placed upon the land. The shift has involved a greater reliance upon the individual surrounding circumstances of the case in question as distinct from any attempt to seek to apply some simple rule or some automatic solution.[131]

In *Anthony v Commonwealth*, telephone cables and power lines permanently installed upon land were held not to be fixtures.[132] The focus of the court's inquiry in that case was the purpose of the annexation. A similar approach was taken in *Neylon v Dickens*, where it was determined that a prefabricated house, helicopter hangar, and meat storage and freezing facilities were not fixtures as there was only a temporary annexation to the land.[133] In *Elitestone Ltd v Morris*,[134] the House of Lords ruled that wooden bungalows that rested on concrete pillars in a rural location were in fact fixtures. Lord Berwick stated:

> Many different tests have been suggested, such as whether the object which has been fixed to the property has been so fixed for the better enjoyment of the object as a chattel, or whether it has been fixed with a view to effecting a permanent improvement of the freehold. This and similar tests are useful when one is considering an object such as a tapestry, which may or may not be fixed to a house so as to become part of the freehold: see *Leigh v. Taylor* [1902] A.C. 157. These tests are less useful when one is considering the house itself. In the case of the house the answer is as much a matter of common sense as precise analysis. A house which is constructed in such a way so as to be removable, whether as a unit, or in sections, may well remain a chattel, even though it is connected temporarily to mains services such as water and electricity. But a house which is constructed in such a way that it cannot be removed at all, save by destruction, cannot have been intended to remain as a chattel. It must have been intended to form part of the realty.[135]

In *National Dairies WA Ltd v Commissioner of State Revenue*,[136] plant and equipment used in a system for milk processing were found to be fixtures. The equipment was extensively connected by pipes so as to form an integrated whole, and mostly fixed to the floor by its own weight. Some items of machinery were bolted to the floor to keep them steady or for safety reasons. While the equipment had been permanently installed, it was readily removable.

A fixture is described as a 'tenant's fixture' when the tenant has a right to remove the fixture in accordance with its lease.[137] The test for determining whether the chattel has become a fixture is the same as for other chattels described above.[138]

---

130 [1986] NSW ConvR ¶55-673.
131 *Palumberi v Palumberi* [1986] NSW ConvR ¶55-673, ¶56-672.
132 *Anthony v Commonwealth* (1973) 29 *Local Government Reports* 61, 71.
133 [1979] 2 NZLR 714.
134 [1997] 1 WLR 687.
135 [1997] 1 WLR 687, 692–3.
136 [2001] WASCA 112.
137 *D'Arcy v Burelli Investments Pty Ltd* (1987) 8 NSWLR 317.
138 *Commissioner of Main Roads v North Shore Gas Co Ltd* (1967) 120 CLR 118.

3.4.4 Finding

A finding dispute may arise where goods have been lost by their true owner and are subsequently discovered by another. The true owner will, of course, have the strongest entitlement to the goods.[139] However, if the true owner cannot be located, then the question of whether the finder or the occupier has the better claim to possessory title would need to be addressed.[140]

An occupier may have possessory rights to a chattel on the basis that they are exercising control over the place where the item was found.[141] The key factor here is the objective manifestation of a desire to exercise control over the relevant land, house or place. If the chattel goods are attached to the land, then the occupier might obtain better title to them than any other finder.[142] However, the finder may acquire better title if the chattel is unattached.[143]

The finder does not acquire an absolute right to title to the goods, but may have a better claim than all others except the true owner.[144] In *Parker v British Airways Board*,[145] a passenger at Heathrow Airport discovered a gold bracelet in the British Airways executive lounge. He handed the bracelet to the British Airways staff at the lounge, but he expressly declared that if the true owner could not be found he would want the bracelet returned to him. The true owner never claimed the bracelet and British Airways subsequently sold it. Parker successfully sued British Airways for the value of the proceeds of that sale. Donaldson LJ, in the English Court of Appeal, compiled a set of principles which might be summarised as follows:

1. The finder of a chattel acquires no rights unless (a) it has been abandoned or lost and (b) the finder takes it into their care and control.
2. The finder of a chattel acquires very limited rights over it if they take it into their care and control with dishonest intent or in the course of trespassing.
3. The finder of a chattel who is lawfully upon the land acquires ownership against all but the true owner.
4. Subject to any contrary agreement, an employee who finds a chattel while acting in the course of their employment is to be taken to find that item on behalf of their employer.
5. The finder is under an obligation to take reasonable and appropriate measures to find the true owner of a chattel.

3.5 Challenging notions of personal property

Recognition of novel property rights and their classification as personal rights present a conundrum where they are sufficiently vexing to resist classification according to traditional

139 *Waverley Borough Council v Fletcher* [1995] QB 334.
140 *Armory v Delamirie* (1722) 93 ER 664.
141 *Corporation of London v Appleyard* [1963] 1 WLR 982.
142 *South Staffordshire Water Co v Sharman* [1896] 2 QB 44.
143 *Waverley Borough Council v Fletcher* [1995] QB 334.
144 *Parker v British Airways Board* [1982] QB 1004.
145 [1982] QB 1004.

norms. The concept of property is not stagnant. Innovation and development are attendant with new concepts and things that challenge concepts of property and personal property rights. For example, 50 years ago software was not sold separately.[146] In the early days of personal computing, software came preinstalled on computer hardware. The move to sell software separately, for an additional fee, was called 'unbundling'. As innovative as it was, unbundling brought unique challenges to legal notions of property rights. Software innovation has continued in gaming, which has given rise to complex issues of virtual property. This section of the chapter considers four developments that have at various stages challenged the boundaries of the common law concept of personal property.

3.5.1 Property rights in software

The classification of property rights surrounding software in the United States has proved controversial and difficult, particularly for the purpose of commercial sales contracts and taxation. In both cases discussed here, tax could be imposed only if the software was found to be tangible property.

In *South Central Bell Telephone Co v Bartheley*,[147] the Supreme Court of Louisiana considered two types of computer software: the switching system and data-processing software. Bell had purchased rights to use the software under a licence. The licence limited the permitted use of the software and included a right to transfer the licence. No ownership interests were acquired. The question before the court was whether the software was tangible property. It was argued that the software was tangible since it was a part of the physical magnetic tape on which it was delivered to Bell. When Bell received this tape, which was of little intrinsic value, it uploaded the software on to its switching system processes and then discarded or reused the tape. In reaching its decision, the court looked to the essence of the transaction rather than the mode of delivery. Hall J stated that the true object of the transaction was revealed by the fact that the software was 'recorded and stored in a physical form upon a physical object',[148] which Bell's computers could then install. Hall J explained that the critical factor was that, once recorded in physical form, the software was 'not merely an incorporeal idea to be comprehended and would be no use if it were'.[149] Rather, the software had been given a physical existence to 'make certain desired physical things happen'.[150] The court held that the computer software was tangible personal property.

The decision in *South Central Bell Telephone Co v Bartheley*[151] was at odds with a range of much earlier cases in which it had been decided that computer software was intangible personal property, including *State v Central Computer Servers Inc*[152] and *Matter of Protest*

146 R L Glass, 'Before the Beginning: The Pre-Software Era' in R L Glass (ed), *In the Beginning: Personal Recollections of Software Pioneers* (IEEE Computer Society Press, Los Alamitos, CA, 1998); B Burton, 'A Personal Recollection: IBM's Unbundling of Software and Services' (2002) 24(1) *IEEE Annals of the History of Computing* 64, 65.
147 (1994) 643 So 2d 1240.
148 (1994) 643 So 2d 1240, 1247.
149 (1994) 643 So 2d 1240, 1247.
150 (1994) 643 So 2d 1240, 1247.
151 (1994) 643 So 2d 1240.
152 (1977) 349 So 2d 1160.

of Strayer.[153] These earlier decisions were founded on the notion that the product being sold was the information in the software, and that any tangible medium used to facilitate the sale was merely incidental.

The question of how to classify software arose again in *Wal-Mart Stores Inc v City of Mobile*, where the Supreme Court of Alabama held that computer software sold by Walmart was tangible personal property. The majority observed that times had changed: mass-produced, off-the-shelf software was prolific.[154] It was marketed in a manner that presumed it would be sold in a tangible medium, not unlike a book.[155] Further, the court's knowledge and understanding of computer software had grown since the early software cases such as *State v Central Computer Servers Inc*.[156]

These cases demonstrate that the law in this area has evolved so as to reveal a greater willingness to classify software as taxable tangible property at least where the software is for standard installation. There remains scope to argue that software is intangible where it is custom designed and delivered in an intangible format. Whether software is classified as tangible or intangible is likely to turn upon considerations such as the complexity of customisation of the software, and the method by which it is sold and delivered to the purchaser.

3.5.2 Virtual property

'Property' refers to the thing that is capable of being owned and is also used to describe the nature of the bundle of rights of ownership in relation to the thing. While the notion of choses in action accommodates intangible and incorporeal property, virtual worlds and the virtual property within them present unique legal challenges. Virtual worlds are 'Internet-based simulated environments that feature software-animated objects and events'.[157] Land and objects that 'exist' only in virtual worlds present new challenges for traditional concepts of property. Legal scholars advocate clarity and recognition of virtual property rights on the basis that they hold personal and economic value, and give rise to disputes and opportunities for crime.[158] Lastowka notes that this is not without controversy: if virtual property is recognised as legal property, it may be among the assets to be divided in divorce proceedings, disposed of by will, and possibly even subject to tax.[159]

The Supreme Court of the Netherlands, Hoge Raad der Nederlanden, has considered a matter involving both a real-world assault and theft of objects existing within the virtual game

153 (1986) 239 Kan 136.

154 (1996) 696 So 2d 290, 290–1.

155 (1996) 696 So 2d 290, 292.

156 (1996) 696 So 2d 290, 292; see *State v Central Computer Servers Inc* (1977) 349 So 2d 1160.

157 G Lastowka, *Virtual Justice: The New Laws of Online Worlds* (Yale University Press, New Haven, CT, 2010), 9.

158 L B Moses, 'The Applicability of Property in New Contexts: From Cells to Cyberspace' (2008) 30 *Sydney Law Review* 639, 646; G Lastowka and D Hunter, 'The Laws of the Virtual World' (2004) 92 *California Law Review* 1; G Lastowka, *Virtual Justice: The New Laws of Online Worlds* (Yale University Press, New Haven, CT, 2010); C Chambers-Jones, *Virtual Economies and Financial Crime: Money Laundering in Cyberspace* (Edward Elgar Publishing, Cheltenham, UK, 2012).

159 G Lastowka, *Virtual Justice: The New Laws of Online Worlds* (Yale University Press, New Haven, CT, 2010), 12.

world Runescape.[160] The court was required to determine whether theft had occurred in circumstances where two teenagers attacked and threatened a boy with a knife, demanding he hand over virtual objects acquired within the virtual game world. The objects, a mask and an amulet, were associated with power and prestige within the game. The attackers demanded that the boy log into his Runescape game account. The boy's avatar then 'dropped' the amulet and mask within the virtual game arena, and they were immediately 'claimed' by the avatar of one of the attackers. The court recognised that virtual objects were capable of being the subject of theft, and acknowledged that prior to the incident the boy had control over goods of value to him.[161]

The nature of the virtual property varies from one platform to another. It may consist of land, clothing, weapons, or money typically accumulated by the player's avatar. This virtual property may have little value outside the platform. Yet, since the virtual property enhances the status of the player, or is considerably difficult or expensive to attain within the platform, it has value to the player and to other users within the platform. The sheer scale of participation in online virtual reality environments contributes to the creation of increasingly significant virtual economies that may in turn affect real-world economies.[162] Virtual objects, purchased or earned in virtual worlds, may be of considerable value to their owner, or 'player'. Users of virtual worlds are typically subject to an 'in world property model'.[163] End-user licence agreements typically limit remedies in contract law and outline the terms upon which the user may participate in the virtual world, and purchase and use virtual property. Copyright law may be relevant to considerations that involve intellectual property in intangible items. Lastowka and Hunter consider that virtual environments require separate legal treatment: '[V]irtual worlds are jurisdictions separate from our own, with their own distinctive community norms, laws and rights.'[164]

Existing legal frameworks may not adapt well to the unique challenges of virtual property rights.[165] What remedies does the player have if the virtual world is discontinued by its developers, or if the developer decides to shut down the player's account?[166] What remedies might the player have if they become the target of a hacker who steals, damages or usurps their virtual wealth? How should legal systems best address opportunities for money laundering through virtual economies?[167] The struggle that existing legal frameworks may face in

160 Hoge Raad der Nederlanden, LJN BQ9251, Supreme, J. 10/00101, 31 January 2012: http://uitspraken.rechtspraak.nl/.

161 See also S J Horowitz, 'Competing Lockean Claims to Virtual Property' (2007) 20(2) *Harvard Journal of Law and Technology* 443, 443, where Horowitz cites an example of one Chinese gamer killing another over a stolen 'virtual' dragon sabre. See also G Lastowka and D Hunter, 'Virtual Crimes' (2004) 49 *New York Law School Law Review* 293.

162 C Chambers-Jones, *Virtual Economies and Financial Crime: Money Laundering in Cyberspace* (Edward Elgar Publishing, Cheltenham, UK, 2012); V Lehdonvirta and E Castronova, *Virtual Economies: Design and Analysis* (MIT Press, Cambridge, MA, 2014).

163 S J Horowitz, 'Competing Lockean Claims to Virtual Property' (2007) 20(2) *Harvard Journal of Law and Technology* 443, 444.

164 G Lastowka and D Hunter, 'The Laws of the Virtual World' (2004) 92 *California Law Review* 1, 73.

165 See G Lastowka and D Hunter, 'The Laws of the Virtual World' (2004) 92 *California Law Review* 1 for an analysis of these difficulties and how legal frameworks might adapt in order to accommodate virtual property rights.

166 See, for example, *Bragg v Linden Research* (2007) 487 F Supp 2d 593.

167 C Chambers-Jones, *Virtual Economies and Financial Crime: Money Laundering in Cyberspace* (Edward Elgar Publishing, Cheltenham, UK, 2012).

providing answers to these questions becomes apparent when considering the nature of virtual property rights and the objectives of existing laws.[168]

Horowitz says:

> A virtual property right is a property right in a virtual product. While both virtual and intellectual property rights protect interests in non-corporeal things, virtual property rights apply to *rivalous* goods whereas intellectual property rights apply to *nonrivalrous* goods. For example a virtual property right can protect a domain name. While anyone can own a copy of the Beatles' 'White Album' without making others worse off, we cannot all own the same domain name – say www.google.com – without destroying its usefulness. The content of a virtual property right is also different from that of an intellectual property right. Like real property rights, virtual property rights typically provide for the rights to use, to exclude others from using, and to alienate or transfer objects. Intellectual property rights, by contrast, prohibit copying or producing similar ideas, expressions or products.[169]

Bragg v Linden Research[170] involved the virtual world of Second Life. The operator of the virtual world, Linden, had terminated Bragg's user account, alleging that he had violated its terms of service. Bragg instituted proceedings in Pennsylvania to recover US$8000, which represented the balance of his user account at the time it was terminated and the estimated value of virtual property accumulated in Second Life. The matter did not extend beyond interlocutory proceedings and was settled, leaving the legal status of virtual property in doubt.[171]

3.5.3 Commercial exploitation of medical research

Commercial exploitation of medical research in potentially lucrative markets has raised issues as to property rights in the human body. The Supreme Court of California was asked to consider these issues in *Moore v Regents of the University of California*.[172] Moore's spleen had been removed in treatment for leukaemia. Without Moore's knowledge or consent, Moore's doctor and a research assistant developed a potentially valuable cell line from samples of Moore's removed spleen. Commercial markets were estimated to be valued in excess of US$3 billion. Moore instituted proceedings for 13 causes of action, including conversion. Moore claimed that taking and using cell samples from his spleen was an interference with his ownership rights in personal property. Moore claimed a proprietary interest in products created from his cells or the cell line. In a majority decision, the court found that it would be an 'unprecedented extension of liability' to find Moore had property rights that had been infringed.[173] Mosk J dissented, reasoning that recognition of ownership in their own tissues

168 G Lastowka and D Hunter, 'The Laws of the Virtual World' (2004) 92 *California Law Review* 1.

169 S J Horowitz, 'Competing Lockean Claims to Virtual Property' (2007) 20(2) *Harvard Journal of Law and Technology* 443, 444. Emphasis in original.

170 (2007) 487 F Supp 2d 593.

171 C Dougherty, '*Bragg v Linden*: Virtual Property Rights Litigation' (2007) 9(7) *E-Commerce Law and Policy* 1; L Bennett Moses, 'The Applicability of Property in New Contexts: From Cells to Cyberspace' (2008) 30 *Sydney Law Review* 639, 646.

172 (1990) 51 Ca 3d 120.

173 *Moore v Regents of the University of California* (1990) 51 Ca 3d 120, 147. See also *Yearworth v North Bristol NHS Trust* [2010] QB 1.

would give patients an affirmative right of participation in the commercialisation of their tissue for medical development.[174]

3.5.4 Property rights in a spectacle

In *Victoria Park Racing and Recreation Grounds Co Pty Ltd v Taylor*,[175] the High Court considered whether property rights could exist in a spectacle. Victoria Park Racing and Recreation owned a racecourse. Taylor owned land nearby. Taylor had erected a platform upon the land, from which it was possible to observe the racecourse. From the platform, the defendant was able to provide a sufficiently interesting commentary of the activities at the racecourse to be broadcast. Victoria Park Racing claimed the broadcast was negatively impacting upon attendance and revenue. It sought an injunction to prevent the broadcasts. The immediate difficulty was that it was unclear what right had been wronged. Latham CJ explained:

> I find difficulty in attaching any precise meaning to the phrase 'property in a spectacle'. A 'spectacle' cannot be 'owned' in any ordinary sense of that word. Even if there were any legal principle which prevented one person from gaining an advantage for himself or causing damage to another by describing a spectacle produced by that other person, the rights of the latter person could be described as property only in a metaphorical sense. Any appropriateness in the metaphor would depend upon the existence of the legal principle. The principle cannot itself be based upon such a metaphor.
>
> Even if, on the other hand, a spectacle could be said to exist as a subject matter of property, it would still be necessary, in order to provide the plaintiff in this case with a remedy, to show that the description of such property is wrongful or that such description is wrongful when it is widely disseminated. No authority has been cited to support such a proposition.[176]

It was held by a majority that no property rights exist in a spectacle[177] and the plaintiff's right to the knowledge broadcast by the defendants lacked the necessary element of exclusiveness to qualify as property.[178]

Rich J, in dissent, held that there ought to be a limit to the right of overlooking to balance the right of free prospect from one piece of land with the right of profitable enjoyment from another.[179] Rich J considered that the expansiveness of the law ought to adapt and change over time.

> [L]aw grows and ... though the principles of law remain unchanged, yet (and it is one of the advantages of the common law) their application is to be changed with the changing circumstances of the times. Some persons may call this retrogression[;] I call it progression of human opinion. [180]

174 *Moore v Regents of the University of California* (1990) 51 Ca 3d 120, 164–5.
175 *Victoria Park Racing and Recreation Grounds Co Pty Ltd v Taylor* (1937) 58 CLR 479.
176 (1937) 58 CLR 479, 496–7.
177 (1937) 58 CLR 479, 496, 507, 523–4.
178 (1937) 58 CLR 479, 509–10, 514.
179 (1937) 58 CLR 479, 503.
180 (1937) 58 CLR 479, 503, Rich J, citing *R v Ramsay* (1883) 48 LT NS 733, 735.

3.6 Key points

- Personal property is one of the central features of commercial law.
- There are two types of personal property: choses in action and choses in possession.
- 'Choses in action' refers to legal rights, whereas 'choses in possession' refers to tangible personal property.
- Possession is a key incident of ownership. Possession itself can give rise to a type of title in goods. Possessory title will prevail against all others apart from the true owner of the goods.
- The common law recognises tortious interference with possession in the form of trespass, detinue and conversion.
- Personal property rights in goods may be lost through accession, intermixture and the operation of the doctrine of fixtures.

3.7 DISCUSSION QUESTIONS

1. What is property?
2. What is the difference between a chose in action and a chose in possession?
3. What are the different ways in which property allocates ownership? What commonalities can you discern across the various categories of property?
4. What challenge does developing technology pose to existing property law doctrines in Australia?

3.8 FURTHER READING

Gray, K, 'Property in Thin Air' (1991) 50 *Cambridge Law Journal* 252.

Horowitz, S J, 'Competing Lockean Claims to Virtual Property' (2007) 20(2) *Harvard Journal of Law and Technology* 443.

Lastowka, G, *Virtual Justice: The New Laws of Online Worlds* (Yale University Press, New Haven, CT, 2010).

Merrill, T, 'Property and the Right to Exclude' (1998) 77 *Nebraska Law Review* 730.

4

SALE OF GOODS

4.0 Introduction

This chapter deals with the topic of the sale of goods. There are Sale of Goods Acts in each state and territory in Australia, all of them broadly the same in their terms and structure.[1] They are all based on the *Sale of Goods Act 1893* (UK). As such, UK court decisions are very relevant to the interpretation of Australian legislation. The sale of goods is regulated in Victoria by the *Goods Act 1958* (Vic) ('Goods Act') and this chapter uses this Act as a model with which to explore the various issues pertaining to the sale of goods.

The Goods Act mostly codifies the common law relating to the sale of goods. The Goods Act is not a perfect code because the common law still appears to have some operation under certain provisions. The sale of goods is also regulated, in relation to transactions by a corporation to a consumer, by the *Competition and Consumer Act 2010* (Cth) (CCA). The Goods Act covers certain disputes that occur within Victoria. The CCA applies anywhere within Australia, but is limited in operation to corporations and, under certain circumstances, individuals. The CCA covers implied terms in consumer contracts, misleading or deceptive conduct, unconscionable conduct, unfair terms and other like matters in consumer contracts. The Goods Act applies to all contracts for the sale of goods where the basic definitional issues are concerned. Further, the Act covers implied terms in sale of goods contracts that are not covered by the Australian Consumer Law.

This chapter looks at the fundamental requirements of a sale of goods contract. It explores the ways of distinguishing a sale of goods contract from other contracts. It also examines those terms that are implied into sale of goods contracts by the Goods Act. The issues relating to the remedies of buyers and sellers are covered in Chapter 6 on price and delivery.

4.1 Interpreting the Sale of Goods Acts

One of the consequences of the history behind the Sale of Goods Acts and their coverage over so many different jurisdictions is that there are issues regarding interpretation of the statute. As a codifying statute, the 1893 Act presented a unique challenge for the courts of England, drawing together as it did a rich history of past jurisprudence on sale of goods contracts into some seemingly well-settled rules. The approach to interpreting such a statute was discussed in *Bank of England v Vagliano Brothers*,[2] where Lord Herschell stated:

> I think the proper course is in the first instance to examine the language of the statute and to ask what is its natural meaning, uninfluenced by any considerations derived from the previous state of the law, and not to start with inquiring how the law previously stood, and then, assuming that it was probably intended to leave it unaltered, to see if the words of the enactment will bear an interpretation in conformity with this view. If a statute, intended to embody in a code a particular branch of the law, is to be treated in this fashion, it appears to me that its utility will be almost entirely destroyed, and the very

1 See, generally, *Goods Act 1958* (Vic); *Sale of Goods Act 1923* (NSW); *Sale of Goods Act 1896* (Qld); *Sale of Goods Act 1895* (SA); *Sale of Goods Act 1895* (WA); *Sale of Goods Act 1896* (Tas); *Sale of Goods Act 1954* (ACT); *Sale of Goods Act 1972* (NT).

2 [1891] AC 107.

> object with which it was enacted will be frustrated. The purpose of such a statute surely was that on any point specifically dealt with by it, the law should be ascertained by interpreting the language used instead of, as before, by roaming over a vast number of authorities in order to discover what the law was, extracting it by a minute critical examination of the prior decisions, dependent upon a knowledge of the exact effect even an obsolete proceeding such as a demurrer to evidence.[3]

Lord Herschell's obiter comment makes for interesting reading. To a modern lawyer it signifies a mixing of literal and purposive approaches to statutory interpretation at various stages of the interpretive task. Whether that is a sound method of interpretation and construction is another matter altogether. Leaving aside questions of legal technique, there are good reasons to be wary of following Lord Herschell's obiter dicta comments too closely.

For instance, the changing nature of modern commerce makes a literal approach to statutory interpretation rather redundant in the context of the sale of goods. This was recognised by Lord Diplock in *Ashington Piggeries v Christopher Hill Ltd*,[4] where he stated:

> Unless the Sale of Goods Act 1893 is to be allowed to fossilise the law and to restrict the freedom of choice of parties to contracts for the sale of goods to make agreements which take account of advances in technology and changes in the way in which business is carried on today, the provisions set out in the various sections and subsections of the code ought not to be construed so narrowly as to force upon parties to contracts for the sale of goods promises and consequences different from what they must reasonably have intended. They should be treated rather as illustrations of the application to simple types of contract of general principles for ascertaining the common intention of the parties as to their mutual promises and their consequences, which ought to be applied by analogy in cases arising out of contracts which do not appear to have been within the immediate contemplation of the draftsman of the Act in 1893.[5]

An overly narrow and literal approach to interpreting the statute would render the Act otiose. Instead, the Act must be read purposively so as to allow it to continue to do justice between commercial parties. It is possible to discern from the statute and its resultant jurisprudence a concern with concepts of good faith, reasonableness and legitimate expectations. This is quite noticeable in the area of terms implied into sale of goods contracts, where the statute requires that certain standards such as fitness for purpose and correspondence with description must be met so that the legitimate and reasonable expectations of buyers and sellers are met. In this context, fidelity to the commercial ideals pursued by the statute is undeniably preferable to literalism.

Atiyah has also criticised Lord Herschell's approach, which in part eschews the relevance of past case law, as 'likely to produce arbitrary and unpredictable decisions'.[6] The crucial point is that in some parts the Sale of Goods Acts offer little more than a framework that must be fleshed out in particular cases by the past jurisprudence. The literalism that underpins Lord Herschell's approach to the statute is ill equipped for this reality.

3 [1891] AC 107, 144–5.
4 *Ashington Piggeries Ltd v Christopher Hill Ltd* [1972] AC 441.
5 [1972] AC 441, 501.
6 P S Atiyah, J Adams and H MacQueen, *The Sale of Goods* (Pearson, London, 11th edn, 2005), 5.

4.2 Applying the Sale of Goods Act

For the Goods Act to apply, there must be (1) a contract of sale; (2) which relates to goods; (3) the consequence of which property in the goods passes from one party to the other; (4) and the property passes in exchange for money consideration. The money consideration provided for the goods is the price. Section 6 of the Goods Act provides:

> **Sale and agreement to sell**
>
> (1) A contract of sale of goods is a contract whereby the seller transfers or agrees to transfer the property in goods to the buyer for a money consideration called the price. There may be a contract of sale between one part owner and another.
>
> (2) A contract of sale may be absolute or conditional.
>
> (3) Where under a contract of sale the property in the goods is transferred from the seller to the buyer the contract is called a sale; but where the transfer of the property in the goods is to take place at a future time or subject to some condition thereafter to be fulfilled the contract is called an agreement to sell.
>
> (4) An agreement to sell becomes a sale when the time elapses or the conditions are fulfilled subject to which the property in the goods is to be transferred.

In order to apply s 6, we must have a clear understanding of the four elements identified above. In the following section, this chapter explores the meaning of: (1) a contract of sale; (2) goods; (3) distinguishing contracts of sale from other arrangements; and (4) price.

4.2.1 A contract of sale

Section 6(1) of the Goods Act provides that a contract of sale is a contract where the seller transfers or agrees to transfer the property in goods to the buyer in exchange for money. The contract can be oral or in writing. Under s 3 of the Goods Act a 'contract of sale' includes both an agreement to sell and a sale. In a sale the property in goods transfers at the time of the transaction. However, in an agreement for a sale the property transfers in the future or is conditional.[7] In an agreement for sale the completion of the transaction depends on some event occurring. For example, in *Jansz v GMB Imports Pty Ltd*,[8] the event was the ascertainment of tobacco for shipment to the buyer. 'Ascertainment' refers to the separating out and setting aside of the particular goods for a specific transaction from the broad mass of other goods that might have been used for that transaction. In *Jansz*, the relevant transaction was for tobacco; but until the specific lot of tobacco had been identified by the seller, there was no ascertainment. In *Jansz*, the buyer had to give a specific order for tobacco to the seller and the seller had to then put together that order. Until that time the agreement was an agreement for sale. Once the property in the goods was ascertained and transferred, it then would have become a sale. Most often, an agreement to sell will relate to future goods. The term 'future goods' refers to goods that are to be manufactured or acquired by the seller after the making of the contract of sale. For example, in *Jansz* the tobacco needed to be grown. In other situations

7 *Jansz v GMB Imports Pty Ltd* [1979] VR 581. See also *Butler v JSL Racing Pty Ltd* [2014] VSC 509.
8 [1979] VR 581.

a builder might need to build or manufacture something. A present sale of future goods is an agreement to sell the goods. The difference between a sale and an agreement to sell can affect the type of remedies that are available. In a sale, property has passed, and the seller can sue for the price. In an agreement to sell, default by either party might result in damages.

4.2.2 Goods

Section 3 of the Goods Act provides that 'goods' includes all chattels personal, other than things in action and money, and includes emblements and fixtures that are to be severed from the land. Section 5 of the *Sale of Goods Act 1923* (NSW) contains the same definition of 'goods', including the somewhat dated reference to 'emblements'. The term 'emblements' refers to crops that are grown on agricultural land by a tenant who in turn acquires a right to harvest them. A thing in action, or a chose in action, is a legal right, such as a copyright or a debt. As a legal right, a chose in action cannot be physically possessed. In contrast, a chose in possession refers to physical goods to which legal rights of ownership may attach. The term 'chattels' refers to physical objects. Examples of chattels include tables, chairs, cars, dresses and watches. The terms 'chattels' and 'goods' may very well be used interchangeably or in conjunction, such as where a contract refers to 'chattel goods'. As commercial law is often concerned with laws governing commercial activities, it is no surprise that the law of the sale of goods has gained and maintained its significance since the Industrial Revolution. Much of the case law that applies here has its basis in the manufacture and subsequent sale of goods between commercial parties at various ends of the supply chain.

Yet, as technology and commerce change, the established definitions under the Goods Act have come under some strain. In the case of *St Albans City and District Council v International Computers Ltd*,[9] it was held that software, upon which depended the operation of an entire computer system, was in fact 'goods' for the purposes of the applicable Sale of Goods Act. The facts that gave rise to a dispute in *St Albans* were that the sale of the computer system was effectively meaningless unless the software that made the system function was itself operable. Lord Glidewell in *St Albans* resolved the issue by implying that the parties must have intended that the software under the agreement should have worked properly. Thus the relevant Sale of Goods Act applied. In other words, the workability of the computers depended on the workability of the software, so even though the software was not 'goods', a defect in the software meant that there was a defect in the computers, thereby causing the sale of goods legislation to apply.

The decision in *St Albans* does not make sense on a technical level. Computer programs are protected as personal property in the sense that they are protected by copyright law. As such, they are a form of chose in action. To copy a computer program without a licence from the copyright owner will give rise to a suit for copyright infringement. It may well be the case that the interaction between the computer program and the computers is required to make the overall computer system work, as was the case in *St Albans*, but the interrelationship between the two does not necessarily render the software itself 'goods' for the purpose of the Goods Act. Notably, in *Telstra Corporation Ltd v Hurstville City Council*,[10] the High Court found that

9 [1996] 4 All ER 48.
10 (2000) 105 FCR 322.

electromagnetic signals that passed through cables were not goods. That said, in *Telstra* the distinction that the High Court drew was that Telstra was providing information as a service and the electromagnetic signals, which were ancillary to this service, were not goods.

There are fundamentally four types of goods: (1) specific goods; (2) unascertained goods; (3) ascertained goods; and (4) future goods. Specific goods are the particular goods that the parties have agreed will form the subject matter of their contract of sale.[11] Unascertained goods are those that have not been precisely identified as belonging to a particular sale contract, but which still form part of an identifiable class of goods from which the particular goods used for the transaction will be drawn. Ascertained goods are those goods identified, usually from the pool of ascertained goods, in accordance with the contract.[12] These goods are not specific goods at the time of the contract. Future goods are those that will be produced or acquired after the formation of the contract.

4.2.3 Distinguishing a sale of goods contract

A sale of goods contract can be distinguished from other transactions. For example, unlike other legal categories such as bailment or agency, the sale of goods is primarily concerned with the transfer of property from one party to another in exchange for money. In contrast, a bailment may involve a transfer of possession of property from a bailor to a bailee,[13] but the ownership of the property does not change. Similarly, an agency relationship may involve the agent having the power to make representations on behalf of the principal,[14] who may be the owner of the goods, but the agent does not acquire ownership of the goods themselves. Likewise, a sale of goods contract is not concerned with the making of a gift, a barter arrangement or a transfer by deed.

Where there has been some confusion has been in the boundary between a contract for work and incidental materials and a sale of goods contract. The jurisprudential terrain here is confused and often unhelpful. The primary divide lies between one test that focuses upon the substance of the contract and another that concerns itself with the result of the contract. To illustrate the problem, it might be useful to consider the hiring of an artist to paint a portrait. The result of the contract will no doubt be a portrait that the buyer may then proudly display to her friends. However, she would most likely have chosen the artist for his skill and craftsmanship. Therein lies the nub of the problem. It is equally true to say of the contractual arrangements that the end result is a chattel good as it is to say that the substance of the contract is the skill and craftsmanship of the artist. It is not easy to say which description best encapsulates the arrangement between the buyer and the artist. The better view might well be that the contract is one for both work and the sale of goods. However, where a dispute arises before the goods are completed and sold, this may well affect the buyer's ability to recover any advance payment.[15] The difference between the two types of contract can affect when the property passes and, consequently, the available remedies. In a contract for work and materials,

11 See, for example, NSW, s 23; Vic, s 23; WA, s 18; SA, s 18; Tas, s 23; ACT, s 23; NT, s 23.
12 *Re Wait* [1927] 1 Ch 606, 630.
13 See Chapter 8.
14 See Chapter 7.
15 *Hyundai Heavy Industries Co Ltd v Papadopoulos* [1980] 1 WLR 1129.

property only passes once the work has been done. In a contract for sale, the remedy can be the goods. However, in a contract for work, the remedy would be damages.

In *Lee v Griffin*,[16] the court held that if a contract results in the sale of a chattel, then it is a contract for the sale of goods. *Lee* concerned a contract for the manufacture of dentures. In *Lee*, a dentist had contracted to make dentures for a patient, but the patient died after the dentures were made and after rejecting an appointment for a fitting. The dentist sued his patient's estate. In contrast in *Robinson v Graves*,[17] a different approach, focusing on the substance of the contract, was taken in order to identify the nature of the contract. In that case, the court stated:

> If the substance of the contract . . . is that skill and labour have to be exercised . . . and that it is only ancillary to that that there will pass from the artist to his client or customer some materials ... the substance of the contract is the skill and experience of the artist in producing the picture.[18]

In subsequent cases, the two tests have been applied and criticised. For example, in *Deta Nominees Pty Ltd v Viscount Plastics Pty Ltd*,[19] Fullagar J criticised the 'substance of the contract' test. In *Deta Nominees*, the plaintiff contracted with Viscount for the manufacture of a furniture component. Under the contract, property in the component was to pass when it was made and when enough drawers were delivered to Deta. Viscount refused to supply the components and repudiated other aspects of the agreement. The basis of Fullager J's criticism probably lies in the fact that the goods in question were mass-produced and not necessarily purchased for the artistry of the manufacturer. That is, the goods were functional and served no aesthetic purpose. In *Toby Constructions Products Pty Ltd v Computa Bar (Sales) Pty Ltd*,[20] a mass-produced computer system that consisted of both hardware and software was found to be goods within the meaning of the NSW Sale of Goods Act. Rogers J applied the substance of the contract test and in doing so was swayed by the fact that the system was mass-produced and not a one-off painting. In *Pacific Film Laboratories Pty Ltd v Federal Commissioner of Taxation*,[21] Barwick CJ stated:

> Whilst one cannot derive any uniformity of application of principle from these and other like cases ... the question whether or not an agreement is an agreement merely to provide services or an agreement for the sale of goods depends upon the substance of the arrangements between the parties and is not to be resolved by any single criterion.[22]

In *Re Amlink Technologies Pty Ltd and Australian Trade Commission*,[23] the AAT stated:

> It is easy enough to understand how a court might conclude that a contract with an artist to produce a portrait, or with an author to produce a manuscript, qualifies as the supply of know-how or intellectual property and not a contract for the supply of goods – even though the product of the producer's endeavours might be expressed in a physical form.

16 (1861) 1 B&S 272.
17 [1935] 1 KB 579.
18 [1935] 1 KB 579, 587.
19 [1979] VR 167.
20 [1983] 2 NSWLR 48.
21 (1970) 121 CLR 154.
22 (1970) 121 CLR 154, 160.
23 (2005) 86 ALD 370.

> That conclusion is consistent with *Robinson v Graves* and the guidelines. But once the artist has painted the portrait and it is resold, it is likely to be sold as goods. Even more clearly, when the publisher reproduces the manuscript of the author and prints thousands of copies of a book, the copies are almost certainly sold as goods. That reasoning applies in a discussion about software. If the program had been commissioned by the purchaser and written (or even modified) to its specifications, the contract of supply is likely to be a supply of know-how or intellectual property rather than goods. The situation is different once the product is sold as a tangible commodity after being copied or mass-produced. At that point, the products cease to be know-how and become goods.
>
> While one hesitates to describe this product as being available 'off the shelf' given its high price, the *Robinson v Graves* analysis suggests the product is properly characterised as goods. I am satisfied the guidelines are consistent with that approach. What was once know-how has become a commodity marketed in a tangible form. The fact the license agreement places restrictions on the use of the product after sale does not make it much different to music CDs and DVD movies – products that are clearly goods. The requirement for an access code is apparently an innovative attempt to combat piracy which might rob the producers of revenue. It is merely a more sophisticated protection than the regional coding system used in DVDs. That evidence does not change my conclusion. The existence of 24 hour service is also not determinative: help-desks and other forms of round-the-clock assistance are available as part of the purchase price of many goods, such as computers and cars.[24]

In her assessment of the substance of the contract approach, Traves has suggested that regard must be had 'to the relative importance of the work done or the good supplied'.[25] This is a particularly apt way of characterising the test and it effectively captures the essence of much of the jurisprudence. For example, in *Perlmutter v Beth David Hospital*,[26] it was held that a blood transfusion, which was contaminated with the jaundice virus, did not take place under a contract for the sale of goods. The patient had paid for the medical treatment that he received at the hospital and this included an account for the blood itself. In *Perlmutter*, the service provided by the hospital was of paramount importance to the plaintiff at the time of the act and the blood was merely incidental in the overall course of dealings. Similarly, in *Lockett v A & M Charles Ltd*,[27] the supply of a meal in a restaurant was held to be a contract for the sale of goods. The dispute in *Lockett* arose after the plaintiff ordered whitebait for lunch and was taken ill shortly after consuming a small amount of her meal. In *Lockett*, the meal was clearly the focus of the dealing between the parties. In *North East Equity Pty Ltd v Proud Nominees Pty Ltd [No 2]*,[28] a contract concerning the installation of plant and equipment at a carrot processing plant was held to be a contract for work and materials as opposed to a contract for the sale of goods.

Another perspective that might render some assistance in alleviating the doctrinal difficulties in this area of the law is that the more artistic the endeavour, the more likely it is that the

24 (2005) 86 ALD 370, [42]–[43].
25 S Traves, *Commercial Law* (LexisNexis Butterworths Australia, Sydney, 2009), 133.
26 123 NE 2d 792 (1955).
27 [1938] 4 All ER 170.
28 [2008] FCA 1189.

contracting party is paying for work with goods being the result, rather than just paying for goods. The less artistic the endeavour, the more likely that it is a sale of goods contract. This would be consistent with the decisions in *Deta Nominees* and *Toby Constructions*. Particular regard should be had to whether the commodity traded is purely functional or an expression of skill and artistry.

4.2.4 Price

Section 13 of the Goods Act provides:[29]

> **Ascertainment of price**
>
> (1) The price in a contract of sale may be fixed by the contract or may be left to be fixed in manner thereby agreed or may be determined by the course of dealing between the parties.
>
> (2) Where the price is not determined in accordance with the foregoing provisions the buyer must pay a reasonable price. What is a reasonable price is a question of fact dependent on the circumstances of each particular case.

The parties to a contract may elect either to fix a price for the goods prior to their sale, or to rely on an agreed mechanism for determining price. The latter option may be utilised where the parties have ongoing dealings with each other, usually revolving around unascertained goods, and where their ascertainment, weighing and measuring is required in order to determine the price. Section 13(2) will be used only where the contract itself cannot be relied upon to determine the price.[30] Where s 13(2) is used, the ascertainment of the price will depend upon a number of factors such as production cost, market price for like goods, and issues around delivery.[31]

4.3 Terms implied into sale of goods contracts

The Goods Act implies terms into sale of goods contracts. Sections 17–20 deal with sales by description, merchantable quality, fitness for purpose, sale by sample, freedom from encumbrance, and quiet possession. Similar terms can be found in international treaties such as the Convention on Contracts for the International Sale of Goods (CISG).[32] If anything, this reflects how crucial these terms are in assisting the trade in goods to flourish.

In the area of implied terms, there was a fair degree of legislative overlap between the Trade Practices Act (TPA), the Goods Act and the Fair Trading Act. The TPA has now been replaced by the Competition and Consumer Act, which contains the Australian Consumer Law (ACL). The ACL is brought into Victorian law through the new *Australian Consumer Law and*

29 Qld, s 11; NSW, s 13; SA, s 8; WA, s 8; Tas, s 13; ACT, s 13; NT, s 13.
30 *Wenning v Robinson* (1964) 64 SR (NSW) 157.
31 *Watson Brothers v Hornby (Inspector of Taxes)* [1942] 2 All ER 506.
32 See *Castel Electronics Pty Ltd v Toshiba Singapore Pte Ltd* [2010] FCA 1028, [123].

Fair Trading Act 2012 (Vic) (ACLFTA). The ACLFTA limits the operation of the Goods Act through s 32FA to matters that the ACL does not cover. The ACL is confined to consumer transactions. Section 31 of the ACLFTA provides:

> **Application of Goods Act 1958 to contracts of supply**
>
> (1) Sections 17, 18, 19(a) and (b) and 20 of the Goods Act 1958 do not apply to contracts of supply to which Division 1 of Part 3-2 of the Australian Consumer Law (Victoria) applies.

It follows then that ss 17, 18, 19 and 20 of the Goods Act apply to business-to-business contracts. That is, the implied terms scheme under the Goods Act applies to contracts for the sale of goods between traders. The operation of the implied terms scheme under the Goods Act may also be expressly excluded by contract.[33] Section 61 of the Goods Act provides:

> **Exclusion of implied terms and conditions**
>
> Where any right duty or liability would arise under a contract of sale by implication of law it may be negatived or varied by express agreement or by the course of dealing between the parties or by usage if the usage be such as to bind both parties to the contract.

The following sections of the chapter examine ss 17–20 of the Goods Act, which cover sales by description, fitness for purpose, merchantable quality, sale by sample, quiet possession and freedom from encumbrance. While the jurisprudence under ss 17–20 of the Goods Act was developed with equal regard to consumer transactions and dealings between traders, it must be kept in mind that the scheme now applies primarily to transactions between traders.

4.4 Correspondence with description

Section 18 of the Goods Act deals with the implied obligation of correspondence with description.[34] The requirement imposed by s 18 is that where there is a contract for the sale of goods by description, there is an implied condition that the goods shall correspond with the description.[35] The section provides:

> When there is a contract for the sale of goods by description there is an implied condition that the goods shall correspond with the description; and if the sale be by sample as well as by description it is not sufficient that the bulk of the goods corresponds with the sample if the goods do not also correspond with the description.

Section 18 is primarily concerned with whether the goods supplied correspond with the description proffered before the sale took place. As such, the implied obligation of correspondence with description refers to the identity of the goods. In essence, where the buyer has relied upon the description given by the seller, the latter should be held to that representation. Where there is an express contractual provision dealing with compliance with description, there is no

33 *All Saints Estate Pty Ltd v Victorian Alps Wine Co Pty Ltd* [2010] VSC 599. See also *Victorian Alps Wine Co Pty Ltd v All Saints Estate Pty Ltd* (2012) 34 VR 397. Also, *Hogan v BPW Transpec Pty Ltd* [2013] VSC 249.

34 Qld, s 16; NSW, s 18; SA, s 13; WA, s 13; Tas, s 18; ACT, s 18; NT, s 18.

35 See *Cassar v Pegoraro* [2011] VCC 819.

need to use the implied statutory obligation. However, where no such term exists, s 18 may be applied to the contract. There are three key factual issues that arise in applying s 18. They are: (1) determining what is actually comprised in the description; (2) establishing that there has been reliance on the description; and (3) determining whether the goods correspond to the description.

4.4.1 Sale by description

A sale by description can apply to both unascertained and specific goods. However, it will usually be the case that the implied obligation is imposed in relation to specific goods. Where unascertained goods are sold, such contracts of sale will by necessity be sales by description. It is possible that goods can be sold without a description.[36] For example, a Ford car can be sold to a buyer simply on the basis that the car is present at the time of sale. However, it is more than likely that some description will accompany the sale. While the statutory language used by s 18 (and like provisions) does not use the term 'reliance', it is sufficiently clear that the provision cannot be applied unless the buyer has 'relied' upon the description offered by the seller.[37] For example, in *Couchman v Hill*,[38] the plaintiff purchased a heifer described as unserved. It was pregnant and later died from carrying a calf at too young an age. The description as 'unserved' was held to be a condition.

The description does not have to be directly communicated by the seller to the buyer. It is sufficient if the description is contained on the packaging of the goods or on some other sign or label.[39] The fact that the goods have been inspected does not necessarily obviate the existence of a sale by description. For example, in *Elder Smith Goldsbrough Mort Ltd v McBride*,[40] the sale of a 'breeding bull' that had been inspected by the buyer was held to be a sale by description. The bull was sold as a breeding bull, but later proved to be infertile. The sale by description occurred, despite the inspection by the buyer, because the defect in the goods was not detectable upon inspection. In *Elder Smith*, Sheppard J noted that a sale by description may be less arguable where the goods have been inspected. However, his Honour found that this hurdle fell away where the defect was not apparent.[41]

In *Beale v Taylor*,[42] the defendant advertised his car for sale as a 'Herald convertible, white, 1961' and the car was bought by B after examination. Both parties believed the car was a 1961 model, but B discovered soon after the sale that it was made up of two parts that had been welded together, one of which had been a 1961 model. It was held that although Beale had examined the car, he had relied on the description in the advertisement as showing the kind of car he was buying. The model of the car had become part of the way the car was identified. The sale was a sale by description and since the car did not correspond to the description, Beale was entitled to damages for breach of an implied condition.

36 S Traves, *Commercial Law* (LexisNexis Butterworths Australia, Sydney, 2014), 161.
37 *Harlingdon & Leinster Enterprises Ltd v Christopher Hull Fine Art Ltd* [1990] 3 WLR 13.
38 *Couchman v Hill* [1947] 1 All ER 103.
39 S Traves, *Commercial Law* (LexisNexis Butterworths Australia, Sydney, 2014), 161.
40 [1976] 2 NSWLR 631.
41 See *Thornett & Fehr v Beers & Son* [1919] 1 KB 486.
42 [1967] 1 WLR 1192.

The contexts within which a sale by description may occur are many and varied. In *Grant v Australian Knitting Mills Ltd*,[43] Lord Wright stated:

> [T]here is a sale by description even though the buyer is buying something displayed before him on the counter; a thing is sold by description, though it is specific, so long as it is sold not merely as the specific thing but as a thing corresponding to a description, eg, woollen under-garments, a hot water bottle, a secondhand reaping machine, to select a few obvious illustrations.[44]

In *Grant v Australian Knitting Mills*, the buyer contracted dermatitis from woollen underwear that he had purchased. The buyer sued the retailer on the basis that it had breached the implied conditions as to merchantability. The implied condition as to merchantability also requires that there had been a sale by description. Grant had self-selected the underwear from the shelf, but the defect in question – namely, the existence of a chemical-free sulphite – was not discoverable on a basic examination. When the case went on appeal in the Privy Council, the court held that there had been a sale by description, at least to the extent that the description on the box delineates the good and describes the kind of clothing to be bought. Similarly, in the High Court, Dixon J stated:

> When the ground upon which the goods are selected or identified is their correspondence to a description and when, therefore, it may be said that the buyer primarily relies upon their classification or possession of attributes, then, notwithstanding that they are bought as specific goods ascertained and identified, the goods are bought by description. In the ordinary case of a sale over the counter by a shopkeeper to a customer, who calls for an article of a given description, inspects the specimens produced, and buys one, the transaction is a sale by description.[45]

A point of difficulty in *Grant* had been that the absence of direct contact between the buyer and the seller over the contents of the goods made it hard at first blush to establish description. However, the existence of the description on the packaging was held to be sufficient to render the sale one that was made by description. Moreover, the packaging was sufficient to occasion reliance by the buyer.

4.4.2 Reliance

The existence of reliance is pivotal to making out the existence of the obligation of correspondence with description. The case of *Harlingdon & Leinster Enterprises Ltd v Christopher Hull Fine Art Ltd*[46] illustrates the need for the existence of reliance within the implied condition. In *Harlingdon*, a painting was sold from one art dealer to another. The buyer very clearly stated that he wanted to buy a Munter painting. However, at the time of the sale the seller made it very clear that he was not an expert in Munter's paintings. The painting was signed 'Munter', but this was later discovered to have been a forgery. The question that subsequently arose

43 [1936] AC 85.
44 [1936] AC 85.
45 *Australian Knitting Mills Ltd v Grant* (1933) 50 CLR 387, 417.
46 *Harlingdon & Leinster Enterprises Ltd v Christopher Hull Fine Art Ltd* [1990] 3 WLR 13.

before the UK Court of Appeal was whether the name 'Munter' on the painting formed part of the description of the painting on which the buyer relied when deciding to buy it.

In *Harlingdon*, a majority of the Court of Appeal held that the buyer could not have reasonably relied on the name on the painting. The fact that the seller had made it clear that he had no expertise was sufficient to negate the buyer's argument of reliance. Lord Justice Nourse examined the jurisprudence dealing with the concept of reliance within the rule of correspondence with description and found that, despite the existence of some criticisms, the requirement of reliance was central to the implied obligation. Nourse LJ stated:

> In theory it is no doubt possible for a description of goods which is not relied on by the buyer to become an essential term of a contract for their sale. But in practice it is very difficult, and perhaps impossible, to think of facts where that would be so. The description must have a sufficient influence in the sale to become an essential term of the contract and the correlative of influence is reliance. Indeed, reliance by the buyer is the natural index of a sale by description. It is true that the question must, as always, be judged objectively ... For all practical purposes, I would say that there cannot be a contract for the sale of goods by description where it is not within the reasonable contemplation of the parties that the buyer is relying on the description. For those purposes, I think that the law is correctly summarised in these words of Benjamin on Sale, which should be understood to lay down an objective test: 'Specific goods may be sold as such ... where, though the goods are described, the description is not relied upon, as where the buyer buys the goods such as they are.'[47]

The key propositions that emerge from *Harlingdon* are that (1) the requirement of correspondence with description must be judged by having regard to all the circumstances surrounding the transaction; (2) if the circumstances are such as to show that the buyer and seller do not have a common intention, then the obligation cannot be implied; (3) the test for determining whether the obligation can be implied is an objective one and depends upon the facts at hand; and (4) the existence of the implied obligation of correspondence with description is not limited to circumstances where the buyer has not seen the goods. In *Harlingdon*, Nourse LJ made the point that s 13 of the UK legislation, the equivalent of s 18 of the Goods Act, was not confined to situations where the buyer has not seen the goods. The inspection by the buyer in *Harlingdon* would not have displaced the reliance element but for the protestations and clear statements of the seller as to his lack of expertise.

4.4.3 Breaching the condition

Notwithstanding the question of whether the requirement that the goods correspond to their description can be found to exist in a sales contract, there is the issue of whether the condition has in fact been breached. There are two issues that arise here. The first concerns the way in which a court will approach the question of whether correspondence with description has been breached. The second pertains to a further boundary issue concerning the legal rule in that issues of quality may not rise to the level of being matters regarding correspondence with description.

47 [1990] 3 WLR 13, 21.

The case of *Ashington Piggeries Ltd v Christopher Hill Ltd* highlights the approach of the courts in evaluating cases of description.[48] Christopher Hill was a company that sold animal foods. Ashington Piggeries ran a mink farm. Christopher Hill entered into a contract to sell mink food to Ashington. Mr Udall of Ashington then supplied a formula to Christopher Hill for them to make up the food meal called 'King Size'. As Christopher Hill had no particular expertise with respect to mink, it subcontracted the task to Nordsildmel. Under the subcontract, Nordsildmel was required to supply Norwegian herring meal of 'fair average quality of the season' for the compound. The herring meal that Nordsildmel prepared contained the substance dimethyl nitrosamine (DMNA). The existence of the DMNA within the herring meal was not known to any of the parties. The DMNA was toxic to mink and the animals died after they consumed the herring meal.

Understandably, Ashington Piggeries did not pay Christopher Hill for the herring meal. The respondent subsequently sued the appellant for the price of the goods. In response, Ashington Piggeries counter-claimed that the goods did not correspond with purpose, were not fit for purpose and were not of merchantable quality.

The House of Lords held that while there was a sale by description, the implied term had not been breached. The House of Lords found that the description at issue was whether the goods constituted 'herring meal'. The House of Lords reasoned that the toxicity created by the DMNA affected the quality of the herring meal, rather than the identity of the goods as herring meal. The DMNA occurred as a result of the combination of some of the ingredients used to make the herring meal. The existence of the DMNA was not the result of a deliberate action. As Lord Diplock noted:

> [I]t was no one's fault that the Norwegian herring meal which was an ingredient of the compound feeding-stuff for mink made the food poisonous to those animals. At the relevant time the possibility of the chemical reaction which produced the toxic substance DMNA in the course of manufacture of the meal was unthought of. In the then state of knowledge, scientific and commercial, no deliberate exercise of human skill or judgment could have prevented the meal from having its toxic effect upon mink. It was sheer bad luck.[49]

Lord Diplock further set out the basis for finding liability on the following terms:

> If the law of sale of goods is as sensible and simple as it ought to be, the question of law for the court should be: What, if any, responsibility as to the characteristics of the goods to be supplied under the contract would the seller reasonably understand that the buyer believed that he, the seller, was accepting? Or, put in the obverse form: What responsibility as to the characteristics of the goods to be supplied would the buyer reasonably believe that the seller was accepting by entering into the contract? And in the circumstances of the present case that question of law can be reduced to this: Would Hill's reasonable understanding and Udall's reasonable belief be that Hill was accepting responsibility to deliver feeding-stuffs characterised by their being compounded in accordance with the formula provided by the appellants and composed of ingredients

48 [1972] AC 441.
49 [1972] AC 441, 498.

> of the kinds specified and of a quality suitable for use in compound feeding-stuffs for domestic animals and poultry? Or were their respective reasonable understanding and belief that Hill was accepting an additional responsibility that feeding-stuffs so compounded and composed would be suitable for feeding to mink?
>
> So stated, as it seems to me, the question answers itself. The additional responsibility was not one which, in the circumstances of this case, either party would understand or believe that the seller was accepting.[50]

A majority of the House of Lords followed a similar line of reasoning and held that the obligation on Christopher Hill was simply to deliver herring meal. Christopher Hill had not agreed to take on an extra obligation to ensure that the herring meal was specifically suitable for mink.

The decision of the House of Lords in *Ashington Piggeries* illustrates that the difference between deficiencies in quality and identity are crucial in determining whether goods correspond with their description. The line between quality on the one hand and identity on the other may not always be easy to draw. In some circumstances, it may be rather straightforward. For example, if a buyer contracts to buy a horse but receives a donkey instead, the difference is clear enough to show that the two goods are different in identity. However, where a buyer contracts to buy an animal for farm work, expecting to receive a horse but having failed to communicate this desire, and receives instead a donkey, the difference between the two may only be one of quality. Similarly, wine that is undrinkable may be an issue of quality, rather than identity. That is, where a buyer purchases a 2004 Bordeaux wine, and upon opening it discovers that it is oddly unpalatable, the fundamental identity of the good has not changed. All that is altered is the actual state of the wine in relation to its anticipated quality.

The difference between quality and kind was considered by Salmond J in *Taylor v Combined Buyers Ltd.*[51] In *Taylor*, Salmond J stated:

> If I contract to buy 'a cask of port wine', and I receive beer, I am entitled to reject the goods because there has been a breach of the statutory condition of conformity with description. The difference between port wine and beer is not a difference of quality, degree or other unessential attribute, but is a difference of kind. If, however, I contract to buy 'a cask of port wine in sound condition' and I receive a cask of port wine which, upon delivery and examination, is found to be in poor condition I am not entitled to reject the goods on the basis that the goods did not conform to the description under which it was sold. The port wine conforms to the description, inasmuch as the difference between good port wine and bad port wine is merely a difference of quality, state or condition.[52]

In *Edgar v Hector*[53] the supply of imitation chairs was found to breach the condition of description, as the contract in question stipulated that the chairs to be supplied were antique chairs.[54] Similarly, in *Dell v Quilty*,[55] a bull sold as a pedigree bull breached the condition of

50 [1972] AC 441, 502–3.
51 [1924] NZLR 627. See also *Russo v Belcar Pty Ltd* (2011) 111 SASR 459.
52 [1924] NZLR 627, 642.
53 [1912] SC 348.
54 [1912] SC 348.
55 [1924] NZLR 1270.

conformity with description when it was found to be sterile. In *Beale v Taylor*,[56] the sale of a car that was advertised as a 'Herald convertible, white, 1961, twin carbs' was found to breach the condition of conformity with description when it was revealed that the car was in fact two different cars welded together.

4.5 Fitness for purpose

Section 19 of the Goods Act implies a term that the goods must be fit for the purpose for which they are sold.[57] This term denotes a common intention between the buyer and the seller that the goods provided will meet a particular purpose. Where this fails to be the case, the seller may face liability. Section 19(a) provides:

> where the buyer expressly or by implication makes known to the seller the particular purpose for which the goods are required so as to show that the buyer relies on the seller's skill or judgment and the goods are of a description which it is in the course of the seller's business to supply (whether he be the manufacturer or not) there is an implied condition that the goods shall be reasonably fit for such purpose: Provided that in the case of a contract for the sale of a specified article under its patent or other trade name there is no implied condition as to its fitness for any particular purpose . . . .

Section 19 seeks to provide a guarantee that where goods are sold for a given purpose, they will actually be fit for that purpose. There are four elements to s 19: (1) the buyer must have made known, expressly or by implication, the particular purpose for which they wanted the goods; (2) the particular purpose must have been disclosed in such a way that it was clear that the buyer was relying on the seller's skill and judgment; (3) the seller must be in the business of supplying goods of that description; and (4) the goods, if specific, must not be bought under their patent or other trade name.[58]

4.5.1 Particular purpose must be known

The first element places an onus on the buyer to communicate to the seller the purpose for which they require the goods.[59] As the implied term places an obligation on the seller to ensure that the goods are fit for purpose, that obligation cannot be fairly imposed unless the seller knows what the buyer wants. Section 19 uses the language of 'particular purpose', as do all the other Sale of Goods Acts, in setting out the first element of the implied condition of fitness for purpose. This should be taken to mean a reference to a specific purpose.[60] In *Henry Kendall & Sons v William Lillico & Sons Ltd* ('*Hardwick Game Farm* case'),[61] Lord Wilberforce stated: '"particular" in section 14(1) is not used in contrast to "general" or so as to require a quantum of particularity, but more in the sense of "specified" or "stated".'[62]

56 [1967] 1 WLR 1192.
57 Qld, s 17; NSW, s 19; SA, s 14; WA, s 14; Tas, s 19; ACT, s 19; NT, s 19.
58 *Groundhog Sales & Rentals Pty Ltd v Eastern Pearl Corporation* [2012] FCAFC 113.
59 *Tre Cavalli Pty Ltd v Berry Rural Co Operative Society Ltd* [2013] NSWCA 235.
60 P S Atiyah, J Adams and H MacQueen, *The Sale of Goods* (Pearson, London, 11th edn, 2005), 202.
61 [1969] 2 AC 31.
62 [1969] 2 AC 31, 123.

In determining whether the buyer has communicated their purpose to the seller, and whether the latter has taken on that task, a court will look at all the dealings between the parties prior to the sale taking place. This involves looking at the context within which the sale took place, as well as any communications and the like. It is possible to infer the purpose from the circumstances.[63] If the goods are suitable for only one purpose, then it may be inferred that the buyer has made the purpose for which the goods are required known to the seller.[64] In *Frost v Aylesbury Dairy Co Ltd*,[65] a buyer bought from a dairy milk that later turned out to have been contaminated with typhoid. The buyer's wife drank the milk and died. The defendant argued that the buyer had not disclosed the purpose for which the milk was required. The court held that it could reasonably be inferred that the milk had been bought for human consumption. As such, courts will take into account the ordinary purposes for which particular goods are purchased. Similarly, where the buyer has not communicated a purpose for the goods it will be assumed that the goods are being bought for their usual purpose.[66] If the goods are capable of being used for multiple purposes, then the buyer must make known the purpose for which they are required and the goods must suit that purpose.[67]

In *Priest v Last*,[68] the plaintiff bought a hot water bottle from a chemist. A few days after it had been purchased the hot water bottle burst and the plaintiff's wife was scalded. The Court of Appeal found that the hot water bottle had not been fit for purpose at the time that it had been sold. Collins MR stated:

> There are many goods which have in themselves no special or peculiar efficacy for any one particular purpose, but are capable of general use for a multitude of purposes. In the case of a purchase of goods of that kind, in order to give rise to the implication of a warranty, it is necessary to show that, though the article sold was capable of general use for many purposes, in the particular case it was sold with reference to a particular purpose. But in a case where the discussion begins with the fact that the description of the goods, by which they were sold, points to one particular purpose only, it seems to me that the first requirement of the sub-section is satisfied, namely, that the particular purpose for which the goods are required should be made known to the seller.[69]

The purpose must be communicated before the sale takes place. As suggested in the obiter remarks of Collins MR in *Priest v Last*, it will often be clear from the facts that the goods are required for a particular purpose. Nonetheless, it will often make sense for the buyer to clearly communicate the purpose for which the goods are required. In part, this reflects the fact that the implied terms scheme under the Goods Act now applies in business-to-business transactions and a higher degree of precision is expected from sophisticated commercial operators.[70] In *Environmental Systems Pty Ltd v Peerless Holdings Pty Ltd*,[71] the respondent purchased a

63 *Cammell Laird & Co Ltd v Manganese Bronze & Brass Co Ltd* [1934] AC 402.
64 *Priest v Last* [1903] 2 KB 148.
65 [1905] 1 KB 608.
66 *Priest v Last* [1903] 2 KB 148.
67 *Priest v Last* [1903] 2 KB 148.
68 [1903] 2 KB 148.
69 [1903] 2 KB 148, 154.
70 See *Narellan Pools Pty Ltd v Huntsman Chemical Co Australia Pty Ltd* [2010] FCA 267.
71 [2008] 19 VR 358.

regenerative thermal oxidiser (RTO) from the appellant. The respondent made clear to the appellant the purpose for which the RTO was needed. Moreover, the appellant was in the business of supplying RTOs. The RTO did not work effectively and Peerless was awarded damages at trial. On appeal in the Victorian Supreme Court of Appeal, the appellant, Environmental Systems, argued that the respondent had not made known the purpose for which it required the goods. However, Nettle JA found that the evidence clearly indicated that Peerless had communicated its precise requirements for the goods.

The courts will not necessarily construe the purpose for which goods are bought in a broad fashion so as to favour plaintiffs. Nevertheless, this may be an issue of some contention and may depend rather heavily on the facts at hand. In the case of *Heil v Hedges*,[72] a customer sued a butcher, claiming that he had been sold pork meat that was not fit for purpose. The plaintiff had bought pork chops that were infected with a parasitic worm and became ill after eating them. The trial judge found that the pork had been undercooked at the time it was consumed and held that, as it was generally known by the public that pork should be cooked substantially longer than other meats, the meat was fit for purpose at the time of sale. At the time that *Heil v Hedges* was litigated, there were accepted and well-known standards for the cooking of pork meat. Accordingly, on appeal, McNair J found that the pork, when sold, satisfied the implied condition of fitness. However, Atiyah, Adams and MacQueen have cast doubt on whether *Heil v Hedges* is correct. Atiyah et al. have stated:

> [I]t is perhaps doubtful whether *Heil v Hedges* would be followed today; it seems to go too far to treat the failure to cook pork thoroughly as such an unusual thing as to break the chain and relieve the seller of responsibility ... Where more exotic food stuffs are concerned, the duty of the seller must surely be to warn of the dangers.[73]

In *Regal Pearl Pty Ltd v Stewart*,[74] the NSW Court of Appeal took a restrictive approach to 'purpose' in the context of the purchase of frozen prawns. Regal Pearl owned and operated Chinese restaurants in Sydney. In 1997, patrons at Regal Pearl's Coogee restaurant contracted hepatitis after eating contaminated prawns. Regal Pearl had bought the prawns from a wholesaler. In the course of the ensuing litigation, Regal Pearl cross-claimed against the wholesaler on the basis that the prawns were not fit for purpose. It was deduced that the prawns had been contaminated with hepatitis when they were bought, and that the light steaming to which they were subjected did not kill the virus, but that a proper cooking would have done so and rendered them safe for human consumption.

At first instance, the trial judge construed the purpose for which the goods were bought narrowly. That is, the trial judge held that the goods were bought for cooking, rather than steaming, and concluded that on that basis they had been fit for purpose at the time of sale. However, on appeal, Stein JA disagreed with this view of the facts, arguing that the manager of the restaurant, Mr Wong, had given no evidence that suggested the prawns were bought to be cooked but not steamed. Stein JA stated:

72 [1951] 1 TLR 512.
73 P S Atiyah, J Adams and H MacQueen, *The Sale of Goods* (Pearson, London, 11th edn, 2005), 179.
74 *Regal Pearl Pty Ltd v Stewart* [2002] NSWCA 291.

> In my view his Honour stated the relevant purpose too narrowly. Such a limited purpose was never the subject of evidence led by the appellant or the wholesaler. Mr Wong gave no such evidence and the wholesaler led no evidence relating to the purpose. The evidence from the health authorities of their expectation that imported prawns (and other foods) would be cooked and served and that such cooking would destroy the pathogens, was not such as would limit the purpose implied under s 19 of the Sale of Goods Act. The fact remains that the supply of contaminated prawns by the wholesaler to the restaurant was the supply of goods of unmerchantable quality. Moreover, the supply of prawns containing the virus must mean that the prawns were not reasonably fit for the purpose of being sold for human consumption by patrons of the appellant's restaurant. If the prawns had been uncontaminated when supplied, the light steaming by the restaurant would not have led to the plaintiffs contracting hepatitis.[75]

Similarly, Hodgson JA made the point that there were no 'well-known' means by which prawns were to be cooked. As such, the narrow approach to designating the purpose for which the goods could be purchased could not be sustained.

Other factors such as price may also affect the interpretation of the term 'purpose' under the Sale of Goods Acts. Where goods can fit a number of uses, the onus will be on the buyer to communicate a special purpose within that range if one exists. Otherwise, factors such as price and the like may be taken into account. In the *Hardwick Game Farm* case,[76] Lord Reid stated:

> If the object of the disclosure of the particular purpose is, as I think it must be, to give to the seller an opportunity to exercise his skill or judgment in making or selecting appropriate goods, then it is difficult to see how a stated purpose can be a 'particular' purpose if it is stated so widely that it would cover different qualities of goods, because carrying out the purpose in one way would only require a lower quality of goods whereas carrying it out in another way would require a higher quality. Different qualities normally sell at different prices. If a customer sought from a manufacturer or dealer cloth for the purpose of making overcoats the dealer could not know what quality was required. A cut price tailor would not want to pay the price of cloth used in Saville Row, and the tailor in Saville Row would not use the quality which the cut price tailor wants. Unless the seller knew the nature of the buyer's business his only clue to the quality which the buyer wanted would be the price which the buyer was prepared to pay.[77]

Given the fact that the seller is at a disadvantage in knowing the buyer's business, the latter must take active steps to inform the seller of the buyer's requirements. Similarly, if the buyer has some peculiar weakness or idiosyncrasy but fails to disclose this to the seller, there will be no failure to meet the implied condition if the goods later turn out to be unsuitable. In *Griffiths v Peter Conway Ltd*,[78] the plaintiff purchased a tweed coat and later contracted dermatitis. It was discovered that her skin was particularly sensitive and that a normal person would not have contracted dermatitis upon wearing the coat. It was held that the implied condition had not been breached, as the sensitivity of the plaintiff had not been disclosed to the seller and the

75 [2002] NSWCA 291, [100]–[101].
76 [1969] 2 AC 31.
77 [1969] 2 AC 31, 69.
78 [1939] 1 All ER 685.

latter had not been afforded the opportunity to exercise his skill and judgment. Sir Wilfrid Greene MR stated:

> Before the condition as to reasonable fitness is implied, it is necessary that the buyer should make known, expressly or by implication, first of all the particular purpose for which the goods are required. The particular purpose for which the goods were required was the purpose of being worn by a woman suffering from an abnormality. It seems to me that, if a person suffering from such an abnormality requires an article of clothing for his or her use, and desires to obtain the benefit of the implied condition, he or she does not make known to the seller the particular purpose merely by saying: 'The article of clothing is for my own wear.' The essential matter for the seller to know in such cases with regard to the purposes for which the article is required consists in the particular abnormality or idiosyncrasy from which the buyer suffers. It is only when he has that knowledge that he is in a position to exercise his skill or judgment.[79]

As such, the failure to communicate a special need will defeat a claim under fitness for purpose. In *Southern Cross Homes (Broken Hill) Inc v Chapman*,[80] a buyer who had purchased commode chairs argued that they were not fit for purpose as they allowed for leakage into a designated fibreglass base. The South Australian Supreme Court held that this specific purpose had not been made known to the seller. The buyer had only requested a commode chair that would accept commode pots and bedpans.

The principle developed in *Griffiths v Peter Conway* was further expounded by the House of Lords in *Slater v Finning Ltd*.[81] In that case, a buyer bought a camshaft from a manufacturer and it was fitted to their motorised fishing vessel. The camshaft failed at sea and had to be replaced twice. It was later discovered that the problem was that the old engine on the fishing vessel created excessive torsional resonance. This was the reason that the camshaft and its two replacements failed. The buyers lost at first instance and appealed to the House of Lords, where their appeal failed. Lord Keith of Kinkel stated:

> The particular purpose for which the camshafts were here required was that of being fitted in the engine of a vessel which suffered from a particular abnormality or idiosyncrasy, namely a tendency to create excessive torsional resonance in camshafts. The respondents, not being made aware of that tendency, were not in a position to exercise skill and judgment for the purpose of dealing with it. Nor were they in a position to make up their minds whether or not to accept the burden of the implied condition ...[82]

One of the driving principles in commercial law is efficiency. It is inefficient for the seller to unknowingly bear the risks associated with the implied condition of fitness for purpose where it would be quite easy for the buyer to communicate to the seller the particular circumstances in which that risk arises. If the rule on fitness for purpose were construed in that way, then the seller would be forced to adopt costly and inefficient measures to avoid liability. In *Slater v Finning Ltd*,[83] Steyn LJ stated:

79 [1939] 1 All ER 685, 686.
80 [1999] SASC 491.
81 [1997] AC 473.
82 [1997] AC 473.
83 [1996] 3 All ER 398.

> Postulate a firm specialising in the supply of motor car tyres. A customer walks in and asks for a tyre suitable for his car which is parked on the forecourt. The firm supplies a tyre. The car breaks down due to the collapse of the tyre. There was nothing wrong with the tyre. But a defect in the steering mechanism caused the problem. Is the supplier, who was ignorant of the steering problem, liable to the customer because the tyre was unfit for the particular vehicle? If the answer is in the affirmative, such a supplier (if he is unable to disclaim liability) may be forced to resort to time-consuming and expensive investigations of cars to which tyres are to be fitted. Such a view of the law would therefore tend to complicate commonplace transactions. Considerations of everyday commerce militate against the adoption of the argument.[84]

It can be seen that the first element in the implied condition of fitness for purpose is not without accompanying limitations.

4.5.2 Particular purpose must be clearly disclosed

It is a necessary element of the implied condition of fitness for purpose that there must be actual reliance by the buyer on the seller's skill and judgment.[85] The reliance claimed by the buyer must be evident to a reasonable seller at or before the time the contract is formed. The existence of reliance can be inferred from the facts. There does not need to be total reliance.[86] In *Aqua-Marine Marketing Pty Ltd v Pacific Reef Fisheries (Australia) Pty Ltd [No 5]*,[87] a customer cursorily inspected some prawns at a supplier's prawn farm. The customer, Mr Lewis, intended to purchase prawns from the supplier for onsale to Woolworths. Subsequently, when the prawns were supplied to Woolworths they were found to be of inferior quality. The applicant sued and in response the respondent argued that the inspection by Mr Lewis had negatived any reliance. In *Aqua-Marine*, Collier J stated:

> The evidence is that Mr Lewis, during the course of his visit on 9 November 2007, photographed some of the relevant prawns and tasted a number of the relevant prawns. However in the circumstances of this case to suggest that, as a result of conducting this superficial assessment, Mr Lewis or the applicant therefore did not rely on the respondent's skill and judgment in identifying the relevant prawns as suitable for onsale to Woolworths, is in my view ludicrous. I do not consider this case comparable with, for example, the thorough testing conducted over several days in respect of the suitability of timber for piano manufacture in *H Beecham & Co Pty Ltd v Francis Howard & Co Pty Ltd* ... I am not satisfied that, by examining a small number of the relevant prawns from a number of cartons, Mr Lewis satisfied himself, to the exclusion of any reliance on the skill and judgment of the respondent in assessing the relevant prawns, that the prawns were in fact fit for the purpose of onsale to Woolworths. Indeed, it was perfectly reasonable for the applicant to rely on the skill and judgment of the respondent in this regard – as in my view it did – because:

84 [1996] 3 All ER 398.
85 *Roadstar Caravans Pty Ltd v Emjay Products Pty Ltd* [2013] VCC 1921.
86 *Aqua-Marine Marketing Pty Ltd v Pacific Reef Fisheries (Australia) Pty Ltd [No 5]* [2012] FCA 908, [162].
87 [2012] FCA 908.

- The applicant, through Mr Lewis, knew that a major customer of the respondent for its frozen cooked prawns was Coles Supermarkets, which (like Woolworths) would only accept 'A' grade product suitable for resale to consumers.
- During earlier discussions with Mr Con Mitris, Mr Lewis had informed him of the type of product he required for resale to Woolworths.
- Most importantly – from his knowledge of the prawn farming industry, and more specifically from his visit to the respondent's facilities on 9 November 2007, Mr Lewis knew that the respondent had a sophisticated processing facility with a professionally established production line, capable of enabling prawns to be sorted, graded and processed to the relevant standard.[88]

The inference of reliance may be drawn on the basis that the buyer has confidence that the seller has carefully selected appropriate items to supply for sale. In *Grant v Australian Knitting Mills Ltd*, reliance was found to exist where a customer entered a department store and selected goods. Lord Wright stated in that case:

> The reliance will seldom be expressed: it will usually arise by implication from the circumstances: thus to take a case like that in question, of a purchase from a retailer, the reliance will be in general inferred from the fact that a buyer goes to the shop in the confidence that the tradesman has selected his stock with skill and judgment ...
>
> Thus, the question whether the buyer has stated his purpose and has relied on the seller's skill or judgment will be a question of fact to be answered by examining all of the circumstances leading up to the selling transactions ...[89]

The reliance might not need to be reasonable. On this point, Australian authority differs somewhat from the UK law. In *National Engineering Pty Ltd v Wellington Orana Foundry Pty Ltd*,[90] Macready M stated: 'There does not seem to be any basis in law to imply a test of reasonableness on the part of the buyer in determining reliance. Reliance is simply a question of fact and is normally determined by inference from the relevant primary facts.'[91] Whether this is correct is questionable. Atiyah has noted that in the United Kingdom, prior to the *Supply of Goods (Implied Terms) Act 1973*, which amended the *Sale of Goods Act 1893*, 'a court which found that the buyer had acted unreasonably in relying on the seller could always hold that the implied condition was excluded by contrary intention'.[92] Atiyah notes that the amendments to the Sale of Goods Act have rendered this approach untenable and that a court must now find that there has in fact been unreasonable reliance under s 14(3) of the UK Act.[93] Section 19 of the *Goods Act 1958* (Vic) is silent on the point of unreasonable reliance, as are the other Australian Sale of Goods Acts. This divergence is unhelpful, yet the law might not accord with the position of Master Macready in *National Engineering*.

88 [2012] FCA 908, [162].
89 [1936] AC 85.
90 [2003] NSWSC 21.
91 [2003] NSWSC 21, [39].
92 P S Atiyah, J Adams and H MacQueen, *The Sale of Goods* (Pearson, London, 11th edn, 2005), 183.
93 Section 14(3) of the *Sale of Goods Act 1979* (UK) provides 'there is an implied condition that the goods supplied under the contract are reasonably fit for that purpose, whether or not that is a purpose for which such goods are commonly supplied, except where the circumstances show that the buyer does not rely, or that it is unreasonable for him to rely, on the skill or judgment of the seller'.

In *Dowdell v Knispel Fruit Juices Pty Ltd*,[94] the Federal Court suggested that knowledge of a supplier's lack of care would negate the reliance required for the implied condition of fitness for purpose. The facts of *Dowdell* were that Nippy Packing sourced oranges from various suppliers, including the Constas brothers, and in turn supplied those oranges to Nippy's Fruit Juices. Though they were separate companies, both Nippy Packing and Nippy's Fruit Juices were members of the same corporate group. In early 1999, after an outbreak of salmonella poisoning associated with Nippy's Fruit Juices, it was discovered that some of the oranges supplied by Nippy Packing had salmonella and were unfit for human consumption. The contamination was traced to the Constas brothers. Nippy Packing received the oranges from its various suppliers in bins. It then supplied those bins containing the oranges to Nippy's Fruit Juices. Nippy Packing took little or no care to examine the bins. At one stage, Jeff Knispel, of Nippy's Fruit Juices, complained to the Constas brothers about the smell of some of the bins, but little else was done. Unfortunately, it turned out that one of the sheds operated by the Constas brothers had traces of salmonella. As to the question of whether the condition of fitness for purpose could be implied into the contract between Nippy Packing and Nippy's Fruit Juices, Selway J stated:

> Although there was evidence that on one occasion Mr Jeff Knispel had complained to the Constas brothers about a smell from the oranges they had supplied to Packing (although even then it is not suggested that the oranges were refused or returned), it is obvious that Packing exercised little or no skill and judgment in the supply of the oranges. And one effect of the close relationship between Nippy's Fruit Juices and Packing is that it is clear that Nippy's Fruit Juices were perfectly well aware of how Packing obtained and supplied fruit: see *Helicopter Sales* [*Helicopter Sales (Australia) Pty Ltd v Rotor-Work Pty Ltd* (1974) 132 CLR 1] at 11. In this case Nippy's Fruit Juices knew that Packing received the bins of oranges from the growers and then delivered those same bins to Nippy's Fruit Juices. In these circumstances it is not possible to imply a warranty of fitness for purpose into the contract between Nippy's Fruit Juices and Packing.[95]

While Selway J did not find reliance in the relationship between Nippy Packing and Nippy's Fruit Juices, his Honour did find that it existed in the dealings between Nippy Packing and the Constas brothers:

> Pursuant to s 14 of the Goods Act there was an implied condition in each contract that the oranges would be reasonably fit for the purpose of the manufacture of orange juice for human consumption. The purpose for which the oranges were to be used was made known to each of the Constas brothers. They were responsible for picking the fruit and placing it in bins. There is a necessary inference that Packing was relying on the skill and judgment of the respective brother in not supplying fruit which was unsuitable, such as fruit which was mouldy, fruit which had fallen to the ground.[96]

The key point of difference between the two sets of relationships centres upon knowledge. Nippy's Fruit Juices were well aware that Nippy Packing was doing little more than passing on

94 [2003] FCA 851.
95 [2003] FCA 851, [138].
96 [2003] FCA 851, [114].

the bins. This knowledge effectively negated any reliance on skill and care. In contrast, Nippy Packing was entitled to rely on the judgment of the Constas brothers, as they were responsible for picking the fruit and packing the bins. Nippy Packing could have no intimate knowledge of the operations of the Constas brothers other than that which could be gleaned from the supply of the oranges. In contrast, Nippy's Fruit Juices and Nippy Packing were closely related companies. Taken at its highest, the approach of Selway J in *Dowdell* would appear to contradict that of Macready M in *National Engineering*. This contradiction might be avoided if Selway J is taken to have found, although he does not expressly state it upon these terms, that there was no reliance at all by Nippy's Fruit Juices. That in itself is an altogether different thing from reliance existing but being unreasonable on the part of the buyer. Alternatively, if the obiter remarks of Selway J are construed as to suggest that there was no reasonable basis upon which reliance could be found, that might also suggest that unreasonableness can negate reliance.

The idea that unreasonable reliance can still support the existence of the implied condition of fitness for purpose is an altogether unattractive proposition. It sits uneasily with the notions of the willing acceptance of risk on the part of the seller and the knowing exercise of their skill and judgment. Accordingly, where the seller wishes to disclaim the prospect liability, they must make it plain in their dealings with the buyer that the seller's statements cannot be relied upon for fitness for purpose. It may very well be necessary to expressly contract out of the term.

4.5.3 Seller must be in the business of supplying goods of that description

The implied condition will apply where the seller is in the course of selling goods of that description. In *Ashington Piggeries*, it was noted that the effect of this requirement was to protect non-commercial transactions between private persons from liability under the sale of goods legislation.[97] The protection offered to private persons does not afford any great safeguard for commercial operators. A business may still be affected by the implied condition even where it has only sold a particular type of goods once.[98] Similarly, the transactions do not have to be frequent. Irregular transactions, even over a period of years, may still be sufficient to suggest that the seller was in the business of selling goods of that description.[99]

4.5.4 The trade name exception

Liability will be avoided where the goods have been bought under their trade name.[100] The fact that the goods simply bear the trade name of their manufacturer does not activate the operation of the exception.[101] The trade name exception provides that 'in the case of a contract for the sale of a specified article under its patent or other trade name there is no implied

97 *Ashington Piggeries Ltd v Christopher Hill Ltd* [1972] AC 441, 474.
98 *Ashington Piggeries Ltd v Christopher Hill Ltd* [1972] AC 441, 485.
99 *Stevenson v Rogers* [1999] 2 WLR 1064.
100 *Groundhog Sales & Rentals Pty Ltd v Eastern Pearl Corporation* [2012] FCAFC 113, [18]; *Tre Cavalli Pty Ltd v Berry Rural Co Operative Society Ltd* [2013] NSWCA 235.
101 *Refaat v Barry* [2014] VCC 199.

condition as to its fitness for any particular purpose'. The basis of the exception is that where a buyer decides to purchase goods under their trade name, they do so without reference to any representations made by the seller.[102] However, where the seller has made representations as to the suitability of the goods, a mere reference in the sale contract to the trade name will not exclude the implied condition.[103]

4.6 Merchantable quality

While the United Kingdom has abandoned the implied condition that the goods sold shall be of merchantable quality in favour of the more broad-ranging condition that the goods shall be of 'satisfactory quality', the various Australian Sale of Goods Acts retain the condition of merchantable quality. Nonetheless, it is notable that the Australian Consumer Law, whose consumer guarantees provisions mirror the implied terms under Sale of Goods Acts, has adopted the condition of satisfactory quality in s 56 of the ACL.

Section 19(b) of the Goods Act provides:

> ... where goods are bought by description from a seller who deals in goods of that description (whether he be the manufacturer or not) there is an implied condition that the goods shall be of merchantable quality: Provided that if the buyer has examined the goods there shall be no implied condition as regards defects which such examination ought to have revealed.[104]

In effect, where a buyer purchases goods from a seller a condition is implied into the contract that the goods shall be of merchantable quality. There are three elements under the implied condition of merchantable quality. The first is that the goods should have been bought by description. The second is that the seller should deal with goods of that description in the ordinary course of their business. The third is that the buyer must not have examined the goods, or if they did examine the goods, the defect must not have been evident upon examination.

The first element requires that the buyer establishes that there has been a sale by description. As the Goods Act uses the term 'sale of goods by description' in different provisions, it is logical that there should be a uniformity of application in the interpretation of that term.[105] As such, the meaning of the term 'sale by description' under s 19(b) has the same meaning as under s 18.

The second element requires that the seller ordinarily deals in goods of that description. The purpose underlying the second element has often been said to be that of distinguishing between sales that are done in a private capacity and those that are done in a commercial context. In *Ashington Piggeries*, while commenting on the meaning of the phrase 'deals in goods of that description', Lord Guest stated:

---

102 *Baldry v Marshall* [1925] 1 KB 260.
103 *Baldry v Marshall* [1925] 1 KB 260.
104 Qld, s 17; NSW, s 19; SA, s 14; WA, s 14; Tas, s 19; ACT, s 19; NT, s 19.
105 *Taylor v Combined Buyers Ltd* [1924] NZLR 627.

> If the purpose of the qualifying words 'deals in goods of that description' was to confine the section to a dealer in the way of business as opposed to a private capacity, then I think a fair interpretation of the words would be 'who deals in goods of that kind'.[106]

Accordingly, private and non-commercial transactions are exempted from the operation of the condition, but commercial transactions fall squarely within the ambit of the Act. The seller may be dealing with the goods for the first time, but this will not preclude the operation of the provision if the sale takes place in a commercial context.[107]

The third element provides that the condition of merchantable quality does not apply where an examination would have revealed the defect.[108] The examination must be carried out by the buyer. Even where the examination takes place, the condition will apply if the defect could not reasonably have been discovered. There is a slight tension within the law as to the standard of the examination that should have taken place. The authority in *Frank v Grosvenor Motor Auctions Pty Ltd*[109] suggests that whether the defect could reasonably have been discovered depends upon the examination that actually took place. In contrast, *Thornett & Fehr v Beers & Son*[110] suggests that whether the defect could reasonably have been discovered turns upon a full examination. The authority of *Thornett* suggests that a cursory examination, where a full examination was possible, which does not reveal a defect will result in the buyer bearing the risks associated with the transaction.

The question of whether the goods supplied are of merchantable quality is one of fact.[111] As such, merchantable quality is a composite term. A range of factors, such as price, condition, description and the uses for which the good can be employed, is to be taken into account. A price reduction may render goods merchantable. In *BS Brown & Son Ltd v Craiks*,[112] a price reduction meant that cloth that was bought for dresses, and which was not of a good enough quality for that purpose, could be sold instead as industrial fabric. In the *Hardwick Game Farm* case,[113] the sale of contaminated Brazilian groundnut extract was found not to have breached the condition of merchantable quality because the product could be sold at much the same price albeit for a different purpose. As Lord Reid noted in *Hardwick Game Farm*, if the description offered in the contract of sale is vague, then the goods proffered will be of merchantable quality, provided that they are fit for a purpose that falls under that description.

Nevertheless, if the buyer would not have bought the goods knowing their defects, as they would not serve the specific purpose or description clearly identified in the contract of sale, then the goods will not be of merchantable quality. In *Dowdell v Knispell Fruit Juices*, Selway J noted:

> The question of whether there was a breach of the implied condition is to be determined by asking whether a purchaser would purchase the oranges for fruit juice knowing that some of them were affected by salmonella ... The Constas brothers argue that the goods

106 *Ashington Piggeries Ltd v Christopher Hill Ltd* [1972] AC 441, 474.
107 *Ashington Piggeries Ltd v Christopher Hill Ltd* [1972] AC 441, 474.
108 *Eastern Pearl Corporation v Groundhog Sales & Rentals Pty Ltd* [2012] FCA 406.
109 [1960] VR 607.
110 [1919] 1 KB 486.
111 *Medtel Pty Ltd v Courtney* (2003) FCR 182.
112 [1970] 1 WLR 752.
113 [1969] 2 AC 31.

> were 'merchantable' in that a juice manufacturer who pasteurised the juice would still purchase the oranges. And, as I have commented above, even if the juice was not pasteurised it would probably not have caused illness if the juice had not been immediately chilled. And a sanitiser could have been used together with brushing or some other means to remove the wax layer to make the oranges safe. However, as Dr Bentham said in his evidence, even a person who pasteurised the juice would probably not be prepared to take the risk of having salmonella on his or her equipment. This seems to me to be common sense. Certainly if affected oranges were purchased for the purpose of juice production it could be expected that the purchaser, having knowledge that the oranges were affected by salmonella, would expect a very significant reduction in price.[114]

Similarly, in *Regal Pearl v Stewart*, Stein JA stated:

> I have already found that at the time of supply by the wholesaler to the appellant, the prawns were contaminated with HAV [hepatitis A virus]. In that circumstance the prawns were plainly not of merchantable quality and not fit for the purpose for which they were required at the time of supply[;] that is the supply by the appellant to patrons of the restaurant to eat. It is plain that the wholesaler would have been aware of this particular purpose of the sale. The frozen prawns had no other purpose. The wholesaler must have known that the prawns were for human consumption by restaurant patrons. The implication is obvious.[115]

Accordingly, the knowledge of the seller about the context and purpose behind the sale will also be a relevant factor in determining whether the condition of merchantable quality has been breached.

4.7 Sale by sample

The implied condition of a sale by sample ostensibly means that where a sample is offered in the course of negotiation, with the implicit or explicit assurance that the bulk will correspond to the sample, and where the parties intend that the contract is a sale by sample contract, the seller will be found to have breached the term where the bulk does not conform to the sample.

Section 20 of the Goods Act deals with the implied condition of sale by sample.[116] Section 20 of the Goods Act provides:

> (1) A contract of sale is a contract for sale by sample where there is a term in the contract express or implied to that effect.
> (2) In the case of a contract for sale by sample –
>   (a) there is an implied condition that the bulk shall correspond with the sample in quality;
>   (b) there is an implied condition that the buyer shall have a reasonable opportunity of comparing the bulk with the sample;

114 [2003] FCA 851, [118].
115 [2002] NSWCA 291, [95].
116 Qld, s 18; NSW, s 20; SA, s 15; WA, s 15; Tas, s 20; ACT, s 20; NT, s 20.

(c) there is an implied condition that the goods shall be free from any defect rendering them unmerchantable which would not be apparent on reasonable examination of the sample.

A sale does not become a sale by sample contract simply because a sample is offered to the buyer prior to the sale taking place.[117] Section 20(1) serves to restate this limitation by requiring that the parties must have expressly or implicitly required that the contract be a sale by sample contract. The essence of the guarantee offered by a sale by sample was stated by Lord Macnaghten in *Drummond & Sons v E H Van Ingen*:[118]

> [T]he office of a sample is to present to the eye the real meaning and intention of the parties with regard to the subject-matter of the contract which, owing to the imperfection of language, it may be difficult or impossible to express in words. The sample speaks for itself. But it cannot be treated as saying more than such a sample would tell a merchant of the class to which the buyer belongs, using due care and diligence, and appealing to it in the ordinary way and with the knowledge possessed by merchants of that class at the time. No doubt the sample might be made to say a great deal more. Pulled to pieces and examined by unusual tests which curiosity or suspicion might suggest, it would doubtless reveal every secret of its construction. But that is not the way in which business is done in this country. Some confidence there must be between merchant and manufacturer. In matters exclusively within the province of the manufacturer the merchant relies on the manufacturer's skill, and he does so all the more readily when, as in this case, he has had the benefit of that skill before.[119]

Some important principles can be discerned from Lord Macnaghten's statement. First, the sample and the context within which it is offered must reflect the intent of the parties that the contract is to be a sale by sample contract.[120] Second, the buyer must have an opportunity to examine the sale. Those defects that a reasonable examination would reveal cannot later be argued against the seller. However, where a defect could not reasonably have been discerned, the buyer does not lose the benefit of the implied term.[121] Where the bulk does not correspond with the sample, it is no defence to argue that a simple procedure can be applied to the bulk to bring them into the same condition and quality as the sample.[122]

In *Godley v Perry*,[123] the sale of a toy catapult that broke, causing a serious injury to a child, was held to be a breach of a sale by sample contract because the sample that had been shown to the shopkeeper, who later sold the toy to the boy, was superior to the bulk of the catapults that she later received. In *Godley*, the plaintiff sued the shopkeeper. In turn the shopkeeper joined the wholesaler and the importer and pleaded the s 20 equivalent against them. The court held that both the sale by the wholesaler to the shopkeeper and the sale by the importer to the wholesaler were sales by sample, and that the defect within the catapult could not have been discovered on examination.

117 *J S Robertson (Australia) Pty Ltd v Martin* (1956) 94 CLR 30.
118 (1887) 12 App Cas 284.
119 (1887) 12 App Cas 284, 296.
120 *L G Thorne Ltd v Thomas Borthwick & Sons (Australasia) Ltd* (1956) 56 SR (NSW) 81.
121 *Godley v Perry* [1960] 1 WLR 9; *Cameron & Co v Slutzkin Pty Ltd* (1923) 32 CLR 81.
122 *E & S Ruben Ltd v Faire Brothers & Co Ltd* [1949] 1 KB 254.
123 [1960] 1 WLR 9.

In *L G Thorne Ltd v Thomas Borthwick & Sons (Australasia) Ltd*, a sample was offered to the plaintiff in the course of negotiations. The plaintiff was satisfied with the sample and was thus compelled to enter into a contract with the defendant. However, the contract itself contained no reference to the sample. A dispute arose when the bulk of the goods provided were different in quality from the sample. At issue before the High Court was whether the term as to a sale by sample was a term of the written contract. The High Court held that the parol evidence rule applied and that the verbal exchanges as to the sample could not be used to vary the terms of the written contract. Thorne neatly illustrates the limitation that is created by s 20(1) in that, in order for the implied condition to apply, there must first be a term that the contract itself is a sale by sample contract.

4.8 The right to sell, quiet possession and freedom from encumbrance

Section 17(a) of the Goods Act contains a provision imposing an implied condition that the seller has a right to sell the goods.[124] In effect, this requires that the seller either has title or has a right to sell the goods on behalf of the true owner.[125] The purpose of this provision is to ensure that when the buyer purchases goods from the seller they will receive those goods free from any action by a true owner to try to recover those goods. A breach of s 17(a) is a breach of a condition that gives rise to a right in the buyer to treat the contract as repudiated and to claim damages for the breach of the condition.

The facts of *Rowland v Divall*[126] illustrate the application of the implied condition. Divall unwittingly bought a motor car from a thief. Divall later sold the car to Rowland. In turn, Rowland fixed the car up and sold it to Colonel Raildson. Sometime thereafter the police took possession of the car and Raildson sought a refund from Rowland. Having refunded Raildson, Rowland then sued Divall. The Court of Appeal found in favour of Rowland on the basis that he had not received that which he had paid for when he contracted with Divall. In the Court of Appeal, Bankes LJ stated:

> [I]n the present case it cannot possibly be said that the plaintiff received any portion of what he had agreed to buy. It is true that a motor car was delivered to him, but the person who sold it to him had no right to sell it, and therefore he did not get what he paid for – namely, a car to which he would have title; and under those circumstances the use of the car by the purchaser seems to me quite immaterial for the purpose of considering whether the condition had been converted into a warranty. In my opinion the plaintiff was entitled to recover the whole of the purchase money.[127]

As the facts of *Rowland v Divall* indicate, the seller will face liability regardless of whether they knew that there was an impediment to their right to sell the goods. It is possible for a seller to 'perfect' their title and thereby evade liability.[128] For example, a seller might be in the

124 Qld, s 15; NSW, s 17; SA, s 12; WA, s 12; Tas, s 17; ACT, s 17; NT, s 17.
125 *Karlshamms Oljefabriker v Eastport Navigation Corporation ('The Elafi')* [1982] 1 All ER 208.
126 [1923] 2 KB 500.
127 [1923] 2 KB 500, 504.
128 *Patten v Thomas Motors Pty Ltd* (1965) 66 SR (NSW) 459; *Denis Geary Motors v Hunter Street Finance* [1979] Qd R 207.

practice of selling goods to customers before title has actually been transferred to them. The seller might be in the habit of doing this because they need the monies received from the customer to pay the true owner for the goods. The implied condition that the seller has the right to sell is not constrained strictly to ownership. A seller may breach the condition where other rights and obligation affect the goods. For example, in *Niblett Ltd v Confectioners' Materials Co Ltd*[129] a seller sold goods that had a trademark upon them. The goods belonged to the seller, but the trademark belonged to a third party who subsequently sued for infringement. It was held that the seller had breached the implied condition.

The perfecting of title will nullify the liability that arises where a seller has sold goods without having the right to sell them. In *Butterworth v Kingsway Motors*,[130] the seller was a hirer of a car under a hire-purchase agreement. She sold the car before she had fully paid for it. The car was subsequently bought and sold several times. In each subsequent sale, the implied condition that the seller has the right to sell was breached. The ultimate buyer became aware of this defect and sought a remedy from his immediate seller. Shortly thereafter, the first seller paid all the monies under the hire-purchase agreement and perfected her title. This then fed down the chain of titles, perfecting each title. Nonetheless, in *Butterworth v Kingsway Motors Ltd*, the purchase price was repaid to the buyer and the immediate seller, Kingsway Motors, recovered some damages from the person who had sold it the car.

The implied warranty that the buyer shall have quiet possession is somewhat related to the implied condition that the seller has the right to sell the goods. In *Microbeads AG v Vinhurst Road Markings Ltd*,[131] in reference to the equivalent UK provision, Denning LJ stated: 'The words "a right to sell the goods" mean not only a right to pass the property in the machines to the buyer, but also a right to confer on the buyer the undisturbed possession of the goods.'[132] The implied warranty as to quiet possession requires that the buyer's possession of the goods shall not be disturbed by others as a result of an act or omission on the part of the seller.[133] In *Rubicon Computer Systems Ltd v United Paints Ltd*,[134] the sale of a computer system in which a time-lock had been wrongfully installed resulted in a breach of the warranty of quiet possession when the time-lock was later activated, thereby denying the buyer access to the computer system. For example, in *Niblett Ltd v Confectioners' Materials Co Ltd*, the failure to resolve the trademarks issue meant that the buyer was denied their right to quiet possession. Similarly, the warranty as to quiet possession may be breached where goods are sold to a buyer while the immediate seller has not paid for the goods themselves.[135] The implied warranty to quiet possession exists both at the time of sale and immediately thereafter.[136] Given their relationship, it will often be the case that the implied warranty to quiet possession will be pleaded

129 [1921] 3 KB 387.

130 [1954] 1 WLR 1286. See also *Sirius Shipping Corporation v Ship 'Sunrise'* [2006] NSWSC 398.

131 [1975] 1 All ER 529.

132 [1975] 1 All ER 529, 531.

133 *Microbeads AG v Vinhurst Road Markings Ltd* [1975] 1 All ER 529; *Niblett Ltd v Confectioners' Materials Co Ltd* [1921] 3 KB 387.

134 [2000] 2 TCLR 454.

135 *Healing (Sales) Pty Ltd v Inglis Electrix Pty Ltd* (1968) 121 CLR 584; *Keetley v Quinton Pty Ltd* (1991) 4 WAR 133.

136 *Keetley v Quinton Pty Ltd* (1991) 4 WAR 133.

alongside the implied condition that the seller has the right to sell the goods. In *Howell v Richards*,[137] Lord Ellenborough stated:

> The covenant for quiet enjoyment is an assurance against the consequences of a defective title, and of any disturbances thereupon. For the purpose of this covenant, and the indemnity it affords, it is immaterial in what respects, and by what means, or by whose acts the eviction of the grantee or his heir takes place.[138]

This assurance has been somewhat strictly construed. The strictness with which the implied warranty is applied is evident in the case of *Microbeads AG v Vinhurst Road Markings Ltd.*[139] In *Microbeads*, the buyer bought a road-marking device from two Swiss companies. Unbeknown to both the buyer and the sellers, an English company had applied for a patent for a road-marking machine. The patent had not been granted at the time of the sale, but it was granted some months later. The buyer found the road-marking device to be unsatisfactory and refused to pay for it. The Swiss sellers sued for the price and the buyer counter-claimed on the basis that the implied warranty as to quiet possession had been breached. The sellers claimed that in order for the warranty to have been breached the defect must have existed at the time of sale. However, the English Court of Appeal disagreed. With respect to s 12(2) of the *Sale of Goods Act 1893*, the equivalent of s 17(b) of the *Goods Act 1958* (Vic), Lord Denning stated:

> It seems to me that when a buyer has bought goods quite innocently and later on he is disturbed in his possession because the goods are found to be infringing a patent, then he can recover damages for breach of warranty against the seller. It may be the seller is innocent himself, but when one or other must suffer, the loss should fall on the seller: because, after all, he sold the goods and if it turns out that they infringe a patent, he should bear the loss. In the present case the Prismo company can sue for infringement now and stop the buyer using the machines. That is a clear disturbance of possession. The buyer is not able to enjoy the quiet possession which the seller impliedly warranted that he shall have. There is a breach of section 12(2).[140]

While the seller had the right to sell the goods, as there was no impediment on title at the time of sale, the later grant of the patent placed the seller in breach of the implied warranty of quiet possession. In some respects, *Microbeads* is a harsh decision, but the logic of the English Court of Appeal places the burden of loss upon the seller in circumstances where both the buyer and seller were unaware of any impending problem with quiet possession. The corollary of this line of reasoning is that the burden might then be displaced where the buyer has cause to suspect that there may be some future difficulty with the quiet possession of the goods.

Section 17(c) also provides an implied warranty that the goods are free from encumbrance. The effect of the implied warranty is that the goods will be free from any charge or encumbrance in favour of any third party not declared or known to the buyer before or at the time when the contract is made. In the unreported South Australian case of *Steinke v Edwards*,[141] the plaintiff

137 (1809) 11 East 633.
138 (1809) 11 East 633, 642.
139 [1975] 1 All ER 529.
140 [1975] 1 All ER 529, 531.
141 Unreported, Local Court of Adelaide, SD Ronald SM, 1935. See R Newman, 'Sale of Goods – Implied Condition of Free of Charge' (1935) 8 *Australian Law Journal* 368.

bought a car from the defendant and then resold it. As the previous owner still owed unpaid taxes, the car was liable to be seized by the state. The car was subsequently seized and the plaintiff was forced to pay the tax so that the car could be returned to the immediate buyer. The plaintiff then successfully sued the defendant. The Special Magistrate of the Adelaide Local Court held that a 'charge or encumbrance' could be defined to include a tax and that at the time the sale took place there was an implication that the car was free from any charge or encumbrance.

4.9 Key points

- For the Goods Act to apply, there must be (1) a contract of sale; (2) which relates to goods; (3) the consequence of which property in the goods passes from one party to the other; and (4) the property passes in exchange for money consideration.
- The Goods Act implies terms into sale of goods contracts. Sections 17–20 deal with sales by description, merchantable quality, fitness for purpose, sale by sample, freedom from encumbrance, and quiet possession.
- Section 18 of the Goods Act deals with the implied obligation of correspondence with description.
- Section 19 of the Goods Act implies a term that the goods must be fit for the purpose for which they are sold.
- Section 19(b) of the Goods Act provides that where goods are bought by description from a seller who deals in goods of that description (whether they be the manufacturer or not) there is an implied condition that the goods shall be of merchantable quality.
- Section 20 of the Goods Act deals with the implied condition of sale by sample.
- Section 17(a) of the Goods Act contains a provision imposing an implied condition that the seller has a right to sell the goods.
- Section 17(b) of the Goods Act entitles the buyer to the quiet possession of the goods.
- Section 17(c) also provides an implied warranty that the goods are free from encumbrance.

4.10 Discussion questions

1. Why does the Goods Act imply terms into goods contracts?
2. What is the meaning of 'correspondence with description'? How has it been defined in the case law?
3. What does it mean to say that goods must be fit for the purpose for which they are sold? What is sale by sample, and what are the leading cases on this matter?
4. What is the meaning of 'quiet possession' and 'free from encumbrance'? Is there any overlap between these rules?

4.11 FURTHER READING

Brown, I, 'The Swing of the Pendulum from Caveat Venditor to Caveat Emptor' (2000) 116 *Law Quarterly Review* 537.

5

TRANSFER OF PROPERTY

5.0 Introduction

This chapter deals with the legal issues associated with the transfer of property and title in sale of goods contracts. The various state and territory Sale of Goods Acts regulate the way in which property is transferred from a seller to a buyer. However, there are circumstances where the parties to a contract of sale will be unclear as to when property will pass between them. Under these circumstances, the transfer of property will need to be regulated by one of the five general rules set out in the Sale of Goods Act. Similarly, there may be circumstances under which a non-owner will purport to transfer ownership in goods. Should this occur, the law will have to seek to do justice between one of two innocent parties: the true owner and the third party buyer without notice. The various Sale of Goods Acts contain rules determining when one party or the other prevails. For the purposes of this chapter, the sale of goods legislation referred to will be the *Goods Act 1958* (Vic) ('Goods Act').

This chapter commences with a brief overview of the categories of goods. The overview highlights the importance of classifying goods in order to identify the basic rules for the passing of title. The chapter then examines the five statutory presumptions that apply under the Goods Act, before examining the exceptions to the nemo dat principle. Finally, the chapter provides a brief overview of the common law relating to retention of title. A further discussion on retention of title is contained in Chapter 9 on the *Personal Property Securities Act 2009* (Cth).

5.1 Categories of goods

Identifying the actual nature of a good is vital to determining the question of when property should pass. There are four categories of goods: (1) specific goods; (2) unascertained goods; (3) ascertained goods; and (4) future goods.

5.1.1 Specific goods

Section 3 of the Goods Act provides that the phrase 'specific goods' means goods identified and agreed upon at the time a contract of sale is made.[1] These are the identifiable goods that are unique and subject to the contract. It will ordinarily be the case that where specific goods are the subject of a contract of sale, property will pass when the contract for the sale of the goods has been made.[2] It is possible for specific goods to be future goods. The parties to a contract of sale may also agree among themselves as to when property will pass.

5.1.2 Unascertained goods

The Goods Act does not define unascertained goods. Generally, the term 'unascertained goods' refers to goods that are not agreed on, specified or identified, at the time of making

1 *Goods Act 1958* (Vic), s 3; *Sale of Goods Act 1923* (NSW), s 3; *Sale of Goods Act 1896* (Qld), s 3; *Sale of Goods Act 1895* (SA), s 60; *Sale of Goods Act 1895* (WA), s 60; *Sale of Goods Act 1896* (Tas), s 3; *Sale of Goods Act 1954* (ACT), s 5; *Sale of Goods Act 1972* (NT), s 5.

2 *McPherson, Thom, Kettle & Co v Dench Brothers* [1921] VLR 437.

the contract.[3] For example, in *Carlos Federspiel & Co SA v Charles Twigg & Co Ltd*,[4] a buyer made a contract with a seller to purchase cycles and tricycles. The seller subsequently went bankrupt before the goods had been delivered to the buyer. At the time of the contract, the goods still had to be manufactured. Accordingly, at the time that the contract was made the goods were unascertained goods by description. Section 21 of the Goods Act provides that where there is a contract for the sale of unascertained goods, no property in the goods is transferred to the buyer unless and until the goods are ascertained. These can be generic goods or goods sold ex bulk. It is not possible to transfer property in unascertained goods.[5] Property will pass in unascertained goods when they become ascertained.[6]

5.1.3 Ascertained goods

Ascertained goods are those identified 'in accordance with the agreement after the time a contract of sale is made'.[7] They are not specific goods, because they are identified only after the contract is made. For example, if a farmer has a vast number of eggs in bulk and agrees to sell some to a buyer, the exact eggs that will belong to the buyer will not be known until the farmer has separated the requisite eggs from the bulk.

5.1.4 Future goods

Section 3 of the Goods Act provides that 'future goods' are the goods that are to be manufactured or acquired by the seller after the making of the contract for sale.[8] They include goods not yet in existence, as well as goods existing but not yet acquired by the seller. Section 10 of the Goods Act provides that where a contract for sale deals with future goods, it is an agreement to sell goods.

5.1.5 The importance of classifying goods

The nature of goods determines when property passes. As such, it is important to understand the nature of the classification of goods, as this will affect the remedies that are available to both the buyer and the seller. Sections 21–33 of the Goods Act deal with the transfer of property in sale of goods contracts. 'Property' in the Goods Act generally means property in goods. Although the terms 'title' and 'property' can have different meanings depending on the context in which they are used, they can generally be used interchangeably. The transfer of property is important because risk prima facie passes with property. Once property passes, buyers can lose the right to reject those goods. Similarly, the party with property can sue for

3 *Re Goldcorp Exchange Ltd (in rec)* [1995] 1 AC 74, 90; *Jansz v GMB Imports Pty Ltd* [1979] VR 581.

4 [1957] 1 Lloyd's Rep 240.

5 *Re Goldcorp Exchange Ltd (in rec)* [1995] 1 AC 74, 90; *Jansz v GMB Imports Pty Ltd* [1979] VR 581; *Hughes v Australian Competition and Consumer Comission* (2004) 247 FCR 277.

6 *Karlshamms Oljefabriker v Eastport Navigation Corporation ('The Elafi')* [1982] 1 All ER 208. See also *THC Holding Pty Ltd v CMA Recycling Pty Ltd* (2014) 101 ACSR 202.

7 *Re Wait* [1927] 1 Ch 606.

8 Qld, s 3; NSW, s 3; SA, s 60; WA, s 60; Tas, s 3; ACT, s 5; NT, s 5.

damages to the goods. If the buyer has property in the goods, they can pass title. Moreover, the seller can sue for the price only after property has passed.

5.2 Transfer of property presumptions

Section 22 of the Goods Act provides that where there is a contract for the sale of specific or ascertained goods, property will pass when the parties intend it to pass.[9] Section 22(2) provides that in determining when the parties intended property to pass, regard must be had to the terms of the contract, the circumstances of the case and the conduct of the parties. Accordingly, s 22 prioritises the intent of the parties in determining when property is to pass. If the circumstances are such that the intent of the parties can be ascertained, then there will be no need to apply the statutory presumptions that are contained in s 23 of the Act. Section 23 provides for five presumptions that apply in the absence of evidence as to intent. The question of which specific presumption will apply depends upon the relevant circumstances.

Section 23 of the Goods Act states:

> **Rules for ascertaining intention**
>
> Unless a different intention appears the following are rules for ascertaining the intention of the parties as to the time at which the property in the goods is to pass to the buyer:
>
> Rule 1. Where there is an unconditional contract for the sale of specific goods in a deliverable state the property in the goods passes to the buyer when the contract is made, and it is immaterial whether the time of payment or the time of delivery or both be postponed.
>
> Rule 2. Where there is a contract for the sale of specific goods and the seller is bound to do something to the goods for the purpose of putting them into a deliverable state the property does not pass until such thing be done and the buyer has notice thereof.
>
> Rule 3. Where there is a contract for the sale of specific goods in a deliverable state, but the seller is bound to weigh measure test or do some other act or thing with reference to the goods for the purpose of ascertaining the price, the property does not pass until such act or thing be done and the buyer has notice thereof.
>
> Rule 4. When goods are delivered to the buyer on approval or on 'sale or return' or other similar terms the property therein passes to the buyer –
>
> (a) when he signifies his approval or acceptance to the seller or does any other act adopting the transaction;
>
> (b) if he does not signify his approval or acceptance to the seller, but retains the goods without giving notice of rejection, then if a time has been fixed for the return of the goods on the expiration of such time and if no time has been fixed on the expiration of a reasonable time. What is a reasonable time is a question of fact.
>
> Rule 5. (1) Where there is a contract for the sale of unascertained or future goods by description and goods of that description and in a deliverable state are unconditionally appropriated to the contract either by the seller with the assent of the buyer or by the

9 Qld, s 21; NSW, s 23; SA, s 18; WA, s 18; Tas, s 23; ACT, s 23; NT, s 23.

buyer with the assent of the seller, the property in the goods thereupon passes to the buyer. Such assent may be express or implied and may be given either before or after the appropriation is made.

(2) Where in pursuance of the contract the seller delivers the goods to the buyer or to a carrier or other bailee (whether named by the buyer or not) for the purpose of transmission to the buyer and does not reserve the right of disposal he is deemed to have unconditionally appropriated the goods to the contract.

5.2.1 Rule 1

Rule 1 of s 23 provides:

> When there is an unconditional contract for the sale of specific goods in a deliverable state, the property in the goods passes to the buyer when the contract is made, and it is immaterial whether the time of payment or the time of delivery, or both, is or are postponed.

There are three elements to Rule 1. First, there must be an unconditional contract. Second, the contract must be for the sale of specific goods. 'Specific goods' are the goods identified and agreed upon at the time the contract of sale is made.[10] Third, the specific goods must be in a deliverable state. The term 'deliverable state' refers to the state that the goods must be in under the contract so that the buyer would be bound to take delivery of them.[11] If these three elements are met, then property will pass when the contract is made regardless of the time of delivery or payment.

In *McPherson, Thom, Kettle & Co v Dench Brothers*,[12] the sale of a heifer at an auction was held to be a sale made under an unconditional contract. The buyer had successfully bid on the heifer. However, the heifer disappeared before delivery. Subsequently, the seller sued for the price. Clause 1 of the auction rules stated that '[a]ll lots shall be at risk of purchaser after the fall of the hammer'. Clause 2 of the auction rules stated that if the purchaser did not pay for the goods, they could then be retaken by the seller and resold. The buyer argued that the effect of cl 2 was to make the contract conditional. It was held that cl 2 did not suspend cl 1 or make the contract conditional; instead, the effect of cl 2 was merely to provide a means for resolving a contingent scenario. Accordingly, the conditions of sale meant that property passed after the hammer fell at the auction.

5.2.2 Rule 2

Rule 2 provides:

> When there is a contract for the sale of specific goods and the seller is bound to do something to the goods for the purpose of putting them into a deliverable state, the property does not pass until such thing is done and the buyer has notice thereof.

10 *Re Renovation Boys Pty Ltd (admins apptd)* [2014] NSWSC 340, [13].
11 *Underwood Ltd v Burgh Castle Brick & Cement Syndicate* [1922] 1 KB 343.
12 [1921] VLR 437.

Notwithstanding the precondition of there being a contract of sale, there are effectively three elements to Rule 2. These are: (1) the sale must pertain to specific goods; (2) the seller must be bound to do something to those goods in order to render them deliverable; and (3) the seller must then notify the buyer.[13]

The contract must require that the seller does something to the goods. Once this has been done, the goods will be deliverable under the contract.[14] 'Notice' under Rule 2 most likely means actual notice.[15] In *Worcester Works Finance Ltd v Cooden Engineering Co Ltd*,[16] a case regarding nemo dat, Lord Denning MR stated: '[T]he word "notice" here means actual notice[;] that is to say, knowledge of the sale or deliberately turning a blind eye to it. Our commercial law does not like constructive notice.'[17] Lord Denning MR made his remarks in the context of the *Sale of Goods Act 1893* (UK). As the Goods Act is based upon the 1893 UK Act, it is quite likely that the sentiments of Lord Denning MR should colour the interpretation of notice under Rule 2. The case of *Wallace v Safeway Caravan Mart*[18] demonstrates the parameters of Rule 2. In *Wallace*, the buyer purchased a caravan on the condition that the seller would install a shower and deliver the caravan. However, it was stolen before the work was complete. As the caravan was not in a deliverable state, the property and the risk had not passed. In order for Rule 2 to apply, the caravan would have to have been both fixed and delivered before it would have been in a deliverable state.

5.2.3 Rule 3

Rule 3 provides:

> When there is a contract for the sale of specific goods in a deliverable state, but the seller is bound to weigh, measure, test or do some other act or thing with reference to the goods for the purpose of ascertaining the price, the property does not pass until such act or thing is done and the buyer has notice thereof.

The operation of Rule 3 requires that there must be (1) a sale of specific goods; (2) in a deliverable state; with (3) the requirement that the seller weigh, measure, test or do some similar act to the goods; and that (4) the buyer must be given notice when this is done. If these requirements are met, then property will pass. This rule covers 'situations where specific goods are bought, but the extent or quality is not known and the actual price cannot be known until either the extent or quality are known'.[19] In *Nanka-Bruce v Commonwealth Trust Ltd*,[20] it was held that the weighing, measuring or testing must be done to determine the price. Rule 3 will not apply if the weighing, measuring or testing is done merely to satisfy the customer with regard to quality.[21]

13 *Underwood Ltd v Burgh Castle Brick & Cement Syndicate* [1922] 1 KB 343.
14 *Re Renovation Boys Pty Ltd (admins apptd)* [2014] NSWSC 340.
15 *Worcester Works Finance Ltd v Cooden Engineering Co Ltd* [1972] 1 QB 210, 218.
16 [1972] 1 QB 210.
17 [1972] 1 QB 210, 218.
18 (1975) 3 QL 224.
19 *National Coal Board v Gamble* [1959] 1 QB 11.
20 [1926] AC 77.
21 *Nanka-Bruce v Commonwealth Trust Ltd* [1926] AC 77.

5.2.4 Rule 4

Rule 4 provides that when the goods are delivered to the buyer on approval or 'on sale or return' or other similar terms, the property therein passes to the buyer either:

- when the buyer signifies the buyer's approval or acceptance to the seller, or does any other act adopting the transaction; or
- if the buyer does not signify approval or acceptance to the seller but retains the goods without giving notice of rejection, and if a fixed time passes, or if there is no fixed time, when a reasonable time passes.

'Reasonable time' under Rule 4 is a question of fact that must be determined on the basis of the circumstances of the case.[22] The term 'approval or sale', or any similar phrase, means that the buyer can decide whether to accept the goods.[23] For a sale on approval situation to exist, it must be the intention of the parties that the goods are given to the buyer with the discretion to approve or disapprove of them.[24] If the buyer sells the goods to a customer, this will be an act that signifies approval.[25]

5.2.5 Rule 5

Rule 5 provides:

> (1) Where there is a contract for the sale of unascertained or future goods by description and goods of that description in a deliverable state are unconditionally appropriated to the contract either by the seller with the assent of the buyer or by the buyer with the assent of the seller, the property in the goods thereupon passes to the buyer. Such assent may be express or implied and may be given either before or after the appropriation is made.

Alternatively:

> (2) Where in pursuance of the contract the seller delivers the goods to the buyer or to a carrier or other bailee (whether named by the buyer or not) for the purpose of transmission to the buyer and does not reserve the right of disposal they are deemed to have unconditionally appropriated the goods to the contract.

Rule 5 requires that (1) there must be a contract for the sale of unascertained or future goods by description; (2) goods of that description in a deliverable state are ascertained; (3) those goods are then unconditionally appropriated to the contract; (4) by either the buyer or the seller with the other's assent. With these conditions met, the property then passes.[26]

22 *Kirkham v Attenborough* [1897] 1 QB 201.
23 *Cammell Laird & Co Ltd v Manganese Bronze & Brass Co Ltd* [1934] AC 402; *Re Ferrier; Ex parte The Trustee v Donald* [1944] 1 Ch 295.
24 *London Jewellers Ltd v Attenborough* [1934] 2 KB 206.
25 *Poole v Smith's Car Sales (Balham) Ltd* [1962] 1 WLR 744.
26 See *Eastern Well Service No 2 Pty Ltd v Campac (Australia) Pty Ltd* [2010] QSC 350.

Appropriation occurs where the relevant goods are clearly attached to the contract between the two parties.[27] The ascertained goods must belong to the relevant contract. It might be difficult to determine which goods have been appropriated to a contract, although this does not mean that appropriation has not occurred. In *Crouch v Adams*,[28] White J stated:

> There is an important distinction between there being no appropriation of goods to a contract and its being impossible now to determine what goods were appropriated to an individual contract. It does not follow that because the liquidator cannot now determine which machines were appropriated to which contract, that no appropriation occurred. If there were an appropriation, the property in the machines, both at law and in equity, passed to the individual buyers. If there were not, then, in my view, property in the machines, both at law and in equity, remained with the company.[29]

Subsequently, in the case *Re Renovation Boys Pty Ltd (admins apptd)*,[30] Black J agreed with the principle espoused in *Crouch v Adams*. *Renovations Boys* involved a company in receivership with goods that had been paid for by customers. The administrators sought to exercise an equitable lien over those goods in order to recover from the customers the costs of storing and attending to the goods. In *Renovation Boys*, Black J found that the property had passed to the customers even though it was difficult to determine which goods belonged to each contract. Black J stated:

> [P]roperty in category 'A' stock passed to customers upon the Company's allocation of goods to the relevant purchase order, consistent with the facts that the relevant customers had paid for the goods in full, the Company had undertaken an act of allocation in respect of an item to a customer, although the particular items was [*sic*] not then or now individually identifiable, and those goods are available for collection and would have been collected or delivered, had the Company not been placed in administration.[31]

However, the goods in question must not simply have been separated from the bulk of the seller's goods for use in future transactions or for some other purpose. They must have been set aside, with the buyer's assent, for the specific transaction between the buyer and the seller.[32] Once this has occurred, property will pass to the buyer. The buyer's assent to the appropriation does not need to coincide with the time of the appropriation.[33] The assent can be given before or after the appropriation.[34] In *Renovation Boys*, Black J stated that 'consent may be given in advance and without knowledge of the particular item to be appropriated'.[35] The assent may be express or implied.[36]

27 *Carlos Federspiel & Co SA v Charles Twigg & Co Ltd* [1957] 1 Lloyd's Rep 240.
28 [2006] NSWSC 1029.
29 [2006] NSWSC 1029, [38].
30 [2014] NSWSC 340.
31 [2014] NSWSC 340, [21].
32 *Matthew Short & Associates Pty Ltd v Riviera Marine (International) Pty Ltd* [2001] NSWCA 281.
33 *Carlos Federspiel & Co SA v Charles Twigg & Co Ltd* [1957] 1 Lloyd's Rep 240; *Aldridge v Johnson* (1857) 7 El & Bl 885.
34 *Crouch v Adams* [2006] NSWSC 1029; *Pignataro v Gilroy* [1919] 1 KB 459.
35 [2014] NSWSC 340, [19].
36 *Pignataro v Gilroy* [1919] 1 KB 459.

5.3 Transfer by a non-owner (nemo dat)

In most sales situations, the person who sells the goods to the buyer will either be the true owner of the goods or a person with proper authority to sell them on behalf of the owner. However, there may well be occasions where a sale takes place and the seller is neither the true owner nor the owner's agent to sell. In these cases, there are invariably two wronged parties: (1) the true owner, who has been deprived of their property; and (2) the innocent buyer, who now finds that the goods they have purchased are claimed by another. Accordingly, a legal dispute will arise between the true owner and the innocent third party buyer.

In order for the third party buyer to have a reasonable chance of retaining the goods, they must be innocent of any knowledge that the seller did not have title to the goods or authority to sell. This is sometimes expressed as 'buying in good faith, without notice'. The particular difficulty that the innocent buyer faces appears in the form of the nemo dat principle. This principle is that a person who purports to sell something can transfer a title that is no better than that which they actually possess.[37] In effect, a seller without title or authority to sell can only give possession. The rule here is the embodiment of the Latin maxim *nemo dat quod non habet*. While this chapter is confined to discussing the nemo dat principle within the context of sale of goods transactions, it can also be applied to the sale of a chose in action.[38] The nemo dat rule is well entrenched in the various Sale of Goods Acts.[39]

For example, in Victoria, the primary rule on nemo dat is contained in s 27 of the Goods Act. Section 27 provides:

> **Sale by person not the owner**
>
> Subject to the provisions of this Part and of any express enactment where goods are sold by a person who is not the owner thereof and who does not sell them under the authority or with the consent of the owner, the buyer acquires no better title to the goods than the seller had unless the owner of the goods is by his conduct precluded from denying the seller's authority to sell.

There are three primary elements to s 27. First, the sale must be done by a person who is not the true owner of the goods or someone with authority to deal with the goods. Second, the general presumption will be that the buyer gains no better title than the seller. Third, the general presumption will be displaced where it is evident that the true owner should be precluded from denying the seller's authority by their own conduct.

Section 27 encapsulates the balancing act that the various Sale of Goods Acts attempt to play between the nemo dat rule and the various applicable exceptions. In *Bishopsgate Motor Finance Corporation Ltd v Transport Brakes Ltd*,[40] Lord Denning summarised the principles at play by stating:

---

37 *Hollins v Fowler* (1875) LR 7 HL 757; *Bishopsgate Motor Finance Corporation Ltd v Transport Brakes Ltd* [1949] 1 KB 322.

38 See *Palin v Vetterli* [2013] NSWSC 893; *Southern British National Trust Ltd v Pither* (1937) 57 CLR 89; *Ghirardi v Allregal Corporation Pty Ltd* [2001] WASCA 366.

39 See Vic, s 27; NSW, s 26(1); SA, s 21(1); Qld, s 24(1); WA, s 21(1); Tas, s 26(1); ACT, s 26(1); NT, s 26(1).

40 [1949] 1 KB 322.

> In the development of our law, two principles have striven for mastery. The first is for the protection of property: no one can give a better title than he himself possesses. The second is for the protection of commercial transactions: the person who takes in good faith and for value without notice should get a good title. The first principle has held sway for a long time, but it has been modified by the common law itself and by statute so as to meet the needs of our own times. The modification here in question is one conferred by the common law itself.[41]

Commercial certainty should be allowed to prevail where the conduct of the true owner is such that there is significant merit in denying them the right to reclaim their property. Such a situation can only arise where the true owner has contributed to the wrongful sale through a lack of care, wrongful conduct or some other similar act. The exceptions to the nemo dat rule provide a means for balancing commercial certainty on the one hand and the protection of property on the other. There are five generally recognised categories of exceptions to the nemo dat rule: (1) estoppel; (2) sale under a voidable title; (3) sale by a mercantile agent; (4) seller in possession; and (5) buyer in possession. The categories of exceptions to the nemo dat rule are not closed and miscellaneous exceptions may arise.[42]

5.3.1 Estoppel

Section 27 of the Goods Act provides for an estoppel exception to the nemo dat rule by virtue of the phrase 'unless the owner of the goods is by his conduct precluded from denying the seller's authority to sell'. In effect, estoppel is incorporated into nemo dat by the contingent rule in s 27 that the owner's conduct might preclude the right to sell.[43] The consequence of a finding by a court that the estoppel exists is that the true owner is disentitled from asserting their ownership and from denying the third party's ownership.[44] The third party ultimately acquires full ownership of the goods by virtue of the estoppel. The estoppel exception does not merely prevent the true owner from reclaiming their goods; it effectively transfers ownership from the true owner to the innocent third party buyer.[45] The estoppel must be founded in the behaviour and conduct of the true owner. For example, there may have been a representation by the true owner that was relied upon by the purchaser.[46] Merely entrusting another with possession of the goods is not sufficient on its own to constitute a representation.[47] For silence to amount to an estoppel, there must have been a recognisable duty of care owed to the third party buyer.[48]

The critical issue here is the conduct and circumstances giving rise to the estoppel. There are two ways in which the estoppel can arise: (1) by representation; or (2) by negligence. The representation would be from the true owner to the effect that the seller is the true owner or

41 [1949] 1 KB 322, 336. See also *Pearson v Rose & Young Ltd* [1950] 2 All ER 1027.
42 S Traves, *Commercial Law* (LexisNexis Butterworths Australia, Sydney, 2016), 275.
43 *Associated Midland Corporation v Sanderson Motors Pty Ltd* [1983] 3 NSWLR 395.
44 *Eastern Distributors Ltd v Goldring* [1957] 2 QB 600; *Associated Midland Corporation v Sanderson Motors Pty Ltd* [1983] 3 NSWLR 395.
45 *Eastern Distributors Ltd v Goldring* [1957] 2 QB 600.
46 *Eastern Distributors Ltd v Goldring* [1957] 2 QB 600.
47 *Central Newbury Car Auctions Ltd v Unity Finance Ltd* [1957] 1 QB 371.
48 *Moorgate Mercantile Co Ltd v Twitchings* [1977] AC 890.

has authority. Negligence would be where the seller permits the appearance of ownership. The basis for the estoppel exception can be found in *Lickbarrow v Mason*,[49] where Ashurst J stated: 'Wherever one of two innocent persons must suffer by the acts of a third, he who has enabled such third person to occasion the loss must sustain it.' The essential idea formulated by Ashurst J has been a thread running through the estoppel cases in nemo dat. Nevertheless, his rather broad formulation has not been brazenly applied and has attracted criticism.[50] As such, the operation of the estoppel exception to nemo dat depends upon the satisfaction of key requirements.

5.3.1.1 Estoppel by representation

Estoppel by representation draws rather heavily on the doctrine of apparent authority in agency law. In essence, where the true owner arms another party with the means of representing to an innocent purchaser that they have the authority to sell the relevant goods, the true owner will be estopped from asserting their right of ownership. There must be a representation that the non-owner has the right to sell the goods.[51] The typical case of estoppel by representation is exemplified by the facts in *Kulkarni v Manor Credit (Davenham) Ltd*,[52] where the claimant sought to buy a Mercedes car under a hire-purchase agreement from a company. Unbeknown to the claimant, the company was acting fraudulently and the true owner of the car was Manor Credit, which had allowed the company to take possession of the car. Additionally, Manor Credit had not interceded at any point prior to the dispute, although it knew the company was engaging in a hire-purchase business, to indicate that it was the true owner. While *Kulkarni v Manor Credit* was decided on other grounds, it illustrates a situation where a true owner permits another to hold themselves out as having the authority to sell the goods. Particular scrutiny must be given to the conduct of the true owner.

The case of *Eastern Distributors v Goldring*[53] is the leading authority on estoppel by representation. In *Eastern Distributors*, Murphy, the owner of a van, let Coker, a dealer, pretend that the van was his for the purpose of Murphy obtaining finance from Eastern Distributors for the purchase of the van and another car. Coker pretended that Murphy had paid a deposit for both vehicles. Murphy signed the paper for both vehicles, but Eastern Distributors authorised finance only for the van. Murphy sold the van to Goldring. Murphy also did not pay any instalments. Eastern Distributors sued for the van.

The Court of Appeal held that the UK equivalent of s 27 created a type of estoppel. The court held that even though there had been no real sale to Coker, the representation by Murphy via Coker could preclude Murphy from asserting ownership. While Coker had made the relevant representation, Murphy had been privy to it and was thus bound by effect of the representation. In an important speech, Devlin LJ stated:

> The apparent ownership or authority has generally taken the form of arming the agent with some indicia which made it appear that he was either the owner or had the right to

49 (1787) 2 Term Rep 63.

50 See *Mercantile Bank of India Ltd v Central Bank of India Ltd* [1938] AC 287; *Sheik Ali Ahmend Al-Thani v Bradshaw & Webb (Sales) Ltd* (unreported, Queens Bench Division, 30 March 1988).

51 *Eastern Distributors Ltd v Goldring* [1957] 2 QB 600.

52 [2010] All ER (D) 120.

53 [1957] 2 QB 600.

> sell. In our judgment the principle applies to any form of representation or holding out of apparent ownership or the right to sell. It is embodied in s. 21 (1) of the Sale of Goods Act, 1893, which provides:
>
> > ... where goods are sold by a person who is not the owner thereof, and who does not sell them under the authority or with the consent of the owner, the buyer acquires no better title to the goods than the seller had, unless the owner of the goods is by his conduct precluded from denying the seller's authority to sell.
>
> This section expresses the old principle that 'apparent authority to sell is an exception to the maxim nemo dat quod non habet; and it is plain from the wording that if the owner of the goods is precluded from denying authority, the buyer will in fact acquire a better title than the seller'.[54]
>
> We doubt whether this principle, which is sometimes referred to ... as common law estoppel, ought really to be regarded as part of the law of estoppel. At any rate it differs from what is sometimes called 'equitable estoppel' in this vital respect that the effect of its application is to transfer a real title and not merely a metaphorical title by estoppel.[55]

Even though Devlin LJ doubted whether the doctrinal rule could properly be described as 'estoppel', it certainly operated as such a rule would operate, by preventing the true owner from resiling from his representation. In addition, the estoppel by representation effectively transfers ownership from the true owner to the innocent buyer. In *Lloyds & Scottish Finance Ltd v Williamson*,[56] the English Court of Appeal held that the actions of the appellant, a hire-purchase company, in allowing its agent to sell a motor car as if he were the true owner, were bound by the representation that it had made. The appellant had done more than simply allow the agent to possess the car. The appellant had furnished the agent with the authority to sell as if he were the owner. The buyer was completely unaware that the appellant was the true owner. Lord Justice Salmon stated:

> In the present case the principal did much more than merely put Peerless in possession of the motor car. He did what he could to induce any person buying the car from Peerless to believe that Peerless were the owners of the motor car by authorising Peerless to sell it as owners. As a result, the defendant Mr. Lunt obtained a good title at common law. This is not because of the operation of a true estoppel, for the defendant Mr. Lunt obtained a real title which he could properly transfer. The plaintiffs are not merely estopped as between themselves and the defendant Mr. Lunt from calling evidence to show that they are the true owners of the grey Jaguar.[57]

In both *Lloyds & Scottish Finance* and *Eastern Distributors*, the representation made by the true owner was in effect that the agent was the real owner of the relevant goods. A similar situation occurred in *Whelan Kartaway Pty Ltd v G & C Weatherburn Pty Ltd (in liq)*,[58] where a

---

54 Goods Act, s 27.
55 [1957] 2 QB 600, 610–11.
56 [1965] 1 WLR 404.
57 [1965] 1 WLR 404, 410.
58 [2002] NSWSC 677.

representation that a hoist attached to a vehicle had been supplied and serviced by the plaintiff was found to amount to a representation that the hoist was owned by whoever owned the vehicle. In the NSW Supreme Court, Sperling J held that any reasonable person would assume that the phrase 'supplied and serviced by [Whelan Kartaway]' would mean that the hoist was owned by the owner of the vehicle.

Quite apart from representations as to ownership, it is also possible that the true owner, by their conduct, may represent that an agent has the authority to sell the goods. In the NSW Supreme Court, in *Motor Credits (Hire Finance) Ltd v Pacific Motor Auctions Pty Ltd*,[59] Walsh J held that allowing an agent to have possession of the cars at its premises where they were displayed for sale amounted to a representation that the agent at least had the authority to sell them.

5.3.1.2 Estoppel by negligence

Negligence by the true owner can allow the seller to create the appearance of ownership. Under these circumstances, the buyer will be justified in assuming that the seller is the owner or has the requisite authority to sell the goods. However, negligence stands in stark contrast to a representation, in that the former requires an absence of action. Given the primacy that the common law has traditionally afforded to ownership and property rights, as amply demonstrated by the nemo dat maxim itself, the inaction and the context within which it occurs must be sufficient to justify transferring ownership from the true owner to the buyer. Accordingly, the owner must at least owe the buyer a duty of care.[60] This duty must have been breached by the owner and the breach must have caused the buyer to buy the goods from the seller.[61] Often the owner will not owe a duty to a third party buyer. A mere lack of prudence on the owner's part will be insufficient to support an estoppel by negligence.[62]

The competing principles that are at play in estoppel by negligence were summarised in *Moorgate Mercantile Co Ltd v Twitchings*,[63] where Lord Wilberforce said in his dissenting judgment:

> English law has generally taken the robust line that a man who owns property is not under any general duty to safeguard it and that he may sue for its recovery any person into whose hands it has come ... He is not estopped from asserting his title by mere inaction or silence, because inaction or silence, by contrast with positive conduct or statement, is colourless: it cannot influence a person to act to his detriment unless it acquires a positive content such that that person is entitled to rely on it. In order that silence or inaction may acquire a positive content it is usually said that there must be a duty to speak or to act in a particular way, owed to the person prejudiced, or to the public or to a class of the public of which he in the event turns out to be one ... I think that the test of duty is one which can safely be applied so long as it is understood what we mean ... whether, having regard to the situation in which the relevant transaction occurred, as known to both parties, a

59 (1962) 79 WN (NSW) 685.

60 *Johnson Matthey (Australia) Ltd v Dascorp Pty Ltd* (2003) 9 VR 171.

61 *Johnson Matthey (Australia) Ltd v Dascorp Pty Ltd* (2003) 9 VR 171.

62 *Moorgate Mercantile Co Ltd v Twitchings* [1977] AC 890. See also *Rosecell Pty Ltd v JP Haines Plumbing Pty Ltd* [2015] NSWSC 1238.

63 *Moorgate Mercantile Co Ltd v Twitchings* [1977] AC 890.

> reasonable man, in the position of the 'acquirer' of the property, would expect the 'owner' acting honestly and responsibly, if he claimed any title in the property, to take steps to make that claim known to, and discoverable by, the 'acquirer' and whether, in the face of an omission to do so, the 'acquirer' could reasonably assume that no such title was claimed.[64]

In estoppel by negligence, many of the fundamental principles of tort, such as duty and breach, perform a vital role in demarcating the line between retaining ownership and being estopped from reclaiming title. The decision of the House of Lords in *Moorgate Mercantile* neatly sets out the requirements of duty and breach. This has greatly influenced the development of estoppel by negligence.[65] The sum total of the failure of the true owner to take due care to assert ownership, in circumstances where a duty is owed to the prospective buyer, is that the silence or acquiescence may have the same effect as a representation.[66] That is, the overall characterisation of the negligence or omission is that it amounts to a representation. As such, if the buyer has been misled by the state of affairs that the true owner has allowed, the latter will be estopped from later demurring from their own effective representation and asserting ownership.

In *Thomas Australia Wholesale Vehicle Trading Co Pty Ltd v Marac Finance Australia Ltd*,[67] Kirby P, as his Honour then was in the NSW Court of Appeal, suggested in dissent that imposing a duty of care ran counter to the true meaning of the s 27 equivalent in the Sale of Goods Act. However, both Glass and McHugh JJA, as the latter then was, disagreed with this approach to the provision. Similarly, the dissenting view of Kirby P in *Thomas Australia* was considered, but not followed, by Redlich J in *Johnson Matthey (Australia) Ltd v Dascorp Pty Ltd*.[68] A case of estoppel by negligence will inevitably require a nexus between the true owner and the buyer.[69] The true owner must owe a duty of care either to the buyer or to the class of persons to whom the buyer belongs.

In *Johnson Matthey* the failure to prevent the theft of gold, which was sold to the buyer by the employee who stole it, was found not to amount to an estoppel by negligence. The plaintiff in *Johnson Matthey*, the true owner, was unaware of the thefts at the time that they occurred and had no knowledge that the thief's accomplice was selling the gold to the defendant. In finding for the plaintiff, Redlich J stated:

> The buyer relying upon estoppel by negligence must establish a representation arising from a failure to act in circumstances where the owner had a duty to do so to ensure that the buyer was not misled. I am satisfied no representation arises from any negligent conduct on the plaintiff's part. It took no step to clothe anyone with the appearance of a right to sell its gold. It neither knew nor could it be said should have known that a large amount of its gold was likely to be offered for sale in the market place.[70]

64 [1977] AC 890, 903–4.
65 *Johnson Matthey v Dascorp* (2003) 9 VR 171; *Republic of India v India Steamship Co* [1998] AC 878; *Tradax Export SA v Dorada Compania Naviera SA* [1982] 2 Lloyd's Rep. 140.
66 *Johnson Matthey (Australia) Ltd v Dascorp Pty Ltd* (2003) 9 VR 171.
67 (1985) 3 NSWLR 452.
68 (2003) 9 VR 171.
69 *Cadbury Schweppes plc v Halifax Share Dealing Ltd* [2006] EWHC 1184 (Ch).
70 (2003) 9 VR 171, [62].

5.3.2 Mercantile agent

A mercantile agent is a person who sells or deals with goods on behalf of the owners. Where the relevant legislation operates, good legal title will be conferred on the purchaser. Under the Goods Act, the relevant provisions are ss 65–81. Section 67 sets out the essential concept of a mercantile agent.[71] It states:

> Where a mercantile agent is entrusted as such with the possession of any goods or the documents of title to any goods any sale pledge or other disposition of the goods made by him in the ordinary course of business of a mercantile agent shall subject to the provisions of this part be as valid as if he was expressly authorised by the owner of the goods to make the same: Provided that the person taking under such disposition acts in good faith and has not at the time of the disposition notice that the person making the disposition has not authority to make the same.

Section 67 deals with the authority of a mercantile agent. It deems an apparent agency in some cases. In these cases, the owner will be estopped from denying the agent had authority to sell and an innocent third party buyer will acquire title in the goods. While s 67 deems apparent agency to arise in certain circumstances, this does overlap with s 27 to some extent. That is, if the innocent third party buyer can prove an apparent agency independently of s 67, then they will also be able to rely on s 27 as an exception to nemo dat. Mercantile agents may also be referred to as 'factors'. They are in the business of passing title to goods that others have entrusted to them for sale. A mercantile agent is defined in s 65 as 'a mercantile agent having in the customary course of his business as such agent authority either to sell goods or to consign goods for the purpose of sale or to buy goods or to raise money on the security of goods or documents of title'.

There are three essential elements of s 67. First, the mercantile agent entrusted in possession 'as such'. That is, the possession must be provided by the owner or authorised agent. Further, this must be given to the mercantile agent in their role as a mercantile agent and not as a friend or in some other capacity. Second, the sale that transpires must be a disposition in the ordinary course of business of a mercantile agent. Third, the third party buyer must be innocent in that they have no notice and are acting in good faith.

It follows, then, that where a mercantile agent has possession of the relevant goods and sells the goods to a bona fide buyer who has no knowledge of any wrongdoing, the latter acquires ownership.[72] In *Pearson v Rose & Young Ltd*,[73] Denning LJ stated: 'Parliament has not protected the true owner if he has himself consented to a mercantile agent having possession of them, because, by leaving them in the agent's possession, he has clothed the agent with apparent authority to sell them, and he should not, therefore, be allowed to claim them back from an innocent purchaser.'[74]

The three elements of s 67 may each prove controversial in a mercantile agent case. With respect to the first element, which posits that the mercantile agent is entrusted with possession

71 Qld, s 3; NSW, ss 5, 6; SA, s 4; ACT, s 6.
72 *Lowther v Harris* [1927] 1 KB 393.
73 [1950] 2 All ER 1027.
74 [1950] 2 All ER 1027, 1031.

'as such', this effectively requires that the goods must be entrusted by the owner, or a person authorised by the owner, with the actual consent to possession by the mercantile agent in that capacity. The mercantile agent may have only one principal, or they may have several.[75] What matters is that they must be acting as a mercantile agent. Accordingly, ordinary personal and non-commercial dealings would be precluded from the operation of s 67. For example, if a person loans their car to their neighbour, this would not be entrusting the neighbour with possession of the vehicle as a mercantile agent even if the neighbour was ordinarily in the business of buying and selling cars. Nevertheless, some boundary issues may arise between sale and other purposes. In the case of *Pearson v Rose & Young*, Denning LJ suggested that the line might be drawn so as to require that '[t]he owner must consent to the agent having them for a purpose which is in some way or other connected with his business as a mercantile agent. It may not actually be for sale. It may be for display or to get offers ...'[76] In the formulation offered by Denning LJ, some tangential connection to a sales context is sufficient to satisfy the requirement that there has been possession as such. In contrast, where goods are put in for repair, where the repairer also sells similar goods, the element may not be satisfied.[77]

The second element requires that any disposition must be in the ordinary course of the business of the mercantile agent. The satisfaction of this element may necessitate an examination of the actual business of the relevant mercantile agent. As such, it might be rather context driven. A sale at a substantial undervalue may not be in the ordinary course of the business.[78] A transaction may be valid if it is something that directly relates to the running of the business.[79] There should be nothing that puts the buyer on inquiry as to the validity of the sale.[80] In *Oppenheimer v Attenborough & Son*,[81] the Court of Appeal held that the pledge of diamonds by a diamond broker was a valid transaction as a mercantile agent, even though only diamond merchants usually pledged diamonds. In *Mercedes-Benz Financial Services Australia Pty Ltd v New South Wales*,[82] a false invoice was prepared by the mercantile agent wrongly suggesting that a luxury tax was incorporated in the sales price. The NSW Supreme Court found that these were not the actions of a mercantile agent acting in the ordinary course of their business. White J stated:

> No question arises in this case about trading hours or the place of business of ECS. Nonetheless, the question is whether ECS acted 'in other respects in the ordinary way in which a mercantile agent would act, so that there [was] nothing to lead the [purchaser] to suppose that anything wrong was being done' (*Oppenheimer v Attenborough & Son* per Buckley LJ at 231), and whether ECS acted 'as a mercantile agent would act if he were

75 *Mahumarakalage Edward Andrew Cooray v The Queen* [1953] AC 407; *Lloyds Bank Ltd v Bank of America National Trust & Savings Association* [1938] 2 All ER 63.
76 [1950] 2 All ER 1027, 1032.
77 *Staffs Motor Guarantee Ltd v British Wagon Co Ltd* [1934] 2 KB 305; *Oppenheimer v Frazer & Wyatt* [1907] 1 KB 519.
78 *Mercedes-Benz Financial Services Australia Pty Ltd v New South Wales* [2011] NSWSC 1458, [93]; *Heap v Motorists' Advisory Agency Ltd* [1923] 1 KB 577, 590.
79 *Oppenheimer v Attenborough & Son* [1908] 1 KB 221.
80 *Magnussen v Flanagan* [1981] 2 NSWLR 926, 934.
81 [1908] 1 KB 221.
82 [2011] NSWSC 1458.

> carrying out a transaction which he was authorized by his master to carry out' (per Lord Alverstone CJ at 227).
>
> In the present case ECS, at Mr Turner's request, supplied a false invoice that purportedly showed that luxury car tax was included in the purchase price of $600,000. There was no evidence that that is the way a motor car dealer would act if it were carrying out a transaction it was authorised by its principal to carry out. In other words, MBFS has not shown that a motor car dealer, if acting in the ordinary course of business, would falsely state that luxury car tax was included in the purchase price when it was not. The onus was on MBFS to establish that the sale was made in the ordinary course of business of a mercantile agent.[83]

In *Mortgage Loan & Finance Co of Australia v Richards*,[84] the plaintiff gave a trader named Jacobs some jewellery to sell on 'sale or return'. The terms of the possession were that if the jewellery was not sold within six months, Jacobs was required to return the jewellery to Mortgage Loan in good order. The contract between Mortgage Loan and Jacobs declared that the former had property in the jewellery. The jewellery was given to Jacobs at less than its actual cost and he was permitted under the contract to sell it at whatever price he wanted. The listed price would then need to be paid to Mortgage Loan. Jacobs pledged jewellery with Richards. The trial judge held that Jacobs was not a mercantile agent. On appeal it was argued that because this was an isolated transaction and there was no evidence as to past business that Jacobs previously carried on, he could not be regarded as a mercantile agent. Halse Rogers J held that 'there is nothing to prevent a man who has never before carried on business as a mercantile agent become instanter such agent ... by virtue of the terms of the transaction in which particular goods are entrusted to him'. The court noted that a mercantile agent's business had to begin as such at some point, and that there was no reason as to why their first transaction should not fall within the ambit of the Act.

The third element requires that the third party buyer must be innocent. This requires that the buyer must act in good faith and have no actual notice of any wrongdoing. In the case of *Associated Midland Corporation v Sanderson Motors Pty Ltd*,[85] it was held that good faith connotes honesty. However, a lack of care is not, in itself, sufficient to deprive a buyer of good faith. Nonetheless, if the failure to take due care is coupled with other circumstances, such as incidents that might have put a more prudent buyer on inquiry, then a lack of good faith may be established.[86] More recently, in *Itaoui v Yamaha Motor Finance Australia Pty Ltd*,[87] Schmidt J endorsed the approach of the court in *Sanderson* to the issue of the buyer's innocence.[88]

The case of *Lowther v Harris*[89] offers a useful illustration of the mercantile agent exception to the nemo dat rule. Lowther owned two pieces of tapestry – Aubusson and Leopard tapestries. Lowther engaged Barton Prior as his agent with respect to the tapestries and other

83 [2011] NSWSC 1458, [94]–[95].
84 (1932) 32 SR (NSW) 50.
85 [1983] 3 NSWLR 395.
86 [1983] 3 NSWLR 395, 401.
87 [2009] NSWSC 1363.
88 [2009] NSWSC 1363, [36].
89 [1927] 1 KB 393.

items. However, Lowther specifically limited the authority that he gave to Barton Prior. Under the authority given to him by his principal, Prior could not complete a sale or make delivery without Lowther's permission. Lowther then purchased premises where he kept the tapestries and other items. With regard to these premises, Lowther allowed another man, Urwin, to stay there as the lessee. Prior was also permitted to live there from time to time. Prior also operated two stores nearby and would bring customers to view items at Lowther's house. Yet, in most cases, the persons who came to view the items were not aware that they were owned by someone other than Prior.

It later transpired that Prior fraudulently took the tapestries from the house and sold them to Harris. For his part, Harris was unaware of the circumstances. The circumstances surrounding the tapestries differed in crucial ways. With regard to the Aubusson tapestry, Prior told Lowther that he would be able to sell the tapestry for a certain price. This statement was a lie, but Lowther, who was unaware of the truth of the matter, agreed to the 'sale' and gave his consent for Prior to remove the tapestry from the house to complete the sale. Prior then gave the tapestry to his brother to deliver to Harris's business in order to complete the sale. Harris was told that it was being sold on behalf of Lowther. Harris purchased it and then onsold it to another buyer.

Prior took the Leopard tapestry without permission. Prior again delivered the tapestry to his brother, who then sold it to Harris on his behalf. Harris subsequently onsold the Leopard tapestry. When Lowther discovered what had happened, he sued Harris for conversion.

The court found that, notwithstanding the lie that Lowther had been told, Prior sold the Aubusson tapestry in his role as a mercantile agent. In contrast, by taking the Leopard tapestry without consent Prior had not been acting as a mercantile agent. The absence of consent to possession in his capacity as a mercantile agent precluded the exception from being applied to the sale of the Leopard tapestry.

5.3.3 Sale under voidable title

Sale by person with voidable title serves as an exception to the nemo dat rule if the sale occurs before the true owner voids the relevant transaction.[90] Under s 29 of the Goods Act, if person A sells to person B, and for some reason A has the right to void the contract to B, A may lose title if B in the interim sells the goods to person C before A has avoided their contract with B. In order for this exception to be made out, person C must be acting in good faith and should be wholly unaware of any defect in B's title. Section 29 provides:

> When the seller of goods has a voidable title thereto but his title has not been avoided at the time of the sale the buyer acquires a good title to the goods provided he buys them in good faith and without notice of the seller's defect of title.[91]

90 A contract is voidable where it has been procured by fraud, by misrepresentation, or by some other wrong that creates in the innocent contracting party a right to void the contract. The contract is not regarded as void *ab initio*; rather, it is at the discretion of the innocent party as to whether to avoid the contract.

91 Qld, s 25; NSW, s 27; SA, s 23; WA, s 23; Tas, s 28; ACT, s 27; NT, s 27.

If person A has avoided their contract with person B, then person C will not acquire good title to the goods. Section 29 is subject to the operation of the estoppel requirement, and an argument for an estoppel by representation may succeed if person A has failed to do any conduct that might vitiate the representation. The relevant act of repudiation under s 29 can be manifested through conduct clearly indicating intention to repudiate. This may be effective even if A is not able to communicate this to B. In *Car & Universal Finance Co Ltd v Caldwell* (discussed below), sufficient acts of avoidance included going to the bank, police and a car association to try and have the car returned.

In *Car & Universal Finance*,[92] Caldwell sold Norris a car that Norris paid for with a personal cheque. Norris took the car, but the cheque bounced. As soon as Caldwell discovered this, he went to the police and attempted to locate Norris and the car. However, Caldwell could not locate Norris. The car was subsequently sold to a bona fide third party. The issue that arose for dispute in *Car & Universal Finance* was whether the defendant had avoided the contract and therefore recovered title before the sale to the bona fide buyer. As Caldwell had notified the police and had attempted to notify Norris but could not find him, the issue was whether there could be avoidance without communication. At trial, Denning MR answered this question in the affirmative at least in the circumstances where communication was simply not possible. The case was then appealed to the Full Court of the Court of Appeal, who agreed with Lord Denning MR on this issue. In the Court of Appeal, Sellers LJ stated:

> The general rule ... is that where a party is entitled to rescind a contract and wishes to do so the contract subsists until the opposing party is informed that the contract has been terminated. The difficulty of the seller in this case was that, when he learnt of the fraud ... he could not without considerable delay find either the fraudulent buyer or the car ... Where a contracting party could be communicated with ... [i]t would be unlikely that a party could be held to have disaffirmed a contract unless he went so far as to communicate his decision so to do ... But in circumstances such as the present case the other contracting party, a fraudulent rogue who would know that the vendor would want his car back as soon as he knew of the fraud, would not expect to be communicated with as a matter of right or requirement and would deliberately, as here, do all he could to evade any such communication being made to him ... In such exceptional contractual circumstances, it does not seem to me appropriate to hold that a party so acting can claim any right to have a decision to rescind communicated to him before the contract is terminated ... If he cannot communicate his decision he may still satisfy a judge or jury that he had made a final and irrevocable decision and ended the contract ... [H]e can do so 'if he at once, on discovering the fraud, takes all possible steps to regain the goods, even though he cannot find the rogue nor communicate with him'.[93]

The decision by Norris to deliberately disappear made locating him nigh on impossible. Under these circumstances, the Court of Appeal felt it appropriate that the law must allow the innocent party to exercise his right of rescission in a manner otherwise than by a communication or the act of repossession. As Lord Upjohn noted, 'to hold otherwise would be to allow a

92 [1965] 1 QB 525.
93 [1965] 1 QB 525, 549–51.

fraudulent contracting party by his very fraud to prevent the innocent party from exercising his undoubted right'.

5.3.4 Seller or buyer in possession after sale

Section 30 provides that title will pass to an innocent third party buyer if a sale occurs after the seller is left in possession of the goods, or the documents of title for the goods, after the property has passed to the buyer.[94] Section 30 applies only where there has been an initial sale between the seller and the buyer but the buyer lets the seller remain in possession of the goods. Under s 30, the seller must have continuous possession of the goods.[95] The seller's possession of the goods does not need to be in their capacity as a seller.[96] The seller may retain the goods as a bailee for the buyer.[97] The effect of s 30 is that if the seller then sells the goods to a bona fide third party buyer, the latter receives good title to the goods. Title may pass where the seller has given constructive possession to a third party buyer.[98] In *Crouch v Adams*,[99] the seller remained in possession of the goods after sale and subsequently entered into a new management agreement with a new buyer who purchased the goods in good faith and without notice. Physical delivery did not take place, but the signing of a new management agreement was found to amount to constructive delivery and receipt.[100]

Section 31 provides that where the buyer has possession of the goods or of documents of title for the goods before property has passed to the buyer, and they then subsequently sell the goods to an innocent third party, the latter will obtain good title.[101] Section 31 applies to both contracts of sale and agreements to sell, provided that the buyer has taken possession of the goods before property has passed.[102] Under s 31, the seller must have consented to the buyer having possession of the goods.[103] The seller's consent to the buyer's possession must not have been procured by fraud.[104]

The case of *Pacific Motor Auctions v Motor Credits*[105] illustrates the 'seller in possession' exception. Under a written agreement, Motordom was Motor Credits' agent to buy used vehicles on the proviso that the purchases were first authorised by Motor Credits. If they were authorised, then Motordom could purchase the vehicles in its own name without disclosing that it was buying them on behalf of Motor Credits. Motor Credits would then pay Motordom 90 per cent of the price of the vehicle and obtain ownership and Motordom was to remain in possession as bailee only. Motordom would then sell the vehicles on behalf of Motor Credits

94 Qld, s 27(1); NSW, s 28(1); SA, s 25(1); Tas, s 30(2); ACT, s 29(2); NT, s 28(2).
95 *Worcester Works Finance Ltd v Cooden Engineering Co Ltd* [1972] 1 QB 210.
96 *Pacific Motor Auctions Pty Ltd v Motor Credits (Hire Finance) Ltd* [1965] 2 All ER 105.
97 *Pacific Motor Auctions Pty Ltd v Motor Credits (Hire Finance) Ltd* [1965] 2 All ER 105.
98 *Michael Gerson (Leasing) Ltd v Wilkinson* [2001] 1 All ER 148, *Crouch v Adams* [2006] NSWSC 1029.
99 [2006] NSWSC 1029.
100 [2006] NSWSC 1029, [27].
101 Qld, s 27(2); NSW, s 28(2); SA, s 25(2); WA, s 25(1); Tas, s 30(1); ACT, s 29(1); NT, s 28(1).
102 *Orix Australia Corporation Ltd v Peter Donnelly Automotive Pty Ltd* [2007] NSWSC 977.
103 *National Employers' Mutual General Insurance Association Ltd* [1990] 1 AC 24, 62; *Newtons of Wembley Ltd v Williams* [1964] 1 WLR 1028.
104 *National Employers' Mutual General Insurance Association Ltd* [1990] 1 AC 24, 33; *Newtons of Wembley Ltd v Williams* [1964] 1 WLR 1028.
105 [1965] 2 All ER 105.

and could retain a commission from any sales. Further, Motor Credits could take possession of the vehicles at any time. In practice, Motordom would buy cars in its own name without Motor Credits' authority.

Motordom would then contact Motor Credits and ask if it could display the cars for sale. If Motor Credits accepted, it would then send a cheque for 90 per cent of the cost of cars to which, consequently, it would obtain title. Motordom would then retain possession and could resell in its own name and with the right to receive commission. Eventually, Motordom got into financial difficulties and Motor Credits withdrew Motordom's authority to sell.

Later the same day, Motordom sold 29 cars to Pacific Motor Auctions. Sixteen of the 29 cars had been paid for by Motor Credits. The contract stated that the car was the seller's 'sole property, free from any other interest, and that the seller had good right and title to sell it'.

The NSW Supreme Court held that there was continuity of possession. In the court's view, the legal manner in which possession was held was not relevant. In the High Court, Taylor J disagreed with the notion that there had been continuity of possession on the basis that the legal character of the possession had changed from ownership to bailment. The matter went on appeal to the House of Lords where their Lordships reinstated the decision of the Supreme Court. Lord Pearce stated:

> There is . . . no doubt about the general intention of the original provision and the general mischief at which it was aimed. It was intended as a protection to innocent purchasers in cases where estoppel gave insufficient protection.[106]

Lord Pearce further stated:

> It is plainly right to read the section as inapplicable to cases where there has been a break in the continuity of the physical possession . . . What is the justification, however, for saying that a person does not continue in possession where his physical possession does continue, although the title under or by virtue of which he is in possession has changed? He did not consider there was any reason for placing such an artificial limitation on the application of the provision . . . There is . . . the strongest reason for supposing that the words 'continues . . . in possession' were intended to refer to the continuity of physical possession regardless of any private transactions between the seller and purchaser which might alter the legal title under which the possession was held.[107]

In *Gamer's Motor Centre (Newcastle) Pty Ltd v Natwest Wholesale Australia Pty Ltd*,[108] the possession of delivery receipts was held to be sufficient to pass title to an innocent third party buyer in circumstances where the original buyer had physical possession of the cars but had sold them to the third party buyer. The appellant, Gamer's Motor Centre, sold and delivered cars to a retail dealer. The dealer then sold those cars to Natwest, who paid 90 per cent of the price and received delivery receipts. The dealer was then required to sell the cars to customers on Natwest's behalf. The agreement between the dealer and Natwest stipulated that the latter would pay the remaining 10 per cent to the dealer once the sales occurred. The agreement also stipulated that each car was Natwest's unencumbered property. However, the dealer had not

106 [1965] 2 All ER 105, 110.
107 [1965] 2 All ER 105, 112.
108 (1987) 163 CLR 236.

paid Gamer's Motor Centre, the original seller, and when the dealer failed to make payment Gamer's seized the cars. Natwest sued for their recovery. A majority of the High Court held that as Natwest had received the delivery receipts, it had also received constructive delivery of the goods. As such, the s 31 equivalent was enlivened and title in the cars had passed to Natwest.

5.4 Retention of title

Retention of title clauses are often referred to as Romalpa clauses pursuant to the decision in the English Court of Appeal in *Aluminium Industrie Vaassen BV v Romalpa Aluminium Ltd*.[109] Romalpa clauses exist because of the desire of the seller to retain property in goods to the exclusion of the buyer, in the event that the buyer does not pay for the goods or where the buyer goes bankrupt. The purpose of these clauses is to ensure that there is some form of commercial certainty for the seller so that they can minimise their risks in sale transactions. As Spink and Ong note:

> A retention of title clause enables the unpaid sellers to escape from the economic malaise of unsecured creditors. Such a clause can protect the creditor against the prejudicial effect of 'hiving down' in the event that the debtor-buyer is a corporation and a receiver is appointed against the corporation which can secure performance of other obligations and liabilities owing by the debtor-buyer . . .[110]

The fear that most sellers would have is that in the event of the buyer's bankruptcy they, as unsecured creditors, would be a low priority when compared to the buyer's secured creditors. As such, it is necessary to employ a legal instrument in contracts of sale to protect against that possibility. Under the law, parties are able to employ Romalpa clauses because the various Goods Acts allow for property to pass when the parties intend for it to pass. For example, in Victoria s 22 of the Goods Act provides that property passes when it is intended to pass. Provided that the relevant Romalpa clause is a part of the contract between the buyer and the seller, it will have a good prospect of being enforced as intended.

Retention of title clauses are now part of the scheme set up by the *Personal Property Securities Act 2009* (Cth) (PPSA). The PPSA scheme and its application to retention of title clauses is set out in Chapter 9. Section 254 of the PPSA preserves the common law as it relates to retention of title clauses. However, it is quite likely that the PPSA scheme now effectively ousts the operation of the common law in relation to most of the longstanding issues surrounding retention of title clauses.

5.5 Retention of title clauses and the common law

This section provides a brief overview of the common law in relation to retention of title clauses. To illustrate the ways in which the legal complexities surrounding the use of a

109 [1976] 1 WLR 676.

110 P M Spink and C A Ong, 'Substance versus Form: Anglo-Australian Perspectives on Title Financing Transactions' (2004) 63 *Cambridge Law Journal* 199, 206.

Romalpa clause can arise, it is useful to consider a basic fact situation in which a retention of title may be employed.[111] Consider that we have a company A. Let us imagine that company A sells timber and engages to do so with company B. Obviously, company A would be concerned about the risk of not receiving full payment from company B. Thus, as part of the sales contract company A may include a Romalpa clause such as that used in *Associated Alloys v ACN 001 452 106 Pty Ltd*.[112] The attraction of this clause is that it purports to cover a number of different situations, all of which might reasonably occur at some point in the future. So, company A is being prudent and is acting to safeguard its interests.[113] If company B agrees to the clause, then it validly forms part of the contract.[114]

Upon receipt of the goods, company B may contract to onsell them to company C. Alternatively, company B may contract with company C, such that the former is bound to use the timber to manufacture some other good, before selling that to the latter. For the purposes of the exercise, assume that neither company B nor company C has paid its respective immediate seller. If company C acquires possession of the newly manufactured timber goods, it would be impossible for company A to retain those goods. However, company A may, under the common law or equity, wish to trace into the debt that company C owes to company B. Further, if company B were to go bankrupt, a dispute would likely arise between the administrator and company A. This would most likely be the case if company B still had timber which it had received from company A but which has not been transformed into another good, or where company B is owed payment by company C. The stage would be set for a typical Romalpa dispute.

There are several difficulties that attend the application of Romalpa clauses under the common law. First, despite the stated intent of the parties, property in the goods in question may actually pass.[115] In this respect, the particular terms of the retention of title clause are of paramount importance. In the various cases that have come before the courts, different clauses have been involved. It follows that the legal issues in dispute have varied along with the respective clauses. It is important also to look at all the facts surrounding the case – in particular, the way that the parties have, or have not, given effect to the retention of title clause. As Williams J noted in *Puma Australia v Sportman's Australia*:

> In my view the terms of the agreement are of critical importance, and little assistance is gained by using technical terms such as trustee, bailment and conversion in defining the rights and obligations of the parties. The court can, and will, give effect to an agreement governing commercial relationships and providing that legal and equitable rights and remedies should co-exist.[116]

111 Further, it is useful to use the clause in *Associated Alloys v ACN 001 452 106 Pty Ltd (in liq)* (2000) 202 CLR 588 as an example.

112 (2000) 202 CLR 588.

113 Which obviously corresponds with the basic principle of economics that persons act rationally in their own perceived self-interest.

114 Even if company B had not read the clause, but had just signed the contract containing the clause, the law dictates that they would still be bound by its terms: *Toll (FGCT) Pty Ltd v Alphapharm Pty Ltd* (2004) 219 CLR 165.

115 *Rondo Building Services Pty Ltd v Casaron Pty Ltd* [2002] QDC 128.

116 [1994] 2 Qd R 159, 174.

Given that Romalpa clauses now try to cover a variety of contingencies, it is likely that the types of clause employed by parties will be multifaceted and that several subclauses will be involved. It has not been unknown for Romalpa clauses to use the terms 'bailment', 'agent', 'trustee' and 'conversion' in various subparagraphs. There is an obvious contradiction here in that a buyer cannot simultaneously be both a bailee, with a duty to return the property, and an agent with the right to sell the goods on behalf of the principal. Where a seller has decreed the buyer to be an agent who holds the proceeds of any sale of the goods on trust for the seller, the property may well pass.

Second, there has been some judicial opinion which suggests that the effect of a Romalpa clause, depending upon its construction, may give rise to a security or to a charge.[117] This issue arose in *Armour v Thyssen Edehlstahlwerke AG.*[118] However, Lord Keith of Kinkel held that no security arose because the creditor never passed title in the goods.[119] Third, if a trust arrangement is intended, there is also the danger that it may not have eventuated.[120] This particular problem has two parts: the question of whether the trust has been validly formed under law, and whether the trust is possible in fact. The latter part was at issue in *Associated Alloys Pty Ltd v ACN 001 452 106 Pty Ltd*[121] when the High Court gave consideration to the meaning of the word 'proceeds' in the proceeds subclause of the relevant Romalpa clause.

Fourth, if a trust has in fact been created, or if some other fiduciary relationship exists, then the issue of tracing, either under the common law or at equity, is enlivened. Fifth, given that the seller under a Romalpa clause is a creditor, there are sound legal policy reasons for consideration to be given to the legitimate interests of all the buyer's other creditors. This particular difficulty is the matter that the *Chattel Securities Act 1987* (Vic),[122] the Corporations Act and the new PPSA would seek to address. Finally, in constant attendance to the subject of Romalpa clauses is the task of contractual interpretation. Where the parties are in dispute and the courts are called upon to resolve the matter, the multifaceted nature of the modern Romalpa clause, with its variety of contingencies a milieu of legal concepts, can pose significant interpretative problems.

The Australian High Court's decision in *Associated Alloys* illustrates many of the issues that are at stake with respect to Romalpa clauses. In *Associated Alloys* the plaintiff, Associated Alloys, had been trading with Metropolitan Engineering and Fabrications Pty Ltd for a period of 15 years.[123] During the course of dealings between the parties, Associated Alloys attached reservation of title clauses to its invoices. These clauses were quite detailed and purported to have a legal effect beyond mere retention of title.

117 *Re Bond Worth Ltd* [1979] 3 WLR 629.

118 [1991] 2 AC 339. See also *Clough Mill Ltd v Martin* [1985] 1 WLR 111.

119 [1991] 2 AC 339, 351.

120 *Associated Alloys Pty Ltd v ACN 001 452 106 Pty Ltd (in liq)* (2000) 202 CLR 588.

121 (2000) 202 CLR 588.

122 Sections 7(1) and 3(1) of the *Chattel Securities Act 1987* (Vic) were at issue in *General Motors Acceptance Corporation Australia v Southbank Traders Pty Ltd* (2007) 227 CLR 305. In *General Motors*, the High Court held that s 3(1), which defined the term 'security interest', was capable of application to the seller of goods under a conditional sale. Section 7(1) allowed an unregistered security interest to be extinguished in the event that goods were sold to a third party buyer for value in good faith without notice.

123 The parties traded from 1981 to 1996 until Metropolitan went into receivership and then liquidation. At that point, Metropolitan became ACN001 452 106 (in liq).

The clause in *Associated Alloys* serves as a useful example for the overall Romalpa problem. It provided:

> (1) It is expressly agreed and declared that the title of the subject goods/product shall not pass to the [buyer] until payment in full of the purchase price. The [buyer] shall in the meantime take custody of the goods/product and retain them as the fiduciary agent and bailee of the [seller].
> (2) The [buyer] may resell but only as a fiduciary agent of the [seller]. Any right to bind the [seller] to any liability to any third party by contract or otherwise is, however, expressly negatived. Any such resale is to be at arm's length and on market terms and, pending resale or utilisation in any manufacturing or construction process, is to be kept separate from its own, properly stored, protected and insured.
> (3) The [buyer] will receive all proceeds, whether tangible or intangible, direct or indirect, of any dealing with such goods/product in trust for the [seller] and will keep such proceeds in a separate account until the liability to the [seller] shall have been discharged.
> (4) The [seller] is to have power to appropriate payments to such goods and accounts as it thinks fit notwithstanding any appropriation by the [buyer] to the contrary.
> (5) In the event that the [buyer] uses the goods/product in some manufacturing or construction process of its own or some third party, then the [buyer] shall hold such part of the proceeds of such manufacturing or construction process as relates to the goods/product in trust for the [seller]. Such part shall be deemed to equal in dollar terms the amount owing by the [buyer] to the [seller] at the time of the receipt of such proceeds.

From mid-1995, Metropolitan entered into contracts with a Korean company, Lucky Goldstar, for the manufacture of steel products. The completion of the Lucky Goldstar contracts required Metropolitan to purchase steel from Associated Alloys. All of the steel provided by Associated Alloys was used by Metropolitan to manufacture products for the Lucky Goldstar contracts.

In 1996, Metropolitan went into receivership and then liquidation. At that point, it owed Associated Alloys US$197 911.29. Further, Lucky Goldstar owed Metropolitan $2 048 500. Associated Alloys' claim at first instance was rejected by Bryson J in the NSW Supreme Court on the basis that the monies owing to Associated Alloys constituted an unregistered charge over Metropolitan's book debts.[124] Under the then s 266 of the Corporations Law, the charge was void for want of registration. An appeal to the NSW Court of Appeal failed on the same basis.[125] The High Court granted special leave to appeal.

In dispute before the High Court was the subclause that purported to create a trust relationship between the buyer and the seller. Both the Supreme Court at first instance and the Court of Appeal had found that the proceeds subclause had instead created a charge over the book debts. The view that the Court of Appeal took was that the proceeds clause was liable to frustration, were it to be interpreted upon its bare terms, as the buyer could simply elect to not receive the proceeds of the sale of the seller's goods. That is, once the subsale had occurred, the buyer gained a book debt. If the buyer wished to defeat the seller's interest,

124 *Associated Alloys Pty Ltd v Metropolitan Engineering & Fabrications Pty Ltd* (1996) 20 ACSR.
125 *Associated Alloys Pty Ltd v Metropolitan Engineering & Fabrications Pty Ltd* (1998) 16 ACLC 1633.

the buyer could assign the book debt to another party, thereby never receiving the actual proceeds and frustrating the seller's interests. Accordingly, for reasons of business efficacy, the Court of Appeal decided that the proceeds clause created a charge over the book debts.

The High Court was not convinced by this reasoning. The High Court noted that the language of the parties was not inexplicit.[126] It disagreed with the Court of Appeal's view that the proceeds subclause had to be construed as a charge for reasons of efficacy. The High Court observed that were the term 'proceeds' to be construed to refer to book debts or monies received as payment, the buyer could still frustrate the interests of the seller.[127] Moreover, the High Court placed particular emphasis on the clear language of the parties. The majority stated:

> The reasonable operation of the Proceeds Subclause is effected, as a matter of necessity, by the implication of the above contractual term providing for the discharge of the debt when a trust is constituted under the Proceeds Subclause 'equal in dollar terms [to] the amount owing by the [Buyer] to the [Seller] at the time of the receipt of such proceeds'. This clause is capable of clear expression and is so obvious, as a means of effectuating the commercial interests of the parties, that if the subject had been raised with them they would have replied 'of course'.[128]

The court found that an agreement to create trust had arisen from the subclause. However, the court found that no proceeds, at least as it construed the term 'proceeds', could be found to exist with respect to the clause.[129] On this basis, the High Court found that the trust did not properly come into operation.

The High Court's decision in *Associated Alloys* can be seen as both praiseworthy and puzzling. The court's approach to the interpretation of the parties' intent to create a trust displays a commonsense approach to the task of contractual interpretation. However, there has been justifiable criticism of the rather artificial way in which the court dealt with the term 'proceeds' in the subclause.[130] It seems strange, given that a trust relationship creates fiduciary duties and that a fiduciary relationship should allow the seller to trace into the buyer's debts, that the High Court should rule that 'proceeds' cannot relate to book debts. Further, given that Gummow J, during the special leave application, noted that 'proceeds' is a commercial term, it seems unusual that the court would then ascribe to the term a meaning that is somewhat limited in its commercial operation.[131]

126 (2000) 202 CLR 588, 605.

127 (2000) 202 CLR 588, 602.

128 (2000) 202 CLR 588, 610.

129 The High Court was of the view that the term 'proceeds' should not apply to debts. See, further, D Ong, 'Romalpa Clauses and the Issues Concerning (i) the Meaning of "the Proceeds" Received by the Buyer; (ii) the Buyer's Credit Period; and (iii) the Charge/Trust Dichotomy in Relation to "the Proceeds"' (2000) 12(2) *Bond Law Review* 148.

130 See D Ong, 'Romalpa Clauses and the Issues Concerning (i) the Meaning of "the Proceeds" Received by the Buyer; (ii) the Buyer's Credit Period; and (iii) the Charge/Trust Dichotomy in Relation to "the Proceeds"' (2000) 12(2) *Bond Law Review* 148. See also D Solomons, 'The Regulation of Romalpa Clauses: The Limitations of Equity' (2008) 16 *Insolvency Law Journal* 69. Also T Carlin, '*Associated Alloys Pty Ltd v ACN 001 452 106 Pty Ltd*: A Commentary and Analysis' (2002) 30 *Australian Business Law Review* 106.

131 *Associated Alloys Pty Ltd v ACN 001 452 106 Pty Ltd (in liq) S65/1999* [1999] HCATrans 613 (7 December 1999).

Much of the common law around Romalpa clauses was contentious for quite some time. Nevertheless, given the emergence of the PPSA scheme, the problems posed by the common law are now largely redundant. Chapter 9 explores the issues around the PPSA in greater depth.

5.6 Key points

- There are four categories of goods: (1) specific goods; (2) unascertained goods; (3) ascertained goods; and (4) future goods.
- Ordinarily, property will pass when the parties intend it to pass under the contract of sale.
- However, s 23 of the *Goods Act 1958* (Vic) contains five presumptions that apply where the parties have not stipulated when property is to pass.
- A sale by a non-owner who lacks the authority to sell will ordinarily have no effect unless one or more of the exceptions to the nemo dat rule apply to the transaction.
- Retention of title is now covered by the *Personal Property Securities Act 2009* (Cth).

5.7 DISCUSSION QUESTIONS

1. What are the different types of goods? Could any of these categories of goods overlap?
2. What are the five presumptions as to the transfer of property?
3. What is the concept of nemo dat?
4. How does estoppel operate in a nemo dat context?
5. What is the general concept of retention of title, and why would firms seek to apply it in a commercial context?

5.8 FURTHER READING

Ong, D, 'Romalpa Clauses and the Issues Concerning (i) the Meaning of "the Proceeds" Received by the Buyer; (ii) the Buyer's Credit Period; and (iii) the Charge/Trust Dichotomy in Relation to "the Proceeds"' (2000) 12(2) *Bond Law Review* 148.

6

PRICE AND DELIVERY

6.0 Introduction

This chapter considers the central role of price in a contract for the sale of goods. In particular, it examines its role in the contract's certainty of terms, the exceptions to this requirement, and the operation of those exceptions. The statutory provisions for determining a price in a contract that is silent on this term are examined, as are the leading cases. Contracts for the sale of goods are defined and distinguished from contracts in which goods are exchanged partly for a money consideration and partly in exchange for other goods. The chapter also examines when such an agreement may constitute a contract for the sale of goods, and when it constitutes a barter contract. The performance of the contract of sale is then examined in terms of the reciprocal obligations of payment and delivery. The wrongful performance of both payment and delivery is considered – for example, in the case of incorrect goods, and mixed deliveries of partially correct and partially incorrect goods – as well as the special case of delivery by instalments. The chapter then examines the remedies available to the buyer and the seller for breaches of payment or delivery, depending on whether the breach is of a condition or a warranty, and the defences to claims by either party against the other.

6.1 Price

There are Sale of Goods Acts in each state and territory in Australia, all of which deal with price and delivery and are broadly the same in their terms and structure.[1] For example, s 6(1) of the *Goods Act 1958* (Vic)[2] defines a contract for the sale of goods as one in which the transference of, or agreement to transfer property in, the relevant goods occurs for a money consideration called the price.

> **Sale and agreement to sell**
>
> (1) A contract of sale of goods is a contract whereby the seller transfers or agrees to transfer the property in goods to the buyer for a money consideration called the price. There may be a contract of sale between one part owner and another.

The contract may fix the price of the goods that are the subject of the sale. Where the contract does not fix the price, it may expressly provide that the price is to be ascertained in an agreed manner, or is to be determined by a course of dealing between the parties.[3] If s 13(1) does not apply because the contract neither fixes a price, nor provides a mechanism whereby the price may be determined, s 13(2) is triggered. Section 13(2) provides only that 'the buyer must pay a reasonable price' and defines what is reasonable as 'a question of fact dependent on the circumstances of each particular case'.

1 See, generally, *Goods Act 1958* (Vic); *Sale of Goods Act 1923* (NSW); *Sale of Goods Act 1896* (Qld); *Sale of Goods Act 1895* (SA); *Sale of Goods Act 1895* (WA); *Sale of Goods Act 1896* (Tas); *Sale of Goods Act 1954* (ACT); *Sale of Goods Act 1972* (NT).

2 See the equivalent provisions in state Acts: Qld, s 4; NSW, s 6; SA, s 1; WA, s 1; Tas, s 6; ACT, s 6; NT, s 6.

3 *Goods Act 1958* (Vic), s 13(1).

Ascertainment of price

(1) The price in a contract of sale may be fixed by the contract or may be left to be fixed in manner thereby agreed or may be determined by the course of dealing between the parties.

(2) Where the price is not determined in accordance with the foregoing provisions the buyer must pay a reasonable price. What is a reasonable price is a question of fact dependent on the circumstances of each particular case.[4]

The provisions in the Sale of Goods Acts contradict the otherwise strict legal maxim that 'there cannot be a contract to make a contract' (an agreement to agree), and that the courts will not interpose a contract between parties who have not agreed to make one between themselves. However, case law has recognised that the strict application of the maxim may produce injustice since, in various business sectors, sophisticated parties commonly contract to sell or purchase goods that are to be delivered a considerable time after the execution of the contract in order to secure sources and outlets of supply. In a volatile market, the parties prefer not to fix a price so as to avoid the situation where all the risk is borne by the seller in a falling market, or by a purchaser in a rising market. These parties typically conclude contracts in the belief that it is mutually understood that they have entered a binding relationship with enforceable rights. The contractual maxim that agreements to agree are not binding, however, undermines their expectations that their rights will be recognised.

In *May & Butcher Ltd v The King*[5] the plaintiff, a dealer in war surplus equipment, agreed to purchase from the Crown all tents surplus to government requirements for a specified period of time – that is, for agreement in the future. The parties left the price to be agreed upon from time to time. The parties further provided for arbitration in the event of a dispute in agreed terms that '[i]t is understood that all disputes with reference to or rising out of this agreement will be submitted to arbitration in accordance with the provisions of The Arbitration Act, 1889'.[6]

The plaintiff brought its action against the Crown when, after several shipments of equipment had been delivered at an agreed price, it refused to continue shipping the equipment. The Crown's defence was that the contract failed as an agreement because it lacked an agreed price for the goods. The plaintiff submitted, relying on s 9 of the English Sale of Goods Act,[7] which is similar in its terms to the current Australian legislation, that the agreement impliedly settled the price for the goods at a reasonable price, and that the arbitration clause provided for arbitration of its reasonableness.

The court rejected the argument. Lord Warrington of Clyffe observed that because the parties were silent about the price, the court would not be engaged in implying a reasonable price but in an exercise of inserting 'a stipulation contrary to that for which [the parties] had bargained' into the contract and therefore substituting its price for the parties' agreement which

4 NSW, s 13; SA, s 8; WA, s 8; Tas, s 13; ACT, s 13; NT, s 13; Qld s 11.

5 [1934] 2 KB 17 (HL 1929).

6 [1934] 2 KB 17, 18.

7 *Sale of Goods Act 1952* (UK): '(1) The price in a contract of sale may be fixed by the contract, or may be left to be fixed in a manner thereby agreed, or may be determined by the course of dealing between the parties. (2) Where the price is not determined in accordance with the foregoing provisions the buyer must pay a reasonable price . . .'

would be 'to contradict the express terms of the document which they have signed'.[8] The House of Lords held that the arbitration clause could not be used to bring certainty to the price because the clause only governed the concluded agreement, and was inoperative in the absence of a price and therefore a contract.[9] In the well-known words of Viscount Dunedin: 'To be a good contract there must be a concluded bargain, and a concluded contract is one which settles everything that is necessary to be settled and leaves nothing to be settled by agreement between the parties.'[10]

The arguments rejected in *May and Butcher* were admitted in *Foley v Classique Coaches Ltd*.[11] A bus company and a garage owner entered an agreement whereby the bus company purchased land from the garage owner for cash and on the condition that the bus company purchase all the petrol for its operations from the garage owner. The price of the petrol was to be agreed in writing from time to time. The same agreement contained the arbitration clause: 'If any dispute or difference shall arise on the subject matter or construction of this agreement the same shall be submitted to arbitration in the usual way in accordance with the provisions of the Arbitration Act, 1889.' After three years of purchasing petrol from the garage owner at an agreed price, the bus company refused to purchase any more. In its defence, it relied on *May & Butcher Ltd v The King*. The trial judgment finding for the garage owner was confirmed by the Court of Appeal. The judge at trial constructed the agreement as implying that a reasonable price was to be inferred in the absence of an agreement on a price between the parties. The Court of Appeal approved the construction on the basis of factors powerfully demonstrating an intention to bind the parties even in the absence of a price, agreement about which was reserved for future agreement – namely that, immediately the agreement was made, title to the lot vested in the defendant and the contract was thereby substantially performed, such that implying a reasonable price for the petrol was employed to give business efficacy to the agreement.[12]

Foley v Classique Coaches Ltd is authority for the proposition that terms relating to essential matters that the parties have not expressly dealt with may be implied into the contract.[13] The application of a reasonable price where the parties have not otherwise agreed in accordance with s 13 is an exception to the principle which requires there to be certainty of terms as between the contracting parties. Contracts that specify criteria for determining matters to be agreed, or in which the application of machinery provisions can supply the omitted term, are more likely to be upheld than contracts relying on the implication of a reasonable price in the absence of express agreement. Furthermore, where the parties have significantly performed a commercial agreement, or where the contract has been largely performed by one of the parties, it is more likely that a reasonable term will be implied to give effect to the parties'

8 [1934] 2 KB 17, 22.

9 [1934] 2 KB 17, 22.

10 [1934] 2 KB 17, 21.

11 [1934] 2 KB 1. *Australia & New Zealand Banking Group Ltd v Frost Holdings Pty Ltd* [1989] VR 695; *Moonlighting International Pty Ltd v International Lighting Pty Ltd* [2000] FCA 41; *Wenning v Robinson* (1964) 64 SR (NSW) 157; *Roehlen v Mikhail* [2018] VSC 121.

12 *Foley v Classique Coaches Ltd* was applied in *National Coal Board v Galley* [1958] 1 All ER 91.

13 See also *W & J Investments Ltd v Commissioner of Taxation* (1987) 16 FCR 314; *Whitehouse Properties Pty Ltd v Bond Brewing (NSW) Ltd* (1992) 28 NSWLR 17; *Hall v Busst* (1960) 104 CLR 206; *Austotel Pty Ltd v Franklins Selfserve Pty Ltd* (1989) 16 NSWLR 582.

intentions,[14] or to avoid injustice to the party who had performed the agreement but was unable to enforce the contract.[15] On the other hand, where the contract is executory on both sides, it is unlikely that an implied undertaking to pay a reasonable amount will be inferred.[16]

An agreement to agree on a price may therefore be construed as an agreement to pay a reasonable price. Sargent LJ in *Chillingworth v Esche*[17] observed that the absoluteness of the maxim that there cannot be an agreement to enter an agreement extends too far, and is better understood as stating that there cannot be an agreement 'to enter into an indeterminate contract', whereas 'the court will enforce a contract to enter into a determinate agreement'.[18] In *Hillas & Co Ltd v Arcos Ltd*,[19] an option to purchase timber did not provide for a price to be paid but was held binding because it provided that an official price list was to be used to calculate the price of the timber. A material issue was whether a clause in an agreement to 'contemplate a future bargain the terms of which remained to be settled' was enforceable. According to Lord Wright, certain trades 'record the most important agreements in crude and summary fashion; modes of expression sufficient and clear to them in the course of their business may appear to those unfamiliar with the business far from complete or precise'. His Lordship held that while courts were not in a position to conclude a contract on behalf of the parties, or to construct contracts beyond the meaning of the words used in them, judges should 'interpret contract language fairly and broadly', consistent with the maxim that '[w]ords are to be so understood that the subject-matter may be preserved rather than destroyed'.

The *Goods Act 1958* (Vic) at s 14 provides:

Agreement to sell at valuation

(1) Where there is an agreement to sell goods on the terms that the price is to be fixed by the valuation of a third party, and such third party cannot or does not make such valuation, the agreement is avoided: Provided that if the goods or any part thereof have been delivered to and appropriated by the buyer he must pay a reasonable price therefor.

(2) Where such third party is prevented from making the valuation by the fault of the seller or buyer the party not in fault may maintain an action for damages against the party in fault.

A contract to sell goods or assets at a price to be fixed by valuation is sufficiently certain to constitute an enforceable agreement, and obviates the need to invoke statutory provisions that the sale be for a reasonable price.[20]

14 *F & G Sykes (Wessex) Ltd v Fine Fare Ltd* [1967] 1 Lloyd's Rep 53; *Foley v Classique Coaches Ltd* [1934] 2 KB 1; *Hempel v Robinson* [1924] SASR 288; *Sudbrook Trading Estate Ltd v Eggleton* [1983] 1 AC 444; *Hillas & Co Ltd v Arcos Ltd* (1932) 147 LT 503.

15 *Shire of Yea v Roberts* (1879) 5 VLR (E) 222; *Hall v Busst* (1960) 104 CLR 206.

16 *Pua Hor Ong v Wu You Yang Pty Ltd* (2008) 103 SASR 9.

17 [1924] 1 Ch 97.

18 [1924] 1 Ch 97, 100. In *Chillingworth v Esche* the determinate contract was the renewal of a lease. In the Canadian case of *Post v Bean* (1947) 20 MPR 168 (NBCA, 1946); aff'd [1947] 3 DLR 513 (Can S Ct), the Court of Appeal of New Brunswick held that the grant of a lease for fishing rights was too uncertain to be enforceable. See the remarks of Michaud CJQB at (1947) 20 MPR 168, 192, 193.

19 (1932) 147 LT 503.

20 Goods Act, s 13(2). See *Wenning v Robinson* (1964) 64 SR (NSW) 157 in which a contract for the sale of stock 'at valuation' was held to constitute a sufficiently fixed price not necessitating resort to the equivalent of s 13(2).

Where a reasonable price is to be determined, it is 'a question of fact dependent on the circumstances of each particular case'.[21] The proper basis for determining a reasonable price is the current reasonable value. For instance, in *Watsons Brothers* v *Hornby (Inspector of Taxes)*,[22] the issue was the proper basis for assessing the income for taxation purposes of two different parts of the poultry breeding business: an egg-producing part; and a hatchery selling day-old chicks (which were liable for tax under different schedules of the income tax legislation), when some of these chicks were transferred to and became part of the farm stock. Watsons sought to claim the loss between the market price of the chicks as stock (4d) and the cost of producing each transferred chick (7d). At issue was: at what value should the chicks be transferred from the hatchery to the farm? The Crown argued that the transfer was not between separate persons because the farm and the hatchery merely represented two activities of the same person, and a loss could not be made by transferring a loss between those activities. The Crown submitted that the cost to the hatchery was the production cost, not the difference between what it cost the business and what it could be sold for. Macnaghten J held that the hatchery and the farm were separate entities, and the basis of calculating the price of the chicks, and the amount to be credited, was the 'reasonable price' referred to in s 8 of the sale of goods legislation.[23] Macnaghten J further found that the relevant market for determining 'market value' for a taxpayer who sold the same items in two markets was the market in which those goods, as a matter of course, would be sold.

6.2 Sale of goods and barter

The basic nature of a contract of sale is that the seller agrees to transfer property in goods to the buyer in exchange for money. The money serves as consideration for the transfer of property. However, if the consideration is not money, but consists wholly or partly of goods, work, rent, or valuable consideration other than money, the question arises as to whether a contract effects a sale or a barter. If the consideration for the sale of goods is not money, the contract may constitute a barter or an exchange external to the sale of goods legislation. However, if the transaction is one whereby goods on the one hand are exchanged for goods and money on the other, and consideration other than money constitutes only part of the total consideration, the legislation may continue to apply because some money has changed hands.

Contracts of barter are treated analogously to contracts of sale in accordance with the civil law principle *permutatio vicina est emptioni*.[24] Common examples of sales of this kind include the purchase of a motor vehicle involving both cash consideration and the trade-in of the purchaser's current vehicle.[25] The courts have taken divergent approaches in clarifying the nature of the transaction. One approach has it that the situation involves two separate

21 Goods Act, s 13(2).

22 [1942] 2 All ER 506.

23 The approach in *Watson v Hornby* was approved by the House of Lords in *Sharkey v Wernher* [1956] AC 58 (HL).

24 *Institutions of Justinian*, Book 19. *Halsbury's Laws of England* (Butterworth & Co, London, 3rd edn, 1952), vol 34, 6. '*Permutatio*' is an innominate contract whereby there is no obligation until one of the two exchanging parties has done what they have promised. In contracts of sale, the obligation is independent of part performance.

25 See *Aldridge v Johnson* (1857) 7 El & Bl 885.

reciprocal sales whereby the parties are both selling goods to each other, with the price of each good setting off the price of the other.[26] Clearly, taking this view of the matter, the sale of goods legislation applies to both transactions.

In *Messenger v Greene*,[27] the defendant was supplied by the plaintiff with supplies, and the plaintiff was supplied by the defendant with peeled pulpwood. After giving credit for the value of the supplied pulpwood, the plaintiff sued for the balance due of the price of the supplies. Doull J held the transaction not to be a barter. Rather, '[w]hat was done in this case was that the storekeeper agreed to sell provisions to the defendant at regular prices, and the defendant agreed to sell and the plaintiff to buy pulpwood to approximately the amount of the store bill, the accounts to be off-set'.[28] In *Hands v Burton*,[29] the plaintiff agreed to take the defendant's horse for 30 guineas, and the defendant agreed to take the plaintiff's brother's horse for 14 guineas; it was further agreed that the defendant should pay only the difference. In his judgment, Le Blanc J observed that 'the agreement was in effect this: the plaintiff says, I will buy your (the defendant's) horse for 30 guineas, and you shall buy my brother's horse for 14 guineas, and the 14 guineas which you are to pay shall be reckoned as part of the 30 which you are to receive'.[30]

Because such an approach is not always realistic, another has developed in which the new car (say) represents the principal goods sold under a contract of sale, included within which is a second subsidiary agreement for the traded-in goods, to adjust the price of the goods if the purchaser delivers to the seller a vehicle to be traded in. Although reference is made to a principal and subsidiary agreement, there is only one sale, and not two. Because the seller in accepting the traded-in vehicle releases the purchaser of part of the debt owing to the seller for the new vehicle, the consideration for the vehicle is not money and therefore does not fall within the sale of goods legislation.[31] In *G J Dawson (Clapham) Ltd v H & G Dutfield*,[32] the plaintiff agreed to supply two used lorries valued at £475 to the defendant and to take £250 in cash and two other lorries in part exchange. Hilbery J held that 'here there were not two purchases, but one transaction'.[33] It was further held that the contract was one of sale because the vehicles had been valued, and because the parties had very nearly decided the price of the goods in conversation.[34]

In *Hands v Burton*, Lord Ellenborough CJ examined the position when the defendant paid the cash difference between the two sets of lorries, but failed to deliver his lorries:

> The action in such circumstances is not one in detinue, and therefore no demand is necessary. Nor are the plaintiffs bound to claim the lorries. The defendants were merely given the right to satisfy £225 of the purchase price by the delivery of the lorries within

26 *Davey v Paine Brothers (Motors) Ltd* [1954] NZLR 1122.
27 [1937] 2 DLR 26 (NSCA).
28 [1937] 2 DLR 26 (NSCA), 27.
29 (1808) 9 East 349.
30 (1808) 9 East 349, 350.
31 *Warmings Used Cars Ltd v Tucker* [1956] SASR 249.
32 [1936] 2 All ER 232.
33 [1936] 2 All ER 232.
34 Agreements for part-exchange involving valued goods have been held to constitute a contract of sale in *Forsyth v Jervis* (1816) 1 Stark 437. Where two vehicles valued at the same price were involved, the transaction was said to attract the application of the Sale of Goods Act: *Davey v Paine Brothers (Motors) Ltd* [1954] NZLR 1122.

> one month or thereabouts. Such an arrangement does not deprive the plaintiffs of their right to the purchase price in cash.[35]

In one line of cases, unless an element of price can be discerned from the parties' agreement, their contract cannot be regarded as a sale. In *Flynn v Mackin & Mahon*,[36] the second defendant agreed to supply the first defendant with a new car. In exchange, the first defendant promised to pay £250 and to trade in his own model to the second defendant. The transaction was arranged for an agreed time and place; however, en route to the meeting the second defendant was involved in an accident in which the plaintiff passenger was injured. The High Court found that the second defendant driver drove negligently, but that the case against the first defendant could not be put to the jury because title in the vehicle had not passed to him when the accident occurred. The Supreme Court agreed (Walsh and Budd JJ and Fitzgerald CJ concurring), finding that the transaction between the defendants was a barter and not a sale, such that the transfer of ownership would only be effective upon delivery of the vehicle. The reason the transaction was a barter rather than a sale was that while evidence was presented that the parties had agreed to transfer the new vehicle for money plus another vehicle, no evidence was forthcoming that the parties had agreed on a price for the new vehicle, and had therefore not assigned a value to either.

Other cases can be distinguished from *Flynn* on the basis that they are concerned with a transfer of goods that had been valued at a pre-determined specific price. The agreement in *Aldridge v Johnson*[37] was said to constitute a sale because the parties had valued the chattels exchanged in the transaction: the plaintiff agreed to transfer bullocks valued at £192 and to pay £23 in cash to a third party in return for barley valued at £215.[38] It is arguable that the agreement would have been a contract of barter had the chattels involved in the exchange not been valued.[39] *Bull v Parker*[40] adopted the more flexible approach whereby the parties' omission to value the goods in the transaction is not fatal to the construction of the contract if the value of the goods is apparent. In that case, old riding equipment and £2 was exchanged for new equipment, but without the equipment being valued. The apparent value of the goods allowed the court to deduce a price for the goods (in this case, £4). The court's approach in *Bull v Parker* follows the common-sense path of treating the contract as a sale if the parties do – for example, by implicitly fixing a notional price for the new goods in the set-off permitted against the book or market price of the new goods.

6.3 Performance of the contract

Payment and delivery of the goods are governed by s 35, which provides that:

> Unless otherwise agreed, delivery of the goods and payment of the price are concurrent conditions (that is to say) the seller must be ready and willing to give possession of the

35 (1808) 9 East 349, 350. See also *Forsyth v Jervis* (1816) 1 Stark 437; *Saxty v Wilkins* (1843) 11 M&W 622.
36 [1974] IR 101.
37 *Aldridge v Johnson* (1857) 7 El & Bl 885.
38 The vehicles exchanged in *G J Dawson (Clapham) Ltd v H & G Dutfield* [1936] 2 All ER 232 had also been valued: transfer of two used lorries for £475, £250 in cash and two other lorries in part exchange.
39 *Benjamin's Sale of Goods* (Sweet & Maxwell, London, 1974), 26.
40 *Bull v Parker* (1842) 2 Dowling NS 345.

> goods to the buyer in exchange for the price, and the buyer must be ready and willing to pay the price in exchange for possession of the goods.

The seller must be ready and willing to deliver the goods; and, concurrently, the purchaser must be ready and willing to accept and pay for the goods. The concurrency of the duties of seller and buyer may be displaced by the parties contracting on other terms.

The Act sets out both general and special rules as to delivery of the goods. The general rules of delivery are set out in s 36, which provides:

> (1) Whether it is for the buyer to take possession of the goods or for the seller to send them to the buyer is a question depending in each case on the contract express or implied between the parties. Apart from any such contract express or implied the place of delivery is the seller's place of business if he have one and if not his residence: Provided that if the contract be for the sale of specific goods which to the knowledge of the parties when the contract is made are in some other place then that place is the place of delivery.
>
> (2) Where under the contract of sale the seller is bound to send the goods to the buyer, but no time for sending them is fixed, the seller is bound to send them within a reasonable time.
>
> (3) Where the goods at the time of sale are in the possession of a third person there is no delivery by seller to buyer unless and until such third person acknowledges to the buyer that he holds the goods on his behalf: Provided that nothing in this section shall affect the operation of the issue or transfer of any document of title to goods.
>
> (4) Demand or tender of delivery may be treated as ineffectual unless made at a reasonable hour. What is a reasonable hour is a question of fact.
>
> (5) Unless otherwise agreed, the expenses of and incidental to putting the goods into a deliverable state must be borne by the seller.

Special rules govern delivery when the parties engage a carrier to transport goods. These are set out at s 39, which provides:

> (1) Where in pursuance of a contract of sale the seller is authorized or required to send the goods to the buyer, delivery of the goods to a carrier, whether named by the buyer or not, for the purpose of transmission to the buyer is prima facie deemed to be a delivery of the goods to the buyer.
>
> (2) Unless otherwise authorized by the buyer, the seller must make such contract with the carrier on behalf of the buyer as may be reasonable, having regard to the nature of the goods and the other circumstances of the case. If the seller omit so to do, and the goods are lost or damaged in course of transit, the buyer may decline to treat the delivery to the carrier as a delivery to himself or may hold the seller responsible in damages.
>
> (3) Unless otherwise agreed, where goods are sent by the seller to the buyer by a route involving sea transit under circumstances in which it is usual to insure, the seller must give such notice to the buyer as may enable him to insure them during their sea transit, and if the seller fails to do so the goods shall be deemed to be at his risk during such sea transit.

As a general rule, the seller must deliver the exact quantity of goods at the time when they have contracted to deliver. Section 37 governs situations where the wrong quantity of the goods is supplied, subject to trade usage, any special agreement made between the parties, or any course of dealing that the parties may have had.[41] Section 37 provides:

> (1) Where the seller delivers to the buyer a quantity of goods less than he contracted to sell the buyer may reject them, but if the buyer accepts the goods so delivered he must pay for them at the contract rate.
> (2) Where the seller delivers to the buyer a quantity of goods larger than he contracted to sell the buyer may accept the goods included in the contract and reject the rest, or he may reject the whole. If the buyer accepts the whole of the goods so delivered he must pay for them at the contract rate.
> (3) Where the seller delivers to the buyer the goods he contracted to sell mixed with goods of a different description not included in the contract, the buyer may accept the goods which are in accordance with the contract and reject the rest, or he may reject the whole.

Where only a portion of the goods under the agreement has been delivered in accordance with the contract, the buyer may by right under sub-s (1) reject them. Section 37 sets out a strict duty with regard to quantity.

It is clearly open to parties to deal with the matter by the contract. This might be done in a number of ways. Where the words 'more or less', or 'about' or other similar terms or statements qualify a contract for the delivery of a specified quantity, the delivered quantity will be subject to a reasonable latitude, on condition that any definite maximum or minimum limit expressed in the contract is delivered.

If the subject matter of a contract is a complete cargo or the remaining cargo, or a whole set or bulk lot, and the contract contains a statement or representation as to an approximation or estimation of the probable quantity, the discrepancy allowable in the quantity is subject to greater latitude.[42] The case of *Euphoric Pty Ltd v Ryledar Pty Ltd*[43] raised issues of whether the correct quantity of goods had been delivered by the seller to the buyer. The goods in question were petroleum products that expand and contract in response to ambient temperature variations. The buyer submitted that the contract of sale contained an implied term whereby the volume was to be tested at the point of delivery when the temperature, and therefore the volume, was to be lower, thereby reducing the cost of the goods. Palmer J examined the issue by referring to s 33(1) of the *Sale of Goods Act 1923* (NSW). His Honour observed:

> Under this section, it was open to Ryledar to measure the volume of petroleum delivered in each case against the volume ordered. If the measurement showed that the volume delivered was less than the volume ordered, Ryledar could reject the delivery. Alternatively, it could accept the volume delivered and pay at the contract rate but then it would

41 *Goods Act 1958* (Vic), s 37(4).

42 See *In re Harrison & Micks, Lambert & Co.* [1917] 1 KB 755; see also *Halsbury's Laws of England* (LexisNexis Butterworths, London, 2010), vol 25, 212–15; M Chalmers, M Mark and J Mance, *Chalmers' Sale of Goods Act, 1893: Including the Factors Acts 1889 & 1890* (Butterworths, London, 7th edn, 1910), 86, 209.

43 [2006] NSWSC 2.

> bear the onus of showing that the volume delivered was not the volume ordered and loaded: see eg *Canberra Washed Sand Pty Ltd v Ro-Mix Concrete Pty Ltd* (1976) 11 ACTR 1 at 7–8. Ryledar has uniformly accepted the volumes delivered by Euphoric but it has not even attempted to discharge the onus of showing that any one of these volumes was less than the volume ordered and loaded.[44]

Palmer J also observed that s 36 of the same Act provides for situations where deterioration is either in the nature of the types of goods traded, or a necessary incident of the manner of storing or transporting those goods under the contract, and cites Professor Sutton's conclusion that, in those circumstances, the buyer accepts such risk. On the other hand, 'if deterioration [is] attributable to inherent faults or unusual characteristics in the goods an inquiry must be made into whether the condition or quality of the goods has been warranted and the period or point of time to which such warranty relates'.[45]

Palmer J continued:[46]

> 'To deteriorate' means 'to grow worse in character; to become lowered or impaired in quality or value; to degenerate': *Oxford English Dictionary*. I think that, from a purchaser's viewpoint, it is legitimate to say that a tanker load of petroleum which it has purchased has 'deteriorated' during transport because it has contracted to a smaller volume than that paid for and is therefore of less value to it than when it was loaded at the refinery. However, I do not think it essential that this case fit squarely into the words of s 36 [of the] Sale of Goods Act. In my opinion, the section states a general proposition of law as to how risk of deterioration inherent in the nature of the goods or in the nature of their transportation is to be borne, which may be applied by analogy in the present case.
>
> Here, Euphoric, having sold the petroleum, agreed by cl 5.1 and 5.2 to deliver it to Ryledar's sites. By cl 5.4, the delivery was to be at Euphoric's own risk. However, as both buyer and seller well knew, there was a risk but not a certainty, inherent in the very nature of petroleum products, that there would be contraction in the volumes to be delivered due to variations in temperature necessarily incident to the course of transit. The Supply Agreement does not expressly or implicitly provide which of the seller or buyer is to bear that risk. Consistently with the policy evinced in s 36 [of the] Sale of Goods Act, it should be the buyer who bears the risk. Correspondingly, if there was an expansion in the volume delivered to the buyer between the time of loading and the time of delivery, then it should be the buyer who gains the benefit.[47]

General contractual principles require strict compliance with a term pertaining to performance of the agreement, otherwise a party will be in breach.[48] This is subject to the parties

44 [2006] NSWSC 2.

45 [2006] NSWSC 2, [144], per Palmer J, citing Professor K Sutton on this section in *The Laws of Australia*, 'Sale of goods', Chapter 4, para 27.

46 Referring to s 36 of the NSW Act, the Victorian equivalent of which provides: 'Where the seller of goods agrees to deliver them at his own risk at a place other than that where they are when sold, the buyer must nevertheless unless otherwise agreed take any risk of deterioration in the goods necessarily incident to the course of transit' (s 40).

47 [2006] NSWSC 2, [147].

48 *Bellgrove v Eldridge* (1954) 90 CLR 613, 617, per Dixon CJ, Webb and Taylor JJ; *Highmist Pty Ltd v Tricare Ltd* [2005] QCA 357, [41], per Keane JA (Gerrard and Cullinane JJA agreeing).

agreeing on only 'substantial' or 'reasonable' performance, and to the common law maxim *de minimis non curat lex* – the law is not concerned about trifling matters – which deals with cases in which a buyer attempts to reject goods by reason of a minute departure from the contractual description. The principle recognises the unavoidability of variation, and allows for some flexibility in relation to the quantity of goods, in the performance of some commercial contracts. The only qualification to the strictness of s 37 imposing an obligation on the seller to supply the correct quantity of goods is where the principle of *de minimis non curat lex* may be applied to a breach of contract.

The two stages of the court's analysis are: (1) the court must decide whether the shortfall or excess can be regarded as being slight (*de minimis*); and (2) it must decide whether it would be unreasonable to allow the buyer to reject under all of the circumstances.[49] This principle may apply only where the quantity is very small, because the tender of a wrong quantity is evidence that the seller is unready and unwilling to perform the contract. The seller has no right to obligate the buyer to pay for a quantity of goods not agreed to under the contract; but equally, the seller is not entitled under sub-s 37(2) to reject the entire delivery where the deviation from the quantity stipulated under the contract is trifling.

Examples of its application include the leading case of *Shipton, Anderson & Co v Weil Brothers & Co.*[50] The contract at issue in *Shipton* concerned the sale of 4950 tons of wheat, but the seller delivered an excess of 55 pounds. It was held that the excess above the stipulated limit was too insignificant to entitle the buyer to reject the goods.

In *Arcos Ltd v E A Ronaasen & Sons*,[51] on the other hand, the buyer was held entitled to reject staves measuring nine sixteenths of an inch in thickness instead of a one half inch thickness as stipulated under the contract of sale. The cases are distinguishable on their facts. The deviation in the first case imposed no burden on the buyer, but in the second case rendered the staves unsuitable for their intended purpose.

6.4 Delivery by instalments

Where buyer and seller have agreed for goods to be delivered by instalments, s 38 provides:

> (1) Unless otherwise agreed, the buyer of goods is not bound to accept delivery thereof by instalments.
>
> (2) Where there is a contract for the sale of goods to be delivered by stated instalments which are to be separately paid for, and the seller makes defective deliveries in respect of one or more instalments, or the buyer neglects or refuses to take delivery of or pay for one or more instalments, it is a question in each case depending on the terms of the contract and the circumstances of the case whether the breach of contract is a repudiation of the whole contract or whether it is a severable breach giving rise to a claim for compensation but not to a right to treat the whole contract as repudiated.

49 See J L Yap, 'No Trifling Matter: The De Minimis Principle in Relation to the Delivery of the Wrong Quantity of Goods under Hong Kong Law' (2008) *International Journal of Private Law* 1(1/2), 222.

50 [1912] 1 KB 574.

51 [1933] AC 470.

Take the situation where a bulk carrier contracted to ship a certain amount of liquid natural gas to an overseas port. If the waterways were restricted in their capacity to permit shipping beyond a certain size and the shipping company was required to utilise several vessels to remove the cargo, it would be implicit in the contract that delivery would be undertaken in instalments. After loading, the separate cargoes may all arrive at their destination at the same time. It is not clear that delivery is thereby by instalment, or that any particular cargo constitutes less than the quantity contracted for.

6.5 Remedies of the buyer

6.5.1 Remedies available to the buyer

A breach of condition gives rise to a right of rescission, which means for the buyer that they may, as a specific instance of the general right of contractual rescission, reject the goods delivered.[52] The right to rescind the contract and reject the goods is not available in all jurisdictions. In Victoria, Queensland, Tasmania, Western Australia and the Northern Territory, for instance, the buyer may reject goods only if they have not accepted either all or part of the goods, or the property does not consist of specific goods property in which has passed to them.[53] If the goods are unascertained goods, the buyer may not reject them once they have accepted the goods or a part of the goods. Otherwise, the breach is treated as being of a warranty not giving rise to a right of rescission, rather than a condition. In New South Wales, South Australia and the Australian Capital Territory, the buyer loses the right only when the goods have been accepted.

A rescission has the effect of restoring the parties to the positions they occupied prior to entering the contract of sale. However, if only a warranty is breached, subject to a contractual term providing otherwise, the innocent party may only claim damages for the offending party's breach, and the buyer is not permitted to reject the goods. When the time for the property to pass is not provided for in the contract, property in specific goods in a deliverable state, by s 23, r 1 of the Goods Act, passes to the buyer when the contract is made.

The injustice that may result from the buyer not being able to inspect the goods prior to entering the contract may be ameliorated by applying the principle that goods must be accepted if property in them is to pass.[54]

Under s 42 of the Goods Act, a buyer may be deemed to have accepted the goods when the buyer either:

> ... intimates to the seller that he has accepted them, or, subject to section 41, when the goods have been delivered to him and he does any act in relation to them which is inconsistent with the ownership of the seller, or when after the lapse of a reasonable time he retains the goods without intimating to the seller that he has rejected them.

Section 41 provides that the buyer is not deemed to have accepted goods that they have not previously examined 'unless and until he has had a reasonable opportunity of examining them

52 *Kwei Tek Chao v British Traders & Shippers Ltd* [1954] 2 QB 459.
53 Qld, s 14(3).
54 *Taylor v Combined Buyers Ltd* [1924] NZLR 627, 650.

for the purpose of ascertaining whether they are in conformity with the contract'.[55] And s 41(2) provides that '[u]nless otherwise agreed when the seller tenders delivery of goods to the buyer he is bound on request to afford the buyer a reasonable opportunity of examining the goods for the purpose of ascertaining whether they are in conformity with the contract'.

Whether s 42 should be read subject to s 41 is an important question in the context of commercial dealings where the buyer, for any number of business-related reasons, does not take delivery of, and therefore does not inspect, the goods. It has now been stipulated that, under a contract of sale, the buyer cannot be expected to determine whether they will accept or reject goods without having first inspected them. The buyer retains the contractual right to reject the goods once they are received. The buyer holds property in the goods subject to the condition that they shall revest in the seller if upon examination they are not in accordance with the contract, and the buyer exercises the right to reject the goods.[56] In *Kwei Tek Chao v British Traders & Shippers Ltd*, Devlin J (as his Lordship then was) said:

> I think that the true view is that what the buyer obtains, when the title under the documents is given to him, is the property in the goods, *subject to the condition* that they revest if upon examination he finds them to be not in accordance with the contract. That means that he gets only conditional property in the goods, the condition being a condition subsequent.
>
> If the property passes conditionally the only ownership left in the seller is the reversionary interest in the property in the event of the condition subsequent operating to restore it to him. It is that reversionary interest with which the buyer must not, save with the penalty of accepting the goods, commit an inconsistent act ... The seller's reversionary interest entitles him, immediately upon the operation of the condition subsequent, that is, as soon as opportunity for examination has been given, to have the goods physically returned to him in the place where the examination has taken place ...
>
> In any event he said 'money will only be recoverable on the ground of a total failure of consideration where the contract is discharged'.[57]

Sections 41 and 42 are to be read as qualifying the buyer's deemed acceptance: a buyer who has not examined the goods is not deemed to accept the goods unless they have had a reasonable opportunity of examining them. Acting in a manner inconsistent with the seller's continued ownership is no longer deemed acceptance unless the buyer has been afforded a reasonable opportunity to inspect the goods.

The issue of the buyer's deemed acceptance was raised in *E Hardy & Co (London) Ltd v Hillerns & Fowler*[58] in which s 35 of the *Sale of Goods Act 1893* (UK) was held not to be limited by s 34. The buyer purchased Rosario or Santa Fe wheat, which was shipped from Argentina to Hull, England under CIF (cost, insurance, freight; see Section 6.5.3 of this chapter) terms. The shipment arrived on 18 March, but was not reported until 20 March. On 21 March the buyer resold and forwarded the wheat to a sub-buyer. The buyer had not examined the wheat prior to the sale and dispatch of the goods. However, the buyer undertook an inspection of the

55 Section 41(1).

56 *J S Robertson (Australia) Pty Ltd v Martin* (1956) 94 CLR 30, 59; *Kwei Tek Chao v British Traders & Shippers Ltd* [1954] 2 QB 459, 487–8.

57 *Kwei Tek Chao v British Traders & Shippers Ltd* [1954] 2 QB 459, 475 (emphasis added).

58 [1923] 2 KB 490.

goods on 23 March, found them not to be Rosario or Santa Fe wheat, and rejected them. The goods, at this stage in transit to the sub-buyers, were recalled by the buyers.

The issue that arose was whether the buyer had, after delivery, committed an act inconsistent with the continued ownership of the seller in accordance with s 34(b) of the English Act. The issue arises in the context of the workings of commercial transactions and their consistency with the buyer's right to examine goods. Specifically, if the buyer had insufficient time to inspect the goods prior to their being onsold to the sub-buyer, can they act in such a way that is inconsistent with the seller's continued ownership?

At the dispute before the arbitration board the buyer argued that the machinery of s 34 was required to be completed before s 35 could be triggered. The board held that the notice of rejection was given within a reasonable time, entitling the buyer to reject the goods. The seller appealed the board's decision to the Court of Appeal, arguing that the buyer's act in selling the goods to the sub-buyer was an act inconsistent with the ownership of the seller, which stripped the buyer of the right of rejection. The court rejected the submission that s 35 is operative before the reasonable time allowed to the buyer to examine the goods has expired. The buyer cannot be deemed to accept the goods before having had a reasonable time to examine them. If, however, the buyer intimated to the seller that he had accepted the goods, then they are accepted notwithstanding that the acceptance occurs before the expiry of a reasonable time for inspection. In this case, onselling the goods and parting with their possession by delivering them to the sub-buyer is inconsistent with the seller's ownership. The buyer's rejection entitles the seller to have the goods at their immediate disposal, and defeating the seller's right of resuming possession is deemed acceptance of the goods.

The Court of Appeal held:

> There was no doubt that, after delivery was taken under the documents, there was a period during which the buyers could hold the possession, and hold the possession in a position which was neutral as to the rights of property, and as long as they retained the possession on that footing the buyers quite plainly had the right to reject. But if they transferred the possession after it had in fact been handed to them, in circumstances inconsistent either with the goods remaining at that time the property of the sellers, or inconsistent with the goods being eventually restored to the sellers, the buyers did an act which was inconsistent with the ownership of the sellers.[59]

Acceptance will also be deemed under s 37 'when the goods have been delivered to the buyer and the buyer does any act in relation to them which is inconsistent with the ownership of the seller'. Acceptance will only be deemed if the goods have first been delivered to the buyer. A buyer who resells the goods they have agreed to purchase prior to their delivery will not have accepted them. On the other hand, if the buyer delivers the purchased goods to the sub-buyer they may have accepted them. It has, however, been held that a buyer is a buyer in possession if they have requested the seller to deliver the goods directly to the sub-buyer.

In *E & S Ruben Ltd v Faire Brothers & Co Ltd*,[60] a buyer who requested the seller to set aside the goods at the seller's premises and subsequently deliver the goods directly to the sub-buyer was held to have taken constructive delivery from the seller to the buyer at the seller's

59 [1923] 2 KB 490, 496.
60 [1949] 1 KB 254.

premises. The buyer accepted the goods. *Four Point Garage Ltd v Carter*[61] applied *Ruben v Faire*. In that case, the buyer asked the seller to deliver a car directly to a sub-buyer. The court held that the buyer was in constructive possession by means of the actual delivery to the sub-buyer, and the buyer was a buyer in possession by constructive possession while the sub-buyer gained actual possession.

Ruben v Faire was also considered in *Hammer & Barrow v Coca-Cola*.[62] In that case, the contract for the Christchurch-based plaintiff seller to supply the defendant buyer with yoyos included a clause whereby the plaintiff agreed to deliver a portion of the yoyos – which the defendant had onsold to sub-buyers before the defendant had taken delivery of any – to the sub-buyer's premises in Auckland. The plaintiff argued that the defendant had accepted the goods by reselling and delivering them to the sub-buyer. The court held that delivery directly from seller to sub-buyer could not constitute acceptance of the goods if the contract contemplated that the sub-buyer's premises were the place of examination prior to the buyer's acceptance. The plaintiff retained the right to have the goods returned to the sub-buyer's premises in case of rejection, and the defendant was entitled to reject the goods delivered to the sub-buyer's premises. Richmond J stated:

> [P]ossession of the goods on the part of [the sub-buyer] must be regarded as subject to the exercise by [the buyer] of its rights of examination and rejection. In effect, and whether the matter be regarded from the point of view of the ownership in the goods or the possession of the goods, I do not think that [the buyer] had . . . divested itself of the power to return the goods to [the seller].[63]

6.5.2 Purchaser's acceptance of the goods

A purchaser who has accepted goods may be prevented from rescinding the contract, although they retain the right to claim damages. The acceptance of the purchaser is deemed in the following circumstances:

(a) the purchaser intimates to the seller that the purchaser has accepted the goods;[64]
(b) the goods have been delivered and the purchaser does any act which is inconsistent with the ownership of the seller;[65] or
(c) the purchaser retains the goods for a 'reasonable time' without rejecting the goods.[66]

The test of acceptance based on the buyer's doing any act inconsistent with the seller's continued ownership of the goods requires the goods to be delivered to the place where inspection is to take place in accordance with the contract. An act inconsistent with the seller's continued ownership is an act that prevents the seller exercising their right to have rejected

61 [1985] 3 All ER 12.
62 [1962] NZLR 723.
63 [1962] NZLR 723, 731.
64 *Sale of Goods Act 1923* (NSW), s 38(1), based on *Sale of Goods Act 1979* (UK), s 35(1)(a).
65 *Sale of Goods Act 1923* (NSW), s 38(1), based on *Sale of Goods Act 1979* (UK), s 35(1)(b).
66 *Sale of Goods Act 1923* (NSW), s 38(1), based on *Sale of Goods Act 1979* (UK), s 35A(2).

goods returned to the place of examination provided for under the contract.[67] In the case of an agreement between buyer and seller in which goods are onsold by the buyer to a sub-buyer, the sub-buyer's premises are the place for examination of the goods. Under such an agreement, the seller's right to have the goods returned to the sub-buyer's premises preserves their ownership, and neither the onselling of the goods nor the goods being dispatched to the sub-buyer constitutes an act inconsistent with the continued ownership of the seller. A buyer may do an act inconsistent with the seller's continued ownership of the goods if they onsell the product knowing that the product is defective. In *Harnor v Groves*,[68] the buyer onsold some, and themselves used some, flour after having become aware that the sacks of flour did not meet the requirements under the contract. Where the contract is one for delivery of goods by instalment, the rules of acceptance apply to each separate instalment.[69]

In relation to the application of the principle that a purchaser will be held to have accepted goods where the purchaser has retained the goods for a 'reasonable time', the Full Court of the South Australian Supreme Court in *Russo v Belcar Pty Ltd*[70] has noted that:

> The courts have traditionally very much borne in mind practical commercial considerations such as the need for finality of transactions which, in the context of s. 35 [of the South Australian Sale of Goods Act], requires that there be a relatively short period within which sellers may be satisfied that the goods have been 'accepted'.[71]

From this approach the court discerned two interrelated principles.[72] Referring to the learned works of Atiyah,[73] Sutton[74] and Benjamin,[75] the court stated that '[t]he first is that "a reasonable period" may be found to have expired even though a latent fault is present and could not have been detected during that period'.[76] The second principle is that 'subject to the caveat constituted by the first principle above, what is "a reasonable time" will very much depend on all the facts of the particular case'.[77]

In accordance with *Russo v Belcar*, the buyer's rejection must consist of a 'clear and unequivocal' act taking into account 'the whole of the buyer's conduct'[78] and their communications.[79] A buyer is deemed to have affirmed the contract if their act is not unequivocal or they

---

67 *Kwei Tek Chao v British Traders & Shippers Ltd* [1954] 2 QB 459; *Hammer & Barrow v Coca-Cola* [1962] NZLR 723.

68 (1855) 15 CB 667.

69 M G Bridge, *The Sale of Goods* (Oxford University Press, Oxford, UK, 1998), 12-062.

70 (2011) 111 SASR 459, [96].

71 Section 35 provides: 'The buyer is deemed to have accepted the goods when he intimates to the seller that he has accepted them, or (subject to s 34 of this Act) when the goods have been delivered to him, and he does any act in relation to them which is inconsistent with the ownership of the seller, or when, after the lapse of a reasonable time, he retains the goods without intimating to the seller that he has rejected them.'

72 (2011) 111 SASR 459, [96].

73 P S Atiyah, *The Sale of Goods* (Longman, Essex, UK, 10th edn, 2001), 510–11.

74 K Sutton, *Sales and Consumer Law* (Lawbook Co, Sydney, 4th edn, 1995), 587–8.

75 M Bridge (ed), *Benjamin's Sale of Goods* (Sweet & Maxwell, London, 7th edn, 2006), 629–30.

76 (2011) 111 SASR 459, [97].

77 (2011) 111 SASR 459, [100].

78 (2011) 111 SASR 459, [101], citing M Bridge (ed), *Benjamin's Sale of Goods* (Sweet & Maxwell, London, 7th edn, 2006), 613.

79 *Graanhandel T Vink BV v European Grain & Shipping Ltd* [1989] 2 Lloyd's Rep 531, 533.

have not rejected the goods.[80] In *Vargas Pena Apezteguia y Cia SAIC v Peter Cremer GmbH & Co*,[81] Saville J stated that 'a clear and unequivocal rejection is one where buyers indicate that they want and will have nothing more to do with the goods'.[82]

If, after a buyer knows of a defect in the goods, they are induced to retain the goods on the basis of the seller's representation that the defects will be made good, the question arises as to whether the buyer has accepted the goods. In *Attorney-General (Botswana) v Aussie Diamond Products Pty Ltd [No 3]*,[83] the seller, Aussie Diamond Products, under a contract of sale, was to deliver and commission a drilling rig to Botswana in July 2004. The rig required numerous repairs and modifications, which the seller undertook successfully, at the buyer's request and at their own expense. However, the buyer purported to rescind the contract in December 2007 for the seller's failure to commission the rig. The Western Australian Supreme Court held that s 11 of the *Sale of Goods Act 1895* (WA), under which a buyer who has accepted goods under a contract of sale may only treat a breach of condition as a breach of warranty, applied. A manufacturer's obligation, under a sale of goods contract, to commission equipment it supplied was a warranty and not a condition, for which the buyer was not entitled to reject the goods and rescind the contract. It further held that, having paid the purchase price in advance, the buyer who failed to reject the goods on the basis that the goods were defective, was not entitled to terminate the contract. The court found that s 34 of the Act – which provides the buyer with a reasonable opportunity to examine the goods in order to ascertain their conformity with the contract – did not apply, as the rig was in the buyer's possession or control for at least one year and three months prior to purporting to reject it. Further, under s 35 of the Act, a buyer is deemed to have accepted goods if, after the lapse of a reasonable time, they retain the goods without intimating to the seller that they are rejecting them. In this case, the court found that 21 months constituted 'the lapse of a reasonable time' sufficient to satisfy the conditions of acceptance under the section, and affirmation of the continued existence of the contract. Nor was the buyer induced 'by the seller's representations to retain and not to reject the goods'.

In *JAD International Pty Ltd v International Trucks Australia Ltd*,[84] JAD claimed that International Trucks, through one of its employees, misrepresented the age, history and quality of the engine installed in a Kenworth truck which it purchased for $86 000, and that the misrepresentation breached an implied condition of the agreement that entitled it to rescind the contract. The court held that whether a right to rescission remained open following the performance of a contract for the sale of goods was governed by s 6(1) of the *Misrepresentation Act 1972* (SA), which provides:

> Where a misrepresentation has been made by reason of which any party to a contract would, but for any one or more of the following considerations –
>
> (a) that the misrepresentation has become a term of the contract;
> (b) that the contract has been performed; or

80 *Graanhandel T Vink BV v European Grain & Shipping Ltd* [1989] 2 Lloyd's Rep 531.
81 [1987] 1 Lloyd's Rep 394.
82 [1987] 1 Lloyd's Rep 394, 398.
83 [2010] WASC 141.
84 (1994) 50 FCR 378.

> (c) that conveyances, transfers or other documents have been registered at any public registry office in pursuance of the contract,
>
> be entitled to rescind the contract, that contracting party shall be entitled to rescind the contract notwithstanding that consideration or those considerations.

However, the court further held that the effect of s 6(1) was that the right to rescind a contract was only preserved where it would otherwise have been previously lost due to the occurrence of one of the events specified in sub-s (a), (b) or (c). The statute had not otherwise displaced the principle that the right of rescission could be lost by the buyer either accepting the goods or not rescinding the contract within a reasonable time. That is to say, the buyer loses the right to rescind the contract for misrepresentation when they either accept or affirm the contract. If the buyer, either expressly or implicitly, by words or conduct, elects to retain goods they know are faulty, their acceptance will be irrevocable.

The contract was governed by the South Australian *Sale of Goods Act 1895*, s 35, which provides:

> The buyer is deemed to have accepted the goods when he intimates to the seller that he has accepted them, or (subject to s 34 of this Act) when the goods have been delivered to him, and he does any act in relation to them which is inconsistent with the ownership of the seller, or when, after the lapse of a reasonable time, he retains the goods without intimating to the seller that he has rejected them.

Any delay in exercising the right of rescission was potentially but not necessarily fatal to it, since s 34 of the Act provides that a buyer who has not previously examined the goods will have a 'reasonable opportunity of examining them for the purpose of ascertaining whether they are in conformity with the contract'.

The court assessed as strong the evidence that, although rescission was open to the applicant in this case, they had accepted the goods and had affirmed, and not lawfully rescinded, the contract.[85] The court referred to the judgment of Pearce J in *Long v Lloyd*.[86] In that case, it was held that the plaintiff should have a reasonable time in which to test certain representations made to him regarding a lorry's fuel consumption. His Honour said: 'Until he had had such an opportunity it might well be said that he had not accepted the lorry, always assuming of course, that he did nothing inconsistent with the ownership of the seller. An examination of the facts, however, shows that on any view he must have accepted the lorry before he purported to reject it.' In the instant case, although the applicant did not examine the Kenworth truck, it had a reasonable opportunity to do so and was on notice, by virtue of the vehicle's appearance, that it was not of the expected quality. Judgment was therefore for the respondent that the purported rescission of the agreement was void.

The buyer is not bound to return rejected goods to the seller if they have rightfully refused to accept goods delivered to them as long as they have intimated that refusal to accept them to the seller.[87]

85 Referring to the case of *Long v Lloyd* [1958] 1 WLR 753. The purchaser had accepted the lorry and thereby his right of rescission (if any) had been barred by his acceptance.

86 [1958] 1 WLR 753.

87 Section 43.

6.5.3 Acceptance and free on board (FOB), or cost, insurance, freight (CIF) contracts

The usual contract for the carriage of goods by sea is a free on board (FOB) or cost, insurance, freight (CIF) contract. The seller's responsibilities under an FOB contract are to deliver the goods on board the ship and to pay the expenses associated with doing so. Thereafter, all expenses are borne by the buyer. Property in the goods passes to the buyer once the goods are on board.

The seller's responsibilities under a CIF contract are more extensive. The seller arranges for the goods to be shipped, pays for their shipment, insures and pays for the policy of insurance, and tenders shipping documents to the buyer. Property in the goods passes to the buyer when the buyer has obtained the relevant documents of title. The buyer is entitled, nonetheless, to reject the goods, which will revert to the seller if on inspection they breach the contract. The rejection of the goods on inspection is a condition subsequent.

The buyer does not accept the goods by pledging them, or making them subject to a 'string' contract, since the seller retains their reversionary interest despite them. The seller is immediately entitled to have the goods returned to them at the place inspection is to occur upon the triggering of the condition subsequent (the opportunity to examine the goods).

6.5.4 Remedies for breach of a warranty implied by the Sale of Goods Act

A seller who has breached a warranty is entitled to damages. If the buyer has accepted goods after the seller's breach of a condition, the buyer is entitled only to damages. Section 59 of the Goods Act provides:

> **Remedy for breach of warranty**
>
> (1) Where there is a breach of warranty by the seller or where the buyer elects or is compelled to treat any breach of a condition on the part of the seller as a breach of warranty, the buyer is not by reason only of such breach of warranty entitled to reject the goods; but he may –
>
> (a) set up against the seller the breach of warranty in diminution or extinction of the price; or
>
> (b) maintain an action against the seller for damages for the breach of warranty.
>
> (2) The measure of damages for breach of warranty is the estimated loss directly and naturally resulting in the ordinary course of events from the breach of warranty.
>
> (3) In the case of breach of warranty of quality such loss is prima facie the difference between the value of the goods at the time of delivery to the buyer and the value they would have had if they had answered to the warranty.
>
> (4) The fact that the buyer has set up the breach of warranty in diminution or extinction of the price does not prevent him from maintaining an action for the same breach of warranty if he has suffered further damage.

Section 59(2) deals with the measure of damages for a breach of warranty. That loss is the 'loss directly and naturally resulting in the ordinary course of events'. In other words, s 59(2) incorporates the common law test of remoteness of damage into the statutory regime, and echoes the language of Alderson B in *Hadley v Baxendale*[88] that loss is the amount 'arising naturally, i.e. according to the usual course of things, from such breach of contract itself, or such as may reasonably be supposed to have been in the contemplation of both parties, at the time they made the contract, as the probable result of the breach of it'.[89] What the parties contemplated at the time of entering the contract is a question of fact in the circumstances of the case.

Section 59(3) permits the recovery of damages for the difference in value between the quality of the goods as warrantied and the actual quality of the goods. The buyer may recover damages if they are required to undertake rectification or modification to make the goods answer the warranty, even if the work has been neither performed nor paid for.[90]

The burden of proof lies on the person who wishes to adopt another measure of damages. This may be the buyer or the seller. However, it is more common for the buyer to seek to displace the presumption in order that they might recover losses other than the diminution in value. Often a commercial buyer will have either onsold the goods or at least have contemplated onselling them. The buyer is entitled to recover damages in respect of those lost profits if the seller knows that the buyer intended to resell the goods and ought reasonably to have contemplated that a breach as to description or quality would be likely to cause the buyer a loss of profit on the resale or potential resale.[91]

In a case of a series of 'string' contracts, the courts will also consider the possibility that the ultimate buyer will seek damages from the immediate seller who will in turn seek indemnity from their immediate seller, and so on. In such a situation, the damages and costs paid by the buyer will be included in the calculation of damages for the seller's breach of the original contract.[92]

6.5.5 Remedy for defective instalment deliveries

Under an agreement to supply goods by instalment, an issue may arise as to whether the buyer is entitled to reject the whole contract amount, or only to be compensated for the defective goods supplied under the relevant instalment or instalments. Section 38 provides:

> **Instalment deliveries**
>
> (1) Unless otherwise agreed, the buyer of goods is not bound to accept delivery thereof by instalments.
>
> (2) Where there is a contract for the sale of goods to be delivered by stated instalments which are to be separately paid for, and the seller makes defective deliveries in respect of one or more instalments, or the buyer neglects or refuses to take delivery of or pay for one or more instalments, it is a question in each case depending on the

88 (1854) 9 Exch 341.

89 For the application of this principle, see *Victoria Laundry (Windsor) Ltd v Newman Industries Ltd* [1949] 1 All ER 997 and, in the House of Lords, *Koufos v C Czarnikow Ltd ('The Heron II')* [1967] 3 All ER 686.

90 See *Zuvela v Geiger* [2007] WASCA 138, [39], citing *Bellgrove v Eldridge* (1954) 90 CLR 613, 620 and *Hyder Consulting (Australia) Pty Ltd v Wilh Wilhelmsen Agency Pty Ltd* (2002) 18 BCL 122. On the basis that the court may depart from s 54(3) measures of damages for divergence from warrantied quality where appropriate, see *Zuvela v Geiger* [2007] WASCA 138, [3].

91 *Bence Graphics International Ltd v Fasson UK Ltd* [1997] 1 All ER 979.

92 *Bence Graphics International Ltd v Fasson UK Ltd* [1997] 1 All ER 979.

> terms of the contract and the circumstances of the case whether the breach of contract is a repudiation of the whole contract or whether it is a severable breach giving rise to a claim for compensation but not to a right to treat the whole contract as repudiated.

A *de minimis* breach in the context of the entire contract will not constitute a repudiation and not give rise to a right of termination on the part of the buyer. The breach must be sufficiently serious to enable the buyer to terminate. That is, the breach must be both of a certain size or quantity within the context of the contract as a whole, and have a certain probability of being repeated during the performance of the remainder of the contract.[93]

6.5.6 Damages for non-delivery or delayed delivery

Section 57 provides:

> **Damages for non-delivery**
>
> (1) Where the seller wrongfully neglects or refuses to deliver the goods to the buyer the buyer may maintain an action against the seller for damages for non-delivery.
>
> (2) The measure of damages is the estimated loss directly and naturally resulting in the ordinary course of events from the seller's breach of contract.
>
> (3) Where there is an available market for the goods in question the measure of damages is prima facie to be ascertained by the difference between the contract price and the market or current price of the goods at the time or times when they ought to have been delivered, or if no time was fixed then at the time of the refusal to deliver.

The failure of the seller to comply with the stipulated time of delivery entitles the buyer to a claim for damages against the seller. The measure of damages is 'the estimated loss directly and naturally resulting in the ordinary course of events from the seller's breach of contract' (s 57(2)). Damages are measured as the difference between the price at which the goods were purchased under the contract and their market or current price at the time they were to be delivered. If no fixed time for delivery was stipulated under the contract, the price of the goods is measured as at the time delivery was refused (s 57(3)).

An available market is a reference to the existence of an immediate buyer for the goods at the time and place where the goods are to be delivered.[94] The concept of an available market cannot be said to exist where the price of commodities is controlled by such mechanisms as trade protection policies or price maintenance agreements. In other words, commodity prices in an available market are dictated purely by the economics of supply and demand determining the price at which a buyer could be found, whether it was equal to, or greater or less than, the contract price. In the absence of an available market, damages are measured by reference to what a reasonable person, having regard to their own benefit and bearing in mind the risks to them, would have paid for the goods at the time and place they were to be sold.[95]

93 *Maple Flock Co Ltd v Universal Furniture Products (Wembley) Ltd* [1934] 1 KB 148, 157.
94 *Charter v Sullivan* [1957] 2 QB 117; *Waugh v Harper* [1937] St R Qd 327.
95 K Sutton, *Sales and Consumer Law* (Lawbook Co, Sydney, 4th edn, 1995), 655.

If the contract makes time of the essence, delayed delivery is a basis for rescinding the contract. However, if the delayed delivery is accepted, damages may be claimed. Damages are to be measured as the difference between the market value of the goods at the time for delivery under the contract and at the time they were in fact delivered.

Lost profits may not generally be claimed for delayed delivery or non-delivery.[96] However, an exception is that lost profits may be claimed where the goods have been purchased in the course of practising a trade.[97] The exception is based on the parties having reasonably contemplated such a loss since the goods bought in trade do not render profit too remote. In *Williams Brothers v Agius Ltd*,[98] the claimant had contracted to purchase coal at a certain price under a contract of sale, and further to sell that coal at a certain price under another contract. The House of Lords calculated damages not on the basis of compensation for the plaintiff's loss when the defendant failed to deliver the coal, but at the greater sum calculated on the basis of the increased price of coal at the tme of the breach. The Court of Appeal in *Slater v Hoyle & Smith Ltd*[99] applied the House of Lords' reasoning, awarding the plaintiff damages based on the difference in market value at the time of delivery between the defective cotton and cotton conforming to the quality requirements of the contract.

6.5.7 Remedy for specific performance

A court may order specific performance of a contract if the seller has failed to deliver specific or ascertained goods. Section 58 provides:

> **Specific performance**
>
> In any action for breach of contract to deliver specific or ascertained goods the court may if it thinks fit on the application of the plaintiff by its judgment direct that the contract shall be performed specifically without giving the defendant the option of retaining the goods on payment of damages. The judgment may be unconditional or upon such terms and conditions as to damages payment of the price and otherwise as to the court may seem just, and the application by the plaintiff may be made at any time before judgment.

Additionally, the order may impose conditions such as that the seller pay the buyer damages, or the price of the goods, or other orders to do justice in the circumstances. The court has discretion to award specific performance and will generally award damages to compensate the buyer, unless the goods were unique or otherwise of a special quality or nature, or a peculiar value, such that damages will not compensate for their loss.[100] Where an award of money is adequate compensation, an award of specific performance will not be ordered. However, where damages would not put the party in as advantageous a position as if the agreement had

96 *Williams Brothers v Agius Ltd* [1914] AC 510.

97 *Mahinder Singh v Acme Sawmills Ltd* (1958) 14 DLR (2d) 361.

98 *Williams Brothers v Agius Ltd* [1914] AC 510.

99 *Slater v Hoyle & Smith Ltd* [1920] 2 KB 11. In these cases, the remedy may substitute for the infringed right of sale and represent the value of the right. See also *Wrotham Park Estate Co Ltd v Parkside Homes Ltd* [1974] 1 WLR 798 and *Experience Hendrix LLC v PPX Enterprises Inc* [2003] EWCA Civ 323 for cases expressing the 'hypothetical bargain' measure of damages.

100 *Dougan v Ley* (1946) 71 CLR 142.

been specifically performed,[101] the court may use specific performance as a means of doing 'more perfect and complete justice'.[102]

6.6 Remedies of the seller

The seller is principally concerned for the buyer to accept the goods delivered to them and to pay for them. The remedies it may pursue against the buyer include an action on the price and actions effective against the goods themselves, such as a lien, a stoppage of the delivery, or a right of resale. Section 45 of the Goods Act provides:

> **Definition of unpaid seller**
>
> (1) The seller of goods is deemed to be an *unpaid seller* within the meaning of this Part –
>
> (a) when the whole of the price has not been paid or tendered;
>
> (b) when a bill of exchange or other negotiable instrument has been received as conditional payment, and the condition on which it was received has not been fulfilled by reason of the dishonour of the instrument or otherwise.
>
> (2) In this Division the term 'seller' includes any person who is in the position of a seller, as for instance an agent of the seller to whom the bill of lading has been indorsed or a consignor or agent who has himself paid or is directly responsible for the price.

Section 46 provides:

> **Unpaid seller's rights**
>
> (1) Subject to the provisions of this Part and of Part II and of any Act in that behalf, notwithstanding that the property in the goods may have passed to the buyer, the unpaid seller of goods as such has by implication of law –
>
> (a) a lien on the goods for the price while he is in possession of them;
>
> (b) in case of the bankruptcy of the buyer a right of stopping the goods in transitu after he has parted with the possession of them;
>
> (c) a right of re-sale as limited by this Part.
>
> (2) Where the property in goods has not passed to the buyer the unpaid seller has in addition to his other remedies a right of withholding delivery similar to and co-extensive with his rights of lien and stoppage in transitu where the property has passed to the buyer.

6.6.1 The price

Section 55 provides:

> **Action for price**
>
> (1) Where under a contract of sale the property in the goods has passed to the buyer, and the buyer wrongfully neglects or refuses to pay for the goods according to the terms of the contract, the seller may maintain an action against him for the price of the goods.

101 *Harnett* v *Yeilding* (1805) 2 Sch & Lef 549, 553, per Lord Redesdale.

102 *Tito v Waddell [No 2]*, [1977] Ch 106, 322, per Megarry VC; *Wilson* v *Northampton & Banbury Junction Railway Co* (1874) 9 Ch App 279, 284, per Lord Selborne. The passage was quoted by Dixon J in *Dougan v Ley* (1946) 71 CLR 142, 150.

(2) Where under a contract of sale the price is payable on a day certain irrespective of delivery, and the buyer wrongfully neglects or refuses to pay such price, the seller may maintain an action for the price although the property in the goods has not passed and the goods have not been appropriated to the contract.

The seller may sue the buyer for the price of the goods when property in the goods has passed to the buyer who has refused to pay for the goods. If payment for the goods is due at a specified time, independently of delivery, the seller may sue for the price if the buyer fails to pay, regardless of whether the goods have been appropriated to the contract, or property in the goods has passed to the buyer.

6.6.2 Damages for non-acceptance

Section 56 provides:

Damages for non-acceptance

(1) Where the buyer wrongfully neglects or refuses to accept and pay for the goods the seller may maintain an action against him for damages for non-acceptance.

(2) The measure of damages is the estimated loss directly and naturally resulting in the ordinary course of events from the buyer's breach of contract.

(3) Where there is an available market for the goods in question the measure of damages is prima facie to be ascertained by the difference between the contract price and the market or current price at the time or times when the goods ought to have been accepted, or if no time was fixed for acceptance then at the time of the refusal to accept.

A buyer who wrongfully neglects or refuses to accept and pay for the goods entitles the seller to claim damages against the buyer for non-acceptance. Damages are measured as the estimated loss directly and naturally resulting, in the ordinary course of events, from the buyer's breach of contract. Where a market for the goods is available, damages are measured as the difference between the contract and market or current price of the goods at the time acceptance of the goods was required. If no time for acceptance is specified in the contract, damages are measured at the time the acceptance of the goods was refused.

6.6.3 Unpaid seller against the goods

Section 46 provides:

Unpaid seller's rights

(1) Subject to the provisions of this Part and of Part II and of any Act in that behalf, notwithstanding that the property in the goods may have passed to the buyer, the unpaid seller of goods as such has by implication of law –

(a) a lien on the goods for the price while he is in possession of them;

(b) in case of the bankruptcy of the buyer a right of stopping the goods in transitu after he has parted with the possession of them;

(c) a right of re-sale as limited by this Part.

(2) Where the property in goods has not passed to the buyer the unpaid seller has in addition to his other remedies a right of withholding delivery similar to and co-extensive with his rights of lien and stoppage in transitu where the property has passed to the buyer.

If the buyer does not pay for the goods, the seller may pursue a number of remedies depending on who is currently in possession of the goods, and whether or not property in the goods has passed. Remedies include a lien against the goods, stopping the goods in transit, and reselling the goods in question. In the case of goods property in which has not passed, the seller may withhold delivery of the goods.

6.6.4 Lien or right to retain the goods

Section 47 provides:

Unpaid seller's lien

(1) Subject to the provisions of this Part the unpaid seller of goods who is in possession of them is entitled to retain possession of them until payment or tender of the price in the following cases, namely –
  (a) where the goods have been sold without any stipulation as to credit;
  (b) where the goods have been sold on credit but the term of credit has expired;
  (c) where the buyer becomes bankrupt.

(2) The seller may exercise his right of lien notwithstanding that he is in possession of the goods as agent or bailee for the buyer.

A lien is a right to retain possession of goods until they have been paid for. The remedy therefore requires the seller to be in actual possession of the goods, regardless of the capacity they exercise in retaining possession. They may, for example, be a seller in possession of the goods, or the goods may be bailed to them for the buyer.

The circumstances in which the seller may exercise their right are when:

(a) the goods have been sold without any stipulation as to credit;
(b) the goods have been sold on credit, but the term of credit has expired; or
(c) the buyer becomes insolvent.

A buyer is insolvent when they have ceased paying their debts in the ordinary course of business, or are unable to pay their debts when and as they become due.

Section 49 provides for circumstances when the right to retain goods is lost. Section 49 provides:

Termination of lien

(1) The unpaid seller of goods loses his lien thereon –
  (a) when he delivers the goods to a carrier or other bailee for the purpose of transmission to the buyer without reserving the right of disposal of the goods;
  (b) when the buyer or his agent lawfully obtains possession of the goods;
  (c) by waiver thereof.

> (2) The unpaid seller of goods having a lien thereon does not lose his lien by reason only that he has obtained judgment for the price of the goods.

Section 48 provides:

> **Part delivery**
> Where an unpaid seller has made part delivery of the goods he may exercise his right of lien on the remainder unless such part delivery has been made under such circumstances as to show an agreement to waive the lien.

An unpaid seller who has part delivered goods may exercise their right of lien on the goods still to be delivered unless part delivery constitutes a waiver of that lien.

6.6.5 Withholding delivery

If property in the goods has not passed to the buyer, the unpaid seller is entitled to withhold delivery of the goods. The right to withhold delivery is comparable to and overlaps with the unpaid seller's right of retention and *stoppage in transitu* once property has passed to the buyer. Section 50 provides:

> **Right of stoppage in transitu**
> Subject to the provisions of this Part and of Part II of this Act when the buyer of goods becomes bankrupt the unpaid seller who has parted with the possession of the goods has the right of stopping them in transitu that is to say he may resume possession of the goods as long as they are in course of transit and may retain them until payment or tender of the price.

Section 51 enables a determination as to whether the goods are in transit for the purposes of the Act. It provides:

> **Duration of transit**
> (1) Goods are deemed to be in course of transit from the time when they are delivered to a carrier by land or water or other bailee for the purpose of transmission to the buyer until the buyer or his agent in that behalf takes delivery of them from such carrier or other bailee.
> (2) If the buyer or his agent in that behalf obtains delivery of the goods before their arrival at the appointed destination the transit is at an end.
> (3) If after the arrival of the goods at the appointed destination the carrier or other bailee acknowledges to the buyer or his agent that he holds the goods on his behalf and continues in possession of them as bailee for the buyer or his agent the transit is at an end, and it is immaterial that a further destination for the goods may have been indicated by the buyer.
> (4) If the goods are rejected by the buyer and the carrier or other bailee continues in possession of them the transit is not deemed to be at an end even if the seller has refused to receive them back.

(5) When goods are delivered to a ship chartered by the buyer it is a question depending on the circumstances of the particular case whether they are in the possession of the master as a carrier or as agent to the buyer.

(6) Where the carrier or other bailee wrongfully refuses to deliver the goods to the buyer or his agent in that behalf the transit is deemed to be at an end.

(7) Where part delivery of the goods has been made to the buyer or his agent in that behalf the remainder of the goods may be stopped in transitu unless such part delivery has been made under such circumstances as to show an agreement to give up possession of the whole of the goods.

Exercising the right of stoppage in transitu is governed by s 52, which provides:

Exercise of stoppage in transitu

(1) The unpaid seller may exercise his right of stoppage in transitu either by taking actual possession of the goods or by giving notice of his claim to the carrier or other bailee in whose possession the goods are. Such notice may be given either to the person in actual possession of the goods or to his principal. In the latter case the notice to be effectual must be given at such time and under such circumstances that the principal by the exercise of reasonable diligence may communicate it to his servant or agent in time to prevent a delivery to the buyer.

(2) When notice of stoppage in transitu is given by the seller to the carrier or other bailee in possession of the goods he must re-deliver the goods to or according to the directions of the seller. The expenses of such re-delivery must be borne by the seller.

The right is claimed by the unpaid seller taking actual possession of the goods, or giving notice that they have been so claimed by a person in possession of the goods, such as a carrier or a bailee of the goods. Such a notice requires the person in possession to redeliver the goods to the seller, or to another person or location in accordance with the seller's instructions, at the seller's expense.

Section 53 governs circumstances in which the seller's right of lien or stoppage of the goods in transit may be affected by acts of the buyer. Circumstances that may affect the seller's rights include where there has been a bona fide, for value and without notice, subsale of the goods by the buyer, or where the buyer has pledged to deliver goods. Section 53 provides:

Effect of sub-sale or pledge by buyer

Subject to the provisions of this Part and of Part II the unpaid seller's right of lien or stoppage in transitu is not affected by any sale or other disposition of the goods which the buyer may have made unless the seller has assented thereto.

Subsections (3) and (4) of s 54 provide for the seller's right of resale of the goods. They state:

(3) Where the goods are of a perishable nature or where the unpaid seller gives notice to the buyer of his intention to re-sell, and the buyer does not within a reasonable time pay or tender the price, the unpaid seller may re-sell the goods and recover from the original buyer damages for any loss occasioned by his breach of contract.

(4) Where the seller expressly reserves a right of re-sale in case the buyer should make default, and on the buyer making default re-sells the goods, the original contract of sale is thereby rescinded but without prejudice to any claim the seller may have for damages.

The resale rescinds the original contract in the first two circumstances, entitling the unpaid seller to sue for damages for the buyer's breach of contract.[103]

6.7 Key points

- The essence of a contract of sale is that the seller should transfer, or agree to transfer, property in goods to the buyer for a money consideration called the price.
- Payment and delivery of the goods are governed by s 35 of the Goods Act.
- The Goods Act sets out both general and special rules as to delivery of the goods. The general rules of delivery are set out in s 36.
- In the context of a contract for the sale of goods, a seller's duty is to deliver the goods, and a buyer's duty is to accept and pay for them, according to the terms of the contract.
- The seller is principally concerned for the buyer to accept the goods delivered to them and to pay for them. The remedies it may pursue against the buyer include an action on the price, and actions effective against the goods themselves, such as a lien, a stoppage of the delivery or a right of resale.

6.8 DISCUSSION QUESTIONS

1. What is the meaning of 'price' under the sale of goods legislation?
2. What does 'delivery' mean under the sale of goods legislation?
3. What are the duties of the buyer?
4. What are the duties of the seller?
5. What remedies might the seller pursue against the buyer?

6.9 FURTHER READING

Goldberger, J, 'Mistake in the Formation and Performance of Contracts: Remedial Options under Australian Law' (2009–10) *Commercial Law Quarterly* 23(4), 15.

Gutteridge, H C, 'Contracts and Commercial Law' (1935) *Law Quarterly Review* 91.

Howard, M, 'Contracts Expressly Providing for Further Agreement' (1977) *Otago Law Review* 4, 14.

103 *R V Ward Ltd v Bignall* [1967] 1 QB 534, interpreting s 48 of the *Sale of Goods Act 1893*, which concerned resale by unpaid sellers of goods, and addressing the difficulties raised by and concluding that *Gallagher v Shilcock* [1949] 2 KB 765 was wrongly decided, correcting the difficulties created by that case.

7

AGENCY LAW

7.0 Introduction

This chapter covers the common law of agency in Australia. Agency is a legal relationship of great utility in commercial life. In essence, an agent acts on behalf of another person, known as the principal, in order to achieve things that the principal finds difficult or inconvenient to do themselves.[1] The chapter deals with the definition of an agent, the law pertaining to the formation of an agency relationship, the duties of the agent and the principal, and the liability of agents and principals to third parties.

7.1 Agency

The legal concept of agency exists because commercial convenience demands that it must exist. It is impracticable for a principal to attend directly to all commercial matters that arise in the course of their business. Accordingly, some responsibilities must be delegated to agents who can then manage the affairs of the principal. As Professor Tan has noted, an agency relationship has the practical effect of multiplying the legal personality of the principal.[2] There are three primary players in the agency relationship. The first is the agent, who acts on behalf of the principal. The second is the principal, who needs an agent in order to perform certain tasks. The third is the third party with whom the agent deals on behalf of the principal. Generally, an agent will have the capacity to bind a principal in contract with a third party.[3] In return, the agent will owe a fiduciary duty to the principal.[4]

The term 'agent' is often used in commercial life and its overuse is apt to mislead.[5] In *International Harvester Co of Australia Pty Ltd v Carrigan's Hazeldene Pastoral Co*,[6] the High Court stated that agency is 'a word used in law to connote an authority or capacity in one person to create legal relations between a person occupying the position of principal and third parties'.[7] Similarly, in *Petersen v Moloney*,[8] the High Court stated that an agent is 'a person who is able, by virtue of authority conferred upon him, to create or affect legal rights and duties as between another person, who is called his principal, and third parties'.[9]

An agency relationship is invariably created by consent.[10] In *Garnac Grain Co Inc v H M F Faure & Fairclough Ltd*,[11] Lord Pearson stated:

1 A J Kerr, *The Law of Agency* (Butterworths, Durban, 3rd edn, 1993).
2 C-H Tan, 'Unauthorised Agency in English Law' in D Busch and L J Macgregor (eds), *The Unauthorised Agent: Perspectives from European and Comparative Law* (Cambridge University Press, Cambridge, UK, 2009).
3 *International Harvester Co of Australia Pty Ltd v Carrigan's Hazeldene Pastoral Co* (1958) 100 CLR 644. See also *Australian Competition and Consumer Commission v Flight Centre Travel Group Ltd* (2016) 261 CLR 203.
4 F M B Reynolds, *Bowstead & Reynolds on Agency* (Sweet & Maxwell, London, 18th edn, 2006), [1–001]. See also *Hospital Products Ltd v United States Surgical Corporation* (1984) 156 CLR 41, 71–2.
5 *Scott v Davis* (2000) 204 CLR 333, 338; *Colonial Mutual Life Assurance Society Ltd v Producers & Citizens Co-operative Assurance Co of Australia Ltd* (1931) 46 CLR 41, 50.
6 (1958) 100 CLR 644.
7 (1958) 100 CLR 644, 652.
8 (1951) 84 CLR 91.
9 (1951) 84 CLR 91, 94. See also *Perpetual Trustee Co Ltd v Burniston [No 2]* (2012) 271 FLR 122.
10 *Tonto Home Loans Australia Pty Ltd v Tavares* (2011) 15 BPR 29,699; *Alliance Craton Explorer Pty Ltd v Quasar Resources Pty Ltd* (2013) 296 ALR 465.
11 [1968] AC 1130.

> The relationship of principal and agent can only be established by the consent of the principal and the agent. They will be held to have consented if they have agreed to what amounts at law to such a relationship, even if they do not recognise it themselves and even if they have professed to disclaim it ... But the consent must have been given by each of them either expressly or by implication from their words and conduct.[12]

In *Branwhite v Worcester Works Finance Ltd*,[13] Lord Wilberforce made a similar point, stating:

> [W]hile agency must ultimately derive from consent, the consent need not necessarily be to the relationship of principal and agent itself (indeed, the existence of it may be denied), but may be to a state of fact upon which the law imposes the consequences which result from agency.[14]

The one exception to the rule regarding consent is the doctrine of agency of necessity, which is discussed below, wherein an 'agent' may act on behalf of a principal in an emergency situation. Both the agent and the principal must have legal personality in order for an agency relationship to be established. A person will not be regarded to be an agent under the law simply because that person and the alleged principal declare that person to be the 'agent'.[15] Similarly, an agency relationship can exist even where the parties to that relationship have expressly declared that there is no agency.[16] That is, the question of whether an agency relationship exists is a question of substance rather than of form.[17] In *Sran v Minister for Immigration*,[18] Nichols J stated: '[W]hether an agency relationship is constituted is to be assessed having regard to what can be said to be the "nature" of the agreement between the alleged principal and the purported agent, or even the exact circumstances of the relationship, rather than simply just having regard to the "language" used by them.'[19] In *International Harvester*, the High Court articulated the importance of focusing on the substance of the relationship in assessing whether it is one of agency or not:

> Agency is a word used in the law to connote an authority or capacity in one person to create legal relations between a person occupying the position of principal and third parties. But in the business world its significance is by no means thus restricted. In *W.T. Lamb and Sons v. Goring Brick Co. Ltd.* (1932) 1 KB 710 the agreement under the consideration of the Court of Appeal was described by Scrutton L.J. thus 'By this particular agreement the respondents, therein called the "manufacturers", the makers of the bricks, appoint the "merchants", the buyers of the bricks from them and sellers of the bricks to builders and contractors, "sole selling agents of all bricks and other materials manufactured at their works" (1932) 1 KB, at p 717'. Greer L.J. was led by this language to say 'It is somewhat remarkable that, notwithstanding the numerous cases in which the difference

12 [1968] AC 1130, 1137.
13 [1969] 1 AC 552.
14 [1969] 1 AC 552, 587. See also *Re Victoria Station Corporation Pty Ltd (admins apptd)* (2018) 56 VR 26.
15 *Beazely v Seed & Grain Sales Moree Pty Ltd* (1988) 4 BPR 9,529.
16 *South Sydney District Rugby League Football Club Ltd v News Ltd* (2000) 177 ALR 611.
17 *South Sydney District Rugby League Football Club Ltd v News Ltd* (2000) 177 ALR 611; *International Harvester Co of Australia Pty Ltd v Carrigan's Hazeldene Pastoral Co* (1958) 100 CLR 644; *Petersen v Moloney* (1951) 84 CLR 91.
18 (2014) 283 FLR 391.
19 (2014) 283 FLR 391, [50].

> between a buyer and an agent has been pointed out, there are still innumerable persons engaged in business who do not understand the simple and logical distinction between a buyer and agent for sale, but are content to treat the two words as synonymous. However, I can only read this contract as meaning that the manufacturers undertake, as they say in par. 3, to supply goods to the persons whom they call "selling agents" in return for the price mentioned in par. 2' (1932) 1 KB, at p 720. But as Lord Herschell said in a much quoted observation[:] 'No word is more commonly and constantly abused than the word "agent". A person may be spoken of as an "agent", and no doubt in the popular sense of the word may properly be said to be an "agent", although when it is attempted to suggest that he is an "agent" under such circumstances as create the legal obligations attaching to agency that use of the word is only misleading.'[20]

In the case of *International Harvester*, the respondent was advised by the appellant at an agricultural show to deal with their 'agent', Hassan Co, in Gunnedah if they wished to buy a hay baler that the appellant had manufactured. The respondent duly contacted Hassan Co and arranged to buy a hay baler. The agreement between Carrigan's and Hassan for the hay baler included an express warranty. There were difficulties in operating the machine and Carrigan's eventually sued on the basis of the express warranty. In their suit, Carrigan's claimed that Hassans were the agents of International Harvester. The High Court disagreed, pointing out that the mere use of the term 'agent' did not make the relationship between Hassan and International Harvester one of agency. Instead, International Harvester manufactured the machines and sold them to Hassan who then resold them in its own right.

In *Petersen v Moloney*,[21] an estate agent was instructed to find a purchaser for the house of a homeowner. The estate agent found the purchaser and thereafter received from him the purchase monies for the house. After the contract was completed and the purchaser was installed as the registered proprietor, the vendor brought a suit claiming payment of the unpaid purchase price. Unbeknown to the purchaser, the estate agent had no authority to collect the purchase money and had not passed on the money he had received to the vendor. The High Court found that there was no evidence in the dealings between the parties to suggest that the estate agent had the authority to receive money on behalf of the vendor. As such, the High Court's ruling in *Petersen v Moloney* illustrates that an agency relationship that exists with respect to one particular purpose does not necessarily extend to other purposes and activities.[22]

Recent cases have demonstrated the importance of focusing on the substance of the relationship between the parties in order to determine that an agency relationship exists. In *Perpetual Trustees Australia Ltd v Schmidt*,[23] the respondent was induced by a conman to invest in property developments. In order to finance the investments, the respondent, Schmidt, sought a loan from Perpetual Trustee Australia. Three intermediaries were involved in procuring the loan. Schmidt claimed in part that one of the intermediaries, Violet Home Loans Australia Pty Ltd (VHLA), acted unconscionably and was the agent of Perpetual Trustees. In assessing the matter, Forrest J found that VHLA effectively acted as agent for Perpetual Trustees

20 (1958) 100 CLR 644, 652.
21 (1951) 84 CLR 91.
22 See also *Rockcote Enterprises Pty Ltd v F S Architects Pty Ltd* [2008] NSWCA 39.
23 [2010] VSC 67.

by finding loan applicants and preparing loan applications. Moreover, VHLA assumed further responsibilities on Perpetual Trustees' behalf after the loan was granted. Forrest J stated:

> The totality of the relationship demonstrates that VHLA was, in truth, the agent of Perpetual. VHLA sought out the borrower and ensured that the documentation was in order and in compliance with the parameters (which included the provision of at least one document addressed directly to Perpetual). It was, unlike an independent contractor, required to comply with directions given by Perpetual ... The loan contract, and its administration, I think, exposed the true nature of the relationship and the one that subsisted in fact. Once it was entered into by the borrower, VHLA handled, on behalf of Perpetual, all aspects of the management of the loan repayments, accounts, statements, and any defaults.[24]

In *South Sydney District Rugby League Football Club v News Limited*,[25] an agency relationship was found to exist between the National Rugby League (NRL) and a News Limited subsidiary despite express statements to the contrary. Finn J noted that while there could be genuine reasons as to why parties might seek to avoid an agency relationship, the courts would have to have regard to the substance of the commercial relationship rather than the form. On this point, Finn J noted that 'it is difficult to conceive of a relationship of purportedly independent parties that involves so great a degree of dominance by one and subservience by the other'.[26] Fundamentally, substance triumphs over form in agency law.[27] The true question is then whether the substance of the relationship manifests a consent between the parties to an agency relationship. Finn J stated:

> The consents so given need not necessarily be to a relationship that the parties understand, or even accept, to be that of principal and agent. It is sufficient if 'they have agreed to what amounts in law to such a relationship'; notwithstanding that they may have 'artfully disguised' it by express disclaimers.
>
> It is legitimate for parties to avoid the 'unwanted consequences' of a particular category of legal relationship by seeking to cast it in a form that takes it outside that category of relationship. But whether or not they are successful in achieving that end does not depend simply upon whether, in an express provision of their agreement, they attribute or deny to their relationship a particular legal character – be this, for example, employer and employee[,] principal and principal[,] or principal and agent or partners. The parties cannot by the mere device of labelling, no matter how genuinely intentioned, either confer a particular legal character on a relationship that it does not possess or deny it a character that it does possess.[28]

Professor Dal Pont has stipulated that the following aspects are key to an agency relationship:

> There are at least two essential elements of an agency relationship: the *consent* (or assent) of both principal and agent; and the *authority* given to the agent by the principal to act on

24 [2010] VSC 67, [154].
25 (2000) 177 ALR 611.
26 (2000) 177 ALR 611, [155].
27 *Technology Leasing Ltd v Lennmar Pty Ltd* [2012] FCA 709.
28 (2000) 177 ALR 611, [133]–[134].

the principal's behalf. A third element found in some conceptions of an agency relationship is the principal's *control* over the agent's actions.[29]

In the following sections, the issue of authority is explored with regard to actual authority, actual implied authority and ostensible authority. Similarly, even where authority does not initially exist it might later be found to exist through the subsequent conduct of the principal.

7.2 Actual authority

There are two main forms of actual authority in agency law: (1) actual express authority; and (2) actual implied authority. The fundamental inquiry at issue within actual authority concerns the scope of authority under the agency relationship rather than whether the relationship exists or not. This depends upon the nature of the consent provided by both the principal and the agent. In *Equiticorp Finance Ltd (in liq) v Bank of New Zealand*,[30] Clarke and Cripps JJA stated: '[A]ctual authority arises where a principal grants, and an agent accepts, authority for the agent to perform specific tasks on behalf of the principal – in short there must be a consensual agreement between the principal and the agent.'[31] Consent is the basis for actual authority. The consent can be drawn from the express words used by the parties in a contract, a set of instructions, a verbal exchange or from some other document. In *Poulet Frais Pty Ltd v The Silver Fox Co Ltd*[32] the Full Federal Court stated: 'Actual authority requires the consent of both the principal and the agent but the manifestation of consent may be express or implied.'[33]

7.2.1 Actual express authority

In a situation of actual express authority, the principal will directly grant authority to the agent to perform certain acts. Both the agent and the principal will be aware of the actual express authority. The consent underpinning the authority will most likely be set out in some written form. Ordinarily, the terms of the actual express authority will be set out in a contract between the parties. For example, if P agrees to a contract with A stipulating that A will find buyers on P's behalf, then the parties have agreed to an agency relationship. The subsequent actions of A in attempting to find buyers on P's behalf will probably fall within the actual express authority as set out in the contract. Whether every given act of A falls within this authority may depend upon the construction of the contract.[34]

7.2.2 Actual implied authority

Actual implied authority is the second form of actual authority. As with actual express authority, actual implied authority arises from the consent of the principal to the actions of

29 G Dal Pont, *Law of Agency* (LexisNexis Butterworths Australia, Sydney, 2nd edn, 2008), 4.04.
30 (1993) 32 NSWLR 50.
31 (1993) 32 NSWLR 50, [132].
32 (2005) 220 ALR 211.
33 (2005) 220 ALR 211, [124].
34 *Codelfa Construction Pty Ltd v State Rail Authority of New South Wales* (1982) 149 CLR 337.

the agent.[35] However, the consent is not expressly stated, but is instead manifested from the actions of the parties or as a necessary implication drawn from the terms of their agreement.[36] In cases where actual implied authority arises as a matter in dispute, a court must examine the conduct of the parties and draw the relevant inferences from that conduct.[37] In *Equiticorp*, Clarke and Cripps JJA stated: '[W]here the question is whether the agent has implied authority to act in a particular way the court directs its attention to the conduct of the parties in order to decide whether the inference of authority should be drawn.'[38]

In *Freeman & Lockyer v Buckhurst Park Properties (Mangal) Ltd*,[39] a director of a company acted in the position of manager even though he had not been appointed to that role. The other directors were aware of his actions and raised no objections. The director then engaged some architects to undertake work. When the architects sought payment, the other directors protested that the director had no relevant authority. The court found that the director had both actual implied authority and ostensible authority. Diplock LJ stated:

> An 'actual' authority is a legal relationship between principal and agent created by a consensual agreement to which they alone are parties. Its scope is to be ascertained by applying ordinary principles of construction of contracts, including any proper implications from the express words used, the usages of the trade, or the course of business between the parties. To this agreement the contractor is a stranger; he may be totally ignorant of the existence of any authority on the part of the agent. Nevertheless, if the agent does enter into a contract pursuant to the 'actual' authority, it does create contractual rights and liabilities between the principal and the contractor.[40]

As Diplock LJ noted, where actual implied authority is concerned the court's focus must be on the relationship between the agent and the principal. The effect that the principal's conduct has on the third party, which is a crucial factor in ostensible authority, is of far less relevance when considering actual implied authority.

In *Hely-Hutchinson v Brayhead Ltd*, Richards was a director of Brayhead Ltd. It was alleged that he acted as the company's de facto managing director and committed it to a contract with Hely-Hutchinson. Richards frequently made decisions without seeking the authority of the board of directors but would later inform them of his actions. The board of directors of Brayhead knew of Richards' conduct, but whenever it had arisen they had failed to discipline him.

Ultimately, Richards signed some letters that created obligations that the company did not want to honour. In the Court of Appeal, it was found that Richards had actual implied authority. The court said this authority arose because of his past dealings. In this case, the board of directors had acquiesced to Richards committing the company to contracts without checking with the board and later just informing the board at meetings. This created actual implied authority. Lord Denning stated:

35 *Hely-Hutchinson v Brayhead Ltd* [1968] 1 QB 549.

36 *Crabtree-Vickers Pty Ltd v Australian Direct Mail Advertising & Addressing Co Pty Ltd* (1975) 133 CLR 72. See also *Powercor Australia Ltd v Pacific Power* [1999] VSC 110.

37 *Hely-Hutchinson v Brayhead Ltd* [1968] 1 QB 549; *Bank of New Zealand v Fiberi Pty Ltd* (1992) 8 ACSR 790.

38 (1993) 32 NSWLR 50, [132].

39 [1964] 2 QB 480.

40 [1964] 2 QB 480, 502.

> [A]ctual authority may be express or implied. It is express when it is given by express words, such as when a board of directors pass a resolution which authorises two of their number to sign cheques. It is implied when it is inferred from the conduct of the parties and the circumstances of the case, such as when the board of directors appoint one of their number to be managing director. They thereby impliedly authorise him to do all such things as fall within the usual scope of that office. Actual authority, express or implied, is binding as between the company and the agent, and also as between the company and others, whether they are within the company or outside it . . .
>
> Apply these principles here. It is plain that Mr. Richards had no express authority to enter into these two contracts on behalf of the company: nor had he any such authority implied from the nature of his office. He had been duly appointed chairman of the company but that office in itself did not carry with it authority to enter into these contracts without the sanction of the board. But I think he had authority implied from the conduct of the parties and the circumstances of the case. The judge did not rest his decision on implied authority, but I think his findings necessarily carry that consequence. The judge finds that Mr. Richards acted as de facto managing director of Brayhead. He was the chief executive who made the final decision on any matter concerning finance. He often committed Brayhead to contracts without the knowledge of the board and reported the matter afterwards.[41]

What matters with actual implied authority is that the consent is manifested over a period of time. Cases such as *Freeman* and *Hely Hutchinson v Brayhead* contain situations wherein the actions of the agent are initially unauthorised, but over time the principal's continued acquiescence demonstrates a real consent to the requisite level of authority.

In her treatment of agency law, Traves suggests that there are four types of actual implied authority: incidental authority, usual authority, customary authority, and that which is established by the conduct of the principal and the agent.[42] The terms 'usual authority' and 'customary authority' are often used interchangeably.[43] 'Usual authority' connotes the level of authority that is generally conferred upon a person acting in a particular position within a given field of commerce.[44] Whereas Traves suggests that incidental authority falls under the aegis of actual implied authority, Fisher suggests that implied authority, also known as incidental authority, is a separate category of authority.[45] Whether the distinction between actual implied authority and incidental authority is of much consequence is another matter altogether. Nonetheless, it would appear that Traves offers the better view on the matter, as incidental authority is after all authority genuinely conferred upon the agent by the principal, but which has not been expressly stated. It must then be implied from the express statement of authority.

41 [1968] 1 QB 549, 584.
42 S Traves, *Commercial Law* (LexisNexis Butterworths Australia, Sydney, 4th edn, 2016), 82–4.
43 S Fisher, *Agency Law* (Butterworths, Sydney, 2000), 37.
44 *Watteau v Fenwick* [1893] 1 QB 346.
45 See S Traves, *Commercial Law* (LexisNexis Butterworths Australia, Sydney, 4th edn, 2016), 82–4 and S Fisher, *Agency Law* (Butterworths, Sydney, 2000), 38.

7.3 Ostensible authority

Ostensible authority is sometimes referred to as apparent authority or agency by estoppel. The latter term reflects the estoppel concept that informs the doctrine of ostensible authority. It is a well-established rule that where a principal represents to a third party that an agent has authority to act on behalf of the principal, and the third party, in reliance of that representation, alters their position through dealings with the agent, the principal will be bound to the third party.[46] In effect, the principal is estopped from resiling from the representation that they have made where to do so would result in some detriment to the third party.[47]

The essential principle is that clear statements made in a commercial context should bind the principal where they invite and occasion reliance. In *Technology Leasing Ltd v Lennmar Pty Ltd*,[48] Cowdroy J stated: '[T]he doctrine of ostensible authority is related to estoppel, in the sense that it is intended to prevent parties from acting inconsistently with representations they have made about another's authority that others have relied upon to their detriment.'[49] Similarly, in *Thanakharn Kasikorn Thai Chamkat (Mahachon) v Akai Holdings Ltd (in liq)*,[50] Lord Neuberger stated: 'In a commercial context, absent dishonesty or irrationality, a person should be entitled to rely on what he is told: this may occasionally produce harsh results, but it enables people engaged in business to know where they stand.'[51]

A simple illustration of an ostensible authority situation would occur where a principal in company X has represented through words or conduct that an agent has a level of authority that is higher than that which really exists. A third party who seeks to deal with company X might then conduct business with that agent in reliance of that representation. Having then concluded a contract with the agent between themselves and company X the third party would then seek to enforce the contract. If company X believes that the contract is unfavourable it may seek to deny it. This would cause obvious detriment to the third party who may have foregone other opportunities. Provided that there are no rules in the articles of incorporation of company X strictly forbidding the agent's conduct, then it is likely that the third party can hold company X to the contract. In *Freeman and Lockyer v Buckhurst Park Properties (Mangal) Ltd*,[52] Lord Diplock stated:

> If the foregoing analysis of the relevant law is correct, it can be summarised by stating four conditions which must be fulfilled to entitle a contractor to enforce against a company a contract entered into on behalf of the company by an agent who had no actual authority to do so. It must be shown: (a) that a representation that the agent had authority to enter on behalf of the company into a contract of the kind sought to be enforced was made to the contractor; (b) that such representation was made by a person or persons who had

46 *Hely-Hutchinson v Brayhead Ltd* [1968] 1 QB 549; *Crabtree-Vickers Pty Ltd v Australian Direct Mail Advertising & Addressing Co Pty Ltd* (1975) 133 CLR 72.

47 *Bishopsgate Motor Finance Corporation Ltd v Transport Brakes Ltd* [1949] 1 KB 322; *Fry v Smellie* [1912] 3 KB 282.

48 [2012] FCA 709.

49 [2012] FCA 709, [149].

50 [2010] HKCFA 64.

51 [2010] HKCFA 64, [52]–[62]. See also *LNOC Ltd v Watford Association Football Club Ltd* [2013] EWHC 3615 (Comm); *Newcastle International Airport v Eversheds* [2013] PNLR 5.

52 [1964] 2 QB 480.

> 'actual' authority to manage the business of the company either generally or in respect of those matters to which the contract relates; (c) that he [the contractor] was induced by such representation to enter into the contract, i.e., that he in fact relied on it; and (d) that under its memorandum or articles of association the company was not deprived of the capacity either to enter into a contract of the kind sought to be enforced or to delegate authority to enter into a contract of that kind to the agent.[53]

In many respects, ostensible authority is an unavoidable feature of commercial life. It will not always be practicable for an agent to check with their principal as to whether a particular transaction is expressly authorised. The extent of an agent's authority might become blurred, as their authority might grow the longer they are employed by a principal as an agent. Moreover, an agent might knowingly exceed the limits of their authority in good faith so as to allow the agent's principal to gain the benefit of an advantageous transaction.[54] Similarly, a third party will not always be able to check with the principal as to whether the agent has in fact been conferred with the level of authority that they appear to possess.

7.3.1 General principles of ostensible authority

There are three elements to ostensible authority. The first element is that there must be a representation from the principal to the third party in relation to the agent's authority.[55] A representation can be manifested in a number of ways such as words, conduct, job title or a course of dealings.[56] The second element is that there must be reliance on the part of the third party.[57] This reliance must be genuine.[58] The third party should not be wilfully blind to any indications that the agent might not have the authority that they at first appeared to possess.[59] In *Pourzand v Telstra Corporation Ltd*,[60] McLure P stated: '[T]here can be no reasonable reliance when the circumstances are such as to put a person on inquiry as to whether the agent has the relevant authority.'[61] The third element is that the third party must have suffered some detriment.[62] The detriment may be as simple as signing a contract, as this would represent undertaking a legally binding obligation and would also result in the third party forgoing the opportunity of contracting elsewhere.[63]

53 [1964] 2 QB 480, 502.

54 C-H Tan, 'Unauthorised Agency in English Law' in D Busch and L J Macgregor (eds), *The Unauthorised Agent: Perspectives from European and Comparative Law* (Cambridge University Press, Cambridge, UK, 2009), 187.

55 *Pacific Carriers Ltd v BNP Paribas* (2004) 218 CLR 451; *Attorney-General (Ceylon) v Silva* [1953] AC 461. See also *Williams Group Australia Pty Ltd v Crocker* [2016] NSWCA 265.

56 *Egyptian International Foreign Trade Co v Soplex Wholesale Supplies Ltd ('The Raffaella')* [1985] 2 Lloyd's Rep 36; *British Bank of the Middle East v Sun Life Assurance of Canada (UK) Ltd* [1983] 2 Lloyd's Rep 9. Reproduced with permission of Informa Law, London.

57 *Rama Corporation Ltd v Proved Tin & General Investments Ltd* [1952] 2 QB 147.

58 *Armagas Ltd v Mundogas SA* [1986] 1 AC 717; *Tipperary Developments Pty Ltd v Western Australia* [2009] WASCA 126; *Pourzand v Telstra Corporation Ltd* [2014] WASCA 14, [84].

59 *Lysaght Brothers & Co Ltd v Falk* (1905) 2 CLR 421; *Alliance & Leicester Building Society v Edgestop Ltd* [1993] 1 WLR 1462; *Cavenagh Investment Pte Ltd v Kaushik Rajiv* [2013] 2 SLR 543.

60 [2014] WASCA 14.

61 [2014] WASCA 14, [84].

62 *Arctic Shipping Co Ltd v Mobilia AB ('The Tatra')* [1990] 2 Lloyd's Rep 51.

63 *Arctic Shipping Co Ltd v Mobilia AB ('The Tatra')* [1990] 2 Lloyd's Rep 51.

A fundamental limitation applies to ostensible authority in that an agent cannot self-authorise.[64] However, it is possible that an agent who does not have the authority to complete a particular act may have the authority to convey the principal's consent as to that act.[65] As will be discussed below, the English Court of Appeal's decision in *First Energy (UK) Ltd v Hungarian International Bank* seems to run a fine line between respecting this limitation and advancing the proposition that an agent may make an 'assisted representation'.[66] The Singapore Supreme Court of Appeal in *Skandinaviska Enskilda Banken AB (Publ), Singapore Branch v Asia Pacific Breweries (Singapore) Pte Ltd*[67] delivered a stern rebuke to the decision in *First Energy*. Similarly, other cases that have considered *First Energy* have invariably confined it to its peculiar facts; this underlines the fundamental limitation on the ability of an agent to make representations as to their own authority.

7.3.2 Representation

The principal must make a representation to the third party, or to a class of persons to whom the third party belongs, that the agent has a certain level of authority.[68] This representation may take a variety of forms. In *Freeman*, Diplock LJ stated:

> The representation which creates 'apparent' authority may take a variety of forms of which the commonest is representation by conduct, i.e., by permitting the agent to act in some way in the conduct of the principal's business with other persons. By so doing the principal represents to anyone who becomes aware that the agent is so acting that the agent has authority to enter on behalf of the principal into contracts with other persons of the kind which an agent so acting in the conduct of his principal's business has normally 'actual' authority to enter into.[69]

The representation can be made by words, conduct, course of dealings, description, silence, or by the principal equipping the agent with the accoutrements of authority such as a job title and facilities.[70] In *Prospect Industries*, an issue arose as to whether the possession of a business card amounted to a representation. In that case, the agent had made it plain to the third party that he no longer represented the alleged principal and in fact he had crossed out the principal's details on the front of the card and written his new contact details on the back of the business card.

The principal does not need to intend that the representation will be relied upon by the third party.[71] That is, the principal may be negligent in making the representation.[72] In such a situation, the actions of the principal and surrounding circumstances would be such that the

64 *Armagas Ltd v Mundogas SA* [1986] 1 AC 717.

65 *Egyptian International Foreign Trade Co v Soplex Wholesale Supplies Ltd ('The Raffaella')* [1985] 2 Lloyd's Rep 36. Reproduced with permission of Informa Law, London.

66 [1993] 2 Lloyd's Rep 194. Reproduced with permission of Informa Law, London.

67 [2011] 3 SLR 540.

68 *International Paper Co v Spicer* (1906) 4 CLR 739. See also *Brown v Tavern Operator Pty Ltd* (2018) 98 NSWLR 586.

69 [1964] 2 QB 480, 503–4.

70 *Pacific Carriers Ltd v BNP Paribas* (2004) 218 CLR 451; *Egyptian International Foreign Trade Co v Soplex Wholesale Supplies Ltd ('The Raffaella')* [1985] 2 Lloyd's Rep 36, reproduced with permission of Informa Law, London; *British Bank of the Middle East v Sun Life Assurance of Canada (UK) Ltd* [1983] 2 Lloyd's Rep 9; *Prospect Industries Pty Ltd v Anscor Pty Ltd* [2003] QSC 296.

71 *Pacific Carriers Ltd v BNP Paribas* (2004) 218 CLR 451.

72 *Essington Investments Pty Ltd v Regency Property Pty Ltd* [2004] NSWCA 375.

principal's actions or statements will amount to a representation. An element of knowledge may very well be required in such circumstances. For example, in *Freeman & Lockyer*, the company was well aware of the actions of its director, but never raised any objections. In contrast, in *Pacific Carriers v BNP Paribas*, the bank was unaware of what its senior officer had specifically done, but it was aware that she was in a position to use the company seal and to deal with third parties. Any private instructions given by the principal that might limit the authority of the agent will have no effect on the question of ostensible authority unless they are known by the third party.

Fundamentally, the question that has to be addressed is whether the principal has held out the agent as having the requisite level of authority so as to justify the third party's subsequent dealings with that agent. That is, the holding out must be sufficient enough to constitute a representation. In the section below, two primary ways in which a representation may be made are discussed. The category of representations is not closed.

7.3.2.1 Representation from a course of dealings

The representation upon which the third party relies can arise from a course of dealings. In *Armagas Ltd v Mundogas SA*,[73] Lord Keith of Kinkel stated: '[O]stensible general authority may also arise where the agent has had a course of dealing with a particular contractor and the principal has acquiesced in this course of dealing and honoured transactions arising out of it.'[74] Lord Keith's obiter remark raises the possibility that a representation can be drawn from the principal's conduct over a period of time. That is, if the principal knows that the agent is acting beyond their authority in their dealings with the third party, but ratifies each dealing, then eventually this conduct can form a representation to the third party as to the substance of the agent's authority. There is an obvious overlap here between actual implied authority and ostensible authority. Provided that the third party never learns that the agent lacks authority prior to entering into an agreement procured by the agent on the principal's behalf, then the third party can justifiably claim that the principal's actions amount to a representation.

In *Darrell McGregor (Contractor) Ltd v Mountain Lake Holdings Ltd*,[75] the appellant was hired by the respondent to work on a proposed development. The appellant did work at the behest of a company known as PL Design Ltd, which had been tasked by the respondent with the development. The appellant was ultimately not awarded a contract by the respondent and subsequently refused to remove fill from the development site. The fill had been placed there on the instructions of Mr Lewis of PL Design Ltd. The respondent had to remove the fill at its own expense and sued the appellant to recover its costs. The appellant argued that Mr Lewis had ostensible authority to act on behalf of the respondent. The court found that the course of dealings between the respondent and PL Design Ltd, wherein the latter was allowed to carry on a range of dealings with third party contractors in relation to the development, was sufficient to amount to a representation.

73 [1986] 1 AC 717.
74 [1986] 1 AC 717, 777.
75 [2006] NZHC 591.

7.3.2.2 Representation arising from a job title, holding a particular office or other indicia of authority

A representation can be manifested from a job title or office. A certain level of authority may be imputed to a person who holds a particular position within an organisation. A third party may rely on the appearance of authority created by the job title or position. In *British Bank of the Middle East v Sun Life Assurance of Canada (UK) Ltd*,[76] the principal's decision to provide its employee with the title of 'branch manager' was deemed sufficient to be a representation as to authority. It is important to keep in mind that the third party is not privy to the inner workings of the principal's company and thus will be unaware of any limitations on the agent's authority. A course of conduct taken by the principal can strengthen the representation that is said to flow from the agent's occupancy of a particular position.

There are three cases that quite neatly illustrate the possibility that a representation might arise from a job title, particular office or other similar conduct. The first case is that of *Pacific Carriers v BNP Paribas*,[77] where an agent of the respondent signed letters of indemnity in her capacity as a senior bank officer. The holding out by BNP Paribas was found to arise from the decision to let her sign the letters. BNP Paribas had a client, known as the New England Agricultural Trading Company (NEAT). NEAT hired Pacific Carrier to transport a shipment of legumes from Australia to India. NEAT was required by Pacific Carriers to provide it with a letter of indemnity. NEAT sought this letter from BNP Paribas. At first, Paribas rejected this request. However, Ms Dhiri, a senior officer at BNP Paribas, signed two letters of indemnity as a witness to the signatures of NEAT officers. In doing so, she affixed the bank's seal. As a result, it would have appeared to a third party that she was signing as an officer of BNP Paribas rather than as a witness. Pacific subsequently suffered a loss and sought to enforce the indemnity against BNP Paribas. The dispute reached the High Court, which found the respondent to be liable for ostensible authority. The High Court stated:

> The importance to a third party, such as Pacific, of the difference between a bank's signature to a letter of indemnity in the capacity of an indemnifying party, and a bank's signature by way of verification of the signature of another party, should have been, and was, obvious to Mr Ryan (although he was not personally involved in this transaction), Mr Kavanagh, and Ms Dhiri. They all accepted, in their evidence, the importance that attached to the capacity in which the bank was lending its name to the documents. Ms Dhiri was the natural and appropriate person to whom Pacific's request for signature of the documents by the bank was directed. If the role of the bank was to be merely that of authentication of NEAT's signature, then she was also the appropriate person to sign and stamp the documents on behalf of the bank. If the role of the bank was to be that of an indemnifying party, she was not the appropriate person. There were no procedures within BNP under which she was to seek legal advice about the manner and form of BNP's signature, or take other steps to see that it was communicated to Pacific that the only role the bank was willing to undertake was one of authentication. She was placed in a position to sign and stamp the documents, and send them to NEAT and Pacific, but

76 [1983] 2 Lloyd's Rep 9.
77 (2004) 218 CLR 451.

> without any internal check upon their final form and, in particular, without any qualification or limitation of the capacity in which the bank was participating in the transaction.[78]

The failure of BNP Paribas to put in place safeguards concerning Ms Dhiri's signature was fatal to their case. In *BNP Paribas*, the High Court effectively found the respondent liable for the foreseeable consequences of their agent's actions in signing the letters. The use of the company's seal gave the letter a sign of authority. This seal, coupled with Ms Dhiri's position within the organisation, amounted to a representation of authority. It was particularly significant that Ms Dhiri was an officer of the bank who appeared to have the authority to deal with matters such as those raised by NEAT and Pacific Carriers by dint of her position in the bank. By arming her with the company's seal and a position in which she could deal with matters such as those pertaining to the letters of indemnity, BNP Paribas had effectively held out Ms Dhiri as having the authority to bind it in such matters.

In the case of *Egyptian International Foreign Trade Co v Soplex Wholesale Supplies Ltd* (*'The Raffaella'*),[79] a letter of guarantee signed by an agent was held to bind a principal as the agent had been held out as being a manager that could handle matters of this nature. The letter had been produced by the agent after several days of negotiation at the bank's premises. The letter contained the bank's seal and the signature of the agent. The agent in question in *The Raffaella* held the job description of manager of the documentary credits department. Browne-Wilkinson LJ stated:

> It is important to bear in mind that the doctrine of holding out is a form of estoppel. As such, the starting point is that the principal must be shown to have made a representation, which the third party could and did reasonably rely on, that the agent had the necessary authority. The relevant enquiry, therefore, in all cases is whether the acts of the principal constitute a representation that the agent had a particular authority and were reasonably so understood by the third party. This requires the court to consider the principal's conduct *as a whole*. In many cases, the holding out or representation by the company consists solely of the fact that the company has invested the agent with a particular office, e.g., 'managing director' or 'secretary' . . . where, as in the present case, the holding out is alleged to consist of a course of conduct wider than merely describing the agent as holding a particular office, although the authority normally found in the holder of such an office is very material, it must be looked at as part and parcel of the whole course of the principal's conduct in order to decide whether the totality of the principal's actions constitute a holding out of the agent as possessing the necessary authority.[80]

In *The Raffaella*, the principal had sought to argue that the job title of the agent alone could not support the alleged level of ostensible authority. This argument was unsuccessful because the Court of Appeal assessed the manager's job title in light of all the other relevant circumstances of the case. The remarks of Browne-Wilkinson LJ in *The Raffaella* suggest that the job title or other indicia of authority sets up the basis for finding a representation, but that there must be some other contributory conduct on the part of the principal to substantiate the actual representation. In *The Raffaella*, the agent had been granted authority to deal with the third

78 (2004) 218 CLR 451, [43].
79 [1985] 2 Lloyd's Rep 36. Reproduced with permission of Informa Law, London.
80 [1985] 2 Lloyd's Rep 36, 43. Reproduced with permission of Informa Law, London.

party on a wide range of matters, the letter was provided at the bank's premises, and the bank's seal was attached to the letter.

In *Prospect Industries v Anscor Pty Ltd*,[81] a third party unsuccessfully attempted to argue that the use of a business card by a putative agent bound the principal to a contract. In *Prospect Industries*, the agent in question had worked for the alleged principal in the past. However, at the time that he met Mr Hope, a director of the plaintiff company, he was engaged in part-time employment with the principal. However, when Woodrow, the alleged agent, met with Mr Hope he did not attend as a representative of the principal. At trial there was some disagreement about what took place at the meeting. In his decision, Phillippides J found that the business card had been proffered to Mr Hope, but that he understood that Woodrow and his companion were there representing ANZCorp. In particular, Phillippides J found that the fact that Hope had written 'ANZCORP' on the business card highlighted that understanding. Consequently, there was no holding out by the alleged principal.

7.3.3 Representation by an agent

As a general rule, an agent cannot self-authorise.[82] Any representation as to ostensible authority must emanate from the principal or someone authorised by the principal to delegate the requisite level of authority.[83] Nonetheless, it is possible that a principal may put the agent in a position to make the actual representation of authority by making other representations that make the agent's assertions seem credible. In *Crabtree-Vickers Pty Ltd v Australian Direct Mail Advertising & Addressing Co Pty Ltd*,[84] the High Court stated:

> There are circumstances where the actual representation of authority may be made by the agent but in such cases it will be found that the relevant representation is made by the principal (or by the person to whom the principal has given actual authority) either by a previous course of dealing or by putting the agent in a position or by allowing him to act in a position from which it can be inferred that his actual representation of authority in himself is in fact correct. It is therefore always necessary to look at the conduct of the principal (or the person to whom he has actually delegated authority).[85]

This line of reasoning has proved attractive in a handful of cases. It does stand to reason that a principal's representations that establish the credibility of a particular agent will reinforce any statement that the agent then makes to the third party. This is particularly true in light of the fact that the third party is not privy to the true level of authority conferred upon the agent by the principal. If a principal authorises an agent to make representations about a transaction, but not the authority to enter into the transaction, there is a real danger that the agent may

81 [2003] QSC 296.

82 *Armagas Ltd v Mundogas SA* [1986] 1 AC 717; *New Zealand Tenancy Bonds Ltd v Mooney* [1986] 1 NZLR 280, 284; *Attorney-General (Ceylon) v Silva* [1953] AC 461, 479; *Fay v Miller, Wilkins & Co* [1941] Ch 360, 365; *Freeman & Lockyer v Buckhurst Park Properties (Mangal) Ltd* [1964] 2 QB 480, 505; *Bankfield Farm Ltd v Hart & MacFarlane as Trustees of the Harvest Trust* [2009] NZCA 297.

83 *Freeman & Lockyer v Buckhurst Park Properties (Mangal) Ltd* [1964] 2 QB 480; *Australia & New Zealand Banking Group Ltd v Frenmast Pty Ltd* (2013) 282 FLR 351.

84 (1975) 133 CLR 72.

85 (1975) 133 CLR 72, 78.

represent that they have been authorised to enter into the transaction. In *The Raffaella*, Browne-Wilkinson LJ endorsed the idea of an assisted representation by the agent. This, in turn, set the stage for the English Court of Appeal's rather controversial decision in *First Energy (UK) Ltd v Hungarian International Bank*. In *The Raffaella*, Browne-Wilkinson LJ stated:

> It is obviously correct that an agent who has no actual or apparent authority either (a) to enter into a transaction or (b) to make representations as to the transaction cannot hold himself out as having authority to enter into the transaction so as to [a]ffect the principal's position. But, suppose a company confers actual or apparent authority on X to make representations and X erroneously represents to a third party that Y has authority to enter into a transaction; why should not such a representation be relied upon as part of the holding out of Y by the company? By parity of reasoning, if a company confers actual or apparent authority on A to make representations on the company's behalf but no actual authority on A to enter into the specific transaction, why should a representation made by A as to his authority not be capable of being relied on as one of the acts of holding out?[86]

Subsequently, in *Armagas*, the court expressed doubt as to the likelihood of a principal being bound to a transaction where the third party knew that the agent could not enter into the specific transaction, but where the agent could make representations about the transaction. Lord Keith of Kinkel stated:

> It must be a most unusual and peculiar case where an agent who is known to have no general authority to enter into transactions of a certain type can by reason of circumstances created by the principal reasonably be believed to have specific authority to enter into a particular transaction of that type.[87]

Subsequently, in *First Energy* the English Court of Appeal relied upon the obiter remarks in both *Armagas* and *The Raffaella* in finding a bank to be bound by the representations made by one of its branch managers.[88] First Energy was a company that specialised in heating systems. First Energy sought financing from Hungarian International Bank (HIB). First Energy was aware that Mr Jamison, the Manchester branch manager of HIB, had no authority to authorise the funding that it required and that he would need to seek the approval of HIB's head office in London. HIB granted First Energy an initial credit facility. First Energy then sought an additional facility. Mr Jamison wrote to First Energy offering the further facility. The head office of HIB subsequently decided that it would not provide further financing to First Energy. The English Court of Appeal found that Mr Jamison had the ostensible authority to communicate the purported decisions of the head office in London. In his decision, Steyn LJ reviewed the decisions of *Armagas* and *The Raffaella* and stated:

> It seems to me that the law recognises that in modern commerce an agent who has no apparent authority to conclude a particular transaction may sometimes be clothed with apparent authority to make representations of fact. The level at which such apparent authority could be found to exist may vary and generalisation will be unhelpful.[89]

86 [1985] 2 Lloyd's Rep 36, 43. Reproduced with permission of Informa Law, London.
87 [1986] 1 AC 717, 779.
88 [1993] 2 Lloyd's Rep 194, 203. Reproduced with permission of Informa Law, London.
89 [1993] 2 Lloyd's Rep 194, 204. Reproduced with permission of Informa Law, London.

It should be noted that Steyn LJ's characterisation of the actions of the plaintiff company, and its particular position of vulnerability as a third party, underpins his decision in *First Energy*. In the view of Steyn LJ, First Energy had acted honestly and reasonably. Steyn LJ stated:

> A theme that runs through our law of contract is that the reasonable expectations of honest men must be protected. It is not a rule or a principle of law. It is the objective which has been and still is the principal moulding force of our law of contract. It affords no licence to a judge to depart from binding precedent. On the other hand, if the prima facie solution to a problem runs counter to the reasonable expectations of honest men, this criterion sometimes requires a rigorous re-examination of the problem to ascertain whether the law does indeed compel demonstrable unfairness.[90]

This particular passage of Steyn LJ's decision has been quoted in a number of cases. However, the English Court of Appeal's holding in *First Energy* has repeatedly been noted and then distinguished on its facts by other courts in subsequent cases. This suggests that many courts view the decision in *First Energy* as somewhat troublesome. In *Kilcran, in the matter of Allco Finance Group Ltd (recs and mgrs apptd) (in liq) v Gothard*,[91] the Federal Court noted that the *First Energy* principle is 'very fact sensitive'.[92] Some support for *First Energy* emerged in *Kelly v Fraser*,[93] where Lord Sumption stated:

> It is clear from the judgments in *First Energy* that the Court of Appeal regarded their approach in that case as being wholly consistent with the law stated by Lord Keith in *Armagas Ltd v Mundogas SA*. In the Board's opinion, they were right to regard them as consistent. Lord Keith's speech remains the classic statement of the relevant legal principles. An agent cannot be said to have authority *solely* on the basis that he has held himself out as having it. It is, however, perfectly possible for the proper authorities of a company (or, for that matter, any other principal) to organise its affairs in such a way that subordinates who would not have authority to approve a transaction are nevertheless held out by those authorities as the persons who are to communicate to outsiders the fact that it has been approved by those who are authorised to approve it or that some particular agent has been duly authorised to approve it. These are representations which, if made by someone held out by the company to make representations of that kind, may give rise to an estoppel. Every case calls for a careful examination of its particular facts.[94]

However, in *Skandinaviska Enskilda Banken AB (Publ), Singapore Branch v Asia Pacific Breweries (Singapore) Pte Ltd*,[95] the Singapore Court of Appeal directly attacked the Court of Appeal's decision in *First Energy*. The case of *Skandinaviska v Asia Pacific Breweries* concerned an elaborate fraud perpetrated by a finance manager. Chia Teck Leng was the finance manager for the Singaporean subsidiary of Asia Pacific Breweries (APBS). APBS was a blue-chip company. Skandinaviska was a commercial bank. The Singapore branch of Skandinaviska (SEB) sought to establish a commercial relationship with APBS. Chia was an inveterate

90 [1993] 2 Lloyd's Rep 194, 196. Reproduced with permission of Informa Law, London.
91 [2014] FCAFC 6.
92 [2014] FCAFC 6, [78].
93 [2012] 3 WLR 1008.
94 [2012] 3 WLR 1008, 1016.
95 [2011] 3 SLR 540.

gambler, although his employer was unaware of his gambling habits. Chia devised a scheme to cheat SEB and other foreign banks out of SG$117.1 million. Chia was able to carry out the fraud because he was not supervised adequately by senior management at APBS. The issue that arose at trial was whether APBS had held Chia out as having authority to represent to SEB and the other banks that it had accepted its offer of credit facilities. SEB relied heavily upon the English Court of Appeal's decision in *First Energy*. SEB argued that while Chia did not have the authority to enter into a contract for credit facilities, he may have had authority to represent that APBS had agreed to such facilities.

The Singapore Supreme Court of Appeal found in favour of APBS. The court distinguished *Skandinaviska* from *First Energy* on the basis that in the latter case Mr Jamison had a high level of authority as the branch manager of the Manchester branch of Hungarian International Bank.[96] In contrast, Chia had less authority, as he was a finance manager. Further, SEB could quite easily have contacted the senior management of APBS, but failed to do so. Accordingly, there had been no holding out.

The Singapore Supreme Court of Appeal found that the principle in *First Energy* had no application to the dispute in *Skandinaviska*.[97] Nonetheless, the court went out of its way to make a series of criticisms of the decision in *First Energy*. The court stated that *First Energy* may have departed too radically from established authority.[98] The court found that unless *First Energy* was confined to its particular facts, which depended upon Mr Jamison's ostensible authority as the Manchester branch manager to communicate the decisions of the London branch, it would cause doctrinal difficulty.[99] In particular, the court took issue with the way in which the English Court of Appeal had treated the particular representation made by Mr Jamison about the London branch's decision as if it were like any other representation made by an agent.[100] In *Skandinaviska*, Chan Sek Keong CJ stated:

> [A] representation by an agent that his principal has approved a transaction is not like other representations. A representation as to the principal's approval of a transaction goes to the heart of the agency relationship. While an agent may possess authority (whether actual or ostensible) to make general representations pertaining to a certain transaction (such as, for example, a representation about the condition of the goods involved in a sale transaction), this authority, in a situation where the agent *does not* also possess authority (whether actual or ostensible) to enter into the said transaction on the principal's behalf, *cannot* include authority to make the specific representation that the principal has approved that transaction. To argue that an agent has authority to represent that his principal has approved a transaction – which is, in effect, authority to bind the principal to the transaction – because he (the agent) has authority to make general representations about the transaction and, hence, also has authority to represent that his principal has approved the transaction is contrary to the established principle that there cannot be self-authorisation by an agent. Of course, if an agent has been conferred authority, whether actual or ostensible, to make the *specific* representation that his principal has approved a

96 [2011] 3 SLR 540, [51].
97 [2011] 3 SLR 540, [54].
98 [2011] 3 SLR 540, [57].
99 [2011] 3 SLR 540, [58].
100 [2011] 3 SLR 540, [59].

> transaction (which authority Mr J was found to have in *First Energy*), he would also have been vested with at least ostensible authority to enter into the transaction on his principal's behalf. But, if the agent merely has authority to make *general* representations about the transaction and does not have any authority (whether actual or ostensible) to enter into the transaction on the principal's behalf, it is not possible for him to give himself such authority by falsely representing that his principal has approved the transaction, which representation carries with it the implication that the principal has given him (the agent) the requisite authority to bind the principal to the transaction.[101]

There is much to be said for the Singapore Court of Appeal's decision in *Skandinaviska*. In some respects, the English Court of Appeal's decision in *First Energy* creates a 'back alleyway' that allows an agent to circumvent the rule against self-authorisation. The decision in *Skandinaviska* draws a line between the ability of an agent to make general representations about a transaction and their ability to make a representation that specifically relates to entering into the transaction. This distinction preserves the estoppel basis of ostensible authority.

It might be worthwhile to approach the problem posed by *First Energy* by considering the very basic mechanics of a common law doctrine. While agency law is a body of law, ostensible authority itself is a doctrine that exists within it. In turn, every doctrine is made up of a series of interrelated legal rules. A simple taxonomy would be that a doctrine consists of a primary rule, secondary rules and limiting rules. The primary rule would be the core rule within that doctrine. The secondary rules are all the related subrules within the doctrine that apply within all the subcategories of the doctrine itself. Limiting rules would be those rules that demarcate the boundaries of the other legal rules. This taxonomy of legal rules, with three basic categories, is perhaps somewhat simplistic. Yet it is a workable model from which to advance our understanding of important areas of the common law. The relationship between the legal rules within a doctrine might be mostly stable, but it is not immune to change. We might well resolve the question of how a doctrine should develop by examining the relationship between the legal rules.

In the area of ostensible authority, the rule that says that ostensible authority exists where a principal represents that an agent has a certain level of authority, and a third party relies on that representation to their detriment, might be regarded as a primary rule. The primary rule obviously has quite a number of secondary rules. These secondary rules are the rules concerning representations, reliance and detriment. However, the primary rule is bounded by an important limiting rule: namely, that an agent cannot self-authorise. The relationship between the primary rule and the limiting rule is quite crucial. Where that relationship is thrown out of balance, by the emergence of a new secondary rule that threatens to render the limiting rule otiose, then the doctrine has slipped its moorings.

We must remember that the doctrine itself exists because there is a recurrent legal problem that it can meaningfully address. As the case law suggests, it has been a continuing problem in commercial life that principals have unwittingly intimated to third parties that their agents have more authority than they really possess. When the doctrine loses contact with the fundamentals of that problem, it needs to be reined in. The rule in *First Energy* plays fast and loose with the limiting rule that agents cannot self-authorise, and it also plays scant attention to the

101 [2011] 3 SLR 540, [59].

concept of reliance. The rule might well have made sense in the Court of Appeal with regard to the immediate dispute with which it was concerned, but it adds little for coherency in a wider doctrinal context.

Taken at its broadest point, Lord Steyn's dictum in *First Energy* threatens to overwhelm the doctrine of ostensible authority. The doctrine itself draws on two ideas, reliance and responsibility, in setting up its constituent rules. The role of reliance is quite easy to see in that the doctrine itself prevents the principal from resiling from representations that have been relied upon. However, the doctrine deals with the notion of responsibility in two different ways. First, the principal bears responsibility for the representation that they make. Second, the principal bears no responsibility where the agent self-authorises. The latter is a fundamental limitation. The rule in *First Energy*, although no doubt doing great justice in that particular case, bears too closely to the limitation and muddies the waters with regard to the notion of responsibility that underpins the doctrine of ostensible authority. In sum, the views of Chan Sek Keong CJ in *Skandinaviska* should be preferred over the decision in *First Energy*.

7.3.4 Reliance

The third party must rely upon the representation made by the principal.[102] Moreover, the third party's reliance on the representation made by the principal must be reasonable.[103] The element of reliance establishes a causal connection between the actions of the principal and the subsequent conduct of the third party.[104] This is consistent with the estoppel-based nature of ostensible authority.[105] The principal will be estopped from resiling from their representation where the third party reasonably relied upon it to their detriment. In *The Raffaella*, Lord Browne-Wilkinson stated the main inquiry of ostensible authority as being whether the principal had made a representation as to the agent's authority and whether this had been 'reasonably so understood by the third party'.[106] If the third party is aware that the agent is acting outside the scope of their authority, then there is no binding contract with the principal.[107] In the case of *Combulk Pty Ltd v TNT Management Pty Ltd*,[108] Neaves, Beaumont and Burchett JJ stated:

> It is well established that it is not within the scope of an agent's authority to bind his or her principals by a contract which, although made ostensibly on their behalf, is, to the knowledge of the other party, really made for his or her own benefit, even though the contract is of a kind which he or she had general authority to make; and that, therefore, when an agent purports to make such a contract, and the party with whom he or she is dealing is aware of the circumstances, the principal is not bound.[109]

102 *Armagas Ltd v Mundogas SA* [1986] 1 AC 717.
103 *Rama Corporation Ltd v Proved Tin & General Investments Ltd* [1952] 2 QB 147.
104 *Overbrooke Estates Ltd v Glencombe Properties Ltd* [1973] 3 All ER 511.
105 *Lysaght Brothers & Co Ltd v Falk* (1905) 2 CLR 421.
106 [1985] 2 Lloyd's Rep 36, 41. Reproduced with permission of Informa Law, London.
107 *Bloomenthal v Ford* [1897] AC 156; *Lloyds Bank Ltd v Chartered Bank of India, Australia & China* [1929] 1 KB 40; *Criterion Properties plc v Stratford UK Properties LLC* [2004] UKHL 28.
108 (1993) 113 ALR 214.
109 (1993) 113 ALR 214, [15].

Actual knowledge will suffice to prevent reliance. However, knowledge that does not amount to actual knowledge may still be sufficient to prevent reliance. Where the third party knows that the agent is doing something that is not consistent with the principal's interests,[110] or where the agent has made a promise that is outside their authority and which would be unlikely to have been approved by the principal,[111] there can be no justifiable reliance. It may very well be that if there are circumstances to put the third party upon inquiry as to the bona fides of the transaction, and if they refrain from making further inquiries for fear of learning the truth, then they will not be able to substantiate the element of reliance.

In *Cavenagh Investment Pte Ltd v Kaushik Rajiv*,[112] a defendant's reliance on the representations of an agent was found to be unreasonable. Dr Kaushik responded to an advertisement offering an apartment for lease. When Dr Kaushik made enquiries, he was met by Razali, who purported to be the agent of the owner. Razali showed Dr Kaushik and his wife the apartment and negotiated with them over details of the lease. When this was agreed, Razali then sought that the rent be paid to him. Dr Kaushik refused and requested that Razali produce a letter of authorisation from the owner. In truth, the apartment was owned by Cavenagh Investments, which in turn was a company whose sole director and shareholder was Ms Ching Mun Fong. The apartment had been left vacant by Ms Ching. She had entrusted its general care to a property management company. Razali was merely an employee of that property management company.

Razali forged a letter that appeared to be signed by Ms Ching. Thereafter, the rent was paid to Razali by Dr Kaushik's employer. The fraud was subsequently discovered when other employees of the property management company visited the apartment and were shocked to discover that it was occupied. Subsequently, the plaintiff sued Dr Kaushik for trespass to property. Dr Kaushik contended that the lease had been a valid one and that Razali had been clothed with ostensible authority by the plaintiff. The only real basis for this argument lay in the appearance created by Razali's possession of the keys and his ability to enter the apartment and its complex. Chan Seng Onn J stated:

> Whether or not a state of affairs created by allowing an agent to act in a certain way amounts to a representation sufficient to create ostensible authority is a question which must be decided and determined on the specific facts of each case. I am of the view that equipping an agent with the keys to a property does not amount to a representation that the agent has authority to enter into leases on the landlord's behalf. Landlords in Singapore commonly hand property agents the keys to their properties for the purpose of conducting viewings for prospective tenants and for other ministerial acts. I do not think that in doing so, these agents are therefore clothed with the ostensible authority to enter into leases with third parties on behalf of the landlords. When all is said and done, a reasonable prospective tenant would be satisfied only if the landlord himself gives approval for a lease. Such was in fact the case here. Dr Kaushik was not satisfied with Razali or anyone else signing the lease. He specifically insisted that Madam Ching, whom he had identified as the director of the true landlord, sign the Tenancy Agreement.

110 *Armagas Ltd v Mundogas SA* [1986] 1 AC 717.
111 *Alliance Acceptance Co Ltd v Oakley* (1987) 48 SASR 337.
112 [2013] 2 SLR 543.

> Dr Kaushik cannot now contend that the equipping of Razali with the keys and access cards to the Property amounts to a representation by the Plaintiff of Razali's authority to enter into the lease on its behalf, as Dr Kaushik himself did not at the relevant time read such a representation to be so.[113]

The fact that Dr Kaushik himself did not accept Razali's first attempt at signing a lease, and insisted that Ms Ching should sign, demonstrated that he was aware of both limits on Razali's authority and that he could not solely rely on statements made by Razali about Ms Ching's intentions. Nonetheless, while the plaintiff had claimed $352 000 as damages, Chan J awarded her only a nominal sum on the basis that she would otherwise have left the apartment vacant.

7.3.5 Detriment

Some form of detriment must be present in order for ostensible authority to be established.[114] In *The Tatra*,[115] the court stated that 'the only form of detriment that has to be shown . . . is the entering into the contract'.[116] Accordingly, where the third party alters its position by signing a contract, then detriment will be established.[117] The doctrine of ostensible authority thus differs slightly from conventional forms of estoppel in that actual detriment does not actually need to be shown.

7.4 Ratification

An agent may do an act that is not authorised by the principal. However, the third party with whom the agent has dealt will believe that the transaction was authorised by the principal. When this occurs, the principal will have the option of ratifying the act done by the agent. The act of ratification means that the principal accepts the actions of the agent and will honour the obligations created by the agent. Ratification works retrospectively so that the principal is able to assess whether or not it is in their interests to adopt the act or transaction entered into by their agent.[118] Where transactions are entered into subject to ratification, the doctrine of ratification does not apply as the third party will have been aware that the principal has not as yet agreed to the transaction.[119]

While there are different judicial formulations of the precise elements required to apply the doctrine of ratification, it can be said that there are six essential elements of the doctrine of ratification. First, the agent must have acted for the principal in entering into the relevant transaction or doing the particular act.[120] Second, the agent must have had a competent principal.[121] Third, the principal must be capable of doing the relevant act

113 [2013] SGHC 45, [24].
114 *Rama Corporation Ltd v Proved Tin & General Investments Ltd* [1952] 2 QB 147.
115 *Arctic Shipping Co Ltd v Mobilia AB ('The Tatra')* [1990] 2 Lloyd's Rep 51.
116 [1990] 2 Lloyd's Rep 51, 59.
117 *Hoare v McCarthy* (1916) 22 CLR 296.
118 *Life Savers (Australasia) Ltd v Frigmobile Pty Ltd* [1983] 1 NSWLR 431.
119 *Watson v Davies* [1931] 1 Ch 455.
120 *Firth v Staines* [1897] 2 QB 70.
121 *Firth v Staines* [1897] 2 QB 70; *Trident General Insurance Co Ltd v McNiece Brothers Pty Ltd* (1987) 8 NSWLR 270.

themselves.[122] Fourth, the principal must ratify the act, although this need not be communicated to the third party.[123] Fifth, the principal must have full knowledge of all the circumstances of the relevant transaction at the time of ratification.[124] Sixth, the principal must ratify the whole of the transaction.[125]

In *Suncorp Insurance & Finance v Milano Assicurazioni Spa*,[126] Waller J summarised the law of ratification as follows:

> The law on this aspect so far as material seems to me to be as follows:
>
> (i) Where an act is done (as it was here) by a person in the name of another and that person does not have authority, then the person in whose name it was done may ratify by adopting the transaction (see Bowstead 15th ed. pp. 51 and 52).
>
> (ii) In order that a person may be held to have ratified an act done without his authority, it is necessary that at the time of the ratification, he should have full knowledge of all the material circumstances in which the act was done, unless he intended to ratify and take the risk whatever the circumstances may have been. (See Bowstead art. 16, p. 64.) The commentary makes clear however that this principle, designed to protect the principal from being held too readily to have ratified acts of his agent, is less strict in the contractual context than it is in a tort context.
>
> (iii) Ratification may be express or implied, and will be implied whenever the conduct of the person in whose name a transaction has been entered into is such as to show that he adopts the transaction in whole or in part; mere acquiescence or inactivity may be sufficient . . . It seems to me that it should not be open to a principal, who to the outside world by his conduct, or that of his duly authorized agents, appears to have adopted a transaction to be able to prove subjectively that in fact he had not, any more than such a principal would be able to prove subjectively that he did not intend to adopt a transaction when he does an act e.g. accepts the payment of money, which objectively adopts the transaction.
>
> (iv) A principal may wish to ratify a transaction for commercial reasons so as to preserve his commercial reputation. It is in such circumstances that it seems to me that it should be possible for the principal to ratify as against the third party but not waive any breach of duty as against the agent. There seems no reason to me why the principal should not be able to make his position clear in this regard, in that there are two distinct but connected contractual relations. There is the contract which the agent has purported to make for the principal, and the contract between the agent and the principal.

122 *Keighley, Maxsted & Co v Durant* [1901] AC 240; *Presentaciones Musicales SA v Secunda* [1994] 2 All ER 737.

123 *Borg v Northern Rivers Finance Pty Ltd* [2004] QSC 29.

124 *Taylor v Smith* (1926) 38 CLR 48.

125 *Suncorp Insurance & Finance v Milano Assicurazioni Spa* [1993] 2 Lloyd's Rep 225, reproduced with permission of Informa Law, London; *Commercial Banking Co of Sydney Ltd v Mann* (1960) 34 ALJR 293.

126 [1993] 2 Lloyd's Rep 225.

(v) Ratification can also be by a duly authorized agent ... There is no doubt that ratification can be effected by an agent but that agent must be duly authorized either expressly or by virtue of being held out as having such authority ...
(vi) The adoption of part of a transaction operates as a ratification of the whole.[127]

The agent must represent to the third party that they are acting on behalf of the principal.[128] The existence of the principal must be disclosed even if the exact identity of the principal is not known by the third party.[129] The agent must not appear to be acting for themselves. In *Watson v Swann*,[130] an agent took out an insurance policy ostensibly on his own behalf. The principal later tried to invoke the policy but was unsuccessful as the policy appeared to have been taken for the benefit of the agent alone. In this sense, the doctrine of ratification differs greatly from the doctrine of the undisclosed principal, as in the latter the agent need not purport to be acting for a principal at the outset of the transaction. In the case of *Keighley, Maxsted & Co v Durant*,[131] Lord Macnaghten stated:

> As a general rule, only persons who are parties to a contract, acting either by themselves or by an authorized agent, can sue or be sued on the contract. A stranger cannot enforce the contract, nor can it be enforced against a stranger. That is the rule; but there are exceptions. The most remarkable exception, I think, results from the doctrine of ratification as established in English law. That doctrine is thus stated by Tindal C.J. in *Wilson v. Tumman*: 'That an act done, for another, by a person, not assuming to act for himself, but for such other person, though without any precedent authority whatever, becomes the act of the principal, if subsequently ratified by him, is the known and well-established rule of law. In that case the principal is bound by the act, whether it be for his detriment or his advantage, and whether it be founded on a tort or on a contract, to the same effect as by, and with all the consequences which follow from, the same act done by his *previous* authority.' And so by a wholesome and convenient fiction, a person ratifying the act of another, who, without authority, has made a contract openly and avowedly on his behalf, is deemed to be, though in fact he was not, a party to the contract.[132]

The agent must also have a competent principal. This does not necessarily require the agency relationship between the agent and the principal to be in existence at the time the relevant act occurs.[133] Instead, an identifiable principal, who can assume both the obligations to the third party and the agency relationship with the agent, must be in existence.[134] The principal should be capable of doing the relevant act under the law.[135] An act that is forbidden by law cannot be ratified.[136]

127 [1993] 2 Lloyd's Rep 225, 234–5. Reproduced with permission of Informa Law, London.
128 *Keighley, Maxsted & Co v Durant* [1901] AC 240.
129 *Watson v Swann* (1862) 11 CB (NS) 756.
130 (1862) 11 CB (NS) 756.
131 [1901] AC 240.
132 [1901] AC 240, 246–7.
133 G Dal Pont, *Law of Agency* (LexisNexis Butterworths Australia, Sydney, 2nd edn, 2008), 119.
134 *Celthene Pty Ltd v W K J Hauliers Pty Ltd* [1981] 1 NSWLR 606.
135 *Trident General Insurance Co Pty Ltd v McNiece Brothers Pty Ltd* (1987) 8 NSWLR 270.
136 *Crabtree-Vickers Pty Ltd v Australian Direct Mail Advertising & Addressing Co Pty Ltd* (1975) 133 CLR 72.

The principal may ratify the agent's act. This may be done by the principal themselves or through their agents.[137] There is no strict requirement that the ratification should be communicated to the third party. Indeed, based on the strength of the agent's representations, the third party is likely to be unaware that ratification was even required. In *Harrison's & Crossfield Ltd v London & North-Western Railway Co*,[138] the court stated that 'ratification does not rest upon estoppel. It need not be communicated to the party alleging it. Ratification is a unilateral act of the will.'[139] In contrast, where the principal does not wish to ratify the agent's act, this must be communicated promptly to the third party.[140]

The principal should be aware of all the relevant facts at the time of ratification.[141] Where the principal lacks knowledge, because the agent has deceived the principal or has been careless in relaying information, the ratification may be nullified.[142] In *Taylor v Smith*,[143] an erroneous overpayment by the principal's solicitor was found not to be ratified simply by the silence of the principal. The principal was unaware of the true circumstances and would not otherwise have consented to the payments.

There are three primary limitations on the doctrine of ratification. The first is that the principal must ratify the relevant act within a reasonable time.[144] It is not possible to identify clearly what will suffice as a reasonable time. This limitation must be applied with regard to the facts of the relevant matter. Second, the principal must have been able to legally perform the act that they subsequently choose to ratify.[145] Where a time limit exists for the doing of a given act the ratification cannot occur after that time has expired. Moreover, where an estate has vested, it cannot be divested from a third party.

Third, ratification may be prevented where it would result in some unjustifiable harm to a third party.[146] Where the third party seeks to withdraw from the contract, the principal may still ratify the contract.[147] This can result in harm to the third party, particularly if it is clear that it is difficult or impossible to perform the contract in question. In this area of the law, there is a conflict between the decisions of *Kidderminster Corporation v Hardwick*[148] and *Bolton Partners v Lambert*.[149] The inconsistency between the two cases centres on the question of whether ratification can occur after the third party has attempted to withdraw from the contract. Wherever a third party indicates that it is unwilling to go through with a contract, it will most likely suffer some injury if it is forced to uphold that contract. In *Kidderminster*, an agent, acting outside their authority, agreed to a contract with a third party. The third party told the agent it could not complete the contract, but the principal sought to ratify and enforce it. The Court of Exchequer held that the ratification came too late. In *Bolton Partners*, the third

137 *Re Portuguese Consolidated Copper Mines Ltd* (1890) 45 Ch D 16.
138 [1917] 2 KB 755.
139 [1917] 2 KB 755, 758.
140 *Prince v Clark* (1823) 107 ER 70.
141 *Tobin v Melrose* [1951] SASR 139; *Sinclair v Hudson* (1995) 9 BPR 16,259.
142 *Taylor v Smith* (1926) 38 CLR 48.
143 (1926) 38 CLR 48.
144 *Life Savers (Australasia) Ltd v Frigmobile Pty Ltd* [1983] 1 NSWLR 431.
145 *Bird v Brown* (1850) 154 ER 1433.
146 *Adams v Elphinstone* (1993) 2 Tas R (NC) N14.
147 *N M Superannuation Pty Ltd v Hughes* (1992) 27 NSWLR 26.
148 (1873) LR 9 Ex 13.
149 (1889) 41 Ch D 295.

party offered to take up a lease. An agent of the plaintiff, acting without authority, purported to accept the offer. The third party sought to withdraw their offer, but the plaintiff ratified their agent's acceptance. The court in *Bolton Partners* held that the lease could still be enforced. The decision in *Bolton Partners* conflicts with that of *Kidderminster*. As Pearson et al. have noted, the decision in *Bolton Partners* makes no reference to *Kidderminster* and may have been decided *per incuriam*.[150]

Notwithstanding the conflict between *Bolton Partners* and *Kidderminster*, ratification may not be permissible where it would cause an injury to a third party. In *Davison v Vickery's Motors Ltd (in liq)*,[151] Isaacs J outlined the basis for this rule. Isaacs J considered the relevant jurisprudence, including *Bolton* and *Kidderminster*, and stated:

> On the assumption that the Company has itself purported to ratify, the following propositions are all that are necessary in this case: – (1) The general rule is that no person can become a party to a bilateral contract unless he enters into it personally or by an authorized agent. (2) An exception is recognized where a person ratifies an agreement made by another as for him but without his antecedent authority. (3) On ratification, and not before, the agreement is as a general rule deemed by a fiction to have been made by his antecedent authority to the person actually making it. (4) Fictions, however, are not arbitrary. They are not allowed to work an injury; their operation is to prevent a mischief or to remedy an inconvenience that might result from the general rule of law. (5) Where, therefore, an injury would be caused by the operation of the fiction, it cannot be invoked to alter the general course of the law. (6) An injury would be caused in this case certainly by the known basis of the agreement having disappeared followed by the withdrawal of Davison from the agreement.[152]

As ratification is a legal fiction, to allow it to operate where it would materially injure another party is not consistent with the common law's goal of fairness and justice. Moreover, where a third party has had sufficient time to think the matter over and to seek to withdraw from the contract, there may, on the specific facts of the matter, be an arguable case that ratification has not taken place in time.

7.5 The doctrine of the undisclosed principal

The doctrine of the undisclosed principal entails a situation where an agent, acting within the scope of their authority, contracts with a third party on behalf of the agent's principal, but the third party is unaware that the agent has a principal.[153] In this situation, the principal may, subject to some exceptions, step forward and take on the benefits of the contract. For the doctrine to operate, the contract should not expressly preclude the possibility that the agent is

150 G Pearson, S Fisher, E Peden and G J Tolhurst, *Commercial Law* (Lawbook Co, Sydney, 3rd edn, 2010), 255.

151 (1925) 37 CLR 1.

152 (1925) 37 CLR 1, 19.

153 *Maynegrain Pty Ltd v Compafina Bank* [1982] 2 NSWLR 141; *Tehran-Europe Co Ltd v S T Belton (Tractors) Ltd* [1968] 2 QB 545.

acting in their capacity as an agent for a principal.[154] Either the principal or the agent may sue or be sued on the contract.

The rationale that lies behind the doctrine of the undisclosed principal is that of commercial convenience. While it is somewhat unusual for a third party to find themselves bound in contract to a principal that they were unaware of at the time they entered the agreement, the doctrine does circumvent the need for the principal to require their agent to enforce the contract with the third party. In *Tehran-Europe Co Ltd v ST Belton (Tractors) Ltd*,[155] Lord Denning stated:

> It is a well-established rule of English law that an undisclosed principal can sue and be sued upon a contract, even though his name and even his existence is undisclosed, save in those cases when the terms of the contract expressly or impliedly confine it to the parties to it. This rule is an anomaly, but is justified by business convenience.[156]

The doctrine is an exception to the rule of privity of contract.[157] The doctrine will most likely arise in cases where the principal requires that the agent should purchase a particular commodity on the principal's behalf. In that situation, the agent might approach the seller without disclosing that the purchase is being done on behalf of the principal. The doctrine of the undisclosed principal is available to all principals.[158] In *Tehran-Europe*, the Court of Appeal overruled previous dicta that had excluded foreign principals from utilising the doctrine.[159]

The principal must disclose their existence in order to sue on the contract.[160] Where the contract is drafted so as to preclude the admissibility of materials outside the contract or to suggest that the agent and third parties are the only true parties to the contract, the principal may be unable to intervene.[161] The existence of the principal does not free the agent from the prospect of contractual liability.[162] Once the principal is disclosed, the third party may choose to sue either the agent or the principal.[163] Where the agent has rights against the third party, those rights exist subject to the superior rights of the principal.[164] In essence, any remedy that the agent obtains as against the third party is held on behalf of the principal.

In *Siu Yin Kwan v Eastern Insurance Co Ltd*,[165] Lord Lloyd stated the legal requirements for the doctrine of the undisclosed principal to apply:

> For present purposes the law can be summarised shortly. (1) An undisclosed principal may sue and be sued on a contract made by an agent on his behalf, acting within the scope of his actual authority. (2) In entering into the contract, the agent must intend to act

154 *Maynegrain Pty Ltd v Compafina Bank* [1982] 2 NSWLR 141.
155 [1968] 2 QB 545.
156 [1968] 2 QB 545, 552.
157 *Keighley, Maxsted & Co v Durant* [1901] AC 240.
158 *Tehran-Europe Co Ltd v S T Belton (Tractors) Ltd* [1968] 2 QB 545.
159 *Tehran-Europe Co Ltd v S T Belton (Tractors) Ltd* [1968] 2 QB 545, 553.
160 *Siu Yin Kwan v Eastern Insurance Co Ltd* [1994] 2 AC 199.
161 *Finzel, Berry & Co v Eastcheap Dried Fruit Co* [1962] 1 QB 370.
162 *Allen v F O'Hearn & Co* [1937] AC 213; *Elder Smith Goldsbrough Mort Ltd v McBride* [1976] 2 NSWLR 631.
163 *Basma v Weekes* [1950] AC 441.
164 *Maynegrain Pty Ltd v Compafina Bank* [1982] 2 NSWLR 141.
165 [1994] 2 AC 199.

> on the principal's behalf. (3) The agent of an undisclosed principal may also sue and be sued on the contract. (4) Any defence which the third party may have against the agent is available against his principal. (5) The terms of the contract may, expressly or by implication, exclude the principal's right to sue, and his liability to be sued. The contract itself, or the circumstances surrounding the contract, may show that the agent is the true and only principal.[166]

The five elements set out by Lord Lloyd must be present in order for the doctrine to apply. The agent must have been acting within the scope of their authority.[167] This also means that the agent must have been an agent for the relevant principal at the time that the contract with the third party was made.[168] The agent must intend to act for the principal. However, this intention may be unexpressed insofar as the third party is concerned and regard must be had to the common intention of the principal and the agent.[169] As noted, the agent of the undisclosed principal may sue on the contract.[170] This doctrinal principle stems from the first element as set out by Lord Lloyd. In *Maynegrain Pty Ltd v Compafina Bank*,[171] Hope JA noted that the rights and liabilities of the principal and the agent were not held jointly, but rather were available as alternatives. Any defence that the third party can raise against the agent is also available against the principal. Where the terms of the contract exclude the existence of a principal, the undisclosed principal cannot intervene.

There are two key limitations that apply to the doctrine of the undisclosed principal. The first, as stated above, is that the contract made between the agent and the third party should not be such as to exclude the existence of a principal.[172] Where an agent expressly represents to the third party that they are acting on their own behalf or by other statements leads the third party to believe that this is in fact the case, then the doctrine cannot apply.[173] In *Humble v Hunter*,[174] the agent entered into a charter party as the 'owner of the good ship or vessel called The Ann'. Later the agent's mother, the true principal, sought to sue but she was denied. Lord Denman CJ stated that the doctrine of the undisclosed principal 'cannot be applied where the agent contracts as principal; and he has done so here by describing himself as "owner" of the ship'.[175] In contrast, in *White v Baycorp Advantage Business Information Services Ltd*,[176] the use of standard terms in a contract, even where they specifically referred to the agent, did not displace the application of the doctrine as other terms left open the possibility of an undisclosed principal. The court in *White v Baycorp Advantage* also made the point that the use of usual commercial terms in a contract did not indicate that they were employed because the identity of one of the parties was a major issue in agreeing to the contract.[177] The corollary

166 [1994] 2 AC 199, 207.
167 *Keighley, Maxsted & Co v Durant* [1901] AC 240.
168 *Construction Engineering (Australia) Pty Ltd v Hexyl Pty Ltd* (1985) 155 CLR 541.
169 *The Astyanax* [1983] 2 Lloyd's Rep 109.
170 *Maynegrain Pty Ltd v Compafina Bank* [1982] 2 NSWLR 141.
171 [1982] 2 NSWLR 141.
172 *White v Baycorp Advantage Business Information Services Ltd* (2006) 200 FLR 125; *Humble v Hunter* (1848) 12 QB 310.
173 *Greer v Downs Supply Co* [1927] 2 KB 28.
174 (1848) 12 QB 310.
175 (1848) 12 QB 310, 312.
176 (2006) 200 FLR 125.
177 (2006) 200 FLR 125, [86].

of this is that if specific terms are drafted and make special mention of the agent as one of the two exclusive parties to the contract, then the application of the doctrine will be displaced.

The second is that where the identity of the parties is crucial to the third party, an undisclosed principal cannot intervene if the third party either would not have contracted with that principal or wished only to contract with the agent.[178] In certain classes of contracts, the identity of the other party may well be crucial. Leases are a good example of such contracts, as they often involve entrusting property to another party for their use. Similarly, where a third party would not have contracted with a particular person, for whatever reason, the use of an agent and the doctrine of the undisclosed principal is not appropriate.[179]

7.6 Agency by operation of law

The law permits an agency to arise in times of emergency under the guise of the doctrine of agency by necessity. As such, the law recognises that there may be times where an agent must act without authority to safeguard the vital interests of the principal. This may arise in situations where one spouse is abandoned by the other and must purchase essential items to take care of the remaining family.[180] It may also arise where the property of the principal has to be saved by the agent such that the latter must take charge of the property.[181] The doctrine of agency of necessity does not require a pre-existing agency relationship between the putative agent and principal. What must exist is that the property of the principal is in peril and the putative agent is forced to act in order to save that property.

Historically, the doctrine of the agency of necessity arose out of situations where a shipmaster found himself with cargo in a faraway location without any prospect of contacting the owner of the cargo.[182] Initially, the doctrine only applied to maritime matters. Subsequent developments extended the doctrine to also cover emergencies arising on land. Notably, the doctrine applied in situations of deserted spouses, where the abandoned spouse, usually the wife, had to pledge the husband's credit in order to look after their children and home.

In *The Pa Mar* case, a particular test for agency of necessity was laid out.[183] However, that test applied to shipping, and it would need to be adapted to apply to different scenarios. In *The Pa Mar*,[184] Clarke J stipulated the criteria in terms of 'salvage':

> (i) it is necessary to take salvage assistance; and
> (ii) it is not reasonably practicable to communicate with the cargo-owners or to obtain their instructions; and
> (iii) the master or ship owners act bona fide in the interests of the cargo; and
> (iv) it is reasonable for the master or ship owner to enter into the particular contract . . .

178 *Carberry v Gardiner* (1936) 36 SR (NSW) 559.
179 *Dyster v Randall & Sons* [1926] Ch 932.
180 *Burns Philp & Co v Gillespie Brothers Pty Ltd* (1947) 74 CLR 148.
181 *Sims & Co v Midland Railway Co* [1913] 1 KB 103.
182 *Sims & Co v Midland Railway Co* [1913] 1 KB 103.
183 [1999] 1 Lloyd's Rep 338.
184 *Tsavliris Salvage (International) Ltd v Guangdong Shantov Overseas Chinese Materials Marketing Co ('The Pa Mar')* [1999] 1 Lloyd's Rep 338, 341.

The test set out by Clarke J can be restated so as to apply to all situations of emergency, regardless of whether they involve salvage or other maritime affairs. Furthermore, the third and fourth requirements can be amalgamated on the basis that whether it is reasonable for an agent to enter into a given contract is an indication of whether that agent has been acting bona fide in the interests of the principal. Accordingly, an agency of necessity arises where:

(a) there is a necessity to incur expenditure to preserve the principal's property and safeguard the principal's interests;[185] *and*

(b) there exists a commercial impossibility or extreme difficulty of communicating with the principal;[186] *and*

(c) the 'agent' acted bona fide in the interests of the principal.[187]

All three elements must be present. The first element requires the existence of some emergency and the necessity to take action to preserve the principal's interests.[188] The emergency must be externally driven, and it must relate to some harm to the goods.[189] The emergency cannot relate to mere commercial or financial matters.[190] Similarly, the agent is not empowered to deal with the principal's property simply because it has become inconvenient.[191] In general, where the property is in physical danger the emergency exists and the agent may act.[192] With perishable goods, this may occur where the threat of deterioration arises.[193] For example, if foodstuffs are being shipped from port to port and delivery is held up such that deterioration begins to occur, the party carrying the goods might have to seek an immediate buyer lest the goods deteriorate completely and become unsaleable.

The second element requires that it is impossible to communicate with the principal.[194] This second requirement has also been expressed as extending to situations where it is 'practically impossible to get the owner's instructions in time'.[195] In previous times, before the rapid advancement of communication technologies, it might have been completely impossible to contact the principal.[196] However, given the current state of technology it is highly unlikely that it will be impossible to contact the principal.[197] Nevertheless, there may be situations where communication is virtually impossible, such as where a principal is in a physically remote area or is incapacitated in some way.[198] There may also be situations where the principal simply does not respond.[199] The second element may be satisfied under these circumstances.

185 *Burns Philp & Co v Gillespie Brothers Pty Ltd* (1947) 74 CLR 148.
186 *China-Pacific SA v Food Corporation of India* [1982] AC 939.
187 *The Gratitudine* [1801] 164 ER 450.
188 *The Pa Mar* [1999] 1 Lloyd's Rep 338.
189 *Sachs v Miklos* [1948] 2 KB 23; *Springer v Great Western Railway* [1921] 1 KB 257.
190 *John Koch Ltd v C & H Products Ltd* [1956] 2 Lloyd's Rep 59.
191 *Sachs v Miklos* [1948] 2 KB 23.
192 *Palmer v Stear* (1963) 113 LJ 420.
193 See, for example, *Springer v Great Western Railway* [1921] 1 KB 257.
194 *China-Pacific SA v Food Corporation of India* [1982] AC 939.
195 *Sims & Co v Midland Railway Co* [1913] 1 KB 103, 112.
196 See, for example, *The Gratitudine* [1801] 164 ER 450.
197 See T Vollans, 'Global Technology and Modern Commercial Agency of Necessity' (2008) 3(3) *Journal of International Commercial Law and Technology* 188.
198 *China-Pacific SA v Food Corporation of India* [1982] AC 939.
199 *Graanhandel T Vink BV v European Grain & Shipping Ltd* [1989] 2 Lloyd's Rep 531.

The third element requires that the agent is acting bona fide in the interests of the principal.[200] The dominant motive of the agent must be to secure the interests of the principal.[201] This does not preclude the possibility that the agent may also benefit in some way. The agent must be reasonable and prudent in acting in the principal's interests. If the agent, in trying to save the principal's property, strikes some highly unreasonable bargain and runs up costs that far outweigh the value of the goods, then it is unlikely that they are acting bona fide. In contrast, if the agent makes reasonable and appropriate arrangements and saves the goods from harm, then it is highly likely that they are acting bona fide.[202]

7.7 The duties of agents and principals

7.7.1 The duties accompanying an agency relationship

An agent may be subject to duties under contract and the general law. An agency that is created by contract will impose contractual duties on the agent.[203] The agency will then be subject to obligations of reasonableness and good faith in the discharge of its contractual duties.[204] Notwithstanding the specific duties created under the contract, the agent will have fiduciary obligations towards the principal.[205] The agent will owe a basic duty of care to the principal in carrying out their duties under the agency.[206] The agent must exercise skill, care and diligence in carrying out their duties.[207] An agent must act in accordance with their instructions.[208] This includes a duty not to exceed those instructions.[209] The agent owes a duty of allegiance to the principal and the principal's interests.[210] The agent must disclose material information to the principal.[211] The specific duties required of the agent will draw their colour from the context of the particular agent–principal relationship. The agent must avoid a conflict of interest.[212] The agent must account to the principal.[213] The agent must also not take bribes.[214]

A principal has three primary duties towards their agent. The first is to indemnify the agent with regard to losses or liabilities incurred in the course of the agency.[215] The second is to reimburse the agent for any costs that they incur in order to carry out their duties.[216] The third

200 *The Gratitudine* [1801] 164 ER 450; *China-Pacific SA v Food Corporation of India* [1982] AC 939.

201 *China-Pacific SA v Food Corporation of India* [1982] AC 939.

202 *James Phelps & Co v Hill* [1891] 1 QB 605.

203 *Jones v Canavan* [1972] 2 NSWLR 236.

204 *South Sydney District Rugby League Football Club Ltd v News Ltd* (2000) 177 ALR 611.

205 *Breen v Williams* (1996) 186 CLR 71.

206 *Chaudhry v Prabhakar* [1989] WLR 29.

207 *Daniels v Anderson* (1995) 37 NSWLR 438; *Commonwealth Bank of Australia v Friedrich* (1991) 5 ACSR 115.

208 *Donellan v Watson* (1990) 21 NSWLR 335.

209 *Waugh v H G Clifford & Sons* [1982] Ch 374.

210 *Daniels v Anderson* (1995) 37 NSWLR 438.

211 *Provincial Insurance Australia Pty Ltd v Consolidated Wood Products Pty Ltd* (1991) 25 NSWLR 541.

212 *Thornley v Tilley* (1925) 36 CLR 1.

213 *Walker v Corboy* (1990) 19 NSWLR 382.

214 *Attorney-General (Hong Kong) v Reid* [1994] 1 AC 324.

215 *Anglo Overseas Transport Ltd v Titan Industrial Corporation (UK) Ltd* [1959] 2 Lloyd's Rep 152; *Re Parker* (1882) 21 Ch D 408.

216 *Dolphin v Harrison, San Miguel Pty Ltd* (1911) 13 CLR 271; *Taylor v Robinson* (1818) 129 ER 536; *Re Parker* (1882) 21 Ch D 408.

is to remunerate the agent for their services.[217] Where the agent has been unpaid for services, a right of lien over the principal's goods may also arise.[218] This right of lien will normally be restricted to goods that relate to the agency itself.[219] The right of remuneration will usually be covered by the contract between the agent and the principal. Where no such contract exists, the duty may not arise.

7.7.2 Liability of the agent

Where an agent acts without authority, and where no ostensible authority is subsequently found or ratification does not occur, the agent may face liability to a third party. For example, in a situation where an agent contracts for an undisclosed principal, believing that they are within the parameters of their authority, the agent may find themselves personally bound in contract to the third party when it turns out that the agent lacks authority. Similarly, an agent may contract for a principal without disclosing the exact identity of that principal. If this occurs, then it will become a question of construction as to whether the agent avoids personal liability. In *McNally v Jackson*,[220] Dwyer J stated:

> My view of the law is that the agent is liable if he does not disclose the existence of a principal. If he does disclose the existence and does not disclose the name of the principal, that mere non-disclosure of the name is not, in itself, sufficient to make him liable on a contract. Where a contract is in writing, and where it is incorporated in a document, it is that document which should be looked to, and if it says nothing in qualification of the agent, there is a personal liability. I think it is the accepted law now that, in the matter of agency, a signature which merely describes a man as an agent may not be enough, but if the body of the agreement shows that the position in which the person contracts is as an agent for a principal, then it should be normally assumed at least *prima facie*, that the person so described did contract on behalf of the principal, if, of course, that is the actual fact. Put in another way, it amounts to this, that if a man signs himself agent, that might merely be a term of description, but if he contracts as agent, that rather negatives personal responsibility. Of course that is subject to the overriding doctrine that, although a man purports to contract as agent, if he is, in fact, the real principal, he is personally liable.[221]

In ordinary circumstances, where both parties know that the agent is contracting on behalf of a principal, that should be sufficient to protect the agent from liability. Nonetheless, if the contract is drafted so as to suggest that the agent is the sole party to the contract, they may not be able to avoid liability.[222] It is easy enough to see how this might arise in a sales context. For example, if an agent wishes to purchase goods on behalf of their principal, they may approach a third party who has those goods. The agent might then enter a contract for sale with the third party. The agent might very well intend to purchase the goods and to pass them

217 *Dolphin v Harrison, San Miguel Pty Ltd* (1911) 13 CLR 271; *Smith v Stallard & French* [1919] WALR 19.
218 *Taylor v Robinson* (1818) 129 ER 536; *John D Hope & Co v Glendinning* [1911] AC 419.
219 *Dixon v Stansfield* (1850) 10 CB 398.
220 (1938) 42 WALR 27.
221 (1938) 42 WALR 27.
222 *Sun Happiness* [1994] 1 Lloyd's Rep 381.

on to the agent's principal for subsequent reimbursement. Yet if, in the immediate contract with the third party, the terms of the agreement do not admit the existence of a principal or describe the purpose of the agent in entering the contract, the third party is entitled to hold the agent bound to that contract. It would be unfair if the agent could simply contract with a third party and then escape any liability, particularly if no claim of ostensible authority could be made out against the principal and if ratification was not forthcoming.

7.7.3 Breach of warrant of authority

The agent who makes a representation to a third party that they are acting within their authority, when they know that they are not, is effectively breaching their warrant of authority.[223] Moreover, the breach of the agent's warrant of authority can happen unwittingly if the agent inadvertently or carelessly exceeds their authority.[224] In *Yonge v Toynbee*,[225] a solicitor acted for a client in a defamation matter. Unbeknown to the solicitor, the client was later declared insane. When the action was struck out, the defendant sought to sue the solicitor on the basis that he had no authority to act for their client. The solicitor was held to be liable. In contrast to the situation in *Yonge v Toynbee*, where the agent was completely unaware that they had come to lack authority, there may be situations where agents knowingly misrepresent that they have authority to act for a principal in anticipation of later acquiring the requisite level of authority. However, an agent cannot self-authorise; thus, without more, the principal can bear no liability where the agent has exceeded their authority.[226] In *Rummery v Dorsman*,[227] Sheller JA set out the basic requirements of the doctrine:

> The doctrine applies where one person expressly or by implication holds himself or herself out as having competent authority to do an act and thereby draws another party into a reciprocal engagement. The essentials are (1) assertion of authority; (2) inducement by asserting; (3) transaction which but for that assertion the other party would not have entered into. Where they coexist there is a warranty.[228]

In *Leggo v Brown & Dureau Ltd*,[229] Isaacs J stated that no positive belief on the part of the third party needed to be established. Nonetheless, if the third party is fully aware that the agent has no authority, then the doctrine will not apply.[230] Leaving aside issues of belief, provided that there has been (1) an assertion of authority; (2) an inducement stemming from that assertion; and (3) a resulting contract, then where the agent has acted without any authority, the principal will not be bound to the resulting contract and the agent will be liable to the third party. The primary case in which the doctrine of breach of warrant of authority was established was *Collen v Wright*,[231] where an agent represented that he was acting on behalf of a landowner.

223 *Cro Travel Pty Ltd v Australia Capital Financial Management Pty Ltd* [2018] NSWCA 153.
224 *Yonge v Toynbee* [1910] 1 KB 215.
225 [1910] 1 KB 215.
226 *First Sport Ltd v Barclays Bank Plc* [1993] 3 All ER 789.
227 [1996] ANZ ConvR 513.
228 [1996] ANZ ConvR 513, [13].
229 (1923) 32 CLR 95.
230 *Brownett v Newton* (1941) 64 CLR 439.
231 (1857) 120 ER 241.

The agent then purported to sign a lease with the plaintiff on the landowner's behalf. When the landowner discovered what had happened, he denied the lease. The plaintiff then successfully sued the agent. As *Collen* indicates, the principle underpinning the doctrine is that where a third party has acted to their own detriment on the basis of representations made by the agent, the third party should have a right of action against the agent. As Fisher has noted, the elements of breach of warrant of authority 'closely shadow the elements of agency by estoppel'.[232]

The authority that the agent purports to have must pertain to an identified or identifiable principal. If the principal misrepresents their true identity, this does not necessarily create liability on the part of the agent. An interesting subset of cases has recently emerged, mainly in relation to land transactions, wherein a fraudster poses as another person and dupes both the agent and the third party in a land fraud. After the fraudster has been apprehended or has absconded, the third party might then seek redress against the agent. In *Excel Securities plc v Masood*,[233] a man attempted to borrow from a company that was in the business of providing short-term commercial loans. He presented himself as if he were the owner of a specific property. In fact, he had stolen the identity of the true owner. The solicitors who acted on his behalf were unaware of the fraud that he was perpetrating. When the fraud was discovered, the plaintiff sought to sue the solicitors for breach of warrant of authority. The action failed, as they had indeed acted for the person who presented himself to the third party as the principal, notwithstanding that he had misrepresented his true identity. The basis of the decision in *Excel Securities* was stated by Judge Hegarty QC:

> [T]he court should not readily impose upon a person rendering professional services an absolute, unqualified obligation amounting, in effect, to a guarantee of his client's identity and title. The risk that the law has sought to address by the implication of a warranty of authority is that the agent may not have the authority which he claims; and the justification for such an allocation of risk is that the agent is in much the better position to know or ascertain whether he has the requisite authority. But the risks against which Excel is seeking to be protected in these proceedings are the commercial risks involved in lending to a person who may not be all that he claims to be. For my part, I can see no justification why risks of this kind should be transferred from the shoulders of a commercial concern such as Excel on to those of a professional firm such as BM Solicitors.[234]

The decision in *Excel Securities* was followed in *Stevenson v Singh*,[235] where a firm of solicitors unwittingly acted for a fraudster in a property scam. The facts of *Excel Securities* can be contrasted with those of *Penn v Bristol & West Building Society*,[236] where solicitors acted for both a husband and wife, but failed to check whether the wife had actually authorised the relevant transaction. As the wife's consent could have been ascertained by a simple phone call or a brief meeting, the solicitors were liable for breaching their warrant of authority.

232 S Fisher, *Agency Law* (Butterworths, Sydney, 2000), 155.
233 [2010] Lloyd's Rep PN 165.
234 [2010] Lloyd's Rep PN 165, [102]. Published by Informa Law, London. Reproduced with kind permission of Informa Law.
235 [2012] EWHC 2880 (QB).
236 [1997] 1 WLR 1356.

7.8 Termination of agency

An agency relationship can be terminated by either of the parties. The principal can revoke the authority that they have given to the agent. Likewise, the agent can inform the principal that they no longer wish to work for the principal. Alternatively, an agency relationship can expire where the purpose for which the agent was retained has been achieved. For example, if a principal retains an agent in order to facilitate the sale of a house, the agency relationship ends when the house has been sold. Where the principal has terminated the agency relationship, they must inform interested third parties if they know that the third parties still believe that the agent is working for the principal.[237] Notwithstanding termination of the agency by the consent of the parties, an agency relationship will be terminated by law where the principal has (1) died; (2) been declared insane; or (3) been declared bankrupt.

7.9 Key points

- Agency is a legal relationship in which an agent acts on behalf of another person, known as the principal, in order to achieve things that the principal finds difficult or inconvenient to do themselves.
- There are three primary forms of authority under agency law: actual express authority, actual implied authority and ostensible authority.
- Authority can also be retrospectively conferred upon an agent under the doctrine of ratification.
- The doctrine of ostensible authority requires a representation as to authority, reliance by the third party and detriment.
- The doctrine of the undisclosed principal entails a situation where an agent, acting within the scope of their authority, contracts with a third party on behalf of the agent's principal, but the third party is unaware that the agent has a principal.
- The law permits for an agency to arise in times of emergency under the guise of the doctrine of agency by necessity.
- An agent may be subject to duties under contract and the general law.
- An agent who makes a representation to a third party that the agent is acting within their authority, when they know that they are not, is effectively breaching their warrant of authority.

7.10 DISCUSSION QUESTIONS

1. Why do agency relationships exist? What commercial purpose do they serve?
2. What is the difference between the different forms of authority within agency law?
3. Could the doctrine of ostensible authority extend too far and impose liability upon principals in circumstances that might be regarded as unfair?

237 *Klement v Pencoal Ltd* [2000] QCA 152.

4. What is the doctrine of ratification?
5. What is the purpose of the law on breach of warrant of authority? How does it allocate risk between the relevant parties?

7.11 FURTHER READING

Dal Pont, G E, *Law of Agency* (LexisNexis, Sydney, 2nd edn, 2008).

Tan, C-H, 'Unauthorised Agency in English Law' in D Busch and L J Macgregor (eds), *The Unauthorised Agent: Perspectives from European and Comparative Law* (Cambridge University Press, Cambridge, UK, 2009).

8

BAILMENT

8.0 Introduction

This chapter examines the topic of bailments. It sets out the basic concept of a bailment and the required factors that must be in place for a bailment relationship to exist. The chapter then examines sub-bailments, the categories of bailment, the duties common to all bailments, and the relationship between bailment and other legal categories. The issues pertaining to bailments and the *Personal Property Securities Act 2009* (Cth) are discussed in Chapter 9.

8.1 Bailment

Although it might be regarded as a somewhat unglamorous arrangement, a bailment is one of the most common legal relationships in the commercial world. A business that manufactures goods, or which buys and sells goods, must invariably rely upon a carrier to move those goods from one location to another. Whenever there is a situation wherein goods belonging to one person are entrusted to another person for a given purpose, there will always be a degree of risk involved. That risk centres on the carriage and safekeeping of those goods. It is within this context that the law of bailment has evolved.

In essence, a bailment is a legal relationship where one person, known as the bailor, permits their goods to be taken into the possession of another person, known as the bailee, so that the bailee can carry out a task assigned by the bailor.[1] The task required by the bailor may be that the bailee holds the goods for safekeeping, or does work on the goods or transports them to some other party. Ordinarily, the bailor must either deliver the goods to the bailee or arrange to have them delivered to the bailee. In *Hobbs v Petersham Transport Co Pty Ltd*,[2] Windeyer J stated:

> A bailment comes into existence upon a delivery of goods of one person, the bailor, into the possession of another person, the bailee, upon a promise, express or implied, that they will be re-delivered to the bailor or dealt with in a stipulated way.[3]

Halsbury's Laws of England offers an extended definition of bailments.[4] There are in effect two parts to this definition: a traditional version and a more modern version.[5] *Halsbury's* states:

> A bailment, traditionally defined, is a delivery of personal chattels on trust, usually on a contract express or implied that the trust shall be duly executed and the chattels redelivered in either their original or an altered form as soon as the time or use for or condition on which they were bailed shall have elapsed or been performed. Under modern law, bailment arises whenever one person, the bailee (here alleged to be the defendants) is voluntarily in possession of goods belonging to another person, the bailor (here alleged to be the plaintiffs).[6]

1 *Hobbs v Petersham Transport Co Pty* Ltd (1971) 124 CLR 220. See also *Big Top Hereford Pty Ltd v Thomas* (2006) 12 BPR 23,843. See, further, *Redox v Swan Hill Chemicals Pty Ltd* [2018] VCC 531.
2 124 CLR 220.
3 124 CLR 220, 238.
4 *Halsbury's Laws of England* (LexisNexis Butterworths, London, 4th edn, 2005).
5 S Traves, *Commercial Law* (LexisNexis Butterworths Australia, Sydney, 2009), 249.
6 *Halsbury's Laws of England* (LexisNexis Butterworths, London, 4th edn, 2005), [1801].

The more traditional definition exists in the first sentence with reference to the delivery of chattels on trust and to contract. Bailments have now emerged as a defined area of law with no particular requirement that a contract must be in place in order for obligations to arise on the part of the bailee and the bailor.[7] That is, a bailment is a legal relationship that does not depend upon the existence of a contract.[8] Given the different types of bailment that might arise, such as bailments for reward and gratuitous bailments, the general definition of a bailment must be broad enough to cover all the relevant categories without excluding any given type of bailment.

The idea of bailment is a longstanding one in Western legal thought. The notion of a bailment first arose in Roman law.[9] In *Morris v C W Martin & Sons Ltd*,[10] Lord Diplock stated that 'the legal concept of bailment as creating a relationship which gives rise to duties owed by a bailee to a bailor is derived from Roman law and is older in our common law than the legal concept of parol contract'. However, the genesis of the modern law of bailment began with the decision of Holt CJ in *Coggs v Bernard*,[11] wherein his Honour held that a private carrier should be regarded under the law as a bailee of the goods that had been delivered to him. The driving force behind the development of this area of the law was that where one party had entrusted goods to another for the purposes of carriage or the like, it should then follow that some manner of responsibilities and duties must fall upon the latter.

8.2 The requirements of bailment

For a bailment to exist, certain requirements must be satisfied. As a general prerequisite, the bailor must be in possession of goods. This need not be actual possession; it may be constructive possession or de facto possession. The subject matter of the bailment must be some type of goods or other chattel.[12] In *Federal Commissioner of Taxation v United Aircraft Corporation*,[13] the High Court held that the transfer of knowledge could not amount to a bailment. Latham CJ stated:

> I am unable to regard the communication of information as constituting a transfer of property ... Knowledge is valuable, but knowledge is neither real nor personal property. A man with a richly stored mind is not for that reason a man of property.[14]

Accordingly, even though the High Court's decision in *United Aircraft Corporation* and the sentiments behind it must now be regarded as rather dated, it is highly unlikely that a bailment will extend to intangible assets such as intellectual property. There has been some suggestion that the principles of bailment can be applied to commercial relationships wherein intangible

---

7 *Parastatidis v Kotaridis* [1978] VR 449, [455]; *Morris v C W Martin & Sons Ltd* [1966] 1 QB 716.

8 *K H Enterprise (Cargo Owners) v Pioneer Containers (Owners) ('The Pioneer Container')* [1994] 2 AC 324.

9 W S Holdsworth, *A History of English Law* (Sweet & Maxwell, London, 5th edn, 1942), vol 7, 453.

10 [1966] 1 QB 716.

11 (1703) 92 ER 107.

12 *Federal Commissioner of Taxation v United Aircraft Corporation* (1943) 68 CLR 525.

13 (1943) 68 CLR 525.

14 (1943) 68 CLR 525, 534.

assets are entrusted between one party and another.[15] It is at least clear that information, and in particular intellectual property, is a bona fide species of personal property. Nonetheless, with the exception of confidential information, most forms of intellectual property, such as copyright, trademarks and patents, are statutorily created forms of property, and do not fit readily within the parameters of bailment as it has been developed within the common law.

Similarly, the bailor must require that the bailee deliver or care for the goods in some manner. This might arise in a variety of contexts. For example, a bailor may deliver their car to a repairer so that the latter may complete repair work on the vehicle. In this situation, the bailor must entrust the vehicle to the bailee who will then redeliver it to the bailor. In *Ultzen v Nichols*,[16] a situation wherein a coat was left in the care of the proprietor of a restaurant was held to amount to a bailment. A bailment might arise where goods have been lost and are later found and are redelivered to the true owner.[17] In such a situation, there is initially no intent on the part of the bailor to enter into a bailment relationship, but once the goods have been lost the bailor has a legitimate expectation that the finder, who becomes a bailee by finding and taking possession of the goods, will voluntarily surrender them to the true owner.[18]

Leaving aside the prerequisites that bring about the need for a bailment, there are four primary elements that must be satisfied. First, the goods must either be delivered to the bailee or possession must be transferred to the bailee in some other way.[19] Second, the bailee must voluntarily accept responsibility for the goods.[20] Third, the bailee must exercise due care and skill in handling the goods.[21] Fourth, the bailee must be under some obligation to deliver or return the goods that have been bailed to them.

In *Hobbs v Petersham Transport Co*, Windeyer J articulated the definition of bailment in such a manner as to suggest that delivery was a requirement for bailment to exist. In strict terms, this is not accurate. Invariably, it will be the case that the bailor delivers the goods to the bailee, but this need not be the case. For example, in *Parker v British Airways Board*[22] a person lost a brooch in an airport transit lounge. Mr Parker found the brooch and brought it to the attention of British Airways who controlled the lounge. Under these circumstances, a bailment by finding was formed the moment that Mr Parker found the brooch and took it into his care. There was no actual delivery in this case. What occurred was that Mr Parker voluntarily assumed control of the brooch.

It is notable that in other cases the judiciary has been careful not to use the term 'delivery' in defining the concept of a bailment. In *Carlton International plc v Crayford Freight Services Ltd*,[23] the Federal Court stated:

---

15 N Palmer and P Kohler, 'Information as Property' in N Palmer and E McKendrick (eds), *Interests in Goods* (Lloyd's of London Press, London, 1993), 187.

16 [1894] 1 QB 92.

17 *Parker v British Airways Board* [1982] QB 1004; *W D & H O Wills (Australia) Ltd v State Rail Authority of New South Wales* (1998) 43 NSWLR 338.

18 *Parker v British Airways Board* [1982] QB 1004.

19 *Midlands Silicones Ltd v Scruttons Ltd* [1959] 2 QB 171, 189.

20 *Hobbs v Petersham Transport Co Pty Ltd* (1971) 124 CLR 220; *W D & H O Wills (Australia) Ltd v State Rail Authority of New South Wales* (1998) 43 NSWLR 338.

21 *Hobbs v Petersham Transport Co Pty Ltd* (1971) 124 CLR 220; *Gilchrist Watt & Sanderson Pty Ltd v York Products Pty Ltd* [1970] 3 All ER 825.

22 [1982] QB 1004.

23 (1998) 162 ALR 119.

> It is well settled that to constitute a bailment there must be a transfer of possession of the goods from one person to another without any intention on the part of the bailor to transfer the ownership of the goods to the bailee. The bailee receives the goods for the purpose of fulfilling the instructions of the bailor, which may be to keep the goods in safe custody or to carry the goods from one place to another or to do something to the goods and then return them.[24]

What must happen is that the bailor must transfer the possession of the goods in question into the possession of the bailee. The bailee must have possession in some form in order for the obligations of a bailment to arise.[25] In *Matthew Short & Associates Pty Ltd v Riviera Marine (International) Pty Ltd*,[26] a claim for a bailment failed on the grounds that the putative bailee never received possession. Riviera Marine had made arrangements for the transport of a boat. It contracted with Short to arrange for the transfer of the boat on to a low loader. In turn, Short hired Campbell to transfer the boat. Campbell's driver drove the boat under a bridge and damaged it. Riviera claimed against Short on the basis that he was a bailee. The NSW Court of Appeal held that Short did not have possession of the boat and as such was not a bailee.

The bailee must also voluntarily accept possession of the goods. That is, a bailment requires the knowledge and consent of the bailee. The principle that the bailee must have knowledge of the bailor is illustrated by the case *Marcq v Christie Manson & Woods Ltd*.[27] In *Marcq*, the claimant was the true owner of a painting that was stolen from him in 1979. The defendants received the painting in 1997 from a Mr Schuenemann, who instructed that the painting be sold at auction. When the painting went unsold at auction, it was returned to Mr Schuenemann. The claimant, upon hearing of the auction, sued the defendant for both conversion and breach of duty under a bailment. The claimant argued that the defendant was a bailee and that, as such, Christie's owed duties to him. Tuckey LJ in the Court of Appeal rejected the claimant's argument that some form of bailment had formed on the basis that the putative 'bailee' had no knowledge of the existence of the alleged head bailor. In reaching this decision, Tuckey LJ, with whom the rest of the Court of Appeal agreed, was of the view that while Christie's was a bailee for reward for Mr Schuenemann, there was no bailment relationship of any sort between the claimant and Christie's. As Tuckey LJ observed, 'If you are to owe duties to someone else you should know or at least have some means of knowing of his existence.'[28]

In *W D & H O Wills (Australia) v State Rail Authority of New South Wales*,[29] a container-load of cigarettes was stolen from a locked building that was leased by the State Rail Authority. The appellant argued that the respondent was negligent and had failed to fulfil the terms of a bailment or a sub-bailment. The sub-bailment argument was pressed on the grounds that TNT, which was carrying the goods, had arranged for the goods to be locked in a shed in the building. The NSW Court of Appeal rejected the bailment argument. The short extract below from Mason P sets out the basis upon which the appellant's bailment argument was rejected:

---

24 (1998) 162 ALR 119.
25 *Ashby v Tolhurst* [1937] 2 KB 242.
26 [2001] NSWCA 281.
27 [2004] QB 286.
28 [2004] QB 286, [50].
29 (1998) 43 NSWLR 336.

> Relying on *The Pioneer Container* [1994] 2 AC 324, the appellant contended in its written submissions that the trial judge had erred in not finding that SRA was bailee or sub-bailee of Wills' goods. It is unclear whether this submission was pressed, but I shall address it. It appears to be the case that the appellant accepts that any possible bailment to SRA consequent upon the carriage of the container by rail from Melbourne to Sydney came to an end when SRA relinquished control over the container that was unloaded at the Contrans site. Thereafter TNT was the sole bailee, at least initially. However, a bailment or sub-bailment to SRA is said to have arisen when Mr Sirimanee agreed with TNT for the goods to remain overnight at the Terminal. I would reject this submission. The arrangement simply constituted or confirmed TNT as bailee (cf *Hobbs v Petersham Transport Co Pty Ltd* (1971) 124 CLR 220 at 237–8, but SRA was a stranger to that arrangement. The goods in the container were placed under TNT's exclusive control and locked in its shed.
>
> Alternatively, Wills submitted that SRA became bailee or sub-bailee when (as is likely) the container was driven out of the shed in the middle of the night and parked in the general area of the Terminal as the thieves unloaded its contents. It is true that a finder can become a bailee without an antecedent relationship with the owner of goods, but it is quite unrealistic to regard SRA as being in an equivalent position simply because the land it occupied was the place where the goods were transferred from the container by the thieves. The latter activity took less than 1½ hours. It is unlikely that the cigarettes ever touched the ground as they passed from the container to the thieves' own truck. In any event, the necessary handing over of control to the putative bailee or sub-bailee was absent, as was any assumption of such control: cf *Buchanan & Co Ltd v Hay's Transport Services* [1972] 2 Lloyd's Rep 535 at 542.
>
> It is one thing to conclude that it is not a prerequisite of a bailment that the bailor should have consented to the bailee's possession of the goods. It is something entirely different to hold that a bailment or sub-bailment can come about in the absence of possession, consent or knowledge as regards the alleged bailee or sub-bailee. Proof of bailment may reverse the onus of proof as regards negligence, but the bailment itself must first be established. It was not established here.[30]

In *State Rail Authority*, the simple control of the building pursuant to the lease did not give rise to any special knowledge or consent to goods that were stored in the building. A similar principle can be gleaned from *Big Top Hereford Pty Ltd v Thomas*,[31] where ownership of a particular parcel of land did not make the owner a bailee simply because he consented to the agistment of cattle on his land. An agistment is an arrangement to graze cattle on land in exchange for payment to the landowner. The agistment arrangement could be regarded as a licence or a bailment, depending upon the degree of control exerted by the landowner. The NSW Supreme Court held that the arrangement was a licence. The court stated:

> An agreement for the agistment of livestock may take different legal forms. It may involve a bailment, if the owner of the stock has no right to enter the land on which the stock will be grazed and is not responsible for their care[;] in that case[,] the owner of the property on which the stock are agisted is the bailee and has possession of the cattle, and must take reasonable and proper care of the stock. Or it may involve a licence, by which the owner

30 (1998) 43 NSWLR 338, 353–4.
31 [2006] NSWSC 1159.

> of the cattle has permission to graze his cattle on the licensor's land and to enter the land to care for them. In such a case, the owner of the stock retains possession of the cattle while they are on the licensor's land. Or it may involve a lease, if exclusive possession of the land is granted.
>
> An important distinction between bailment and licence is whether the agistor (land-owner) undertakes responsibility for care of the stock. In the present case, I favour the view that the agistment was a licence.[32]

Once the bailee is voluntarily in possession and has consented to their role in the bailment, then the obligations of reasonable care and the requirement to deliver or return the goods will be incumbent upon the bailee. In Section 8.5 of this chapter, the common duties of all bailments are discussed.

8.3 Sub-bailment

A sub-bailment occurs where the bailor delivers the goods to the bailee who in turn finds another person to carry out the task, or part of the task, that the bailor had allocated to the bailee.[33] For example, a furniture maker in Sydney may contract with a transportation company to carry furniture from Sydney to Melbourne. The furniture maker is the bailor and the transportation company the bailee. The transportation company may then contract with a private truck owner to carry the furniture from its premises to the Melbourne delivery address. The private truck owner is the sub-bailee. The transportation company is both a bailee, in terms of its relationship with the furniture maker, and a bailor, in terms of its arrangement with the private truck owner. The furniture maker is the head bailor. The agreement between the furniture maker and the transportation company is the principal bailment, whereas the arrangement between the transportation company and the private truck owner is a collateral bailment.

There are some legal requirements that must be satisfied in order to give effect to the sub-bailment. The sub-bailee must know of the existence of the head bailor.[34] The sub-bailee must know of the existence of the head bailor at the time that it takes possession.[35] In order for the sub-bailment to form, the initial bailee must first have possession of the goods.[36] In terms of possessory rights, the sub-bailee has an immediate right to possession of the goods.[37] When the sub-bailment comes into existence, the sub-bailee will owe a duty of care to the bailor.[38] There does not need to be a contract between the sub-bailee and the bailor in order for a duty to be owed.[39] Where a dispute arises between the sub-bailee and the bailor, the sub-bailee

32 (2006) 12 BPR 23,383, [36]–[37].
33 *Sandeman Coprimar SA v Transitos y Transportes Integrales SL* [2003] EWCA Civ 113.
34 *The Pioneer Container* [1994] 2 AC 324.
35 *The Pioneer Container* [1994] 2 AC 324.
36 *Matthew Short & Associates Pty Ltd v Riviera Marine (International) Pty Ltd* [2001] NSWCA 281.
37 *Brambles Security Services Ltd v Bi-Lo Pty Ltd* (1992) Aust Torts Reports ¶81-161.
38 *Gilchrist Watt & Sanderson Pty Ltd v York Products Pty Ltd* [1970] 1 WLR 1262.
39 *Gilchrist Watt & Sanderson Pty Ltd v York Products Pty Ltd* [1970] 1 WLR 1262; *The Pioneer Container* [1994] 2 AC 324.

may rely upon their contract with the bailee in order to limit or avoid liability so long as the bailor had authorised the bailee to agree to the sub-bailment contract.[40]

The leading case on sub-bailments is *The Pioneer Container*.[41] In this case, the Privy Council settled two crucial issues pertaining to sub-bailees. The first was whether a bailor would be bound by the terms of a sub-bailment signed by the bailee. The second was whether the sub-bailee could be liable to the head bailor.

In *The Pioneer Container*, two of the three sets of plaintiffs had authorised their carriers to sub-contract 'on any terms'. The carriers then entered a sub-bailment that included a clause providing that any dispute was to be settled in Taiwan. The vessel sank and the cargo was lost. The plaintiffs then sought to sue in Hong Kong. The High Court of Hong Kong ruled that the jurisdiction clause was valid but exercised its discretion to hear the matter in Hong Kong as the proceedings were time-barred in Taiwan. The defendant ship owners appealed and the Hong Kong Court of Appeal ruled that the clause was valid and that the plaintiffs had erred in failing to bring proceedings in Taiwan. The matter was appealed to the Privy Council. As to the question of whether the bailor would be bound by the terms of the sub-bailment, after a lengthy discussion Lord Goff of Chieveley stated:

> It must be assumed that, on the facts of the case, no direct contractual relationship has been created between the owner and the sub-bailee, the only contract created by the sub-bailment being that between the bailee and the sub-bailee. Even so, if the effect of the sub-bailment is that the sub-bailee voluntarily receives into his custody the goods of the owner and so assumes towards the owner the responsibility of a bailee, then to the extent that the terms of the sub-bailment are consented to by the owner, it can properly be said that the owner has authorised the bailee so to regulate the duties of the sub-bailee in respect of the goods entrusted to him, not only towards the bailee but also towards the owner.[42]

With regard to the question of whether the bailee would be liable to the bailor, Lord Goff stated:

> [A] sub-bailee can only be said for these purposes to have voluntarily taken into his possession the goods of another if he has sufficient notice that a person other than the bailee is interested in the goods so that it can properly be said that (in addition to his duties to the bailee) he has, by taking the goods into his custody, assumed towards that other person the responsibility for the goods which is characteristic of a bailee.[43]

8.4 Categories of bailment

It is widely acknowledged that there are several different categories of bailment, but there is a lack of consensus on the true nature of the taxonomy. In *Coggs v Bernard*,[44] Holt CJ identified

40 *The Pioneer Container* [1994] 2 AC 324.
41 [1994] 2 AC 324.
42 [1994] 2 AC 324, 339.
43 [1994] 2 AC 324, 342.
44 (1703) 92 ER 107.

six categories of bailment. These were: (1) *depositum* – a delivery of goods by bailor to bailee to be kept for the use of the bailor; (2) *commodatum* – a situation where goods are lent by the bailor to the bailee for free; (3) *locatio et conductio* – where the goods are left with the bailee on a for hire basis; (4) *vadium* – where goods are left as security for some transaction; (5) where the bailor gives the goods to the bailee for a particular purpose and for a reward; and (6) where the bailee does something to the goods on behalf of the bailor without receiving any reward.[45]

These six categories outlined by Holt CJ are now somewhat out of date. In effect, there are now two main categories of bailment. These are bailments for reward and gratuitous bailments. The basic requirements and subcategories associated with bailments for reward and gratuitous bailments are set out below.

Notwithstanding the two main categories of bailment, there are some other categories of bailment that warrant a brief explanation. In the main, these are sub-bailments, substitutional bailments, bailments by attornement and quasi-bailments. The category of sub-bailments has been set out above in Section 8.3. A substitutional bailment occurs where a bailee who has possession of the goods gives possession of the goods to another bailee on the direction of the bailor.[46] In this situation, there is no contractual relationship between the first bailee and the second bailee, so a sub-bailment does not form. The second bailee is directly responsible to the bailor. A bailment by attornement occurs where the bailee holds the goods to fulfil an order by a person other than the original bailor.[47] For example, a seller might house a particular set of goods at their warehouse. After the sale of those goods, the buyer might pay an extra fee to the seller to store the goods at the warehouse for a while longer or so that a sub-buyer can pick them up later. In this situation, the character of the seller's possession has changed and they are now a bailee to the buyer.

Refers to a situation where a putative bailee undertakes to the bailor that they will carry out particular tasks, but hires another party to deal with these goods.[48] In this situation, the putative bailee is referred to as the quasi-bailee and never gains possession of the goods. In *Hobbs v Petersham Transport Co Pty Ltd*, Windeyer J pointed out that an assumption that had been made at trial, that the defendant was a bailee, was incorrect because the defendant never actually handled the goods in question.[49]

8.4.1 Gratuitous bailment

In a gratuitous bailment, the bailee will perform certain acts in relation to the bailor's goods without receiving compensation. The bailee's obligations will commence once the bailee acquires possession of the goods. Thereupon the bailee will be liable in tort for any damage to the goods. There are three sub-categories of gratuitous bailments: deposit, mandate, and gratuitous loan for use.

45 *Coggs v Bernard* (1703) 2 Ld Raym 909, 912.
46 *China-Pacific SA v Food Corporation of India* [1982] AC 939.
47 *Dublin City Distillery (Great Brunswick Street Dublin) Ltd v Doherty* [1914] AC 823.
48 *Westrac Equipment Pty Ltd v 'Assets Venture'* (2002) 192 ALR 277.
49 (1971) 124 CLR 220, 237.

A deposit arises where the bailor leaves goods with the bailee on the basis that the bailor may regain possession of the goods on demand. The bailee receives no reward for keeping the goods in their possession. Once the bailee has taken possession of the goods they are under an obligation to keep them safely and return them when required. If the bailee cannot fulfil these obligations, they must demonstrate that they are not at fault. For example, in *Phipps v New Claridge's Hotel Ltd*,[50] a hotel guest gave his dog to one of the hotel employees. The dog was subsequently lost and the court held that the New Claridge's Hotel, as bailee of the dog, bore the burden of proving that it was not negligent.

A deposit can be made out of necessity, where external events force the bailor to give possession of the goods to the bailee.[51] A deposit can occur through a mistake if the bailor believes that the bailee is another person who is entitled to possession. A deposit by mistake can arise if the bailor is not in a fit state. In *R v Reeves*,[52] the bailor was intoxicated and allowed a friend to take his watch from his person. When the watch was not returned, the friend was found to be a bailee and was convicted of larceny. Goods may also be deposited by accident. In *Nicholson v Chapman*,[53] the court held that where a bailor had floated timber down a river in order to send it to a saw mill and it had accidentally washed up on a river bank, the 'bailee' was not entitled to recover for expenses incurred in retrieving the timber. A gratuitous bailment by deposit can also arise where the bailee finds goods that the bailor has lost. Once the bailee finds the goods and takes them into their possession, they are bound to try to locate the true owner and to surrender the goods to them if they are found. The finder must also take reasonable care of the goods while they are in their possession.

A gratuitous bailment can also form through a mandate. Under a mandate the bailee has possession of the goods with the consent of the bailor on the basis that the bailee will do some work to the goods while they are in the bailor's possession. In this form of bailment, the bailee is effectively volunteering to do work for the bailee and will receive no reward for their services. Once the bailee has possession, they are under an obligation to comply with the terms of the bailment. Depending upon the terms of the bailment, the bailee may be entitled to recover some costs associated with the work on the goods.

In a gratuitous loan for use, the third type of gratuitous bailment, the bailor gives the goods to the bailee for the benefit of the latter. The bailor receives no compensation in return.

8.4.2 Bailment for reward

A bailment for reward occurs where both parties receive some form of benefit, monetary or otherwise, from the bailment transaction.[54] For example, a bailor might make arrangements with a bailee that the latter is to hold the former's goods in safekeeping for a particular period of time. In return, the bailor will pay the bailee a sum of money and receive the corresponding benefit of having the goods securely stored. Strictly speaking, a bailment for reward does not

50 (1905) 22 TLR 49.
51 *Isaac v Clark* (1615) 80 ER 1143.
52 (1859) 5 Jur NS 716.
53 (1793) 126 ER 536.
54 N E Palmer, *Palmer on Bailment* (Lawbook Co, Sydney, 2nd edn, 1991), 525.

require that either party receives money.[55] It is sufficient that the respective parties derive some form of benefit from the transaction.[56] The reward does not have to be conferred directly on to either party; it may be assigned to a party that they nominate.[57]

There are four types of bailment for reward. These are: (1) custody for reward; (2) hire of work and labour; (3) hire; and (4) pledge. These various forms of bailment for reward are discussed below.

A bailment of custody for reward involves the bailee keeping the goods of the bailor safe in return for some form of compensation.[58] The bailee will take custody of the goods for a temporary period and make them available to the bailor when that period expires or as otherwise required.[59] The bailee is under a duty to take reasonable care of the goods in their possession.[60] If the goods are destroyed or stolen by the actions of a third party, the bailee cannot answer the bailor's claim for compensation simply by pointing out that the bailee was not directly at fault.[61] Instead, the bailee must demonstrate that the loss was not caused by their negligence.[62] In *Pitt Son & Badgery Ltd v Proufelco SA*,[63] the appellant was a bailee who stored greasy wool at their storage shed. The respondent was the bailor and had bought the wool. While it was stored at the shed, a young drifter stuffed paper into a hole in the shed and set fire to the paper. The greasy wool ignited and was destroyed along with the shed. There had been fencing around the shed, but it was not sufficient to prevent intruders from entering the premises. In the High Court, Gibbs CJ stated:

> It can hardly be denied that the appellant's duty required it to take reasonable care to keep out intruders who might misappropriate or damage the wool. Because of the size and weight of the bales the risk of theft was slight, but, when regard is had to the value of the wool, it is impossible to say that no precautions needed to be taken. It may also have been true that the risk of damage by intruders was slight, but it was foreseeable that, under modern conditions, there might be intruders who might, in one way or another, cause damage to the wool. It was the duty of the appellant to take reasonable care to prevent damage of that kind. In deciding what was reasonable, regard must, of course, be had to the difficulty and expense of the possible precautions. The provision of a secure fence is so obvious a precaution and so comparatively inexpensive to provide, that failure to provide it was negligent.[64]

The other justices of the High Court agreed with Gibbs CJ. Even though the risk of damage was slight, the appellant had failed to take adequate measures to secure the premises, and the bailed goods, against a foreseeable risk. It followed then that the appellant could not discharge the onus of proof that they had taken reasonable steps to care for the bailed goods.

A hire for work and labour is a bailment for reward wherein the bailee undertakes to work on the goods in exchange for some benefit.[65] For this bailment to occur, the goods must be

55 *Bryce v Hornby* (1938) 82 SJ 216 (KB).
56 *Sanderson v Collins* [1904] 1 KB 628; *Murphy v Hart* (1919) 46 DLR 36; *Martin v Town 'N' Country Delicatessen Ltd* (1963) 42 DLR (2d) 449.
57 *Andrews v Home Flats Ltd* [1945] 2 All ER 698.
58 *Stallard v Great Western Railway Co* (1862) 121 ER 1129.
59 *Alexander v Railway Executive* [1951] 2 All ER 442.
60 *Coldman v Hill* [1919] 1 KB 443.
61 *Davis v Pearce Parking Station Pty Ltd* (1954) 91 CLR 642.
62 *Nibali v Sweeting & Denney (WA) Pty Ltd* (1989) Aust Tort Reports ¶80-258.
63 (1984) 153 CLR 644.
64 (1984) 153 CLR 644, 648.
65 *Morris v C W Martin & Sons Ltd* [1966] 1 QB 716.

delivered into the possession of the bailee.[66] A bailee for hire of work and labour is under a duty to take reasonable care of the goods.[67] Examples of bailments for hire of work and labour include delivering a car to a garage for repair work or leaving a computer with a workshop for repairs. Under the *Competition and Consumer Act 2010* (Cth), the Australian Consumer Law now applies to certain transactions so as to import a standard of due care and skill with regard to the bailee's work.[68]

A hire of chattels for reward occurs where the bailor provides the bailee with a chattel good for use and the bailee in turn compensates the bailor for the use of the goods.[69] The bailor receives some form of benefit in monetary or other terms. In turn, the bailee gets the quiet possession of the goods for the period of hire. The goods must be returned in reasonable condition.[70] The goods given by the bailor must be fit for the purpose of the hire.[71] In *Gemmell Power Farming Co Ltd v Nies*,[72] Jordan CJ stated: '[W]hen one person for value supplies a chattel to another to be used for an agreed or stated purpose, or for a purpose indicated by the nature of the chattel, he impliedly promises, in the absence of some provision to the contrary, that it is reasonably fit for such use.'[73] This principle was affirmed and adopted by the High Court in *Derbyshire Building Co Pty Ltd v Becker*[74] and by the Queensland Court of Appeal in *Townsend v BBC Hardware Ltd*[75] in relation to bailments of hire of chattels for reward.

Under a pledge, the bailor provides goods to the bailee as security for a transaction.[76] In *Askrigg Pty Ltd v Student Guild of the Curtin University of Technology*,[77] Cohen J stated:

> A pledge is a form of security created by a contract which results in a bailment of the subject matter to the creditor which he is entitled to retain until the debt is paid. It requires actual or constructive delivery of the goods to the pledgee.[78]

The bailee must demonstrate that they have received possession in order for the pledge to operate.[79] The goods will remain with the bailee until the bailor fulfils the obligation under the relevant transaction. The bailee may retain the goods during the period of the pledge, and may sell the goods if the bailor has not fulfilled the relevant requirements.[80] However, the goods cannot be converted prior to the bailor failing to perform the relevant duties, such as payment, by the specified date.[81]

66 *James Spittles v Michael's Appliance Services Pty Ltd* (2008) 71 NSWLR 115.
67 *Krieger v Bell* [1943] SASR 153; *Crouch v Jeeves (1938) Pty Ltd* (1946) 46 SR (NSW) 242.
68 See the introduction to Part 2 of this text and Chapter 13.
69 *Derbyshire Building Co Pty Ltd v Becker* (1962) 107 CLR 633.
70 *Hughes v Rooke* [1954] St R Qd 45.
71 *Derbyshire Building Co Pty Ltd v Becker* (1962) 107 CLR 633; *Townsend v BBC Hardware Ltd* [2003] QCA 572; *Cottee v Franklins Self Service Pty Ltd* [1997] 1 Qd R 469.
72 (1935) 35 SR (NSW) 469.
73 (1935) 35 SR (NSW) 469, 475.
74 (1962) 107 CLR 633.
75 [2003] QCA 572.
76 *Askrigg Pty Ltd v Student Guild of the Curtin University of Technology* (1989) 18 NSWLR 738.
77 (1989) 18 NSWLR 738.
78 18 NSWLR 738, 743.
79 *Official Assignee of Madras v Mercantile Bank of India* [1935] AC 53.
80 *Osborne Computer Corporation Pty Ltd v Airroad Distribution Pty Ltd* (1995) 37 NSWLR 382.
81 N E Palmer, *Palmer on Bailment* (Lawbook Co, Sydney, 2nd edn, 1991), 1405–6.

8.5 Common duties of all bailments

As the bailee has possession of the goods of the bailor, it follows that some duties must be imposed upon the bailee to ensure that the goods remain safe and intact. There are three duties that apply to all bailments. The first is the duty to take reasonable care with the goods bailed.[82] The second is the duty to deliver the goods bailed back to the bailor or where the latter may direct.[83] The third is the duty to comply with the terms of the bailment and to not convert the goods.[84]

In general terms, a bailee will be under a duty to take reasonable care of the goods.[85] The duty will arise as an issue if there is any damage or destruction to the goods while they are in the possession of the bailee.[86] If such damage does occur, then the bailee must demonstrate that they were not at fault.[87] A sub-bailee will be in the same position as a bailee when it comes to the duty to take reasonable care. However, a sub-bailee may limit their liability by relying upon a sub-bailment on terms in circumstances where the bailor has consented to the bailee agreeing to terms in prospective sub-bailments.[88]

The English courts have adopted an approach that effectively imposes a duty to take reasonable care in light of the circumstances of the bailment.[89] In *Mitchell v Ealing London Borough Council*,[90] O'Connor J held that a gratuitous bailee is under a duty to take reasonable care of the goods bailed and to deliver them up on demand. Similarly, in *Port Swettenham Authority v T W Wu & Co (M) Sdn Bhd*,[91] Lord Salmon stated:

> [I]n their Lordships' view the onus is always upon the bailee, whether he be a bailee for reward or a gratuitous bailee, to prove that the loss of any goods bailed to him was not caused by any fault of his or of any of his servants or agents to whom he entrusted the goods for safe keeping. Accordingly the onus of proving that the loss of the goods deposited with the defendants for safe custody was not caused by the negligence or misconduct of their servants in the course of their employment, without any doubt, lies on the defendants.[92]

In *Yearworth v North Bristol NHS Trust*,[93] the negligent storage of sperm samples that ultimately perished while in the defendant's care was held to be a breach of bailment.[94]

82 N E Palmer, *Palmer on Bailment* (Lawbook Co, Sydney, 2nd edn, 1991), 529.
83 *John F Goulding Pty Ltd v Victorian Railway Commissioners* (1932) 48 CLR 157.
84 *Morris v C W Martin & Sons Ltd* [1966] 1 QB 716; *Caxton Publishing Co Ltd v Sutherland Publishing Co* [1939] AC 178.
85 N E Palmer, *Palmer on Bailment* (Lawbook Co, Sydney, 2nd edn, 1991), 529.
86 *Westrac Equipment Pty Ltd v 'Assets Venture'* (2002) 192 ALR 277.
87 *Followmont Transport Pty Ltd v Premier Group Pty Ltd* [1999] QCA 232; *Matrix Europe Ltd v Uniserve Holdings Ltd* [2009] All ER (D) 126.
88 *Westpac Banking Corporation v Royal Tongan Airlines* [1996] NSWSC 409; see also K Lewins, 'Sub-Bailment on Terms and the Australian Consumer' (2002) 9(3) *Murdoch E-Law Journal* 37.
89 *China-Pacific SA v Food Corporation of India* [1982] AC 939.
90 [1979] QB 1, 6.
91 [1979] AC 580.
92 [1979] AC 580, 589.
93 [2010] QB 1.
94 See, further, J Lee, '*Yearworth v North Bristol NHS Trust* [2009]: Instrumentalism and Fictions in Property Law' in S Douglas, R Hickey and E Waring, *Landmark Cases in Property Law* (Hart Publishing, Oxford, UK, 2015), 25. See also *Re Cresswell* [2018] QSC 142.

The approach of the English courts appears to be generally accepted in Australia. While the High Court in *Pitt Son & Badgery Ltd v Proufelco SA* did not specifically endorse any English authorities, the tenor of the decision of Gibbs CJ, with whom the court agreed, is generally consistent with the English authorities. In *W G H Nominees Pty Ltd v Tomblin*,[95] Zelling J stated that the formula of reasonable care as demanded by the circumstances of the case was 'obviously correct'. As Traves has noted, this approach drew support in *Bowden v Lo*[96] and *Graham v Voigt*.[97] In *Bowden v Lo*, a tenant departed from a premises where his goods were stored without paying a significant amount of unpaid rent. The landlord, Lo, took possession of the premises and by extension took possession of the tenant's goods. Though the landlord was initially an involuntary bailee, he later consented to this role and used possession of the goods as security for the unpaid rent. The tenant, Bowden, subsequently paid the arrears and regained possession of the premises. He found that some of his goods were missing. In the NSW Supreme Court, relying in part on *Mitchell v Ealing*, Hodgson CJ found that Lo as bailee owed a duty of reasonable care to Bowden. More recent decisions of *Santos Coffee Co Pty Ltd v Direct Freight Express Pty Ltd*[98] and *Pangallo Estate Pty Ltd v Killara 10 Pty Ltd*[99] also provide support for this approach.

There has been an approach in the past that a gratuitous bailee will only face liability for gross negligence.[100] The English courts have rejected this approach.[101] However, in *Kehoe v Williams*,[102] McLellan J affirmed the traditional approach. It remains to be seen whether *Kehoe* is an anomalous decision or whether Australia courts will adopt a position on the liability of gratuitous bailees that is at odds with their English counterparts. There is much to commend the view of the English courts that a common-sense approach should be adopted and that where a gratuitous bailee has consented to a bailment, they should be held to a reasonable standard of care. Nonetheless, given that most bailments that are litigated tend to be bailments for reward, this matter might not be settled soon.

The proposition that the duty to take reasonable care will depend upon the context in which the bailment occurs requires a consideration of the goods bailed and the circumstances in which they are stored. In *China-Pacific SA v Food Corporation of India*,[103] Lord Diplock held that a bailee had a duty to preserve the integrity of his perishable cargo even though the type of bailment under which he acted had changed. Lord Diplock stated:

> The bailment which up to the conclusion of the salvage services had been a bailment for valuable consideration became a gratuitous bailment; and so long as that relationship of bailor and bailee continued to subsist the salvors, under the ordinary principles of the law of bailment too well known and too well established to call for any citation of authority, owed a duty of care to the cargo owner to take such measures to preserve the salved wheat from deterioration by exposure to the elements as a man of ordinary prudence

95 (1985) Aust Tort Reports ¶80-740.
96 (1998) NSW ConvR ¶55-868.
97 (1989) 95 FLR 146. See S Traves *Commercial Law* (LexisNexis Butterworths Australia, Sydney, 2009), 260. See also *Glebe Island Terminals v Continental Seagram* (1993) 40 NSWLR 206, 228.
98 [2008] NSWDC 235.
99 [2007] NSWSC 1528.
100 *Coggs v Bernard* (1703) 92 ER 107.
101 *Garlic v W & H Rycroft Ltd* [1982] CAT 277 (CA).
102 [2006] NSWSC 326.
103 [1982] AC 939.

> would take for the preservation of his own property. For any breach of such duty the bailee is liable to his bailor in damages for any diminution in value of the goods consequent upon his failure to take such measures; and if he fulfils that duty, he has, in my view, a correlative right to charge the owner of the goods with the expenses reasonably incurred in doing so.[104]

In contrast, an attempt to rely upon this argument in relation to the bailment of a ship was found by the Supreme Court of Victoria in *Challenge Charter Pty Ltd v Curtain Brothers (Qld) Pty Ltd*[105] to be 'audacious' and without foundation. In *Challenge Charter*, the bailor had failed to pay for the maintenance of his ship and sought to impose a duty to do so on the bailee through the duty to take reasonable care. In *Challenge Charter*, Gillard J drew a distinction between the cargo of wheat in *China-Pacific* and the ship by pointing out that the former was quite prone to deterioration if exposed to the elements while the latter was not. Gillard J stated:

> Wheat is a natural product which will rapidly deteriorate when exposed to the elements, reaching the point when it can no longer be used for consumption. The deterioration of a ship is different. It is part and parcel of a natural process over time and falls into the category of wear and tear. It can be arrested by suitable measures and the rate of deterioration accordingly minimised.[106]

His Honour found that a prudent ship owner would have sought to prevent the deterioration. As such, the duty could not be shifted on to the bailee. Other attempts to expand the duty of reasonable care have been similarly unsuccessful. In *All Covers & Accessories Pty Ltd v Sidawi*,[107] the Victorian Supreme Court held that a bailee was not under a duty to inform a bailor that it did not have insurance to cover the goods bailed in the event of their destruction. Mr Sidawi had left his boat with the appellant so that the latter could do work on the boat. During the time that the boat was with the appellant a fire destroyed his factory workshop. Mr Sidawi's boat was also destroyed in the fire. At first instance, a magistrate held that the appellant was under a duty to inform Mr Sidawi that he did not have insurance. The appellant subsequently appealed to the Supreme Court of Victoria, which held that the duty to inform the bailor of the bailee's lack of insurance was not an ordinary part of the bailee's duties under a bailment. Mukhtar J stated:

> If the bailee is not an insurer of the goods, and is under no duty to insure goods, then the question whether he was bound to warn that there was no insurance can only arise in the same way as the law of negligence ordinarily considers cases where there is an alleged failure to warn (or an inadequate warning) about a foreseeable or unreasonable risk to person or property.[108]

Under the laws of negligence, there may be situations where one party must warn another party about a foreseeable risk. In the context of a bailment, this would translate to a duty on the part of the bailee to warn the bailor that the premises at which it contemplated that the goods

104 [1982] AC 939, 960.
105 [2004] VSC 1.
106 [2004] VSC 1, [219].
107 (2012) 36 VR 113.
108 (2012) 39 VR 113, [47].

would be stored was inadequate for the purpose. However, in the absence of those circumstances the bailee's primary duty is to take reasonable care of the goods that have been bailed. Mr Sidawi had sought to rely upon the principle of reasonable care in order to extend the duties of the bailee. The court found this to be an argument that extended the duties of the bailee too far and without any basis in authority. Mukhtar J concluded:

> The respondent's thesis was that the notion of reasonable care for the bailed goods goes beyond the physical care and protection of the goods, especially where the goods were of an unusually high value. The notion of reasonable care can, it was submitted, extend to steps necessary generally to looking after the bailor's interests.
>
> In my view that is far too broad an extension to countenance. There is, as I have endeavoured to show, no authority to support it ... It clashes with the settled law that a bailee is not an insurer and is under no duty to ensure. Nor do I see a principled basis to make the extension, certainly not on the exiguous facts of this case. Even accepting that circumstances may arise arousing a duty to warn in a bailment case under the general laws of negligence, then consistently with the duties of bailee, it would be a duty to warn about hazards to the goods, for to go beyond that and require the bailee to warn about matters affecting the bailor's interests in the goods imposes an assumption of responsibility by the bailee for something more than the goods as bailed.[109]

While the duty to take reasonable care with the goods bailed may seem at face value to be a simple proposition, it does seem likely that there will be cases that will legitimately test the boundaries of the duty. Cases like *Challenge Charter* and *Sidawi* go rather too far in attempting to extend the duty. Nonetheless, given that the duty to take reasonable care depends upon the circumstances of the bailment, the task of mapping out the limits of the duty will be a question of fact and degree as cases arise.

A bailee is also under a duty to deliver the goods that have been bailed to them. This duty is fundamental to the bailment relationship. To some extent, the duty to take reasonable care and the duty to deliver the goods are interlinked, but they are distinct and separate duties.[110] In *Jackson v Cochrane*,[111] McPherson J stated that it was 'the primary duty of the bailee to redeliver the chattel bailed to the bailor or as the bailor may direct'.[112] Similarly, in *Santos Coffee Co*, the court stated:

> Bailment involves the redelivery of a specific thing in its original or some altered form to the bailor in accordance with the terms of the bailment. It is necessary that the goods themselves, either in altered or original form, are returnable and not merely some other goods of equivalent character or value. There must be a clear physical heredity between what has been delivered to the bailor and what must be returned.[113]

If the bailee is unable to redeliver the goods bailed or to deliver them as directed through no fault of their own, then they will not have failed to comply with the duty. In *John F Goulding Pty Ltd v Victorian Railway Commissioners*, Starke, Dixon and McTiernan JJ held that the duty

109 (2012) 36 VR 113, [61]–[62].
110 *John F Goulding Pty Ltd v Victorian Railway Commissioners* (1932) 48 CLR 157.
111 [1989] 2 Qd R 23.
112 [1989] 2 Qd R 23.
113 [2008] NSWDC 235, [14].

to redeliver 'was not absolute but qualified' and that it would not be breached 'if the defendants were disabled from delivery through destruction or loss of the goods which reasonable care and skill on their part could not avoid'.[114] However, if a misdelivery were to arise, the bailee might still face liability as they would have dealt with the goods in a manner that is contrary to the terms of the bailment.[115] In *John F Goulding*, a failure to correct the loss of possession on the part of the defendant gave rise to liability. The High Court held that 'even if the defendants had lost possession of the goods without negligence on their part but by the exercise of reasonable care they might have regained them, their failure to deliver them to the plaintiff would not be excused'.[116]

The duty to comply with the terms of the bailment and to not convert the goods bailed is closely related to the foregoing two duties incumbent upon the bailee. In essence, a bailee must comply with the terms of the bailment and should not intentionally interfere with the bailor's property rights.[117] This duty is applicable where the bailee's failure to comply with the terms of the bailment results in the loss or destruction of the goods bailed. A failure to comply with the duties of the bailment can amount to a wrongful interference with the goods.[118] In *Lancashire & Yorkshire Railway Co, London & North Western Railway Co & Graeser Ltd v MacNicoll*,[119] Atkin J defined conversion as follows:

> [D]ealing with goods in a manner inconsistent with the right of the true owner amounts to a conversion, provided that it is also established that there is also an intention on the part of the defendant in so doing to deny the owner's right or to assert a right which is inconsistent with the owner's right.[120]

This definition was cited with approval by Lord Porter in *Caxton Publishing Co Ltd v Sutherland Publishing Co*,[121] who added that 'another way of reaching the same conclusion would be to say that conversion consists in an act intentionally done inconsistent with the owner's right, though the doer may not know of, or intend to challenge, the property or possession of the true owner'.[122] In turn, this definition was endorsed by Lord Diplock in the course of defining a bailee's duties in *Morris v C W Martin & Sons Ltd*,[123] in a case where the plaintiff sent a mink stole to a furrier for cleaning. The furrier explained to the plaintiff that he could not do the task himself and sent it to the defendant, C W Martin & Sons, for cleaning. While in the possession of C W Martin, the mink stole was stolen by a junior employee. The plaintiff sued for conversion. Lord Diplock stated:

> One of the common law duties owed by a bailee of goods to his bailor is not to convert them, i.e., not to do intentionally in relation to the goods an act inconsistent with the

114 48 CLR 157, 166.
115 *Jackson v Cochrane* [1989] 2 Qd R 23.
116 48 CLR 157, 166.
117 *Morris v C W Martin & Sons Ltd* [1966] 1 QB 716; *Caxton Publishing Co Ltd v Sutherland Publishing Co* [1939] AC 178, 202.
118 *Schwarzchild v Harrods* [2008] All ER (D) 299.
119 (1918) 88 LJKB 601.
120 (1918) 88 LJKB 601, 605.
121 [1939] AC 178.
122 [1939] AC 178, 202.
123 [1966] 1 QB 716.

> bailor's right of property therein ... This duty, which is common to all bailments as well as to other relationships which do not amount to bailment, is independent of and additional to the other common law duty of a bailee for reward to take reasonable care of his bailor's goods. Stealing goods is the simplest example of conversion.[124]

The Court of Appeal duly found that the defendants were in breach of their duty of care to take reasonable care of the goods and to not convert them. It was no answer to the plaintiff's case that the defendant had an exemption clause in their contract with the furrier (sub-bailee).

It is important to note that conversion requires an intent to deprive the true owner of the goods of their right to possession. In *Morris v C W Martin*, this requirement was satisfied by the theft of the mink stole. The act of theft required intent and purpose in the actions of the junior employee. In contrast, in *Santos Coffee Co Pty Ltd v Direct Freight Express Pty Ltd*, an arrangement between the plaintiff and the defendant was such that the plaintiff sent pallets of their product to their customers via the defendant. As such, the goods bailed to the defendant as bailee were both the plaintiff's product and the pallets on which they were carried. Under the arrangement between the parties the defendant was to return empty pallets to the plaintiff. For its part, the plaintiff was sourcing the pallets from a third party. For two years the defendant only intermittently returned pallets. The plaintiffs ignored this omission despite the fact that they had to source more pallets. Eventually the plaintiffs sued and based their claim in part on conversion. The NSW District Court stated:

> Conversion entails an intentional dealing with chattels in a manner repugnant to the 'owner's' immediate right to possession. In addition, there must be an intention to deprive the 'owner' of its immediate right to possession. It is not conversion to transfer possession otherwise than for the purpose of affecting the 'owner's' immediate right to possession ... Even if there was a bailment of the pallets, there are two impediments to Santos's claim in conversion. First, Direct did not deal with the pallets in a manner repugnant to Santos's right to possession. It delivered them to third parties, as required by the transport agreement. Second ... the necessary intention was absent as there was no deliberate or positive act of withholding pallets.[125]

The failure to redeliver the pallets to the plaintiff occurred as a result of the lack of care on the part of the defendants and the plaintiff's customers. Technically, the pallets could still be recovered, even though little effort had been expended to this end. Moreover, the defendant's dealings with the pallets were consistent with the wishes of the plaintiff. There had only been neglect in recovering them from the plaintiff's own customers. The absence of any intent to deprive the plaintiff of rightful possession was fatal to their claim in bailment.

8.6 Bailment and other legal relationships

Bailment can share attributes with other legal categories. Yet bailment is distinct from categories such as agency, trusts, contract and licence. In this section, we will address the key distinctions between bailment and other legal relationships and categories.

124 [1966] 1 QB 716, 732.
125 [2008] NSWDC 235, [18]–[19].

8.6.1 Bailment and agency

An agency relationship exists where an agent undertakes tasks on behalf of a principal. An agency relationship is based on consent in that both the agent and the principal consent to the particular agency between them. Both bailment and agency are legal relationships that serve the ends of commercial convenience. However, an agency relationship has a multiplier effect with regard to the principal's legal personality by allowing them to contract with multiple parties simultaneously. The agent has the power to contract with third parties on behalf of the principal. In contrast, a bailee does not have the legal power to represent the bailor in contractual dealings with third parties. A bailment is most likely confined to the carriage of goods, whereas the scope of an agent's authority depends upon the consent and conduct of the principal. It is true that both bailments and agency relationships may impose fiduciary obligations. It is clear that an agent owes a fiduciary obligation to their principal. However, it is less clear as to whether a bailee owes a fiduciary obligation to the bailor.[126] Instead, the existence of fiduciary obligations in the context of a bailment may well depend upon the specific circumstances of the dealings between the relevant parties.

8.6.2 Bailment and trust

A trust relationship arises where the equitable title to property is vested in one party (the beneficiary) while the legal title is vested in another (the trustee). A trust relationship may arise over real and personal property. In contrast, a bailment involves no separation of ownership from one party to another, merely the transfer of possession, and bailments are confined to those forms of personal property that are choses in possession.

8.6.3 Bailment and licence

As a bailment may arise where goods are stored at premises controlled by another, there have been cases where the distinction between a bailment and a licence has become important. In *Palmer v Toronto Medical Arts Building Ltd*,[127] a man gave his car to an attendant at a parking lot. The man had previously parked his car at the parking lot without dealing with the attendants. When he sought to recover his car, he found that it had been stolen. He sued the owner of the parking lot, claiming that there had been a bailment. The Ontario Court of Appeal held that the relationship between the parties was one of licensee–licensor, rather than that of bailor–bailee. The plaintiff had permission to park his car in the parking lot, but he retained possession of the vehicle.

In *Zweeres v Thibault*,[128] the plaintiff rented a room and stored furniture at the defendant's premises. The plaintiff later found that her furniture had been damaged by damp and rats. The plaintiff sued on the basis that the relationship between the parties was one of bailment. The court found that the defendant had sufficient power to exclude all others from the premises,

126 *Brambles Security Services Ltd v Bi-Lo Pty Ltd* (1992) Aust Torts Reports ¶81-161, 61,275.
127 [1960] OR 60 (Ont CA).
128 23 A2d 529 (US Vt SC 1942).

apart from the plaintiff, and that there was sufficient grounds to regard the situation as one of a bailment. The fact that the plaintiff could have removed the goods at any time did not preclude the possibility that the relationship was one of a bailment.

In essence, the degree of control over the goods sets the distinction between a bailment and a licence.[129] A licence amounts to a permission to enter and use an area, whereas a bailment involves a transfer of possession and an acceptance of a duty of care.[130]

8.6.4 Bailment and contract

The existence of a bailment does not depend upon the existence of a contract. A contract requires offer, acceptance, consideration, capacity and the intention to create legal relations. The existence of a bailment does not depend upon the formation doctrines of contract law. Nonetheless, an agreement for a bailment may be such as to also constitute a contract, as the two are not mutually exclusive.[131] Where a bailment has been created by a contract, the application of common law principles will depend upon the terms of the contract. In *Hill v Reglon Pty Ltd*,[132] Beazley JA stated:

> Where the bailment is created by contract, the extent to which the common law principles continue to apply depends upon a construction of the contract . . . Common law rights are only excluded or overridden by the terms of the contract if the clearest of terms to that effect are used: see also *Waterways Authority of New South Wales v Coal & Allied (Operations) Pty Limited* [2007] NSWCA 276. A clause that merely gives a right to terminate by notice for breach of the contract of bailment does not have that effect: *Union Transport Finance Ltd v British Car Auctions Ltd* [1978] 2 All ER 385 at 391 per Bridge LJ . . . In *Union Transport Finance Limited v British Car Auctions Ltd*, Bridge LJ stated the proposition in these terms:
>
>> . . . it would be perfectly possible to introduce into a contract of bailment a term expressly limiting the manner in which the bailee's right to possession as against the bailor could be terminated . . . It seems to me that it would require the clearest express terms to have that effect. A clause which merely gives a right to terminate by notice for any breach of the contract of bailment could not possibly, in my judgment, be construed as having that effect. Its purpose is to enhance the rights of the bailor and not to curtail them.[133]

Fundamentally, where parties enter into a contractual relationship the parameters of that relationship are invariably demarcated by the contract itself.[134] In *Tomlin v Ford Credit Australia*,[135] McDougall J stated: 'Where the parties have agreed that a particular thing under the contract may be done by one of them in its uncontrolled discretion, the law

129 *Robertson v Stang* (1997) 38 CCLT (2d) 62.
130 N E Palmer, *Palmer on Bailment* (Lawbook Co, Sydney, 2nd edn, 1991).
131 *Parastatidis v Kotaridis* [1978] VR 449.
132 [2007] NSWCA 295.
133 [2007] NSWCA 295, [46].
134 *Tomlin v Ford Credit Australia Ltd* [2005] NSWSC 540, [124]–[129]; *Tai Hing Cotton Mill Ltd v Liu Chong Hing Bank Ltd* [1986] AC 80, 107.
135 [2005] NSWSC 540.

should be slow to remake their bargain by imposing a duty of care the effect of which would be to fetter that contractually uncontrolled discretion.'[136] A common law obligation that is inconsistent with the terms of the contract cannot normally displace the clear intentions of the parties.[137]

8.7 Key points

- A bailment is a legal relationship where one person, known as the bailor, permits their goods to be taken into the possession of another person, known as the bailee, so that the bailee can carry out a task assigned by the bailor.
- For a bailment to exist, certain requirements must be satisfied. As a general prerequisite, the bailor must be in possession of goods. This need not be actual possession; it may be constructive possession or de facto possession.
- The bailee must also voluntarily accept possession of the goods. That is, a bailment requires the knowledge and consent of the bailee.
- A sub-bailment occurs where the bailor delivers the goods to the bailee, who in turn finds another person to carry out the task, or part of the task, that the bailor had allocated to the bailee.
- There are three duties that apply to all bailments: (1) the duty to take reasonable care with the goods bailed; (2) the duty to deliver the goods bailed back to the bailor, or to where the latter may direct; and (3) the duty to comply with the terms of the bailment and to not convert the goods.

8.8 DISCUSSION QUESTIONS

1. What purpose does the law of bailment serve? Who are the relevant parties to a bailment, and how is risk allocated among them?
2. What are the primary requirements of a bailment?
3. How do you define the duties of a bailment, and how might they be breached?
4. How should risk be allocated between the parties in the context of a sub-bailment?
5. What are the different types of possession that arise in the context of a bailment?

8.9 FURTHER READING

Palmer, N E, *Palmer on Bailment* (Lawbook Co, Sydney, 2nd edn, 1991).

136 [2005] NSWSC 540, [124].
137 *Simms Jones Ltd v Protochem Trading NZ Ltd* [1993] NZLR 369, 377.

9

PERSONAL PROPERTY SECURITIES ACT

9.0 Introduction

This chapter concerns the system for creation and enforcement of security interests over personal property. It considers the operation of the *Personal Property Securities Act 2009* (Cth) (PPSA, or 'the Act'), examining (1) the Act's purpose and overall design, (2) the definition of security interests, (3) the kinds of security interests it governs; (4) what constitutes the taking of good security, including explanation of the concepts of attachment and perfection of interests; (5) the extinguishment rules; (6) the fate of certain proprietary interests such as fixed and floating charges under the Act; and (7) the principles and rules of priority of interests as they operate under the Act.

The chapter explains how the Act approaches the recognition of a security interest as a matter of substance rather than form. Recent amendments to the PPSA are also examined. In order to facilitate readers' understanding, we have used a series of short examples to illustrate some abstract concepts as well as the application of some complex provisions, and have attempted to explain the policy rationale and objectives underlying the different parts of the PPSA where appropriate. Emerging PPSA law cases are referred to where relevant.

9.1 What is the Personal Property Securities Act?

The *Personal Property Securities Act 2009* (Cth), along with the *Personal Property Securities (Consequential Amendment) Act 2009* (Cth), is the Commonwealth legislation that replaces 77 existing Commonwealth, state and territory Acts with a single, national law. The PPSA represents a major step in the development of Australian commercial law, and it affects many important aspects of commercial law, such as banking law, sale of goods law, the law on hire purchase, intellectual property law, the law of restitution, the law relating to assignments, insolvency law, and property law.[1] The PPSA applies throughout Australia through various states' Personal Property Securities (Commonwealth Powers) Acts. The PPSA also introduces the Personal Property Securities Register (PPSR), a national online register for the registration of security interests, replacing multiple security-related registers such as those registering company charges, bills of sale, crop liens, motor vehicle securities and stock mortgages.[2]

The PPSA is based on Canadian and New Zealand interpretations of the Article 9 regime of the Uniform Commercial Code (UCC) of the United States. The Australian PPSA was enacted in 2009 and came into effect on 30 January 2012. New Zealand enacted a PPSA in 1999, more than a decade earlier than Australia.[3] The New Zealand PPSA closely follows the text of the Canadian (Saskatchewan) PPSA.[4] Australia has taken a more freewheeling approach. It takes

1 See A Duggan and D Brown, *Australian Personal Property Securities Law* (LexisNexis Butterworths Australia, Sydney, 2nd edn, 2016), xv.

2 C Wappett, 'Background and Overview of Personal Property Securities Law in Australia' in *Essential Personal Property Securities in Australia* (LexisNexis Butterworths Australia, Sydney, 2013), [1.50].

3 *Personal Property Securities Act 1999* (NZ).

4 *Personal Property Security Act RSS 1993*, c P-6.2. The Canadian (Saskatchewan) PPSA is based on a model statute drafted by the Western Canada Personal Property Security Act Committee. All the common law provinces and territories, with the exception of Ontario, have enacted substantially similar

the Canadian (Saskatchewan) model as its starting point. However, it is distinct from this model in a number of significant ways, particularly with regard to drafting and substance.[5] The PPSA was conceived to completely overhaul how all security interests over property are created, perfected and enforced. The exception to this is for security interested over land, fixtures, water rights and certain statutory licences. The PPSA fundamentally alters the law relating to security interests in personal property, regulating the creation, registration and enforcement of securities in personal property. It also changes the law regarding determination of priorities by establishing codified priority rules that rely on the concepts of 'attachment', 'enforceability' and 'perfection'.[6] The PPSA further expands the scope of 'security interest' definition to include PPS leases and retention of title (ROT) arrangements.[7] Like its counterparts in the US and Canada, the Australian PPSA adopts a unitary concept of 'security interest' based on function rather than form and abolishing the distinction between security in the traditional sense and title-retention devices serving a security purpose.[8]

More specifically, the PPSA's changes to the common law are accompanied by new terminology and novel concepts. For example:

- A 'security interest' has two elements: (1) secured property (collateral), and (2) secured monies (obligations).[9] Collateral satisfies the debtor's obligations if the debtor fails to satisy them.[10] The PPSA 'concerns itself with personal property in which there is a security interest'.[11] It also focuses on the substance rather than the form of a transaction, and is centrally concerned with whether the security interest secures the performance of a debt or an obligation. Under the PPSA, 'assets are available for realisation by creditors if a "security interest" has been "perfected" by the person who has such an interest'.[12] A creditor who holds a perfected security interest has priority over other creditors.[13] The substantive

legislation. See also A Duggan, 'The Australian PPSA from a Canadian Perspective: Some Comparative Reflections' (2011) 40(1) *Monash University Law Review* 59–60.

5 See also A Duggan, 'The Australian PPSA from a Canadian Perspective: Some Comparative Reflections' (2011) 40(1) *Monash University Law Review* 59–60. (Duggan provided a detailed comparison of the PPSA in Australia and Canada.)

6 See R North, 'The New Zealand Personal Property Securities Act: Growing Pains' (2005) 11 *Canterbury Law Review* 123, cited by Thynne & Macartney, 'Australia: The PPSA Priority Rules: Lessons from Abroad', *Mondaq*, 31 August 2011.

7 See R North, 'The New Zealand Personal Property Securities Act: Growing Pains' (2005) 11 *Canterbury Law Review* 123, cited by Thynne & Macartney, 'Australia: The PPSA Priority Rules: Lessons from Abroad', *Mondaq*, 31 August 2011.

8 Pre-PPSA law depended to a great extent on doctrinal distinctions between forms of secured transactions. See A Duggan and D Brown, *Australian Personal Property Securities Law* (LexisNexis Butterworths Australia, Sydney, 2nd edn, 2016), xvi.

9 See D Barlin, '*Personal Property Securities*' (Wentworth Selborne Chambers, 2012), 8: https://www.13wentworthselbornechambers.com.au/.

10 See M Bennett, 'Practical Problem Caused by the Personal Property Securities Act' (Wentworth Selborne Chambers, 2013), 4: https://www.13wentworthselbornechambers.com.au/.

11 See M Bennett, 'Practical Problem Caused by the Personal Property Securities Act' (Wentworth Selborne Chambers, 2013), 4: https://www.13wentworthselbornechambers.com.au/.

12 See M Bennett, 'Practical Problem Caused by the Personal Property Securities Act' (Wentworth Selborne Chambers, 2013), 4: https://www.13wentworthselbornechambers.com.au/.

13 See M Bennett, 'Practical Problem Caused by the Personal Property Securities Act' (Wentworth Selborne Chambers, 2013), 4: https://www.13wentworthselbornechambers.com.au/.

approach to registered security interests means that title no longer determines rights over assets. In fact, a person may create a security interest in personal property they do not own.

- All personal property that is the subject of a security interest is now known as collateral. Collateral also has an extended definition. Section 10 of PPSA provides that collateral may include personal property described by registration of a security interest regardless of whether the security interest has attached. Section 161 extends the definition of collateral to include personal property described in a registered financing statement before or after a security agreement is made or a security interest has attached to the property.
- A retention of title (*Romalpa*) security interest is now known as a purchase money security interest (PMSI).
- Under the PPSA, retention of title is considered only another security interest within the meaning of s 12, requiring sellers to comply with the PPSA (not simply its retention of title) to ensure protection against non-payment, and registration to provide the vendor or financier with priority against competing security interests. Previously, transactions subject to retention of title clauses protected sellers or financiers by delaying the transfer of title in (but not possession of) goods to the buyer, enabling sellers of financiers to retain ownership over the goods until certain conditions – usually, that the goods had been paid for – were satisfied. Retention of title clauses defeated claims by purchasers and third parties subject to the nemo dat ('no one [can] give what one does not have') provisions of the sale of goods legislation, enabling sellers to recover goods should the buyer become insolvent or bankrupt.
- A PPS lease is a lease of personal property for more than two years.[14] However, vehicle leases that were entered into prior to 1 October 2015 are categorised as a PPS lease if they are for a period of 90 days.[15] A fixed and floating charge is known as a circulating asset or, sometimes, a general security agreement (GSA).
- The charger, borrower or mortgagor of personal property is now the *grantor* – that is, the person who either owns or has an interest in the personal property to which the security interest is attached, and who gives the security interest.
- The charge, or person to whom the security interest is given, is the *secured party*. The secured party may be a financier, mortgagee, charge, lender, supplier under a retention of title arrangement, or lessor.
- The charge document is the security agreement.

14 The minimum period for a lease or bailment to qualify as a PPS lease was previously an indefinite period, or a term or terms of one year or more. The *Personal Property Securities Amendment (PPS Leases) Act 2017* (Cth) modifies the meaning of a 'PPS lease' under s 13 of the PPSA. It extends the minimum duration of a PPSA lease to more than two years (from more than one year) and stipulates that a lease of an indefinite term will not be deemed to be a PPS lease unless and until the lease term 'runs' for a period of more than two years. The change came into effect on 20 May 2017. The change means that leases and bailments entered into after 20 May 2017 are subject to the new PPS lease definition. See also https://www.ppsr.gov.au/legislation/pps-lease-change-2017. It is noteworthy that the changes only apply to leases and bailments entered into on and after 20 May 2017. The previous law will continue to apply to leases and bailment arrangements entered into before this date.

15 The repeal section of s 13(1)(e) of the PPSA came into effect in October 2015. This amendment does not operate retrospectively, meaning that any lease or bailment of serialised goods for more than 90 days that was entered into prior to 1 October 2015 still gives rise to a security interest that must be registered on the PPS Register in order to properly protect the interest.

9.1.1 What happens to existing security arrangements?

The PPSA and the PPS Register commenced in Australia in 2012. Security interests already registered on other existing registers prior to the commencement date, such as Australian Securities and Investments Commission (ASIC) charges and motor vehicle encumbrances, were automatically migrated to the PPS Register.[16] Subject to 'retention of title', any security interests that already existed at or before their commencement were 'transitional security interests'.

However, subject to retention of title, all security interests in existence prior to the commencement date that were not at the time registrable (eg retention of title clauses or PPS leases, and chattel mortgages) were 'transitional security interests'. The transitional period extended over two years, and ended in January 2014. During the transitional period, existing security interests were deemed 'temporarily perfected' and given two years to be registered on the PPS Register (or to be otherwise perfected) so that the perfected security interest and priority against other secured parties are maintained.[17] Since the transitional period ended on 30 January 2014, all provisions under the PPSA will 'now apply to all security interests, including security interests created before 30 January 2014'.[18]

9.2 What does the PPSA apply to?

The PPSA applies to 'security interests' in 'personal property'. 'Personal property' is an extremely broad category that includes both tangible and intangible property. It is defined in s 10 ('The Dictionary'), which relevantly provides as follows:

> '[P]ersonal property' means property (including a licence) other than:
>
> (a) land; or
> (b) a right, entitlement or authority that is:
> (i) granted by or under a law of the Commonwealth, a State or a Territory; and
> (ii) declared by that law not to be personal property for the purposes of this Act.
>
> Note: This Act does not apply to certain interests even if they are interests in personal property (see section 8).

Under s 10, examples of personal property include stock in trade, inventory, goods of all kinds, raw materials, livestock, marketable securities, shares, investment instruments, accounts, certain contractual rights, intellectual property and receivables. Effectively, personal property is everything except land, and certain statutory rights. Section 10 also states that '"land" includes all estates and interest in land, whether freehold, leasehold or chattel, but does not include fixtures'. Through the breadth of s 10, the PPSA provides scope to recognise the importance of new classes of property such as those associated with advanced technology (software, code and programs), and intellectual property rights.

16 See F Gibson, *Overview of the Personal Property Securities Act* (Grain Trade Australia, Sydney), 4.
17 PPSA, Chapter 9.
18 Gordon & Jackson, 'PPSA – Updates and Interesting Cases', 1: https://svensonbarristers.com.au/.

Generally speaking, personal property does not include real property or fixtures to land: PPSA, s 8(1)(j), *Forge Group Power Pty Ltd (in liq) v General Electric International Inc* (2016) 305 FLR 101, [76]–[84] (Hammerschlag J). In *Power Rental Op Co Australia, LLC v Forge Group Power Pty Ltd* (2017) 93 NSWLR 765, the court further examined the concept of a fixture adopted in the PPSA.

POWER RENTAL OP CO AUSTRALIA, LLC *v* FORGE GROUP POWER PTY LTD (IN LIQ) (RECS AND MGRS APPTD) (2017) NSWLR 765

Issue: The concept of a fixture adopted in the PPSA.

Facts: General Electric (GT) leased turbines to Forge Group Power (Forge). GE, as lessor, did not perfect its security interest registration under the PPSA. Later, Power Rental (PR) replaced GE as lessor. Forge went into voluntary administration, then into liquidation. At first instance, the NSW Supreme Court had found that 'the lease vested in Forge on administration under s267, and so it acquired title to the turbines: *Forge Group Power Pty Limited v General Electric International Inc* [2016] NSWSC 52'.[19] PR (in GE's place) appealed, and argued that the turbines were 'fixtures' and so they fell outside the scope of the PPSA.

Decision: The Court of Appeal dismissed the appeal. It held that '(1) the first instance decision was correct in holding that the definition of "fixtures" in the PPSA is in line with the common law meaning of "fixtures", which requires "a determination of both the degree of annexation of an item to the land, and the purpose of annexation"; and (2) the first instance decision also correctly applied the common law test, and correctly found that the turbines were not fixtures'.[20]

Moreover, s 8 lists property interests not captured by the definition of personal property and therefore not governed by the PPSA regime. The personal property regime does not apply with respect to:

- any right of set-off or right of combination of account (s 8(1)(d));
- rights under general law or under the relevant state and federal statutes in relation to the control, use or flow of water (s 8(1)(i));
- a lien, charge or any other interest in personal property that arises under the relevant state or federal statutes (other than the PPSA), unless the person who owns the property in which the interest is granted agrees to the interest (s 8(1)(b));
- a lien, charge or any other interest in personal property that is created, arises or is provided by operation of the general law (s 8(1)(c));
- certain interests in property created under the *Bankruptcy Act 1966* (Cth) (s 8(1)(g));

19 S Pemberton, *Digest of PPSA Cases* (last updated: 10 December 2019), 46.
20 S Pemberton, *Digest of PPSA Cases* (last updated: 10 December 2019), 46.

- an interest in a fixture (s 8(1)(j)); or
- particular statutory rights granted by a relevant state or federal statute which are declared not to be personal property for the purposes of the PPSA (s 8(1)(k)).

Personal property under the PPSA is extremely broadly defined at s 10. The reason for such classification is that different types of personal property are differently categorised and subject to particular security interests to which different rules apply. These rules may relate to, for example, the mode of perfection relevant to the particular property, or whether or not it is subject to extinguishment.

9.3 What is a 'security interest'?

The PPSA will only be applicable once a security interest related to personal property is identified. Therefore, identifying such a security interest is a necessary condition for triggering the application of the PPSA. A security interest is defined in s 10 of the PPSA by reference to s 12. Section 12(1) provides a simple definition, which the remaining subsections expand and modify. Section 12 of the PPSA identifies either 'in substance' (sub-s (1), sub-s (2) providing examples) or 'deemed' (sub-s (3)) classes of security interests.

A PPSA 'security interest' is defined in s 12(1) of the PPSA in the following terms:

> **12 Meaning of security interest**
>
> (1) A security interest means an interest in personal property provided for by a transaction that, in substance, secures payment or performance of an obligation (without regard to the form of the transaction or the identity of the person who has title to the property).

The two essential elements required to be identified to determine whether or not a security interest exists pursuant to the PPSA are that there is:

- secured property (ie collateral); and
- secured monies (ie the obligation).

The Explanatory Memorandum to the Personal Property Securities Bill 2009 (Cth), 10, provides:

> A security interest in personal property arises from a transaction that in substance secures the payment or performance of an obligation. The interest in the personal property, taken as security for a loan or other obligation, is a security interest. The Bill would apply to transactions which have the effect of securing a payment or other obligation, regardless of the form of the transaction, the nature of the debtor or the jurisdiction in which the personal property or parties are located (subject to specified exceptions).

The Explanatory Memorandum stresses a substance over form test, or *functional approach*. It is not relevant to the creation of a security interest which entity has title to it, as the entity creating the interest need not have title.

A PPSA security interest is determined to exist once the following elements have been established:

- that the security interest in question relates to personal property; this may be satisfied by the grantor (debtor) being either the owner or being in possession of the relevant property. Where the grantor is in possession, a security interest may be created over property owned by another;
- that the security interest is the subject of a consensual transaction in which the debtor agrees to provide a security interest in favour of the secured party by means of an enforceable security agreement, and that if the security interest is to be enforceable against third parties the agreement must be in writing (s 20);
- that the agreement creates either legal or equitable proprietary rights in favour of the secured party (creditor/grantee); and
- that the agreement in substance secures the payment of a debt or performance of an obligation.[21]

The 12 types of transactions that would be considered as creating a security interest are set out in s 12(2) of the PPSA:

(a) a fixed charge;
(b) a floating charge;
(c) a chattel mortgage;
(d) a conditional sale agreement (including an agreement to sell subject to retention of title);
(e) a hire purchase agreement;
(f) a pledge;
(g) a trust receipt;
(h) a consignment (whether or not a commercial consignment);
(i) a lease of goods (whether or not a PPS lease);
(j) an assignment;
(k) a transfer of title; and
(l) a flawed asset arrangement.

These are examples of transactions that 'in substance' would be security interests if they satisfy the essential element of a security interest. That element is given in s 12(3), which provides that a transaction is a security interest if it secures payment, or secures the performance, of an obligation.

9.4 Deemed security interests

Pursuant to s 12(3), the PPSA is more expansive than traditional concepts of security interest. Some interests are deemed to be security payments even if the transaction does not secure the payment or performance of an obligation.

21 See, generally, J Harris and N Mirzai, *The Annotated Personal Property Securities Act 2009 (Cth)* (CCH Australia Ltd, North Ryde, 2011), [12.5.1].

Section 12(3) provides:

> A security interest also includes the following interests, whether or not the transaction concerned, in substance, secures payment or performance of an obligation:
>
> (a) the interest of a transferee under a transfer of an account or chattel paper;[22]
> (b) the interest of a consignor who delivers goods to a consignee under a commercial consignment;[23]
> (c) the interest of a lessor or bailor of goods under a PPS lease.[24]

The inclusion of interests under arrangements of consignment, bailment, supply or lease signals the policy behind the PPSA to protect third parties who mistake, or are misled into believing, that the grantor's, bailee's, consignee's or hirer's possession of the goods signifies ownership.

Where the financier or business consigns, bails, supplies or leases goods and seeks to protect its position through its ownership of the goods in question, it will need to register its interest in order to achieve the maximum protection afforded to it under the PPSA. Section 109 of the PPSA provides that the enforcement provisions in Part 4 of the PPSA do not apply to deemed security interests unless the relevant financiers or businesses secure the payment or performance of an obligation.

The following example illustrates one of the main implications of the PPSA's application to a lease agreement. We assume that a leasing company (Lessor) rents heavy equipment, and a construction company (Lessee/Contractor) wins a two-year government contact to build a new road. Lessee (the construction company/Contractor) leases a bulldozer from Lessor (the leasing company) for the duration of the contract at a monthly rental of $1000 and on the understanding that Lessee (the construction company/ Contractor) will return the bulldozer to Lessor (the leasing company) at the end of the two years. In this case, the contact between Lessor and Lessee is a true lease, and it does not in substance secure payment or performance of an obligation owning by Lessee to Lessor. Nevertheless, it is a PPS lease and so the PPSA applies. As a result, Lessor should register a financing statement through the PPSR. Otherwise, it will be at risk if, for example, Lessee (the construction company) wrongfully sells the bulldozer to a third party transferee, or gives a security in the bulldozer to a third party financier.[25] See also *Re Maiden Civil (P&E) Pty Ltd; Albarran v Queensland Excavation Services Pty Ltd* (2013) 277 FLR 337.

---

22 'Chattel paper' is defined in s 10 of the PPSA and includes a writing that evidences both a monetary obligation and a security interest in or lease of specific goods – for example, a hire-purchase agreement or lease.

23 'Commercial consignment' is defined in s 10 of the PPSA.

24 'PPS lease' is defined in s 13 of the PPSA.

25 A Duggan and D Brown, *Australian Personal Property Securities Law* (LexisNexis Butterworths Australia, Sydney, 2nd edn, 2016), 79.

RE MAIDEN CIVIL (P&E) PTY LTD; ALBARRAN *v* QUEENSLAND EXCAVATION SERVICES PTY LTD (2013) 277 FLR 337 (THE FIRST MAJOR DECISION UNDER THE PPSA)

Facts: The lessor (Queensland Excavation Services Pty Ltd (QES)) failed to register a financing statement. The lessee (grantor – Maiden Civil (P&E) Pty Ltd (Maiden)) gave a security interest in the equipment to another financier (Fast Financial Solutions Pty Ltd (Fast Financial)), which registered a financing statement.

Decision: (1) For the purpose of the PPSA, the lessor (QES)'s interest in the goods was a security interest; and (2) the lessor (QES)'s failure to register a financing statement resulted in its security interest being subordinated to the competing perfected security interest registered by another financer (Fast Financial).

9.5 What is not covered by the PPSA?

Some arrangements are expressly 'carved out' of the new PPSA regime. Section 12(5) of the PPSA provides:

> A security interest does not include:
>
> (a) a licence;
>
> (b) an interest of a kind prescribed by the regulations for the purposes of this section.

Section 12(6) expressly excludes subordination agreements from the PPSA:

> A security interest is not created only by an agreement or undertaking to do either of the following:
>
> (a) to postpone or subordinate a person's right to payment or performance of all or any part of a debtor's obligation to another person's right to payment or performance of all or any part of another of the debtor's obligations;
>
> (b) to postpone or subordinate all or any part of a secured party's rights under a security agreement to all or any part of another secured party's rights under another security agreement with the same grantor.

Section 61 of the PPSA is relevant here.

> (1) A secured party may (in a security agreement or otherwise) subordinate the secured party's security interest in collateral to any other interest in the collateral.
>
> (2) The subordination:
>
> (a) is effective according to its terms between the parties; and
>
> (b) may be enforced by a third party if the third party is the person, or one of a class of persons, for whose benefit the subordination is intended.

The items expressly excluded from being a 'security interest' are:

- the interests of a seller who has shipped goods under a negotiable bill of lading unless the parties have otherwise evidenced an intention to create or provide for a security interest in the goods: s 8(1)(a);
- the security interest or other interest in personal property arising by operation of law (such as a lien, or charge): s 8(1)(b) and (c);
- interests in land or payments in connection with land: s 8(1)(f);
- the transfer of accounts for collection purposes: s 8(1)(f);
- the transfer of an account or negotiable instrument to satisfy existing indebtedness: s 8(1)(f);
- interests in fixtures: s 8(1)(j); and
- superannuation interests: s 8(1)(jb).

9.6 The creation of a security interest

The taking of good security under the PPSA requires financiers to observe and implement the three-stage PPSA process. Security interests cannot be enforced unless they:

- attach to the collateral – which makes the security interest enforceable against the grantor (s 19);
- are enforceable against third parties – which usually will require an agreement in writing which is signed or otherwise adopted by the grantor, but may be effected by the secured party having possession or being in control of the collateral (s 20); and
- are perfected (s 21).

Perfection is the key step under the PPSA. Attachment and perfection are both required to provide the intended 'priority' to 'provide protection against wrongful sale by the grantor', and to ensure that 'the security interest will survive the grantor's insolvency' where interests compete for the same collateral.[26] For most security interests, perfection will be effected by registration on the PPSR; although in some cases possession or control may suffice.

9.6.1 Attachment

Attachment is one of the central concepts of the PPSA determining when creditors acquire an interest in specified property, and therefore who, among competing interests, assumes priority. For the interest to attach, the PPSA requires the following: (1) there must be a valid security agreement; (2) the secured party (creditor/grantee) must give value for the security interest: s 19(2)(b); (3) the grantor (debtor) must have rights in the collateral: s 19(2)(a); and (4) no agreement to postpone the time of attachment has been entered into: s 19(3).[27]

26 See D Barlin, 'Personal Property Securities' (Wentworth Selborne Chambers, July 2012), 5: https://www.13wentworthselbornechambers.com.au/.

27 In *Australian Personal Property Securities Law* (LexisNexis Butterworths Australia, Sydney, 2nd edn, 2016), 106, A Duggan and D Brown outline three requirements that must be met before a security interest can be attached to collateral: (1) there must be a valid security agreement; (2) the secured party must give value for the security interest; and (3) the grantor must have rights in the collateral.

The PPSA itself does not define attachment. Attachment is, helpfully, defined in the Explanatory Memorandum as '[t]he creation of a security interest in personal property which could be enforced against that property'. Section 10 defines 'attaches' to have 'the meaning given by section 19'.[28]

More specifically, s 19(1) of the PPSA provides that 'a security interest is enforceable against a grantor in respect of particular collateral only if the interest has attached to the collateral'.

The effect of the attachment of a security interest to personal property is that it (1) limits the grantor's rights in the collateral by the rights of the secured party; and (2) enables the secured party to enforce its security interest against the collateral (s 19(1)).[29]

Further, the 'attachment rule' is set out in s 19(2). Attachment requires the grantor and secured party to have entered into a legally binding agreement under which the security interest in particular personal property is created. Section 19(2) of the PPSA governs how the attachment of a security interest is established.

> A security interest attaches to collateral when:
>
> (a) the grantor has rights in the collateral, or the power to transfer rights in the collateral to the secured party; and
>
> (b) either:
>
> (i) value is given for the security interest; or
>
> (ii) the grantor does an act by which the security interest arises.

Section 19(2)(a) makes it a precondition to attachment that the grantor has rights or the power to transfer rights in the collateral to the secured party. Consistent with the policy of the PPSA, attachment does not depend on the grantor being the owner of, or having title to, the collateral. The requirement is satisfied, for example, where the grantor is the owner, or is in possession, of the collateral, or has the 'power to transfer rights in the collateral' (s 19(2)). In other words, a security interest may attach to collateral that the grantor does not own. This marks a break from the pre-PPSA law, which applied (subject to certain exceptions) the nemo dat principle.[30]

Attachment has particular significance for holders of security interests under s 12(3). Where goods have been leased to lessees, consigned to commercial consignors, or supplied under conditional sale agreements such as being subject to retention of title clauses, parties can no longer rely on the fact of ownership but must under the PPSA register their security interest in order to maximise their protection.[31] Under the same circumstances, grantors have rights for the purpose of attachment once they have obtained possession of the goods (s 19(5)).

Under s 19(2)(b)(i), a secured party may 'give value' by lending money on the value of the security. 'Value' is defined to mean 'consideration that is sufficient to support a contract' and includes 'an antecedent debt or liability'.[32] The most common way that s 19(2)(b)(ii) may be enlivened is by executing a security agreement with the secured party. Interest attaches when

28 Explanatory Memorandum to the PPS Bill 2009, 6.

29 Explanatory Memorandum to the PPS Bill 2009, [2.9]. In order for a security interest to be enforceable against *third parties*, the security interest would need to be attached and perfected.

30 N Mirzai and J Harris, *The Annotated Personal Property Securities Act 2009 (Cth)* (Wolters Kluwer, Sydney, 3rd edn, 2018), 132.

31 See, for example, *Waller v New Zealand Bloodstock Ltd* [2006] 3 NZLR 629.

32 Section 10.

the parties execute the security agreement.[33] The security interest is attached to the collateral regardless of whether the relevant asset is the subject of regular or routine trade, dealing or disposal. Further, the concept of crystallisation has no meaning under the PPSA, which does not distinguish between fixed and floating charges, or security interest.

Parties to the security agreement may contract out of s 19(2). The time when the security interest attaches to the collateral is dealt with in s 19(3) and (4) of the PPSA:

> (3) Subsection (2) does not apply if the parties to a security agreement have agreed that a security interest attaches at a later time, in which case the security interest attaches at the time specified in the agreement.
>
> (4) To avoid doubt, a reference in a security agreement to a floating charge is not a reference to an agreement that the security interest created by the floating charge attaches at a time later than provided under subsection (2).

Section 19(3) provides that attachment may occur at a time agreed by the parties, who may specify in their agreement that the security interest is to attach at a later time. Section 19(4) provides that an agreement for the purposes of s 19(3) is not constituted by the parties agreeing to a floating charge (s 19(4)).

9.6.2 Attachment and perfection

Under the PPSA, attachment alone is insufficient for the security interest to be enforceable against third parties, or for a security interest to gain priority over other security interests in the same property. Security interests will be enforceable against third parties and prevail against competing security interests, and other interests in the relevant personal property, only if they are attached to the collateral and perfected.[34] Perfection also protects the holder of the security interest in the event of insolvency of the grantor.

Section 20 of the PPSA provides:

> **20 Enforceability of security interests against third parties**
>
> **General rule**
>
> (1) A security interest is enforceable against a third party in respect of particular collateral only if:
>
> (a) the security interest is attached to the collateral; and
>
> (b) one of the following applies:
>
> (i) the secured party possesses the collateral;
>
> (ii) the secured party has perfected the security interest by control;
>
> (iii) a security agreement that provides for the security interest covers the collateral
>
> in accordance with subsection (2) ...

33 In *Royal Bank of Canada v Radius Credit Union* Ltd [2010] SCC 48, Charron J applied (at [31]) the dictum of Gonthier J in *Sparrow Electric* (at [63]) to the effect that the PPSA interest attaches when the agreement is executed by the parties.

34 See *Graham v Portacom New Zealand Ltd* [2004] 2 NZLR 528, [12].

Written security agreements

(2) A security agreement covers collateral in accordance with this subsection if:
  (a) the security agreement is evidenced by writing that is:
    (i) signed by the grantor (see subsection (3)); or
    (ii) adopted or accepted by the grantor by an act, or omission, that reasonably appears to be done with the intention of adopting or accepting the writing and
  (b) the writing evidencing the agreement contains:
    (i) a description of the particular collateral, subject to subsections (4) and (5); or
    (ii) a statement that a security interest is taken in all of the grantor's present and after-acquired property; or
    (iii) a statement that a security interest is taken in all of the grantor's present and after-acquired property except specified items or classes of personal property.

The secured party must therefore also have either possession or control of the collateral (s 20(1)), or a written security agreement signed or accepted by the grantor (s 20(2)).

The main rule for perfection is contained in s 21. Section 21 of the PPSA provides:

(1) A security interest in particular collateral is perfected if:
  (a) the security interest is temporarily perfected, or otherwise perfected, by force of this Act; or
  (b) all of the following apply:
    (i) the security interest is attached to the collateral;
    (ii) the security interest is enforceable against a third party;
    (iii) subsection (2) applies.
(2) This subsection applies if:
  (a) for any collateral, a registration is effective with respect to the collateral; or
  (b) for any collateral, the secured party has possession of the collateral (other than possession as a result of seizure or repossession); or
  (c) for the following kinds of collateral, the secured party has control of the collateral:
    (i) an ADI account;
    (ii) an intermediated security;
    (iii) an investment instrument;
    (iv) a negotiable instrument that is not evidenced by a certificate;
    (v) a right evidenced by a letter of credit that states that the letter of credit must be presented on claiming payment or requiring the performance of an obligation;
    (vi) satellites and other space objects.

  Note: For what constitutes possession and control of collateral, see Part 2.3.
(3) A security interest may be perfected regardless of the order in which attachment and any step mentioned in subsection (2) occur.
(4) A single registration may perfect one or more security interests.

By combined effect, ss 20 and 21 determine the security interest to be 'perfected' when:

- 'the security interest is "attached" to collateral and is "enforceable against third parties"; and
- the secured party has either:
  - registered its interest on the PPSR;
  - taken possession of the collateral; or
  - with respect to certain collateral, taken control of collateral (that is, if it is sub-section 21(2) property)'.[35]

Depending on the type of collateral, perfection may occur:

- by registration of a 'financing statement' in a PPSR;
- by the secured party taking possession of collateral other than by seizure or repossession;
- where the secured party has control of the collateral; or
- if it is temporarily perfected in certain situations, such as where there is a change or transfer of collateral, or otherwise perfected by force of the provisions elsewhere in the PPSA (s 21).[36]

Perfection is a means of ensuring that third parties are adequately and publicly notified of any existing security interest, so that they take collateral subject to that interest.

A contest between security interests emerges when more than one is attached to a collateral. Determining priorities between competing security interests is governed by rules supplied by the PPSA. Perfection determines priority between competing security interests. Interests must be perfected in order to benefit from the priority rules. Under the PPSA regime, security interests with the higher priority may be enforced before the security interests of other parties.

The consequences of unperfected securities include that a subsequent purchaser or lessee of collateral may take free of an unperfected security interest (s 43) and a perfected security interest may take priority over an earlier but unperfected security interest (s 55(3)).

'Unperfected' securities are:

- 'subordinated to the interests of a creditor that has seized the collateral;
- subordinated to a perfected security in the same collateral; and
- subordinated to the buyer/lessee of the collateral'.[37]

The main reasons for 'perfection' are to ensure that:

- 'the intended priority of competing security interests is preserved;
- the secured party is protected if the grantor becomes insolvent;
- it protects against taking free or extinguishment provisions under the PPSA'; and
- an unperfected security interest vests in a debtor upon insolvency.[38]

35 See D Barlin, 'Personal Property Securities' (Wentworth Selborne Chambers, July 2012), 15: https://www.13wentworthselbornechambers.com.au/.

36 See D Barlin, 'Personal Property Securities' (Wentworth Selborne Chambers, July 2012), 15–16: https://www.13wentworthselbornechambers.com.au/.

37 See D Barlin, 'Personal Property Securities' (Wentworth Selborne Chambers, July 2012), 14: https://www.13wentworthselbornechambers.com.au/.

38 See D Barlin, 'Personal Property Securities' (Wentworth Selborne Chambers, July 2012), 14: https://www.13wentworthselbornechambers.com.au/.

'Perfection' is essential because it makes it possible for a secured party to achieve priority against competing security interests.[39] It also protects the secured party in the case of the insolvency of a debtor, or becoming bankrupt.[40] That is, the claimant's security interest must have been perfected when they entered the transaction if they are to be afforded the protection of a secured party's interest in collateral.

As mentioned above, s 21(2) establishes the three methods available to a secured party seeking to perfect their interest: (1) registration – s 21(2)(a); (2) possession – s 21(2)(b); and (3) control – s 21(2)(c).

9.6.2.1 Perfection by registration

After the security interest is attached to the collateral and the requirements of s 19(2) are satisfied, the secured party usually protects their interest in the property by means of registration on the PPS Register (s 21(2)(a)).

Part 5.3 of the PPSA sets out the specific requirements for registration. One of the most important mechanisms for perfecting a security interest is the registration of a financing statement in which the security interest is described; and in nearly all cases this is the means by which perfection will be achieved. The financing statement is defined in s 10 as 'data registered (or that is to be registered) pursuant to an application for registration under subsection 150(1)'.

The financing statement is to contain a description of the collateral subject to the security interest, details of the secured party and, for collateral which is consumer property and not required to be described by a serial number, the details of the grantor; but if the consumer property is required to be described by a serial number, the grantor's details are not required (s 153(1)). Whether collateral may or must be described by a serial number is set out in reg 2.2 of Schedule 22 to the *Personal Property Securities Regulations 2010* (Cth). It is the financial statement that represents notice of the existence of a security interest in the collateral. Collateral is considered registered from the time its description under the financing statement in relation to the secured party can be searched on the register (s 160). The registration time is important because of the priority given to perfection by registration (s 55).

9.6.2.2 Perfection by possession

Possession is another means by which a secured party may perfect their interest in the collateral. It is defined in the PPSA in the following terms:

> **24 Possession**
>
> **Possession by one party exclusive of possession by others**
>
> (1) A secured party cannot have possession of personal property if the property is in the actual or apparent possession of the grantor or debtor, or another person on behalf of the grantor or debtor.

39 See D Barlin, 'Personal Property Securities' (Wentworth Selborne Chambers, July 2012), 14: https://www.13wentworthselbornechambers.com.au/.

40 See D Barlin, 'Personal Property Securities' (Wentworth Selborne Chambers, July 2012), 14: https://www.13wentworthselbornechambers.com.au/.

(2) A grantor or debtor cannot have possession of personal property if the property is in the actual or apparent possession of the secured party, or another person on behalf of the secured party.

Timing rule for possession of goods transported by common carrier

(3) A grantor or debtor to whom goods are transported by a common carrier acquires possession of the goods only when the earlier of the following occurs:
  (a) the grantor or debtor, or another person at the request of the grantor or debtor, actually acquires possession of the goods;
  (b) the grantor or debtor, or another person at the request of the grantor or debtor, acquires possession of a document of title to the goods.

Possession of certain negotiable instruments

(4) A person (the first person) has possession of a negotiable instrument that is not evidenced by an electronic record if, and only if, the first person, or another person on behalf of the first person, takes physical possession of the instrument.

Note: For possession of investment instruments, see subsection 24(6).

Possession of chattel paper that is evidenced electronically

(5) A secured party has possession of chattel paper that is evidenced by an electronic record if, and only if:
  (a) a single authoritative copy of the record exists which is unique, identifiable and unalterable (except as set out below); and
  (b) the authoritative copy identifies the secured party as the transferee of the record; and
  (c) the authoritative copy is communicated to, and maintained by, the secured party or the secured party's agent; and
  (d) copies or revisions of the record that change the transferee of the authoritative copy can be made only with the participation of the secured party; and
  (e) each copy of the authoritative copy (or any copy of such a copy) is readily identifiable as a copy that is not the authoritative copy; and
  (f) any revision of the authoritative copy is readily identifiable as an authorised or unauthorised copy.

Possession of investment instruments

(6) Despite subsections (1) and (2), a person (the possessor) has possession of an investment instrument that is evidenced by a certificate if, and only if:
  (a) the certificate specifies the person who is entitled to the investment instrument; and
  (b) a transfer of the investment instrument may be registered on books maintained for that purpose by or on behalf of the issuer (or the certificate states that a transfer of the instrument may be so registered); and
  (c) any of the following applies:
    (i) the possessor has possession of the certificate;

(ii) another person (other than the grantor or the debtor) has possession of the certificate on behalf of the possessor;

(iii) the registered owner (who is not the grantor or debtor) of the investment instrument acknowledges in writing that he, she or it has possession of the investment instrument on behalf of the possessor.

The concept of possession as outlined in s 24 differs from the common law. It does not, for example, include constructive possession. Further, possession is conceived in terms of exclusivity, such that the possession by one party (grantor or secured party) excludes the possibility of possession by the other (s 24(1) and (2)). Perfection stems from the fact of the secured party coming into possession of the collateral and does not require further formalities to be completed. The security interest remains perfected as long as it is in the party's possession and continuously perfected in accordance with the requirements of s 56. Perfection of the security interest ends, for example, if the secured party transfers possession of the collateral, even temporarily, to the other party, and resumes with repossession. The possibility of temporary and brief, prolonged or even permanent discontinuity, even if inadvertent, makes the caution of registration prudent.

9.6.2.3 Perfection by control

Some types of personal property can defeat the security provided by prior registration on the PPSR, or possession, by taking 'control' of the property, even if the party has notice of the prior interest. Only certain types of property that are not tangible are capable of control. They include (s 21(2)(c)(i)–(v)):

- ADI (authorised deposit-taking institution) accounts;
- intermediated securities;
- investment instruments;
- letters of credit; and
- uncertified negotiable instruments.

Moreover, one class of tangible property is also included – namely, satellites and other space objects: s 21(2)(c)(vi). Control of these properties is governed by rules set out in ss 25–29.

Section 27 of the PPSA focuses on the control of investment instruments, such as shares. Under s 27, a person has control of an investment instrument if (and only if) one of the following occurs:[41]

- a person (other than a debtor or a grantor of the security interests themselves) becomes the registered owner of the investment instrument; or
- if the investment instrument is evidenced by a certificate the person takes possession of the certificate and has the power to either:
  - transfer the instrument to themselves or to another person; or
  - otherwise deal with the instrument; or

41 M Bennett, 'Practical Problem Caused by the Personal Property Securities Act' (Wentworth Selborne Chambers, 2013), 20: https://www.13wentworthselbornechambers.com.au/.

- if the investment instrument is not evidenced by a certificate, the secured party and debtor or grantor must agree that the secured party is able to initiate or control sending instructions by which the investment instrument could be transferred or otherwise dealt with; or
- if the investment instrument is not evidenced by an instrument, a person may also control it where:
  - the registered owner (who is not the debtor or grantor) acknowledges in writing that the investment instrument is held on behalf of the person, or the investment instrument is registered to a third party on behalf of the person; and
  - there is an agreement by which the person has the power to direct the transfer of or otherwise deal with the investment instrument.'

A secured party will most likely not become the registered owner of a secured asset. The secured party will therefore seek control over an investment instrument by securing the right to deal with it, and by possession of any certificates evidencing the instrument. Retaining the right to deal with an investment instrument does not grant the debtor or grantor exclusivity in dealing with the instrument. The secured party retains control over the investment instrument.

Further, the ranking of creditors, and distinguishing between competing security interests, is specified by rules under the PPSA. The rules provide that, as stated at s 57(1) of the PPSA: 'A security interest in collateral that is currently perfected by control has priority over a security interest in the same collateral that is currently perfected by another means.'

Perfection of a security interest by 'control' will therefore beat any other form of perfection.

- Where security interests that are both perfected by control are in competition, s 57(2) of the PPSA provides that the first in time prevails. Further, neither knowledge nor notice of a competing security interest is relevant in resolving priority disputes using the principal priority rules under the PPSA.
- Security interests perfected by control are not trumped by purchase money security interests, even though the latter are sometimes said to have 'super-priority', in that a perfected PMSI has priority over all non-PMSIs (even if that non-PMSI is earlier or has been perfected) in matters of competition between interests.
- However, security interests perfected by control and PMSIs only compete when s 21(2) property is collateral – including lending for shares, derivatives and other financial products. Otherwise, PMSI operates with a broader range of personal property extending beyond those enumerated at s 21(2).

9.7 Vesting in the grantor

Part 8.2 of the PPSA provides that when a grantor becomes insolvent, unperfected security interests vest in the grantor (s 267). The circumstances under which this occurs include when:

- a 'winding-up' order is made or a resolution is passed winding up a company; or
- an administrator is appointed to a company, or a company executes a deed of company arrangement; or
- an individual becomes bankrupt.

A supplier who supplies goods under a retention of title clause will have a security interest in the goods by virtue of the retention of title under the PPSA. If the purchaser of the goods is declared insolvent while in possession of the goods and the supplier has not registered their interest, the supplier's security interest vests in the purchaser as grantor. The supplier loses thereby its ownership of the goods, which are available to satisfy the purchaser's creditors.

Not all security interests are affected by this 'vesting' rule (s 268). For example, transfers of chattel paper and accounts, and commercial consignments are exempt. Section 267 is designed to 'vest in' insolvent grantors interests held by mortgagees, charges, and the ownership interest in the secured parties in retention of title sales. This also includes PPS leases and bailments that are not exempted by s 268.

9.8 Specific rules that apply to the proceeds from collateral

Under the PPSA, a party with a security interest in collateral is able to claim an interest in the proceeds of a sale of that collateral where the party to whom they are transferred deals with and receives proceeds from them prior to having paid the original supplier, or security interest holder, as long as the grantor had an interest in the proceeds, or the power to transfer rights in the proceeds to the secured party (s 31(3)).

Section 31 in Part 2.4, Division 2 of the PPSA defines 'proceeds' as a variety of identifiable and traceable personal property. It includes any personal property that may have been derived either directly or indirectly from a dealing involving the original collateral, or proceeds from a dealing with it (s 31(1)(a)). The definition makes it clear that proceeds include not only first-generation proceeds but also second- and subsequent generation proceeds.

Duggan and Brown provide an example of second- and subsequent generation proceeds.[42]

EXAMPLE

Facts: Secured Party (SP/Creditor/Grantee) holds a security interest in Grantor (Debtor)'s inventory, Grantor sells an item of inventory to Customer, in the ordinary course of business, on 90-day terms. At the end of the 90 days, Customer pays Grantor by cheque. Grantor cashes the cheque and uses the money to buy office supplies.

Analysis: Grantor's sale to Customer gives rise to money obligation owing by Customer to Grantor (an 'account', under PPSA s 10). The account is first-generation proceeds of the original collateral. Customer's payment discharges the account, but now SP has a claim to the cheque ('negotiable instrument', under PPSA, s 10) as first-generation proceeds of the account and second-generation proceeds of the original collateral.

42 A Duggan and D Brown, *Australian Personal Property Securities Law* (LexisNexis Butterworths Australia, Sydney, 2nd edn, 2016), 338–9.

Of this example, Duggan and Brown state: '[T]he cashing of the cheque terminates SP's interest in the cheque, but SP acquires an interest in the cash as proceeds of the cheque and likewise, when Grantor spends the cash on the office supplies, SP acquires an interest in the office supplies as proceeds of the cash.'[43]

Proceeds also include any rights to an insurance payment, or other payments by way of compensation where the original collateral is destroyed or damaged; and, in the case of intellectual property, the rights of a licensor to receive payments under a licence agreement: s 31(1)(b)–(e).

The person with a security interest in the proceeds and the person with rights in or who has dealt with the proceeds need not have been in a fiduciary relationship for the proceeds to be traced (s 31(2)).

Section 32 provides:

32 Proceeds – attachment

Continuation of security interest in collateral, and attachment to proceeds

(1) Subject to this Act, if collateral gives rise to proceeds (by being dealt with or otherwise), the security interest:
  (a) continues in the collateral, unless:
    (i) the secured party expressly or impliedly authorised a disposal giving rise to the proceeds; or
    (ii) the secured party expressly or impliedly agreed that a dealing giving rise to the proceeds would extinguish the security interest; and
  (b) attaches to the proceeds, unless the security agreement provides otherwise.

Note 1: The effect of paragraph (a) is to extinguish the security interest in the collateral if the secured party expressly or impliedly authorised the dealing mentioned.

Note 2: A transferee can also take the collateral free of the security interest because of the operation of another provision of this Act (for example, under Part 2.5).

Enforcement of security interest against collateral and proceeds

(2) If the secured party enforces a security interest against both collateral (other than an investment instrument or an intermediated security) and proceeds, the amount secured by the security interest in the collateral and proceeds is limited to the market value of the collateral immediately before the collateral gave rise to the proceeds.

Note: For the enforceability of a security interest against a third party in relation to proceeds, see also subsection 20(6).

(3) However, subsection (2) does not apply if, at the time of the transfer of the collateral, the transferee has actual or constructive knowledge that the transfer was in breach of a security agreement that provides for the security interest in the collateral.

43 A Duggan and D Brown, *Australian Personal Property Securities Law* (LexisNexis Butterworths Australia, Sydney, 2nd edn, 2016), 338–9.

(4) To avoid doubt, subsection (2) does not affect any right the secured party may have to recover the amount secured without enforcing the security interest.

Priority of proceeds

(5) For the purposes of section 55 (default priority rules), the time of registration or possession in relation to original collateral, or the time of perfection of a security interest in original collateral, is also the time of registration, possession or perfection in relation to the proceeds of the original collateral.

Note: The effect of subsection (5) is that the security interest in the proceeds has the same default priority as the security interest in the original collateral.

The PPSA maintains the vendor's claim. However, the vendor must still compete with other interest holders for priority. Whether the vendor achieves priority ranking will depend on factors such as the identity of the other creditors (in particular, whether banks or financial institutions are included among them), and the location of proceeds of the sale. The identity of other creditors is relevant where a bank or financial institution controls the purchaser's account and holds a general security interest over the purchaser's assets, including the proceeds of onsold goods. The vendor has priority where the proceeds appear in a general account.

9.9 Extinguishment rules under the PPSA

The common law provided for circumstances where a non-owner could nevertheless pass good title to a bona fide purchaser having no knowledge or notice that the seller lacked the capacity to pass title and who provided good value where the exceptions to the nemo dat principle applied.

Similarly, the PPSA in Part 2.5 provides 'taking free' rules for determining the circumstances under which a buyer or lessee of personal property may take it free of the security interest to which the goods in question are subject. Part 7.4 of the PPSA provides that the taking free rules do not exclude the operation of consistent state and territory laws.

Whether or not the PPSA has limited the scope of operation of the nemo dat rules in various sales of goods legislation remains an unresolved issue.[44]

9.9.1 Unperfected security interest

Section 43 of the PPSA is the main extinguishment rule. It provides:

43 Taking personal property free of unperfected security interest

Main rule

(1) A buyer or lessee of personal property, for value, takes the personal property free of an unperfected security interest in the property.

44 See, further, D McGill, 'Transfer of Title by a Non-owner: The Personal Property Securities Act 2009 (Cth) Exceptions to the Nemo Dat Rule' (2011) 39 *Australian Business Law Review* 209, 225.

Exception

(2) Subsection (1) does not apply if the unperfected security interest was created or provided for by a transaction to which the buyer or lessee is a party, unless the personal property concerned is of a kind prescribed by the regulations for the purposes of this subsection.

By sub-s (1), a buyer or lessee of collateral will take the property free of any security interest from a supplier or financier who fails to perfect their interest – for example, by registering it on the PPS Register. The provision makes the secured party responsible for perfecting their security. Subsection (2) provides the exception that the buyer or lessee will not take free of the security interest if they were a party to the transaction that created or provided the security interest.

EXAMPLE

Facts: A purchaser of equipment or machinery obtains finance for the purchase from a financial institution that fails to register its interest in the equipment or machinery, and the purchaser subsequently sells it to a third party,

Application: The third party will take the equipment and machinery free of the financial institution's interest.[45]

Perfecting the security interest is not conclusive, as other extinguishment rules may apply, allowing a purchaser or lessee to take property free of a perfected security interest.

9.9.2 Perfected security interests

9.9.2.1 Defects in serial numbers

Section 44 of the PPSA provides as follows:

44 Taking personal property free of security interest if serial number incorrect or missing

Main rule

(1) A buyer or lessee of personal property takes the personal property free of a security interest in the property if:

(a) the regulations provide that personal property of that kind may, or must, be described by serial number in a registration; and

(b) searching the register, immediately before the time of the sale or lease, by reference only to the serial number of the property, would not disclose a registration that perfected the security interest.

45 See the example given in the Explanatory Memorandum to the PPS Bill 2009, [2.72].

Exceptions

(2) Subsection (1) does not apply if:

(a) the buyer or lessee holds the personal property:

(i) as inventory; or

(ii) on behalf of a person who would hold the collateral as inventory; or

(b) the security interest was created or provided for by a transaction to which the buyer or lessee is a party, unless the personal property concerned is of a kind prescribed by regulations for the purposes of this paragraph.

(3) Within the period of 24 months after the registration commencement time, subsection (1) does not apply if the security interest is a transitional security interest, other than:

(a) a migrated security interest in a motor vehicle; or

(b) a migrated security interest in a watercraft within the meaning of the regulations.

Section 44 demonstrates some of the rigidity of the PPSA in relation to inaccurate registration. The provision is one of several that aim to deter the negligent lodgment of financing statements.[46] The main rule under sub-s (1) provides, in effect, that a buyer or lessee of serial numbered collateral takes free of a security interest perfected by registration unless the financing statement correctly discloses the serial number.[47] Serial number is defined in s 10 as 'in relation to collateral . . . a serial number by which the regulations require, or permit, the collateral to be described in a registration'. The register may not disclose the registered security interest either because it was not registered, or because it was not properly registered. Non-disclosure resulting from a secured party negligently registering the wrong serial number allows a buyer or lessee of the collateral to take free of the security interest.

Determining whether personal property must or may be registered is governed by the rules in reg 2.2 of Schedule 1 to the PPS Regulations. Collateral that must be described by a registered serial number is property that is described as consumer property that falls into certain categories of intangible property, motor vehicles and watercraft (reg 2.2(1)(a) of Schedule 1 to the PPS Regulations). If the same collateral is described as commercial property, reg 2.2(1)(c) determines that it may be described by serial number. Regulation 2.2(1)(a)(i) and (b) determines that aircraft must always be described by serial number.

Whether collateral is consumer or commercial property is determined by the definition provided in s 10 of the PPSA. The definition of consumer property is 'personal property held by an individual, other than personal property held in the course or furtherance, to any degree, of carrying on an enterprise to which an ABN has been allocated'; while commercial property is 'personal property other than consumer property'.

Under the exceptions provided in s 44(2), the main rule does not apply either (1) where the buyer or lessee is a dealer ('holds the property as inventory') after the sale, either for

46 N Mirzai, and J Harris, *The Annotated Personal Property Securities Act 2009 (Cth)* (Wolters Kluwer, Sydney, 3rd edn, 2018), 236.

47 A Duggan, and D Brown, *Australian Personal Property Securities Law* (LexisNexis Butterworths Australia, Sydney, 2nd edn, 2016), 279.

themselves or on behalf of someone else; or, (2) where the buyer or lessee was a party to the security interest agreement: s 44(2). Section 10 defines 'inventory' as personal property that, in the course of an enterprise to which an ABN has been allocated, is held either for sale or lease; to be provided under a contract of service; is held as raw materials or as work in progress; or is held, used or consumed by the person as materials.

9.9.2.2 Motor vehicles

Under circumstances as set out in s 45 of the PPSA, a motor vehicle may be taken free from a security interest. Section 45 provides:

> **45 Taking motor vehicles free of security interest**
>
> **Incorrect or missing serial number**
>
> (1) A buyer or lessee, for new value, of a motor vehicle of a kind prescribed by the regulations for the purpose of this section, takes the motor vehicle free of a security interest in the motor vehicle if:
> (a) the regulations provide that motor vehicles of that kind may, or must, be described by serial number; and
> (b) there is a time during the period between the start of the previous day and the time of the sale or lease by reference to which a search of the register (by reference otherwise only to the serial number of the motor vehicle) would not disclose a registration that perfected the security interest; and
> (c) the seller or lessor is:
> (i) the person who granted the security interest; or
> (ii) if the person who granted the security interest has lost the right to possess the motor vehicle, or is estopped from asserting an interest in the motor vehicle – another person who is in possession of the motor vehicle.
>
> (2) Subsection (1) does not apply if:
> (a) the secured party is in possession of the motor vehicle immediately before the time of the sale or lease; or
> (b) the motor vehicle is bought at a sale held by or on behalf of an execution creditor; or
> (c) the buyer or lessee holds the motor vehicle:
> (i) as inventory; or
> (ii) on behalf of a person who would hold the motor vehicle as inventory; or
> (iii) the buyer or lessee buys or leases the motor vehicle with actual or constructive knowledge of the security interest.
>
> **Taking from prescribed persons**
>
> (3) A buyer or lessee, for new value, of a motor vehicle of a kind prescribed by the regulations for the purpose of this section takes the motor vehicle free of a security interest in the motor vehicle if:
> (a) the regulations provide that motor vehicles of that kind may, or must, be described by serial number; and

(b) the seller or lessor is in a class of persons prescribed by the regulations for the purposes of this subsection.

(4) Subsection (3) does not apply if:

(a) the secured party is in possession of the motor vehicle immediately before the time of the sale or lease; or

(b) the motor vehicle is bought at a sale held by or on behalf of an execution creditor; or

(c) the buyer or lessee holds the motor vehicle:

(i) as inventory; or

(ii) on behalf of a person who would hold the motor vehicle as inventory; or

(d) the buyer or lessee buys or leases the motor vehicle with actual or constructive knowledge that the sale or lease constitutes a breach of the security agreement that provides for the security interest.

The general rule provides that when purchasing or leasing a motor vehicle, if a search of the register would not disclose a registration in the period between the start of the day previous to the sale and the time of the sale, and the seller or lessor is either the person who granted the security interest, or is in possession of the motor vehicle, the vehicle may be taken free of any security interest (s 45(1)).

If the buyer or lessee is purchasing the vehicle from a licensed motor vehicle trader ('prescribed person' under reg 2.2 of the PPS Regulations), the vehicle is taken free of any security interest without the need to search the PPS Register (s 45(3)). The circumstances in which s 45(3) does not apply is provided in s 45(4): (1) the secured party is in possession of the vehicle at the time of the sale or lease; (2) the vehicle is bought at a sale held by or on behalf of an execution creditor; (3) the buyer or lessee is a dealer; or (4) the buyer or lessee has actual or constructive knowledge that the sale or lease breaches the security agreement.[48] Even if the dealer is merely the bailee of vehicles as inventory owned by another entity that has registered its security interest, neither the potential purchaser nor the purchaser's financier need search the register even if they are aware of the arrangement since this knowledge will not amount to 'actual or constructive knowledge that the sale constitutes a breach of the security agreement'.[49]

9.9.2.3 Collateral sold or leased in the ordinary course of business

Section 46 of the PPSA provides as follows:

46 Taking personal property free of security interest in ordinary course of business

Main rule

(1) A buyer or lessee of personal property takes the personal property free of a security interest given by the seller or lessor, or that arises under section 32

48 A Duggan, and D Brown, *Australian Personal Property Securities Law* (LexisNexis Butterworths Australia, Sydney, 2nd edn, 2016), 284.

49 See Explanatory Memorandum to the PPS Bill 2009, [2.87].

(proceeds–attachment), if the personal property was sold or leased in the ordinary course of the seller's or lessor's business of selling or leasing personal property of that kind.

Exceptions

(2) Subsection (1) does not apply if:
  (a) in a case in which personal property of that kind may, or must, be described by serial number – the buyer or lessee holds the personal property:
    (i) as inventory; or
    (ii) on behalf of a person who would hold the collateral as inventory; or
  (b) in any case – the buyer or lessee buys or leases the personal property with actual knowledge that the sale or lease constitutes a breach of the security agreement that provides for the security interest.

The main rule provides that personal property is *taken free of security interest* given by the grantor (seller or lessor), or otherwise under s 32 of the PPSA, if the buyer or lessee acquires or leases the property in the ordinary course of the seller's or lessor's business, when that business is to sell or lease property of that kind (s 46(1)). Under the circumstances, it is the seller or lessor who bears the risk of there being unknown security interests in respect of the goods the subject of the transaction.

RE RENOVATION BOYS PTY LTD [2014] NSWSC 340

Issues: The buyer in ordinary course provision (PPSA, s 46) – issues on sale to buyer.

Facts: The inventory had been supplied to a retailer (the grantor) on retention of title terms, and the supplier had registered a financing statement. Customers had paid in full for goods. The retailer (the grantor) had allocated goods by description to the customers in its computer system, but had not yet delivered the goods to them. There were sufficient items in stock to fill all orders that had been entered in the system.[50]

Decision: The court held that 'the allocation of goods on the computer system, coupled with the customers' payment for them and the terms of the sale contracts, was enough for property to have passed under ss 21–23 of the *Sale of Goods Act 1923* (NSW)'.[51] Since the goods had been 'sold' (the property had been passed), the customers were entitled to rely on the 'taking free' rules under the PPSA, s 46(1).[52]

50 S Pemberton, *Digest of PPSA Cases* (last updated: 10 December 2019), 49.
51 See also S Pemberton, *Digest of PPSA Cases* (last updated: 10 December 2019), 49.
52 A Duggan and D Brown, *Australian Personal Property Securities Law* (LexisNexis Butterworths Australia, Sydney, 2nd edn, 2016), 296.

The rule under s 46(1) does not apply if in the case where (1) the personal property may or must be described by serial number, the buyer or lessee holds the property as inventory after the sale, either on their own behalf or for someone else (s 46(2)(a)); or (2) in any case where the buyer or lessee has actual knowledge that the sale or lease constitutes a breach of the security agreement that creates the security interest (s 46(2)(b)).

WAREHOUSE SALES PTY LTD (IN LIQ) *v* LG ELECTRONICS AUSTRALIA PTY LTD [2014] VSC 644

Issue: The buyer in ordinary course provision (PPSA, s 46) – whether a sale to a related company is necessarily outside the ordinary course of business.

Facts: The grantor was a whitegoods dealer that acquired its inventory from various suppliers on conditional sale (retention of title terms). It sold goods direct to the public, but it also commonly sold goods to a related company, which, in turn, sold them to the public.

Decision: The court held that the sales to the related company were in the ordinary course of the grantor's business, and that therefore the related company acquired the goods free of the inventory suppliers' security interests.

9.9.2.4 Personal, domestic or household property – low-value transactions

Section 47 of the PPSA provides as follows:

47 Taking personal, domestic or household property free of security interest

Main rule

(1) A buyer or lessee of personal property, for new value, that the buyer or lessee intends (at the time of purchase or lease) to use predominantly for personal, domestic or household purposes takes the personal property free of a security interest in the property if the market value (worked out at the time each part of the total new value is given) of the total new value given for the personal property is not more than:
   (a) $5,000; or
   (b) if a greater amount has been prescribed by regulations for the purposes of this subsection – that amount.

Exceptions

(2) Subsection (1) does not apply if:
   (a) the personal property is of a kind that the regulations provide may, or must, be described by serial number in a registration; or
   (b) the buyer or lessee buys or leases the personal property with actual or constructive knowledge that the sale or lease constitutes a breach of the security agreement that provides for the security interest; or

(c) at the time the contract or agreement providing for the sale or lease is entered into, the buyer or lessee believes, and it is actually the case, that the market value of the personal property is more than:
   (i) $5,000; or
   (ii) if a greater amount has been prescribed by regulations for the purposes of this paragraph – that amount.

Under the main rule, *the buyer or lessee* who acquires the property for new value not exceeding $5000 and intends to use the bought or leased property predominantly for personal, domestic or household use takes the property *free of security interests* in it.

The practical benefit to consumers of this rule is that it enables them to make purchases of relevant goods to the value of $5000 without the inconvenience of searching the PPS Register. Section 10 of the PPSA defines 'new value' as 'value other than value provided to reduce or discharge an earlier debt or liability owed to the person providing the value'. The market value of the total new value for the property must not exceed $5000.

The exceptions to the rule are that it does not apply if:[53]

(a) the personal property (the disputed collateral) may or must be described by a serial number, such as a motor vehicle;

(b) the buyer or lessee buys or leases the personal property has actual or constructive knowledge that the sale or lease constituted a breach of the relevant security agreement; or

(c) at the time the sale or lease was entered into, the buyer or lessee believes, and it is actually the case, that the market value of the personal property is more than $5000.

9.10 Determining priority

Under the PPSA, priority between competing security interests is determined legislatively. The legislation does not distinguish between competing security interests whether they are legal or equitable, fixed or floating, ownership or less than ownership. Indeed, ownership under the PPSA is one of many competing security interests along with charges and hypothecations.

The PPSA provisions dealing with the issue of priority between competing security interests in Part 2.6 are default rules. They apply generally unless specific rules elsewhere in the Act apply or the parties have agreed to a different order of priorities.

The default priority rules are contained in s 55 of the PPSA.[54] The section provides as follows:

Default priority rules

(1) This section sets out the priority between security interests in the same collateral if this Act provides no other way of determining that priority.

53 PPSA, s 47(2).

54 For a detailed discussion of these rules, see A Bull, 'Purchase Money Security Interests and the Default PPSA Priority Rules: An Overview' (2011) 26(10) *Australian Banking and Finance Law Bulletin* 167–72.

Note: For other rules about priorities, see the following:

(a) the remaining provisions of this Part;

(b) Chapter 3 (agricultural interests, accessions and commingling);

(c) Part 9.4 (transitional application of this Act).

Priority between unperfected security interests

(2) Priority between unperfected security interests in the same collateral is to be determined by the order of attachment of the security interests.

Perfected security interest has priority over unperfected security interest

(3) A perfected security interest in collateral has priority over an unperfected security interest in the same collateral.

Priority for perfection in other ways

(4) Priority between 2 or more security interests in collateral that are currently perfected is to be determined by the order in which the priority time (see subsection (5)) for each security interest occurs.

(5) For the purposes of subsection (4), the priority time for a security interest in collateral is, subject to subsection (6), the earliest of the following times to occur in relation to the security interest:

(a) the registration time for the collateral;

(b) the time the secured party, or another person on behalf of the secured party, first perfects the security interest by taking possession or control of the collateral;

(c) the time the security interest is temporarily perfected, or otherwise perfected, by force of this Act.

(6) A time is a priority time for a security interest only if, once the security interest is perfected at or after that time, the security interest remains continuously perfected.

Note: A security interest in the proceeds of original collateral has the same default priority as the security interest in the original collateral (see s 32(5)).

PPSA adopts a 'first-in-time' rule. The key priority rules under the PPSA are as follows:

- unperfected security interests rank in order of attachment (s 55(2)); priority as between unperfected security interests is given in accordance with the order of attachment of the security interests so that the first in time takes priority over those attached later;
- a perfected security interest takes priority over an unperfected security interest in the same collateral (s 55(3));
- perfection by *control* has priority over *perfection* of a security interest by any other method (s 57);
- priority between perfected security interests amongst themselves, and unperfected security interests amongst themselves, is determined on a first-in-time basis;
- two or more competing perfected security interests rank in order of priority of time, such that priority will be given to the interest perfected first in time (s 55(4)). This time is called 'priority time' and by definition means (1) the earliest of the time of registration, (2) the time the secured party first took possession or control of the collateral, or (3) the time the security interest is temporarily perfected, or otherwise perfected by the PPSA (s 55(5)(a)–(c));

- a purchase money security interest has priority over a non-purchase money security interest (s 62(1)).

9.11 Purchase money security interest – special priority rules

In some cases, priority is governed by the application of special priority rules. A purchase money security interest is a category of security interest created when a secured party provides finance to the grantor to acquire the collateral. It includes, for example, retention of title arrangements, certain leases and bailments of goods, and commercial consignments of goods. PMSI receives different priority rule treatment similar to its significance in priority terms prior to the PPSA regime. The special priority rules reflect the 'traditional priority accorded to ownership interests' and 'to security taken to secure amounts used to purchase the subject of the security'.[55]

9.11.1 Definition: Purchase money security interests

PMSI is defined in s 14(1) of the PPSA as any of the following:

(a) a security interest taken in collateral, to the extent that it secures all or part of its purchase price;

(b) a security interest taken in collateral by a person who gives value for the purpose of enabling the grantor to acquire rights in the collateral, to the extent that the value is applied to acquire those rights;

(c) the interest of a lessor or bailor of goods under a PPS lease;

(d) the interest of a consignor who delivers goods to a consignee under a commercial consignment.

Seller's PMSI: Section 14(1)(a) relates to where a seller takes a security interest (SI) in goods it sells to the buyer to secure payment of the purchase price. Formally speaking, the seller does not 'take a security interest' in the case of a retention of title agreement; rather, it reserves title. But s 14 must be read alongside s 12(3), which in effect assimilates title reservation arrangements with security interests in the strict sense: see Sections 9.3–9.4 of this chapter (deemed security interests). It follows that the seller's interest under a retention of title agreement is a PMSI within the meaning of s 14(1)(a).[56]

Lender's PMSI: Section 14(1)(b) deals with an equivalent three-party transaction, where a lender (Party 1) lends money to a buyer (Party 2) to finance a purchase from a seller

55 See M Bennett, 'Practical Problem Caused by the Personal Property Securities Act' (Wentworth Selborne Chambers, 2013), 22: https://www.13wentworthselbornechambers.com.au/.

56 A Duggan and D Brown, *Australian Personal Property Securities Law* (LexisNexis Butterworths Australia, Sydney, 2nd edn, 2016), 234.

(Party 3), and the lender (Party 1) takes an SI in the goods purchased to secure repayment of the loan.[57]

> ***Example of lender's PMSI:*** ABC Bank (Party 1) lends money to a buyer (Party 2) to finance a purchase of a car from a car dealer (Party 3), and the bank (the lender/Party 1) takes an SI in the car (the goods) purchased to secure repayment of the loan.

Lessor and bailors of PPS leases – s 14(1)(c): PPS leases are defined extensively under s 13. By virtue, interests arising from PPS leases are PMSIs. This is because a lessor or bailor effectively arms the debtor with a proprietary interest in the underlying collateral – namely, possession – without which any other SI over that particular collateral cannot attach and thus cannot be perfected: s 21.[58]

Commercial consignments – s 14(1)(d): Commercial consignments are discussed under s 12(3). Like PPS leases, by virtue of the instrument itself, commercial consignments constitute PMSIs.[59]

9.11.2 Priority

The priority accorded PMSI has been described as a 'super-priority' in respect of the collateral in the sense that it takes precedence over all other security interests perfected either by registration or possession (s 62). Section 62 of the PPSA provides as follows:

> **Scope**
>
> (1) This section sets out when a perfected purchase money security interest that is granted by a grantor in collateral or its proceeds has priority over a perfected security interest that is granted by the same grantor in the same collateral, but that is not a purchase money security interest.
>
> Note: This section is subject to section 57 (perfection by control).
>
> **Inventory**
>
> (2) The purchase money security interest has priority if:
>
> (a) the purchase money security interest is in inventory or its proceeds; and
>
> (b) the purchase money security interest is perfected by registration at the time:
>
> (i) for inventory that is goods – the grantor, or another person at the request of the grantor, obtains possession of the inventory; or
>
> (ii) for any other kind of inventory – the purchase money security interest attaches to the inventory; and

57 A Duggan and D Brown, *Australian Personal Property Securities Law* (LexisNexis Butterworths Australia, Sydney, 2nd edn, 2016), 234.

58 N Mirzai and J Harris, *The Annotated Personal Property Securities Act 2009 (Cth)* (Wolters Kluwer, Sydney, 3rd edn, 2018), 109.

59 N Mirzai and J Harris, *The Annotated Personal Property Securities Act 2009 (Cth)* (Wolters Kluwer, Sydney, 3rd edn, 2018), 109.

(c) the registration that perfects the purchase money security interest states, in accordance with item 7 of the table in section 153, that the interest is a purchase money security interest.

Note: This subsection is subject to sections 64 (non-purchase money security interest in accounts) and 71 (chattel paper).

Personal property other than inventory

(3) The purchase money security interest has priority if:

(a) the interest is in personal property, or its proceeds, other than inventory; and

(b) the purchase money security interest is perfected by registration before the end of 15 business days after whichever of the following days applies:

(i) for goods – the day the grantor, or another person at the request of the grantor, obtains possession of the property;

(ii) for any other property – the day the interest attaches to the property; and

(c) the registration that perfects the purchase money security interest states, in accordance with item 7 of the table in section 153, that the interest is a purchase money security interest.

Note: The period mentioned in paragraph (b) may be extended by a court under section 293.

The fact that a security interest is a PMSI does not ensure its super-priority without other steps being taken. First, the *financing statement* through which the PMSI is registered as a security interest must state that it is a PMSI. In other words, if a secured party (SP) holds a PMSI, but failed to make the PMSI disclosure in the financing statement, the SP loses its super-priority status: PPSA, s 153(1), Table, Item 7, *PPS Regulation 2010* (Cth), reg 5.5, Schedule 1, cl 3.1.

More specifically, the PMSI will *only* attain super-priority in relation to:

- *inventory that comprises goods*, if registered prior to the grantor obtaining possession; and
- *inventory of other kinds*, if registered prior to attachment (s 62(2) of the PPSA); and
- for *personal property that is not inventory*, in the case of *goods*, if registered within 15 business days after the grantor obtains possession; and
- for *any other property* within 15 days after the interest attaches (s 52(3) of the PPSA).

Inventory is defined in s 10 of the PPSA as follows:

[I]nventory means personal property (whether goods or intangible property) that, in the course or furtherance, to any degree, of an enterprise to which an ABN has been allocated:

(a) is held by the person for sale or lease, or has been leased by the person as lessor; or

(b) is held by the person to be provided under a contract for services, or has been so provided; or

(c) is held by the person as raw materials or as work in progress; or
(d) is held, used or consumed by the person, as materials.

Security interests are at risk of being defeated by 'silent' equipment PMSIs that emerge on the PPSR within 15 business days, but do not show on the PPSR at the time of the search. This is because equipment PMSIs may be registered any time within 15 business days.[60]

ALLIED DISTRIBUTION FINANCE PTY LTD *v* SAMWISE HOLDINGS PTY LTD [2017] SASC 163

Issues: PMSI priority contest; effect of PPSA on transactions where secured party retains title.

Facts: In 2012, Commercial Distribution Finance Pty Ltd (CDF) (SP1/lender1) provided floorplan finance over motorbikes to Bill's Motorcycles (BM) (grantor/debtor). It retained ownership of the motorbike and registered a PMSI. In June 2014, BM (grantor) granted an all present and after-acquired property (AllPAAP) security interest to Samwise (SP2), which perfected its interest by registration. In March 2016, Allied Distribution Finance Pty Ltd (ADF) (SP3/lender2) entered into a floorplan finance agreement with BM (grantor), ADF (SP3/lender) registered a PMSI, and CDF transferred the motorcycles to ADF (SP3/lender2). ADF (SP3/lender2) claimed its PMSI had priority over Samwise (SP2)'s interest.

Analysis: This case depended on whether ADF (SP3/lender2) interest was perfected by possession at the time the grantor (Samwise) obtained possession of the inventory (the motorbikes): s 62(2)(b)(i).

In his judgment, Blue J made it clear that, in the PPSA, the reference to a grantor obtaining 'possession' of goods that are inventory (in s 62(2) regarding PMSI priority) is a reference to the grantor obtaining possession of that very inventory as a grantor of the PMSI and not in some other capacity.

Decision: The court held that the PMSI held by ADF had priority. In s 62(2)(b)(i), 'obtains possession of the inventory' meant obtaining possession of the inventory in question as grantor of the relevant PMSI. This happened when Samwise became a grantor of the security interest, which was held by ADF rather than 'at the earlier point when Samwise had first obtained possession of the motorbikes under the financing arrangement with CDF, or any other earlier point when it granted another security interest (such as the interest granted to Samwise)'.[61]

The court further commented on the effect of the PPSA on security transactions in which a secured party (grantee) retained ownership. The court held that 'the PPSA treated such transactions as if the property were owned by the grantor and the financier held security, but

60 See M Bennett, 'Practical Problem Caused by the Personal Property Securities Act' (Wentworth Selborne Chambers, 2013), 23: https://www.13wentworthselbornechambers.com.au/.
61 See S Pemberton, *Digest of PPSA Cases* (last updated: 10 December 2019), 2.

did not actually deem the property to be owned by the grantor'.[62] Moreover, the financier retained legal ownership 'for the purpose of enforcing general law rights against the person having possession (the grantor) and against strangers (persons other than those having competing security interests in the property)'.[63]

Lesson: The PMSI provisions in the PPSA afford priority to security holders who provide to the grantor the means of acquiring the grantor's interest in the personal property over other security holders as it is equitable to do so, but a security holder must follow the rules in the PPSA to enjoy PMSI priority. In particular, the SI must be registered on the Personal Property Securities Register before the time the grantor obtains possession of the goods if they are inventory, and the SI must be registered within 15 business days of the grantor obtaining possession of the goods if they are not inventory.[64]

9.12 Important developments and changes

9.12.1 PPSA review

As required by s 343 of the PPSA, the Attorney-General announced a review of the PPS Act in April 2014.

> **Review of operation of Act**
>
> (1) The Minister must cause a review of the operation of this Act to be undertaken and completed within 3 years after the registration commencement time.
> Note: For registration commencement time, see section 306.
>
> (2) The persons who undertake the review under subsection (1) must give the Minister a written report of the review.
>
> (3) The Minister must cause a copy of the report of the review under subsection (1) to be tabled in each House of the Parliament within 15 sitting days of the day on which the report is given to the Minister.

The Final Report on the review was released before Parliament in 2015. In line with the terms of reference for the review, the report examines:[65]

- the effects of the reforms introduced by the PPSA;
- the level of awareness and understanding of the PPSA at all levels of business;

62 See S Pemberton, *Digest of PPSA Cases* (last updated: 10 December 2019), 2.
63 See S Pemberton, *Digest of PPSA Cases* (last updated: 10 December 2019), 2.
64 K Lee, 'The Personal Property Securities Act Turns 6 on 30 January 2018' (Legal Know-How, 25 January 2018): https://www.saiglobal.com/.
65 Attorney-General's Department, *Statutory Review of the Personal Property Securities Act 2009*: https://www.ag.gov.au/; see also B Whittaker, *Review of the Personal Property Securities Act 2009 Final Report* (2015), vii (Terms of Reference): https://www.ag.gov.au/.

- the incidence and causes of non-compliance with the PPSA;
- opportunities for minimising regulatory and administrative burdens, including cost; and
- opportunities for further efficiencies in the PPSA regime, including simplification of the PPSR and its use.

The report also examines:[66]

- the scope and definitions of personal property covered by the PPSA;
- the desirability of introducing thresholds for the operation of the PPSA regime in respect of particular types of personal property;
- the interaction of the PPSA with other legislation; and
- any other relevant matters.

Extensive consultation with stakeholders has been undertaken during the review process. A total of 171 submissions and responses have been received, and they came from a range of stakeholders, including 'industry organisations, individual businesses, law firms and law societies, Government bodies representing business, consumer and privacy interests, and members of the academic legal community'.[67]

This report has introduced 29 pages of detailed recommendations in relation to how to improve the PPSA, including how to simplify the Act and the PPSR.[68] The government was preparing its response to the review at the time of writing.[69]

9.12.2 PPS lease change 2017

As mentioned above, a change to the legislation regarding PPS leases occurred in 2017. The *Personal Property Securities Amendment (PPS Leases) Act 2017* (Cth), which commenced on 20 May 2017, revised the concept of a 'PPS lease' under s 13. The Amendment Act extends the minimum duration before leases and bailments become PPS leases under the PPS Act 'from more than one year, to more than two years'. Leases with an indefinite term will 'not be deemed to be PPS leases unless and until they "run" for a period of more than two years'.[70]

This change does not affect agreements entered into prior to 20 May 2017. In other words, the changes only apply to leases and bailments entered into after the changes commenced. For leases and bailments entered into prior to the changes, the law remains unchanged and registrations should proceed for these leases and bailments as usual.

In relation to fixed-term PPS leases entered into after 20 May 2017, the changes mean that those who enter into leases (and bailments) for two years or less will no longer need to be registered because the leases will not be deemed as PPS leases. If a lease agreement is entered

66 Attorney-General's Department, *Statutory Review of the Personal Property Securities Act 2009*: https://www.ag.gov.au/.

67 See *Review of the Personal Property Securities Act 2009 Final Report* (2015), 502–30: https://www.ag.gov.au/.

68 All the recommendations are listed separately at the end of the review report, in Annexure E. See *Review of the Personal Property Securities Act 2009 Final Report* (2015), 502–30.

69 Attorney-General's Department, 'Statutory Review of the Personal Property Securities Act 2009': https://www.ag.gov.au/.

70 PPSR, PPS Lease change 2017 (under the 'What are the changes' session): https://www.ppsr.gov.au/.

into after 20 May 2017, and is for more than two years, the lease agreement will be deemed as a PPS lease, and it should be registered. However, if the lease agreement is 'for two years or less, but exceeds the agreed term, it will become a PPS lease when it extends beyond two years, and should be registered at that time'.[71]

In respect of indefinite-term PPS leases entered into after 20 May 2017, these changes mean that leases (and bailments) with an indefinite term will not be deemed as PPS leases unless they have been operated for more than two years. For example, if a car is leased for an 'indefinite term' under a lease agreement concluded after 20 May 2017, and is returned to the lessor after 23 months (less than two years), the car was never the subject of a PPS lease. If it was returned after 25 months (more than two years), it would have been deemed as the subject of a PPS lease.[72]

9.12.3 Importance of ABN versus ACN

Although errors in PPSR registration are common, an increased number of businesses are beginning to understand the importance of registering their security interests.[73] Some errors can be fatal and result in the loss of their assets. For example, in January 2017, the NSW Supreme Court confirmed that an administrative error made by Alleasing Pty Ltd in its PPSR registrations resulted in the loss of assets valued at $23 million (crushing and screening equipment and associated parts).

RE ONESTEEL MANUFACTURING PTY LTD (ADMINS APPTD) (2017) 93 NSWLR 611

Issues: Defective registrations – ABNs; extension of time; and constitutional validity.

Facts: Alleasing Pty Ltd (Alleasing) leased equipment to OneSteel Manufacturing Pty Ltd (OneSteel), and made PPSR registrations by reference to OneSteel's ABN rather than its ACN. Later, on 7 April 2016, OneSteel went into administration. Alleasing lodged new financing statements, and amended its original registrations to include the correct ACN details on 17 June 2016. Alleasing sought:

'(1) a declaration that its security interest was validly perfected; or

(2) a declaration that section 267 of the PPSA was invalid as it would result in an acquisition of property other than on just terms, which is prohibited by section 252B of the PPSA; and

(3) alternatively, pursuant to section 588FM of the *Corporations Act 2001* (Cth) (Corporations Act) an order fixing the registration time at the time of the Amended Registration.'[74]

71 See 'Compliance: New PPSR Rules', in *CCF WA ONSITE Q3 2017*, 18: www.ccfwa.com.au/.

72 For more examples, see 'Compliance: New PPSR Rules', in *CCF WA ONSITE Q3 2017*, 18: www.ccfwa.com.au/.

73 K Payne and G Scott, 'Court Confirms Importance of ABN vs ACN Distinction on PPSR Registrations', *Insolvency and Reconstruction* (Hall & Wilcox, 3 February 2017): https://hallandwilcox.com.au/. See also A Leslie, 'The Importance of Effective PPSA Registrations' (Vincents, 2017): https://vincents.com.au/.

74 See A Borland and J O'Farrell 'The ABCs of ABNs and ACNs under the PPSA: The Irreparable Effects of Defective PPSR Registrations': https://www.millsoakley.com.au/.

Decision:

(1) The court held that Alleasing's interests had vested. The PPSR registrations were defective because they were not made against the ACN but the ABN. This defect resulted in ineffectiveness of the registration under s 165(b) because a search of the PPSR against the ACN would not have discovered the original registration. The court also considered the registrations ineffective as 'seriously misleading' under s 164(1)(a), and held 'it was irrelevant that the administrators in fact had discovered them by a search against the ABN'.[75]

(2) The court rejected Alleasing's arguments that 'vesting gave rise to an acquisition of property other than on just terms contrary to s 51(xxxi) of the Constitution, consistently with *White v Spiers Earthworks Pty Ltd* [2014] WASC 139', and also 'noting that vesting under s 267 did not involve the grantor taking property of the secured party but, rather, the consequence of an incident to which all PPS leases were subject'.

(3) The court refused the claim that Alleasing can apply under the Corporations Act, s 588FM to fix a later time for registration. The court held that 'an extension under s 588FM could only save a security interest from vesting under s 588FL where registration occurred after the time required by s 588FL(2)(b) but before the "critical time" at which administrators were appointed, not (as had occurred here) where registration had not occurred at all by the critical time. And it could only save a security interest from vesting under s 588FL, not (as had occurred here) from vesting under s 267 of the PPSA.'[76]

Lesson: The court's decision in this case is 'a timely reminder of the importance of secured parties ensuring that their security interests are properly registered on the PPSR and the potentially significant consequences of failing to do so'.[77] It is also important for lessors to 'register their security interests on the PPSR within the statutory timeframe and include all of the prescribed information'.[78]

9.13 Key points

- The PPSA applies to 'security interests' in 'personal property'.
- The PPSA will only be applicable once a security interest related to personal property is identified. A security interest is defined in s 10 of the PPSA by reference to s 12.
- Security interests cannot be enforced unless they (1) attach to the collateral that makes the security interest enforceable against the grantor; (2) are enforceable against third parties; and (3) are perfected.

75 S Pemberton, *Digest of PPSA Cases* (last updated: 10 December 2019), 35–6.

76 S Pemberton, *Digest of PPSA Cases* (last updated: 10 December 2019), 35–6.

77 K Payne and G Scott, 'Court Confirms Importance of ABN vs ACN Distinction on PPSR Registrations', *Insolvency and Reconstruction* (Hall & Wilcox, 3 February 2017): https://hallandwilcox.com.au/. See also A Leslie, 'The Importance of Effective PPSA Registrations' (Vincents, 2017): https://vincents.com.au/.

78 K Payne and G Scott, 'Court Confirms Importance of ABN vs ACN Distinction on PPSR Registrations', *Insolvency and Reconstruction* (Hall & Wilcox, 3 February 2017): https://hallandwilcox.com.au/. See also A Leslie, 'The Importance of Effective PPSA Registrations' (Vincents, 2017): https://vincents.com.au/.

- The perfection of a security interest has a direct impact on 'the priority it has relative to other security interests in the collateral and its status in the event of the insolvency or bankruptcy of the grantor'.[79]

9.14 DISCUSSION QUESTIONS

1. What are some of the features of the PPSA that make it a different system from the prior law for security over personal property?
2. What are the elements of the definition of a security interest under the PPSA?
3. What are some of the forms of personal property that are excluded by the PPSA?
4. How are supplies of goods under retention of title arrangements covered by the PPSA?
5. What is the difference between attachment and perfection of a security interest?
6. What forms of property may be used as collateral?
7. How is priority determined between two perfected secured parties?
8. What is a PMSI? What advantages apply to classifying a security interest as a PMSI under the PPSA?
9. How might a priority contest be determined between a general security interest in all present and after acquired property and a perfected PMSI?

9.15 PROBLEM QUESTION

Alex has recently traded in his old BMW X5 for a value of $75 000 and purchased a new BMW X5 from ABC Motors for $100 000 (with $75 000 coming from the trade-in and the balance provided by finance from ABC Motors). The salesman at ABC Motors ran a PPSR search using the Vehicle Identification Number (VIN) for the trade-in car and for Alex as grantor, and nothing showed up.

In fact, the vehicle is collateral for finance obtained by Alex from CarLease Ltd. However, CarLease Ltd made an error when it recorded its interest on the PPSR for the vehicle by mixing up two numbers in the VIN. ABC Motors registered a security interest against Alex's new vehicle, and recorded the VIN correctly. Alex then gave the vehicle to David (his son) as a birthday gift. David has an outstanding bank loan covering all present and after acquired property with Ozland Bank Ltd (with a proper PPSR registration). When David defaults on his bank loan, Ozland seizes the new vehicle.

ABC Motors sold Alex's trade-in vehicle to Grace for $85 000, and provided Grace with finance for the purchase. ABC Motors correctly recorded a security interest in Grace's vehicle on the PPSR.

79 See Personal Property Securities Register, *PPSR Overview*: https://www.ppsr.gov.au/.

Who has priority to the two vehicles (the new $100 000 BMW X5 and Alex's original trade-in vehicle) under the Personal Property Securities Act? How about if David is a taxi driver, mainly uses the new BMW X5 as a taxi, and always deposits his taxi income into his bank account with Ozland Bank?

9.16 FURTHER READING

Aitken, L, 'Personal Property Security, Equitable Interests and Priority' (August 2011) *Australian Banking and Finance Law Bulletin* 31.

Allan, D E and Wappett, C C, 'Personal Property Security Bill (The Bond Bill)' (2002) 14 *Bond Law Review* 132.

Clarke, C J, 'The Threshold Requirements of the PPSA: Does s 12 Require an Interest in rem in Order to Create a Security Interest?' (2016) 27 *Journal of Banking and Finance Law and Practice* 6.

Duggan, A and Brown, D, *Australian Personal Property Securities Law* (LexisNexis Butterworths Australia, Sydney, 2nd edn, 2016).

Mirzai, N and Harris, J, *The Annotated Personal Property Securities Act 2009 (Cth)* (Wolters Kluwer, Sydney, 3rd edn, 2018).

Shtein, O and Hustler, P, 'What Becomes of the Fixed and Floating Charge under the PPSA?' (December 2010) *Australian Banking and Finance Law Bulletin* 74.

Steicke, K and Spurritt, M, 'Security over Bank Deposits under the Personal Property Securities Act' (October 2011) *Australian Banking and Finance Law Bulletin* 76.

Wappett, C, 'Competing Interests in Leased Collateral under the PPSA' (2015) 24 *Australian Property Law Journal* 255.

Whittaker, B, *Review of the Personal Property Securities Act 2009 Final Report* (March 2015): https://www.ag.gov.au/.

Widdup, L, 'The Vesting of PPSA Security Interests: A Critical Look at the Critical Time' (2015) 24 *Australian Property Law Journal* 345: https://www.ag.gov.au/.

10

CONTRACTS OF GUARANTEE

10.0 Introduction

This chapter explores the topic of contracts of guarantee. Contracts of guarantee are utilised in a range of consumer and business contexts to minimise a lender's risk in situations where the borrower lacks sufficient assets to utilise as security, or where money is lent to inherently risky ventures. Guarantees enable access to credit in situations where the borrower lacks a credit history or cannot secure a loan because they do not have appropriate collateral. A lender to a corporation will require a guarantee because of the risks posed by the nature of business itself, and by use of the corporate structure preventing financiers' access to assets vested in shareholders and beneficiaries. Guarantees reduce the cost of borrowing by reducing the lender's risk in providing loaned money, and relieving the lender of the need to undertake costly risk assessments. Such costs would otherwise be passed on to the borrower through increased interest rates on borrowings.[1]

The incidence of the use of third-party guarantees in Australia has not been accurately assessed. However, information provided by institutional lenders suggests that guarantees more often secure business loans rather than personal consumer loans.[2] According to Lovric and Millbank, guarantees may secure up to 75 per cent of loans to small businesses, although the reported figures vary enormously.[3] Indeed, more recent figures from the Reserve Bank of Australia indicate that Australian businesses are financed by approximately 40 per cent debt, composed largely of loans from financial institutions (which will invariably be secured).[4]

In most instances of lending to businesses, financial institutions will require guarantees because businesses in general will tend to lack either the capital or assets to provide security for lending. Recent data from the Australian Small Business and Family Enterprise Ombudsman indicates that small to medium-sized enterprises (SMEs) do indeed experience difficulty obtaining loan finance because traditional lenders regard such lending as risky.[5] This hesitance is primarily due to the fact that most SMEs lack fixed assets against which to secure loans, are sensitive to macroeconomic trends, and are often perceived as lacking the skills and resources to handle finance in a sophisticated manner.[6] Data from the Australian Bankers' Association[7]

1 See Australian Trade Practices Commission, *Guarantors: Problems and Perspectives* (Discussion Paper, 1992), 16–18.

2 J Lovric and J Millbank, *Darling, Please Sign This Form: A Report on the Practice of Third Party Guarantees in New South Wales* (NSW Law Reform Commission and University of Sydney, Research Report 11, 2003), [4.48].

3 J Lovric and J Millbank, *Darling, Please Sign This Form: A Report on the Practice of Third Party Guarantees in New South Wales* (NSW Law Reform Commission and University of Sydney, Research Report 11, 2003), [4.49]–[4.50]. The figure of 75 per cent was provided by a bank; an estimate of 70 per cent was provided by a representative body; a small lender reported requiring guarantees in 39 per cent of cases; while another small lender reported seeking guarantees for only 5 per cent of loans made.

4 Christopher Kent, Assistant Governor (Financial Markets), 'The Availability of Business Finance' (Speech delivered at the 30th Australasian Finance and Banking Conference, University of New South Wales, 13 December 2017).

5 Australian Government, Australian Small Business and Family Enterprise Ombudsman, *Barriers to Investment: A Study into Factors Impacting Small to Medium Enterprise Investment* (November 2017), 3.

6 Australian Government, Australian Small Business and Family Enterprise Ombudsman, *Barriers to Investment: A Study into Factors Impacting Small to Medium Enterprise Investment* (November 2017), 3–4.

7 Australian Bankers' Association, 'The Small Business Sector in Australia – Economic Report' (May 2016).

and submitted as part of the Royal Commission into Misconduct in the Banking, Superannuation and Financial Services Industry,[8] indicates that just under half of all small businesses have a business loan facility (excluding credit cards) and around one million loans have been provided to small businesses.

Contracts of guarantee have proven problematic for a number of reasons. First, many persons who become guarantors do not understand the nature and function of the guarantee agreement they have entered;[9] accordingly, they lack sufficient awareness of the consequences for them following the borrower's default on the loan.[10] Many, if not most, guarantors are in a close personal relationship with the borrower. Consequently, the guarantor may be manipulated by either the borrower or the lender, or, because the relationship is one based on trust, ignore the potential risks, failing to submit the agreement to the analysis or subject it to the enquiries they would have made had they been entering an arm's length commercial agreement. Even when guarantors have sought the information they require, they may enter an improvident transaction in order to preserve the relationship.

In *Watt v State Bank of New South Wales*, Higgins CJ and Crisp J observed that parents are vulnerable to their children in the context of contracts of guarantee, not because they lack knowledge of the nature of the transaction or are mistaken as to the potential consequences, but because 'love of their children' produces a 'desire to help and protect them, to advance their interests, to maintain a close relationship, to avoid causing disappointment, hurt or distress, to maintain the relationship [which] may all make it difficult to say "no"'.[11]

10.1 The nature of the obligations

A guarantee is a binding promise of one person to be answerable for the present or future debt or obligation of another in case that person defaults.[12] There are three parties involved in a contract of guarantee:[13]

8 A Godwin, J M Paterson and N Howell, Background Paper 10 – Credit for Small Business: An Overview of Australian Law Regulating Small Business Loans, *Royal Commission into Misconduct in the Banking, Superannuation and Financial Services Industry*, 7 May 2018.

9 A J Duggan, *The Law of Guarantee in Australia* (Australian Finance Conference Ltd and Australian Equipment Lessors Association Inc, Sydney, 4th edn, 1998), [1.1] states that many guarantors are of the belief that they are no more than the referee for a borrower. See also J Lovric and J Millbank, *Darling, Please Sign This Form: A Report on the Practice of Third Party Guarantees in New South Wales* (NSW Law Reform Commission and University of Sydney, Research Report 11, 2003), [3.71]–[3.73]; *Commercial Bank of Australia Ltd v Amadio* (1983) 151 CLR 447; *Permanent Mortgages Pty Ltd v Vandenbergh* (2010) 41 WAR 353; *Hanna v Raoul* [2018] NSWCA 201.

10 J Lovric and J Millbank, *Darling, Please Sign This Form: A Report on the Practice of Third Party Guarantees in New South Wales* (NSW Law Reform Commission and University of Sydney, Research Report 11, 2003), [3.44]–[3.49], report that even those guarantors who understand that they are personally securing the borrower's loan with their own money or assets do not believe that they have assumed a considerable risk, in part because some guarantors labour under the misapprehension that guarantees will not be called upon in case of default.

11 [2003] ACTCA 7, [22].

12 See *Sunbird Plaza Pty Ltd v Maloney* (1988) 166 CLR 245, 256. See also *Yeoman Credit Ltd v Latter* [1961] 1 WLR 828; *Direct Acceptance Finance Ltd v Cumberland Furnishing Pty Ltd* [1965] NSWR 1504.

13 In *Allcott Hire Pty Ltd v Silk* [2016] NSWSC 1135, [52], Rothman J described contracts of guarantee as 'three-party agreements'.

- the *principal debtor (or principal)* – the party promising to do something;
- the *creditor* – the party to whom this promise is made; and
- the *guarantor/surety* – the party undertaking to be liable should the promisor (principal debtor) fail to adhere to the agreement.

The guarantee is the undertaking that the debt shall be paid.[14] In *Jowitt v Callaghan*[15] Jordan CJ described the nature of the guarantee in the following terms:

> The contract of guarantee or suretyship is a contract between two persons which is intended by them to secure the performance of the obligation of a third person to one of them. The existence, present or future, of the obligation of a third person, and an intention in the parties to the contract to secure the performance of that obligation, are essential features of the contract of guarantee. If these elements are present, the contract is one of guarantee whether the promise be collateral to the promise of a principal obligor and in the nature of a distinct and separate promise to perform the principal obligation if it does not, or whether it be a joint promise with the principal obligor by virtue of which an immediate obligation is assumed to the obligee which is joint with that of the principal obligor (in which case there is a suretyship in equity though not at common law); and whether the promise be a promise to be personally liable if the principal obligor does not perform the obligation, or the promise merely that certain property of the promisor shall be a security for the performance of the principal obligation.[16]

As Mason CJ stated in *Sunbird Plaza Pty Ltd v Maloney*, guarantees are not restricted to the payment of debts but extend to a 'wide range of obligations',[17] the performance of which may currently, or at some future time, be required under a contract. It is merely common to speak of the parties to a guarantee relationship as creditor, guarantor and principal debtor because the majority of guarantees are given in relation to the payment of debts. The obligation in question is not restricted to contracts, but may include obligations arising from a bailment, a tort, or an unsatisfied judgment.[18]

10.2 The nature of the obligations under a contract of guarantee

The obligations owed by the parties to a contract of guarantee depend upon the parties' respective positions and, of course, the terms of the contract itself. What follows is a general outline of the nature of the various obligations arising from a guarantee.

14 *Campbell v McIsaac* (1873) 9 NSR 287.
15 (1938) 38 SR (NSW) 512.
16 (1938) 38 SR (NSW) 512–16. This definition is 'well settled' in Australian law: *Beagle Holdings Pty Ltd v Equus Financial Services Ltd* [2000] WASC 27, [50]. For a recent affirmation, see *Nannup Timber Processing Pty Ltd v Minister for Commerce* [2014] WASC 438.
17 (1988) 166 CLR 245, 245.
18 *Moschi v Lep Air Services Ltd* [1973] AC 331, 347–8.

10.2.1 Principal debtor

The principal debtor owes a primary obligation to the creditor. The obligation is primary in that the principal debtor is ultimately liable to the guarantor, who has rights against the principal debtor to be reimbursed for the payment made to the creditor arising from the principal debtor's default.[19] However, unless otherwise provided in the contract of guarantee, the creditor is not obligated to pursue the principal debtor prior to proceeding against the guarantor; they may proceed against the guarantor as soon as the principal debtor has defaulted.[20]

To use an example, if John takes out a home loan with a bank, he has a primary obligation to the bank (as creditor). As with most lenders, the bank will likely require a guarantor if John does not have a sufficient cash deposit or assets to borrow the balance of the purchase price. If John's friend Nora agrees to guarantee the loan, and John defaults, the bank can promptly pursue Nora directly.

10.2.2 Guarantor/surety

The guarantor owes a secondary obligation to the creditor. The obligation is secondary in that it only exists if the principal debt (or other obligation) remains enforceable; that is, the secondary obligation coexists with the principal debtor's liability to the creditor either currently or in the future.[21]

To use the earlier example, once John pays his loan off, there is no longer an enforceable debt and his primary obligation to the bank is discharged, meaning that Nora's secondary obligation to the bank is discharged as well.

Under a contract of guarantee, the guarantor does not assure the creditor that the principal debtor will fulfil their obligations under the contract;[22] nor do they arrange the contract's performance.[23] The nature of a guarantee is such that the guarantor's obligation arises immediately after the principal debtor defaults, unless otherwise determined by the contract of guarantee.[24] The contract may provide that a demand be issued to the guarantor prior to their liability for the principal debtor's obligation arising. However, such a requirement must be expressly provided for in the contract and will not be implied.[25]

19 *Sunbird Plaza Pty Ltd v Maloney* (1988) 166 CLR 245, 254.
20 *Sunbird Plaza Pty Ltd v Maloney* (1988) 166 CLR 245, 255.
21 *McDonald v Dennys Lascelles Ltd* (1933) 48 CLR 457, 479–80.
22 *Blashki v Utara* (2003) Aust Contract R ¶90-159.
23 *Sunbird Plaza Pty Ltd v Maloney* (1988) 166 CLR 245, 256.
24 *Moschi v Lep Air Services Ltd* [1973] AC 331, 356–7.
25 *M S Fashions Ltd v Bank of Credit & Commerce International SA (in liq) [No 2]* [1993] Ch 425, 436.

The case of *McDonald v Dennys Lascelles Ltd* illustrates the secondary nature of the guarantor's obligation.[26] In March 1925, Besley purchased a parcel of land in Victoria on an instalment contract, with title to be transferred upon payment of the final instalment in April 1931. In June 1927, Besley on-sold the land to the Rye Grazing Company Pty Ltd. Under this second contract, the purchaser agreed to pay a £6000 deposit, and four further instalments: three annual instalments of £1000, and £14 462 as a final instalment on 24 January 1931. The contract also provided that time was of the essence, and that the purchaser would forfeit the deposit and the contract would be rescinded if they were in default of payment. After paying the first two instalments, the purchaser sought an extension of time for payment of the third instalment, until 24 January 1931, the date the final instalment was due to be paid.

In August 1929, Besley assigned his interest in the land to Dennys Lascelles Ltd, which agreed to the extension of time (for payment of the third instalment) on the basis of a guarantee that the payment would be made on 24 January 1931 executed in their favour by McDonald and Holdsworth, the directors of Rye Grazing Company. When the purchaser failed to pay both the instalment for which they sought an extension of time and the final instalment, Dennys Lascelles moved to enforce the guarantee against the purchaser. The first contract was rescinded in April 1931, and two months later Rye Grazing Company sought to rescind the second contract on the basis that it could not effectively pass title in light of the failure of the first contract. In other words, Rye Grazing Company argued the guarantee could not continue to be enforceable in light of the first contract's termination.

The High Court held by majority that, as the original contract did not provide otherwise, the effect of its termination was that the vendor had to return any instalments paid, and there was no longer any liability on the purchaser to pay the outstanding instalments. This was because the contract did not unconditionally vest in the vendor the right to retain its money.[27] The guarantee was simultaneously extinguished when the original contract was rescinded. The court reasoned that the unenforceability of the principal debt meant that 'the groundwork of the accessory obligation [had] disappeared'.[28] Dixon J concluded that 'wherever the principal is discharged, in whatever manner it may be, not only by actual payment or a compensation, but also by a release, the surety is discharged likewise'.[29] Put another way, given that the purchaser was not liable to make future payments under the discharged contract, neither was the guarantor.

10.2.3 The guarantor's collateral obligation is co-extensive

In general, an agreement will constitute a guarantee only if the guarantor's and the principal debtor's liabilities are co-extensive.[30] That is, the guarantor will be equally liable for the whole

26 For more recent cases discussing this seminal authority, see: *Geeveekay Pty Ltd v Director of Consumer Affairs Victoria* (2008) 19 VR 512; *MSD Securities Pty Ltd v MFB Properties (NQ) Pty [No 2]* [2018] 2 Qd R 51.

27 '[The vendor's] title to retain the money has been considered not to be absolute but conditional upon the subsequent completion of the contract': (1933) 48 CLR 457, 477.

28 (1933) 48 CLR 457, 467.

29 (1933) 48 CLR 457, 479–80.

30 *Yeoman Credit Ltd v Latter* [1961] 1 WLR 828; *Biscayne Partners Pty Ltd v Valance Corporation Pty Ltd* [2003] NSWSC 874.

amount for which the principal debtor is liable. This fundamental principle is nevertheless subject to the parties' agreement: the contract of guarantee may provide otherwise.[31]

Returning to the earlier example of John and Nora, it is customary for a guarantor in such situations to guarantee only a *portion* of the loan. As such, it is likely that Nora will only guarantee a smaller agreed sum – that is, a part of the entire amount John has borrowed from the bank.

Co-extensive liability may also be lacking in certain situations. For example, a guarantor will generally not be liable where the principal debtor's obligation is discharged, altered in a significant way from that which the guarantor secured, or otherwise legally determined (brought to an end).[32] There are exceptions to this general proposition. As mentioned earlier, the contract of guarantee may provide otherwise and change the nature of the guarantor's obligation. In addition, the guarantor's obligation will not be legally determined (extinguished) by bankruptcy, liquidation of a company, entry into a scheme of arrangement, or a company's placement into official management.[33] The guarantee would be futile and its very purpose would be frustrated if it could not operate in such situations.

Co-extensive liability requires that the guarantor's liability not be of a kind different from the principal debtor's.[34] Similarly, co-extensive liability also requires that the guarantor's liability not exceed, replace or terminate the principal debtor's liability.[35]

In the case of *Direct Acceptance Finance Ltd v Cumberland Furnishing Pty Ltd*,[36] a recourse agreement[37] between a financier and a dealer purporting to guarantee customers' liabilities provided that if in the opinion of the financier a customer's account was unsatisfactory, the dealer was required to pay the financier the amount due on the contract between the financier and the customer, except for any monies already paid by the customer. It was contended that the agreement did not constitute a guarantee because it demonstrated a lack of co-extensive liability between both the dealer's and the customer's liabilities. The court agreed, holding that the recourse agreement was not a guarantee for two reasons: (1) because under the agreement the financier had recourse to the dealer even where the customer had not

31 *Perry v National Provincial Bank of England* [1910] 1 Ch 464.

32 *McDonald v Dennys Lascelles Ltd* (1933) 48 CLR 457; *Jowitt v Callaghan* (1938) 38 SR (NSW) 512; *Ankar Pty Ltd v National Westminster Finance (Australia) Ltd* (1987) 162 CLR 549; *Commercial Banking Co of Sydney Ltd v Patrick Intermarine Acceptance Ltd (in liq)* (1978) 52 ALJR 404.

33 See *Helou v Mulligan Pty Ltd* (2003) 57 NSWLR 74; *Jowitt v Callaghan* (1938) 38 SR (NSW) 512; *Quainoo v New Zealand Breweries Ltd* [1991] 1 NZLR 161; *Hill v Anderson Meat Industries Ltd* [1971] 1 NSWLR 868; [1972] 2 NSWLR 704; *Commercial Banking Co of Sydney Ltd v Gaty* [1978] 2 NSWLR 271; *Gan v Sanders* (1994) 15 ACSR 298; *Re Care Builders Pty Ltd* (1997) 23 ACSR 754; *Ehrenfeld v Oriana Nominees Pty Ltd* [1999] WASCA 222; *Ex parte Jacobs; Re Jacobs* [1875] 10 Ch 211; *Re London Chartered Bank of Australia* [1893] 3 Ch 540.

34 *Duncan, Fox & Co v North & South Wales Bank* (1880) 6 App Cas 1.

35 *Direct Acceptance Finance Ltd v Cumberland Furnishing Pty Ltd* [1965] NSWR 1504; *Permanent Trustee Co of New South Wales Ltd v Hinks* (1934) 34 SR (NSW) 130; *Yeoman Credit Ltd v Latter* [1961] 1 WLR 828; *St George Wholesale Finance Pty Ltd v Spalla* (2000) 181 ALR 682.

36 [1965] NSWR 1504.

37 A recourse agreement is a legal agreement vesting in a lender the right to claim pledged collateral in the event that the borrower is unable to satisfy the associated debt obligation.

defaulted; and (2) the court held that even if the customer did default, the financier could require the dealer to pay an amount greater than that owed by the customer. In the event of a customer's default, liability was limited to instalments due and unpaid, whereas the dealer's liability was calculated on the basis of the contract running to its full term.

10.2.4 Continuing versus limited/specific guarantees

Under a contract of continuing guarantee, a guarantor secures the performance of a principal debtor over a course of future transactions, whereas a limited or specific guarantee guarantees the performance of a single transaction (normally where the principal debtor has a fixed liability).[38] As such, the distinction affects the guarantor's liability. Under a specific guarantee a guarantor's liability will be extinguished even when the principal debtor continues to be indebted to the creditor, provided the debt for the fixed liability is met; or if the guarantee secures a single transaction, provided the subject goods are paid for, irrespective of non-payment for subsequent supplies of goods.[39] A continuing guarantee usually involves the principal debtor purchasing goods on credit or borrowing money to be repaid over a period of time. A continuing guarantee without a specified duration is a guarantee without a limitation of time.[40] Contracts of guarantee may provide for a period of notice or stipulate a time limit. However, this gives rise to problems of precisely when the guarantor's liability arose.

The principles for the construction of either continuing or limited/specific contracts of guarantee are nevertheless consistent. The terms of any agreement are given their ordinary and natural meaning, and are interpreted in the context of the contract as a whole.[41] Where there is some ambiguity in the instrument of guarantee as to whether it provides for a specific transaction or ongoing transactions, courts will determine the guarantee to be continuing if the guarantee refers to future transactions.[42] If there is no reference to a series of transactions, and the words of the agreement are neutral with respect to the guarantee being fixed or continuing, the court may have regard to the circumstances of the transaction. Factors

---

38 *Turner Manufacturing Co Pty Ltd v Senes* [1964] NSWR 692; *Parr's Banking Co Ltd v Yates* [1898] 2 QB 460. Technically speaking, a guarantee is not specific merely because it is limited. The agreement may indicate the ongoing nature of the obligations despite a limit being set to liability. For example, an upper limit of liability may be set but the guarantor covers transactions within that limit. A guarantee for future transactions will not be limited absent specific provisions to that effect, even where the contract specifies that the guarantee has an upper limit which is not specified: *Caltex Oil (Australia) Pty Ltd v Alderton* (1964) 81 WN (Pt 1) NSW 297. Nor will such a contract be considered uncertain. This is not the same as a guarantee that refers specifically to an upper limit that has not been specified because of the parties' inability to agree. Where a contract specifies an upper limit by the words 'up to [money amount]' or 'to [money amount]', the guarantee will not be interpreted as meaning that the guarantee is triggered by the principal debtor's debt reaching that limit. But where the limit refers to the advanced rather than the guaranteed amount, the creditor is in breach if they advance an amount in excess of the limit and the guarantee is void: *Philips v Astling* (1809) 2 Taunt 206. However, courts have on occasion preferred constructions more favourable to the creditor: *Queensland National Bank Ltd v Queensland Trustees Ltd* (1899) 9 QLJ 282.

39 *Heffield v Meadows* (1869) LR 4 CP 595.

40 *Coles v Pack* (1869) LR 5 CP 65.

41 *Andar Transport Pty Ltd v Brambles Ltd* (2004) 217 CLR 424; *Royal Botanic Gardens & Domain Trust v South Sydney City Council* (2002) 186 ALR 289. The general principles for the construction of contracts of guarantee will be explored in greater depth later in this chapter (see Section 10.4).

42 *Nicholson v Paget* (1832) 1 C & M 48; *See v Farey* (1889) 10 LR (NSW) 72, 75.

suggesting a guarantee is continuing include a business requiring or previously receiving continuous supplies, or the fact the guarantee would be nugatory unless it ensured future transactions.

That a guarantee is continuing may be evident from words used to identify the nature of the guarantee (such as a reference to the contract as a 'continuing security'), or a reference to guaranteeing 'any goods' supplied or 'all monies' advanced to the principal debtor from time to time.[43] Terms utilising this type of language are known as 'all monies' or 'all debts' clauses.[44] All monies clauses are designed to ensure that the mortgagor or guarantor will be liable for all sums owed by the debtor (or other nominated party) to the creditor.[45] To cover all possible eventualities, these clauses are generally drafted comprehensively.[46] The breadth of the all monies clause in *Re Bankrupt Estate of Murphy; Donnelly v Commonwealth Bank of Australia Ltd* was held sufficient to entitle a creditor to rely on it to recover monies stolen by the principal debtor from the guarantor.[47]

As Collier notes,[48] the courts have held the following debts to fall within the ambit of particular all monies clauses (and therefore falling within the scope of the guarantor's liability):

- the legal costs of the creditor, where the creditor was joined as a co-defendant with the debtor in an action by a third party;[49]
- liabilities of the principal debtor itself as surety for the debts of others;[50]
- the liabilities of the debtor under a cross-guarantee;[51]
- bills paid out by the bank on behalf of the debtor;[52]
- obligations incurred by the debtor under a later transaction with the creditor, where both the relevant transaction and the obligations were of a kind within the purview of the ongoing banking arrangements and the subject of the original agreement;[53]
- contingent liabilities;[54] and

43 *Mason v Pritchard* (1812) 170 ER 1210; *National Bank of Nigeria Ltd v Awolesi* [1964] 1 WLR 1311; *Paradise Constructors Pty Ltd v Lofts Quarries Pty Ltd* [2003] VSC 370; *Re Piccolo; McVeigh v National Australia Bank Ltd* [1999] FCA 386; affirmed in *McVeigh v National Australia Bank Ltd* (2000) 278 ALR 429. All monies clauses may also be referred to as 'all debts', 'all accounts', 'all obligations' and 'all moneys' clauses. In the United States, they are commonly referred to as 'dragnet clauses'.

44 See, generally, B Collier, '"All Debts" Clauses in Commercial Contracts of Guarantee: Principles of Construction and Limitations on the Ambit of Clauses of This Nature' (1998) 24(1) *Monash University Law Review* 7.

45 *National Bank of New Zealand Ltd v West* [1978] 2 NZLR 451.

46 See *Hall v Westpac Banking Corporation* (1987) 4 BPR 97,303, 97,580.

47 (1996) 140 ALR 46.

48 The following list of examples is extracted from B Collier, '"All Debts" Clauses in Commercial Contracts of Guarantee: Principles of Construction and Limitations on the Ambit of Clauses of This Nature' (1998) 24(1) *Monash University Law Review* 7, 10.

49 *Estoril Investments Pty Ltd v Westpac Banking Corporation* (1993) 6 BPR 13,146.

50 *Catley Farms Ltd v ANZ Banking Group (NZ) Ltd* [1982] 1 NZLR 430.

51 *Coghlan v S H Lock (Australia) Ltd* (1987) 8 NSWLR 88.

52 *Westpac Banking Corporation v George Comanos* (unreported, NSW Supreme Court, Cole J, 26 March 1993).

53 *Fountain v Bank of America National Trust & Savings Association* (1992) 5 BPR 11,817; *Re Rudd & Son; Re Fosters & Rudd Ltd* (1986) 2 BCC 98, 955; *Bank of Scotland v Wright* [1991] BCLC 244.

54 *Re Rudd & Son; Re Fosters & Rudd Ltd* (1986) 2 BCC 98, 955; *Bank of Scotland v Wright* [1991] BCLC 244.

- foreign exchange facilities, where the all debts clause clearly included debts incurred in the provision of banking facilities by the creditor.[55]

Courts are willing to enforce appropriately broad all monies clauses where the actual language used demonstrates that intention.[56] However, the courts are also willing to read down wide clauses not only to preserve the width of the operation of some words but also to avoid their having an effect they were not intended to have from the point of view of an ordinary guarantor using those words.[57] In *McVeigh v National Australia Bank Ltd*, Kenny J considered an all monies clause containing an agreement by the guarantor to pay 'any amounts' owed by, and upon the default of, the principal debtor to be 'plainly enough intended ... to cover all eventualities' regardless of whether it was in fact 'the common intent of the parties at the point of execution'.[58]

The intentions of the parties are crucial in determining whether a guarantor is liable under an all monies clause. Intentions are to be ascertained in the light of the surrounding circumstances, and the commercial purpose the guarantee is intended to secure.[59] Where the clause falls unequivocally within the scope of the guarantee, the courts evince no hesitation in enforcing it.[60] If, however, a contextual interpretation produces ambiguity, the all monies clause would be construed *contra proferentem* – that is, in favour of the guarantor.[61] As Young J explained in *Australia & New Zealand Banking Group Ltd v Comer*, the courts will read down very wide all monies obligations 'so that the wide words have some operation but do not include situations that would never have been contemplated by the ordinary [guarantor] by the use of the words'.[62]

Terms that arise conventionally within the context of all debts guarantees include references to all 'costs, charges and expenses'. Interpreted broadly, a reference to the costs of the creditor in relation to the debt includes the creditor's costs where the creditor has faced suit in relation to the debtor's account.[63] A reference to the guarantor having to pay 'all costs, charges, expenses and payments' is restricted to include only those properly incurred. Unjustifiable costs that impose an unreasonable burden on the debtor or the guarantor may not be recovered.[64] Where a guarantee imposes on the guarantor a liability to pay the creditor on

55 *Bank of India v Trans Continental Commodity Merchants Ltd & Patel* [1983] 2 Lloyd's Rep 298.

56 See, for example, Kirby P in *Smith v Australia & New Zealand Banking Group Ltd* (1996) NSW ConvR ¶55-774, ¶55-937.

57 *Australia & New Zealand Banking Group Ltd v Comer* (1993) 5 BPR 97,404, 11,758, per Young J; *Burke v State Bank of New South Wales* (1994) 37 NSWLR 53.

58 (2000) 278 ALR 429, [82].

59 *Meldov Pty Ltd v Bank of Queensland* (2015) 18 BPR 35,313; *Olympic Holdings Pty Ltd v Windslow Corporation Pty Ltd (in liq)* (2008) 36 WAR 342; *McVeigh v National Australia Bank Ltd* (2000) 278 ALR 429, [83]. See also *Estoril Investments Pty Ltd v Westpac Banking Corporation* (1993) 6 BPR 13,146; *Australia & New Zealand Banking Group Ltd v Comer* (1993) 5 BPR 11,748; *Jageev Pty Ltd v State Bank of New South Wales* (1996) 2 ACCR 396.

60 *State Bank of South Australia v MacIntosh; Halwood Corporation Ltd v State Bank of South Australia* (unreported, NSW Supreme Court, Young J, 31 May 1995, Equity Divison).

61 *Australia & New Zealand Banking Group Ltd v Comer* (1993) 5 BPR 11,748, 11,758.

62 *Australia & New Zealand Banking Group Ltd v Comer* (1993) 5 BPR 11,748, 11,758.

63 *Estoril Investments Pty Ltd v Westpac Banking Corporation* (1993) 6 BPR 13,146.

64 McLelland J in *Elders Trustee & Executor Co Ltd v Eagle Star Nominees Ltd* (1986) 4 BPR 97,256, 9,208.

the default of the debtor 'on any account whatever', the term is to be subject to a construction premised on the circumstances in which the guarantee was given, with particular attention paid to the consideration given by the bank in exchange for the guarantee. Although 'account' is a term of wide meaning, its meaning is not unrestricted.[65] The phrase 'on any account whatsoever' was considered in *Skylink International Courier Pty Ltd v Grellman*.[66] It was held that construction of the phrase required it to be considered in the context of the deed's other provisions. In particular, the provision in the deed that interest was required to be paid on 'moneys hereby secured' was seen to restrict the liability that the security contemplated.

The use of all monies clauses may be affected by the operation of statute or other instruments. For example, s 55 of the *National Credit Code* requires guarantees to comply with any regulations made under the Code. Pursuant to s 55(3), such regulations may concern the content of guarantees or the way they are expressed. Part 7 of the Australian Banking Association's *Banking Code of Practice 2020*[67] also regulates the manner in which financial institutions may issue and enforce contracts of guarantee. Finally, an all monies clause within a contract of guarantee may prompt a review for fairness under state legislation such as the *Contracts Review Act 1980* (NSW).

10.2.5 Personal liability of the guarantor

Guarantors are not required to be personally liable for the principal debtor's performance of their obligation.[68] They may, for example, provide a 'pledge, mortgage or charge' over property as security for the debtor's performance as well as pledging their personal credit.[69] Personal liability or personal credit was found not to be an essential element of suretyship in a number of cases. In *Re Conley*, Greene MR identified the function of a surety as originating from the same source as a 'security' and therefore that another party's performance may be secured other than personally.[70] In *Jowitt v Callaghan*,[71] Jordan CJ found that, so long as the guarantor secured the existing or future obligation of the principal debtor, the guarantor may promise either 'to be personally liable' or 'that a certain property of the promisor shall be security for the performance of the principal obligation'.[72]

65 *National Bank of New Zealand Ltd v West* [1978] 2 NZLR 451.
66 Unreported, NSW Supreme Court, Needham J, 21 September 1987.
67 The vast majority of banks with a retail presence in Australia are signatories to the Code, since this is a condition of Australian Banking Association membership.
68 *Re Conley; Ex parte Trustee v Barclays Bank Ltd* [1938] 2 All ER 127; *Edwards v Lennon* (1866) 6 SCR (NSW) Eq 18; *Bolton v Salmon* [1891] 2 Ch 48; *Smith v Wood* [1929] 1 Ch 14; *Jowitt v Callaghan* (1938) 38 SR (NSW) 512.
69 *Re Conley; Ex parte Trustee v Barclays Bank Ltd* [1938] 2 All ER 127, 138–9.
70 *Re Conley; Ex parte Trustee v Barclays Bank Ltd* [1938] 2 All ER 127, 131–2.
71 *Jowitt v Callaghan* (1938) 38 SR (NSW) 512.
72 *Jowitt v Callaghan* (1938) 38 SR (NSW) 512, 157, citing *Re Conley; Ex parte Trustee v Barclays Bank Ltd* [1938] 2 All ER 127.

10.2.6 Guarantee as security for whole or part of the debt

The distinction between a guarantee being for the whole debt but with a limit as to the guarantor's liability, or for part of the debt to the creditor, has serious implications for the guarantor. If the latter, the guarantor may share in the securities that the debtor provided the creditor in the principal transaction proportionate to the guarantor's payment to the creditor (relative to the whole debt). However, the guarantor will have no such right if the guarantee is for the whole debt.[73] Similarly, where the principal becomes insolvent, a guarantee for a part of the debt will entitle the guarantor to dividends in the proportion of the principal debt to the whole debt.[74] Further, co-guarantors who guarantee separate parts of a whole debt have no right of contribution as against each other.

The importance of the distinction makes it necessary to understand how contracts will be constructed. A guarantor is prima facie guaranteeing only part of the debt where the guarantee is continuing, the balance varies, but the liability is limited. The presumption may be rebutted by specific words in the contract of guarantee that the guarantee is for the whole debt.[75]

10.2.7 Must the guarantor pay the whole sum upon the principal debtor's default?

If the whole sum is payable on default by the terms of the guarantee, the natural enquiry that follows is whether the guarantor has to pay the total sum that has become payable. There is authority providing that, if the guarantee is for each sum as it falls due, the guarantor is not liable for the principal sum but for the periodic payments.[76]

10.2.8 What if a voidable guarantee is set aside?

If a voidable contract of guarantee is rescinded or set aside by court order, the guarantor avoids liability. But where the principal is able to affirm the contract, the law is uncertain. The situation centres on the question of whether the guarantor can rely on the principal's right to avoid the voidable contract. On the one hand, it has been argued that the guarantor should not be permitted to take advantage of a defence open to the principal.[77] On the other, it is argued that in the case of fraud and unconscionable conduct the guarantor should be advantaged by the principal's defence.[78] However, in consumer transactions, the argument has been made that the guarantor should be permitted to rely on any defence, unrestricted by whether the principal has a defence.[79]

73 *Gedye v Matson* (1858) 25 Beav 310.
74 *Barclay's Bank Ltd v TOSG Trust Fund Ltd* [1984] 1 All ER 628, 641.
75 *Re Sass; Ex parte National Provincial Bank of England Ltd* [1896] 2 QB 12. See also *Ulster Bank Ltd v Lambe* [1966] NI 161, 165.
76 *Parker v Bayly* [1927] GLR 265.
77 S Williston, *A Treatise on the Law of Contracts* (Baker, Voorhis & Co, Mount Kisco, NY, 3rd edn, 1957), 1218.
78 J Steyn, 'Guarantees: the Co-extensiveness Principle' (1974) 90 *Law Quarterly Review* 246.
79 Law Reform Commission of British Columbia, *Report on Guarantees of Consumer Debts* (1979) 86–9, recommendations 34, 42.

10.2.9 What if the contract of guarantee is unenforceable?

The law is similarly uncertain in the case of unenforceable contracts. Where the creditor may have their right of recovery against the principal debtor statute-barred, but have retained a right of action against the guarantor, the guarantor is liable.[80] However, if the principal contract cannot be enforced because of failures to comply with statutory requirements, the guarantor may not be liable because the principal is not.[81] Other cases have subsequently restricted this very broad basis upon which the guarantor avoids liability to the provisions of a particular statute.[82]

10.2.10 The potential impact of the estoppel doctrine

The doctrine of estoppel can be used to widen a guarantor's liability,[83] limit that liability,[84] or enforce a guarantee.[85] Evidence was admitted in *Amalgamated Investment & Property Co Ltd (in liq) v Texas Commerce International Bank Ltd*[86] to show that, on the basis of the estopped party's action or inaction, it induced in the other party an assumption as to a state of affairs[87] – namely, that the guarantee was to discharge all the principal's indebtedness – and the bank reorganised its financial affairs on the basis of the truth of the assumption, establishing an estoppel by convention.

10.3 Formation of the contract of guarantee

10.3.1 Situations in which a contract of guarantee may arise

The contract of guarantee may arise in one of three situations:

1. Creditor and principal debtor agree from the outset that the guarantor's liability is secondary and principal liability rests with the principal debtor. In some cases the same instrument will record the joint or several obligations of the principal debtor and guarantor, but usually the guarantor's obligations are recorded separately.[88]
2. Co-debtors may agree that one will assume the primary liability as primary debtor and the other the secondary liability as guarantor. The creditor is not a party to this contract.

80 *Carter v White* (1883) 25 Ch D 666, 672.
81 *Eldridge & Morris v Taylor* [1931] 2 KB 416, 418–20, which involved the *Moneylenders Act 1927* (UK).
82 *Temperance Loan Fund Ltd v Rose* [1932] 2 KB 522 also concerned the *Moneylenders Act 1927* (UK).
83 *Amalgamated Investment & Property Co Ltd (in liq) v Texas Commerce International Bank Ltd* [1982] QB 84.
84 *National Westminster Finance NZ Ltd v National Bank of NZ Ltd* [1996] 1 NZLR 548.
85 *Amalgamated Investments & Property Co Ltd (in liq) v Texas Commerce International Bank Ltd* [1982] QB 84.
86 [1982] QB 84.
87 *UDT v Beech* [1972] 1 Lloyd's Rep 546, 552.
88 See *Duncan, Fox & Co v North & South Wales Bank* (1880) 6 App Cas 1.

One co-debtor is guarantor for the other, but the creditor may treat both as principal debtors.[89]

3. In the third case a form of constructive guarantee arises in equity. Then, two debtors have primary and secondary liability for a debt that is the debt of only one of them. No contract of guarantee exists, but the secondary debtor will have a right of reimbursement against the first debtor in case the second pays it.[90]

Absent a contract, a gratuitous promise to pay the debt or liability of another may produce a guarantee by estoppel where a party acted unconscionably in inducing the assumption of guarantee and the creditor too acts on the same assumption.[91] The determination of a contract of guarantee depends on the substance of the agreement between the parties and on the conduct of the parties.

Whether a contract of guarantee exists is a question of fact in the circumstances of the case. No particular words are required in the formation of the agreement, but the agreement must be evinced by unequivocal words.[92] It is not sufficient that the parties refer to the agreement between them as a contract of guarantee, since even the specific use of the word may not confer substance on the agreement.[93] In that case, the court will look to the actions of the parties in the circumstances and take into account such things as the types of persons involved and whether they are professionals or less experienced, and the effect of the agreement on the persons it impinges upon.[94] Courts may also sidestep the parol evidence rule and allow extrinsic evidence to be introduced so as to determine who the parties are, and what relationships and obligations exist between them.[95]

10.3.2 Formation under principles of contract law

Contracts of guarantee are governed by the general principles of contract law explored in Chapter 1, as well as the law of equity. In line with fundamental principles of contract law, nothing further is required to establish the contract of guarantee than the agreement of the parties as a manifestation of their clear intention.[96] Most such contracts are executed between creditor and guarantor.[97]

89 *Duncan, Fox & Co v North & South Wales Bank* (1880) 6 App Cas 1, 11–12.

90 *Duncan, Fox & Co v North & South Wales Bank* (1880) 6 App Cas 1, 13.

91 *Amalgamated Investment & Property Co Ltd (in liq) v Texas Commerce International Bank Ltd* [1981] 2 WLR 554, 574. See also *Duncan, Fox & Co v North & South Wales Bank* (1880) 6 App Cas 1, 12.

92 *Bradley Brothers v Scott* [1923] NZLR 1050; *M'Iver v Richardson* (1813) 1 M & S 557.

93 *Re Denton's Estate; Licences Insurance Corporation & Guarantee Fund Ltd v Denton* [1904] 2 Ch 178; *Re Australian & Overseas Insurance Co Ltd* [1966] 1 NSWR 558, 565.

94 *German v Norton* (1887) 8 LR (NSW) 479, 466. The court applied the test of whether a reasonable person in the position of the creditor would act upon the agreement as if it were a guarantee.

95 See Hodgson J admitting extrinsic evidence to identify parties and clarify liabilities in *AGC (Advances) Ltd v West* (1984) 5 NSWLR 590. The parol evidence rule stipulates that where parties intended a contract to be wholly in writing, all of the terms they have agreed upon are to be found within the written agreement and cannot be varied by reference to extrinsic materials: *Goss v Nugent* (1833) 110 ER 713; *Codelfa Construction Pty Ltd v State Rail Authority of New South Wales* (1982) 149 CLR 337. Ambiguity in the critical terms of the contract is one exception to the rule and the courts will generally permit extrinsic evidence as an interpretative aid. See, further, Section 10.4.2.

96 *Dane v Mortgage Insurance Corporation Ltd* [1894] 1 QB 54.

97 *Duncan, Fox & Co v North & South Wales Bank* (1880) 6 App Cas 1, 11.

The guarantor usually makes the offer to enter a contract of guarantee, and must do so in clear and definite terms[98] which clearly demonstrate that the party's intention is to enter a legally binding agreement. The offer is made to the creditor,[99] who has a reasonable time to accept the offer provided the offeror is in a position to accept it. In *Coulthart v Clementson*,[100] it was decided that an offer could not be accepted where the creditor had notice of the death of the offeror, while the guarantor may revoke the offer at any time prior to acceptance.[101]

Where an issue arises as to whether or not such an agreement has arisen, courts examine the constituting documentation and the operative circumstances. An equivocal statement may suffice where the course of dealings unambiguously binds the parties. In *Sorby v Gordon*,[102] the words 'I am quite willing to guarantee the first shipment' were considered sufficient given the conduct of the parties. In some circumstances, conduct alone may constitute the guarantee.[103] The nature and conditions upon which the guarantee is given will depend on the offer, including whether there has been a breach,[104] or whether the guarantor can expect to be discharged upon a change of principal debtor. For example, the terms of the contract may allow for survival of the guarantee despite a change of principal.

The effectiveness of acceptance follows normal contractual principles. That is to say the acceptance must be communicated either within a specified time or, if none is specified, within a reasonable time. However, the terms of the offer may be taken to have waived the requirement for express communication by implication,[105] although this conclusion cannot be reached when communication is required under the agreement.[106]

Where the creditor relies on actions constituting acceptance, dispensing with the need for express acceptance will depend on the creditor acting precisely in compliance with the terms of the offer.[107] Acceptance by conduct requires both that the offeree know of the offer and that their actions show that they are relying on it, such as when goods are supplied on a contract to guarantee payment for a supply of goods.[108]

Guarantees may be general or special. A guarantee in general terms can be accepted by any person with knowledge of it and who acts reliantly on it. But a special guarantee can only be accepted and entered into by the person the offeror intends to contract with. If the special offer is ambiguous about the party with whom the guarantee will be entered, extrinsic evidence may be used to identify the addressee of the offer.[109] In certain circumstances the court may order rectification where the guarantee is addressed to the wrong company.[110]

98 *Van Wart v Carpenter* (1861) 21 UCQB 320.
99 *A A Davidson Pty Ltd v Seabrook* (1931) 37 ALR 156.
100 (1879) 5 QBD 42.
101 *Offord v Davies* (1862) 12 CBNS 748.
102 (1874) 30 LT 528.
103 *Deutsche Bank AG v Ibrahim* [1992] 1 Bank LR 267, where property title deeds were deposited with a bank as security for an overdraft.
104 *Blest v Brown* (1862) 4 De G F & J 367.
105 *Sorby v Gordon* (1874) 30 LT 528.
106 *Mozley v Tinkler* (1835) 1 Cr M & R 692.
107 *Luck v Ilsa* [1951] QSR 281.
108 *Smith v Passmore* (1883) 4 LR (NSW) 274.
109 *Boral Resources (Qld) Pty Ltd v Donelly* [1988] 1 Qd 506, where a guarantee was addressed to a group of companies and evidence admitted to determine which particular company the principal debtor was trading.
110 On the requirements of rectification see *Pukallus v Cameron* (1982) 56 ALJR 907.

Offers made to one of two or more persons must be accepted by one of those persons so that the guarantor may be fully informed of their responsibilities, including to whom they owe their obligations, or else be entitled to evade liability.[111]

Contracts of guarantee are simple contracts like any other. As such, unless executed as a deed, they must be supported by consideration.[112] The creditor must exchange something of sufficient legal value in order to 'purchase' the guarantor's promise to answer for the principal debtor's obligation. Although the guarantor attains no direct 'benefit' from a suretyship arrangement (as the creditor does), the creditor incurs a detriment by financially accommodating the principal debtor or refraining from suing them for outstanding debts at the request of the guarantor.[113]

10.3.3 Formal requirements

In jurisdictions where the *Statute of Frauds 1677* (or an equivalent) applies, a contract of guarantee is not enforceable unless it or a memorandum or written note of the same is reduced to writing and signed by the guarantor (or an authorised representative). The *Statute of Frauds* is an old English statute that effectively required particular classes of agreement – such as contracts of guarantee, or for the sale of land – to be in writing and signed by the party to be charged by the agreement. The statute sought to address the incidence of fraud and perjury in England at the time by mandating that contracts of particular significance and value be recorded in writing.[114]

The *Statute of Frauds* has for the most part been repealed by state and territory legislation; however, many provisions have been re-enacted in other statutes such as s 56 of the *Property Law Act 1974* (Qld) and s 6 of the *Mercantile Law Act 1935* (Tas), both of which require contracts of guarantee to be recorded in writing and signed. If, however, a party gives an oral guarantee, they may be precluded from relying on the *Statute of Frauds* or equivalent provisions to prevent enforcement of the guarantee if the doctrine of estoppel applies.[115] Where neither the *Statute of Frauds* nor an equivalent or other statute imposing a writing requirement applies, a legally valid guarantee can theoretically be issued verbally.

In the case of credit contracts, s 55 of the *National Credit Code* (Schedule 1 to the *National Consumer Credit Protection Act 2009* (Cth)) requires contracts of guarantee to be in writing and signed by the guarantor.

111 *Lott v Collins* (1869) 8 SCR (NSW) 104, involving an offer made to a lessee or lessor but not accepted by either. However, the result of that case is disputed: see J O'Donovan and J Phillips, *The Modern Contract of Guarantee* (Lawbook Co, Sydney, 1992), 40–1.

112 *Coghlan v S H Lock (Australia) Ltd* (1987) 8 NSWLR 88. See, further, Chapter 1.

113 *Murphy v Timms* [1987] 1 Qd R 550; *Edlin v Williams* [2000] ANZ ConvR 43.

114 M Giancaspro and C Langos, *Understanding Contract Law: A Practical Guide* (LexisNexis Butterworths Australia, 2016), 194.

115 *Tipperary Developments Pty Ltd v Western Australia* (2009) 38 WAR 488.

10.4 Construction of the contract of guarantee

10.4.1 Current approaches to interpretation of guarantees

Where the words of an agreement, including a contract of guarantee, are unambiguous, the court is bound to give effect to them, even if it is to be suspected that the parties intended something contrary to the words employed.[116] Neither inconvenience nor even injustice to the parties will empower the court to amend an unambiguous agreement. The court may only intervene where the language of an agreement lends itself to at least two contradictory constructions.[117] Then the preferred meaning is that which avoids 'capricious, unreasonable, inconvenient or unjust'[118] results even if, in so constructing the agreement, the meaning given to it 'is not the most obvious, or the most grammatically accurate'.[119]

The approaches taken to the construction of contracts of guarantee have been varied. On the one hand, the courts have generally construed contracts of guarantee *strictissimi juris* (strictly according to their terms), in favour of the guarantor.[120] Alternatively, contracts of guarantee have been interpreted like all other commercial agreements, in the light of the expectations, customs and traditions of the business to which they apply, and in order to secure their effectiveness.[121] It is a presumption of construction that the parties do not intend their agreement to operate unreasonably and produce a commercially irrational result.[122] Further, if the parties did intend an unreasonable operation of their agreement, 'it is essential that that intention be made abundantly clear'.[123] Where a detailed analysis of the words of a commercial agreement is likely to yield a result contrary to sound business or commercial sense, that interpretation is to be rejected,[124] and a reasonable and commercial operation of the guarantee is to be presumed to have been meant.[125]

116 *Australian Broadcasting Commission v Australasian Performing Right Association Ltd* (1973) 129 CLR 99; *Precious Metals Australia Ltd x Xstrata (Schweiz) AG* [2005] NSWSC 141.

117 *Peppers Hotel Management Pty Ltd v Hotel Capital Partners Ltd* (2004) 12 BPR 22,879, [69].

118 *Peppers Hotel Management Pty Ltd v Hotel Capital Partners Ltd* (2004) 12 BPR 22,879, [69].

119 *Australian Broadcasting Commission v Australasian Performing Right Association Ltd* (1973) 129 CLR 99, 110.

120 *Eastern Counties Building Society v Russell* [1947] 1 All ER 500; *Ankar Pty Ltd v National Westminster Finance (Australia) Ltd* (1987) 162 CLR 549, 561; *Chan v Cresdon Pty Ltd* (1989) 168 CLR 242, 256; *Credit Suisse AG, Sydney Branch v Springsure Property Holdings Pty Ltd (in liq)* [2017] QSC 142.

121 *Andar Transport Pty Ltd v Brambles Ltd* (2004) 217 CLR 424; *Royal Botanic Gardens & Domain Trust v South Sydney City Council* (2002) 186 ALR 289; *Pearson v Goldsbrough Mort & Co* [1931] SASR 320; *Mason v Pritchard* (1810) 12 East 227. See also *Mineralogy Pty Ltd v BGP Geoexplorer Pte Ltd* [2017] QSC 219.

122 *Fitzwood Pty Ltd v Unique Goal Pty Ltd (in liq)* [2001] FCA 1628; *Electricity Generation Corporation v Woodside Energy Ltd* (2014) 251 CLR 640.

123 *Peppers Hotel Management Pty Ltd v Hotel Capital Partners Ltd* (2004) 12 BPR 22,879, [69].

124 *Maggbury Pty Ltd v Hafele Australia Pty Ltd* (2001) 210 CLR 181, 248, per Gleeson CJ, Gummow and Hayne JJ.

125 *Maggbury*; *Upper Hunter County District Council v Australian Chilling & Freezing Co Ltd* (1968) 118 CLR 429; *Australian Broadcasting Commission v Australasian Performing Right Association Ltd* (1973) 129 CLR 99. See also *Vodafone Pacific Ltd v Mobile Innovations Ltd* [2004] NSWCA 15; *Club Hotels Operations Pty Ltd v CHG Australia Pty Ltd* [2005] NSWSC 998.

The current approach recognises two guiding principles: (1) that the ambiguous instrument should be resolved in favour of the guarantor (ie *contra proferentem*);[126] and (2) that construction is not based solely on the terms of the contract of guarantee but also on the fact that the parties negotiated an agreement in a commercial setting to which effect ought to be given.[127] With respect to the second principle, if the guarantor is a compensated professional, a less strict and more business-like interpretation of the contract is arguably justified. While the latter approach has found some support, and courts may take it into account, authority favours the general rule of contractual construction for guarantees.[128] The rationale for this approach was provided in *Ankar Pty Ltd v National Westminster Finance (Australia) Ltd* by Mason ACJ, Wilson, Brennan and Dawson JJ in the following terms:

> At law, as in equity, the traditional view is that the liability of the surety is *strictissimi juris* and that ambiguous contractual provisions should be construed in favour of the surety. The doctrine of *strictissimi juris* provides a counterpoise to the law's preference for a construction that reads a provision otherwise than as a condition.[129]

In *Chan v Cresdon Pty Ltd*,[130] the High Court confirmed that this approach now represented 'a settled principle governing the interpretation of contracts of guarantee'.[131] The principle does not circumvent the respect that ought to be had to the wording of an agreement deliberately chosen to be wide in its ambit; nor does it ignore the need to resort to evidence from the surrounding circumstances prevalent at the time of execution as an aid to the construction of an agreement.[132]

10.4.2 Extrinsic evidence as an interpretative aid

Ambiguities in the contract of guarantee may be resolved using evidence of the surrounding factual circumstances. This is true despite the requirement pursuant to the *Statute of Frauds* that requires the guarantees, terms and the parties to it to be in writing.[133] Before extrinsic evidence will be admissible the contract will have to admit of a real ambiguity, because evidence will not be admitted in contradistinction to the plain meaning of the text of the agreement. In *Royal Botanic Gardens & Domain Trust v South Sydney City Council*,[134] Gleeson CJ, Gaudron, McHugh, Gummow and Hayne JJ stated that it 'is appropriate to have regard to more than internal linguistic considerations and to consider the circumstances with reference to which the words in question were used and, from those circumstances, to discern

126 *Mason v Pritchard* (1810) 12 East 227; *Coghlan v S H Lock (Australia) Ltd* (1987) 8 NSWLR 88; *Ankar Pty Ltd v National Westminster Finance (Australia) Ltd* (1987) 162 CLR 549; *Chan v Cresdon Pty Ltd* (1989) 168 CLR 242; *Andar Transport Pty Ltd v Brambles Ltd* (2004) 217 CLR 424.

127 *Eastern Counties Building Society v Russell* [1947] 1 All ER 500, 560–1.

128 *Eastern Counties Building Society v Russell* [1947] 1 All ER 500, 560–1.

129 (1987) 162 CLR 549, 561.

130 (1989) 168 CLR 242.

131 (1989) 168 CLR 242, 256.

132 See *Coghlan v S H Lock (Australia) Ltd* (1987) 8 NSWLR 88, 92.

133 1677 (UK), 29 Car II, c 3, s 4. See, further, Section 10.3.3.

134 (2002) 186 ALR 289.

the objective which the parties had in view'.[135] The facts that may be drawn on are wide but may include evidence of the negotiations between the parties and the developmental stage of the agreement, the nature of the parties, the purpose of the guarantee, and the commercial context in which the guarantee was to operate.[136]

The use of evidence of surrounding circumstances has been judicially criticised on a number of grounds. Further, the use of evidence in the negotiation phase has been held unhelpful on the basis that it reflects changing intentions and shifting expectations, rather than assisting with the interpretation of the settled agreement. Notwithstanding, pre-contractual obligations do often reveal firm intentions that are ultimately recorded in the instrument.[137]

10.4.3 The recital

The recital is the portion of the guarantee, traditionally located at its beginning, which outlines its purpose and provides other pertinent information. It may be used to interpret the scope of the guarantor's liability, but will not generally justify an alteration of liability that is clearly expressed in the body of the agreement. The role the recital plays stems from the fact that it forms part of the guarantee, and because it may contain conditions forming the basis of the agreement. Where the agreement is not clearly expressed, the words of the recital may prevail in interpreting the scope of the guarantor's liability.[138] However, the proper approach is to interpret the whole of the agreement as defining and limiting the scope of the guarantee.[139]

The guarantee may be limited to certain types of principal transaction, which often are identified in the recital.[140] Where the recital is at odds with the substance of the guarantee, which provides for a wider type of guaranteed activity,[141] there is authority that the broader view ought to be taken.[142] Courts have had regard to extrinsic evidence to determine the breadth of the transaction types referred to by the guarantee.[143]

The guarantor will not be liable in respect of the principal debtor's default on a different transaction from the one guaranteed. In cases of ambiguity, this is resolved in favour of the guarantor. In *Chan v Cresdon Pty Ltd*[144] the High Court took a restrictive view of the transaction for which the guarantor was liable. It held that the term 'under the lease' referred to in the

135 (2002) 186 ALR 289, [10]. See also *Codelfa Construction Pty Ltd v State Rail Authority of New South Wales* (1982) 149 CLR 337, 352.

136 *MCA International BV v Northern Star Holdings Ltd* (1991) 4 ACSR 719. See also *Pressn v Simmonds* [1971] 1 WLR 1381, 1384–5.

137 *Reardon Smith Line Ltd v Yngvar Hansen-Tangen* [1976] 1 WLR 989, 995–6.

138 *Pearsell v Summersett* (1812) 4 Taunt 593. The Privy Council has even said in one case that the words of the recital must qualify those of the agreement in substance: *Australian Joint Stock Bank v Bailey* [1899] AC 396, 400.

139 See *Tucker v Broadlands International Finance Ltd* (unreported, NSW Court of Appeal, Priestley JA, 12 September 1986), 9. See also *Bank of India v Trans Continental Commodity Merchants Ltd & Patel* [1982] 1 Lloyd's Rep 506, 512.

140 *United Dominions Trust Ltd v Beech* [1972] 1 Lloyd's Rep 546.

141 *Bank of India v Trans Continental Commodity Merchants Ltd & Patel* [1982] 1 Lloyd's Rep 506. See also the decision on appeal: [1983] 2 Lloyd's Rep 298, 300.

142 [1982] 1 Lloyd's Rep 506, 512.

143 See, for example, the meaning of bills of exchange in *Dalgety Ltd v John H Hilton Pty Ltd* [1981] 2 NSWLR 169, 173.

144 (1989) 166 CLR 242.

guarantee could only be a registered legal lease, not a common law or equitable lease. The former did not arise on the facts, although the latter did.[145]

10.4.4 Consideration clause

The consideration will be referred to when interpreting the entire contract of guarantee if it is for a specific consideration.[146] A consideration inconsistent with the liability expressed in the agreement is problematic, but it has been said that construction of the agreement is controlled by the consideration clause.[147] On the other hand, there is also authority for the consideration clause not being able to limit the breadth of the liability on the operative parts of the agreement.[148] Again, the court will decide the parties' intentions by interpreting the document in the light of all the evidence, rather than by adopting a firm rule of construction.

10.4.5 Resolving discrepancies between guarantee and principal transaction

The guarantor's liability and the principal agreement are equivalent in extent. However, agreements may be so drafted that they are not corresponding obligations. For example in *Perrott v Newton King Ltd*,[149] the court found that the interest due on money 'owing' – which was the principal's obligation – was not equivalent to the interest due on money that 'remain[s] unpaid' – which was the guarantor's liability. The guarantor's obligation was discharged after the principal's bankruptcy since money was no longer owing. The guarantor's liability is determined by the wording of the guarantee and not the principal agreement,[150] regardless of the effect it has on the liability.[151] There is said to exist a principle of co-extensiveness by which courts will attempt to equalise the guarantor's liability to the principal's, unless by express words the guarantor's liabilities were made greater.[152]

10.4.6 Is the guarantor liable for interest under the principal transaction?

Unless expressly provided for, the guarantor's responsibility for the capital debt and interest on unpaid amounts is a question of construction of the contract. In determining whether the guarantee was intended to cover interest payments, the court may consider evidence of the circumstances in which the agreement was purportedly performed. In *Fahey v MSD Spiers Pty*

145 See also *Yulin Pty Ltd v Japan Building Projects (Australia) Pty Ltd* (1991) ANZ ConvR ¶390.
146 *Tucker v Broadlands International Finance Ltd* (unreported, NSW Court of Appeal, Priestley JA, 12 September 1986), 9.
147 *Scholefield Goodman & Sons Ltd v Gange* (unreported, NSW Supreme Court, Sheppard J, 4 December 1979).
148 *Bank of India v Trans Continental Commodity Merchants Ltd & Patel* [1982] 1 Lloyd's Rep 506. See also the decision on appeal: [1983] 2 Lloyd's Rep 298, 300.
149 [1993] NZLR 1131.
150 [1993] NZLR 1131, 1157.
151 [1993] NZLR 1131, 1157–8.
152 *Stadium Finance Co Ltd v Helm* (1965) 109 SJ 471.

Ltd,[153] the plaintiff was able to demonstrate that the guarantor had actual knowledge that the terms of supply included an interest payment.

Actual awareness of an interest payment can be more readily demonstrated when the guarantee is expressed in those terms than when expressed in more general terms. Of course, if the interest payment appears as a term of the guarantee it is an incorporated obligation whether or not the guarantor's obligation is expressly stated, or whether or not the guarantor has knowledge of it.[154] The extent of the guarantor's liability for interest is also subject to construction.

A limited guarantee may be limited to the extent of both the capital sum and the interest payable on it. However, limited guarantees are normally expressed to be limited only with respect to the capital, but liable for interest that accrues on that limited capital amount.[155] If the guarantee is expressly for the interest only, and not the principal, it will not be interpreted as making the guarantor liable for interest payable on the principal amount that is outstanding because that would make the guarantor liable for all interest payments into the future, and force them to discharge their liability only by paying the principal.[156]

The guarantor's liability for interest payment will cease when the principal debtor's liability for the principal ceases.[157] The principal's bankruptcy or winding up will also affect the guarantor's liability for interest payments on the principal debt. This is because, the judgment being handed down, the interest is no longer payable on the terms of the contract but under the rules of court.[158] As the cause of action for a recovery in debt no longer exists once it has merged with the judgment the money being guaranteed cannot be recovered as a debt. This is, of course, subject to the terms of the guarantee making the guarantor liable for payments of interest on the principal beyond the date by which it is fixed by the judgment.

If the guarantor is bankrupt or wound up, no interest is payable from that date. Again the cause of action is merged with the judgment, and interest cannot be recovered after the date of judgment unless otherwise expressly provided for under the contract by the exclusion of the doctrine of merger.[159] Whether the guarantor can in equity avoid payment for interest arrears of payment, which have accumulated because of the creditor's inaction, has been met with opposing responses. For example, in *Dawson v Raynes*[160] the guarantor was relieved, but not in *David Securities Pty Ltd v Commonwealth Bank of Australia*,[161] although to do so would appear to fly in the face of the established principle that the creditor is under no obligation to seek payment from the principal.[162]

---

153 [1975] 1 NZLR 240.
154 *Ackerman v Ehrensperger* (1846) 16 M & W 99.
155 *Bank of Adelaide v Lorden* (1970) 127 CLR 185; *Daw Banking Corporation v Mahnakh Spinning & Weaving Corporation & Bank Mellat* [1983] 2 Lloyd's Rep 561; *Meek v Wallis* (1872) 27 LT 650.
156 *Ruddenklau & Gardner v Charlesworth* [1925] NZLR 161.
157 *Bank of Adelaide v Lorden* (1970) 45 ALJR 49.
158 *Eagle Star Trustee Ltd v Tai Ping Trading Co Pty Ltd* (unreported, NSW Supreme Court, Powell J, 30 October 1990).
159 *McDonald v Scobie* [1980] Qd R 477.
160 (1826) 2 Russ 466.
161 (1990) 23 FCR 1. See also *Hong Kong Bank of Australia Ltd v Larobi Pty Ltd* (1991) 23 NSWLR 593.
162 *David Securities Pty Ltd v Commonwealth Bank of Australia* (1990) 23 FCR 1.

10.4.7 Is the guarantor liable for the creditor's costs?

If the contract of guarantee does not expressly or impliedly make the guarantor responsible for the costs of enforcing the principal debt, the guarantor is unlikely to be responsible for it on other grounds. Similarly, the guarantor will not be liable for costs that arise otherwise than due to a breach of the principal agreement.[163] The contract may provide for costs to be paid – for example, when awarded by way of court order – but this payment would be based on an obligation under the guarantee.[164]

A guarantor may be liable for the costs incurred by the creditor in taking action against the principal debtor if the guarantee is expressed to cover money owed 'on any account whatsoever', or even in suing the principal where the agreement requires money to be recovered by institution of such a suit.[165] Expenses incurred for enforcing the security against a debt is a step that will be covered by a general guarantee,[166] provided it is a reasonable proceeding[167] and the guarantee specifically provides for it. Such expenses arise because of the breach and are necessitated by the breach.

10.4.8 Are the guarantor's obligations secured?

Some guarantees can take the form of a security such as a third-party mortgage, or equitable mortgage, as when the guarantor agrees to provide such security when required by the mortgagee to discharge their obligations.[168] Guarantees may include clauses allowing creditors to create a charge upon default against the guarantor. The creditor could thereby attach the debt to the real and personal property of the guarantor, becoming a secured creditor.[169]

10.4.9 What if there is a mistake in the contract of guarantee?

An uncorrected mistake may limit the scope of the guarantor's liability. Mistakes may include mistaking the parties – principal or creditor. The mistake may be able to be rectified if the parties' common intentions at the time of execution of the guarantee can be determined. However, it must be convincingly proved that the agreement as embodied did not represent those intentions,[170] and not simply that the parties failed to see the financial consequences of their actions.[171]

163 *Hoole Urban District Council v Fidelity & Deposit Co of Maryland* [1916] 1 KB 25.
164 [1916] 1 KB 25, 29–30.
165 *Guenard v Coe* (1914) 17 DLR 47, 51.
166 *Maunsell v Egan* (1846) 9 Ir Eq R 283.
167 *Hatch, Mansfield & Co Ltd v Weingott* (1906) 22 TLR 366.
168 *Fountain v Bank of America National Trust & Savings Association* (1992) 5 BPR 11,817, where the reference to 'successive transactions' and 'new obligations' secured the guarantee as well as the original contract.
169 *Murphy v Wright* (1992) 5 BPR 11,734.
170 *Elders Lensworth Finance Ltd v Australian Central Pacific Ltd* [1986] 2 Qd R 364, 368.
171 *Elders Lensworth Finance Ltd v Australian Central Pacific Ltd* [1986] 2 Qd R 364, 368.

10.4.10 What if the contract of guarantee is defective?

Where no principal contract is concluded, there can be no guarantee. This is true both on contract principles and on the principle of co-extensive liability that governs guarantees.[172] The principal contract may be void, voidable or unenforceable for various reasons. Purported contracts may be void for a number of reasons. For example, they may be illegal contracts prohibited by statute and so cannot be enforced against the guarantor.[173] It may also be illegal for reasons of public policy, such as where the guarantee is for a sum that is a penalty.[174] The court may also declare contracts void on the basis of legislation granting them power to set contracts aside.[175]

In some Australian jurisdictions, legislation provides that where a person who has reached the age of majority (18 years) guarantees a minor's performance of their contractual obligations, the adult is bound to the guarantee to the extent they ordinarily would be if the minor was not a minor.[176] In other jurisdictions, the common law rules apply, making a minor's contract merely voidable so that if the minor either rescinds or fails to ratify the transaction the guarantor is released from their obligation.[177] However, the guarantor remains liable where the minor retains the benefit of the contract, or where the property returned after repudiation by the minor of the contract has decreased in value.[178]

10.5 Revocation of guarantees

The parties to a guarantee may stipulate that the guarantee may be revoked and how the revocation is to be effected. For the guarantor's revocation to be effective, it must occur in the manner stipulated in the guarantee.[179] An effective revocation relieves the guarantor of future liability[180] under the guarantee, but not (except in the case of total failure of consideration[181]) the liabilities accrued up to the time of revocation, unless the guarantee expressly provides for the revocation to have an alternative effect.

All guarantees may be revoked by the guarantor before the creditor provides consideration, provided the guarantee makes no provision for revocation and has not been formed by a deed under seal.[182] A continuing guarantee (which, as discussed earlier, pertains to a series of transactions, and not to one specific transaction) may at any time be revoked by the guarantor as to future transactions by notice to the creditor.[183] Transactions that have already been

172 *Lakeman v Mountstephen* (1874) LR 7 HL 17, 24–5.

173 *Heald v O'Connor* [1971] 1 WLR 497.

174 *Citicorp Australia Ltd v Hendry* (1985) 4 NSWLR 1.

175 See, for example, *Contracts Review Act 1980* (NSW), s 7(1).

176 *Minors (Property and Contracts) Act 1970* (NSW), s 47; *Minors Contracts (Miscellaneous Provisions) Act 1979* (SA), s 5; *Minors Contracts Act 1988* (Tas), s 4; *Credit Act 1984* (Vic), s 140; *Credit Act 1984* (WA), s 140.

177 *Land & Homes (WA) v Roe* (1936) 39 WALR 27.

178 *Land & Homes (WA) v Roe* (1936) 39 WALR 27.

179 *Commercial Bank of Australia Ltd v Cavanaugh* (1980) 7 NTR 12.

180 *Commercial Bank of Australia Ltd v Cavanaugh* (1980) 7 NTR 12.

181 *Baltic Shipping Co v Dillon* (1993) 176 CLR 344.

182 *North British & Mercantile Insurance Co v Kean* (1888) 16 OR 117.

183 *Coulthart v Clementson* (1879) 5 QBD 42; *Lloyd's v Harper* (1880) 16 Ch D 290; *Ronan v Australia & New Zealand Banking Group Ltd* (2000) 2 VR 531, 550.

completed in accordance with the continuing guarantee prior to the revocation continue to bind the guarantor. However, future transactions occurring after the revocation do not bind the guarantor. Clearly, the effectiveness of the revocation assumes that the principal debtor's obligations to the creditor are divisible, separate and distinct.[184]

The effect of the death of a guarantor is the revocation of the continuing guarantee, provided no other effective agreement to the contrary exists. The revocation is only effective on the transaction entered into after the guarantor's death; whereas the guarantor's liability continues in effect for all transactions entered into prior to the guarantor's death. Those guarantees will be satisfied by the guarantor's heirs and are to be satisfied out of the guarantor's estate. Further, the death of a guarantor will not discharge the liability of co-guarantors where their liability is joint and several.[185]

10.6 Distinguishing guarantees from similar commercial transactions

10.6.1 Indemnities

A contract of indemnity is 'a contract by one party to keep the other harmless against loss'[186] independently of the continuing liability of the principal debtor. The obligation under an indemnity has no legal relationship to another's debt. Compared with a contract of guarantee, a liability is assumed under an indemnity regardless of whether the primary debtor defaults on their obligation.

Whether a contract is an indemnity or a guarantee is a matter of construction in each case. References to 'guarantee' or 'indemnity' are suggestive, if not entirely determinative,[187] of the parties' intentions. There will be more confidence in proper ascertainment of the nature of the document if the words are used repeatedly[188] or in significant places such as document headings.[189] Determining whether the contract is for indemnification or guarantee, however, will always require an ascertainment of the nature of the agreement.[190]

In some cases the distinction may be clear from the words of the agreement. Where the document of guarantee involves ambiguous words, or otherwise raises doubt as to the nature of the obligation, courts will determine whether the provisions of the agreement evince a lack of co-extensive liability of the obligations of the debtor, compared with the party entering the agreement, as against the creditor.[191] If the promisor is liable as against the creditor under different circumstances or for a greater amount, compared with the debtor, the agreement is more likely to constitute an indemnity.[192]

184 *Lloyd's v Harper* (1880) 16 Ch D 290, 314.
185 *Beckett & Co v Addyman* (1882) 9 QBD 783.
186 *Yeoman Credit Ltd v Latter* [1961] 1 WLR 828, 830–1.
187 *Total Oil Products (Australia) Pty Ltd v Robinson* [1970] 1 NSWR 701.
188 *Heald v O'Connor* [1971] 1 WLR 497, 503.
189 *Goulston Discount Ltd v Clark* [1967] 2 QB 493, 498.
190 *Yeoman Credit Ltd v Latter* [1961] 1 WLR 828, 830–1.
191 [1961] 1 WLR 828, 830–3.
192 *Direct Acceptance Finance Ltd v Cumberland Furnishing Pty Ltd* [1965] NSWR 1504, 1509.

Where the contract preserves the promisor's liability simultaneously to extending the time the debtor has to perform their obligation, the contract is likely to be a guarantee. Under a contract of indemnification, the provision would be unnecessary.[193] Where the parties understand the contract between creditor and debtor to be void, the promisor is likely to have entered a contract of indemnity. The reason is that a guarantee is dependent on a principal obligation. In these circumstances the parties could not have intended to have entered an agreement without legal effect.

Some modern contracts that secure the obligation of a promisor are difficult to classify easily as either guarantees or indemnities. Simple guarantees that unambiguously secure the performance of the principal debtor's obligation are still in use and readily classifiable. Other so-called guarantees preserve the guarantor's liability in certain circumstances, even where the guarantor would normally be discharged, such as the variation of the principal contract or where the principal is no longer liable. Such contracts are not likely to be treated as guarantees.

Another form of guarantee specifically preserves the liability of the guarantor in circumstances where the principal is no longer liable to the creditor. Classification may depend on the reason for the principal no longer being liable. Where they have been released by the creditor, the secondary contract is treated as a guarantee.[194] Where the contract is void, it has been treated as an indemnity.[195]

Still other contracts may be mixed in nature, containing elements of both an indemnity and a guarantee. If the contract preserves the promisor's liability under a delimited range of conditions despite the principal being relieved of their obligations, it may be a guarantee combining the effects of indemnification.[196] Such contracts frequently contain clauses entitling the creditor to treat the guarantor as the principal debtor, thereby preserving their liability even in circumstances where they would have otherwise been discharged.[197] Nevertheless, contracts that are essentially guarantees do not become indemnities merely by virtue of a clause of this nature.[198]

Some contracts may expressly contain promises for the promisor to both indemnify and to guarantee. Courts have most commonly interpreted the agreement as containing separate obligations – both guarantees and indemnities.[199] The relationship of these separate obligations will need to be scrutinised because the dominant form the obligation takes is likely to impede the effectiveness of the other obligation. In *Citicorp Australia Ltd v Hendry*, the principal obligation was void for being a penalty. The guarantee, which was dependent on the principal liability, was unenforceable, as was the indemnity. Courts have also interpreted such contracts as guarantees rather than indemnities, particularly where the agreement indicates the existence of a principal obligation, and the promisor's liability is triggered by the default of the principal obligation.[200]

193 *Western Credit Ltd v Alberry* [1964] 2 All ER 938, 940.
194 *Bank of Adelaide v Lorden* (1970) 127 CLR 185.
195 *Alliance Acceptance Co Ltd v Hinton* (1964) 1 DCR (NSW) 5.
196 *General Surety & Guarantee Co Ltd v Francis Parker Ltd* (1977) 6 Build LR 18, 21.
197 *Fletcher Organisation Pty Ltd v Crocus Investments Pty Ltd* [1988] 2 Qd R 517.
198 *Citicorp Australia Ltd v Hendry* (1985) 4 NSWLR 1, 20.
199 *Citicorp Australia Ltd v Hendry* (1985) 4 NSWLR 1, 20.
200 *Citicorp Australia Ltd v Hendry* (1985) 4 NSWLR 1.

10.6.2 Warranties

Although the terms 'warranty' and 'guarantee' are frequently used interchangeably, their distinction ought to be preserved. A warranty is a contract as to the title, quality and quantity of the thing being sold, or that it is as it has been represented, and unrelated to the obligations of third parties. In contrast, a guarantee is a contract binding one person to another for the performance of a third party's promise.

10.6.3 Insurance

Under a contract of insurance, an insurer agrees to pay an insured a certain sum of money on the occurrence of an insured event. That event may be a debtor's default. When it is, the insurance contract resembles a guarantee. However, guarantees and insurance are essentially different types of contract. An insurance contract is not an agreement for an insurer to pay on the default of a third party, but to pay in the event of a loss.[201] An insurance payout is an indemnification against the actual loss, not the amount insured, so that anything salvaged is credited to the insurer and is not used to benefit the insured.

Contracts of insurance are usually effected through insurance policies issued in response to an insurance proposal presented to the insurer by the insured, the proposal becoming the basis of the contract. By contrast, as long as parties assume the roles of creditor, principal debtor and guarantor, the manner in which the guarantee is effected is immaterial. Because the insurance contract is effected formally, and usually on particular forms related to the type of insurance being purchased, it may be distinguishable from a guarantee, which generally needs only to be evidenced in writing to be enforceable without further formality and without the need for words, phrases or language of any particular kind.[202]

Compared with a contract of guarantee, a contract of insurance incorporates the exercise of utmost good faith (*uberrimae fides*) between the parties. The requirement reflects an essential distinction between the types of agreement that insurance contracts and guarantees are. An insurance contract is formed by the insured bringing a risk to be covered to the insurer, in return for which coverage the insurer sets a price. The price is entirely dependent on the insured disclosing all matters relevant to the insurer's decision whether or not to bear the risk, so the insurer depends on the insured's dealing in good faith. The creditor, on the other hand, is not bound to reveal what they know of the debt to the guarantor, nor to explain the nature of the risk they are undertaking.[203]

10.7 Vitiating factors – setting aside guarantees

Guarantees may be set aside where the creditor has taken advantage of the guarantor. The same fact situation may permit one or more of these to be raised in seeking the remedy of rescission. The equitable remedy of rescission is discretionary.

201 See, for example, *Dane v Mortgage Insurance Corporation Ltd* [1894] 1 QB 54, 60.
202 *Phoenix Assurance Co Ltd v Wren* [1950] SASR 89.
203 But see s 56 of the *National Credit Code*, discussed at Section 10.9.2 below.

10.7.1 Duress

The guarantee is voidable if it has been acquired through duress active upon the guarantor either directly or indirectly – for example, on their goods. Duress may take many forms, including where the guarantor, or their family, has faced actual or threatened violence, or has been threatened with or in fact experienced deprivation of liberty.[204] Contracts of guarantee have been vitiated in circumstances where a person has been threatened that their son will be prosecuted if they do not enter a guarantee;[205] where company directors have been threatened with prosecution against family members;[206] and where a person has been threatened with the destruction of or damage to their property.[207]

The doctrine of economic duress is a broad principle that may be relied upon to set aside contracts of guarantee. Pressure to enter into a contract will become duress when it goes 'beyond what the law is prepared to countenance as legitimate', and '[p]ressure will be illegitimate if it consists of unlawful threats or amounts to unconscionable conduct'.[208] Pressure, no matter how great, nevertheless falling short of this will not amount to economic duress.[209] In *Wardley Australia Ltd v McPharlin*,[210] a guarantor who signed a contract to further secure a debtor's loan when the creditor threatened to enforce its securities against a guarantor unless further security was provided was found not to have entered the agreement under duress because the creditor's tactics, although unforgiving, were aimed at doing no more than seeking to enforce their legal rights in a manner authorised by the agreement and permitted by law. If, however, the creditor exercises their rights contrary to the agreement or the law, they may be using illegitimate pressure, and the guarantee may be vitiated. Further, if the creditor's actions are *mala fides* (in bad faith) and they do not honestly believe that they are acting in a manner countenanced by the agreement or the law, their conduct may amount to duress against the guarantor.

10.7.2 Unconscionability

Courts will provide equitable relief against bargains obtained unconscionably where a party to a transaction was under a special disability or disadvantage in dealing with the other party, such that there was no reasonable degree of equality between them.[211] This disability or disadvantage must have been sufficiently evident to the stronger party to make it unfair in the circumstances for them to have procured or accepted the weaker party's assent. In such cases, the stronger party bears the onus of proving that the transaction was fair, just and reasonable.[212]

204 *Barton v Armstrong* [1976] AC 104; *Williams v Bayley* (1866) LR 1 HL 200.
205 *Public Service Employees Credit Union Co-op Ltd v Campion* (1984) 75 FLR 131.
206 *Mutual Finance Ltd v John Wetton & Sons Ltd* [1937] 2 KB 389.
207 *Hawker Pacific Pty Ltd v Helicopter Charter Pty Ltd* (1991) 22 NSWLR 298.
208 *Crescendo Management Pty Ltd v Westpac Banking Corporation* (1988) 19 NSWLR 40, 46.
209 *Crescendo Management Pty Ltd v Westpac Banking Corporation* (1988) 19 NSWLR 40, 46.
210 (1984) 3 BPR 9,500.
211 For a detailed discussion of unconscionable conduct, see Chapter 16.
212 *Commercial Bank of Australia Ltd v Amadio* (1983) 151 CLR 447. This case concerned a contract of guarantee in favour of the defendant bank and is discussed fully in Chapter 16.

10.7.3 Undue influence

When the guarantor enters the contract of guarantee as a result of 'the improper use of the ascendancy acquired by one person over another for the benefit of himself or someone else' such that the acts of the guarantor 'are not, in the fullest sense of the word, his free voluntary acts',[213] the contract can be avoided. The enquiry is focused on the independence of the guarantor's will rather than their knowledge of the agreement. The undue influence does not necessarily consist of any particular act of the creditor, but rather of an array of contributing factors that collectively exert an influence.[214]

Some relationships give rise to a presumption of undue influence, while undue influence will have to be inferred where the relationship between the parties falls outside the established categories. The relationships in which undue influence presumptively arises are those between parent and child, guardian and ward, doctor and patient, solicitor and client, priest and parishioner, and trustee and beneficiary. The presumption does not apply in the cases of employer and employee, principal and agent, and landlord and tenant; nor in the case of spouses, in which judicial policy allows for inherent affection and trust to be expressed by way of the giving of guarantees.[215]

If influence is not presumed, an actual influential relationship may still be proved. The influence of a husband at the time of the transaction over an intelligent, capable and otherwise independent wife was demonstrated in *Bank of Credit & Commerce International SA v Aboody*.[216] In *Lloyds Bank Ltd v Bundy*,[217] an elderly man, unconversant in business, secured a guarantee in favour of a bank loan made to his son's business against his only asset, a farmhouse. During an interview arranged between the bank manager, the guarantor and the debtor, the guarantor demonstrated completed reliance on the creditor bank's advice. The bank advised the guarantor on the risks of the transaction by referring specifically, and in some detail, to the state of the business. The son's business collapsed five months later and the bank terminated its overdraft facilities and called on the father's security. The court held that the relationship between the bank and the defendant was one of virtually complete dependency and trust, founding a fiduciary duty.

The presumption of undue influence reverses the burden of proof such that the party who is presumed to have exerted the influence must lead evidence to rebut the presumption. The burdened party may discharge the onus by demonstrating that the party entered the agreement freely, expressing their own unconfined or untainted judgment; and that the party's understanding was informed as to the nature, effect and consequences of the agreement. Showing that the guarantor was provided with independent advice[218] may be a factor in discharging the burden, but is not in itself sufficient.[219]

213 *Union Bank of Australia v Whitelaw* [1906] VLR 711, 720.

214 *Allcard v Skinner* (1887) 36 Ch D 145, 181: 'some unfair and improper conduct, some coercion from the outside, some overreaching, some form of cheating, and generally, though not always, some personal advantage.'

215 *Yerkey v Jones* (1939) 63 CLR 649, 675.

216 [1989] 2 WLR 759.

217 [1975] QB 326.

218 *Re Brocklehurst (Deceased)* [1978] Ch 14.

219 See *Goldsborough v Ford Credit Australia Ltd* (1989) ASC ¶55-946, where the lack of independent advice did not upset the validity of the guarantee.

10.7.4 Does a creditor have a general duty to explain?

There exists a range of judicial statements as to whether or not a creditor is burdened with the general duty to explain the nature of a transaction to a guarantor. On one approach, a creditor bank that fails to advise a customer may be liable in negligence.[220] Another approach is that the creditor is under a general duty to advise the guarantor when the guarantor is in a position of presumed undue influence, or there is evidence of actual undue influence, or where a difference between the creditor's and guarantor's knowledge raises evidence of unconscionable dealing.[221] Yet another approach relieves the creditor of any general duty to provide either financial or legal advice to the guarantor.[222] While the creditor may be under no general obligation to provide the advice, or to ensure that the guarantor seeks and receives it, they may be obliged to advise the guarantor to seek it, and allow time to receive and consider it.[223]

As explained further at Section 10.9.2, s 55 of the *National Credit Code* imposes disclosure obligations on the part of credit providers, requiring them to provide to prospective guarantors documentary information explaining their rights and obligations as guarantor.

10.7.5 The importance of the guarantor receiving independent advice

Understanding what constitutes independent legal advice is central to the creditor's arguments in cases of potential undue influence and unconscionability. This is because both the presumption of undue influence and unconscionability can be rebutted by the provision of independent legal advice. A solicitor advising a guarantor must be acting solely for the guarantor, and not working for either the creditor or the debtor, in order to ensure as far as possible that their decision is independent and free from the influence of either.[224] To ensure independence, officers of neither the creditor nor the debtor should be present when the guarantor is being advised.[225] The solicitor must do more than simply read the provisions of the guarantee instrument to the guarantor and ask the guarantor if they have any questions. The solicitor's reading must be accompanied by some explanation,[226] including of any unusual or peculiar provisions.[227] Once read and explained, the guarantor may also be given an opportunity to read and consider the guarantee in private.[228]

The creditor is able to rely on the solicitor to regard it as their professional duty to advise the guarantor appropriately. Accordingly, the guarantee will be enforceable even if the solicitor

220 *Shotter v Westpac Banking Corporation* [1988] 2 NZLR 316.

221 *Commonwealth Bank of Australia v McGlynn* (unreported, NSW Supreme Court, Gile J, 15 November 1994), 19.

222 *Beneficial Finance Corporation Ltd v Karavas* (1991) 23 NSWLR 256, 276.

223 *Commercial Bank of Australia Ltd v Amadio* (1983) 151 CLR 447, 469.

224 *Nolan v Westpac Banking Corporation* (1989) 51 SASR 496; *McNamara v Commonwealth Trading Bank of Australia* (1984) 37 SASR 232.

225 *Nolan v Westpac Banking Corporation* (1989) 51 SASR 496; *Bank of Credit & Commerce International SA v Aboody* [1989] 2 WLR 759.

226 *Bester v Perpetual Trustee Co Ltd* [1970] 3 NSWR 30, 35–6.

227 *Collier v Moreland Finance Corporation (Vic) Pty Ltd* (1989) ASC ¶55-716, 58,433.

228 *Bester v Perpetual Trustee Co Ltd* [1970] 3 NSWR 30, 33.

has been negligent in their duty towards the guarantor.[229] Guarantors should be informed of the alternatives available to them,[230] including the option of not entering the guarantee transaction at all,[231] the risks attendant on providing the guarantee,[232] and the consequences of defaulting on it.[233] It is not sufficient that independent advice is given to the guarantor if the creditor does not provide the guarantor with all the relevant information.[234] Without being fully informed of the relevant circumstances[235] of the transaction, the guarantor will not be in a position to make necessary enquiries.[236] In some circumstances, the advice required to be given to guarantors includes financial as well as legal advice. In *Beneficial Finance Corporation Ltd v Karavas*,[237] the debtors relied on their business to generate the profit to service the loan the subject of the guarantee, on which they defaulted. The court held that the guarantor should have been provided with a risk assessment of the viability of the business.

10.8 Discharging the liability of the guarantor

10.8.1 Discharge by performance

When, as is usually the case, a guarantor undertakes to guarantee a principal debtor's performance of a particular obligation under a contract, and the principal debtor completely performs that obligation, the guarantor is discharged from further obligation. However, the guarantor's obligations may extend beyond completion if, for example, the guarantee requires acknowledgment or certification of performance.

10.8.2 Payment by principal debtor to creditor in satisfaction of the principal obligation

The principal's performance must in fact be made in satisfaction of their obligation under the principal contract. Where a principal makes payment from funds that have been forwarded to them by the guarantor, a question of interpretation arises as to whether the payment is made by the principal to the creditor, or whether the payment is made by the guarantor to the creditor through the agency of the principal.

The importance of the distinction lies in the fact that where the principal obligation is guaranteed by multiple guarantors, in the first case all guarantors are discharged, but in the

229 *Comino v Manettas; Cooney v Manettas* (unreported, NSW Court of Appeal, Mahoney, Sheller and Cripps JJA, 5 March 1993).
230 *Bester v Perpetual Trustee Co Ltd* [1970] 3 NSWR 30, 33.
231 *Giorgi v European Asian Bank AG* (unreported, NSW Supreme Court, Young J, 21 February 1989).
232 *Farnham v Orrell* (1989) NSW ConvR ¶55-443.
233 *Robinson v ANZ Banking Group Ltd* (1990) ASC ¶55-979, 58,896.
234 *Guthrie v ANZ Banking Group Ltd* (1989) ANZ ConvR ¶221.
235 *Inche Noriah v Shaik Allie Bin Omar* [1929] AC 127, 136.
236 *Brusewitz v Brown* [1923] NZLR 1106, 1117.
237 (1991) 23 NSWLR 256. The case was decided under the *Contracts Review Act 1980* (NSW).

second only the guarantor who makes the payment is discharged.[238] In *Mahoney v McManus*,[239] the High Court found that the principal's payment to the creditor from the guarantor's funds did not discharge their obligations under the principal contract. Normally, the guarantor will make payments in satisfaction of the obligations under the guarantee.

Payments by the creditor to the debtor discharge the guarantee if they represent 'good and satisfactory payment'.[240] Good and satisfactory payment will not be satisfied where the guarantor treats a debt previously owing by the creditor to the debtor as discharging the principal debt.[241] Neither is the assignment of means of payment sufficient. The payment in discharge of the guarantor's obligation must be an actual payment, not an organisation of finances that extinguishes a debt and treats it as a credit. However, if the subject of the guarantee is a particular account and it is closed, the guarantor's obligation is discharged even if the principal remains indebted to the creditor.[242]

If the debtor does not make the payment before the creditor realises securities against the debt, and the creditor subsequently refuses to accept the payment, it is no defence for the guarantor to plead that the payment was refused under the circumstances.[243]

10.8.3 An unfair preference under the Corporations Law[244]

If the debtor is bankrupt, a payment to a creditor may represent a payment over other creditors. In Australia, the guarantor will be treated as discharged even if the sum paid is a preference that is later repaid to the trustee in bankruptcy by the creditor.[245] In such cases the particular wording of the guarantee is essential to the result.[246] If the guarantee makes specific provision for the recovery by the trustee in bankruptcy of unfair preferences, the guarantor will not be discharged.[247]

Prior to 23 June 1993, directors of companies who were also guarantors of the debtor company's obligations could nevertheless have been liable to the liquidator by the operation of

238 *Mahoney v McManus* (1981) 55 ALJR 673. The High Court construed the agreement and payment as constituting a payment to the creditor by the guarantor with the principal debtor as agent. The decision and its reasoning has been criticised in *State Bank of NSW Ltd v Nepean Indoor Sports Centre Pty Ltd* (unreported, NSW Supreme Court, Rolfe J, 28 April 1995).

239 (1981) 55 ALJR 673.

240 *Pritchard v Hitchcock* (1843) 6 M & Gr 151, 166.

241 *Harrison v Nettleship* (1833) 2 My & K 423.

242 *National Bank of New Zealand v Mee & Reid (Executors of Cramond)* (1885) 3 NZLR (CA) 188.

243 *Williamson v Tait* (1892) 18 VLR 649.

244 An unfair preference is essentially a payment or transfer of property made by a company (which will imminently become insolvent) to a specific creditor where that creditor receives more for an unsecured debt than they would have received had the creditor been required to prove for the debt in the winding up of the company: *Corporations Act 2001* (Cth), s 588FA(1).

245 *Commonwealth Bank of Australia v Carruthers* [1964–1965] NSWR 1197. The matter concerned the treatment of a payment under s 95 of the *Bankruptcy Act 1924* (Cth), which was distinguished from its English counterpart by Manning J, who refused to follow English authority that yielded a contrary result. The English legislation refers to an intention to prefer the creditor, whereas the Australian legislation only refers to the effect of preferring the creditor. However, neither statute considers the effect of the preferential payment on the discharge of the guarantor's obligation.

246 *Commercial Bank of Australia Ltd v Carruthers* [1964–1965] NSWR 1197, 1204.

247 *Commercial Bank of Australia Ltd v Carruthers* [1964–1965] NSWR 1197, 1204.

the Corporations Law, s 567(5), which sets out the three conditions under which the liquidator is entitled to recover property from the director. The circumstances are now governed by s 588FH, which is in similar terms. However, the cases decided under s 567(5) remain relevant to the new governing provision.

Section 567(5) provided as follows:

> Where:
>
> (a) a disposition of property is made by a company before the commencement of Part 5.7B and within 6 months before the relation-back day in relation to a winding up of the company;
>
> (b) the disposition of property confers a preference upon a creditor of the company; and
>
> (c) the disposition of property has the effect of discharging an officer of the company from a liability (whether under a guarantee or otherwise and whether contingent or otherwise) . . .

The effect of this section was to ensure directors met their obligations as guarantors by not disposing of assets to selected creditors. Section 567 did not require that the director's intention be established, only that their actions had the effect of preferring particular creditors; nor does it excuse the director who acts in good faith by making dispositions ignorant of the company's financial position.[248] Section 588FH has the same purpose as s 567(5), but additionally refers specifically to discharging the 'liability . . . of a related entity of the company'.

10.8.4 Appropriation of payments and securities

A guarantor is not entitled to direct that a payment from a debtor is made in preference to other liabilities of the debtor and in discharge of the guarantee. The debtor has the primary right of such appropriation. If they have more than one debt they may appropriate a payment to any one of them regardless of whether other debts are guaranteed. A debtor's appropriation may be inferred from the surrounding circumstances. A payment received from a debtor in response to a demand can be inferred to be a payment in relation to the debt for which the demand was made.[249] If the debtor does not appropriate payment by stipulating the debt in respect of which the payment is made, the creditor is freed to do so.

A guarantor can bind the creditor by demonstrating that the debtor has made a payment that is appropriated to the guaranteed obligation.[250] If the guarantor is the victim of a fraud orchestrated in secret between the creditor and the principal debtor the guarantee may be vitiated and the guarantor discharged from meeting their obligation under it.[251] However, whether the existence of an arrangement between creditor and principal should ever discharge the guarantor is a controversial matter. The creditor is under no general obligation to disclose

248 *Matthews v Geraghty* (1986) 43 SASR 576.
249 *Shaw v Picton* [1825] 107 ER 1226.
250 *Simson v Ingham* (1823) 2 B & C 65.
251 *Vivian v Eynon* [1927] GLR 447.

to the guarantor how they intend to appropriate any particular payments,[252] nor the existence of loans other than those guaranteed.[253] Second, the debtor has a right of appropriation, but if they fail to exercise it, the creditor then has the right and may exercise it at their complete discretion.

10.8.5 Discharge by the creditor's release of the principal debtor

A creditor who decides to release the debtor from further obligation despite the debt not having been paid thereby also discharges the guarantor of their obligation,[254] nor is the principal indebted to the guarantor. Such an agreement must be legally binding. Therefore, if it is to be a contract, consideration must be provided for it.

A covenant of the creditor not to sue the debtor may be construed as a release of the guarantor and may contain words to that effect. However, a simple covenant not to sue without reserved rights does not release the guarantor.[255] The reason for this may be because the principal's debt to the creditor still exists, but the parties have entered an agreement not to enforce it. However, the effect on the guarantor is exactly the same as if the agreement were a release. On the grounds of both policy and logical consistency the guarantor's release seems the preferable conclusion.

Nevertheless, there are circumstances in which the creditor's rights against the guarantor are preserved despite the release of the creditor. This may be because it is specifically provided for in the agreement between creditor and debtor, or in the contract of guarantee, or because the guarantee does not contain a reservation of rights clause preserving the liability of the creditor.[256] However, reservations of rights clauses are not effective in absolute or unconditional releases and are treated as void.[257]

Further, parol evidence cannot be admitted to demonstrate the preservation of a right against the guarantor.[258] But parol evidence can be admitted where there is no clear absolute release to determine whether the creditor retains a right of action against the guarantor[259] or where there is no written contract to evidence the transaction and the creditor's rights against the guarantor.[260]

If the reservation of rights clause appears in the contract of guarantee the creditor's right of action against the guarantor may thereby be preserved. In *Perry v National Provincial Bank of England*,[261] the guarantor claimed release from their obligation to the bank that had released the debtor from liability, but the bank refused on the basis of a clause in the mortgage

252 *Bank of Nova Scotia v Neil* (1968) DLR (2d) 357.
253 *Goodwin v National Bank of Australasia Ltd* (1968) 117 CLR 173.
254 *Cragoe v Jones* (1873) LR 8 Exch 81; *Jowitt v Callaghan* (1938) 38 SR (NSW) 512; *Hancock v Williams* (1942) 42 SR (NSW) 252.
255 See *Mallett v Thompson* (1804) 5 Esp 178 confirmed in *Deanplan Ltd v Mahmoud* [1992] 3 All ER 945.
256 *Cole v Lynn* [1942] 1 KB 142.
257 *Webb v Hewitt* (1857) 3 K & J 438, 442.
258 *Lewis v Jones* (1825) 4 B & C 506.
259 *Mercantile Bank of Sydney v Taylor* (1891) 12 LR (NSW) 252; on appeal: [1893] AC 317.
260 *Mercantile Bank of Sydney v Taylor* (1891) 12 LR (NSW) 252; on appeal: [1893] AC 317.
261 [1910] 1 Ch 464.

document that was the subject of this case permitting the bank to make compositions and arrangements with the debtor. The court held that the guarantor liability was preserved. This decision has been conclusively adopted in Australia in *Bank of Adelaide v Lorden*.[262]

Consumer credit legislation renders the guarantor's and debtor's liability co-extensive. As a result, any reservation of rights clause is thereby rendered ineffective. Neither are the provisions excludable.

10.8.6 Discharge by novation

The effect of novation is the extinguishment of an obligation with another raised in its place. When a third party is substituted for the principal debtor, new obligations replace existing obligations such that the parties to the former agreement are released. The guarantor's obligations are fully discharged by the novation.[263] The most common form of novation involves company mergers and takeovers such that the new entity takes over as debtor from the old.

However, there will be no novation unless all parties intend the effect of releasing the debtor from their obligations and having them replaced by the third party, and the agreement is supported by consideration. If the creditor there explicitly and impliedly indicates that there was to be no substitution, the guarantor's obligations are preserved. Creditors cannot preserve rights against the guarantor after novation even if the guarantee provides a promise that the guarantor remain liable for the debts of the old company[264] because the old company's liability had ended absolutely and a new entity in its place renders it impossible to reserve rights against the guarantor.[265]

10.8.7 Termination following the creditor's breach

The contract or statute may confer upon the principal debtor a right of termination. If a purchaser under a contract of sale exercises a right of rescission, the guarantor's liability is discharged[266] with respect to obligations accruing after the date of effective termination. Similarly, the guarantor is discharged of obligations that arise subsequent to a creditor's breach of contract when the debtor accepts the creditor's repudiation of the contract and elects to terminate,[267] but is not relieved of meeting those obligations that have already accrued. However, if the creditor's breach is non-repudiatory, the guarantor is not discharged from their obligations unless the terms of the contract are also terms of the guarantee.[268] The discharge of the guarantor may not occur automatically; it may in some circumstances be necessary for the guarantor to elect to be discharged and to notify the creditor in breach of this intention.[269]

262 (1970) 127 CLR 185.

263 *Commercial Bank of Tasmania v Jones* [1893] AC 313.

264 *Re Mount Costigan Lead & Silver Mining Co Ltd* (1896) 17 LR (NSW) Eq 80.

265 (1896) 17 LR (NSW) Eq 80, 91.

266 *Insurance Office of Australia Ltd v Burke Pty Ltd* (1935) 35 SR (NSW) 438.

267 The debtor must be sure that the right to terminate exists. The obligation violated must be shown to be a condition (or perhaps an intermediate term breached in a significant manner), as opposed to a warranty sounding only in damages: *Ankar Pty Ltd v National Westminster Finance (Australia) Ltd* (1987) 162 CLR 549; *Scott v Forster Pastoral Co Pty Ltd* (2000) 35 ACSR 294. See, further, Chapter 1.

268 *National Westminster Bank plc v Riley* [1986] FLR 213, 223.

269 *Scott v Forster Pastoral Co Pty Ltd* (2000) 35 ACSR 294.

10.8.8 Termination following the principal debtor's breach

The termination of a principal agreement on its terms discharges the principal and thereby the guarantor from liability accruing after the date of termination. However, whether the guarantor's liabilities are discharged when the creditor terminates for the principal's breach and the principal remains liable in damages to the creditor remains an open question. On the basis that the guarantee is taken as protection against the breach, liability continues. Alternatively, the extinguishment of the principal contract on the creditor's termination for the principal's breach should equally determine (end) the contract of guarantee.

The differences in approach may be accounted for by contracts of guarantee being of two types. In one, the guarantor who ensures the principal's payment will be liable to pay when the debtor fails to. In the second, the guarantor who undertakes to ensure the principal's performance of their obligations is in breach of the contract of guarantee when the principal fails so to perform.[270]

The different categories of guarantee give rise to different causes of action. In the first case, the creditor may sue for a debt or sum of money. In the second, they may sue for damages for breach of contract, although a liquidated sum may be appropriate where this can be ascertained. If the guarantor ensures payment of the obligation under the principal contract, the effect of termination is to discharge the guarantor.[271] If the guarantor ensures performance of the contract and is thereby in breach of the contract of guarantee, they are liable for damages measured as the amount recoverable from the principal by the creditor.[272] If the accrued payments under the principal contract can be recovered by the principal despite their breach, the guarantor is discharged from the obligation to pay it.[273] Whether the guarantor is liable in damages to the creditor, however, appears to depend on whether the contract of guarantee incorporates the obligation to ensure the principal's performance of the contract, or only to guarantee the due payments.[274]

10.8.9 Variation of the contract of guarantee

Generally, an alteration of the principal contract agreed between the creditor and principal debtor discharges the guarantor who has not agreed to the new form assumed by the primary obligation.[275] Because the guaranteed obligations no longer exist, the guarantor has no responsibilities and their securities are released. The equitable principle embodied in this rule is strictly applied. The strictness of the application is apparent in the fact that a variation with the possibility of prejudice (even without actual prejudice) will discharge the guarantor. On the other hand, if the creditor is able to show that the variation is 'insubstantial' and there is 'no

270 See *Sunbird Plaza Pty Ltd v Maloney* (1988) 166 CLR 245, 256. See also *Moschi v Lep Air Services Ltd* [1973] AC 331, 344–5.

271 *Moschi v Lep Air Services Ltd* [1973] AC 331, 334–5, approved in *Keene v Devine* [1986] WAR 217, 222–3.

272 *Moschi v Lep Air Services Ltd* [1973] AC 331, 339. The same principles are applied in Australia: see *Nangus Pty Ltd v Charles Donovan Pty Ltd (in liq)* [1989] VR 184, and *Womboin Pty Ltd v Savannah Island Trading Pty Ltd* (1990) 19 NSWLR 364.

273 See *McDonald v Dennys Lascelles Ltd* (1933) 48 CLR 457. Cf *Hyundai Heavy Industries Co Ltd v Papadopoulos* [1980] 1 WLR 1129.

274 *Moschi v Lep Air Services Ltd* [1973] AC 331.

275 *Hancock v Williams* (1942) 42 SR (NSW) 252.

possible prejudice' to the guarantor, or it benefits the guarantor, the guarantor may remain bound.[276] It is not required that the variation of the principal contract be material before the courts will nullify the guarantee.[277] As the plurality in *Holme v Brunskill* noted:

> According to the English cases, the principle applies so as to discharge the surety when conduct on the part of the creditor has the effect of altering the surety's rights, unless the alteration is unsubstantial and not prejudicial to the surety. The rule does not permit the courts to inquire into the effect of the alteration. The consequence is that, to hold the surety to its bargain, the creditor must show that the nature of the alteration can be beneficial to the surety only or that by its nature it cannot in any circumstances increase the surety's risk, eg, a reduction in the debtor's debt or in the interest payable by the surety. The mere possibility of detriment is enough to bring about the discharge of the surety.[278]

For the contract to be released, the contract that is varied must be the contract that is guaranteed and not another, even closely related, contract.[279] An insubstantial variation to a contract may include, for example, clarifications and corrections of minor errors,[280] some alterations to notification requirements,[281] variations permitting securities to be held in certain accounts and for some of them to be realised,[282] and an assignment of the principal transaction to another creditor. Variations may benefit the guarantor: for example, a reduction of the principal's debt or the interest rate on that debt,[283] where the debtor provides the creditor with a (or a further) security.[284]

10.8.10 Discharge by operation of law

Where the principal debtor becomes bankrupt, or undergoes winding up, being placed into official management or entering a scheme of company arrangement, the guarantor's obligations will not thereby be determined. This is because the creditor may nevertheless potentially enforce the primary obligation.[285]

However, if the principal contract is discharged by operation of law, such as where the principal transaction is terminated by the trustee of a bankrupt principal[286] or the liquidators of

276 *Ankar Pty Ltd v National Westminster Finance (Australia) Ltd* (1987) 162 CLR 549, 559; *Valstar v Silversmith* [2009] NSWCA 80; *Pritchard v DJZ Constructions Pty Ltd* (2012) 16 BPR 31,141.

277 Compare H A de Colyar, *A Treatise on the Law of Guarantees and of Principal and Surety* (Butterworth & Co., London, 3rd edn, 1897), 396 on this point with *Holme v Brunskill* (1878) 3 QBD 495, 505–6, and *Chatterton v Maclean* [1951] 1 All ER 761.

278 (1878) 3 QBD 495, 559.

279 *Town of Truro v Toronto General Insurance Co* (1973) 38 DLR (3rd) 1, 8.

280 *Bond v Hong Kong Bank of Australia Ltd* (1991) 25 NSWLR 286, 297–8.

281 *Sanderson v Aston* (1873) LR 8 Exch 73.

282 *Bank of South Australia v Benjamin* (1892) 14 ALT 159.

283 *Ankar Pty Ltd v National Westminster Finance (Australia) Ltd* (1987) 162 CLR 549, 560.

284 *Traders Group Ltd v Brewster* (1968) 2 DLR (3d) 390, 395–6.

285 *Helou v Mulligan Pty Ltd* (2003) 57 NSWLR 74; *Jowitt v Callaghan* (1938) 38 SR (NSW) 512. See, further, Section 10.2.1.

286 *Bankruptcy Act 1966* (Cth), s 135(5A); *Stacey v Hill* [1901] 1 KB 660, where a lease terminated on bankruptcy relieved the guarantor of paying further rent.

companies being wound up terminate contracts,[287] then the principal is relieved of their obligations under the principal contract and the guarantor is relieved of theirs under the guarantee.

The consequences for the guarantor override anything to the contrary in disclaimers purporting to provide that legislation is to take effect without affecting the rights and liabilities of any other person except the bankrupt, or a person other than the company undergoing the winding up.

This exception is necessary to avoid the contradictory consequence that a released principal would nevertheless be required to indemnify the guarantor.[288] A disclaimer will not, however, protect the original lessee who assigns a lease[289] and who remains liable as a principal and therefore is not affected by the disclaimer.[290] Similarly the guarantor of the original lease remains liable for its performance.[291]

If the consent of the court is required to effect a disclaimer, the court will look to the consequences the disclaimer will have on other parties in exercising its discretion. In particular, it will consider the prejudice to the creditor of relieving the guarantor of their obligations.[292] Where the decision does not require court approval but rests with the liquidator, it will not be displaced unless it is exercised *mala fides* (bad faith).[293]

The effect of discharging a principal agreement by operation of law is to relieve both principal and guarantor of all accrued and future obligations.[294] Contracts of guarantee may effectively include terms that the guarantor's liability continues unaffected even when the principal is relieved under the principal agreement by operation of law. However, the clauses will not be effective where they conflict with the operation of consumer credit legislation. Then the guarantor is liable for an amount not exceeding the principal debtor's liability.

10.9 Statutory regulation of guarantees and the creditor's conduct

10.9.1 *Australian Securities and Investments Commission Act 2001* (Cth)

Guarantees are affected by a range of statutes. Misleading or deceptive conduct in relation to financial services, for example, is prohibited under Part 2, Division 2 of the *Australian Securities and Investments Commission Act 2001* (Cth) ('ASIC Act'). As such, parties are forbidden from engaging in conduct that may mislead or deceive a party with respect to any aspect of a guarantee arrangement, as in *Money v Westpac Banking Corporation*[295] where the

287 *Corporations Act 2001* (Cth), ss 568(1), 568(1B).
288 *Stacey v Hill* [1901] 1 KB 660, 664.
289 *Warnford Investments Ltd v Duckworth* [1979] 1 Ch 127, 137–8.
290 *Warnford Investments Ltd v Duckworth* [1979] 1 Ch 127, 137–8.
291 *Warnford Investments Ltd v Duckworth* [1979] 1 Ch 127, 137–8.
292 *Re Katherine et Cie Ltd* [1932] 1 Ch 70.
293 *Re Hans Place Ltd* [1992] BCC 737.
294 *Unity Finance Ltd v Woodcock* [1963] 1 WLR 455.
295 (1988) ATPR (Digest) ¶46-034.

defendant bank requested the borrower to sign a mortgage contract securing the amount loaned when in fact the contract actually provided security for an unlimited amount. The bank's failure to draw the borrower's attention to the unlimited nature of the security, when it was clear the borrower assumed the advances would not exceed the nominated amount, constituted misleading or deceptive conduct under s 52 of the now defunct *Trade Practices Act 1974* (Cth) (now s 18 of the *Australian Consumer Law*). The provisions of Part 2, Division 2 of the ASIC Act cannot be contracted out of.

Where financial services form the subject of a consumer transaction, Subdivision E sets out the implied terms of agreement. To give an example, s 12ED(1) of the ASIC Act provides that every contract for the supply of financial services by a person to a consumer in the course of a business contains an implied warranty that: (a) the services will be rendered with due care and skill; and (b) any materials supplied in connection with those services will be reasonably fit for the purpose for which they are supplied.

10.9.2 National Credit Code

The *National Credit Code* is contained in Schedule 1 to the *National Consumer Credit Protection Act 2009* (Cth). Both credit contracts and guarantees associated with credit contracts (s 8) fall within the ambit of the operation of the *National Credit Code* ('the Code'). Credit contracts are defined at s 4 of the Code. Section 55 sets out the writing requirements to be complied with under the Code. At s 56, the Code requires that disclosures with respect to guarantees be made pre-contractually, including the provision of a copy of the credit contract and a document (in the prescribed form) explaining the guarantor's rights and obligations. The concept of co-extensive liability, as discussed at Section 10.2.3, is reflected in s 60(1) of the Code, which reads as follows:

> A guarantee is void to the extent that it secures an amount, in relation to a credit contract to which this Code applies, that exceeds the sum of the amount of the liabilities of the debtor under the credit contract and the reasonable expenses of enforcing the guarantee, or any lesser amount agreed between the credit provider and the guarantor

Section 61 allows, however, for a guarantor's liability to increase in certain circumstances.

10.9.3 *Contracts Review Act 1980* (NSW)

The *Contracts Review Act 1980* (NSW) permits the courts, upon an examination of the circumstances in which a contract was made, to vary, refuse to enforce, or strike down the contract (or one or more of its provisions) where the contract or provision in question is deemed unjust.[296] Similar provisions are contained in ss 76–77 of the *National Credit Code*. The statute therefore lends itself to parties alleging that a contract of guarantee, in whole or in part, is unjust. Indeed, according to Lindgren, applications under this Act by disgruntled

296 *Contracts Review Act 1980* (NSW), s 7(1). 'Unjust' is defined in s 4 of the Act as including 'unconscionable, harsh or oppressive'.

guarantors have been quite common.[297] The relief offered by the Act is provided 'for the purpose of avoiding as far as practicable an unjust consequence or result'.[298] However, a person cannot access relief under the Act in relation to a contract so far as it was entered into 'in the course of or for the purpose of a trade, business or profession' carried on by the applicant.[299] The majority of guarantors will not provide guarantees as a profession or trade and so will be able to apply for relief under the Act. The Crown, corporations, and public or local authorities are also excluded from the ambit of the Act.[300]

The court is to determine the unjustness of a contract or provision by having regard to the public interest and the circumstances of the case.[301] The court is to be guided by 'the general policy of the law ... that people should honour their contracts'.[302] Contracts are not to be set aside because they are contrary to a party's interest, because they were entered into without the party having received independent advice, or because the party lacks the means to perform the contract. Rather, the court should consider whether the terms are fair and reasonable, and whether the party entered into the contract using their free judgment.[303]

Section 9(2) of the Act sets out the matters the court is to consider in determining the justness or otherwise of the contract. This section provides:

> Without in any way affecting the generality of subsection (1), the matters to which the Court shall have regard shall, to the extent that they are relevant to the circumstances, include the following:
>
> (a) whether or not there was any material inequality in bargaining power between the parties to the contract,
>
> (b) whether or not prior to or at the time the contract was made its provisions were the subject of negotiation,
>
> (c) whether or not it was reasonably practicable for the party seeking relief under this Act to negotiate for the alteration of or to reject any of the provisions of the contract,
>
> (d) whether or not any provisions of the contract impose conditions which are unreasonably difficult to comply with or not reasonably necessary for the protection of the legitimate interests of any party to the contract,
>
> (e) whether or not:
>
> (i) any party to the contract (other than a corporation) was not reasonably able to protect his or her interests, or
>
> (ii) any person who represented any of the parties to the contract was not reasonably able to protect the interests of any party whom he or she represented, because of his or her age or the state of his or her physical or mental capacity,

297 K E Lindgren *Vermeesch and Lindgren's Business Law in Australia* (LexisNexis Butterworths Australia, Sydney, 12th ed, 2011), 1092.

298 *Contracts Review Act 1980* (NSW), s 7(1).

299 *Contracts Review Act 1980* (NSW), s 6(2).

300 *Contracts Review Act 1980* (NSW), s 6(1)

301 *Contracts Review Act 1980* (NSW), s 9(1).

302 *Baltic Shipping Co v Dillon* (1991) 22 NSWLR 1, 9.

303 *Australian Societies Group Financial Services v Bogan* (1989) ASC ¶55-938.

(f) the relative economic circumstances, educational background and literacy of:
  (i) the parties to the contract (other than a corporation), and
  (ii) any person who represented any of the parties to the contract,

(g) where the contract is wholly or partly in writing, the physical form of the contract, and the intelligibility of the language in which it is expressed,

(h) whether or not and when independent legal or other expert advice was obtained by the party seeking relief under this Act,

(i) the extent (if any) to which the provisions of the contract and their legal and practical effect were accurately explained by any person to the party seeking relief under this Act, and whether or not that party understood the provisions and their effect,

(j) whether any undue influence, unfair pressure or unfair tactics were exerted on or used against the party seeking relief under this Act:
  (i) by any other party to the contract,
  (ii) by any person acting or appearing or purporting to act for or on behalf of any other party to the contract, or
  (iii) by any person to the knowledge (at the time the contract was made) of any other party to the contract or of any person acting or appearing or purporting to act for or on behalf of any other party to the contract,

(k) the conduct of the parties to the proceedings in relation to similar contracts or courses of dealing to which any of them has been a party, and

(l) the commercial or other setting, purpose and effect of the contract.

The factors the court considers essentially overlap with those to be considered when assessing whether bargains have been procured unconscionably.[304] Indeed, many of the factors in s 9(2) overlap with those considered under the equitable doctrine of unconscionability and the statutory equivalent contained in the *Australian Consumer Law*[305] and *ASIC Act*.[306]

10.9.4 *Banking Code of Practice 2020*

Although it lacks legislative force, the Australian Banking Association's *Banking Code of Practice 2020* comprehensively regulates the manner in which financial institutions may issue and enforce contracts of guarantee. As discussed in Section 10.2.4, the majority of Australian banks (lenders) are signatories to this code and therefore voluntarily agree to be bound by the instrument and its provisions pertaining to guarantees obtained and banking services provided.[307] Signatories agree to accept guarantees only where these are limited to a specific amount or security,[308] and to satisfy certain disclosure and advisory requirements.[309] There are

304 See Chapter 16 where the statutory regimes proscribing unconscionable conduct are discussed.
305 Sections 20–21.
306 Sections 12CA–12CB.
307 See Part 2.
308 *Banking Code of Practice 2020*, cl 94.
309 *Banking Code of Practice 2020*, cll 96–106.

additional provisions as to extensions of existing guarantees[310] and to enforcement of guarantees in the event of debtor default.[311]

In July 2018, the Australian Securities and Investments Commission approved a new *Banking Code of Practice* to replace the 2013 code.[312] The new code came into effect on 1 July 2019 and, for the first time, required all banks to become signatories and fully implement the code by the date of its commencement. Among the changes in the context of guarantees are new protections for guarantors of loans (eg prescribed 'cooling-off' period for prospective guarantors to contemplate the transaction) and a requirement for banks to enforce guarantees only once action has first been taken against the borrower (debtor). A revised edition of the new code came into effect in March 2020 and further strengthened protections for guarantors in response to the Banking Royal Commission that concluded in February 2019.

10.10 Rights of the guarantor

10.10.1 Indemnity from principal debtor

A person who accepts the role of guarantor and who pays the agreed amount under a guarantee to the creditor is entitled to an indemnity from the principal debtor.[313] The guarantor's right of indemnity may be provided for expressly in the contract of guarantee. If so, the contract governs the guarantor's expectations of indemnification. Otherwise, the guarantor's right of indemnity is provided for by an implied contract[314] or an implied term of the contract of guarantee.[315] The guarantor's payment of the creditor need not have benefited the principal debtor,[316] nor need the monies borrowed by the creditor have been for the creditor's benefit,[317] for the guarantor to seek indemnification from the creditor.

A debtor cannot be sued on the contract of indemnity if they had no knowledge of the guarantee. However, where a majority of a debtor company's directors knew that a party intended to guarantee a company debt and acquiesced to it, the guarantee is deemed to have been requested by the company and the guarantor impliedly indemnified by contract of indemnity.[318]

By express agreement, debtor and guarantor can agree that the guarantor can be indemnified even before the guarantor had paid any part of the debt.[319] Otherwise the guarantor must wait until all or some of the debt has been paid before the indemnity can be invoked.[320] A guarantor may pay a debt as soon as it becomes due, but cannot hasten their indemnification by paying it earlier.[321]

310 *Banking Code of Practice 2020*, cll 104–106.
311 *Banking Code of Practice 2020*, Chapter 29.
312 Australian Securities and Investments Commission, 'ASIC Approves the Banking Code of Practice' (Media Release, 18-223MR, 31 July 2018).
313 *Israel v Foreshore Properties Pty Ltd (in liq)* (1980) 30 ALR 631, 636.
314 *Johnson v Royal Mail Steam Packet Co* (1867) LR 3 CP 38, 43.
315 *Israel v Foreshore Properties Pty Ltd (in liq)* (1980) 30 ALR 631, 634–5.
316 *Brittain v Lloyd* (1845) 14 M & W 762.
317 *Bolton v Cooke* (1825) 3 LJOS Ch 87.
318 *Rogers v ANZ Banking Group Ltd* [1985] WAR 304, 313.
319 *Spark v Heslop* (1859) 1 El & El 563.
320 *Stirling v Forrester* [1821] 4 ER 712.
321 *Drager v Allison* (1959) 19 DLR (2nd) 431.

Guarantor and debtor may expressly[322] or impliedly[323] agree to exclude or limit the guarantor's right of indemnity. If the guarantor promises not to enforce the right of indemnity, they may be estopped from insisting upon their right to it.[324]

A guarantor can claim indemnity from the principal debtor once they have paid any amount of the principal debt; they need not have paid the full amount of their liability prior to seeking recovery.[325] A husband is entitled to reimbursement from a wife or a wife's estate for any payments made under a guarantee, and the presumption of advancement (which presumes such transfers to be by way of gift) will not inhibit or restrict that claim, nor will any payment made under the guarantee be presumed to be a gift to the wife.[326]

The right of indemnity is generally enforced by the guarantor bringing an action against the principal debtor for indemnification. If indemnity has been given by two or more debtors, the indemnity may be either joint or several. The only way to determine whether it is joint or several is by a proper construction of the contract of indemnification or the indemnification clause implied into the contract of guarantee.

The *Property Law Act 1958* (Vic), s 81 provides as follows:

> **Effect of covenant with two or more jointly**
>
> (1) A covenant, and a contract under seal, and a bond or obligation under seal, made with two or more jointly, to pay money or to make a conveyance, or to do any other act, to them or for their benefit, shall be deemed to include, and shall, by virtue of this Part, imply, an obligation to do the act to, or for the benefit of, the survivor or survivors of them, and to, or for the benefit of, any other person to whom the right to sue on the covenant, contract, bond or obligation devolves, and where made after the commencement of this Act shall be construed as being also made with each of them.
>
> (2) This section shall extend to a covenant implied by virtue of this Part.
>
> (3) This section shall apply only if and as far as a contrary intention is not expressed in the covenant, contract, bond or obligation, and shall have effect subject to the covenant, contract, bond or obligation, and to the provisions therein contained.
>
> (4) Except as otherwise expressly provided, this section shall apply to a covenant, contract, bond or obligation made or implied after the thirty-first day of January One thousand nine hundred and five.

Accordingly, in the absence of an express provision to the contrary (advanced by way of evidence) two or more debtors promising to indemnify a guarantor do so jointly and severally.

If the creditor sues the guarantor without joining the principal debtor, the guarantor may institute third party proceedings against the debtor to enforce the indemnity. The guarantor's right to sue the debtor for indemnification is not extinguished by a judgment obtained by the creditor against the guarantor for the principal debt. A guarantor may obtain a Mareva

322 *Bradford v Gammon* [1925] Ch 132.
323 *Hungerford v Hungerford* (1708) Gilb Eq Rep 67, 69.
324 *Chadwick v Manning* [1896] AC 231.
325 *Davies v Humphreys* [1840] 151 ER 361.
326 *Re Salisbury-Jones* [1938] 2 All ER 459.

injunction against the debtor to preserve assets that may be used to satisfy a judgment in their favour and to prevent the debtor's assets being moved outside the jurisdiction of the courts or dissipated.

10.10.2 Subrogation

If the principal debtor defaults and the guarantor pays the guaranteed debt, the guarantor is entitled to be subrogated to the rights of the creditor with respect to the debt. This means that the guarantor is entitled to have all of the securities held against the principal debtor by the creditor (in respect of the transaction guaranteed) assigned to them. The guarantor effectively 'stands in the shoes' of the creditor in enforcing the principal debt of the debtor. The equitable foundations of subrogation are based on the following principle:

> No-one ought to profit by another man's loss where he himself has incurred a like responsibility. Any other rule would put it in the power of the creditor to select his own victim; and upon motives of mere caprice of favouritism, to make a common burden a most gross personal oppression. It would be against equity for the creditor to exact or receive payment from one, and to permit, or by his conduct to cause, the other debtors to be exempt from payment.[327]

The right of subrogation may be excluded by express agreement. However, the debtor and creditor cannot disentitle the guarantor to the securities held for the principal debt by agreement among themselves. The exclusion of the right of subrogation may only be effected by an explicit express or implied provision in the contract of guarantee.[328] A guarantor may also be deprived as to title in securities granted by statute.

The right of subrogation becomes available when the creditor has been paid in full.[329] It is not necessary for the guarantor claiming the right of subrogation to the creditor to have discharged the obligation entirely themselves, although they must have made a payment which at least in part reduced the debt.[330] The guarantor's share in the securities once subrogated to the creditor is equal to the contribution they have made in reduction of the debt.[331]

If a guarantor has guaranteed only part of the principal debt, they are entitled to share in the securities held against that debt once that part of the principal debt has been paid.[332] However, a guarantee for the whole debt but for a limited liability has no entitlement to any held security until the entire debt is paid.[333]

Entitlement to the securities means that the guarantor is entitled to them in whatever form they exist, and to the extent that they are held by the creditor,[334] including any substitutions for

327 J Story, *Commentaries on Equity Jurisprudence* (Stevens & Haynes, London, 1884), 315.
328 *Morris v Ford Motor Co Ltd* [1973] 2 All ER 1084.
329 *Duncan, Fox & Co v North & South Wales Bank* (1880) 6 App Cas 1.
330 *Equity Trustees Executors & Agency Co Ltd v New Zealand Loan & Mercantile Agency Co Ltd* [1940] VLR 201, 207.
331 *Gedye v Matson* (1858) 25 Beav 310, 312.
332 *Ward v National Bank of New Zealand Ltd* (1889) 8 NZLR 10.
333 *Re Sass; Ex parte National Provincial Bank of England Ltd* [1896] 2 QB 12.
334 *Jones v Hill* (1893) 14 LR (NSW) Eq 303.

securities accepted by the creditor.[335] However, the guarantor's entitlement is not restricted to the securities held by the creditor for the principal debt, but will include monies that are paid in lieu or as a consequence of the principal debt, such as money paid to reduce the principal debt of a bankrupt debtor.[336] On occasion the right of subrogation entitles the guarantor to any remedy the creditor may have against third parties, such as the right to sue for damages[337] or a breach of contract.[338]

The right of subrogation is lost to the guarantor when the creditor uses the held securities to reduce or discharge the debt of the principal debtor, since the securities are thereby consumed.[339] If the creditor does not realise the securities' full value and the guarantor is prejudiced, the guarantor may be either fully discharged under the circumstances or discharged to the extent they suffered prejudice.

10.10.3 The doctrine of marshalling

If a debtor has two secured creditors, the creditors may be entitled to different monies or assets. In the case where one creditor (say) can access multiple monies or assets and the other creditor only one, the second creditor may require the first to marshal all of the monies or assets by which the first creditor is secured, so that both creditors are paid to the fullest extent possible out of the securities. Where the first creditor has already enforced their rights with respect to the securities, the second creditor may be subrogated to the first in respect of those securities to which only the first has access.[340]

10.11 Contribution from co-sureties

Contribution is based on the law's recognition of the common interest and the common burden shared among co-sureties to the same debt or obligation.[341] A guarantor who discharges the entire obligation to a creditor by payment of a debt has the right to contribution from the others. Because co-suretyship is a common burden, the contribution of each co-surety should be the equal of the others.[342]

Co-sureties may by express agreement modify or exclude their obligations to contribute. However, courts will be reluctant to draw the inference that a right of contribution has been excluded.[343] Courts are also hesitant to conclude that a right of contribution has been impliedly excluded,[344] and the circumstances in which they are likely to do so are extremely restricted.[345]

335 *Ward v National Bank of New Zealand Ltd* (1889) 8 NZLR 10.
336 *Ford v London Chartered Bank of Australia* (1879) 5 VLR 328, 331.
337 *City of Prince Albert v Underwood McLellan & Associates Ltd* (1968) 3 DLR (3rd) 385.
338 *Phillips v Foxall* [1872] LR 7 QB 666, 680–2.
339 *Regina Brokerage & Investment Co v Waddell* (1916) 27 DLR 533 (CA).
340 *Tombs v Roch* (1846) 2 Coll 490, 499–500 on marshalling and its distinction from contribution.
341 *Ellesmere Brewery Co v Cooper* [1896] 1 QB 75, 80.
342 *Mahoney v McManus* (1981) 180 CLR 370, 376.
343 *Cornfoot v Holdenson* [1932] VLR 4.
344 *Bater v Kare* [1964] SCR 206.
345 *Bater v Kare* [1964] SCR 206.

If guarantors have neither expressly nor impliedly agreed to contribute equally, the degree of contribution may be implied from the construction of their intention as contained in the guarantee agreement. The contribution the guarantors intended may be able to be measured against some other known fact, such as their relative shareholding in the debtor company they used to undertake a joint venture.[346]

Because the doctrine of contribution is most likely premised on the sharing of a common obligation, there can be no contribution between guarantors who are not liable under the same common debt[347] and the same common demand[348] for the default of the same debtor.[349] Guarantors cannot seek contribution from company directors when a company incurs debts for which directors are responsible under the Corporations Law.[350] This is because the company debt is primary, but the guarantors' is secondary and contingent upon the company's default.

Guarantors may seek contribution even if they are liable for different amounts of the principal debt and on different terms.[351] Similarly, contribution may be sought even where the guarantors share a common responsibility for only part of the principal debt.[352] There can, however, be no contribution between guarantors responsible in different ways for different parts of the principal debt – for example, in circumstances where the agreement is modified such that each guarantee assumes responsibility for a specific part of a principal debt.[353] However, where guarantors are responsible for the same debt or obligation it is irrelevant, and contribution may be sought, regardless of whether their obligations are joint, joint and several, or several;[354] or whether their guarantees were secured by the same or different instruments;[355] or their obligations were secured at different times;[356] or whether any of them knows the others exist.[357]

The guarantor may claim contribution once they have paid more than their part of the guarantee – for example, (but not only) if they discharge the whole obligation. If a guarantor pays less than the proportion of the debt for which they are responsible, they may claim contribution only if the debtor makes a payment by means of which the guarantor's payment becomes a payment of greater than their share of the debt.[358]

It has also been suggested that a guarantor may seek contribution when they have paid greater than an amount due at the time the payment was made,[359] rather than the right only arising when they have paid more than they are liable for of the whole of the common

346 *Morgan Equipment Co v Rogers [No 2]* (1993) 32 NSWLR 467.
347 *Smith v Cook* [1911] AC 317.
348 *Smith v Cook* [1911] AC 317.
349 *Ellesmere Brewery Co v Cooper* [1896] 1 QB 75, 79.
350 *Corporations Act 2001* (Cth), s 588G.
351 *Molson's Bank v Kovinsky* [1924] 4 DLR 330, 332.
352 *Molson's Bank v Kovinsky* [1924] 4 DLR 330, 332.
353 *Pendlebury v Walker* [1841] 160 ER 1072.
354 *Stirling v Forrester* [1821] 4 ER 712, 717.
355 *Mahoney v McManus* (1981) 180 CLR 370.
356 *Whiting v Burke* (1871) 6 Ch App 342.
357 *Mahoney v McManus* (1981) 180 CLR 370, 376.
358 *Davies v Humphreys* [1840] 151 ER 361.
359 *Rowlatt on Principal and Surety* (Sweet & Maxwell, London, 3rd edn, 1936), 245.

obligation.[360] However, the latter approach is more in accordance with the principles of equity and the manner in which contribution actions are decided in courts of equity:

> [U]ntil the one has paid more than his proportion either of the whole debt, or of that part of the debt which remains unpaid by the principal, it is not clear that he ever will be entitled to demand anything from the other, and before that he has no equity to receive a contribution, and consequently no right of action.[361]

The guarantor may seek contribution if they pay when the debt becomes due but cannot seek contribution if they have paid the debt before being liable to pay.[362] The payment made by the guarantor must have accrued[363] and must have been one for which they (and their co-surety) were legally liable.[364]

10.12 Key points

- A guarantee is a binding promise of one person to be answerable for the present or future debt or obligation of another in case that person defaults.
- The guarantee is the undertaking that the debt shall be paid.
- Guarantees are different from indemnities, warranties and contracts of insurance.
- The three parties to a contract of guarantee are: (1) the principal debtor or principal, which is the party promising to do something; (2) the creditor, which is the party to whom this promise is made; and (3) the guarantor or surety, which is the party undertaking to be liable should the principal debtor fail to adhere to the agreement.
- The principal debtor owes a primary obligation to the creditor, while the guarantor owes a secondary obligation to the creditor. The guarantor's liability is co-extensive, so they will be equally liable for the whole amount for which the principal debtor is liable.
- Contracts of guarantee are governed by the general principles of contract law, the law of equity, and some statutory and other legal instruments.
- Guarantors are not required to be personally liable for the principal debtor's performance of their obligation. Guarantors may, for example, provide a 'pledge, mortgage or charge' over property as security for the debtor's performance as well as pledging their personal credit.
- Contracts of guarantee are generally construed *strictissimi juris* (strictly according to their terms), in favour of the guarantor.
- Guarantees may be set aside on the basis of duress, unconscionability and undue influence.
- A guarantor's liability may be discharged in a number of ways, including by performance, novation, or operation of law. Some variations to contracts of guarantee may also discharge

360 H A de Colyar, *A Treatise on the Law of Guarantees and of Principal and Surety* (Butterworth & Co., London, 3rd edn, 1897), 343–4.
361 *Davies v Humphreys* [1840] 151 ER 361, 168–9.
362 *Maclean v Discount & Finance Co Ltd* (1939) 64 CLR 312, 335.
363 *Lang v Le Boursicot* [1993] 5 BPR 97,406.
364 *McFarlane v Calhoun* (1879) 2 PEIR 283.

the guarantor, as may termination of the contract of guarantee following the creditor's or principal debtor's breach.

10.13 DISCUSSION QUESTIONS

1. What is a guarantee? How does this instrument differ from (a) indemnities, (b) warranties, and (c) insurance?
2. Explain the nature of the primary and secondary obligations of the principal debtor and surety (respectively) under a contract of guarantee.
3. What is the difference between a continuing and a limited/specific guarantee?
4. What factors might serve to vitiate a contract of guarantee?
5. Which statutory instruments regulate contracts of guarantee?

10.14 FURTHER READING

Australian Bankers' Association, *The Small Business Sector in Australia – Economic Report* (May 2016).

Australian Government, Australian Small Business and Family Enterprise Ombudsman, *Barriers to Investment: A Study into Factors Impacting Small to Medium Enterprise Investment* (November 2017).

Godwin, A, Paterson, J M and Howell, N, Background Paper 10 – Credit for Small Business: An Overview of Australian Law Regulating Small Business Loans, *Royal Commission into Misconduct in the Banking, Superannuation and Financial Services Industry*, 7 May 2018.

Lindgren, K E, *Vermeesch and Lindgren's Business Law in Australia* (LexisNexis Butterworths Australia, Sydney, 12th edn, 2011), Chapter 27.

Lovric, J and Millbank, J, *Darling, Please Sign This Form: A Report on the Practice of Third Party Guarantees in New South Wales* (NSW Law Reform Commission and University of Sydney, Research Report 11, 2003).

Traves, S, *Commercial Law* (LexisNexis Butterworths Australia, Sydney, 3rd edn, 2014), Chapter 12.

11

INSURANCE

11.0 Introduction

This chapter considers insurance as the formation of a contract of risk management between two parties: the insurer and the insured. It examines the governance of that relationship of insurance by the statutory regime contained in the *Insurance Contracts Act 1984* (Cth) and relevant amendments under the *Insurance Contracts Amendment Act 2013* (Cth). It addresses the formation and interpretation of the contract of insurance, and the duty of utmost good faith and disclosure, as they apply to both insureds and insurers. The construction of insurance contracts is examined by reference to the principles of interpretation applicable to commercial contracts broadly, and insurance contracts in particular. The chapter also addresses the types of breach commonly encountered in insurance cases. Finally, it considers the remedies available to insureds and insurers for instances of misrepresentation, fraud, non-disclosure, and breach of policy terms.

11.1 The nature of insurance in Australia

The term 'insurance' describes a commercial arrangement that facilitates the transfer of risk at a price. The practice has a relatively obscure history, with evidence of its origins in Europe and the Middle East. The earliest known policy of insurance was issued in Genoa, Italy in 1347 and pertained to a voyage by sea.[1] The insurance industry established itself as a feature of Australia's economic landscape as early as the 1830s.[2] At August 2019, there were 82 institutions authorised to conduct new or renewal insurance business,[3] and 28 institutions authorised to offer life insurance.[4] The distinction between general and life insurance is explained in Section 11.2.2 of this chapter.

The insurance industry as a whole came under scrutiny as part of the Royal Commission into Misconduct in the Banking, Superannuation and Financial Services Industry, established on 14 December 2017. The Commission was initiated by the Governor-General in response to widespread allegations of misconduct on the part of financial institutions and a string of scandals implicating the major Australian banks. Although scope restrictions preclude a full discussion, the Commission's Final Report submitted on 1 February 2019 revealed instances of (among other things) unscrupulous marketing and selling practices, unfair treatment and exploitation of insureds, and dishonest, opaque and slow claims management processes in the insurance industry.[5]

1 W R Vance, 'The Early History of Insurance Law' (1908) 8(1) *Columbia Law Review* 1.

2 I Enright et al, Background Paper No 14 to Royal Commission into Misconduct in the Banking, Superannuation and Financial Services Industry, *General Insurance*, 12 June 2018, 22.

3 Australian Prudential Regulation Authority (APRA), *Register of General Insurance* (12 August 2019). Of these institutions, 14 were restricted to conducting 'run-off' business only (ie acting only as an insurance agent, broker or underwriting agent for other general insurers).

4 APRA, *Register of Life Insurance Companies* (15 October 2010).

5 Commonwealth, Royal Commission into Misconduct in the Banking, Superannuation and Financial Services Industry, *Final Report – Volume 1* (1 February 2019). For a disturbing summary of some of the major issues raised in submissions to the Royal Commission with respect to the insurance sector, see Chanticleer, 'Banking Royal Commission: Insurers' Confession Session Does Not Bode Well', *Australian Financial Review* (online), 10 September 2018; C Yeates and S Danckert, 'Insurers Admit to Hundreds of Cases of Misconduct', *Sydney Morning Herald* (online), 10 September 2018.

A contract of insurance is a contract in which one party (the insurer), in consideration of a sum of money (the premium) undertakes to pay another party (the insured) on the occurrence of a particular event. Such events include accidents, damage to or loss of property, illness, injury or death. The value of the premium will typically depend upon the nature of the insured risk (and the likelihood of a claim being made), the value of what is being insured, and the relevant government levies, duties and taxes that apply.

There are two main sources of insurance law in Australia: (1) the *Insurance Contracts Act 1984* ('the Act'); and (2) the common law, with respect to situations where the Act does not apply. Various state and territory Acts also regulate or otherwise affect different kinds of insurance.

The Act commenced operation on 1 January 1986 and prima facie applies to all 'contracts of insurance' entered into after that date. Section 9(1) provides that certain types of insurance contracts and proposed insurance contracts are not caught by the Act unless otherwise provided by the Act. Excluded contracts include contracts of reinsurance, contracts with friendly societies, certain private health insurance contracts, and contracts to which the *Marine Insurance Act 1909* (Cth) applies.

The purpose of the Act is stated in its preamble as follows:

> An Act to reform and modernise the law relating to certain contracts of insurance so that a fair balance is struck between the interests of insurers, insureds and other members of the public and so that the provisions included in such contracts, and the practices of insurers in relation to such contracts, operate fairly, and for related purposes.

The Act thus serves to fairly balance competing interests and more effectivelty regulate the insurance sector. It does not define a contract of insurance, but provides for a broad range of instruments concluded between parties that may be considered as falling within the purview of the Act. Nevertheless, the description of the contract of insurance at common law identifies its salient and common features. The contract of insurance was described by Sir Robert Megarry VC in *Medical Defence Union Ltd v Department of Trade*[6] in the following terms:

> First, the contract of insurance must provide that the assured would become entitled to something on the occurrence of some event ... second, the event must be one which involves some element of uncertainty ... Third, the assured must have an insurable interest in the subject matter of the contract.[7]

11.2 Classifications of insurance

There are two main ways to classify insurance: one is by distinguishing the benefits provided under the relevant insurance contract; the other is by the nature of the particular event or subject matter being insured.

6 [1979] 2 WLR 686.
7 [1979] 2 WLR 686, 690–1. It should be noted, however, that an insurable interest is no longer a requirement pursuant to s 16 of the Act. See, further, Section 11.3.5 below.

11.2.1 Indemnity and non-indemnity insurance

Indemnity insurance describes insurance that entitles the insured to a specific amount of compensation upon the occurrence of the event(s) defined under the policy. The amount is typically equivalent to and represents the actual loss that has been suffered through the event occurring. A common example is a policy of motor vehicle insurance: if the vehicle is written off in an accident, the insured will typically receive the market value of the vehicle – or perhaps an alternative agreed value – under the policy. Another example is home insurance: if your home burns to the ground, you will normally be able to receive an agreed sum commensurate with its value as a physical structure with fittings. In the first example, the insured event is the accident; in the second example, it is the fire.

Non-indemnity insurance describes insurance that also entitles the insured to compensation upon the occurrence of the event(s) defined in the policy, but which is payable irrespective of whether any loss has actually been incurred by the insured. Classic examples of non-indemnity insurance include life insurance and health insurance. If you take out a life insurance policy and nominate your partner as beneficiary, and then subsequently pass away, your partner can recover the amount insured even though they have suffered no material loss themselves. The benefit will be paid irrespective of the actual losses incurred through your death, and so it will not necessarily be equivalent to the actual loss suffered.

11.2.2 Event or subject matter being insured

A distinction is drawn in the Act between contracts of general insurance and contracts of life insurance.[8] If a contract is not for life insurance, it is a contract of general insurance. A life insurance contract is defined in s 9(1) of the *Life Insurance Act 1995* (Cth) and includes contracts 'for the payment of money on the death of a person or on the happening of a contingency dependent on the termination or continuance of human life',[9] among others.[10] This is perhaps the most commonly known form of life insurance contract.

General insurance contracts include liability insurance (covering third party liability such as professional liability and occupiers' liability), marine insurance,[11] and property insurance (covering such things as damage to or loss of real estate or chattels caused by flood, theft or fire), among others. Some forms of insurance may even pertain to both health matters and general matters. A good example is travel insurance, which may cover personal items damaged or lost while travelling (general insurance) as well as any illness or death that eventuates (health insurance).

8 *Insurance Contracts Act 1984* (Cth), s 11(6).
9 *Life Insurance Act 1995* (Cth), s 9(1)(a).
10 *Life Insurance Act 1995* (Cth), s 9(1)(b)–(g).
11 See *Marine Insurance Act 1909* (Cth).

11.3 Formation of an insurance contract

11.3.1 The policy, and offer and acceptance

While the Act imposes a number of rules specific to insurance contracts, generally speaking, the ordinary principles of contract law also apply. As such, both sources influence the formation of an insurance contract. The contract (or series of contracts) containing the terms of agreement between the insured and the insurer is typically known as the policy.[12] The process leading to the creation of the policy begins, however, with the proposal. The insurer will normally request the party seeking insurance to provide responses to a series of questions.[13] The questions will vary depending upon the type of insurance sought, but are generally designed to assist the insurer to evaluate the risk it is being asked to insure. The subject matter, along with the insured's personal circumstances and insurance history, will certainly be queried.

Submission of the proposal is construed as an offer to the insurer.[14] The insurer may then accept the proposal, extend a counter-offer (eg modify the terms of insurance), or decline the offer to insure. If an insurer declines an offer to enter into a contract of insurance, cancels or opts not to renew an existing contract, or offers to renew on less favourable terms, it must, if the insured so requests in writing, provide the insured with a written statement of its reasons for this decision.[15] If the insurer accepts the proposal, or a counter-offer is accepted, the policy and a *certificate of insurance* will be issued and will typically also include *endorsements*. Endorsements are essentially customised variations to standard-form policies that take account of an insured's particular circumstances and generally extend or limit the standard cover in the policy.

Whether or not agreement has conclusively been reached is determined by an examination of the circumstances in which the offer was made. For example, if the insurer writes to the insured requiring some act to be done before acceptance is effected, the doing of that act may constitute a condition precedent to the creation of the policy. An example of something that may have to be done is the payment of the first insurance premium.[16] In this situation, unless and until the first premium is paid, no binding contract of insurance arises. Alternatively, the specified act may instead operate as a condition precedent not to contract formation but to the *assumption of liability*. In other words, while the policy may provide that it comes into effect either immediately or at a specified time (without performance of any particular act), it may further provide that no liability is assumed until, for example, the first premium is paid.

11.3.2 Consideration

As mentioned above at Section 11.1, the consideration in a contract of insurance subsists in the payment of a premium from the insured to the insurer in return for the insurer's provision of

12 *C E Heath Underwriting & Insurance (Australia) Pty Ltd v Edwards Dunlop & Co Ltd* (1993) 176 CLR 535, 546.

13 When in written form, the document is normally entitled the 'proposal form', 'proposal for insurance' or something similar.

14 See *Montclare v Metlife Insurance Ltd* [2015] VSC 306, [147].

15 *Insurance Contracts Act 1984* (Cth), s 75(1).

16 *Goodwin v State Government Insurance Office (Qld)* [1994] 2 Qd R 15.

insurance cover (and concomitant assumption of risk). However, not all insurance contracts will involve the payment of a premium, so this is not a prerequisite to validity.[17] For example, the insurance arrangement may be embodied in a deed (which requires no consideration)[18] or in a compulsory insurance scheme, such as compulsory third party insurance, which is factored into the cost of motor vehicle registration.

11.3.3 Cover note

Another important feature in the process of insurance contract formation is the cover note. A cover note is a form of interim insurance cover for the period up to the time the proposed insured completes the proposal, or the insurer accepts the insured's offer.[19] The cover note will insure the insured for the period up to the issuing of the policy, or for a certain period of time specified in the cover note (normally 30 days or less), or otherwise until such time as the insurer terminates the cover note. In all other cases, it is implied that the cover note expires after a reasonable period of time has elapsed.[20] Section 38(2) of the Act determines when an insurer ceases to be liable under a cover note after the insured submits the proposal for longer-term insurance.

11.3.4 Parties to the contract

As mentioned above, an insurance contract is between an insurer and the insured. The contract may, however, be exclusively or inclusively for the benefit of third parties. The term 'third party beneficiary' in the context of insurance contracts is defined in s 11(1) of the Act as 'a person who is not a party to the contract but is specified or referred to in the contract, whether by name or otherwise, as a person to whom the benefit of the insurance cover provided by the contract extends'.[21]

A third party beneficiary under a contract of general insurance has a right, under s 48(1) of the Act, to recover from the insurer, in accordance with the contract, the amount of any loss they have suffered notwithstanding that they are not a party to the contract.[22] Accordingly, the Act modifies the rule on privity of contract between the insured and the insurer to allow the third party to recover their covered loss directly from the insurer. The statutory right of recovery conferred upon the third party by s 48 does not, however, make the third party a party to the contract with entitlements under the relevant contract.[23] Rather, it provides standing to claim to a person to whom a policy applies but who is not, in terms, a party to it.[24]

Subject to the insurance contract, third party beneficiaries have, in relation to their claim, 'the same obligations to the insurer as the third party beneficiary would have if the third party

17 *R v Cohen; Ex parte Motor Accidents Insurance Board* (1979) 141 CLR 577, 587–8.

18 See Chapter 1.

19 *Steadfast Insurance Co Ltd v F & B Trading Co Pty Ltd* (1971) 125 CLR 578, 583.

20 *Canberra Pools Pty Ltd v MMI General Insurance Ltd* (2000) 98 FCR 296, [38].

21 Third party beneficiaries are discussed in depth at Section 11.7.

22 *Insurance Contracts Act 1984* (Cth), s 48(1). This right is subject to any defences the insurer claims against the insured: s 48(3). See, further, *C E Heath Casualty & General Insurance Ltd v Grey* (1993) 32 NSWLR 25.

23 *Zurich Australian Insurance Ltd v Metals & Minerals Insurance Pte Ltd* (2009) 240 CLR 391, [24]. See also *Smart v Westpac Banking Corporation* (2011) 282 ALR 400, 402.

24 *GIO Australia Ltd v P Ward Civil Engineering Pty Ltd* [2000] NSWSC 371, [10].

beneficiary were the insured' and 'may discharge the insured's obligations in relation to the loss'.[25] This extends to the duties of disclosure and good faith.[26]

11.3.5 Insurable interest

Prior to the enactment of s 16 of the Act, there was a requirement at common law for an insured to have an insurable interest in the subject matter of an insurance contract at the time of its formation.[27] Broadly defined, an insurable interest was some legal or equitable right or interest in the property that is the subject of the insurance policy.[28] If the insured benefited from the presence of such right or interest, or was prejudiced in some way by its violation, they were deemed to have an insurable interest.

Section 16(1) of the Act dispenses with this common law requirement. It provides that contracts of general insurance are 'not void by reason only that the insured did not have, at the time when the contract was entered into, an interest in the subject-matter of the contract'.[29] Section 17 goes further and provides that an insured can recover under a contract of general insurance notwithstanding the lack of legal or equitable interest in the insured property; rather, the insured needs only prove a pecuniary or economic loss stemming from the property's damage or destruction.

11.4 Construction of insurance contracts

11.4.1 Basic principles

'An insurance policy is a species of commercial contract' to which the ordinary principles of contract law apply.[30] As such, it must be interpreted so as to give the words used within it their ordinary meaning and operation. With the exception of cover notes, insurance contracts are invariably documented. The courts are required to objectively 'discern from the language, structure and apparent purpose of the document what it means' and identify the parties' ostensible common intentions.[31] This assessment should be undertaken with due regard to the nature and type of insurance policy in question, the relevant background facts and circumstances, the commercial and social purposes for which the policy was written, and the context in which the words of the policy appear.[32]

25 *Insurance Contracts Act 1984* (Cth), s 48(2).

26 These duties are discussed later in the chapter. Section 13(3) of the Act expressly provides that the duty of utmost good faith also applies to third party beneficiaries. Section 13(4) further provides that this section applies in relation to third party beneficiaries only *after* the contract is entered into.

27 *Macaura v Northern Assurance Co Ltd* [1925] AC 619; *Truran Earth Movers Pty Ltd v Norwich Union Fire Insurance Society Ltd* (1976) 17 SASR 1.

28 *Lucena v Craufurd* (1806) 2 Bos & PNR 269, 321.

29 A similar provision for life insurance contracts, or other contracts providing for the payment of money on the death of a person by sickness or accident, is found in s 18 of the Act.

30 *Messagemate Australia Pty Ltd v National Credit Insurance (Brokers) Pty Ltd* (2003) 85 SASR 303, 319. See also *McCann v Switzerland Insurance Australia Ltd* (2000) 203 CLR 579. Basic contract law principles are discussed in Chapter 1.

31 *Messagemate Australia Pty Ltd v National Credit Insurance (Brokers) Pty Ltd* (2003) 85 SASR 303, 319.

32 *Messagemate Australia Pty Ltd v National Credit Insurance (Brokers) Pty Ltd* (2003) 85 SASR 303, 319.

11.4.2 Ambiguity and *contra proferentem*

If there is only one meaning in the words used within the policy, this meaning cannot be rejected simply because it produces an unfair or otherwise undesirable result.[33] However, where an alternative construction is more reasonable and more in accord with the probable intentions of the parties, and (importantly) where the words will *bear* such a construction, the courts may depart from a strictly literal interpretation of the policy.[34]

Where, however, the words of an insurance contract are intractably ambiguous and this ambiguity cannot be resolved by reference to dictionaries and logic alone, they will, as a 'last resort', be construed *contra proferentem*.[35] The maxim *verba chartarum fortius accipiuntur contra proferentem* (or simply *contra proferentem*) requires that the ambiguous clauses be construed against the party substantially responsible for drafting the policy.[36] This will, in the vast majority of cases, be the insurer.

This maxim can be justified on a number of bases. First, insurance contracts are typically offered in standard form (ie offered on a 'take it or leave it' basis) and drafted with due regard to legislation, competition, public policy, and the specific circumstances of the insured.[37] Insurers are in the business of assuming risk and are therefore 'usually in a better position than [their] prospective insureds to make sure the policy wording, whether drafted by it or not, clearly and precisely describes the scope of the risk it intends to take on'.[38] Second, insurance policies are rarely plain English documents, frequently suffer from poor and strained expression,[39] and often contain notorious 'fine print'.[40] They might also be comprised of several documents, or require a subtle understanding of the interrelationship between inclusion and exclusion clauses and the hierarchy of policy sections.[41] It is therefore unreasonable to expect insureds, who frequently lack the knowledge and experience to decipher complex documents of insurance, to try and make sense of the same.

33 *Messagemate Australia Pty Ltd v National Credit Insurance (Brokers) Pty Ltd* (2003) 85 SASR 303, 319. The courts will hesitate before departing from a settled meaning of a word or phrase in an insurance contract: *Johnson v American Home Assurance Co* (1998) 192 CLR 266.

34 *Australian Casualty Co Ltd v Federico* (1986) 160 CLR 513, 520; *Messagemate Australia Pty Ltd v National Credit Insurance (Brokers) Pty Ltd* (2003) 85 SASR 303, 319–20.

35 *Messagemate Australia Pty Ltd v National Credit Insurance (Brokers) Pty Ltd* (2003) 85 SASR 303, 320; *McCann v Switzerland Insurance Australia Ltd* (2000) 203 CLR 579, 602.

36 There must be a genuine ambiguity in the wording of the policy, such that no fair and reasonable construction can be derived from the same: *Manufacturers' Mutual Insurance Ltd v Stargift Ltd* (1985) 3 ANZ Ins Cas ¶60-615; cf *Cameron v Commercial Union General Insurance Co Ltd* (1983) 2 ANZ Ins Cas ¶60-542.

37 *Johnson v American Home Assurance Co* (1998) 192 CLR 266, 272–3; *Hammer Waste Pty Ltd v QBE Mercantile Mutual Ltd* [2002] NSWSC 1006, [25].

38 G Pynt, *Australian Insurance Law: A First Reference* (LexisNexis Butterworths Australia, Sydney, 2008), 49.

39 See *Hajjar v NRMA Insurance Ltd* (1985) 3 ANZ Ins Cas ¶60-647.

40 One judge has said of the notorious 'fine print' that 'seldom has the art of typography been so successfully diverted from the diffusion of knowledge to the suppression of it': *Delancey v Insurance Co*, 52 NH 581 (1873), 587–8. See also U Procaccia, 'Readable Insurance Policies: Judicial Regulation and Interpretation' (1979) 14 *Israel LR* 74, 102; A J Liederman, 'Insurance Coverage Disputes in the United States: A Period of Uncertainty for the Insurer' (1986) *LMCLQ* 79, 83–5.

41 In *Guardian Assurance Co Ltd v Underwood Constructions Pty Ltd* (1974) 48 ALJR 307, Mason J referred to the policy at issue as a 'jumble of ill-assorted documents expressed in that distinctive style which insurance companies have made their own' (at 308).

In light of the foregoing, as Kirby J explained in *Johnson v American Home Assurance Co*,[42] in cases of ambiguity in the wording of a policy drafted wholly or substantially by an insurer,

> it is not unreasonable for an insured to contend that, if the insurer proffers a document which is ambiguous, it and not the insured should bear the consequences of the ambiguity because the insurer is usually in the superior position to add a word or a clause clarifying the promise of insurance which it is offering.

In effect, the *contra proferentem* rule holds the drafting party responsible for any ambiguities in their expression and disentitles them from relying upon such ambiguous wording to their advantage. As Pynt notes, production of the policy presupposes that the insurer 'has satisfied itself that the policy wording precisely reflects the risk it intended to take on'.[43] As such, clauses limiting cover will be construed narrowly while clauses extending cover will be construed more liberally.[44] Construction of an insurance contract therefore generally favours the insured. However, the *contra proferentem* rule naturally works both ways and where the insured (or its agent, usually an insurance broker) drafts the policy or special terms to be added to a standard policy, the rule will benefit the insurer.[45]

11.4.3 Notification of specific or unusual terms

The Act specifies that certain specific terms may have to be brought explicitly to the attention of the insured. For example, when determining if an insurer has failed to act in utmost good faith by relying upon a provision of an insurance contract,[46] s 14(3) requires the courts to consider whether any notification (of a kind described in s 37 or otherwise) of the provision was provided to the insured. Section 35(2) also requires insurers seeking to market policies offering less than the standard cover for particular types of insurance contract to provide notice of such limitations in writing. Failing that, the insurer must demonstrate that a reasonable person in the circumstances could have been expected to be aware of the limitations.

There is also a requirement under the Act for unusual terms to be brought to the attention of the insured prior to the insurance contract being entered into. Provision, for example, of a copy of the policy wording will normally suffice.[47] Section 37 provides:

> **Notification of unusual terms**
> An insurer may not rely on a provision included in a contract of insurance (not being a prescribed contract) of a kind that is not usually included in contracts of insurance that provide similar insurance cover unless, before the contract was entered into the insurer clearly informed the insured in writing of the effect of the provision (whether by providing the insured with a document containing the provisions, or the relevant provisions, of the proposed contract or otherwise).

42 (1998) 192 CLR 266, 275.
43 G Pynt, *Australian Insurance Law: A First Reference* (LexisNexis Butterworths Australia, Sydney, 2008), 49.
44 *Hammer Waste Pty Ltd v QBE Mercantile Mutual Ltd* [2002] NSWSC 1006, [25]–[28].
45 *Eastern Associated Coal Corporation v Aetna Casualty & Surety Co* 632 F 2d 1068 (3rd Circ, 1980).
46 See further below at Section 11.5, especially Section 11.5.4.
47 *Hams v CGU Insurance Ltd* (2002) 12 ANZ Ins Cas 61-525.

The threshold for a term to be classified as unusual appears quite high. For example, terms in policies that are notably more restrictive than those found in similar insurance contracts are not necessarily unusual.[48] It seems the relevant term's departure from the standard language utilised in similar insurance contracts must be significant. On the other hand, terms that are so peculiar in operation or effect may be regarded as unusual and require special notice, as with the complex 'burning cost' clause in *Suncorp Metway Insurance Ltd v Mason Place Pty Ltd*.[49] The clause imposed a complicated method of premium adjustment that was said to require 'a reasonably specialist insurance qualification to understand [it] properly'.[50]

11.5 The duty of utmost good faith

11.5.1 Background

At common law, the contract of insurance has long been described as a contract of utmost good faith (*uberrimae fidei*), requiring each party to act honestly and fairly towards one another both in the formation stage of the contract as well as in the performance of obligations and exercise of rights arising under the contract as created. In the seminal case of *Carter v Boehm*[51] Lord Mansfield expressed what is a classic formulation of the principle of utmost good faith:

> Insurance is a contract upon speculation. The special facts upon which the contingent chance is to be computed lie most commonly in the knowledge of the assured only; the underwriter trusts to his representation, and proceeds upon confidence that he does not keep back any circumstances in his knowledge to mislead the underwriter into a belief that the circumstance does not exist ...
>
> The keeping back such circumstance is a fraud, and therefore the policy is void. Although the suppression should happen through mistake, without any fraudulent intention; yet still the underwriter is deceived, and the policy is void; because the risque is really different from the risque understood and intended to be run, at the time of the agreement ... Good faith forbids either party by concealing what he privately knows, to draw the other into the bargain, from his ignorance of that fact and his believing the contrary.[52]

At common law (in situations where the Act does not apply), the duty of utmost good faith is practically synonymous with the duty of disclosure and tends to focus upon pre-contractual behaviour of the insurer and, more particularly, the insured.[53] Only in very few cases has the duty of utmost good faith been successfully applied to post-contractual conduct.[54] The duty of

48 *Dumitrov v S C Johnson & Son Superannuation Pty Ltd* [2006] NSWSC 1372.
49 [2011] QDC 209.
50 [2011] QDC 209, [11].
51 (1766) 3 Burr 1905.
52 (1766) 3 Burr 1905, 1909–10.
53 *Australian Associated Motor Insurers Ltd v Ellis* (1990) 54 SASR 61, 71; K E Lindgren, *Vermeesch and Lindgren's Business Law of Australia* (LexisNexis Butterworths Australia, Sydney, 12th edn, 2011), 1113. See, further, the discussion in *New South Wales Medical Defence Union Ltd v Transport Industries Insurance Co Ltd* (1985) 4 NSWLR 107.
54 K E Lindgren, *Vermeesch and Lindgren's Business Law of Australia* (LexisNexis Butterworths Australia, Sydney, 12th edn, 2011), 1114. For a rare example of post-contractual application of the common law duty of utmost good faith, see *Black King Shipping Corporation & Wayang (Panama) SA v Massie ('The Litsion Pride')* [1985] 1 Lloyd's Rep 437.

utmost good faith at common law arises 'as an incident of the relationship between the parties to the insurance transaction' and not as an implied term of the contract.[55]

The common law principle of *uberrimae fidei* is now reflected in s 13(1) of the Act, which provides:

> **The duty of the utmost good faith**
>
> A contract of insurance is a contract based on the utmost good faith and there is implied in such a contract a provision requiring each party to it to act towards the other party, in respect of any matter arising under or in relation to it, with the utmost good faith.

As such, s 13(1) *does* imply the duty of utmost good faith as a term of every insurance contract (with limited exceptions). It extends to all matters relating to or arising from the contract of insurance.[56] Consequently, it also applies in both the pre- and post-contractual settings, as well as to the settlement of claims.[57]

The inclusion of the prefix 'utmost' connotes 'the most extensive, rather than the greatest, good faith'.[58] A mere measure will not suffice; the highest degree of good faith is mandated.[59] Unhelpfully, the Act fails to define the term 'utmost good faith', so trying to precisely summarise the content of the duty is an enormously difficult exercise. It is perhaps easier to identify instances where the courts have determined certain forms of conduct occurring within the insurance context to violate the duty. Before this, however, some other important provisions of the Act must be mentioned.

Section 12 of the Act provides that Part II (dealing with the duty of utmost good faith) 'is not limited or restricted in any way by any other law, including the subsequent provisions of this Act'. However, it further states that the Part 'does not have the effect of imposing on an insured, in relation to the disclosure of a matter to the insurer, a duty other than the duty of disclosure'. In effect, this provision emphasises the paramountcy of the duty of utmost good faith. It also makes clear that the duty is not interchangeable with the duty of disclosure (which is provided for in s 21),[60] nor does it 'place a higher duty on an insured than is otherwise required under Part IV' of the Act.[61] The pre-contractual duty of disclosure in s 21 cannot, therefore, be extended to impose a post-contractual duty. Ongoing obligations excluded by the Act may be imposed by drafting suitable contract terms.[62]

Section 14(1) of the Act provides that a party cannot rely on a term of a contract if to do so would be to fail to act with the utmost good faith.[63] The Australian Law Reform Commission

55 *Khoury v Government Insurance Office of New South Wales* (1984) 165 CLR 622, 637.

56 *Britton v Royal Insurance Co* (1866) 4 F & F 905; *Banque Financiere v Skandia (UK) Insurance Co Ltd* [1990] 2 Lloyd's Rep 377, 389.

57 Australian Law Reform Commission, *Report on Insurance Contracts* (ALRC, 1982), paragraph 328: 'The duty of good faith applies to all aspects of the relationship between insurer and insured, including the settlement of claims.'

58 *Manifest Shipping Co Ltd v Uni-Polaris Shipping Co Ltd ('The Star Sea')* [2003] 1 AC 469, [44].

59 *Sheldon v Sun Alliance Ltd* (1989) 53 SASR 97, 152.

60 K Sutton, *Insurance Law in Australia* (LBC Information Services, Sydney, 3rd edn, 1999), 102.

61 *CIC Insurance Ltd v Barwon Region Water Authority* (1998) 147 FLR 353, 368.

62 *New South Wales Medical Defence Union Ltd v Transport Industries Insurance Co Ltd* (1985) 4 NSWLR 107.

63 Pursuant to s 14(3), in making this determination, the court shall consider 'any notification of the provision that was given to the insured, whether a notification of a kind mentioned in section 37 or otherwise'.

(ALRC), in its 1982 report on insurance contracts, noted that this provision would 'provide sufficient inducement to insurers and their advisers to be careful in drafting their policies and to act fairly in relying on their strict terms'.[64] Section 14(2) of the Act further provides that sub-s (1) does not limit the operation of s 13.

Section 13(2) provides that a failure to comply with the duty of utmost good faith constitutes a breach of the Act. Breach of the duty is remedied by an order for damages. Where the Act does not apply, an action for a breach of the duty of good faith under the common law of contract may either sound in damages or trigger a right of rescission concluding in an annulment of the contract and a refund of any premiums paid,[65] possibly because the breach is not of an implied term but undermines the nature of the relationship between the parties instigated by the contract.[66] Finally, s 14A of the Act provides that the Australian Securities and Investments Commission (ASIC) has the power to act against an insurer for failure to comply with the duty of utmost good faith.[67]

11.5.2 Content of the duty

Attempting to extrapolate the content and scope of the duty of utmost good faith under s 13(1) of the Act is extremely difficult. As mentioned earlier, the Act fails to define the term 'utmost good faith' and so judicial decisions and academic commentaries have endeavoured to give it meaning over time. It is often said that the concept of good faith 'encompasses notions of fairness, reasonableness and community standards of decency and fair dealings',[68] such that each party is expected to provide the others' interests with at least the same level of protection as they have provided for themselves.[69] If such mutual respect is the substance of good faith, then it clearly does not mark the relationship between insured and insurer as fiduciary in nature.[70]

In *CGU Insurance Ltd v AMP Financial Planning Pty Ltd*,[71] the High Court described the statutory duty of utmost good faith in the following terms:

> [U]tmost good faith may require an insurer to act with due regard to the legitimate interests of an insured, as well as to its own interests. The classic example of an insured's obligation of utmost good faith is a requirement of full disclosure to an insurer, that is to say, a requirement to pay regard to the legitimate interests of the insurer. Conversely, an

64 Australian Law Reform Commission, *Report on Insurance Contracts* (ALRC, 1982), paragraph 51.

65 *Banque Financière de la Cité SA v Westgate Insurance Co Ltd* [1989] 2 All ER 952, 991–7; and on appeal to the House of Lords ([1990] 2 All ER 947, 959).

66 *Smart v Westpac Banking Corporation* (2011) 282 ALR 400, 402, citing *Khoury v Government Insurance Office of New South Wales* (1984) 165 CLR 622, 637.

67 Section 14A(2).

68 M Gill and M Radford, in 'Utmost Good Faith: Section 13 and Breach of Contract' (1994) 10 *Australian Insurance Law Bulletin* 17, 81, suggest that the duty of good faith requires that a party must act with scrupulous fairness and honesty. See also *Vermeulen v SIMU Mutual Insurance Association* (1987) 4 ANZ Ins Cas ¶60-812.

69 D Derrington and R Ashton, *The Law of Liability Insurance* (LexisNexis Butterworths Australia, Sydney, 2nd edn, 2005), 236.

70 *Bristol & West Building Society v Matthew* [1998] Ch 1, 18; *Maksimovic v Royal & Sun Alliance Life Assurance Australia Ltd* [2003] WASC 46, [14]–[19].

71 (2007) 235 CLR 1, 12.

> insurer's statutory obligation to act with utmost good faith may require an insurer to act, consistently with commercial standards of decency and fairness, with due regard to the interests of the insured. Such an obligation may well affect the conduct of an insurer in making a timely response to a claim for indemnity.

The court also made a number of additional and instructive observations that provide further guidance as to what the duty of utmost good faith requires. First, as discussed earlier, utmost good faith 'will usually require something more than passivity: it will usually require affirmative or positive action on the part of a person owing [the] duty'.[72] Parties must therefore demonstrate reasonable affirmative efforts to uphold their duty to their counterparts. Second, 'a lack of utmost good faith is not to be equated with dishonesty only'.[73] The implication here is that a party to an insurance contract need not actually do something outwardly 'dishonest' in order to violate the statutory duty of utmost good faith.

As discussed earlier, it is perhaps easier to identify instances where the courts have determined certain forms of conduct occurring within the insurance context to violate the duty of utmost good faith under s 13(1) of the Act in order to develop a firmer understanding of the content of this duty.

11.5.3 The insured's duty of utmost good faith

Insureds have been held to have breached the utmost duty of good faith in a broad range of circumstances. We will consider some of these in turn.

11.5.3.1 Deliberately providing false responses in an insurance claim form

In *Gugliotti v Commercial Union Assurance Co of Australia*,[74] the insured's car was involved in an accident while being driven by his cousin, and the insured lodged an insurance claim for the damage. In response to the question in the claim form as to whether the driver had in the 12 hours prior to the accident consumed alcohol, the insured answered 'no'. The driver had in fact consumed alcohol within this period. In response to another question as to the driver's blood alcohol reading, the insured gave the answer 'nil' when in fact the driver's blood alcohol level was recorded as being 0.102 per cent. It was held that the insured had provided deliberately false answers for which the insured offered no credible explanation, and that the only conclusion that could be drawn was that the answers were intended to mislead the insurer. Fullagar J agreed with the trial judge that, on the evidence, the insured had breached s 13 of the Act by providing false responses.[75]

11.5.3.2 Failing to advise of proceedings being initiated against the insurer

The duty of utmost good faith imposes a unique obligation upon an insured with respect to legal liability (or legal indemnity) policies. The insured must inform the insurer that legal proceedings have been issued against it. This provides the insurer with the opportunity to conduct the defence and/or seek a settlement. In *UEB Packaging Ltd v QBE Insurance*

72 (2007) 235 CLR 1, 78.
73 (2007) 235 CLR 1, 77–8.
74 (1992) 15 MVR 463.
75 (1992) 15 MVR 463, 472.

(International) Ltd,[76] QBE had insured Kirby against liability that Kirby might incur as bailee of goods owned by UEB. Kirby incurred such liability when fire destroyed Kirby's premises (containing the goods) in 1987. Kirby reported the loss to QBE, before going into receivership the following year. In 1993, UEB initiated proceedings against Kirby and obtained judgment for the sum claimed in 1994. Only then did UEB notify QBE of these proceedings occurring. UEB sought leave to bring an action under s 9 of the *Law Reform Act 1936* (NZ) against QBE directly. The court held that QBE, as insurer, was entitled to avoid the contract. Kirby had breached its obligation of good faith to QBE by not informing it of the proceedings issued against it by UEB. Just as QBE could resist liability to Kirby for this reason, so could it resist liability to UEB. Under s 9, an applicant could not advance a claim against the insurer that was not available to the insured (Kirby). Baragwanath J stated:[77]

> Such principles [of good faith] govern the nature of Kirby's obligation to inform QBE of the fact of service of the proceeding upon it. While no such obligation was stipulated the overriding obligation of good faith made it mandatory that Kirby should inform QBE of the fact of the proceeding in good time to give it the opportunity whether to take over conduct of its defence in exercise of subrogated authority or to seek out-of-court settlement or both.

11.5.3.3 Intentionally withholding information when making a claim to deceive the insurer

In *New Zealand Insurance Co Ltd v Forbes*,[78] the insured, Forbes, was the owner of a truck used for logging purposes. When the truck failed to start, Forbes attempted to push-start it on a downhill slope by releasing the spring brake, which also acted as the emergency brake. The truck crashed and Forbes lodged an insurance claim. In the claim form, Forbes did not refer to the release of the spring brake. It was held at trial that the insured was entitled to recover by reason of the fact that the release of the spring brake was not relevant to the accident's occurrence. However, the decision was reversed in the Court of Appeal, which observed that the insured's intention to defraud when making the claim amounted to a breach of the duty of good faith.

11.5.3.4 Failing to take reasonable steps to minimise the insurer's liability

In *Newnham v Baker*,[79] Derrington J observed that an insured's failure to take reasonable steps to reduce or to minimise the liability of an insurer may amount to a breach of the duty of utmost good faith in particular circumstances.[80] In that case, the insured's claim for reasonable medical expenses following a workplace injury was challenged by the insurer on the basis that he attended a private rather than a public hospital. The policy indemnified the insured for 'reasonable medical expenses'. It was held that, while the insured 'would not be entitled to have hospital treatment without reasonable cause, nor to have extravagant expenses' without

76 (1996) 2 NZLR 467.
77 (1996) 2 NZLR 467, 479.
78 (1988) 5 ANZ Ins Cas ¶60-871.
79 [1989] 1 Qd R 393.
80 [1989] 1 Qd R 393, 398–9.

express stipulation in the policy, no insured in his position could be expected to undertake public hospital treatment where no expenses would be incurred at all.

11.5.3.5 Failing to provide information required by the insurer under the policy terms

In *New South Wales Medical Defence Union Ltd v Transport Industries Insurance Co Ltd*,[81] Rogers J reaffirmed the established principle that an insured may violate the duty of utmost good faith by failing to provide information required by an insurer under the terms of the policy. In such cases, the duty of good faith attaches to the obligation to supply the required information.[82] His Honour referred to *The Litsion Pride* in which the insured failed to disclose that it was sailing to one of the 'excluded' ports, in contravention of the policy's terms. It was thus deemed to have breached the implied duty of good faith.

11.5.3.6 Intentionally making a fraudulent claim

It would seem to go without saying that an insured who knowingly lodges a fraudulent claim is acting in bad faith and contravening s 13. As Gillard J stated in *Insurance Manufacturers of Australia Pty Ltd v Heron*, 'In all cases where a fraudulent claim is made, one can readily infer a breach of the obligation of utmost good faith.'[83]

11.5.4 The insurer's duty of utmost good faith

Actions for breach of the duty of good faith against insurers are less common than those against insureds, although there are still instances where insurers have been deemed to have violated s 13.

11.5.4.1 Failing to explain the significant provisions of the policy and the consequences of breach

In *Australian Associated Motor Insurers Ltd v Ellis*,[84] the respondents breached their comprehensive motor vehicle policy with the insurer by making modifications (fitting alloy wheels) without the insurer's written consent after renewal of the policy. The vehicle was damaged in a collision while being driving by the respondents' 23-year-old daughter. Although the modifications played no part in the collision, had consent for the same been sought from the insurer, it would have imposed a condition excluding liability while the car was driven by a person under the age of 25. The insurer was deemed to have breached the implied duty of utmost good faith through its failure to properly bring to the attention of the insured the consent provision or the consequences of its breach. The brief notification in the proposal form, and the reference within the policy document provided to the respondents, were in themselves insufficient.[85]

81 (1985) 4 NSWLR 107.
82 (1985) 4 NSWLR 107, 110–11.
83 [2005] VSC 482, [66].
84 (1990) 54 SASR 61.
85 Although there is potential for s 37 of the Act, pertaining to notification of unusual terms, to apply in such situations, Cox J held that the clause in question was not unusual and therefore the provision did not apply.

11.5.4.2 Adhering to a narrow definition of a policy term not detailed in the policy

In *Baccanello v ANZ Life Insurance*,[86] it was held that it would be a breach of the insurer's duty of utmost good faith to rely on a narrow definition of 'accident' when the brochure sent to the insured made no mention of such a narrow definition.

11.5.4.3 Failing to inform the insured of conditions precedent to liability to make payment

In *Re Bradley & Essex & Suffolk Accident Indemnity Society*,[87] an insurer refused to pay a workers compensation claim on the basis of the insured's failure to comply with a condition that they keep a wages book. The insurer alleged this was a condition precedent to liability to make payment. Although it was ultimately deemed not to be so,[88] Farwell LJ observed that it was incumbent on insurers to make clear, both in their proposal forms and in their policies, all conditions that will bind the insured, particularly those conditions that are precedent to the insurer's liability to pay.[89] This, it was stated, was consistent with the requirements imposed by the duty of utmost good faith in insurance contracts.[90] It would be very difficult to establish a breach of the duty of utmost good faith on the part of an insurer who had notified the insured of the existence of such a clause.[91]

11.5.4.4 Failing to adhere to the strict terms of the policy

In *Ibrahim v Greater Pacific Life Insurance Co Ltd*,[92] the insurer wrongfully stopped making payments to the insured under a sickness and injury policy, prompting the insured to seek social security payments. The application was successful. The policy was said to provide for deduction of the social security payments received. Brownie J held that the plaintiff was entitled to the insured sum under the policy and that the payments should not have been deducted. The defendant wrongly withheld payment based on an erroneously liberal reading of the policy. His Honour further noted in obiter that if this finding was incorrect, then, by virtue of s 14 of the Act, the defendant's failure to meet its contractual obligations (and prompting the plaintiff to claim social security benefits) was a failure to act with the utmost good faith.

11.5.4.5 Failing to advise that a policy provides inadequate coverage

In *Speno Rail Maintenance Australia Pty Ltd v Hamersley Iron Pty Ltd*, it was suggested in obiter that the duty of good faith may be breached if an insurer represents, at a prospective insured's request, that it will issue a policy that provides the specified level of coverage and it fails to do so.[93]

86 Unreported, South Australian District Court, Lee J, 27 May 1992. A note of the decision appears in 7 ILB No 10, 90.
87 [1912] 1 KB 415.
88 [1912] 1 KB 415, 421–2 (Cozens-Hardy MR), 433 (Farwell LJ).
89 [1912] 1 KB 415, 430–1.
90 [1912] 1 KB 415, 430.
91 *Banks v NRMA Insurance Ltd* (unreported, NSW Supreme Court, Brownie J, 1 September 1988).
92 (1996) 9 ANZ Ins Cas ¶61-330.
93 (2001) 23 WAR 291, 311 (Ipp J), 329 (Wheeler J).

11.5.4.6 Failing to make a decision as to liability within a reasonable time

Insurers may also breach the duty of good faith if they fail to provide with sufficient expediency their reasons for denying a claim. In *Moss v Sun Alliance Australia Ltd*,[94] the plaintiffs claimed on two policies after a fire destroyed their business premises in March 1987. While the insurer acknowledged liability, they disputed the extent of that liability. The insurer finally admitted liability in February 1988 but still failed to make any payments to the plaintiffs. In light of the significant delay, the plaintiffs brought an action against the insurer alleging breach of the insurer's duty of good faith. The insurer alleged that the reason for the delay in payment of the claim was that they were awaiting a police report. It was held that the unreasonably long delay in admitting liability and withholding payment breached their obligations to act in good faith under s 13 of the Act. Bollen J stated that 'prompt admission of liability to meet a sound claim for indemnity and prompt payment is required of an insurer by virtue of its obligation to act with the utmost good faith towards its insured'.[95]

11.5.4.7 Failing to cautiously evaluate a decision to defend, rather than settle, a claim

In *Distillers Co Bio-Chemicals (Australia) Pty Ltd v Ajax Insurance Co Ltd*,[96] the insured was a drugs distributor covered by a public risk policy issued by the insurer. The insured marketed tablets containing the infamous drug thalidomide, the ingestion of which by a pregnant woman was likely to have harmful effects upon the foetus of her unborn child. Claims were brought by or on behalf of children against the insured in respect of congenital deformities caused by their mothers ingesting the tablets. The insurer elected not to undertake the running of the defence or settlement actions in respect of the claims. Stephen J held that an insurer was bound to act in good faith towards the insured by having regard to their interests both in the defence of actions against them and in the settlement of such actions. The duty extended to the insurer's exercise of its power under the relevant policy to grant or withhold consent for the insured to make admissions, offers, promises or payment in connection with any claim, even if it elected not to take over the defence.[97] In exercising their power to withhold consent, the insurer must not have regard to considerations extraneous to the policy of indemnity.[98]

Stephen J further noted that it was improper for the insurer to refuse to consent to a reasonable settlement if they preferred an alternative course of action merely because they would reduce the amount of indemnity they would have to pay. However, it *would* be proper if the insurer refused to consent to a settlement on the grounds that they held a reasonable belief that they would be able to mount an effective and successful defence against the claims of the insured.[99] Importantly, if settlement is preferred, the insurer should consult with the insured and explain the consequences of this process, otherwise they may be found to have acted in bad faith.[100]

94 (1990) 55 SASR 145.
95 (1990) 55 SASR 145, 154. See also *AMP Financial Planning Pty Ltd v CGU Insurance Ltd* (2005) 146 FCR 447, 475.
96 (1973) 130 CLR 1.
97 (1973) 130 CLR 1, 31.
98 (1973) 130 CLR 1, 27.
99 (1973) 130 CLR 1, 31–2.
100 *Horry v Tate & Lyle Refineries Ltd* [1982] 2 Lloyd's Rep 416.

11.5.4.8 Failing to disclose to the insured a conflict of interest

In *ACN 007 838 584 Pty Ltd v Zurich Australian Insurance Ltd*,[101] the insurer instructed solicitors to continue to act for the insured after forming the view that they were not liable to indemnify the insured. This gave rise to a situation of conflict of interest. In such circumstances, the court held, the insurer must advise and consult with the insured and not seek to influence the latter's defence of the proceedings. The failure to do so was deemed to be a breach of s 14 of the Act and might also constitute an election by the insurer to indemnify the insured notwithstanding that the claim might otherwise fall outside the policy.

11.5.4.9 Unreasonably withholding consent to a proposed course of action

At times an insurer and the insured may agree to a particular course of action during the life of an insurance contract, or one may propose particular conduct for the other to consider. In *Hobartville Stud Pty Ltd v Union Insurance Co Ltd*,[102] the plaintiff claimed $500 000 under a policy of insurance for a thoroughbred colt. The colt suffered from a vertebral malformation, and the veterinary opinion obtained by the insured recommended the colt be destroyed for humane reasons. The insurer resisted the claim, arguing that treatment could improve the colt's condition. The insured destroyed the colt. There are implications in the judgment that the insured's discretion in such situations is fettered by s 13 of the Act and that unreasonably withholding consent to a course of action *may* breach the duty of utmost good faith.

11.5.4.10 Failing to identify limits of obligations under a policy and to advise of certain risks

In *Nigel Watts Fashion Agencies Pty Ltd v GIO General Ltd*,[103] an employee injured at his workplace claimed workers compensation benefits from his employer as well as damages from the employer's landlord for common law negligence. The landlord cross-claimed against the employer, seeking indemnity under the lease (a condition of which provided that the lessee would indemnify the lessor against all actions and claims for which the lessor became liable in respect of injuries occurring in its premises). GIO ran the claim for the insured but lost on the cross-claim on the basis of a breach of the lease.

The court equated the statutory duty of utmost good faith to the requirement of candour in circumstances where there was a duty to speak. The court found that GIO had represented to the insured that it would indemnify it. It was further held that the duty of utmost good faith required GIO to communicate early and candidly to their insured the limit of their policy obligations, the liability of the insured, and the risks the insured faced, and that they may need to seek independent advice. It was held that the insurer was not candid in their dealings with the insured on these points.

101 (1997) 69 SASR 374.
102 (1991) 25 NSWLR 358.
103 (1994) 8 ANZ Ins Cas ¶61-235, 75,638.

11.5.4.11 Other miscellaneous scenarios

The courts have also identified other scenarios in which an insured may be found to have breached the duty of utmost good faith. Some examples include: declining a claim without genuine and credible reasons;[104] making unnecessary and/or unreasonable requests for information;[105] failing to disclose information critical to the insured's decision to insure against a particular risk;[106] and drafting policies in complex terms that are not easily understandable for an insured.[107]

11.6 The duty of disclosure

11.6.1 Background

Insureds have a duty to disclose certain matters to the insurer prior to an insurance contract being entered into. The obligation exists both at common law and under s 21 of the Act. The common law duty was far more onerous and required a great deal more of the insured. The relevant test of 'materiality' was formulated by Samuels J in *Mayne Nickless v Pegler*:

> The question is whether [the] information would have been relevant to the exercise of the insurer's option to accept or reject the insurance proposed. It seems to me that the test of materiality is this: a fact is material if it would have reasonably affected the mind of a prudent insurer in determining whether he will accept the insurance, and if so, at what premium and on what conditions.[108]

Under this test the insured's duty of disclosure was to be assessed from the perspective of the 'prudent insurer', and therefore required the insured to seek to understand what is relevant to an insurer's assessment. The consequences of not disclosing facts the insurer considered material was that the insurer was entitled to rescind the contract. The contract was void ab initio, the insurer released from the contract, and premiums refunded to the insured unless their actions were fraudulent.

The statutory form of the duty of disclosure is detailed in s 21 of the Act. This provision reads:

> (1) Subject to this Act, an insured has a duty to disclose to the insurer, before the relevant contract of insurance is entered into, every matter that is known to the insured, being a matter that:
>
> (a) the insured knows to be a matter relevant to the decision of the insurer whether to accept the risk and, if so, on what terms; or
>
> (b) a reasonable person in the circumstances could be expected to know to be a matter so relevant.

104 *Ziogos v FSS Trustee Corporation as Trustee of the First State Superannuation Scheme* [2015] NSWSC 1385.

105 *Haghis Persian Carpet Trading Co v General Accident Insurance Co New Zealand Ltd* (1990) 6 ANZ Ins Cas ¶61-003.

106 *Banque Financiere de la Cite SA v Westgate Insurance Co Ltd* [1989] 2 All ER 952.

107 *Stuart v Guardian Royal Exchange Assurance of New Zealand Ltd [No 2]* (1988) 5 ANZ Ins Cas ¶60-844.

108 [1974] 1 NSWLR 228, 239.

(2) The duty of disclosure does not require the disclosure of a matter:
 (a) that diminishes the risk;
 (b) that is of common knowledge;
 (c) that the insurer knows or in the ordinary course of the insurer's business as an insurer ought to know; or
 (d) as to which compliance with the duty of disclosure is waived by the insurer.
(3) Where a person:
 (a) failed to answer; or
 (b) gave an obviously incomplete or irrelevant answer to; a question included in a proposal form about a matter, the insurer shall be deemed to have waived compliance with the duty of disclosure in relation to the matter.

Under this provision, the requirement of disclosure is assessed by reference to a test with both subjective and objective elements. The subjective element is present in the requirement under s 21(1)(a) that the insured must disclose every matter that the insured knows will be relevant to the decision of whether the insurer will accept the risk and if so on what terms. The objective element exists in the requirement under s 21(1)(b) that the insured must disclose all that which a reasonable person in the circumstances of the insured would know or be expected to know was relevant to the insurer deciding whether or not to assume the risk to enter the contract of insurance.[109] The rationale for this test was explained by the High Court in *CGU Insurance Ltd v Porthouse*:

> A test of disclosure, which operates by reference to both the insured's actual knowledge and the knowledge of a reasonable person in the same circumstances, is calculated to balance the insured's duty to disclose and the insurer's right to information. The insurer is protected against claims where the insured's disclosure is inadequate because the insured is unreasonable, idiosyncratic or obtuse and the insured is protected from exclusion from cover, provided he or she does not fall below the standard of a reasonable person in the same position.[110]

11.6.2 Insurer's duty to notify the insured of duty of disclosure

Section 22 of the Act sets out the insurer's duty to inform the insured of their duty of disclosure under the Act. Information regarding the 'general nature and effect of the duty of disclosure' must be provided to the insured in writing.[111] If the policy is in respect of an eligible contract of insurance as referred to in s 21A or s 21B, then the same written explanation must be provided to the insured with respect to those provisions.[112] If the policy is in respect of a contract of life insurance, the insured must again be notified in writing as to the effect of s 31A.[113] Finally,

109 *Prime Forme Cutting Pty Ltd v Baltica General Insurance Co Ltd* (1990) 6 ANZ Ins Cas ¶61-028.
110 (2008) 235 CLR 103, 118.
111 Section 22(1)(a).
112 Section 22(1)(b).
113 Section 22(1)(c).

written notice must also be given that the duty of disclosure applies until the proposed contract is entered into.[114] Merely providing information as to the insured's disclosure obligations on the proposal form does not make the existence of the insured's duty of disclosure sufficiently well known to them.[115]

An insurer who fails to provide the necessary written explanation to the insured may not thereafter rely on the fact of the insured's non-disclosure (in contravention of s 21) to avoid the contract 'unless [the insured's] failure was fraudulent'.[116] An insurer who fails to discharge their duty to inform the insured of their duty of disclosure does not lose their right to avoid a contract for an insured's misrepresentation.[117]

Section 11(10) provides that if the insurer discharges their obligation under various provisions (including s 22) at the time the policy is entered into, it is unnecessary to comply with the obligation again in relation to renewals, extensions or reinstatements of the policy. Section 11 (10)(b) further provides that the obligation revives where a variation, and hence a new policy, is effected.[118]

11.6.3 When does the duty of disclosure arise?

The insured's duty of disclosure under s 21 arises prior to the parties entering the contract of insurance (including renewals, extensions or variations, subject to s 10),[119] and ceases once the contract has been entered into.[120] Until such time as the insurer accepts the proposal and thereby the risk, the insured must ensure that the proposal form reflects the relevant facts that they know, or a reasonable person would be expected to know, to be relevant, including facts that may have changed in the interim.[121]

Given that the duty under s 21 ceases once the contract is entered into, the violation of a contractual provision requiring the insured to disclose relevant facts during the life of the policy cannot be a breach of s 21. However, this may be remedied under s 54 of the Act as a breach of the insurance policy.[122]

11.6.4 The insured's actual knowledge test (s 21(1)(a))

The duty under s 21(1) applies only to matters *known* to the insured. Section 21(1)(a) specifically draws attention to the insured's actual subjective knowledge in this context. An insured cannot be expected to disclose matters of which they have no knowledge at all.[123]

114 Section 22(1)(d).

115 *Suncorp General Insurance Ltd v Cheihk* (1999) 10 ANZ Ins Cas ¶61-442.

116 Section 22(5).

117 *Dawes Underwriting Australia Pty Ltd v Roth* [2009] NSWCA 152, [40].

118 See *GIO General Ltd v Wallace* [2001] NSWCA 299.

119 Section 11(9); *Lumley General Insurance Ltd v Delphin* (1990) 6 ANZ Ins Cas ¶60-986.

120 *Australian Associated Motor Insurers Ltd v Ellis* (1990) 54 SASR 61; s 12 provides that the duty of good faith implied by s 13 is not to be used to extend the duty of disclosure to omissions made during the currency of the insurance contract.

121 *Prime Forme Cutting Pty Ltd v Baltica General Insurance Co Ltd* (1990) 6 ANZ Ins Cas ¶61-028.

122 See Section 11.11.1.

123 *Joel v Law Union & Crown Insurance Co* [1908] 2 KB 863. However, in some cases, a sufficiently credible opinion may need to be disclosed: *Prepaid Services Pty Ltd v Atradius Credit Insurance NV* (2013) 302 ALR 732. An opinion's relevance to the insurer's acceptance of the risk will depend on factors such

'The terms "known" and "knows" are used in their ordinary sense', and the question of whether a matter is known by the insured is one of fact.[124] The word 'knows' is strong and 'means considerably more than "believes" or "suspects" or even "strongly suspects"'.[125] By extension, the non-disclosure of facts that are genuinely forgotten clearly cannot constitute a breach of s 21.

In some cases, knowledge may be inferred. In *CIC Insurance Ltd v Midaz Pty Ltd*, the court stated: 'If an insured knows matter A which is not in itself relevant to insurance, but the insured should reasonably infer from matter A a further matter B which is so relevant, then the duty to disclose matters A and B arises.'[126]

While some appellate courts have suggested that the 'knowledge of relevant employees and agents, such as insurance brokers, must [also] be taken into account' and will normally suffice for the purposes of s 21 (given that most business transactions are effected through them),[127] the High Court has implied in obiter that this provision is instead restricted to 'the knowledge of the insured, and not of any insurance intermediary' such as an agent or broker.[128] The issue remains open.

An insured need only disclose matters relevant to the insurer's decision to *accept the risk*; s 21 (1)(a) does not extend to considerations (commercial, emotional or otherwise) relevant to the insurer's *assessment of the risk*, or to the entry into or renewal of the insurance contract itself.[129] Importantly, the actual insurer, and not a hypothetical insurer, is who is referred to in s 21.[130]

In *Twenty-First Maylux Pty Ltd v Mercantile Mutual Insurance (Australia) Ltd*,[131] a corporate insured had not disclosed to the insurer that one of their two directors had been convicted of knowingly being involved in the importation, and being in the possession of, cannabis resin. The same director had twice previously given false or misleading answers to questions on proposals for insurance with other insurers regarding prior convictions. The court found that the director believed that disclosure of the fact of criminal conviction would result in either the insurer not issuing the insurance or doing so only under special conditions, and that therefore the director had withheld relevant knowledge, enabling the insurer to avoid the contract under s 28(2).

The duty in s 21 will not, however, be breached where a non-disclosure is remedied prior to the policy being issued. Such was held in *GIO Insurance Ltd v Nader*,[132] where the insured failed to disclose the correct date upon which an accident occurred, with a view to obtaining more favourable cover. The insured subsequently sought to make proper disclosure prior to

as 'the subject matter of the opinion, the identity of the person holding it, the facts or premises upon which it is based and whether those facts or premises are true or believed by the insurer to be true': *Prepaid Services Pty Ltd v Atradius Credit Insurance NV* (2013) 302 ALR 732, 756.

124 *Commercial Union Assurance Co of Australia Ltd v Beard* (1999) 47 NSWLR 735, 745.

125 *Permanent Trustee Australia Ltd v FAI General Insurance Co Ltd (in liq)* (2003) 214 CLR 514, 531. See also *Australian Casualty of Life Ltd v Hall* (1999) 151 FLR 360.

126 (1998) 10 ANZ Ins Cas ¶61-394, 74-186.

127 *Commercial Union Assurance Co of Australia Ltd v Beard* (1999) 47 NSWLR 735, 745; *Lindsay v CIC Insurance* (1989) 16 NSWLR 673; *Macquarie Bank Ltd v National Mutual Life Association of Australasia Ltd* (1996) 40 NSWLR 543, 610–11; *Tosich v Tasman Investment Management Ltd* (2008) 250 ALR 274, 303.

128 *Permanent Trustee Australia Ltd v FAI General Insurance Co Ltd (in liq)* (2003) 214 CLR 514, 531.

129 *Permanent Trustee Australia Ltd v FAI General Insurance Co Ltd (in liq)* (2003) 214 CLR 514, 531–2.

130 *Twenty-First Maylux Pty Ltd v Mercantile Mutual Insurance (Australia) Ltd* (1989) 92 ALR 661, 665.

131 (1989) 92 ALR 661.

132 Unreported, Victorian Supreme Court, Nathan J, 7 April 1994.

the policy being issued. The insurer nonetheless alleged that the insured had breached s 21 by virtue of his prior dishonest conduct. However, Nathan J distinguished the insured's moral turpitude (which was corrected) from cases in which insureds had relied upon deliberate non-disclosures (as in *Twenty-First Maylux*). As such, the case fell outside the ambit of s 21.

11.6.5 The reasonable person test (s 21(1)(b))

Section 21(1)(b) provides an alternative test to determine whether a duty of disclosure arises under s 21(1). This provision requires disclosure of matters that 'a reasonable person in the circumstances' could be expected to know to be relevant to the decision of the insurer whether to accept the risk. As such, it serves partly to address issues of proof that may arise under the subjective s 21(1)(a) test.

It might well be necessary, when determining what a reasonable person could be expected to know, to consider the circumstances affecting the actual insured; however, s 21(1)(b) ultimately turns on consideration of a reasonable person's state of mind and not on the insured's state of mind.[133]

An important matter is what 'circumstances' are relevant under this provision. For example, does one take into account purely *extrinsic* factors (such as the circumstances in which the contract was made) or also consider *intrinsic* factors (such as the insured's personal circumstances, eg business acumen, language skills, culture, etc.)? Leading case law suggests the courts should only consider the former.[134] Relevant extrinsic factors include the mode and informality of discussions preceding entry into the insurance contract, the type of policy in issue, and any exposure to advertising and promotional material.[135]

Amendments to s 21(1)(b) that came into effect on 28 December 2015 have sought to further clarify the position by introducing 'two additional non-exclusive factors' that the court may consider when making a determination under this provision. Section 21(1)(b) now provides that the courts may have regard to factors 'including, but not limited to' (i) the nature and extent of the insurance cover to be provided under the relevant contract of insurance; and (ii) the class of persons who would ordinarily be expected to apply for insurance cover of that kind.

Some cases have considered the extrinsic factors relevant to determinations under s 21(1)(b). In *Delphin v Lumley General Insurance Ltd*,[136] the Western Australian District Court held that a reasonable person in the circumstances in which the insured found herself could have been expected to know that her prior convictions for cultivating cannabis with intent to sell or supply were relevant to the insurer's decision to accept the risk. However, a reasonable person would *not* have been expected to know that the insured's intermittent

133 *GIO General Ltd v Wallace* [2001] NSWCA 299, [23]; *CGU Insurance Ltd v Porthouse* (2008) 235 CLR 103, 118.

134 *CGU Insurance Ltd v Porthouse* (2008) 235 CLR 103, 118; *Twenty-First Maylux Pty Ltd v Mercantile Mutual Insurance (Australia) Ltd* [1990] VR 919; *HIH Casualty & General Insurance Australia Ltd v Dellavedova* (1999) 10 ANZ Ins Cas ¶61-431; *Dew v Suncorp Life & Superannuation Ltd* [2001] QSC 252; *McCabe v Royal & Sun Alliance Life Assurance Australia Ltd* (2003) 12 ANZ Ins Cas ¶90-119; *Stealth Enterprises Pty Ltd v Calliden Insurance Ltd* [2017] NSWCA 71, [41].

135 *Twenty-First Maylux Pty Ltd v Mercantile Mutual Insurance (Australia) Ltd* (1989) 92 ALR 661, 666.

136 (1989) 6 SR (WA) 161.

cannabis and heroin use was so relevant. The use of the premises for cultivation of cannabis involved risk to the premises themselves, and the conviction was material to the honesty and integrity of the plaintiff, such that both would have affected the insured's decision.[137] A reasonable person would not have considered personal drug use to do the same.

More recently, in *Stealth Enterprises Pty Ltd v Calliden Insurance Ltd*,[138] the appellant owned premises from which it operated a brothel. The premises were insured under a policy with the respondent. Following a fire at the premises, the appellant lodged an insurance claim that was denied by the respondent on the basis that the appellant had failed to comply with its duty of disclosure in s 21 of the Act. The appellant did not disclose that its sole director and manager were both members of the Comancheros bikie gang. The respondent argued that this was relevant to its decision to accept the risk given that 'members of the Comancheros, and businesses with which those members were associated, could become targets of bikie gang violence and conflict, resulting in property damage'.[139]

There was no evidence this was something the appellant *knew* to be relevant to the insurer's decision under s 21(1)(a). As such, applying s 21(1)(b), the court considered whether a reasonable person could be expected to know that the appellant's association with the Comancheros was relevant to the insurer's decision to accept the risk. The court found in favour of the appellant. Considering the relevant extrinsic factors, there was no obligation on the appellant to disclose this fact. Meagher JA (with whom Ward JA and Sackville AJA agreed) stated:

> In my view a reasonable person could not to be expected to know that the fact of the brothers' membership without more was so relevant. It may be accepted that such a person could be expected to appreciate that the membership association carried with it the possibility of violence involving members of bikie gangs. However that person is likely to have regarded that as a risk which arose by reason of the nature of the use of the premises and the character of the persons expected to be involved in that use. It was the sort of association the insurer would expect and take into account as part of the general risk of insuring a brothel; and there were no particular circumstances related to the association, such as the making of threats, that took it outside that general risk.[140]

11.6.6 Matters that need not be disclosed under s 21(1)

An insured's general disclosure requirements are qualified. Section 21(2) of the Act provides as follows:

> The duty of disclosure does not require the disclosure of a matter:
> (a) that diminishes the risk;
> (b) that is of common knowledge;

137 (1989) 6 SR (WA) 161, 175–6.
138 [2017] NSWCA 71.
139 [2017] NSWCA 71, [31].
140 [2017] NSWCA 71, [51].

(c) that the insurer knows or in the ordinary course of the insurer's business as an insurer ought to know; or
(d) as to which compliance with the duty of disclosure is waived by the insurer.

This provision effectively codifies a number of the key common law exceptions.[141] Section 21 (2)(a) is scarcely the subject of controversy or litigation. Section 21(2)(b) is more contentious as it is naturally difficult to determine the point at which knowledge can be deemed 'common'. In *Plasteel Windows Australia Pty Ltd v C E Heath Underwriting Agencies Pty Ltd*,[142] the plaintiff sued the insurer of the underwriter of its insurance policy with a third party (Sun Alliance). The plaintiff sought a declaration that C E Heath was bound to indemnify Sun Alliance. Cole J was required to consider the allegedly common practice of NIBA members charging clients undisclosed fees. The practice was exposed via public investigation in 1983 and prompted an educational campaign as to the obligation upon brokers to disclose any fees charged by them to clients. By 1984, the practice had all but ceased. C E Heath and Sun Alliance entered into a contract of insurance in 1986. Sun Alliance did not disclose that it was engaging in this practice at the time. Given that the practice was so rare at the time, it was held that an insurer would not assume from common knowledge that the practice was continuing. Sun Alliance therefore could not rely upon s 21(2)(b) to escape its obligation to disclose its behaviour.

In *Evans v Sirius Insurance Co Ltd*,[143] Beach J observed that, before an insurer could be said to have knowledge of a particular matter under s 21(2)(c), it had to be established that the knowledge was possessed by a 'responsible officer of the company who either appreciated the significance of the knowledge, or should have appreciated its significance'. Specifically, the officer 'must know that the company has before it a proposal for insuring the particular risk and must know, or should know, that the information in his possession is material to the risk or the terms upon which the risk should be insured'.[144]

Merely having records that are a *source* of knowledge is insufficient; the information must be *actually known* to the insurer, otherwise it is too remote.[145] As such, in *Commercial Union Assurance Co of Australia v Beard*,[146] the NSW Court of Appeal held that a newspaper article in the insurer's files did not impute knowledge of the substance of the article. It held that knowledge within the meaning of s 21(2)(c) means 'actual knowledge. The relevant matter must be known to an appropriate officer or agent of the insurer or contained in current official records.'[147] Ordinarily, it was stated, the 'appropriate officers' will be those who are handling the particular insurance on behalf of the insurer.

The digital age has added another layer of complexity to s 21(2)(c), given that voluminous records are now typically kept in electronic databases by most insurers and can be searched fairly efficiently. As such, it might be said that an insurer can more easily be deemed to 'know' electronically stored information (which might be remotely accessible between different

141 See *Carter v Boehm* (1766) 3 Burr 1905.
142 (1990) 19 NSWLR 400.
143 (1986) 4 ANZ Ins Cas ¶60-755, 74,555.
144 (1986) 4 ANZ Ins Cas ¶60-755, 74,555.
145 *Macfie v SGIO (Qld)* (1985) 3 ANZ Ins Cas ¶60-606. See, especially, at 78,688–9.
146 (1999) 47 NSWLR 735.
147 (1999) 47 NSWLR 735, 750.

outlets). However, in *Kotku Bread Pty Ltd v Vero Insurance Ltd*,[148] Applegarth J dismissed this theory, stating:

> The march of the computer does not require insurers to undertake costly searches throughout their records, at a cost which is likely to be passed on to policyholders, to locate information that was acquired years earlier in respect of a proposed transaction that came to nothing in respect of an entity which was not thought to be a client.

In this case, it was held that the employees of the insurer (Vero), who were transitioning Kotku's information from Suncorp to Vero to inform a proposed new policy for insurance of premises, did not know and could not reasonably have been expected to know that another broker had provided information about those premises in 2006, particularly given that the transaction did not proceed at that time.

Finally, under s 21(2)(d), an insurer may waive compliance with the duty of disclosure. This may occur in a number of ways. For example, if an insured provides information that should be sufficient to put the sagacious insurer on notice, and the insurer fails to make further enquiries, the insured may not be culpable under s 21(1). The ALRC, referring to judicial and academic opinion, has stated the test in the following terms:

> If the insurer receives information from the assured or his agent which, by its content or form, should suggest a doubt to the mind of the reasonably prudent insurer and put him on inquiry, then, if he omits to make the check or inquiry, assuming it can be made simply, he will be held to have waived disclosure of the material facts which that inquiry would necessarily have revealed.[149]

In *Devine v Sun Alliance Australia Ltd*,[150] the insurer denied the plaintiff's claim following a fire at his electro-plating business. The insurer alleged that the plaintiff breached his duty of disclosure under s 21 for failing to disclose that he had been charged with a number of criminal offences. The plaintiff wrote to the insurer noting that he had been charged with arson and stating that he had not been cleared of 'this charges' yet. He did not disclose that he had been charged with several other offences, including deception and larceny. Instead, he alleged that the plural 'charges' put the insurer on notice that there might be more than one charge and that its failure to make further enquiries therefore amounted to a waiver under s 21(2)(d). Giles J rejected this argument, holding that the reference to 'this charges' was plainly a reference to the arson charge only, both because of the flow of the letter and 'because the letter was in terms inconsistent with there being any other involvement with the police'.[151]

An insurer may also waive their right under s 21(2)(d) to disclosure by the form or nature of the question or questions asked of an insured. In *QBE Insurance Ltd v Giampolo*,[152] the insurer's proposal form for motor vehicle insurance enquired as to whether the insured had had 'any traffic convictions (excluding parking fines) in the last five years'. The insured had

148 [2012] QSC 109, [174].
149 Australian Law Reform Commission, *Report on Insurance Contracts* (ALRC, 1982), paragraph 160. The Commission cited F Rose, *MacGillivray and Parkington on Insurance Law* (Sweet & Maxwell, London, 7th edn, 1981), paragraph 685f in support of this proposition.
150 Unreported, NSW Supreme Court, Giles J, 18 June 1992.
151 Unreported, NSW Supreme Court, Giles J, 18 June 1992, 14.
152 [1993] ACTSC 106.

received four traffic infringement notices but had only been formally convicted in court twice, and so disclosed only the two convictions. The insurer resisted the claim on the basis that the insured did not disclose all four offences. Higgins J held that the phrasing of the question in the proposal form reasonably led the insured to conclude that information as to traffic infringement notices was not required and that only court convictions were to be disclosed. It would also have done the same to a reasonable person in the circumstances. As such, the insurer was deemed to have waived compliance with the duty of disclosure.

An insurer's failure to ask sufficient questions on a matter for disclosure may also amount to a waiver under s 21(2)(d). In *General Accident Insurance Asia Ltd v Sakr*,[153] the insured took out insurance over two shops and an attached residence from June 1994 to 1995. The insurance covered the buildings, loss of rent, and public liability. One of the shops and the residence became, and remained, vacant from December 1994, as did the other shop from July 1995. The insured phoned the insurer in June 1996 to notify them that the properties had been unoccupied for a long time and to cancel the public liability and loss of rent coverage. In June 1997, the insurer sent a renewal invitation for the amended coverage until June 1998, which was accepted. The policy allowed the insurer to cancel the policy if the premises became and remained unoccupied for 30 days or more after commencement. When fire damaged the premises in September 1997, the insurer denied the claim on the basis that the insured had not provided notice of the unoccupancy.

The Court of Appeal rejected this argument and held that the insurer had waived the obligation of disclosure pursuant to s 21(2)(d). Giles JA, with whom Hodgson JA and Sperling J agreed, stated that 'any deficiency in the appellant's knowledge of the period and currency of unoccupancy was ... due to [the insurer's] waiver of (further) compliance with the duty of disclosure'.[154]

Determining whether the phrasing of a particular question waives disclosure of additional related information is naturally difficult. If the scope of the question is sufficiently narrow so as to indicate, either expressly or by implication, that disclosure of further information is not required, then this will enliven s 21(2)(d) and relieve the insured of the obligation to make further disclosure.[155] Similarly, if the question has directed attention away from disclosure either because of the question asked or by the form that the answer was expected to take, this may also amount to a waiver.[156] The ultimate enquiry, which very much depends upon the nature of the question posed, is whether the insurer consented to the omission of the particular information in issue.[157]

The mere fact that a proposal form includes 'yes/no' questions and thereby limits the form of the answer does *not* necessarily qualify the insured's duty to disclose *other* relevant information. In *Petkovski v Government Insurance Office of New South Wales*,[158] the insured was asked whether keyed window locks existed on all accessible windows to the insured premises.

153 [2001] NSWCA 402.
154 [2001] NSWCA 402, [32]. See also *Petkovski v Government Insurance Office of New South Wales* (unreported, NSW Court of Appeal, Mahoney, Sheller and Cripps JJA, 20 September 1993).
155 *Petkovski v Government Insurance Office of New South Wales* (unreported, NSW Court of Appeal, Mahoney, Sheller and Cripps JJA, 20 September 1993), 4; *Schoolman v Hall* [1951] 1 Lloyd's Rep 139.
156 *Petkovski v Government Insurance Office of New South Wales* (unreported, NSW Court of Appeal, Mahoney, Sheller and Cripps JJA, 20 September 1993), 4.
157 *Synergy Health (UK) Ltd v CGU* [2011] Lloyd's Rep IR 500.
158 Unreported, NSW Court of Appeal, Mahoney, Sheller and Cripps JJA, 20 September 1993.

The insured answered 'yes' despite one window being padlocked on the outside. Mahoney JA opined that the inference to be drawn from the question and optional answers was simply that the insurer sought to know if something satisfying the description of a 'keyed window lock' existed on the windows. As such, further disclosure was waived. The key to the construction of the insurance proposal form is to ask 'whether a reasonable person reading the form would be justified in thinking that the insurer had restricted its right to receive all material information'.[159]

Finally, an insurer may waive the requirement for the insured to disclose particular information where it fails to follow up incomplete or irrelevant answers (eg by requiring the insured to complete them or provide a relevant answer).[160]

11.6.7 Disclosure before contract originally entered into (s 21A)

Section 21A of the Act applies to *eligible contracts of insurance*, defined in reg 6(2) of the *Insurance Contracts Regulations 2017* (Cth) as being one which:

> (a) is for new business; and
>
> (b) is wholly in a class of contracts that is declared to be a class of contracts in relation to which Division 1 of Part V of the Act applies.

In a note to this provision, those classes are defined as being motor vehicle insurance, home buildings insurance, home contents insurance, sickness and accident insurance, consumer credit insurance, and travel insurance. Under reg 6(3), an insurance contract for new business that is not mentioned in reg 6(2) may still be an eligible contract under s 21A where the insurer provides notice of the nature and effect of s 21A to the insured (whether under s 22(1) or otherwise). Section 21A only concerns the original entry into eligible contracts of insurance and does not apply to renewals, extensions, reinstatements or variations of such contracts.[161]

The purpose of s 21A is to assist consumers to better understand their disclosure obligations, particularly with respect to domestic and personal lines insurance,[162] which have often proven problematic. The provision requires insurers to ask specific questions in respect of proposed eligible contracts of insurance. The failure to do so amounts to a deemed waiver of the insured's duty of disclosure.

Section 21A(2)–(4) provides as follows:

> **Position of the insurer**
>
> (2) Before the contract is originally entered into, the insurer may request the insured to answer one or more specific questions that are relevant to the decision of the insurer whether to accept the risk and, if so, on what terms.

---

159 *Wayne Wilkinson Insurance Ltd v Kaiaua Downs Ltd* (1995) 8 ANZ Ins Cas ¶61-248, 75,785–75,786.

160 Section 21(3).

161 Section 21A(1).

162 These types of insurance extend to products such a motor vehicle insurance, health insurance, life insurance, and home and contents insurance. Injury or loss in any of these categories has the potential to leave individuals and families financially ruined, and so ensuring adequate and legally valid coverage is vital, hence the emphasis upon proper disclosure.

(3) If the insurer does not make a request in accordance with subsection (2), the insurer is taken to have waived compliance with the duty of disclosure in relation to the contract.

(4) If the insurer:

(a) makes a request in accordance with subsection (2); and

(b) requests the insured to disclose to the insurer any other matter that would be covered by the duty of disclosure in relation to the contract;

then the insurer is taken to have waived compliance with the duty of disclosure in relation to that other matter.

The effect of s 21A(3) is that if an insurer does not ask the specific questions relevant to its decision to accept the risk, it waives compliance with the insured's duty of disclosure under s 21. This places the onus upon the insurer to ensure it asks the questions appropriate to the particular risk it is contemplating accepting, and prevents it from falling back on the insured's breach of the general duty of disclosure under s 21 as an excuse to avoid liability. Section 21A(4) provides similar protection for the insured in that the insurer cannot, in the event of a dispute, rely upon the general duty of disclosure if a request to disclose any other relevant matters has been made with respect to an eligible contract under s 21A. Further, under s 21A(5), where in response to a request under sub-s (2) and in the provision of answers to specific questions from the insurer, the insured discloses each matter known to them and that a reasonable person could have been expected to disclose in the circumstances, the insured is taken to have complied with the duty of disclosure in relation to that contract.

11.6.8 Disclosure before contract renewed (s 21B)

Section 21B of the Act also applies to eligible contracts of insurance, as defined in s 21A. However, this provision concerns *renewals* of such contracts. It is substantially similar in effect, although under s 21B(3) the insured may, prior to renewal, require the insured to answer further specific questions and/or provide the insured with a copy of any matter previously disclosed (in relation to the contract) and require the insured to disclose any changes to that matter or confirm that there are no changes. Failure to ask such questions or to provide a copy of the previously disclosed matter amounts to a waiver of the insured's duty of disclosure.[163] If an insurer does make a request under s 21B(3) and requires the insured to disclose any other matter that would ordinarily be covered by s 21 in relation to the renewed contract, the insurer is taken to have waived compliance with the duty of disclosure in relation to that other matter.[164] The same goes for requests to update the insurer as to changed circumstances.[165] Subsections (7)–(10) of s 21B reflect the insured's position in each situation and stipulate when the s 21 duty of disclosure has been taken to have been complied with.

As with s 21A, an insurer is obligated under s 22 of the Act to inform the insured in writing as to the general nature and effect of s 21B.

163 Section 21B(4). See also s 21B(12), which clarifies the position with respect to waivers for previous disclosures or failures to disclose.

164 Section 21B(5).

165 Section 21B(6).

11.6.9 Liability of co-insureds

Section 21 does not deal specifically with co-insureds. In certain situations, material non-disclosures may be made by only *one* co-insured. In *Advance (NSW) Insurance Agencies Pty Ltd v Matthews*,[166] the majority of the High Court held that the Act did not distinguish between joint and composite contracts of insurance. Section 21 imposes the duty to disclose material facts on each insured, and not upon the insureds jointly.[167] The knowledge of one insured is thereby imputed to all, and each must endeavour to disclose what all individually know.[168] Therefore, s 28 applies where one co-insured has failed to disclose a material fact, even though the other co-insured was unaware of the non-disclosure.

In some cases the wording of insurance policies may indicate a modification of the insurer's right to deny insurance cover to an innocent co-insured. The insurer's right of avoidance was modified by the terms of the policy in *Sherry v FAI General Insurance Co Ltd (in liq)*.[169] In that case, a partner of the insured firm engaged in fraudulent dealings with the plaintiff's property. The clause in the policy – about claims arising by reason of fraud on the part of the insured or their partners or their employees – was held to have protected the innocent partners of the insured and the companies in which those innocent co-insureds held interests.

11.7 Third parties to the insurance contract

Trident v McNiece Brothers Pty Ltd[170] was a seminal case in which a crane driver not a party to the insurance contract, but named as a person entitled to a benefit under it (as a subcontractor injured on a worksite while under the insured's direction), was able to recover under the policy. The High Court considered that the privity rule should be circumvented in the case of third party beneficiaries. The Act was not in effect at the time the incident occurred and was litigated and so was inapplicable; however, it would have ultimately delivered the same result.

In order to conclusively overcome the limitation of the common law doctrine of privity, and to provide protection for third party beneficiaries under an insurance contract, ss 48 and 48A[171] were inserted into the *Insurance Contracts Act 1984* (Cth).

Section 48(1) of the Act provides:

> **Contracts of general insurance – entitlements of third party beneficiaries**
> A third party beneficiary under a contract of general insurance has a right to recover from the insurer, in accordance with the contract, the amount of any loss suffered by the third party beneficiary even though the third party beneficiary is not a party to the contract.

166 (1989) 166 CLR 606. See also *P Samuel & Co Ltd v Dumas* [1924] AC 431.
167 (1989) 166 CLR 606, 616.
168 (1989) 166 CLR 606, 621.
169 (2003)12 ANZ Ins Cas ¶61-561.
170 (1988) 165 CLR 107.
171 Section 48A pertains specifically to life insurance policies for the benefit of third party beneficiaries.

A third party beneficiary is a person who is not a party to the actual contract but who is 'specified or referred to' within it, whether by name or otherwise, as someone who is entitled to benefit from the insurance cover provided.[172] Identifying third party beneficiaries involves careful construction of the policy.[173] In *Barroora Pty Ltd v Provincial Insurance Ltd*,[174] 'the insured' was defined within the policy as referring to those persons 'so named in the certificates', which only listed the first plaintiff. As such, the second plaintiff was excluded.

Importantly, s 48 does not *alter* rights or obligations, nor extend the scope of coverage under the relevant policy; it merely gives standing to particular non-parties to sue on it and recover the amount of their losses from the insurer in accordance with the terms of the contract (notwithstanding that they are not a party to it).[175]

The third party beneficiary has the same obligations to the insurer, and the same defences as an insurer would have against the insured.[176] Consequently, the insured's violation of the duties of good faith or disclosure may prejudice the third party's claim.[177] As to whether the general acts or omissions of the insured (including breaches of the policy) can also be treated as if they were those of the third party, judicial opinion is slightly less certain. In *C E Heath Casualty & General Insurance Ltd v Grey*,[178] the court suggested that where a policy condition was breached, the consequences for the third party will depend on the precise wording of the policy, and on whether the terms of the policy specified the consequences of such a breach specifically in relation to third parties.

Another relevant and important question is whether third party beneficiaries themselves have any disclosure obligations, as the insured does under s 21. The obligations of third parties under the contract of insurance are limited by the definition of the 'insured' in s 11(1) of the Act, which, while it includes the 'proposed insured', does *not* include third parties.[179] Indeed, Clarke JA (with whom Meagher JA agreed) in *C E Heath Casualty & General Insurance Ltd v Grey* noted that 'there is no obligation to disclose, or not misrepresent, before a contract is entered into, imposed upon a person entitled to recover the amount of a loss pursuant to s 48(1)', and that '[n]othing in s 28 provides that anything he or she does, or fails to do, before the contract is concluded in any way disentitles him or her from successfully maintaining a claim'.[180] However, according to Mahoney JA, in limited circumstances under the *general law* (such as in 'trust cases' involving trustees and 'benefit cases' involving beneficiaries with revocable interests), the principle of utmost good faith may require third parties to make

172 Section 11(1).

173 *Barroora Pty Ltd v Provincial Insurance Ltd* (1992) 26 NSWLR 170, 174. In *New Arabian Horse Association Inc v Olympic Co-ordination Authority* [2005] NSWCA 210, it was held that a reference to a party 'to be named on [the] policy as an interested party' was a reference to the third party beneficiary and attracted the application of s 48.

174 (1992) 26 NSWLR 170.

175 *GIO Australia Ltd v P Ward Civil Engineering Pty Ltd* [2000] NSWSC 371; *General Motors Acceptance Corporation Australia v RACQ Insurance Ltd* [2003] QSC 80; *Zurich Australian Insurance Ltd v Metals & Minerals Insurance Pte Ltd* (2010) 240 CLR 391.

176 See s 48(2)–(3).

177 *Commonwealth Bank of Australia v Baltica General Insurance Co Ltd* (1992) 28 NSWLR 579; *C E Heath Casualty & General Insurance Ltd v Grey* (1993) 32 NSWLR 25.

178 (1993) 32 NSWLR 25.

179 See *C E Heath Casualty & General Insurance Ltd v Grey* (1993) 32 NSWLR 25, 36.

180 (1993) 32 NSWLR 25, 46; applied and approved in *ABN AMRO Bank NV v Bathurst Regional Council* (2014) 309 ALR 445, 772.

disclosure to insurers.[181] It was noted that this will very much depend upon the facts of the individual case and, in any event, was separate entirely to the duty under s 21, which does not apply to third party beneficiaries.

11.8 Misrepresentation

Misrepresentation is provided for under ss 23–27 of the Act. 'Misrepresentation' describes the violation of the insured's duty to provide truthful and accurate responses to an insurer's questions, whether in the proposal form or otherwise. This can be contrasted with the duty of disclosure, which relates to the insured's duty to disclose pertinent information.

Prior to the Act, there existed at common law a practice of including 'basis of the contract' clauses in insurance contracts. In essence, these clauses warranted that the answers given to the questions in the proposal form were true and correct in all respects, and acknowledged that the proposal formed the basis of the contract between the insurer and the insured. Consequently, any inaccuracy in the proposal amounted to a breach of condition in the insurance contract, entitling the insurer to avoid liability.[182]

This position has now been amended by s 24 of the Act, which provides that a statement made by (or attributable to) the insured in or in connection with an insurance contract regarding the existence of a state of affairs 'does not have effect as a warranty but has effect as though it were a statement made to the insurer by the insured during the negotiations for the contract but before it was entered into'. This provision ensures both that insurers cannot avoid the Act's provisions relating to remedies for misrepresentation (through incorporation of representations as terms of the insurance contract) and that the basic rights and obligations of the parties remain the same notwithstanding how they are phrased within the policy.

There is often an association between misunderstanding of a question and a subsequent misrepresentation. While there is no provision addressing ambiguity in an insurer's questions generally, s 23 of the Act does provide some protection for insureds seeking cover when becoming a member of a superannuation, retirement or other group life scheme. If a reasonable person in the circumstances would have understood the question to have the meaning that the insured apparently understood it to have, that is the meaning that will be assigned to the question.

11.8.1 Statements that are not misrepresentations

Section 26(1) provides that a false statement is not a misrepresentation if the person making it believed the statement to be true and a reasonable person in the circumstances would also have believed it to be true. The onus of proof in this regard lies with the insured.[183] The insured, or a reasonable person in their situation, is not to be imbued with knowledge or

181 (1993) 32 NSWLR 25, 37.

182 *Yorkville Nominees Pty Ltd (in liq) v Lissenden* (1986) 160 CLR 475, 480–1.

183 *Plasteel Windows Australia Pty Ltd v C E Heath Underwriting Agencies Pty Ltd* (1990) 19 NSWLR 400, 407; *Sagacious Legal Pty Ltd v Wesfarmers General Insurance Ltd [No 4]* (2010) 268 ALR 108, 120.

understanding they did not have. For example, when providing a response to a query regarding a medical condition, the insured cannot be expected to know as much as a doctor.[184]

Section 26(2) provides that an insured's statement will not be taken to be a misrepresentation unless the insured knew, or a reasonable person in the circumstances could be expected to have known, that the statement would have been relevant to the insurer's decision whether and on what terms to accept the risk. The onus of proof therefore rests upon the insurer.[185] Importantly, this provision makes no assumptions as to the truth or falsity of the insured's statement; it merely clarifies that 'no statement in a proposal is capable of amounting to a misrepresentation unless it satisfies the prescribed test of relevance'.[186]

Section 27 relates to an insured's failure to properly answer the insurer's questions. Pursuant to this section, an insured is not taken to have made a misrepresentation 'by reason only that the person failed to answer a question included in a proposal form or gave an obviously incomplete or irrelevant answer to such a question'. There is some overlap here with the insured's duty of disclosure under s 21. Under s 21(3), where an insured has failed to answer or given an obviously incomplete or irrelevant answer to a question in a proposal form about a matter, the insurer will be deemed to have waived compliance with the duty of disclosure in relation to the matter. The rationale is that information which is plainly incomplete should serve to put an insurer on notice, such that if it fails to inquire, it is deemed to have waived its right to rely upon the insured's misrepresentation to avoid liability.

In *Prepaid Services Pty Ltd v Atradius Credit Insurance NV*, the court held:

> Under the common law the meaning conveyed by the answer to a question in a proposal, and whether that answer is incomplete, is determined objectively by reference to its 'fair and reasonable' construction. The question and answer must be considered together to ascertain the effect of the answer given or statement made; the question by reference to what a reasonable proponent would fairly have understood it to mean and the answer by reference to what that reasonable person would fairly have understood it to convey to the insurer.[187]

The court further observed that the critical words in s 27 are 'by reason only', as they clarify that the provision is directed to misrepresentations arising *solely* because of the insured's failure to answer or their provision of an obviously incomplete or irrelevant answer. Such misrepresentations 'include those made by a negative answer which is inferred only from the fact of the incomplete or partial answer as well as those which result from a contractual term having that effect'.[188]

In *Orb Holdings Pty Ltd v Lombard Insurance*,[189] the defendant described the insured premises as being constructed of 'brick/iron'. While the building had an iron roof and two of its walls were made of brick, the rest of it – including the remaining walls, roof trusses and

184 *NRG Victory Australia Ltd v Hudson* [2003] WASCA 291, [52].

185 *Plasteel Windows Australia Pty Ltd v C E Heath Underwriting Agencies Pty Ltd* (1990) 19 NSWLR 400, 407; *Schaffer v Royal & Sun Alliance Life Assurance Australia Ltd* [2003] QCA 182.

186 *Plasteel Windows Australia Pty Ltd v C E Heath Underwriting Agencies Pty Ltd* (1990) 19 NSWLR 400, 408.

187 (2013) 302 ALR 732, 748. See also *Deaves v CML Fire & General Insurance Co Ltd* (1979) 143 CLR 24.

188 (2013) 302 ALR 732, 749.

189 [1995] 2 Qd R 51.

floor – was primarily constructed from wood. The defendant had written 'As Per Schedule Attached' and 'See Survey Report' on the proposal form. When the building was damaged by fire, the plaintiff insurer denied the claim on the basis of misrepresentation. The defendant argued that the response was 'obviously incomplete' under s 27 and contingent upon reference to the documents referred to by the defendant in the policy. Fitzgerald P (agreeing with Davies JA and Thomas J) found in favour of the insurer, stating that the defendant's handwritten note:

> may have suggested that additional information was or would be available in such a report. However, it would not necessarily follow that the information given was incomplete so that it cannot be said that it was 'obviously incomplete'. It is a quite sensible reading of the note directing attention to the 'Survey Report' that it meant that the report would provide confirmation and perhaps further details of the information contained in the proposal.[190]

It was open to the insurer to infer that the survey report merely confirmed, or expanded upon, the answer given in the proposal form.[191]

11.9 Remedies

Section 33 provides that the remedies for non-disclosure and misrepresentation by the insured, specified in Division 3 of the Act, are exclusive of any right that the insurer has otherwise than under the Act. The effect of this provision is that the insurer cannot by contract possess a greater range of remedies (with respect to non-disclosure and misrepresentation) than those conferred by Division 3. This division therefore operates as an exclusive code of remedies to address these particular forms of conduct.[192]

11.9.1 Non-disclosure and misrepresentation under contracts of general insurance (s 28)

Section 28 applies in situations where the insured failed to comply with the duty of disclosure or made a misrepresentation to the insurer before the contract was entered into. However, it only applies if the insurer would not have entered into the contract, for the same premium and on the same terms, but for the non-disclosure or misrepresentation.[193] Conversely if the insurer would have gone ahead with the contract, even with the non-disclosure or misrepresentation, s 28 will not apply.

Pursuant to s 28(2), if the non-disclosure or misrepresentation was fraudulent, the insurer can avoid the contract.[194] If the non-disclosure or misrepresentation was innocent, the insurer cannot avoid the contract but may, under s 28(3), reduce its liability to the amount that would place it in the position it would have been in without the non-disclosure or misrepresentation.

190 [1995] 2 Qd R 51, 53.
191 [1995] 2 Qd R 51, 53.
192 *Advance (NSW) Insurance Agencies Pty Ltd v Matthews* (1989) 166 CLR 606, 615. See also *Macquarie Underwriting Pty Ltd v Permanent Custodians Ltd* (2007) 240 ALR 519, 524.
193 Section 28(1).
194 Subject to the court's discretion to overlook the fraud under s 31, to be discussed shortly.

As such, s 28 of the Act modifies the common law position that traditionally allowed an insurer to avoid the contract for either a fraudulent or innocent non-disclosure or misrepresentation.

It is critical, under s 28, to establish whether a non-disclosure or misrepresentation is 'fraudulent'. In the case of non-disclosure, it is arguable that it must be deliberate in order to be fraudulent.[195] However, some cases suggest that s 28(2) is *not* restricted to breaches of the duty of disclosure under s 21(1)(a) and that *reckless* non-disclosure (perpetrated without care as to whether the matter was relevant and should be disclosed or not, or without belief in the matter's truth) may suffice.[196] The fact that a reasonable person in the circumstances could be expected to know that a matter not disclosed was relevant for the purposes of s 21(1)(b) may, if deemed reckless, sustain a finding that the misrepresentation by non-disclosure was made without belief in its truth.[197]

In the case of a misrepresentation, the authorities are more settled and suggest that it will be 'fraudulent' where it is perpetrated either deliberately *or* recklessly (without care whether it be true or false).[198] Making a misrepresentation *carelessly* is not sufficient; the insured must be shown to have been 'consciously indifferent' and lacked honest belief in the truth of what was being said.[199]

Unlike s 28(2), which allows the insurer to avoid the contract, s 28(3) of the Act allows for *reduction in liability* under that contract. Section 28(3) provides as follows:

> If the insurer is not entitled to avoid the contract or, being entitled to avoid the contract (whether under subsection (2) or otherwise) has not done so, the liability of the insurer in respect of a claim is reduced to the amount that would place the insurer in a position in which the insurer would have been if the failure had not occurred or the misrepresentation had not been made.

As such, if a non-disclosure or misrepresentation was *innocent*, the contract cannot be void under s 28(2) for want of fraud; however, the liability of the insurer with respect to the claim may be reduced under s 28(3) by the amount that the non-disclosure or misrepresentation prejudiced the insurer. That is to say, liability is reduced by the amount representing the position the insurer would have been in had the misrepresentation or non-disclosure not occurred.[200] This may, as discussed shortly, conceivably reduce liability to *nil*.

Had the insured properly represented or disclosed the relevant fact, the insurer may have done one of three things: (1) they may have not issued the policy at all; (2) they may have issued the policy, but at a higher premium and on condition that the insured adhere to

195 See, for example, *Advance (NSW) Insurance Agencies Pty Ltd v Matthews* (1988) 12 NSWLR 250, 256; cited in *New Cap Reinsurance Corporation Ltd (in liq) v Daya* [2010] NSWSC 1226, [42].

196 *Plasteel Windows Australia Pty Ltd v C E Heath Underwriting Agencies Pty Ltd* (1990) 19 NSWLR 400; *Twenty-First Maylux Pty Ltd v Mercantile Mutual Insurance (Australia) Ltd* (1989) 92 ALR 661, 667; *New Cap Reinsurance Corporation Ltd (in liq) v Daya* [2010] NSWSC 1226, [44].

197 *Plasteel Windows Australia Pty Ltd v C E Heath Underwriting Agencies Pty Ltd* (1990) 19 NSWLR 400.

198 *Advance (NSW) Insurance Agencies Pty Ltd v Matthews* (1987) 4 ANZ Ins Cas ¶60-813; *Plasteel Windows Australia Pty Ltd v C E Heath Underwriting Agencies Pty Ltd* (1990) 19 NSWLR 400; *Von Braun v Australian Associated Motor Insurers Ltd* (1998) 135 ACTR 1; *Prepaid Services Pty Ltd v Atradius Credit Insurance NV* (2013) 302 ALR 732.

199 *Tyndall Life Insurance Co Ltd v Chisholm* (2000) 11 ANZ Ins Cas ¶90-104; *Dawes Underwriting Australia Pty Ltd v Roth* [2009] NSWCA 152.

200 *Zurich Australian Insurance Ltd v Contour Mobel Pty Ltd* [1991] 2 VR 146, 151.

additional terms; or (3) they may have provided cover on the same terms and premium. Under s 28(3), an insurer's liability can therefore feasibly be reduced to nil given that the insurer may not have elected to insure the risk at all if properly informed.[201] In other words, the damage suffered by the insurer is the total amount of the claim made against it. In line with the general principles of contract law, the goal is ultimately to place the insurer in the position it would have been in had truthful disclosure been made.[202]

In many cases, it may even be appropriate to account for a refund of the premium paid (so the insurer does not end up in a better position than it would have been in had proper disclosure or representations been made and cover refused).[203] This would particularly be so where the insured's conduct was innocent.[204]

If the insurer would have accepted the risk but at a different premium, its loss will logically be the difference between the two premiums. That is, its liability will be reduced by the amount of the theoretical increase in premium. If the insurer would have accepted the risk on different terms (whether at the same premium or not), the insurer will be liable to the extent it would have been had the different term(s) been included.

If the insurer seeks a remedy under s 28(3), it bears the onus of proving that it would not have entered into the insurance contract, for the same premium and on the same terms as it did, had the relevant disclosures been made or misrepresentations not been made.[205]

Given that each renewal of a policy amounts to a new contract of insurance, any claims under s 28 must relate to the *current* policy. Where the insured has made claims under past policies, prior to the discovery of the misrepresentation or non-disclosure, the insurer may retrospectively undertake an action in recovery on the basis of contractual mistake.

McNeill v O'Kane[206] illustrates the importance of the insurer providing evidence of how they would have responded had the insured made the relevant disclosures. The insured took out fire insurance for hotel premises and represented that the premises were fitted with a back-to-base (externally monitored) alarm system, which they were not. The insurer tendered as evidence their underwriting guidelines, which expressly required all metropolitan and regional hotels to have back-to-base alarms installed. The insurer's evidence also demonstrated that the guideline criteria were strictly applied in practice. They were thereby able to prove that, had they known of the true circumstances of the hotel, they would not have entered the insurance contract on the same terms and conditions.

201 *Lindsay v CIC Insurance* (1989) 16 NSWLR 673; *Ayoub v Lombard Insurance Co (Australia) Pty Ltd* (1989) 5 ANZ Ins Cas ¶60-933; *Twenty-First Maylux Pty Ltd v Mercantile Mutual Insurance (Australia) Ltd* [1990] VR 919; *Zurich Australian Insurance Ltd v Contour Mobel Pty Ltd* [1991] 2 VR 146; *CIC Insurance Ltd v Midaz Pty Ltd* (1998) 10 ANZ Ins Cas ¶61-394. See also *Unity Insurance Brokers Pty Ltd v Rocco Pezzano Pty Ltd* (1998) 192 CLR 603; *Green v CGU Insurance Ltd* (2008) 67 ACSR 398; *Michail v Australian Alliance Insurance Co Ltd* (2014) 67 MVR 21.

202 *Lindsay v CIC Insurance Ltd* (1989) 16 NSWLR 673, 687. See also Australian Law Reform Commission, *Report on Insurance Contracts* (ALRC, 1982), paragraph 194.

203 *Lindsay v CIC Insurance* (1989) 16 NSWLR 673, 687.

204 See the discussion and authorities cited in D Chantler, 'Insurance and Misrepresentation: The Right to a Return of Premium' (1980) 14(3) *Western Australian Law Review* 237.

205 *Twenty-First Maylux Pty Ltd v Mercantile Mutual Insurance (Australia) Ltd* [1990] VR 919; *Manchester Unity Total Care Building Society v MGICA Ltd* (1991) 6 ANZ Ins Cases ¶61–062; *Bergman v CGU Insurance Ltd* [2016] VSC 81, [145].

206 [2002] QSC 144.

A more recent example is the case of *Michail v Australian Alliance Insurance Co Ltd*.[207] Michail took out insurance for his Aston Martin with Australian Alliance's agent, Shannons Ltd, in July 2010. In May 2011, the vehicle was damaged in an accident and assessed as a 'total loss' under the policy. Michail lodged a claim under his policy but was denied by the insurer, which alleged that he breached his duty of disclosure by failing to disclose his full driving history when completing the proposal form. Michail did not disclose at least six traffic offences, each attracting three demerit points, and one suspension. Shannons alleged that it would not have entered into the policy at all had Michail disclosed these details, so the insurer denied liability under s 28(3) of the Act. The insurer tendered evidence of its own underwriting guidelines and the testimony of its regional manager in support of its claim that full disclosure would resulted in Michail's application being denied as an 'unacceptable risk'.

The Supreme Court of Queensland held in favour of the insurer and dismissed the appeal, finding that, had proper disclosure been made, the insurer would not have accepted the risk at all. As such, its liability under the policy was reduced to nil pursuant to s 28(3) of the Act.

As will be discussed in Section 11.10, the courts have a statutory discretion to overlook, in appropriate circumstances, an insured's fraudulent non-disclosure or misrepresentation, and to allow them to recover all or part of the sum claimed.

11.9.2 Non-disclosure and misrepresentation under contracts of life insurance (s 29)

Section 29 deals generally with non-disclosure and misrepresentation in the context of contracts of life insurance. The provision is substantially similar to s 28, and applies where the insured failed to comply with the duty of disclosure or made a misrepresentation to the insurer before the contract was entered into.[208] However, it does not apply where the insurer would have entered into the contract even if the insured made full disclosure or did not misrepresent any matters, or where the failure or misrepresentation was in respect of the date of birth of one or more of the life insureds.[209]

If the insured's non-disclosure or misrepresentation under s 29(1) was fraudulent, the insurer may avoid the contract.[210] If, however, the non-disclosure or misrepresentation was not fraudulent, the insurer may, within three years after the contract was entered into, avoid the contract.[211] Where the insurer has not avoided the contract, whether under sub-ss (2) or (3) or otherwise, it may by written notice to the insured vary the contract and the sum insured according to the formula specified in s 29(4).[212]

Pursuant to s 29(6), where an insurer has not avoided the contract or has not varied it under sub-s (4), it may by written notice to the insured vary the contract so as to place the insurer in the position (subject to sub-s (7)) in which it would have been if the duty of disclosure had been complied with or the misrepresentation had not been made. This provision effectively

207 (2014) 67 MVR 21.
208 Section 29(1).
209 Section 29(1).
210 Section 29(2).
211 Section 29(3).
212 Section 29(4).

mirrors s 28(3), which applies to contracts of general insurance. However, s 29(6) allows for the contract to be *varied*, whereas s 28(3) only allows for *liability* under the contract to be *reduced*.

In the particular case of a misstatement of age in relation to a life insurance contract, s 30 of the Act provides that the sum insured (including any bonuses) is to be varied to the amount calculated according to the 'standard formula' prescribed by that provision. The insurer cannot, however, avoid the contract for a misstatement of age, even if the misstatement was fraudulent.

11.10 The court's discretion to overlook fraud (s 31)

Fraud on the part of the insured, if made out, entitles the insurer to avoid the contract, whether it be for general insurance[213] or life insurance.[214] However, the court retains a statutory discretion, in appropriate circumstances, to overlook the insured's fraud where it would be 'harsh and unfair' not to do so. In such cases, the court may order an appropriate sum to be paid to the insured. Section 31(1) accommodates this discretion and reads as follows:

> **Court may disregard avoidance in certain circumstances**
>
> In any proceedings by the insured in respect of a contract of insurance that has been avoided on the ground of fraudulent failure to comply with the duty of disclosure or fraudulent misrepresentation, the court may, if it would be harsh and unfair not to do so, but subject to this section, disregard the avoidance and, if it does so, shall allow the insured to recover the whole, or such part as the court thinks just and equitable in the circumstances, of the amount that would have been payable if the contract had not been avoided.

In exercising this broad power, the court must 'have regard to the need to deter fraudulent conduct in relation to insurance'[215] and weigh the extent of the insured's culpability against the 'magnitude of the loss that would be suffered by the insured if the avoidance were not disregarded'.[216] It may, under this provision, also have regard to 'any other relevant matter'. This is a sensitive balancing exercise for the court to undertake, and involves a holistic

213 Section 28(2).

214 Section 29(2).

215 Section 31(3)(a). In *Boekenstein v Tyndall Life Insurance Co Ltd* [1997] NSWSC 38, the insured misrepresented his business income under a disability policy issued in March 1993. Consequently, the insurer unknowingly committed to paying a far higher monthly benefit (over a period which could have lasted up to 30 years) than it would have agreed to in the event of the insured becoming disabled. The amount also exceeded the insured's net income. The insured lodged a claim, citing total disability, in July 1993. The insurer paid two monthly payments before declining further payment, initiating an investigation, and subsequently suing for fraudulent misrepresentation. James J held in favour of the insurer, finding that the insured had made a fraudulent misrepresentation and declining to exercise the discretion under s 31. James J considered that the insured had no incentive to cease being totally disabled under the policy, and that applying s 31 would not deter but rather encourage fraudulent conduct. See also *Von Braun v Australian Associated Motor Insurers Ltd* (1998) 135 ACTR 1.

216 Section 31(3)(b).

evaluation of the circumstances surrounding the insured's fraud. Importantly, disregarding the insured's avoidance does *not* have the effect of reinstating the contract.[217]

Section 31(2) of the Act further qualifies the court's discretion under s 31(1). This provision states:

> The power conferred by subsection (1) may be exercised only where the court is of the opinion that, in respect of the loss that is the subject of the proceedings before the court, the insurer has not been prejudiced by the failure or misrepresentation or, if the insurer has been so prejudiced, the prejudice is minimal or insignificant.

An insured seeking relief under s 31(1) bears the onus of proving that the insured would not be prejudiced by the court's exercise of this discretion.[218] In *Evans v Sirius Insurance Co Ltd*,[219] the insured was ultimately deemed not to have violated the duty of disclosure. Nonetheless, Beach J noted that, even if non-disclosure had been established, his Honour would have exercised the s 31 discretion given that the insured had plainly demonstrated that he was not an astute businessman and that his broker was actually the party who did not disclose the relevant cancellation of a previous policy. Moreover, one of the employees of the insurance company that the defendant eventually acquired was aware of the cancellation, which itself was not material to the risk or the terms upon which it was to be insured. Accordingly, it would have been harsh and unfair to penalise the insured by allowing the insurer to avoid liability when the prejudice to the latter was insignificant.

The application of s 31 is further illustrated by the case of *Von Braun v Australian Associated Motor Insurers Ltd*.[220] The insured fraudulently represented to the insurer that he had paid $70 000 for a Mercedes Benz motor vehicle, which he proposed to have insured for the sum of $65 000. However, the insurer's 'dealer guide' valued the car at around $56 000, and the insurer was also aware that in the previous year another insurance company (NRMA) had insured it for a lower agreed value. Nevertheless, the insurer insured the vehicle for $65 000 and issued a cover note to that effect. The car was subsequently stolen and the insured lodged a claim that the insurer refused, seeking to avoid the contract on the ground that the insured had misrepresented the price of the car.

Higgins J held that the insured's misrepresentation as to the car value would not have affected the insurer's decision to accept the insurance proposal; rather, at most, it would only have affected the *extent* of indemnity offered.[221] The risk of loss or damage to the vehicle was completely unaffected. On the evidence, had the truth been revealed, the insurer would at worst have been prepared to insure the vehicle for at least $56 000. Higgins J felt it was just and equitable in the circumstances to allow the claim as if the agreed value for the car had been $56 000. His Honour explained:

> That figure is chosen, being most favourable to the defendant and least favourable to the plaintiff, to reflect the need to deter the giving of deliberately false information to insurers,

217 Section 31(4).
218 *Plasteel Windows Australia Pty Ltd v C E Heath Underwriting Agencies Pty Ltd* (1990) 19 NSWLR 400, 411.
219 (1986) 4 ANZ Ins Cas ¶60-755.
220 (1998) 135 ACTR 1.
221 (1998) 135 ACTR 1, 13–14.

> even though, had the plaintiff told the truth, the agreed value figure would in all probability have been no less than $60,000. There is a credit to be allowed both for the premium refunded ($700) and the excess ($400). There will, therefore, be judgment for the plaintiff in the sum of $54,900.[222]

11.11 Breaching a term of the policy

The common law position was that an insured's breach of a warranty under an insurance contract entitled the insurer to avoid the contract at its election and sue for damages, even if the breach was trivial, innocent, or not causally connected to the insurer's loss.[223] The term 'warranty' in the insurance context differs from that under the general law of contract,[224] although there are some similarities.[225] A warranty under the law of insurance is one that is of central importance to the contract and materially bears upon the risk of loss (rather than merely describing it), such that damages would be inadequate to remedy its breach.[226]

The ALRC acknowledged the harshness of allowing an insurer to rely upon an insured's breach of a policy term to avoid the contract even where the insurer has suffered little or no prejudice.[227] This injustice was eventually cured through the enactment of s 54.

11.11.1 Circumstances where the insurer may not refuse to pay claims (s 54)

Section 54 balances the insurer's right to a remedy upon the insured's breach of a policy term against the injustice that might arise should the insured's claim be denied in part or entirely, in circumstances where such denial is not proportionate to the prejudice actually suffered by the insurer.[228] Section 54(1) reads as follows:

> Subject to this section, where the effect of a contract of insurance would, but for this section, be that the insurer may refuse to pay a claim, either in whole or in part, by reason of some act of the insured or of some other person, being an act that occurred after the contract was entered into but not being an act in respect of which subsection (2) applies, the insurer may not refuse to pay the claim by reason only of that act but the insurer's

222 (1998) 135 ACTR 1, 14.

223 *Dawsons Ltd v Bonnin* [1922] 2 AC 413, 423; *Bank of Nova Scotia v Hellenic Mutual War Risks Association (Bermuda) Ltd ('The Good Luck')* [1992] 1 AC 233, 262–3.

224 See Chapter 1.

225 See Australian Law Reform Commission, *Report on Insurance Contracts* (ALRC, 1982), paragraph 216.

226 *Bank of Nova Scotia v Hellenic Mutual War Risks Association (Bermuda) Ltd ('The Good Luck')* [1992] 1 AC 233; *HIH Casualty & General Insurance Ltd v New Hampshire Insurance Co* [2001] EWCA Civ 735.

227 Australian Law Reform Commission, *Report on Insurance Contracts* (ALRC, 1982), paragraph 219.

228 See, further, *Maxwell v Highway Hauliers Pty Ltd* (2014) 252 CLR 590, 597, where the High Court observed that one of the specific objects of s 54 was to '[strike] a fair balance between the interests of an insurer and an insured with respect to a contractual term designed to protect the insurer from an increase in risk during the period of insurance cover'. This balance, it was said, was to be struck irrespective of the form of that contractual term.

> liability in respect of the claim is reduced by the amount that fairly represents the extent to which the insurer's interests were prejudiced as a result of that act.

Under s 54(1), if the insured's act could not reasonably be regarded as being capable of causing or contributing to the insurer's loss, the insurer cannot refuse the claim but the amount payable will be reduced to reflect the extent of the insurer's loss. Where the act *could* reasonably be regarded as being capable of causing or contributing to the insurer's loss, s 54(2) applies instead. Section 54(2) reads as follows:

> Subject to the succeeding provisions of this section, where the act could reasonably be regarded as being capable of causing or contributing to a loss in respect of which insurance cover is provided by the contract, the insurer may refuse to pay the claim.

If the insured proves that no part of the insurer's loss was caused by the insured's act, the insurer is barred from refusing to pay the claim by reason only of the act.[229] It would be limited in this case to an action for damages. Alternatively, if the insured proves that their act only *partially* contributed to the insurer's loss, the insurer is entitled to proportionate partial recovery.[230] The Act also prohibits the insurer denying the insured's claim where the latter's act was necessary to protect persons or property, or where it was not reasonably possible for the insured not to act as they did.[231] Importantly, an 'act' in the context of s 54 also includes omissions.[232]

In *Maxwell v Highway Hauliers Pty Ltd*,[233] the High Court noted that s 54:

> takes as its starting point nothing more than the existence of a claim and of a contract the effect of which is that the insurer may refuse to pay that claim by reason of some act which the insured (or someone else) has done or omitted to do after the contract was entered into; it does not postulate a liability of the insurer to pay the claim that has been made.

Establishing a causal connection between the insured's act and the insurer's loss under s 54(1) is a question of fact involving a normative judgment balancing common sense with fairness.[234]

A useful case demonstrating the application of s 54 is *Ferrcom Pty Ltd v Commercial Union Assurance Co of Australia Ltd*.[235] There the appellant insured a mobile crane under an 'unregistered mobile machinery policy' issued by the respondent insurer. The crane was insured against physical loss, destruction or damage. In May 1987, two months after the policy was issued, the appellant arranged for the crane's registration so that it could be driven on public roads to other building sites (a factor that would increase the overall risk of loss or damage). A term in the policy made the insurer's liability conditional on the insured notifying it of any material variation of the circumstances existing at the commencement of the policy.

229 Section 54(3).
230 Section 54(4).
231 Section 54(5).
232 Section 54(6)(a).
233 (2014) 252 CLR 590, 597.
234 *Greentree v FAI General Insurance Co Ltd* (1998) 44 NSWLR 706, 715. See also *National & General Insurance Co Ltd v Chick* (1984) 2 NSWLR 86.
235 (1993) 176 CLR 332.

The appellant did not inform the respondent of the crane's registration. In September 1987, while onsite, the crane overturned and was damaged. The appellant lodged a claim that was denied by the respondent on the basis of the respondent's breach of the term requiring notification of changed circumstances. The insurer would have been entitled to cancel the policy had it been notified of the crane's registration.

The appellant relied upon s 54 as excluding the respondent's right to avoid the policy or deny liability. It argued that its failure to disclose the altered circumstances had not caused the respondent's loss and that, pursuant to s 54(1), the insurer was therefore unable to avoid the claim. Instead, the respondent's liability should be reduced by an amount fairly representing the prejudice it suffered by exposure to the increased risk of damage to the crane. The respondent submitted that it would have cancelled the policy had it known of the crane's registration. The alternative policy it would then have provided would not have covered the accident that occurred.

It was common ground that the appellant's failure to notify the respondent of the crane's registration, whether construed as an act or omission, could not reasonably be regarded as capable of causing or contributing to the loss and was therefore an 'act' under s 54(1). As such, the respondent argued that the extent to which its 'interests were prejudiced' under this provision by the non-notification was to be measured by reference to the position it would have been in had it been notified. That is, the prejudice suffered was the entirety of their exposure to the insured's claim, such that their liability should be assessed as at nil.

The High Court held in favour of the respondent. The prejudice to the respondent in the circumstances was significant. Had it been notified, it would have cancelled the policy. This lost opportunity was brought about by the appellant's non-notification. It was also unable to receive the additional premium that would have been paid under a different policy (had it chosen to issue one). Moreover, the risk of damage to the crane was significantly increased, exposing the respondent to greater liability. As such, the High Court concluded that the amount which 'fairly represented' the prejudice the respondent suffered in losing the opportunity to go 'off risk' was the equivalent of the liability imposed on it entirely. The liability under s 54(1) was therefore reduced to nil.[236]

It is conceivable that a breach of the duty of utmost good faith under s 13 of the Act may be remedied by s 54, but again this entitlement will depend upon the extent to which the insurer's interests are prejudiced by such breach.[237]

11.12 Fraudulent claims (s 56)

A claim is made fraudulently where:

> the insured has a dishonest intent to induce a false belief in the insurer for the purpose of obtaining payment or some other benefit under the policy. As such, where the insured

236 The operation of s 54(1) bears parallels with that of s 28(3). See Section 11.9.1 above. For other case examples involving the application of s 51, see: *Moltoni Corporation Pty Ltd v QBE Insurance Ltd* (2001) 185 ALR 213; *FAI General Insurance Co Ltd v Australian Hospital Care Pty Ltd* (2001) 2041 CLR 641.

237 *Entwells Pty Ltd v National & General Insurance Co Ltd* (1991) 6 ANZ Ins Cas ¶61-059.

> makes a false statement with knowledge in a claim to induce the insurer to meet the claim, the claim is made fraudulently.[238]

Accordingly, unless the insurance contract contains a clause specifically addressing the consequences of fraudulent conduct when making a claim, the insurer must prove intentional deception on the part of the insured.

Common examples of fraudulent claims in practice include falsifying a loss (eg lodging a claim for lost or stolen items that never actually existed), exacerbating or grossly exaggerating the extent of loss to property, and feigning personal illness or injury under a sickness and accident policy. More rarely, one might even fake their death to try to claim under a life insurance policy, as American businessman Jose Lantigua famously did while travelling through Venezuela in 2013 before being caught two years later.[239]

At common law, where an insured's claim is fraudulent, the insurer is entitled to avoid the contract.[240] As discussed, this extends both to the insured *causing* the loss or event insured, and to *exacerbating* or *grossly exaggerating*[241] the relevant loss. The Act has modified this common law position.[242] Section 56 permits the insurer to refuse *making payment* under the contract, but does not allow it to avoid the contract altogether. Section 56(1) thus reads:

> Where a claim under a contract of insurance, or a claim made under this Act against an insurer by a person who is not the insured under a contract of insurance, is made fraudulently, the insurer may not avoid the contract but may refuse payment of the claim.

Where, however, the claim was only partially fraudulent and it would be unfair for payment of the claim to be avoided altogether, the courts retain a discretion to order the insurer to pay an amount it considers reasonable. This discretion is provided for in s 56(2), which states:

> In any proceedings in relation to such a claim, the court may, if only a minimal or insignificant part of the claim is made fraudulently and non-payment of the remainder

238 *Walton v Colonial Mutual Life Assurance Society Ltd* [2004] NSWSC 616, [144]. Approved in *Sgro v Australian Associated Motor Insurers Ltd* (2015) 91 NSWLR 325, 335; *Rolleston v Insurance Australia Ltd* [2016] NSWSC 1561, [96].

239 Lantigua alleged that he was travelling to receive treatment for a rare degenerative brain disease. His wife reported him as having died and been cremated in Venezuela when he was in fact living under a different name in a North Carolina property that she owned. He was discovered by federal agents in 2015 and promptly arrested and charged. In 2017, Lantigua was sentenced to 14 years in prison for insurance fraud, while his wife received probation.

240 *Goulstone v Royal Insurance Co* (1858) 1 F & F 276; *Manifest Shipping & Co Ltd v Uni-Polaris Insurance Co Ltd* [2003] 1 AC 469.

241 Determining whether a claim has been 'grossly exaggerated' is a difficult exercise, although it appears to be a matter of degree; this analysis is informed by sensible judgment in the circumstances. If the estimates given or losses cited are so greatly exaggerated that they cannot be regarded as honest, this will amount to fraud: *Entwells Pty Ltd v National & General Insurance Co Ltd* (1991) 6 ANZ Ins Cas ¶61-059; *Moxia Pty Ltd v AMP General Insurance Ltd* (unreported, Victorian Supreme Court, Beach J, 21 September 1992).

242 Bargaining for more favourable insurance, however, is not fraudulent: *Orakpo v Barclays Insurance Services* [1995] LRLR 443.

> of the claim would be harsh and unfair, order the insurer to pay, in relation to the claim, such amount (if any) as is just and equitable in the circumstances.

When exercising this discretion, the court is required to have regard to 'the need to deter fraudulent conduct in relation to insurance' and may also have regard to 'any other relevant matter'.[243]

Importantly, s 54 does not apply to claims caught by s 56.[244] Section 54(1) may apply where the contract of insurance provides for the forfeiting of all benefits by reason of using false statements to support a claim. It may be similar in effect to s 56(2), which provides that the court may order payment of that part of the claim not affected by the insured's fraud. At the same time, s 56(2) is subject to the policy, enunciated through s 56(3), that the court's discretion should be exercised with a view to deterring fraud. Section 54 applies more broadly to the insured's acts or omissions, whereas s 56 applies specifically to fraudulent conduct. As such, the specificity of s 56 recommends its application over that of s 54 in circumstances involving fraud.

11.13 Expiry and cancellation of insurance contracts (ss 58, 59, 59A and 60)

11.13.1 Expiration

There is no obligation at common law for an insurer to notify an insured that a policy is due for renewal. Section 58(2) of the Act, however, requires an insurer to give an insured (or their agent) written notice within 14 days of the expiration of an existing contract of general insurance. The insurer must also state the time and date of expiry, as well as its intentions with respect to negotiating the renewal or extension of the existing policy. Failure to provide such notice results in cover being automatically extended pursuant to s 58(3) (provided the insured did not obtain alternative insurance from another insurer beforehand). No premium is payable for the extension unless the insured makes a claim.[245]

11.13.2 Cancellation

It is quite common for an insured to cancel a contract of insurance, such as where the particular subject matter insured has been sold, disposed of or destroyed, or where an alternative insurer has offered a better deal. Upon cancellation, the insurer will typically offer a refund of the premium proportionate to the time remaining on the contract, less administrative and related costs. Entitlements will, of course, be determined by the terms of the individual policy.

---

243 Section 56(3).

244 *Walton v Colonial Mutual Life Assurance Society Ltd* [2004] NSWSC 616, [47]. See also *Gugliotti v Commercial Union Assurance Co of Australia* (1992) 15 MVR 463; *Tiep Thi To v AAMI Ltd* (2001) 3 VR 279.

245 Section 58(4). The claim is calculated by use of the formulae specified in s 58(5) and (6).

Where an insurer seeks to cancel a contract for life insurance or general insurance, it must follow the rules set out in ss 59A and 60 of the Act, respectively.[246] As such, unlike the position at common law, an insurer cannot arbitrarily cancel a contract on a whim, even where it purports to include a clause in the policy to this effect.

The Act previously contained no provisions accommodating the cancellation of life insurance contracts. However, the *Insurance Contracts Amendment Act 2013* (Cth) introduced a new s 59A to permit the insurer to cancel where the insured has made a fraudulent claim. The court retains a statutory discretion, 'where it would be harsh and unfair not to do so', to disregard the cancellation and order the insurer to pay such amount of the claim which the court considers 'just and equitable in the circumstances'.[247] It may also order the insurer to reinstate the contract.

Cancellation of contracts of general insurance is addressed through s 60. Section 60(1) provides:

> Where, in relation to a contract of general insurance:
>
> (a) a person who is or was at any time the insured failed to comply with the duty of the utmost good faith;
>
> (b) the person who was the insured at the time when the contract was entered into failed to comply with the duty of disclosure;
>
> (c) the person who was the insured at the time when the contract was entered into made a misrepresentation to the insurer during the negotiations for the contract but before it was entered into;
>
> (d) a person who is or was at any time the insured failed to comply with a provision of the contract, including a provision with respect to payment of the premium; or
>
> (e) the insured has made a fraudulent claim under the contract or under some other contract of insurance (whether with the insurer concerned or with some other insurer) that provides insurance cover during any part of the period during which the first-mentioned contract provides insurance cover;
>
> the insurer may cancel the contract.

Naturally, the insurer remains at risk with respect to any claims lodged prior to cancellation.

Section 59 of the Act outlines the procedure that must be followed in order for the insurer to effect a valid cancellation of an insurance contract. Under s 59(1), an insurer wishing to exercise a right to cancel a contract of insurance must give written notice of the proposed cancellation to the insured. It must, under s 75(1)(b), also provide its reasons for the cancellation at the insured's request.

11.14 Key points

- A contract of insurance is a contract in which one party (the insurer), in consideration of a sum of money (the premium) undertakes to pay another party (the insured) on the occurrence of a particular event. Insurance is therefore a form of 'risk transfer'.

246 Section 63.
247 Section 59A(2).

- At common law, the contract of insurance has long been described as a contract of utmost good faith (*uberrimae fidei*), requiring each party to act honestly and fairly towards one another both in the formation stage of the contract as well as in the performance of obligations and exercise of rights arising under the contract as created. The duty is now enshrined in s 13 of the Act.
- While the Act imposes a number of rules specific to insurance contracts, insurance contracts are still commercial contracts like any other and are therefore also generally subject to the same general principles of contract law.
- Insureds have a duty to disclose certain matters to the insurer prior to an insurance contract being entered into. The obligation exists both at common law and under s 21 of the Act.
- Misrepresentation describes the violation of the insured's duty to provide truthful and accurate responses to an insurer's questions, whether in the proposal form or otherwise. Misrepresentation is provided for under ss 23–27 of the Act.
- Third parties to an insurance contract may also have entitlements under it, even though they are not a party to the agreement itself. Where they are specified or referred to as a beneficiary, whether by name or otherwise, they may have standing to claim.
- The insurer's remedies for non-disclosure or misrepresentation are outlined in ss 28–29 of the Act, while breaches of policy terms and fraudulent claims are addressed through ss 54 and 56, respectively. Generally speaking, fraud entitles an insurer to avoid a contract.

11.15 DISCUSSION QUESTIONS

1. What is a contract of insurance? Which sources of law affect such contracts?
2. How do the courts approach the interpretation of insurance contracts? How does the *contra proferentem* principle operate in situations of intractable ambiguity?
3. What does the duty of utmost good faith require of insurers and insureds?
4. In what circumstances will an insured be excused from disclosing matters under s 21?
5. What are the consequences for the insured's breach of the duties of utmost good faith and disclosure?
6. How might an insurance contract come to an end? Which provisions of the Act affect this process, and how do they do so?

11.16 FURTHER READING

Brownie, J, 'The Duty of Utmost Good Faith, After the Formation of the Contract' (1993) 5 *Insurance Law Journal* 226.

Drummond, S, 'Unconscionable Conduct and Utmost Good Faith' (2003) 14 *Insurance Law Journal* 208.

Gill, M and Radford, M, 'Utmost Good Faith: Section 13 and Breach of Contract' (1994) 10 *Australian Insurance Law Bulletin* 17.

Mann, P, *Mann's Annotated Insurance Contracts Act* (Thomson Reuters, Sydney, 6th edn, 2014).

Mann, P and Drummond, S, 'Utmost Good Faith, Unconscionable Conduct and Other Notions of Fairness – Where Are We Now?' (2017) 29 *Insurance Law Journal* 1.

Pynt, G, *Australian Insurance Law: A First Reference* (LexisNexis Butterworths Australia, Sydney, 4th edn, 2017).

Tarr, A and Tarr, J, 'The Insured's Non-Disclosure in the Formation of Insurance Contracts: A Comparative Perspective' (2001) 50(3) *International and Comparative Law Quarterly* 577.

12

BANKRUPTCY

12.0 Introduction

Insolvencies are the consequence of capitalist economies and the market factors that underpin and drive them, including competitive behaviours and the appetite for and bias towards risk, limited social and material resources (among them, credit), and the asymmetrical relationship of expectation to capacity. Insolvency always has some (and may have vast) private, public, institutional and systemic consequences. The distinction between insolvency as it relates to corporations, and bankruptcy in relation to persons, is made in the Australian Constitution.[1] Insolvency and bankruptcy occur when corporations, businesses or persons are unable to pay their debts when and as they fall due. The term 'bankruptcy' is applicable to personal insolvency, whereas insolvent corporations or businesses go into liquidation. Bankruptcy laws provide the framework within and procedures by which the failure of debtors to pay their debts can be handled in an organised and efficient manner, making similar provisions for corporations, businesses and persons, while at the same time recognising the differences between the subjects of the processes. Case law regarding textually similar provisions therefore should be equally applicable to either personal bankruptcy or corporate insolvency, and courts' decisions should be given wider scope to apply generally. In this chapter, we address the fundamentals of bankruptcy law.

12.1 Overview of the bankruptcy legislation

The purpose of the modern law of bankruptcy in dealing with cases of individuals having no reasonable prospect of paying their debts is, first, to enable a debtor or creditor to initiate proceedings to enable the distribution of the debtor's property among the creditors in the most expeditious and economical way, which usually means paying creditors in proportion to the amount each creditor is owed by the debtor; second, to enable an investigation into the conduct and affairs of the debtor; and, third, to 'enable the debtor to be freed from the burden of accumulated debts so that the debtor can make a fresh start' unless they have acted dishonestly, improperly or inappropriately, or are otherwise guilty of a serious offence.[2] In other words, the rights of individual creditors are suspended in favour of the debtors' interests and the interests of the creditors as a whole. Bankruptcy law modifies the normal laws of debt to alleviate the debtor by organising a compromise between debtors and creditors.

The legal framework that provides for the governance of personal bankruptcy is constituted by the *Bankruptcy Act 1966* (Cth), which contains the rules and procedures governing bankruptcy proceedings from pre-bankruptcy matters to the discharge of the bankrupt and the release of the trustee in bankruptcy (ie the person charged with the administration of the bankruptcy),[3] the Bankruptcy Schedule, the courts' bankruptcy

1 The Australian Constitution, s 51(xxvii) prefers the terminology of 'personal bankruptcy' and 'corporate insolvency'.

2 D Rose, *Lewis's Australian Bankruptcy Law* (Lawbook Co, Sydney, 11th edn, 1999), 1.

3 Other applicable legislation includes: *Bankruptcy (Estate Charges) Act 1997* (Cth); *Personal Property Securities Act 2009* (Cth); *Proceeds of Crime Act 2002* (Cth); and *Cross-Border Insolvency Act 2008*

rules,[4] and the *Bankruptcy Regulations 1996* (Cth).[5] The Bankruptcy Act provides both for the conversion of the debtor's status into that of a bankrupt and for the preservation of the debtor's status to enable debtors and creditors to enter agreements without the requirement for bankruptcy.

The regulations prescribe the more detailed procedure to be followed in the administration of bankruptcies.[6] Much of this has been transferred to Schedule 2, the Insolvency Practice Schedule (Bankruptcy) (IPSB), or the courts' bankruptcy rules. The administration of the legal regime is undertaken by the Australian Financial Security Authority (AFSA) within which resides the Official Trustee in Bankruptcy, the Official Receiver and the Inspector-General in Bankruptcy. The courts having jurisdiction over bankruptcy matters are the Federal Circuit Court of Australia and the Family Court.[7]

The governing legislative regime of corporate bankruptcy comprises the *Corporations Act 2001* (Cth), Schedule 2 to the Corporations Act, and the *Corporations Regulations 2001* (Cth). The regulator responsible for corporate bankruptcies is the Australian Securities and Investments Commission (ASIC). The courts conferred with special jurisdiction over these matters, as provided by s 58AA of the Corporations Act, include (but are not restricted to) the Federal Court of Australia, the state and territory Supreme Courts, and the Family Court.

12.2 The aims and purposes of insolvency law

Bankruptcy laws and proceedings confer the following social benefits:

1. They protect the debtor or company and its assets from undue claims by creditors by placing them under the control and authority of the trustee.
2. They release the debtor, or the company that goes through a deed of company arrangement, or a director whose company is liquidated, from liabilities, allowing the personal debtor a 'fresh start' (referring to both financial and psycho-social relief from past liabilities and events) free of debt.
3. They place restrictions on dealings. Bankruptcy law benefits the community by imposing certain restrictions on bankrupts in their commercial or domestic dealings, such as prohibiting them from obtaining credit above a certain amount without disclosing the

(Cth). The *Insolvency Law Reform Act 2016* (Cth) made substantial changes to the structure of the Act and the processes of bankruptcy, including the regulation of trustees.

4 The courts' bankruptcy rules are the *Federal Court (Bankruptcy) Rules 2016* (Cth) and the *Federal Circuit Court (Bankruptcy) Rules 2016* (Cth), most bankruptcy matters being heard in the Federal Circuit Court with appeals to the Federal Court.

5 Section 315 of the *Bankruptcy Act 1966* (Cth) permits the making of regulations.

6 'Approved forms' that are to be used by bankrupts, trustees, creditors and others are issued by the Inspector-General in Bankruptcy: s 6D.

7 Other tribunals with roles in administering bankruptcy include the Family Court under the *Family Law Act 1975* (Cth), along with provisions contained in the *Family Law Rules 2004* (Cth) pertaining to bankruptcy proceedings, and the Administrative Appeals Tribunal, which may hear appeals to review decisions of the Inspector-General in Bankruptcy under the IPSB, s 96-1.

bankruptcy, and preventing them from pursuing certain occupations while they remain bankrupt or without approval.[8]

4. They support the rule of law in providing an equal, fair and orderly procedure for handling the affairs of insolvent debtors in circumstances where there might otherwise be disordered, unfair retrieval of funds or assets and unlawful and criminal conduct. The law of insolvency serves as a process of ordered and predictable control according to settled rules under the control of a person given legal authority.
5. They align with and accommodate existing rights and other areas of law, substituting the right of creditors to pursue debts with the right to share in the remaining assets of the debtor if any in fact remain.
6. They protect those creditors who take valid security over the debtor's assets, thereby protecting against the debtor's inability to repay and facilitating recovery processes.
7. They ensure equal sharing between creditors – that is, the pari passu principle, which requires all creditors to be treated equally within the respective classes (ie secured, priority and unsecured claims).
8. They investigate and provide accountability by determining why and how companies or individuals became insolvent and whether any unlawfulness was involved. This further feeds into the regulation of business and good governance.
9. They recycle and promote the more productive use of productive assets that are being used to less than full effectiveness by the insolvent person or entity, putting an end to the misuse of capital.
10. They assist in the restructuring of an insolvent business. The Productivity Commission's report *Set-up, Transfer and Closure* (December 2015) states that a more sympathetic insolvency regime is required to better preserve the business idea, encourage further initiatives, promote entrepreneurial business conduct, research and development, accepting business risk as a necessary element for the advancement of ideas. The appropriate objective of an insolvency regime is that it:

    > should be to provide a genuine opportunity for restructure for economically viable companies, without providing incentive for strategic behaviour by debtors and creditors. If restructure is not possible, the insolvency system should aim to provide an efficient (expedient and inexpensive), effective and orderly process for winding up the company. This process should involve consideration of creditors, as well as other stakeholders, and provide certainty regarding future developments. The regime should foster a coordinated approach to recovery of a company or its assets [p 353].

Yet Australia still lags in the recognition and application of the 'restructure first' principles that characterise Chapter 11 proceedings in the US and bankruptcy proceedings in the EU and the UK.

8 Under the *Privacy Act 1988* (Cth), credit agencies cannot retain personal insolvency information for more than five years after the bankruptcy is declared, or for more than two years after the bankruptcy ends. The names of bankrupts remain on the National Personal Insolvency Index (NPII), which also records their discharge from bankruptcy.

12.3 Administration of the Act

12.3.1 General administration

Ministerial responsibility for the administration of the *Bankruptcy Act 1966* (Cth) is vested in the Commonwealth Attorney-General, the Minister for Justice and the Minister for Consumer Affairs.

12.3.2 Inspector-General in Bankruptcy

Under the Act the Minister appoints the Inspector-General in Bankruptcy.[9] The functions of the Inspector-General are to make such inquiries, and undertake such investigations, as the Minister directs, or as the Inspector-General thinks fit with respect to the administration of, or the conduct of a trustee in relation to, a bankruptcy, personal insolvency agreement or an administration under the Act, and a debtor's property that is subject to sequestration.[10] To enable the Inspector-General to fulfil these functions, they have broad powers of investigation and inquiry.[11]

12.3.3 Official Trustee and Official Receiver

The Official Trustee in Bankruptcy is a body corporate[12] capable of acquiring, holding and disposing of real and personal property.[13] The Official Trustee may also act in accordance with an order that relates to the payment of a debt by a person to the Commonwealth or the Commonwealth authority.[14] When a debtor becomes a bankrupt, their property vests, for administrative purposes, in the Official Trustee; however, if a registered trustee is appointed at the time the debtor becomes a bankrupt, the bankrupt's property vests in the registered trustee.[15] The bankrupt's after-acquired property vests immediately upon acquisition in either the Official Trustee or, if appropriate, the registered trustee.[16]

The Official Receiver may exercise the powers and functions of the Official Trustee,[17] and, when doing so, must act in the name of and on behalf of the Official Trustee.[18] Any act or thing done on behalf of or in the name of the Official Trustee by the Official Receiver is deemed to be an act of the Official Trustee.[19]

9 *Bankruptcy Act 1966* (Cth), s 16.
10 Section 50(1).
11 Section 12.
12 Section 18(1).
13 Section 18(2)(b).
14 Section 18(3).
15 Section 58(1). An exception is made in respect of property of the debtor which is subject to an order made under the Proceeds of Crime legislation: s 58A (see *Proceeds of Crime Act 2002* (Cth)).
16 *Bankruptcy Act 1966* (Cth), s 58(1)(b).
17 Section 18(8).
18 Section 18(8AA).
19 Section 18(8A).

12.3.4 Registered trustees

A person (other than the Official Trustee) may only act as a trustee in bankruptcy if they are registered under the Act. To be registered as a trustee, an individual must apply to the Inspector-General.[20] The registered trustee of a debtor may consent to act as trustee of the debtor's estate as specified in the trust instrument filed with the Official Receiver.[21] Upon the debtor becoming bankrupt, that registered trustee becomes, by force of the Act and provided consent has not been revoked, trustee of the bankrupt's estate.[22] The bankrupt's property vests forthwith in the registered trustee who has consented to act as such for the purposes of the petition on which the bankruptcy took place.[23] If there is no registered trustee, the bankrupt's property vests in the Official Trustee.[24] The trustee is the creditors' representative. The trustee's duty is to administer the estate in the interests of creditors subject to the provisions of the *Bankruptcy Act 1966*, directions of the court and meetings of creditors.[25]

12.3.5 Common Investment Fund

The Common Investment Fund, or Common Fund, is opened and maintained by the Official Trustee[26] and is the repository of all monies received by them,[27] with the exception of money they hold pursuant to a court order for the payment of a debt owed by a person to the Commonwealth or a Commonwealth authority,[28] or another order of the court in relation to the control of the debtor's property,[29] or if a registered trustee controls the debtor's property.[30] The Official Trustee must open and maintain accounts for the Common Fund,[31] and cause accounts to be kept showing the amount (if any) in the Common Fund standing to the credit of each estate or fund of a bankrupt or debtor.[32]

12.3.6 Courts exercising bankruptcy jurisdiction

The Federal Court and the Federal Circuit Court have concurrent jurisdiction in bankruptcy.[33] This jurisdiction is exclusive of all other courts except the High Court[34] and the Family Court in

20 Schedule 2, s 20-5(1). The Inspector-General will convene a committee to consider the application (Schedule 2, s 20-10(1)). The committee must reach a decision within 45 business days of the interview (Schedule 2, s 20-20(3)). The applicant may apply to the Administrative Appeals Tribunal for review of a decision of the committee (Schedule 2, s 96-1(a)).
21 Section 156A(1).
22 Section 156A(3)(a).
23 Section 156A(3).
24 Section 58(1).
25 The duties of a registered trustee are enumerated in s 19(1).
26 Section 20B(1).
27 Section 20B(2).
28 Section 20B(8)(a).
29 Section 20B(8)(c).
30 Division 2 of Part X.
31 Section 20B(4).
32 Section 20F.
33 Section 27(1).
34 Section 27(1). See M Sheldon, 'No One Likes to be Excluded – Rethinking the Federal Court's Exclusive Jurisdiction under the Bankruptcy Act' (2012) 20 *Insolvency Law Journal* 87.

relation to property that is part of settlement or spousal maintenance proceedings,[35] or as a result of proceedings being transferred there.[36] However, this provision 'does not ... confer jurisdiction in a criminal matter',[37] or exclude the jurisdiction of state and territory courts in criminal matters[38] that relate to acts of bankruptcy.

12.4 Application of the Act

The *Bankruptcy Act 1966* (Cth) is applicable to all debtors who are individual persons. Persons who are not Australian citizens, and Members of Parliament, are equally subject to the Act by express provision.[39] However, the Act does not permit a sequestration order to be made against, or a debtor's petition to be presented by:

(a) a corporation; or
(b) a partnership or association registered under a law of the Commonwealth, of a State, or of a Territory of the Commonwealth that provides for the winding up of a partnership or association registered under that law.[40]

A limited company cannot therefore be made bankrupt under the *Bankruptcy Act 1966*. This is because the *Corporations Act 2001* (Cth) under which the company was formed provides the necessary machinery for the winding up of an insolvent corporation.[41] Similarly, the Bankruptcy Act does not apply to partnerships or associations, because the state and territory legislation that deals with those entities provides for their winding up.[42] The Act, however, applies to limited partnerships as if they were ordinary partnerships, such that the assets of a limited partnership vest in the trustee when all the general partners of a limited partnership become bankrupt.[43]

12.4.1 Minors

The *Bankruptcy Act 1966* (Cth) applies only to debtors who are individual persons, including minors who have not attained the age of 18 years.[44] However, minors may be declared bankrupt only in respect of debts that may be legally enforced against them.

35 *Bankruptcy Act 1966* (Cth), s 35.
36 Section 35A.
37 Section 27(2)(a).
38 Section 27(2)(b).
39 Section 7(1).
40 Section 7.
41 *Corporations Act 2001* (Cth), Part 5.4.
42 See, for example, Part 5, Division 6 of the *Partnerships Act 1958* (Vic) and Part 10 of the *Associations Incorporation Reform Act 2012* (Vic).
43 *Bankruptcy Act 1966* (Cth), s 7(3).
44 Section 7(1A).

12.4.2 Persons of unsound mind

A person of unsound mind may also be made bankrupt in respect of debts contracted when the person was of sound mind. Persons of unsound mind act through a person authorised or empowered by law to act for them.[45]

12.4.3 Persons in prison

Imprisonment is no protection against bankruptcy.

12.4.4 Partnerships

A creditor of a partnership may present a petition against the partnership if the creditor is entitled to present a petition against any one of the partners in respect of a partnership debt. In recognition of the nature of liability in partnerships making partners individually liable for partnership debts, the petition need not include all of the partners. Any creditor who is entitled to present a petition against a partnership may present a petition against any member or members of the partnership without including the others.[46]

Partnerships are not separate legal entities. Therefore, partnerships do not in themselves become bankrupt; rather, partners in their individual capacity become bankrupts. Therefore, individual partners may present individual petitions. Special provisions apply when partners seek to present a debtors' petition against the partnership. Then the petition may be presented by all the partners, or by a majority of the partners resident in Australia.[47] In *Re Henderson*, the objection that the debtors did not constitute a majority of the members of the partnership because only one half of the partners petitioned, contrary to the jurisdiction requirements of s 56(1), proved fatal to the application. Under the circumstances, neither was the court conferred with power under s 56(7) to direct the Registrar to correct or amend the petition.[48]

A member of a partnership who has executed a personal insolvency agreement must not join in presenting a petition against the partnership unless the agreement has been set aside or terminated, or all the obligations under the agreement have been discharged, or the court has given the member permission to present the petition against the partnership.[49]

The debtor's petition against the partnership must be presented to the Official Receiver,[50] along with a statement of affairs of each partner (and copies of those statements) and a statement (plus copies) of partnership affairs.[51] If the petition does not comply with the approved form, or is not accompanied by a statement of affairs of the partners and the partnership, or if in the considered opinion of the Official Receiver those statements of affairs are inadequate, the petition may be rejected by the Official Receiver.[52]

45 Section 308(c).
46 Section 45.
47 Section 56A(1).
48 *Re Nigel Bruce Henderson and Marlene Henderson; Ex parte a Debtor's Petition* (1985) 9 FCR 353.
49 *Bankruptcy Act 1966* (Cth), s 56A(3).
50 Section 56B(1).
51 Section 56B(3).
52 Section 56B(4).

If either or both the petition was presented against the partnership by some, but not all, members of the partnership, or there is at least one creditor's petition pending against at least one of the members of the partnership, then the Official Receiver must refer a debtor's petition against a partnership to the court for a direction to either accept or reject the petition.[53] The court may direct that the petition be accepted in its referred form, be accepted after suitable amendment, or be rejected.[54] A court may not make directions about a petition that has been presented against a partnership that includes a person to whom a stay applies, or a person who is not a petitioning partner, until those persons have had the opportunity to be heard.[55]

When the Official Receiver accepts a petition that either has or has not been amended under a direction of the court, and notes the fact of acceptance on it, each member of the partnership to whom the petition applies thereby becomes a bankrupt.[56]

12.4.5 Joint debtors

Joint debtors who are not partners may file a petition against themselves.[57] This situation arises, for example, in relation to married couples. The petition is accompanied by a statement of affairs for each debtor and a statement of the debtors' joint affairs.[58]

12.4.6 Compulsory bankruptcy

While the majority of bankruptcies are voluntary, debtors may be bankrupted by court order. A debtor who is unable or has refused to pay a creditor enables the creditor to elect to commence proceedings to bankrupt the debtor. If the creditor exercises this choice, proceedings commence by the presentation of a creditor's petition seeking a sequestration order against the debtor's estate.

It is open to any creditor to petition, including individuals and corporations,[59] or several creditors acting jointly.[60] However, all joint creditors must be joined in a petition for a joint debt.[61] Secured creditors may retain or surrender their security. If the security is retained, the amount for which they petition is the difference between the amount owed and the value of the security. If, after the sequestration order is made, the security is surrendered to the trustee, the secured creditor may petition for the entire quantum of the debt owed to it.

If a sequestration order is made, the debtor becomes a bankrupt and their estate is taken over by a trustee who administers it for the creditors' benefit. It is not necessary for a creditor to pursue the enforcement of a money judgment against the debtor prior to commencing proceedings to bankrupt the debtor.

53 Section 56C(2). The Act provides illustrations.
54 Section 56C(3)(a)–(c).
55 Section 56C(4).
56 Section 56E.
57 Section 57.
58 Section 57(2). The governing provisions largely follow those pertaining to individual debtors: s 57(3)–(7).
59 *Re Oskar* (1984) 55 ALR 717.
60 *Bankruptcy Act 1966* (Cth), s 44(1)(a).
61 *Australian Workers' Union v Bowen [No 1]* (1946) 72 CLR 575.

12.5 Court process

The jurisdiction for making sequestration orders in bankruptcy lies with the Federal Circuit Court and the Federal Court exclusively.[62] Under the Act, creditors must present a petition to the court and file an application and affidavit. The date of the presentation is significant in that it determines the commencement of bankruptcy.[63] A bankruptcy application is heard by the registrar of the court. If an applicant seeks a review of the registrar's exercise of power, the matter is heard *de novo*.[64] Because the hearing of bankruptcy applications entails serious consequences for the debtors' personal rights, strict compliance with procedure is required. Where the debtor is self-represented, the creditor's lawyer must put all relevant matters before the court.[65]

12.5.1 Against whom may a petition be presented?

Petitions may be presented against individual persons, including persons under 18 years of age, and persons who are not Australian citizens.[66]

12.5.2 Partnerships

Where a law provides for the winding up of a partnership or association registered under it, a bankruptcy petition cannot be presented against that entity.[67] However, the Act applies to limited partnerships as if they were ordinary partnerships. When all the general partners of a limited partnership become bankrupt, the assets of the limited partnership vest in the trustee.[68]

A creditor of a partnership may present a petition against the partnership if the creditor is entitled to present a petition against any one of the partners in respect of a partnership debt.[69] As partners are individually liable for partnership debts, the petition may be presented against any partner without the requirement to include other partners.[70] Because partnerships are not separate legal entities apart from their members, sequestration orders can only be made against partners in their individual capacities.

12.5.3 Joint debtors

A creditor's petition may be presented against two or more joint debtors whether they are or are not partners.[71] One petition may, for example, be presented against a jointly liable married

62 Courts generally have sequestration powers to enforce judgments and orders: see, for example, rules 66.10 and 76 of the *Supreme Court (General Civil Procedure) Rules 2015* (Vic).

63 *Bankruptcy Act 1966* (Cth), s 115.

64 The judicial power of the Commonwealth can only be exercised by judges of federal courts or other courts exercising federal jurisdiction: *Zdrilic v Hickie* (2016) 246 FCR 532; *Kimber v The Owners Strata Plan No 48216* [2017] FCAFC 226.

65 *Federal Court of Australia Act 1976* (Cth), s 37N: see *Kimber v The Owners Strata Plan No 48216* [2017] FCAFC 226.

66 See *Bankruptcy Act 1966* (Cth), s 7.

67 Section 7(2)(b).

68 Section 7(3).

69 Section 45(1).

70 Section 45(2).

71 Section 46(1).

couple. If there are multiple respondents to a creditor's petition, the court may make a sequestration order against one or more respondents named in the petition, and the petition may be dismissed or withdrawn against the other or others.[72]

12.5.4 Debt owed of at least $5000

A creditor (or several creditors acting jointly) can present a bankruptcy petition against a debtor only if the debtor owes to the petitioning creditor a single debt of at least $5000, or two or more debts aggregating to at least $5000. The $5000 threshold imposed under s 44(1) is in respect of any debt owing and is independent of the final judgment or order required for the issue of a bankruptcy notice under s 4(1).[73] If a petition is presented jointly by two or more creditors, the debtor must be owing debts amounting to not less than $5000 to two or more creditors.[74] The debts must be a liquidated sum,[75] due and payable either immediately or at a certain future date,[76] and be founded on an act of bankruptcy[77] committed within six months prior to the presentation of the petition.[78] However, the bankruptcy notice need not be based upon those debts.[79]

12.5.5 Australian connection

A debtor against whom a creditor presents a bankruptcy petition in respect of a particular act of bankruptcy must have a specific connection with Australia. The court has jurisdiction over debtors as long as the act of bankruptcy occurred when the debtor was present or ordinarily resident, or had a dwelling or place of business, or was carrying on business either personally or through an agent, or was a member of a firm or partnership that carried on business through partners, agents or managers, in Australia.[80] The requirement that a debtor have a dwelling in Australia will not be satisfied if the debtor owns a property at which they do not reside. However, a connection is established if the debtor is temporarily absent and is able to enjoy the property upon returning.[81] The requirement that a person be carrying on a business is a reference to the debtor's own business, and is not satisfied where the debtor is employed to carry on the business of another, or is in control of a company carrying on a business.[82] Even if

72 Section 46(2) (eg if the creditor has not been able to serve process against all debtors).

73 *Autron Pty Ltd v Benk* (2011) 195 FCR 404.

74 Section 44(1)(a).

75 Both at the time of the commission of the act of bankruptcy and at the date of the presentation of the petition: *McCracken v Phoenix Constructions (Queensland) Pty Ltd* (2013) 210 FCR 149.

76 The effect of an instalment order is to convert an immediately payable debt into a payable debt in the future: *Re Padagas; Ex parte Carrier Air Conditioning Pty Ltd* (1977) 30 FLR 170; *Re Nath; Ex parte Ghysels* (1996) 63 FCR 523. Payment must not be dependent on a future event.

77 As defined in *Bankruptcy Act 1966* (Cth), s 40.

78 Section 44(1)(c). *McCracken v Phoenix Constructions (Queensland) Pty Ltd* (2013) 210 FCR 149.

79 *Emerson v Wreckair Pty Ltd* (1992) 33 FCR 581.

80 *Bankruptcy Act 1966* (Cth), s 43(b)(i)–(iv). See also s 55(2A) in respect of a debtor's petition.

81 *Mathai v Kwee* [2005] FCA 932. Establishing residence is a question of law (*Levene v Inland Revenue Commissioners* [1928] AC 217); residence is not restricted to a single country (*Re Taylor; Ex parte Natwest Australia Bank Ltd* (1992) 37 FCR 194, 198; *Battenberg v Restom* [2007] FCAFC 195.

82 *Bankruptcy Act 1966* (Cth), s 43(b)(iii); see *Turner v Trevorrow* (1994) 49 FCR 566.

the debtor has left Australia and the relevant business has ended, an act of bankruptcy has occurred if the debtor continues to owe debts in Australia.[83]

12.5.6 Vesting of property

The assets of a person who enters bankruptcy are vested in a separate trust estate (the bankrupt estate).[84] A trustee in bankruptcy is appointed to administer the bankrupt estate. The trustee in bankruptcy is either a registered trustee or the Official Receiver in Bankruptcy. The property that formerly belonged to the bankrupt, such as the bankrupt's real property, vests in the trustee as divisible property, except for those assets specifically exempted by s 116 of the Act. Exempted property includes personal and household property, a car under a certain value, superannuation funds and property held by the bankrupt in trust.

12.6 Definitions: Solvency, insolvency, solvent and insolvent

The Corporations Act, s 95A defines 'solvent' and thereby indirectly provides a test for determining insolvency. The Act provides as follows:

> **Solvency and insolvency**
>
> (1) A person is solvent if, and only if, the person is able to pay all the person's debts, as and when they become due and payable.
>
> (2) A person who is not solvent is insolvent.

A person is therefore insolvent by legislative definition if they are unable to pay all of their debts and not any particular debt.[85] However, a person's inability to pay a debt may be indicative (if not definitive) of their insolvency. A temporary lack of funds or a lack of cash in their current account rendering a person unable to pay a, some or even all of their debts does not satisfy the requirement of insolvency. However, a temporary lack of liquidity is to be distinguished from chronic cash flow shortages, whereas reliance on the outcome of speculative ventures,[86] or raising capital by the sale of business,[87] will not contribute to the assessment of solvency. Insolvency is an inclusive assessment of the debtor's financial position. Liquidity at the time the debt is due to be paid is only a factor the court takes into account in consideration

---

83 *Re Vassis* (1986) 9 FCR 518.

84 By contrast, in the case of a company in liquidation a separation arises between assets and their ownership in the sense that the liquidated company continues to exist and retain ownership of its assets while control of the company, and therefore of its assets, passes from the directors and members of the company to the liquidator.

85 Debts are liquidated sums, while claims (eg for damages) become debts only when determined by courts, and so, on the wording of s 95A, are not relevant to insolvency unless so indicated by the nature of the business. An insurer's liabilities to make claims payment, for instance, are unliquidated damages, but material to a determination of the insurer's solvency: *New Cap Reinsurance Corporation Ltd (in liq) v A E Grant* (2008) 221 FLR 164.

86 *Expo International Pty Ltd v Chan* [1979] 2 NSWLR 820, 837.

87 *Re Timbatec Pty Ltd* (1974) 24 FLR 30, 37.

of the debtor's entire financial position, which embraces the debtor's capital-raising capacity, such as its ability to make payment by means of realising money through – among other legitimate means – selling, mortgaging, borrowing, raising unsecured loans, pledging or otherwise dealing with or using their assets.[88] Moreover, the court will interpret a payment as having been made when and as it falls due if it is made within an acceptable time. What is acceptable is assessed by reference to considerations such as the debtor's assets and liabilities, the nature of the debt or debts, the size of the debt or debts, the circumstances of the individual, corporate or business debtor, including the nature of the business conducted by the debtor, and the conduct of creditors.[89] Creditors may alter the terms of repayment so that debts are no longer due and payable at a particular time; however, failing to demand payment of a due and payable debt will not have the same effect.[90]

12.7 Test for insolvency

The solvency or insolvency of a person or corporation may be determined by application of either or a combination of:

- the 'cash flow' or 'commercial' insolvency test; and
- the 'balance sheet' or 'absolute' insolvency test.

The cash flow test proves insolvency if a person or company is unable to pay their or its debts when and as they fall due and payable because their cash or other resources are inadequate to pay creditors at the time that creditors may properly make a demand for payment. Insolvency is proved on the balance sheet test if the person's or company's assets are insufficient to meet its liabilities. Even if a company or person holds assets of a value sufficient to satisfy its creditors, although its cash flow is inadequate, it may nevertheless be insolvent if it is unable to realise monies from those assets either at all or within a time acceptable to the court.[91] A person or company will be insolvent despite adequate cash flow if liabilities exceed assets, unless they are able to apply the cash flow to the payment of and pay their due debts from the liquidation of their assets.[92]

Neither the cash flow nor the balance sheet test is complete or precise. The imprecision of the cash flow test stems from the uncertainties of cash flow, and whether monies can be realised from assets at a particular time. While either may indicate a current lack of liquidity, neither can accurately forecast whether the debtor will continue to be unable to pay their debts. The balance sheet test, on the other hand, depends on the valuation of assets, particularly by reference to liabilities which may themselves be subject to variation, or exist in a form

88 Despite this being in effect the payment of one debt with another, it will suffice to constitute solvency now that the words 'from the debtor's own moneys' has been removed from the definition of insolvency in s 95A.

89 *Sandell v Porter* (1966) 115 CLR 666, per Barwick CJ.

90 *Southern Cross Interiors Pty Ltd v Deputy Commissioner of Taxation* (2001) 53 NSWLR 213.

91 *Re Tweed Garages Ltd* [1962] Ch 406, 410.

92 *Sandell v Porter* (1966) 115 CLR 666.

that is not readily comparable to the value of held assets, or exist in unvalued form, or be contingent upon the occurrence of future events.[93]

While the cash flow test establishes insolvency under the bankruptcy legislation,[94] insolvency is a finding of fact in the context of a consideration of all the circumstances in which the business operates and the situations in which its debts fall due. In other words, factual insolvency is an assessment of a company's financial performance over time relative to the indicators[95] of insolvency in the particular circumstances[96] of each case, and is not a legal definition or the application of an artificially restrictive set of parameters blind to the reality of commercial and financial considerations.

12.8 Scope of the Act: Voluntary and involuntary bankruptcy

The *Bankruptcy Act 1966* (Cth) prescribes creditors' petitions (involuntary bankruptcy) and debtors' petitions (voluntary bankruptcy) as the means by which proceedings may be initiated to administer a debtor's property under the provisions of the Act. A person may therefore become bankrupt in one of two ways.

1. Involuntary bankruptcy, which recognises the right of a creditor to force bankruptcy on a debtor if a debt remains unpaid. Involuntary bankruptcy involves a sequestration order being made by the court on the application of a creditor, resulting in the debtor becoming a bankrupt.
2. Voluntary bankruptcy, in which debtors go bankrupt voluntarily by presenting a debtor's petition to the Official Receiver.[97] The presentation of a declaration under s 54A is an act of bankruptcy.[98] Unless there is a pending application by the creditor to bankrupt the debtor, the petition is accepted and the person becomes bankrupt.

12.8.1 Bankruptcy on creditor's petition

Involuntary bankruptcy may be initiated by one or more creditors on a petition to the court. Creditors are likely to take the initiative in presenting the petition when the debtor is recalcitrant, or has acted dishonestly or fraudulently, or the debt is large. The debtor becomes a

93 For example, a guarantee triggered by the default of the primary debtor: *Hawkins v Bank of China* (1992) 26 NSWLR 562.

94 *Crema Pty Ltd v Land Mark Property Developments Pty Ltd* (2006) ACSR 631.

95 Indicators are provided in ASIC Information Sheet 42: 'Insolvency: A Guide for Directors'; applied in *Lewis v Doran* (2004) 50 ACSR 175; *Australian Securities and Investments Commission v Plymin* (2003) 46 ACSR 126.

96 Indicators must be assessed in the circumstances (eg consistent late payment may be explicable otherwise than by incapacity); debts the subject of enforcement actions may be disputed; see *Hussein v CSR Building Products Ltd* (2016) 246 FCR 62.

97 Approximately 90 per cent of bankruptcies are voluntary: AFSA administrative statistics, 2016/17. There are, however, state and territory variations.

98 *Bankruptcy Act 1966* (Cth), s 40(1)(da).

bankrupt if the court, having considered the petition, make a sequestration order against the debtor's estate.[99]

12.9 Voluntary bankruptcy

12.9.1 Moratorium provisions: Part IV, Division 2A

12.9.1.1 Declaration of intention to present a debtor's petition (s 54A)

The Bankruptcy Act allows debtors contemplating bankruptcy time to consider a range of options that may be available to them. A 21-day moratorium is available against any civil debt recovery process being taken against debtors by their creditors, enabling debtors time to explore options, to seek appropriate advice and to consider the irrevocable consequences of bankruptcy.[100] The benefit of the moratorium is obtained by the debtor presenting to the Official Receiver a *Declaration of Intention to Present a Debtor's Petition*[101] along with a statement of the debtor's affairs.[102] However, a debtor intending to present a debtor's petition is not required to present the declaration of intention in the prescribed form.

Before accepting such a declaration, the Official Trustee must give the debtor information prescribed by the *Bankruptcy Regulations 1996* (Cth).[103] Subject to this requirement, the Official Receiver must accept the declaration if it appears that the debtor is entitled to present it and if it is in the prescribed form.

Certain debtors are, however, disqualified from presenting the declaration. Section 54B excludes a debtor from presenting a declaration under s 54A if a creditor's petition is pending against them, or has been presented but not yet accepted or rejected, if the debtor's property is subject to control under Part X of the Act, or if the debtor has authorised a trustee or solicitor to control their affairs in accordance with s 188 of the Act within the previous six months, or who has presented and had a declaration accepted in the previous 12-month period.[104] The reason for prohibiting a debtor presenting a fresh declaration after the previous one runs out[105] is to prevent debtors abusing the moratorium process. Similarly, debtors may not use the moratorium process to defeat a creditor's petition.[106]

99 Section 43(2).

100 Section 54D; *Bankruptcy Regulations 1996* (Cth), reg 4.11: The debtor must first be given information about the alternatives to and consequences of bankruptcy. For the irreversible effects of bankruptcy, see *Re Smith* [1999] FCA 1755, wherein a bankrupt's application to have her bankruptcy annulled was refused after she had received incorrect advice in relation to a litigation claim against her former partner. The bankrupt claimed to have received incorrect advice to the effect that a litigation claim against her former partner remained hers to pursue despite bankruptcy; an application by her to annul her bankruptcy based on that misunderstanding was refused.

101 Section 54A; AFSA, Form 5.

102 Section 54A(2).

103 Section 54D.

104 Section 54B.

105 Section 54B(f).

106 Section 54B(b).

12.9.1.2 Secured creditors are protected (s 54L)

The provisions under the Act do not affect a secured creditor's right to realise or deal with the security.[107] Secured creditors can generally stand outside the bankruptcy process even at the pre-bankruptcy stage.

A declaration is effective in respect of 'frozen debts',[108] which are defined in general terms as a debt that would be provable in any bankruptcy.[109] A creditor to whom a frozen debt is owed is unable to apply for the issue of 'enforcement process' (s 5(1)) or to enforce a remedy against the debtor's person or property.[110] But a creditor is not prevented from initiating or taking a fresh step in legal proceedings in respect of the debt that are not connected with enforcing a judgment.[111] And importantly, the creditor is still able to commence bankruptcy proceedings against the debtor.

Sheriffs, court registrars and those subject to garnishee orders are prevented from taking their respective enforcement or other such actions.[112]

12.9.2 Bankruptcy on individual debtor's petition

An individual debtor – including non-Australian citizens, Members of Parliament, and persons under the age of 18 years[113] – who is insolvent may present a debtor's petition.[114] They must do so personally, and not on behalf of a debtor under a power of attorney.[115] Some state laws, however, permit administrators to make those whose affairs they have charge of bankrupt.[116] The debtor must be able to show a connection with Australia.[117]

Voluntary bankruptcy involves an insolvent debtor presenting a debtor's petition[118] and filing a statement of affairs with the Official Receiver, either electronically or by post, that lists the debtor's assets and liabilities and discloses other information, along with a copy[119] verified by affidavit.[120] The Official Receiver must accept the petition unless a decision is made to reject it, either by the exercise of their discretion where if it fails to comply with the prescribed form, or because it is not accompanied by a statement of affairs, or the Official Receiver is of the view

---

107 Section 54L.
108 Section 54E(1).
109 Section 5. This does not include liability under a family law maintenance arrangement.
110 Section 54E(2).
111 Section 54E(3).
112 Section 54F, 54G, 54H.
113 Section 7(1).
114 Section 7(2). *Re Mottee* (1977) 16 ALR 129, 135.
115 *Orix Australia Corporation Ltd v McCormick* (2005) 145 FCR 244. Under some state laws administrators may be appointed to look after the affairs of mentally infirm or cognitively impaired persons. For example, in *SAL and JGL* [2016] WASAT 63, administration orders were made under the *Guardianship and Administration Act 1990* (WA) allowing a son to present a debtor's petition on behalf of his father who had suffered a stroke that left him with significant cognitive impairment.
116 *SAL and JGL* [2016] WASAT 63 (orders made under the *Guardianship and Administration Act 1990* (WA)); *Trustee and Guardianship Act 2009* (NSW).
117 *Bankruptcy Act 1966* (Cth), s 55(2A).
118 Section 55(1); AFSA, Form 6.
119 Section 55(2).
120 Section 55(2).

that the statement of affairs is inadequate,[121] or the debtor does not satisfy the criteria of territorial connection through presence, residency or the conduct of business.[122] The act of the Official Receiver in accepting and endorsing a petition and thereby making a person bankrupt is purely administrative[123] and not judicial.

The debtor becomes a bankrupt 'at the first instant'[124] of the day when the Official Receiver, having accepted the declaration, endorses the petition and signs a copy of it.[125] A debtor who has executed a personal insolvency agreement is not, except with the leave of the court, entitled to present a petition against themselves unless the agreement has been set aside or terminated, or all obligations under the agreement have been discharged.[126] If, at the time when a debtor's petition is presented, a creditor's petition against a group of debtors that includes the debtor is already pending against the debtor, the Official Receiver must refer the debtor's petition to the court for a direction to accept or reject it.[127]

If the Official Receiver accepts the declaration, the Official Receiver must notify the creditors disclosed on the debtor's statement of affairs of that acceptance.[128] The debtor can produce the declaration to creditors intending to execute on court judgments, or to the sheriff. Both must take note of the declaration and put any action on hold during the 21-day period. Where a sealed copy is produced to a creditor, the latter cannot apply during the 'stay period' for the issue of any enforcement process, or enforce any remedy against the debtor's person or property in respect of the debt.[129] Broadly, the 'stay period' is the period beginning on the day of acceptance of the declaration and ending on the 21st day after the day of acceptance or, inter alia, the presentation of a creditor's petition or debtor's petition against the debtor, whichever is the earliest.[130] The period of the stay is defined in s 5(1). The period will end when the first in time of the following events occurs:

(a) the period of 21 days ends;
(b) a creditor's petition is petitioned against the debtor or the debtor presents their own petition;
(c) the debtor signs a petition under s 188; or
(d) a sequestration order is made against the debtor.

121 Section 55(3). The Official Receiver has discretion to reject a debtor's petition broadly to prevent abuse of the bankruptcy process (s 55(3AA)). Appeal lies to the Administrative Appeals Tribunal (s 55(3AC)): *Drake v Jones* [2009] FMCA 298).

122 Section 55(2A). A debtor must also provide the Official Receiver with sufficient information to confirm their identity – for example, a passport or driver's licence.

123 *Official Receiver v Walia* [1997] FCA 1190.

124 *Bankruptcy Act 1966* (Cth), s 57A.

125 Section 55(4A). However, the date of commencement of bankruptcy is determined by s 115(1) of the Act.

126 Section 55(6).

127 Section 55(3B).

128 Section 54C(2).

129 Section 54E.

130 Section 5(1).

12.9.3 Partnership debtors

Partnerships are not separate legal entities. Partnerships, therefore, do not themselves become bankrupt; rather, partners become bankrupt in their individual capacity. Creditors may therefore recover debts against individual partners, and individual partners may present individual petitions.[131] The estates of individual partners are also administered separately. Jointly held assets, however, are available for joint and several debts.

12.9.4 Acts of bankruptcy

Formal bankruptcy or liquidation requires a creditor to prove the insolvency of the debtor by establishing that the debtor committed an act of bankruptcy within the six months before the presentation of the creditor's petition to the Official Receiver.[132] Section 40(1) of the *Bankruptcy Act 1966* (Cth)[133] specifies the cases in which a debtor commits an act of bankruptcy. A debtor may be committing an act of bankruptcy if they do any of the things set out in s 40(1)(c) with the intention of defeating or delaying creditors. The onus is upon the creditor to prove the debtor's intention, and must reckon with the fact that the creditor's absence from the country, their dwelling or their business, or in general, is not compatible only with the requisite intention.[134] A debtor commits an act of bankruptcy if the sale of the debtor's property fails to satisfy the court order, suggesting the debtor has insufficient property to realise funds that will satisfy the debts against them. The warrant of execution must be returned to the court registry to prove that the execution was returned unsatisfied.[135] The presentation of a declaration under s 54A is an act of bankruptcy.[136]

The debtor's inability to pay debts must be distinguished from other reasons why debtors may not have paid their debts. An alleged debtor may refuse to pay a debt even though they are able to do so, on the basis of the existence of a bona fide dispute as to whether a debt is in fact owing, or because the debt is acknowledged but the quantum of the debt is in dispute. Further, the debt may be unpaid merely through inadvertence, or because the debtor refuses to pay.[137] The most common act of bankruptcy is the failure to comply with a bankruptcy notice. The ease with which this is provided makes it rare in practice for any reliance to be placed on other methods. The service of a bankruptcy notice on a debtor must be founded on having obtained final judgment against the debtor.

---

131 Section 56A.

132 Sections 43(1)(a) and 44(1)(c).

133 Section 459C(2) of the *Corporations Act 2001* (Cth) permits a creditor or a person otherwise permitted to seek a company's liquidation to rely on a statutory presumption of insolvency. A company is deemed to be insolvent if during the previous three months ending on the day when an application for winding up was made it fails to comply with the terms of a winding-up demand under s 459E, or the execution process issued upon the company on a judgment is returned wholly or partially unsatisfied, or a receiver is appointed or security interests are enforced. Insolvency proceedings may also be based on presumptions available to a liquidator or trustee.

134 *Edge Technology v Wang* [2000] FCA 1586; *Puels v Exelerate Funding Pty Ltd* (2005) 214 ALR 616.

135 *Re Ousley* (1994) 48 FCR 131; *Lewis v Lamb* [2012] FMCA 392.

136 *Bankruptcy Act 1966* (Cth), s 40(1)(da).

137 *Smith v Bone* (2015) 104 ACSR 528.

An act of bankruptcy may occur when a debtor notifies their creditors that they have or will suspend the repayment of debts.[138] Acts of bankruptcy may also arise out of a simple form of insolvency administration known as 'debt agreements'.[139] Section 40(1)(i) provides that an act of bankruptcy may involve the signing of an authority under s 188 of Part X of the Act. The s 188 authority is used by the debtor to attempt to enter a personal insolvency agreement with creditors by putting a proposal to creditors that may be accepted or rejected. If the proposal is rejected, any creditor may petition for bankruptcy and use the signing of the authority as the act of bankruptcy. The authority must be effective for the purposes of Part X in order to create an act of bankruptcy.[140]

An act of bankruptcy occurs if the debtor becomes insolvent as a result of property being transferred under a financial agreement in family law proceedings to which the debtor is a party.[141] The section was introduced in 2005 to overcome the problem of defeating or delaying creditors by using financial agreements to transfer assets.[142]

12.9.5 Bankruptcy notice

Failure by the debtor to comply with a bankruptcy notice is the most frequently utilised 'act of bankruptcy' upon which creditors' petitions are founded. A creditor may apply for a bankruptcy notice from the Official Receiver upon obtaining either final judgment, or an order for payment, against the debtor.[143] That is, the order or judgment must be dispositive of the dispute or finally determinative of the parties' rights.[144] A judgment or order whose execution has been stayed is not final.[145]

The notice requires the debtor to pay, or secure payment of, the amount claimed in the notice owing under the judgment debt within the time specified in the notice (normally, 28 days).[146] The monetary claim must be at least $5000, whether it is based on one or several judgments or orders,[147] and be issued within six years of the date of the judgment or order.[148]

138 *Conn v Hanks* [2001] FMCA 62 (frank oral notification that the debtor had and would have no money with which to pay creditors); compare with more circumspect language not amounting to notice in *Lawry v Mitrou* [2009] FMCA 258.

139 *Bankruptcy Act 1966* (Cth), s 40(1)(ha), (hb), (hc), (hd).

140 *Re Curry* [1992] FCA 619.

141 *Bankruptcy Act 1966* (Cth), s 40(1)(o). In paragraph (o), transfer of property includes a payment of money. Furthermore, a person who does something that results in another person becoming the owner of property that did not previously exist is taken to have transferred the property to the other person: s 40(7).

142 *Official Trustee in Bankruptcy v Galanis* (2017) 52 FamLR 219.

143 *Bankruptcy Act 1966* (Cth), s 40(1)(g).

144 *Gardiner v Gardiner* (1992) 39 FCR 259; *Autron Pty Ltd v Benk* (2011) 195 FCR 404. A later variation of the order or appeal against the judgment does not diminish its finality: *Re Pannowitz; Ex parte Wilson* (1975) 38 FLR 184. *Bankruptcy Act 1966* (Cth), s 40(3) deems certain judgments or orders final for the purposes of s 40(1)(g).

145 Section 40(1)(g); see *Ritson v Commissioner of Police, New South Wales Police Force* [2018] FCCA 916. Judgment is stayed if leave of the court is required to execute it: *Denneby v Reasonable Endeavours Pty Ltd* (2003) 130 FCR 494.

146 See S Kiel-Chisholm, 'Catch Me If You Can: The Effective Service of Bankruptcy Documents in a Changing World' (2010) 18 *Insolvency Law Journal* 197.

147 *Bankruptcy Act 1966* (Cth), s 40(1)(a), (b); see *Lewis v Nortex Pty Ltd (in liq)* (2013) 211 FCR 483.

148 Section 41(3)(c)(i).

The notice also sets out the consequences for non-compliance, which include that a failure by the debtor to comply with the notice will constitute an act of bankruptcy. The act of bankruptcy committed by the debtor may be used to found a petition by any creditor, not just the creditor who issued the bankruptcy notice.

The purpose of the bankruptcy notice is to inform the debtor of the quantum of the creditor's claim and provide the debtor with an opportunity to pay or secure the amount claimed.[149] The notice should be capable of being understood and complied with by the debtor. A bankruptcy notice must be in the prescribed form,[150] and should comply with every other requirement under the Act.[151] Because of the seriousness of the consequences of bankruptcy proceedings for individuals, courts require strict compliance with the Act.[152] Failure to do so may well result in the notice subsequently being held invalid by the court and thus ineffective to ground an act of bankruptcy.[153] However, a misstatement by the creditor as to the amount owing to them does not in and of itself invalidate the notice unless the debtor notifies the creditor within the time allowed for payment that they dispute the validity of the notice on the basis of the misstatement.[154] Nevertheless, circumstances exist where bankruptcy proceedings based on defective notices not contested by the debtor are dismissed.[155]

Service of the bankruptcy notice on the debtor is made in accordance with reg 16.01(1), which includes personal service, postal and courier service, service utilising a document exchange facility, and service by fax or other electronic means. Under reg 16.02(2), the debtor can adduce evidence of non-service, but not of non-receipt.[156] A bankruptcy notice must be properly served and be considerate of the circumstances of the debtor,[157] but appropriate having regard to actions to avoid service taken by the debtor. Substituted service is available by application under s 309 of the Act and appropriate where the debtor has no permanent address, or is taking evasive action to avoid service. To obtain substituted service the creditor must satisfy the court that it is practically impossible to serve the debtor personally, and that the method to be employed will be reasonably effective in bringing the bankruptcy notice to the debtor's attention.[158] Bankruptcy notices are valid for six months from the date of issue, or for such further time as extended by permission of the Official Receiver.

A debtor has 21 days after the date of service to comply with a bankruptcy notice that is served within Australia, or as much time as granted by the court if the court grants leave to serve the notice outside Australia.[159] Failure of a debtor to comply by the end of the 21st day constitutes an act of bankruptcy.[160]

149 *Re Pugliese; Ex parte Chase Manhattan Bank Australia Ltd* (1993) 44 FCR 536.

150 AFSA, Form 1; *Bankruptcy Act 1966* (Cth), s 41(2); *Bankruptcy Regulations 1996* (Cth), reg 4.02(1). Substantial compliance with the form is sufficient: reg 4.02(3).

151 *Bankruptcy Act 1966* (Cth), s 41.

152 See J Allsop, 'Values in Public Law' [2015] *Fed J Schol* 17.

153 *Re Wong; Ex parte Kitson* (1979) 38 FLR 207, 217.

154 *Bankruptcy Act 1966* (Cth), s 41(5).

155 *Buere v Commonwealth Bank of Australia* (2014) 283 FLR 414.

156 *Skalkos v T & S Recoveries Pty Ltd* (2004) 141 FCR 107.

157 See *Debt Collection Guidelines for Collectors and Creditors* (ACCC and ASIC).

158 *Ginnane v Diners Club Ltd* (1993) 42 FCR 90.

159 *Bankruptcy Act 1966* (Cth), s 40(1)(g)(i)–(ii).

160 *Swarbrick v Burge* (2009) 236 FLR 311.

An application may be made to the Federal Circuit Court or the Federal Court to extend time for compliance with a bankruptcy notice the sole source of power for which is provided by s 41(6A).[161] The seriousness of bankruptcy proceedings means that extension orders should not be made without the creditor being notified and having an opportunity to be heard.[162] The decision to grant the extension or not is discretionary guided by consideration being given to the reasons the debtor failed to obtain a stay of judgment, whether the debtor is solvent, any prejudice that may befall the debtors, whether the relation back period is significant, and whether undertakings have been given with respect to the judgment.[163]

Arguably, an application may be made under s 41(6A) for an extension of time for compliance by a creditor. This may occur where the debtor successfully applies to have the notice set aside at trial, and the creditor succeeds on appeal.[164]

The court may extend the time for compliance with a bankruptcy notice after the expiry of the original time in the notice, as long as prior to the time of expiry for compliance they have satisfied the preconditions in s 41(6A). That is, either they have instituted proceedings to set aside the judgment or order for which the notice was issued, or they have made an application to the court to set aside the bankruptcy notice.

The court may refuse to extend the time for compliance under s 41(6C) if, in its opinion, proceedings have not been instituted in good faith or prosecuted with due diligence.

Debtors' most frequent response is to seek to apply to have the bankruptcy notice set aside. The court hears these applications under its general powers,[165] or under the power to extend time for compliance with a notice. Section 306(1) provides that a formal defect will not invalidate proceedings unless the defect is capable of causing substantial injustice incurable by court order.[166] Debtors therefore seek to demonstrate that the notice is substantively defective, or that a formal defect in the notice is capable of causing substantive injustice. Courts have interpreted compliance with the formal requirements of notices strictly, because of the serious consequences of bankruptcy proceedings,[167] but have also acknowledged that such an approach may produce injustices. For example, in *Kyriackou v Shield Mercantile Pty Ltd*, Weinberg J recognised that 'bankruptcy law is often highly technical, and occasionally far removed from common sense'.[168]

While bankruptcy notice must be in the prescribed form,[169] formal deficiencies or irregularities will not invalidate bankruptcy proceedings 'unless the Court ... is of the opinion that a substantial injustice has been caused by the defect'.[170] Bankruptcy notices are rendered invalid

161 *McLean v Australia and New Zealand Banking Group Ltd* (1993) 42 FCR 300, 302.

162 *Sockhill v Deputy Commissioner of Taxation* (2000) 178 ALR 113; *Re Nguyen; Ex parte Commissioner of Taxation* (1995) 54 FCR 403.

163 *Prins v Body Corporate for the Wave CTS* [2013] FMCA 148; *Council for the City of Sydney v Obeid* [2013] FCA 149.

164 *Shepherd v Chiquita Brands (South Pacific) Ltd* (2004) 1 ABC (NS) 610, 623–4.

165 *Bankruptcy Act 1966* (Cth), s 30(1); *Re Sterling; Ex parte Esanda Pty Ltd* (1980) 30 ALR 77; *Re Briggs* (1986) 12 FCR 310.

166 *Bankruptcy Act 1966* (Cth), s 306(1).

167 *Re Walsh* [1982] FCA 250: 'A bankruptcy notice sets in motion a whole process leading to bankruptcy and must, since the proceedings are of a quasi-penal nature, be construed strictly.'

168 *Kyriackou v Shield Mercantile Pty Ltd* (2004) 138 FCR 324.

169 *Bankruptcy Act 1966* (Cth), s 41(2); *Bankruptcy Regulations 1996* (Cth), reg 4.02; AFSA, Form 1.

170 Section 306.

if they have not satisfied an essential requirement of the Act, or mislead debtors as to what they must do to comply with the notice.[171] As the debtor's compliance with the notice is essential, a notice is not merely formally defective, which could reasonably mislead the debtor as to the requirements of compliance. A notice may be capable of reasonably misleading the debtor without the debtor being in fact misled. In determining whether a notice is misleading, the courts may have regard to the circumstances of the case and assess the issue from the point of view of the relevant debtor.[172] Where a bankruptcy notice has been issued to several debtors, it may be invalid in relation to one or more of them.[173]

Examples of defects that have been held capable of misleading a debtor include the creditor's address for the debtor's payment of debts being stated incorrectly[174] and the wrong legal description of the creditor being stated on the notice;[175] however, notices have not been invalidated for minor misdescriptions[176] or spelling errors.[177] Although the court applies an objective test in determining whether a notice is misleading without having to determine whether the debtor was in fact misled, the attributes and circumstances of the relevant debtor are relevant considerations. The bankruptcy notice itself must enable the debtor to understand what steps they must take to comply with it, and the debtor 'is not expected or required to work ... things out for himself'.[178]

Section 41(5) of the Act provides that a bankruptcy notice is not invalidated only because the amount specified on it exceeds the debt due to the creditor, but requires the debtor to dispute the misstatement of the amount by notice to the creditor within the time permitted for payment. Therefore, a notice that overstates the assessment of the sum owed by the debtor is not thereby automatically invalidated.[179] This is because s 41(5) is not a source of power for setting aside notices on the basis that they contain a misstatement alone or assume that misstated notices are invalid in every instance; rather, it is a saving provision by which the court preserves notices from invalidity.[180] However, if the overstatement results from the creditor's failure to deduct amounts paid by the debtor towards the debt, the validity of the notice will not be preserved by the application of s 41(5) of the Act.[181] While the wording of s 41(5) on its face suggests that the debtor's notice is the only requirement to invalidate the notice, it has been interpreted as requiring the debtor to provide the creditor with details of the basis of the dispute.[182] The Full Federal Court has held that on an application to set aside a

171 *Kleinwort Benson v Crowl* (1988) 165 CLR 71; *Adams v Lambert* (2006) 228 CLR 409.

172 *Fuller, in the matter of Alford v Alford* (2017) 252 FCR 168.

173 *Dimasi v Nangiloc Colignan Farms Pty Ltd* (2007) 157 FCR 387.

174 *Kyriackou v Shield Mercantile Pty Ltd* (2004) 138 FCR 324.

175 *Re Hansen* (1985) 4 FCR 590.

176 *Fuller, in the matter of Alford v Alford* (2017) 252 FCR 168.

177 *Viavattene v Birch* [2015] FCCA 2676; however, a substantial misspelling of a debtor's name invalidated a bankruptcy notice against one of several debtors, but not others, in *Dimasi v Nangiloc Colignan Farms Pty Ltd* (2007) 157 FCR 387.

178 *Blackshaw Services Pty Ltd v Cureton* (2003) 1 ABC (NS) 453, 458.

179 See *Re Walsh* [1982] FCA 250. The debtor may dispute the notice: *Croker v Commissioner of Taxation* (2005) 145 FCR 150.

180 *Re Walsh; Olivieri v Stafford* (1989) 24 FCR 413, 428. *Bankruptcy Act 1966* (Cth), s 41(6) is to be read in conjunction with s 41(5) along these same lines.

181 *St George Wholesale Finance Pty Ltd v Spalla* (2000) 181 ALR 682.

182 *Seovic Civil Engineering Pty Ltd v Groenveld* (1999) 87 FCR 120; *James v Deputy Commissioner of Taxation [No 2]* [2010] FCA 677.

bankruptcy notice the court should not go behind the judgment on which the bankruptcy notice was based, notwithstanding that the amount of the judgment debt exceeded the balance actually owing, if the grounds upon which the judgment is challenged are such that, if accepted, they would only support a finding that the amount of the debt should be reduced and would not support a finding that there was in truth no debt at all.[183]

In *Re Clubb; Ex parte Clubb v Westpac Banking Corporation*,[184] the court exercised its discretion in favour of an applicant where the requisite notice had been given three days late because of an oversight by the applicant's solicitor.[185] It was also held that the bankruptcy notice was invalid and must be set aside where it stipulated an excessive amount of interest, because no allowance had been made for the fact that the relevant period included a leap year.[186] However, a bankruptcy notice that requires the judgment debtor to pay a sum that is in fact due at the date of the issue of the bankruptcy notice is valid, notwithstanding that by the time of its service on the debtor the amount due under the judgment has been reduced by payments made after the issue of the notice but before its service. Such payments must be taken into account in determining whether there has been compliance by the debtor with the requirements of the notice (under s 40(1)(g)) but the bankruptcy notice itself is valid.[187]

A creditor may issue a second correct bankruptcy notice if the debtor challenges a prior defective bankruptcy notice. The creditor incurs further costs, but also loses the advantage of the earlier date of the act of bankruptcy and, with it, the date of the commencement of bankruptcy and time during which voidable earlier transactions may have been challenged. The creditor who issues a second notice must identify to the debtor the notice on which they intend to proceed so that the debtor knows with which notice they must comply.

Section 41(7) of the Act provides that the debtor may, prior to the expiration of the 21 days for compliance, apply to the court for an order to set aside the notice on the basis that they have a counter-claim, set-off or cross demand. The extension of time granted under this subsection is 'until and including the day on which the Court determines whether it is ... satisfied' that the debtor has such a counter-claim, set-off or cross demand.[188] The nature of the counter-claim, set-off or cross demand that satisfies the requirements of s 41(7) is set out in s 40(1)(g) as one that equals or exceeds the judgment debt or amount payable under the final order, and which was not able to be set up in the proceeding by which the creditor obtained judgment. It must also be a monetary claim.[189] The provision permits the debtor to present only those matters that could not have been raised previously. Whether a matter could have been set up is a question of law,[190] not of practicality, and not taking advantage of an opportunity to make a claim is not considered being unable to make it.[191]

183 *Emerson v Wreckair Pty Ltd* (1992) 33 FCR 581, 589.
184 (1990) 93 ALR 123.
185 (1990) 93 ALR 123, 125–6.
186 (1990) 93 ALR 123, 129–30.
187 *Walsh v Deputy Commissioner of Taxation* (1984) 156 CLR 337, 340.
188 The debtor need not prove their claim, but only demonstrate that they have 'a claim deserving to be finally determined': *Re Glew; Glew v Harrowell of Hunt & Hunt Lawyers* (2003) 198 ALR 331. However, neither is this satisfied by simply making the claim and showing how it is made out.
189 *Re Brink; Ex parte Commercial Banking Co of Sydney Ltd* (1980) 44 FLR 135, 138.
190 *Tzovaras v Nufeno Pty Ltd* [2003] FCA 1152.
191 *Re Brink; Ex parte Commercial Banking Co of Sydney Ltd* (1980) 44 FLR 135.

12.9.6 Creditor's petition

A creditor has a fixed, non-extendable period of six months after the act of bankruptcy in which to present a petition seeking a sequestration order.[192] The creditor must demonstrate that the debtor owes a debt of at least $5000 or a lesser amount that, with interest, meets the requirement for obtaining a sequestration order.[193] The petition must show the debtor's connection with Australia and that an act of bankruptcy has occurred. One or several persons – including a company[194] – who operate under a firm or business name may proceed or be proceeded against in that name.[195]

The petition must be properly served, and may be served personally or by substituted service under s 309(2) of the Act. Time for the service of the petition lapses 'at the expiration of . . . the period of twelve months commencing on the date of presentation of the petition'.[196] The petition may be extended by the court for a further period of 12 months at any time before the expiration of the 12 months, but cannot be extended beyond 24 months in total.[197]

12.9.7 Hearing of creditor's petition

A debtor who decides to oppose a creditor's petition must file a notice of opposition at least three days prior to the date of the hearing[198] in which they disclose the ground upon which the challenge is based. If the petition is defective in a manner that cannot be remedied, the court will dismiss it.[199] A petition hearing may be adjourned to give the debtor time to pay the debt.[200] However, a defective petition should be dismissed and not adjourned.[201]

A creditor may apply to be substituted for one whose debt has been paid, or for failing to press its petition with sufficient diligence,[202] as long as the debtor owes the substituted creditor a debt of at least $5000 at the date of the act of bankruptcy upon which the petition is based.[203] A substituted creditor continues the petition as if they had been the petitioning creditor from the commencement of the proceedings.

The court has discretion as to whether to make a sequestration order. Section 52(2) provides that, in relation to matters referred to in s 52(1),

192 *Bankruptcy Act 1966* (Cth), s 47(1A); AFSA, Form 6.

193 *Autron Pty Ltd v Benk* (2011) 195 FCR 404.

194 *All Saints Greek Orthodox Grammar School v Tabatos* (2004) 186 FLR 152.

195 *Bankruptcy Act 1966* (Cth), s 307.

196 Section 52(4). The court may by operation of the slip rule extend the petition after the expiry of the initial 12-month period: *Elyard Corporation Pty Ltd v DDB Needham Sydney Pty Ltd* (1995) 61 FCR 385. The error or omission may arise from the inadvertence of the court or a party: *Flint v Richard Busuttil & Co Pty Ltd* (2013) FCR 375.

197 *Bankruptcy Act 1966* (Cth), s 52(5).

198 *Federal Court (Bankruptcy) Rules 2016*, rule 2.06; AFSA, Form 5.

199 *Bankruptcy Regulations 1996* (Cth), reg 4.05(3) requires the petitioning creditor of a petition that has been dismissed to give a copy of the court's order to the Official Receiver within two business days.

200 Regulation 4.05(3) requires the petitioning creditor of a petition that has been adjourned to give a copy of the court's order, or other evidence of the adjournment date, to the Official Receiver within two business days.

201 *American Express International Inc v Held* (1999) 87 FCR 583.

202 *Bankruptcy Act 1966* (Cth), s 49.

203 *McNamara v Langford* (1931) 45 CLR 267; *McCracken v Phoenix Constructions (Queensland) Pty Ltd* (2013) 210 FCR 149.

If the Court is not satisfied with the proof of any of those matters, or is satisfied by the debtor:

(a) that he or she is able to pay his or her debts; or

(b) that for other sufficient cause a sequestration order ought not to be made; it may dismiss the petition.

The court's discretion is wider than its discretion to set aside a bankruptcy notice.[204] The onus is upon the debtor to demonstrate to the court that sufficient reason exists for it to exercise its discretion in the debtor's favour in not making a sequestration order,[205] while the court considers the public interest that attends the resolution of bankruptcy, and creditors' rights,[206] against the seriousness of the consequences of the debtor's bankruptcy.[207]

A debtor may also dispute the validity of a bankruptcy notice at the hearing of the creditor's petition.[208] A finding that the notice is flawed results in the petition being necessarily dismissed since the lack of an act of bankruptcy removes the basis of the petition and the court's jurisdiction.[209] The debtor may challenge the petition on the basis of formal flaws, defective execution or defective service.[210] Formal flaws that are not misleading to the debtor may be remedied under s 306 of the Act.[211]

At the hearing of the creditor's petition the court requires proof that the matters stated in the petition are true, that the petition has been served (unless service has been dispensed with),[212] and that the debt on which the petition is based is still owing.[213] If these matters are proved to the satisfaction of the court, it may make a sequestration order against the estate of the debtor. If, however, the court is not satisfied that these matters have been proved, or that the debtor is able to pay their debts, or that another sufficient cause exists as to why a sequestration order ought not to be made, it may dismiss the petition.[214] While the court has discretion to dismiss petition proceedings even if the debtor is able to pay their debts,[215] the debtor is not entitled to have the petition dismissed on that basis.[216] The debtor may be able, but unwilling, to pay the debt, and 'is perfectly entitled to adopt the role of recalcitrant debtor, and to decline to pay a

204 *Australian Securities and Investments Commission v Forge* (2003) 133 FCR 487.

205 *Ling v Enrobook Pty Ltd* (1997) 74 FCR 19; *Deputy Commissioner of Taxation v Bayeh* (1999) 100 FCR 144.

206 *Rozenbes v Kronhill* (1959) 95 CLR 409, 414.

207 *Russell v ANZ Banking Group Ltd* (1987) 14 FCR 72, 75.

208 It is, however, better practice for the debtor to seek to set aside the notice after it has been served, rather than to wait until the petition hearing. Even a successful dispute at the later stage may result in costs being ordered against the debtor.

209 *National Australia Bank Ltd v Westbrook* [2000] FCA 246; *Re Pollard; Ex parte Lensing Management Pty Ltd* (1991) 33 FCR 284.

210 *Australia & New Zealand Banking Group Ltd v Elferkh* (2000) 92 FCR 195; *Burrell v Connell* (1998) 84 FCR 383.

211 *MacDonald v Official Trustee in Bankruptcy* (2000) 107 FCR 72; *Joan Freedom Rogers Pty Ltd v Prasad* [2000] FCA 1049 (failure to show the date of the petition).

212 *Bendigo & Adelaide Bank Ltd v Feldman* [2013] FCCA 241.

213 *Bankruptcy Act 1966* (Cth), s 52(1).

214 Section 52(2).

215 Section 52(2)(a).

216 *Sarina v Council of the Shire of Wollondilly* (1980) 48 FLR 372, 376–7.

judgment debt if he wishes'.[217] The onus is on the debtor to prove their solvency and their ability to pay all their debts falling due.[218] However, sequestration may be ordered by courts exercising their discretion where, for example, assets are unable to be converted in a reasonable time to pay the debts,[219] or if the debtor fails to act on their capacity to borrow the money to repay their debts.[220]

The court also recognises 'other sufficient cause[s that] a sequestration order ought not to be made'[221] that cannot be circumscribed or limited,[222] and that arise in numerous and variable circumstances. While these engage judicial discretion, the proper approach to s 52(2)(b) is essential if a sequestration order is not to be set aside on appeal.[223] Sufficient cause has been found where there had been no service of an originating process where the creditor's petition depended on the judgment entered in the proceeding,[224] or the petition was invalidly served, or if the debtor has a set-off or cross demand against the creditor[225] that is of sufficient merit to justify an adjournment to enable a debtor to litigate.[226] However, the impecuniosity of debtors is not grounds for the avoidance of sequestration orders;[227] nor is the debtor's illness,[228] or the effect of bankruptcy on the debtor's standing in the community.[229]

The court must be satisfied as to the existence of the petitioning creditor's debt. The High Court has held that, where there are substantial reasons for questioning whether, despite the judgment debt, there was in reality a debt due to the petitioning creditor, the court must go behind the judgment debt to determine the existence or otherwise of the alleged debt.[230] The existence of a judgment against the debtor is only prima facie evidence of the debt and a judgment is never conclusive in bankruptcy. A bankruptcy court may exercise its discretion in deciding not to accept a judgment as satisfactory proof of the debt claimed.[231] There will normally be substantial reasons for the judgment to be questioned and for the court to question the truth of the debt.[232] Nevertheless, a court hearing a bankruptcy petition retains the

217 *Australia & New Zealand Banking Group Ltd v Foyster* [2000] FCA 400. In these cases, creditors do not have recourse to sequestration but can apply other remedies such as execution against property and garnishee proceedings.

218 It is not sufficient to demonstrate that they have assets that, if realised, would exceed their indebtedness: *Trojan v Corporation of the Town of Hindmarsh* (1987) 16 FCR 37.

219 *Re Sanders* [2003] FCA 1079.

220 *Re Capel; Ex parte Caram Finance Australia Ltd* [1998] FCA 372.

221 *Bankruptcy Act 1966* (Cth), s 52(2)(b).

222 *Clyne v Deputy Commissioner of Taxation* (1985) 5 FCR 1.

223 *Totev v Sfar* (2008) 167 FCR 193.

224 *Re Willshire-Smith; Ex parte Randle & Taylor Services Pty Ltd* (1994) 48 FCR 371.

225 *Re James* (1994) 51 FCR 14; *Totev v Sfar* (2008) 167 FCR 193.

226 Although the court will not consider the debtor's claims against third parties (*Ling v Enrobook Pty Ltd* (1997) 74 FCR 19) unless the relationship between the claims is so close as to make them substantially a claim against the petitioner (*McLean v Biztole Corporation* [1996] FCA 773), or where the debtor has reason to believe that a claim they are prosecuting is likely to produce adequate funds to resolve all their outstanding debts in a reasonable period of time (*Maddestra v Penfold Wines Pty Ltd* (1993) 44 FCR 303; *Radich v Bank of New Zealand* (1993) 45 FCR 101; *Re James* (1994) 51 FCR 14).

227 *Re Capel; Ex parte Caram Finance Australia Ltd* [1998] FCA 372; *Re Field* [1977] 3 WLR 937.

228 *Collett v Deputy Commissioner of Taxation* [2001] FCA 426.

229 *Stedman v Deputy Commissioner of Taxation* (2000) 44 ATR 88.

230 *Wren v Mahony* (1972) 126 CLR 212, 225, 232, 238.

231 *Corney v Brien* (1951) 84 CLR 343; *Wren v Mahony* (1972) 126 CLR 212; *Re Longo* (1995) 57 FCR 523.

232 *Culleton v Balwyn Nominees Pty Ltd* (2017) 343 ALR 632.

discretion to go behind even a final hearing against the debtor.[233] Going behind the judgment may be warranted where the judgment was obtained by default,[234] or where fraud or collusion are alleged.[235] A judgment obtained on compromise will justify the court's enquiry only if questions of unfairness or impropriety arise in relation to it.[236] In examining the debt, the court may find that an amount sufficient to found the bankruptcy, even if not all of it, is still owing.[237]

If a bankruptcy notice and the creditor's petition is based on a judgment that is under appeal by the debtor, the hearing of the petition may be adjourned until the appeal is determined, since this is preferable to bankrupting the debtor,[238] provided the debtor can demonstrate that the appeal has a genuine basis and they are honestly pursuing it.

Furthermore, it has been held by the High Court that a debt is not 'still owing' (since it is substituted for a right of proof against the bankrupt's estate) and therefore a sequestration order cannot be made on a creditor's petition where, subsequent to its presentation, the debtor has become a bankrupt by virtue of the Official Receiver's acceptance of the debtor's own petition for bankruptcy.[239] However, where presentation of the debtor's own petition in such circumstances constitutes an abuse of process, the court may annul the bankruptcy thereby resulting, and accordingly enable a sequestration order to be made on the creditor's petition.[240]

12.9.8 Effect of a sequestration order

By the making of a sequestration order, the debtor becomes a bankrupt and remains a bankrupt until they are discharged from bankruptcy or the sequestration order is annulled. On the date of commencement of bankruptcy, the bankrupt's property not being after-acquired property vests in the Official Trustee or in a registered trustee.[241] The Act defines the bankrupt's property broadly and so as to include any rights or powers that would have been enjoyed by the bankrupt over that property had they not become bankrupt.[242] The Act permits the trustee to divide the bankrupt's 'divisible property' among the creditors.[243] Property that the bankrupt acquires, or which passes to the bankrupt, after the commencement of bankruptcy and before the discharge[244] vests in the trustee as soon as it is acquired.[245] The

233 *Ramsay Health Care Australia Pty Ltd v Compton* (2017) 261 CLR 132.
234 *Olivieri v Stafford* (1989) 24 FCR 413.
235 *Corney v Brien* (1951) 84 CLR 343.
236 *Re Longo* (1995) 57 FCR 523.
237 *Re Seghabi* (1994) 52 FCR 303.
238 *Ahern v Deputy Commissioner of Taxation* (1987) 76 ALR 137.
239 *Corney v Brien* (1951) 84 CLR 343.
240 *Clyne v Deputy Commissioner of Taxation* (1984) 154 CLR 589, 598; see also *Compton v Ramsay Health Care Australia Pty Ltd* (2016) 246 FCR 508, [53]–[67].
241 *Bankruptcy Act 1966* (Cth), s 58(1).
242 Section 5(1).
243 Section 116(1). Non-divisible property is retained by the bankrupt: s 116(2).
244 That is, for the duration of the time that a person is bankrupt – in general, three years.
245 *Bankruptcy Act 1966* (Cth), s 58(1); *Piccone v Suncorp Metway Insurance Ltd* (2005) 148 FCR 437, [29]; including property received as part of a bequest to the bankrupt under a will (*Re Pevsner* (1983) 66 FLR 254); or of an equitable interest in a business (*Official Receiver v Delaton Pty Ltd* (1996) 130 FLR 207; *Donelly v McIntyre* [1999] FCA 450); or a lottery winnings (*Randall v Albaugh* [2009] FMCA 475); or money not being income (*Pascoe v Park* [2009] FMCA 1244). As one purpose of the bankruptcy laws is to offer the bankrupt a fresh start, assets acquired after the bankrupt is discharged do not vest: see

bankrupt is able to retain money saved from income,[246] whereas assets acquired by such monies become after-acquired property and vest in the trustee.[247] The trustee may also apply to the court to have certain property transfers made prior to the bankruptcy to be set aside.[248] A court may order a creditor to whom a preference payment has been made to repay it.[249] The vesting of property under s 58 of the Act is subject to the operation of s 58A (concerning property subject to a restraining order or forfeiture order,[250] or a pecuniary penalty order[251]), and s 59A (concerning family law property orders). The property that vests in the trustee is subject to the rights of secured creditors. Where state or territory law requires the vesting of the bankrupt's property in the trustee to be registered, the property vests in the trustee in equity by s 58(1), and pursuant to s 58(2) vests in law when the registration requirements have been complied with.[252] The trustee takes property subject to any valid equitable interest in it.

Section 58(3) provides that a creditor to whom the bankrupt is indebted in respect of any debt provable in bankruptcy cannot enforce any remedy against the person or property of the bankrupt, and is not able to commence any legal proceeding in respect of the debt without the leave of the court and on terms determined by the court.[253] However, the creditor is not required to seek leave of the court to commence legal proceedings upon the annulment of the bankruptcy by the acceptance of a composition by the creditors.[254] The provisions of s 58(3) do not affect the right of a secured creditor to realise or otherwise deal with their security;[255] nor do they prevent a creditor from enforcing any remedy against a bankrupt or their property that is not vested in the trustee of the bankrupt, in respect of any liability of the bankrupt under a maintenance agreement or maintenance order.[256]

12.9.9 Proceedings after a sequestration order statement of affairs

The debtor's property vests in the registered trustee who has given consent to act as trustee of the debtor's estate or, if there is no registered trustee in the Official Trustee in Bankruptcy, as soon as a debtor becomes a bankrupt.[257]

Within 14 days from the date on which a debtor against whose estate a sequestration order has been made is notified of their bankruptcy, they are required to:

N Howell and R Mason, 'Reinforcing Stigma or Delivering a Fresh Start: Bankruptcy and Future Engagement in the Workforce' (2015) 38(4) *University of New South Wales Law Journal* 1529.

246 *Re Gillies; Ex parte Official Trustee* [1993] FCA 289.

247 *Di Cioccio v Official Trustee in Bankruptcy* [2015] FCAFC 30; *Rodway v White* (2009) 233 FLR 262.

248 *Bankruptcy Act 1966* (Cth), ss 120 and 121.

249 Section 122.

250 Section 58A(1).

251 Section 58A(2).

252 Delay in registration will not of itself defeat the trustee's interests, but the trustee's interest may be defeated by waiver, estoppel or laches, or because the bankrupt has suffered some other detriment: *Dixon v Riquero* [2004] FMCA 173.

253 *Bankruptcy Act 1966* (Cth), s 58(3).

254 *Hudson v Sigalla* (2015) 235 FCR 122, [3], [27], [30].

255 *Bankruptcy Act 1966* (Cth), s 58(5).

256 Section 58(5A).

257 Sections 58, 156A(3), 160.

(a) file with the Official Receiver a statement of her or his affairs; and
(b) furnish a copy of the statement to the trustee.[258]

Joint debtors who are made bankrupt are required to submit a joint statement of affairs.[259] The failure of debtors or joint debtors to comply with these requirements is an offence of strict liability.[260] The statements of affairs of bankrupts and joint bankrupts may be inspected, copied and transcribed, in whole or in part, by creditors without a fee, and by any other person for a fee,[261] or by other bankrupts.[262] The Official Receiver must ensure that particular information in the statement that is not to be made available to the public is not made available to any person other than the bankrupt,[263] unless the information is required to be made available by law.[264] If, in the opinion of the Official Receiver, access to the information in the statement of affairs would or would likely jeopardise any person's safety, access to such information may be refused.[265] A debtor who presented a bankruptcy petition against themselves to the Official Receiver must have accompanied the petition with a statement of their affairs in the prescribed form.[266]

Bankrupts are required, immediately upon becoming a bankrupt, to furnish the trustee with their passport and all books in their possession that relate to their examinable affairs. Bankrupts are required to give the trustee any information they require about any of their conduct and examinable affairs, unless they are excused by the trustee or they are prevented from doing so.[267]

12.9.10 Meetings of creditors

The trustee is to convene a meeting of the creditors of a bankrupt:

(a) whenever the creditors so direct by resolution;
(b) whenever so requested in writing by at least one-quarter in value of the creditors; and
(c) whenever so requested in writing by more than one-tenth but less than one-quarter in value of the creditors, and sufficient security for the cost of holding the meeting has been lodged.[268]

Trustees may convene creditors' meetings at any time,[269] the purpose of which meeting is to consider how to deal with the bankrupt's property, without being required to attend such meetings personally, if they appoint a person in writing to represent them.[270] The bankrupt is

258 Section 54(1).
259 Section 54(2).
260 Section 54(3).
261 Section 54(4).
262 Section 54(5).
263 Section 54(6).
264 Section 54(6A).
265 Section 54(7).
266 Section 55.
267 Section 77.
268 Schedule 2, s 75-15(1).
269 Schedule 2, s 75-10.
270 Schedule 2, s 75-25(1). The Act contains detailed provisions regarding notices, agendas and procedures at such meetings: Schedule 2, ss 75-10 to 75-50.

under a duty to attend a meeting of creditors whenever required to by the trustee, and to provide the meeting with information about any of their conduct and examinable affairs as requested.[271]

In administering the bankruptcy, the trustee must take a 'proactive and considered approach' that provides 'transparency and consistency'.[272] The trustee must inform the debtor of their obligations under the Act, and inform the creditors of matters that have been investigated and that are still under enquiry, a statement of affairs, and details of income contributions.[273] The trustee must obtain access to the bankrupt's financial and other records[274] enabling the examination of the relevant dates[275] and the circumstances contributing to and causing the bankruptcy. The bankrupt must deliver books (widely defined and inclusive of such things as computer records) to the trustee.[276] The trustee may apply for a warrant of committal[277] ordering the seizure of the books. The full Federal Court in *Griffin v Pantzer*[278] emphasised that the importance of the trustee having the records to undertake the administration of the bankruptcy overrides the bankrupt's seeking to withhold documents to maintain their privilege against self-incrimination.

12.9.11 Discovery of the bankrupt's property and examination

The trustee, the Official Receiver or a creditor who has proved their debt may apply to the Federal Court, the Federal Circuit Court or the Registrars of those courts to issue a summons for the nominated person (being the bankrupt or any examinable person in relation to the bankrupt) to attend a public examination for the purpose of answering questions about the bankrupt's financial dealings, or give evidence concerning the bankrupt of their examinable affairs.[279] The bankrupt's spouse, family members, friends or business associates may be called for examination. The trustee may require the bankrupt to deliver up any books, including the books of an associated entity of the bankrupt,[280] which may be a natural person, company, entity or trust associated with the bankrupt, and are in the possession of the examinee and which relate to the bankrupt's examinable affairs.[281]

The bankrupt is required to provide the trustee with a copy of the statement of affairs filed after the sequestration order is made, which contains the information about the bankrupt's assets and liabilities the trustee requires to administer the estate. They are also required to

271 Section 77(1)(c), (d).
272 Insolvency Practice Rules (Bankruptcy) (IPRB), Division 41, 'Standards for Registered Trustees'.
273 IPRB, s 70-30.
274 The 'books' referred to in s 5.
275 Noting the importance of determining the date of the act of bankruptcy (s 40) and the commencement of the bankruptcy (s 5) essential for conducting investigations and challenges to transactions and transfers of property.
276 *Bankruptcy Act 1966* (Cth), s 77(1)(a).
277 Section 78(1); or s 130 to search the bankrupt's premises.
278 (2004) 137 FCR 209.
279 The failure to answer questions may be an offence (s 264C) or amount to contempt of court (*Nathan v Burness* (2011) 193 FCR 360).
280 *Bankruptcy Act 1966* (Cth), s 5(1), which may be a natural person, company, entity or trust.
281 Section 81. See A R Keay, 'Bankruptcy Examinations under Section 81 of the Bankruptcy Act' (1992) 17 *University of Queensland Law Journal* 35.

deliver to the trustee all documents relevant to the bankruptcy, including the relevant records of any associated entities.[282]

The Act provides administrative procedures for the investigating trustee, including the issuing of a demand notice,[283] notices that the Official Receiver may issue on behalf of the trustee,[284] and summons issued by the court on the trustee's application.[285]

The bankrupt is required to disclose to the trustee the acquisition of any divisible property,[286] and is forbidden to remove or conceal any of their property.[287] A trustee may apply for an order to seize the non-compliant bankrupt's property,[288] or a warrant for the bankrupt's committal to jail.[289] A trustee who suspects that property is at a particular premises may apply for a warrant to search those premises,[290] and to seize property found there,[291] which may also authorise the seizure of books and property having a connection to the bankrupt's examinable affairs.[292]

Section 77A provides that the trustee may demand the delivery of specific books of an associated entity which the trustee, in their opinion, believes relevant to the investigation.[293] The trustee is permitted under s 77AA to enter premises to search for books and records. Notices may be issued where parties are uncooperative and the trustee believes that it is likely that records are being concealed or may be destroyed.[294] The Official Receiver is empowered by s 77C to require a person to give information and evidence, and to produce relevant books in their possession.[295] The investigative and inquisitorial power under s 77C is such that it must be approached and exercised responsibly, and is closely supervised by the court because of its potential consequences.[296] The invalid parts of notices may be severed, but cannot be rewritten.[297]

Section 81 notices[298] may be applied for by the trustee, the Official Trustee or a creditor.[299] Notices under s 81 require the bankrupt or another person to attend in court to answer

282 Section 77(1)(a)(i).
283 Section 77A.
284 Sections 77AA, 77C, 81A.
285 Section 81.
286 Section 77(1)(f).
287 Section 78(1)(d).
288 Section 78(1).
289 Section 78(1)(f). Neither orders for search nor for arrest are given without the trustee providing compelling reasons.
290 Section 130(1).
291 Section 130(2).
292 Section 5(1) defines 'examinable affairs' widely.
293 Legal professional privilege applies to s 77A notices: *Re Steele* (1994) 48 FCR 236.
294 Legal professional privilege applies to s 77AA notices: *Re Steele* (1994) 48 FCR 236; *Worrell v Woods* (1999) 90 FCR 264.
295 The privilege against self-incrimination applies to s 77C notices, although the court in *Bond v Tuohy* (1995) 128 ALR 595 doubted that the full width of the privilege was available.
296 Section 77C notices may be challenged under ss 30 and 15(5) of the Act. In *C K Nominees v Official Receiver (WA)* (2007) 16 FCR 524, the court found the notices oppressive for covering too extensive a period, seeking classes of documents that were too numerous and too broad, and with arguable connections with the bankrupt.
297 *Re Terry* [1994] FCA 1531; *Re McKee; Ex parte Lavoar Holdings Pty Ltd v Ross* (1996) 71 FCR 156.
298 The public examinations under this provision have been rendered less frequent by the use of s 77C notices. Section 81 examinations may be used subsequent to s 77C notices.
299 Section 81(1).

questions posed by the trustee or their legal representative in a session presided over by a registrar or, possibly, a judge.[300] However, orders for examination may not be made against persons not having residency or being physically present in Australia – although exceptions may be made in the case of Australian citizens.[301] The examinations are public and creditors are able to attend and participate.[302] Under s 81, a 'relevant person'[303] or an 'examinable person'[304] may be examined. An 'examinable person' includes anyone known or suspected to possess the bankrupt's property; believed to be indebted to the bankrupt; able to provide information on the bankrupt or their examinable affairs; or in possession of books related to the bankrupt or their examinable affairs. An application under s 81 may require the person to be examined to produce relevant books.[305]

The registrar may order a person admitting they owe a debt to the bankrupt to pay it;[306] as may an order be made against a person holding the bankrupt's divisible property.[307]

Section 81 grants extensive powers of examination, covering a wide range of matters, and broad categories of persons to be made subject to examination. Questions are permitted to extend to all financial activities ('examinable affairs'[308]) and those of any 'associated entity' of the bankrupt.[309] The scope of the powers of examination carries with it an obligation that they be exercised carefully so as not to unfairly disadvantage the examined person, at the same time as seeking to promote the public interest in ensuring that the bankrupt's estate is administered efficiently and transparently.

Examinations are subject to limitations that they do not abuse the court's process, that the summons is not so wide as to be oppressive,[310] and that the trustee does not use proceedings to fish for evidence[311] or ask questions that are irrelevant or outside the scope of the summons or the Act.[312]

The power under s 81 is further limited by preserving the privilege of non-bankrupt nominees against self-incrimination and legal professional privilege. The bankrupt, however, cannot claim the privilege against self-incrimination[313] and must answer questions and produce books that may tend to incriminate them. The bankrupt's legal professional privilege endures.

300 *Pollack v Lombe* [2004] FCA 362.

301 *Southwell v Maladina* (2002) 194 ALR 51; *Park v Tschannen* (2016) 341 ALR 452.

302 *Bankruptcy Act 1966* (Cth), s 81(2). Subject to any contrary direction, the bankrupt is not excused from answering a question merely because to do so may incriminate them (s 81(11AA)).

303 As the bankrupt is called.

304 Section 5(1).

305 Section 81(1B), including the books of an associated entity.

306 Section 81(12); *Nicholls v Hills* (2004) 136 FCR 201.

307 Section 81(13).

308 The 'examinable affairs' of a person means the person's dealings, transactions, property and affairs, and the financial affairs of an associated entity of the person, in so far as they are relevant to the person, their conduct, dealings, transactions, property or affairs (s 5(1)).

309 Section 81(1B).

310 *Perazzoli v BankSA* [2017] FCAFC 204.

311 *Re Hodder* (1965) 7 FLR 436; *Re Alafaci* (1976) 9 ALR 262.

312 *Hamilton v Oades* (1989) 166 CLR 483.

313 *Bankruptcy Act 1966* (Cth), s 81(11AA).

12.9.12 Duties of a bankrupt

'Material change' means a change in the particulars contained in the statement of affairs that could reasonably be expected to be relevant to the administration of the bankrupt's estate.[314]

12.9.13 Compositions and schemes by bankrupts

A debtor who has become a bankrupt may make a proposal to creditors for:

(a) a composition in satisfaction of her or his debts; or
(b) a scheme of arrangement.[315]

The decision whether to accept the debtor's proposal rests with the creditors who are not bound to accept any arrangement and may insist that the estate be administered in bankruptcy.

12.10 The end of bankruptcy

The end of bankruptcy, or the end of the administration of bankruptcy, refers to the day the bankrupt is discharged or the bankruptcy is annulled. The annulment of bankruptcy may occur by the court exercising its inherent power,[316] or without court order[317] or by agreement of the creditors.[318] Section 153A provides for the annulment of bankruptcy when all of the debts are paid; s 153B annuls bankruptcy by the court's determination that the bankruptcy should not have occurred and arose by error; and s 73 annuls bankruptcy when the compromised amount agreed to by creditors has been paid. Annulment acts retrospectively to put the bankrupt in a position as if the bankruptcy had never occurred – although the bankrupt remains liable for former debts unless the bankruptcy was annulled on the grounds of payment of all debts. Property that had vested in the trustee re-vests in the former bankrupt.

Discharge of a person from bankruptcy, on the other hand, occurs once the bankruptcy period has run its course, and may be extended by the trustee lodging an objection to their discharge.[319] Discharge also releases the bankrupt from bankruptcy; however, the trustee may continue to administer the estate – although the person is no longer bankrupt, even if administration persists and creditors have not been paid. Property that has vested in the trustee remains vested. A person may seek annulment of bankruptcy even after discharge.

12.11 Key points

- The purpose of the modern law of bankruptcy in dealing with cases of individuals having no reasonable prospect of paying their debts is, first, to enable a debtor or creditor to

314 Section 77(2).
315 Part IV, Division 6, ss 73–76.
316 Section 153B. The court has traditionally had this power.
317 Section 153A.
318 Section 73. This is a more recent and now more common approach.
319 Section 149.

initiate proceedings to enable the distribution of the debtor's property among the creditors in the most expeditious and economical way.

- While the majority of bankruptcies are voluntary, debtors may be bankrupted by court order. A debtor who is unable or has refused to pay a creditor enables the creditor to elect to commence proceedings to bankrupt the debtor.
- A person is therefore insolvent by legislative definition if they are unable to pay all of their debts and not any particular debt. However, a person's inability to pay a debt may be indicative (if not definitive) of their insolvency.
- Failure by the debtor to comply with a bankruptcy notice is the most frequently utilised 'act of bankruptcy' upon which creditors' petitions are founded. A creditor may apply for a bankruptcy notice from the Official Receiver upon obtaining either final judgment, or an order for payment, against the debtor.
- The end of bankruptcy, or the end of the administration of bankruptcy, refers to the day the bankrupt is discharged or the bankruptcy is annulled. The annulment of bankruptcy may occur by the court exercising its inherent power, or without a court order or by agreement of the creditors.

12.12 DISCUSSION QUESTIONS

1. What is the legislation that primarily governs bankruptcy? What other legislative schemes are relevant?
2. How is a bankruptcy established under the law?
3. How do voluntary and involuntary bankruptcy differ?
4. What are the consequences of failing to comply with a bankruptcy notice?
5. How can a bankruptcy be ended?

12.13 FURTHER READING

Ramsay, I and Sim, C, 'Personal Insolvency in Australia: An Increasingly Middle Class Phenomenon' (2010) 38(2) *Federal Law Review* 283.

PART 2

AUSTRALIAN CONSUMER LAW

The Australian Consumer Law (ACL) came into operation on 1 January 2011. The ACL is contained in Schedule 2 to the *Competition and Consumer Act 2010* (Cth) (CCA). The ACL is thought to have had a significant impact on commercial life in Australia, where numerous commercial organisations have dealings with consumers. The ACL now regulates those dealings through a variety of legal schemes. Accordingly, it would be untenable to think that any study of commercial law could take place without consideration of the ACL.

This introduction to Part 2 is designed to set the stage for the chapters that follow, which examine various parts of the ACL that are of relevance to commercial law. It is important to keep in mind that commercial law, unlike many other areas of the law, is not driven by a single defining doctrinal idea. Rather, it is driven by the relevance of selected legal topics to commercial life. There are certain ideas that are recurrent within commercial law, such as reasonableness, good faith and bad faith, the need to protect innocent parties, reliance and legitimate expectations. However, none of these ideas defines an entire area of law or forms the basis for the existence of those laws in the first place. Most areas of commercial law exist because the demands of commerce require a set of rules to regulate the interactions of the players within that field. Consumer law is no different, and its centrality to commercial life makes it a proper sub-field for study within commercial law.

This introduction has two sections. The first section examines the rationale for the ACL; the second looks at its operation. The following chapters examine unfair contract terms (Chapter 13), product liability (Chapter 14), consumer guarantees (Chapter 15), unconscionable conduct (Chapter 16), and misleading and deceptive conduct (Chapter 17) under the ACL. These topics are by no means a complete representation of the ACL, but they do cover some of the most contested areas of consumer law and are therefore of immediate importance to most commercial entities that interact with consumers.

The rationale for the ACL

The primary idea behind the ACL is that consumer protection drives efficient markets and safeguards consumer well-being. For a market to operate efficiently and effectively, consumers need to be well informed. Having useful information allows consumers to act in their own best interests. The cumulative effect of informed consumers acting in their own self-interest allows markets to operate efficiently. This means that inefficient entities are pushed out of business, and those that can compete effectively on quality and price will prosper. However, if businesses are able to mislead consumers or to employ other questionable tactics, then the market will not act in a way that promotes efficiency. Where misleading practices prevail, consumers will be misdirected away from efficient businesses towards less scrupulous ones. The particular problem lies in the fact that modern businesses are quite sophisticated and consumers are often time poor and confronted with a morass of information. The mismatch of resources and time between businesses and consumers necessitates that some safeguard measures must exist in order to ensure that markets operate efficiently. The Productivity Commission states:

> The role of consumers in facilitating competition, and promoting well-functioning markets, has long been recognised. In seeking the 'best' value (the good or service and price/quality combination most appropriate for them) consumers not only advance their own self-interest, but also provide signals to suppliers on the product characteristics they

> require. Competition between suppliers, who respond to these signals, can variously lead to lower costs, improved product quality, greater innovation and higher productivity . . .
>
> However, poorly informed consumers send weak and confused signals to the market, limiting the benefits they receive from transactions and reducing gains from competition more generally . . .
>
> In addition to having access to relevant information, consumers need to be sufficiently confident to act on it . . . Confident consumers have the skills needed to deal effectively with suppliers, and obtain what they expect from a transaction, or, if not, to access effective redress mechanisms.
>
> Of course, it is not necessary for all consumers to be well informed and confident to encourage effective competition between firms. Competition will still be robust if there is a sufficient proportion of informed, 'marginal' consumers who are willing to switch suppliers to secure a better deal. That said, as a general rule, competition works best when the bulk of consumers are reasonably well informed and willing to act on that information.
>
> To this end, a key goal of consumer policy is to overcome significant information failures that can hinder effective competition.[1]

The benefit of the ACL is that it sets up a system wherein unethical practices that impede the proper flow of information and the freedom of consumers can be challenged and counteracted. For example, the rule contained in s 18 of the ACL on misleading or deceptive conduct prevents businesses from engaging in practices that might misrepresent the true nature of their product or enterprise. In short, the prohibition on misleading or deceptive conduct is aimed at stopping businesses using disingenuous measures that would cause consumers to make decisions they would not otherwise make. The protection offered by s 18 of the ACL also assists businesses whose reputations are unfairly tarnished by the inaccurate advertising of their competitors. In *Colgate-Palmolive Pty Ltd v Rexona Pty Ltd*,[2] Lockhart J observed that 'it is the plain purpose of the Act to require truthful conduct in the market place and that competition be free and fair'.[3]

The purposes behind the ACL are further set out in the Intergovernmental Agreement for the Australian Consumer Law (IGAACL), which states:

> The objective of the new national consumer policy framework is to improve consumer wellbeing through consumer empowerment and protection, to foster effective competition and to enable the confident participation of consumers in markets in which both consumers and suppliers trade fairly.[4]

The IGAACL further sets out six policy objectives:

(a) to ensure that consumers are sufficiently well-informed to benefit from and stimulate effective competition;

---

1 Productivity Commission, *Review of Australia's Consumer Policy Framework* (Final Report, Canberra, 2008), vol 2, 28.

2 (1981) ATPR ¶40-242.

3 (1981) ATPR ¶40-242, 43,194.

4 Council of Australian Governments, *Intergovernmental Agreement for the Australian Consumer Law*, 3, available at www.consumerlaw.gov.au/.

(b) to ensure that goods and services are safe and fit for the purposes for which they were sold;

(c) to prevent practices that are unfair;

(d) to meet the needs of those consumers who are most vulnerable or are at the greatest disadvantage;

(e) to provide accessible and timely redress where consumer detriment has occurred; and

(f) to promote proportionate, risk-based enforcement.

With regard to the specific policy schemes set up under the ACL, pre-existing regimes are continued while new schemes have been created. The protections offered by s 18 (misleading or deceptive conduct) or ss 20–22 (unconscionable conduct) of the ACL represent a furtherance of the regimes created under the *Trade Practices Act 1974* (Cth). Section 18 is concerned with developing a norm of commercial conduct. That is, s 18 combats misrepresentations, negligent actions, deceitful conduct, passing off, and the like. Similarly, ss 20–22 place an emphasis on the conduct of commercial actors to ensure that they do not engage in conduct that is against good conscience. The Unfair Contract Terms scheme is targeted at the mismatch between sophisticated businesses and individual consumers. The Unfair Contract Terms scheme represents a significant safeguard against harsh and unfair contract terms that may be imposed upon unsuspecting consumers. The consumer guarantees scheme seeks to ensure that the implied terms set out under the Sale of Goods Acts for sale of goods contracts are available for consumers and that their reasonable expectations are met.

The operation of the ACL

The ACL fixes a problem of inconsistency that had emerged in the various Commonwealth, state and territory consumer laws. The old system that existed prior to the ACL was a patchwork of state and federal regulation of consumer affairs. In the main, the Commonwealth had the *Trade Practices Act 1974* (Cth). For their part, the states had their Sale of Goods Acts and Fair Trading Acts. However, there were minor inconsistencies between these various laws. Consequently, the idea of the CCA and the ACL is to have a single unified consumer protection and competition law.

The arrangements between the Commonwealth and the states are necessary due to the constitutional limitations facing the Commonwealth in the area of consumer protection. There is no express constitutional power allowing the Commonwealth to enact laws for consumer protection. In the past, the state and territory Fair Trade Acts have generally compensated for this limitation. However, given the problem that had emerged with regard to uneven protections within different jurisdictions, cooperation was required between the Commonwealth, state and territory governments to set up a unified consumer and competition law system. It followed, then, that the ACL needed to be an application law in all the states and territories in order to create uniformity.

The Explanatory Memorandum to the *Trade Practices Amendment (Australian Consumer Law) Act (No 2) 2010* (Cth) stated:

> The ACL will be a law of the Commonwealth and of each State and Territory. In accordance with the Council of Australian Government's (COAG) 2 October 2008 decision, the ACL will be implemented as an application law, with the Australian Government as the lead legislator. An application law scheme is necessary as the Australian Parliament does not have power to legislate generally with respect to fair trading and consumer protection matters. It has the power to legislate in respect of 'foreign corporations and trading or financial corporations formed within the limits of the Commonwealth', within the meaning of section 51(xx) of the Australian Constitution and in respect of 'trade and commerce ... among the States'; within the meaning of section 51(i) of the Australian Constitution.[5]

In 2010 the Commonwealth Parliament passed both the *Trade Practices Amendment (Australian Consumer Law) Act (No 1) 2010* (Cth) and the *Trade Practices Amendment (Australian Consumer Law) Act (No 2) 2010* (Cth). The Amendment Acts renamed the Trade Practices Act as the CCA, repealed the consumer protection parts of the Trade Practices Act and introduced the ACL into Schedule 2 to the CCA. The ACL in Schedule 2 to the CCA then served as an application law. This allowed the various state and territory governments to enact laws implementing the ACL. For example, Victoria enacted the *Australian Consumer Law and Fair Trading Act 2012* (Vic), and New South Wales amended Part 3 of the *Fair Trading Act 1987* (NSW) to implement the ACL.

The ACL itself has five main chapters. Chapter 1 sets out the basic definitions and interpretation provisions. Chapter 2 sets out general protections for consumers. Section 18 deals with misleading or deceptive conduct, and ss 20–22 deal with unconscionable conduct and the Unfair Contract Terms scheme. Chapter 3 provides specific protections to consumers. This covers certain activities that are regarded as unfair commercial practices, such as pyramid schemes, harassment and bait advertising. The chapter contains the consumer guarantees scheme. Chapter 4 creates a criminal law regime with regard to consumer protection. Chapter 5 is concerned with enforcement and remedies. Notably, the chapter contains a public enforcement regime, which confers significant powers on the ACCC.

5 Explanatory Memorandum, Trade Practices Amendment (Australian Consumer Law) Bill (No 2) 2010 (Cth), [17.4]–[17.6].

13

UNFAIR CONTRACT TERMS

13.0 Introduction

The advent of the Australian Consumer Law (ACL) as a law having uniform application throughout Australia will have a significant impact upon some areas of contract law.[1] Most notably, the ACL will impact upon statutory unconscionability, implied terms in the form of consumer guarantees, misleading or deceptive conduct (the statutory corollary to the common law doctrine of misrepresentation) and unfair contract terms. It is the last topic that is the focus of this chapter: the unfair contract terms regime of the ACL. The unfair contract terms regime is provided for in ss 23–28 of the ACL and sets up a mechanism for whether terms in standard form consumer or small business contracts are unfair.

13.1 The Australian Consumer Law

The ACL is housed in Schedule 2 to the *Competition and Consumer Act 2010* (Cth) (CCA). The purpose of the ACL is to provide a uniform consumer protection law in Australia. Prior to the commencement of the ACL, consumers were protected under a patchwork of federal, state and territory laws. At a federal level, the *Trade Practices Act 1974* (Cth) (TPA) regulated corporate conduct in relation to consumers. Most notably, the TPA had significant legislative provisions in relation to statutory unconscionability, misleading or deceptive conduct, and implied terms in goods contracts.[2] At a state and territory level, Fair Trading Acts and Sale of Goods Acts provided other – and at times overlapping – protections for consumers.

The idea behind the CCA and the ACL, therefore, is to provide a single, unified consumer and competition law. The ACL is a combination of the TPA and state and territory legislations, with new provisions added to give additional protection to consumers.

As the Commonwealth Constitution does not directly empower the Commonwealth to legislate for consumer protection, it has been deemed necessary for the states and territories to apply the ACL through their respective Fair Trading Acts. This process was conceived and agreed to through the Council of Australian Governments (COAG). As such, the ACL is very much the product of state, territory and federal government cooperation.

To implement COAG's plan, the ACL was deemed to be an application law. For example, in Victoria the ACL is applied through the *Fair Trading Act 1999* (Vic), and similar arrangements exist in every other state and territory. The upshot of these legislative arrangements is that the ACL has uniform application throughout Australia.

While the ACL is designed to protect consumers, there are provisions that apply to corporations and those who are carrying on a business. For example, s 22 of the ACL provides protection against unconscionable conduct in relation to business transactions. Similarly, provided that the transaction in question is a consumer transaction, a business may seek the protection of the consumer guarantees regime in Division 1, which recognises that businesses may at times contract as consumers, but might at other times contract for business purposes. The misleading or deceptive conduct (Chapter 2, Part 2.1 of the ACL) and statutory unconscionability

1 For a more detailed study of the ACL, see A Bruce, *Consumer Protection Law in Australia* (LexisNexis Butterworths Australia, Sydney, 2011).

2 For an overview of these schemes within the TPA, see S Fisher, P Ali and G Pearson, *Commercial Law* (Lawbook Co, Sydney, 2010).

(Chapter 2, Part 2.2 of the ACL) provisions in particular set out a general understanding that while businesses are able to be self-interested and do not need to contract in the best interests of others, they must not engage in conduct that is unconscionable and dishonest.

13.2 The unfair contract terms scheme: Rationale and purpose

The maxim *caveat emptor* was well suited to the times when a buyer could inspect a vendor's goods and decide whether they wished to purchase them. However, in the modern marketplace consumers are afforded less time to make decisions about products and are often confronted by pre-prepared contracts that have been put together by sophisticated businesses. The mismatch between unaware consumers and savvy businesses was evident even when the TPA was enacted. In the Explanatory Memorandum to the TPA, the then Senator Lionel Murphy stated:

> In consumer transactions, unfair practices are widespread. The existing law is still founded on the principle known as *caveat emptor* – meaning 'let the buyer beware'. The principle may have been appropriate for transactions conducted in village markets. It has ceased to be appropriate as a general rule. Now the marketing of goods and services is conducted on an organised basis by trained executives. The untrained consumer is no match for the businessman who attempts to persuade the consumer to buy goods or services on terms suitable to the vendor.[3]

In the current marketplace, businesses are even more sophisticated, with significant resources devoted to strategy, marketing and legal matters. Accordingly, it makes sense that some basic protections should be in place to assist consumers and small businesses whenever businesses seek to rely upon unfair terms in a standard form contract. Moreover, the circumstances under which such problems might arise have expanded. In the 21st century, consumers will regularly encounter standard form contracts when they engage in such activities as signing up for a gym membership, online streaming services, a mobile phone contract, car rentals, the purchase of airline tickets, or the purchase of computer software through a click-wrap licence.

The statutory schemes in the TPA provided no direct coverage of unfair terms in a contract. Similarly, though the common law of contracts does have something to say about unfair terms, it is not infallible in this area. Consider, for example, the situation of a man who drove into a private car park, which advertised free parking for two hours subject to 'terms and conditions', obtained a ticket with terms printed on the back, but then overstayed his allowed free parking time by a mere minute and was then given an infringement notice claiming $88 in damages.[4] In this example, the owner of the car park is claiming to be entitled to $88 in damages under

3 Second Reading Speech, Trade Practices Bill 1974 (Cth), *Hansard*, 30 July 1974, pp. 540–1.

4 This example is actually based on a spate of claims for damages by the operators of several car parks against consumers. Over the past few years, a practice has emerged of certain car parks advertising 'free parking for two hours' and then attempting to claim either $66 or $88 in damages from customers if they either overstay or fail to display their tickets. The practice has drawn the attention of the Australian Competition and Consumer Commission (ACCC), the Consumer Law Group and the Victorian government. It has been stated that the commencement of the Australian Consumer Law will effectively end this practice.

contract law. Upon what grounds could the man contest the claim for $88 in circumstances where the likely imposition of such a claim had not been brought to his attention? Traditionally, contract law might deal with such a situation through the use of the 'red hand rule',[5] as applied in the cases of *Thornton v Shoe Lane Parking*[6] and *Interfoto Picture Library v Stiletto Visual Programmes Ltd.*[7] There are rules concerning liquidated damages that might bar a claim for damages of $88 for overstaying in a car park by a mere minute. Alternately, in the case of *Corporation of the City of Adelaide v Adelaide City Fines Pty Ltd*,[8] it was held that the infringement notices that Adelaide Fines was handing out to customers looked too much like official council fines. It was held that Adelaide Fines had engaged in misleading and deceptive conduct.

However, if the term had been brought to the attention of the motorist, then the 'red hand rule' would not apply; and if the claim for damages was printed in a way that did not resemble fine notices imposed by local councils, then a claim of misleading or deceptive conduct would not be available.

There was some speculation when the former provisions of the TPA relating to statutory unconscionability in business and consumer dealings were enacted that their reach would extend beyond that of unconscionability under the common law and equity. However, in practice it has appeared that special disadvantage and substantive unfairness in the contract must be co-requisites in order for a finding of statutory unconscionability to be made. For example, in the leading consumer unconscionability cases of *Australian Competition and Consumer Commission v Lux Pty Ltd*[9] and *Australian Competition and Consumer Commission v Keshow*,[10] the consumers both suffered from special disadvantages. In *Lux*, the consumer was an illiterate and mentally disabled woman. In *Keshow*, the consumers were illiterate and disadvantaged Indigenous women. In both cases, the businesses in question showed a lack of conscience, through their agents, in attempting to procure contracts and retain their benefit in circumstances where to do so would be manifestly unjust.

To return to the example above, it is clearly unfair for a business to seek to claim $88 in damages from a consumer for overstaying in a parking space for a minute. However, neither misleading or deceptive conduct nor statutory unconscionability offer a perfect solution. The common law rules of contract law are of some assistance, but these rules might also be displaced under certain circumstances. Moreover, litigating under either the common law or the ACL might prove costly and time-consuming.

The unfair contract terms regime would offer a seemingly perfect solution in that it offers relatively clear rules on unfairness in contracts. In this sense, the unfair contract terms regime targets the regulatory gap in the former TPA and provides a mostly workable solution to attempts by businesses to impose unfair and harsh terms on consumers. The need for the unfair contract terms regime is aptly demonstrated by the fact that between the interim of the enactment of the unfair contract terms regime of the TPA and the commencement of the CCA

5 The 'red hand rule' states that the more unreasonable a clause is, the greater the notice that must be given of it.
6 [1971] 2 QB 163; see also *Spurling v Bradshaw Ltd* [1956] 1 WLR 461.
7 [1989] QB 433.
8 (2009) 253 ALR 417.
9 [2004] FCA 926.
10 [2005] FCA 558.

and the ACL, both Victoria and New South Wales enacted their own unfair contract terms legislation. The ACL now supersedes both the *Fair Trading Amendment (Unfair Contract Terms) Act 2010* (Vic) and the *Fair Trading Amendment (Unfair Contract Terms) Act 2010* (NSW).[11] Furthermore, several states had unfair contract terms rules in their Fair Trading Acts long before the commencement of the ACL.[12]

In recent jurisprudence, the courts have had the opportunity to develop a set of principles summarising the purpose and rationale of the Unfair Contract Terms scheme.[13] In *Australian Competition and Consumer Commission v CLA Trading Pty Ltd*,[14] Gilmour J stated:

> (a) the underlying policy of unfair contract terms legislation respects true freedom of contract and seeks to prevent the abuse of standard form consumer contracts which, by definition, will not have been individually negotiated: *Jetstar Airways Pty Ltd v Free* [2008] VSC 539 at [112];
>
> (b) the requirement of a 'significant imbalance' directs attention to the substantive unfairness of the contract: *Director-General of Fair Trading v First National Bank plc* [2001] UKHL 52; [2002] 1 AC 481 at [37];
>
> (c) it is useful to assess the impact of an impugned term on the parties' rights and obligations by comparing the effect of the contract with the term and the effect it would have without it: *Director-General of Fair Trading v First National Bank plc* at [54];
>
> (d) the 'significant imbalance' requirement is met if a term is so weighted in favour of the supplier as to tilt the parties' rights and obligations under the contract significantly in its favour – this may be by the granting to the supplier of a beneficial option or discretion or power, or by the imposing on the consumer of a disadvantageous burden or risk or duty: *Director-General of Fair Trading v First National Bank* at 494 [17] per Lord Bingham, applied in *ACCC v ACN 117 372 915 Pty Ltd (in liq) (formerly Advanced Medical Institute Pty Ltd)* [2015] FCA 368 at [950];
>
> (e) significant in this context means 'significant in magnitude', or 'sufficiently large to be important', 'being a meaning not too distant from substantial': *Jetstar Airways Pty Ltd v Free* at [104]–[105] per Cavanough J: Cf. *Director of Consumer Affairs Victoria v AAPT Ltd* [2006] VCAT 1493 at [32]–[33];
>
> (f) the legislation proceeds on the assumption that some terms in consumer contracts, especially in standard form consumer contracts, may be inherently unfair, regardless of how comprehensively they might be drawn to the consumer's attention: *Jetstar Airways Pty Ltd v Free* at [115]; and
>
> (g) in considering 'the contract as a whole', not each and every term of the contract is equally relevant, or necessarily relevant at all. The main requirement is to consider

11 The unfair contract terms regime is now fully within the CCA as part of the ACL.

12 For example, Victoria had a smaller Unfair Contract Terms regime in Part 2B of the *Fair Trading Act 1999* (Vic): see *Director of Consumer Affairs Victoria v Craig Langley Pty Ltd & Matrix Pilates & Yoga Pty Ltd* [2008] VCAT 1332; see also *Director of Consumer Affairs Victoria v Trainstation Health Clubs Pty Ltd (Civil Claims)* [2008] VCAT 2092.

13 See *Australian Competition and Consumer Commission v Chrisco Hampers Australia Ltd* (2015) 239 FCR 33.

14 [2016] FCA 377, [54].

terms that might reasonably be seen as tending to counterbalance the term in question: *Jetstar Airways Pty Ltd v Free* at [128].

13.3 The operation of the unfair contract terms scheme

The unfair contract terms regime is found in Chapter 2, Part 2.3 of the ACL. The scheme is contained within ss 23–28. Section 23(1) provides that a term will be void if it is unfair and if the contract is a standard form contract. Either the consumer/small business party to the contract or the ACCC may apply for a declaration from a court that the term is void. It is important to note that the larger contract itself is not considered to be void ab initio. However, if an essential term is found to be void, and where this raises serious issues of uncertainty or incompleteness, the prospect of the contract as a whole being void ab initio also arises.

There are effectively three primary requirements that need to be satisfied under the unfair contract terms regime:

(a) the contract in question must be a consumer or small business contract;[15]

(b) the contract must be a standard form contract;[16] and

(c) the term in question must be unfair.[17]

With regard to the above:

(a) Section 23(3) deals with the requirements of a consumer contract and s 23(4) deals with the requirements of a small business contract.

(b) The term 'standard form contract' is not defined in the ACL; however, s 27(1) sets up a rebuttable presumption that a pre-prepared consumer contract or small business contract is a standard form contract.

(c) There are four requirements that must be met before a contract term will be declared to be unfair, and these are discussed below.[18] Section 25(1) sets out a series of examples in which a term might be considered to be unfair.

13.4 Consumer and small business contracts

Section 3 of the ACL provides that a person is a consumer if they buy goods for less than $40000; or where the goods are of a kind ordinarily acquired for personal, domestic or household use or consumption; or where the goods consist of a vehicle or trailer acquired

15 See ACL, s 23(3)–(4).
16 See ACL, s 27.
17 See ACL, ss 24–25.
18 See below, Section 13.6.

for use principally in the transport of goods on public roads. However, s 23(3) in Chapter 2, Part 2.3 of the ACL, offers an arguably narrower definition and it is important, in the context of the unfair contract terms regime, to remember that the two definitions are conceptually and legally separate. The unfair contract terms regime contained in Chapter 2, Part 2.3 has a narrower field of operation than the general term 'consumer' in the ACL.

In effect, s 23(3) confines the unfair contract terms regime to situations where the goods are of a kind ordinarily acquired for personal, domestic or household use or consumption, and to dealings in land. It provides:

> A *consumer contract* is a contract for:
> (a) a supply of goods or services; or
> (b) a sale or grant of an interest in land;
> to an individual whose acquisition of the goods, services or interest is wholly or predominantly for personal, domestic or household use or consumption.

Note also that in the Explanatory Memorandum to the *Trade Practices Amendment (Australian Consumer Law) Act (No 2) 2010* (Cth), it was stated that the regime is restricted to 'business to consumer transactions as the provisions apply only to a consumer contract in which at least one of the parties is an individual'.[19] The regime was extended by the *Treasury Legislation Amendment (Small Business and Unfair Contract Terms) Act 2015* (Cth) to cover 'small business contracts' in addition to business to consumer transactions (as set out in s 23(4) of the ACL). Section 23(4) applies to small business contracts entered into or renewed after 12 November 2016. Sections 23(4)–(5) provide:

> (4) A contract is a small business contract if:
> (a) the contract is for a supply of goods or services, or a sale or grant of an interest in land; and
> (b) at the time the contract is entered into, at least one party to the contract is a business that employs fewer than 20 persons; and
> (c) either of the following applies:
> (i) the upfront price payable under the contract does not exceed $300,000;
> (ii) the contract has a duration of more than 12 months and the upfront price payable under the contract does not exceed $1,000,000.
> (5) In counting the persons employed by a business for the purposes of paragraph (4)(b), a casual employee is not to be counted unless he or she is employed by the business on a regular and systematic basis.

Sections 23(4)–(5) were applied by the Federal Court of Australia in *Australian Competition and Consumer Commission v JJ Richards & Sons Pty Ltd*[20] and *Australian Competition and Consumer Commission v Servcorp Ltd*.[21] In both of these cases, the Federal Court (with the consent of both parties) declared that a series of contract terms were unfair and imposed

19 Explanatory Memorandum, *Trade Practices Amendment (Australian Consumer Law) Act (No 2) 2010* (Cth), [5.15].
20 [2017] FCA 1224 ('*JJ Richards*').
21 [2018] FCA 1044 ('*Servcorp*').

obligations that would prevent future breaches of s 23 of the ACL. The types of provisions that will fall foul of the s 23 requirements will be discussed in more detail below.

13.5 A standard form contract

Under the unfair contract terms regime, the contract in question must be a standard form contract. This allows for a relatively wide scope of coverage over pre-prepared contracts that businesses seek to employ in consumer transactions. The Australian Competition and Consumer Commission has stated in its *Guide to the Unfair Contract Terms Law*:[22]

> [I]n broad terms a standard form contract will typically be one that has been prepared by one party to the contract and is not subject to negotiation between the parties – that is, it is offered on a 'take it or leave it' basis.[23]

The ACCC notes in its Guide that such contracts are invariably found in the context of consumer transactions relating to telecommunications, gym memberships, finance, domestic buildings and motor vehicles. However, this list is not closed and a standard form consumer contract might be found to exist in any number of consumer transaction situations.

The existence of the rebuttable presumption in s 27 – that a pre-prepared consumer contract or small business contract is a standard form contract – seeks to account for the power imbalance between sophisticated businesses, which have had time to prepare the contract, and the consumer or small business who receive the contract on a 'take it or leave it' basis:

> **27 Standard form contracts**
>
> (1) If a party to a proceeding alleges that a contract is a standard form contract, it is presumed to be a standard form contract unless another party to the proceeding proves otherwise.
>
> (2) In determining whether a contract is a standard form contract, a court may take into account such matters as it thinks relevant, but must take into account the following:
>
> (a) whether one of the parties has all or most of the bargaining power relating to the transaction;
>
> (b) whether the contract was prepared by one party before any discussion relating to the transaction occurred between the parties;
>
> (c) whether another party was, in effect, required either to accept or reject the terms of the contract . . . in the form in which they were presented;
>
> (d) whether another party was given an effective opportunity to negotiate the terms of the contract that were not the terms referred to in section 26(1);
>
> (e) whether the terms of the contract (other than the terms referred to in section 26 (1)) take into account the specific characteristics of another party or the particular transaction;
>
> (f) any other matter prescribed by the regulations.

22 ACCC, *A Guide to the Unfair Contract Terms Law* (Commonwealth of Australia, Canberra, July 2010).
23 ACCC, *A Guide to the Unfair Contract Terms Law* (Commonwealth of Australia, Canberra, July 2010), 4.

Section 27(2) lists a number of factors for the courts to take into consideration in determining whether a contract is a standard form contract. Crucially, paras (b) and (c) refer to whether a contract has been prepared before any discussion between the parties, and whether a party has been required to effectively either accept or reject the terms; while para (d) refers to whether a party has been able to negotiate the terms of the contract. It seems highly likely that where a consumer has been able to negotiate the terms of a contract, it will not be found to be a standard form contract. In the *Director of Consumer Affairs Victoria v Craig Langley Pty Ltd & Matrix Pilates & Yoga Pty Ltd (Civil Claims)*,[24] decided under the then Victorian unfair contract terms legislation, Harbison J stated:

> [T]erms of a consumer contract which have been the subject of genuine negotiation should not be lightly declared unfair. This legislation is designed to protect consumers from unfair contracts, not to allow a party to a contract who has genuinely reflected on its terms and negotiated them, to be released from a contract term from which he or she later wishes to resile . . .[25]

13.6 'Unfair' terms

Whether a term in a standard form contract will be held to be unfair will depend upon the application of s 24. In effect, there are four requirements under s 24 that must be satisfied before a term can be held to be unfair:

1. The court must take into account whether the term is transparent.
2. The term must cause a significant imbalance in the parties' rights under the contract.
3. The term must not be reasonably necessary to protect the interests of the party that benefits from the term.
4. The term must cause a detriment to the consumer.

The requirement that a court must have regard to whether a contract term is transparent is contained in s 24(2), and in s 24(3) it is stipulated that a term is transparent if it is expressed in reasonably plain language, legible, presented clearly and readily available to any party affected by the term.

Whether a term causes a significant imbalance in the parties' rights under a contract will depend upon the facts of the particular case. The ease with which the business might alter terms or evade obligations to a consumer will likely influence any finding in relation to this requirement. In the *Director of Consumer Affairs Victoria v Craig Langley Pty Ltd & Matrix Pilates & Yoga Pty Ltd (Civil Claims)*,[26] it was held that clauses allowing a gym to avoid performance but not allowing the member to either sue the gym or cancel their membership were unfair.

24 [2008] VCAT 1332. See also *Australian Competition and Consumer Commission v Servcorp Ltd* [2018] FCA 1044.

25 [2008] VCAT 1332. See also *Australian Competition and Cconsumer Commission v Servcorp Ltd* [2018] FCA 1044, [66].

26 [2008] VCAT 1332.

In the UK case of *Director General of Fair Trading v First National Bank*,[27] when considering legislation similar to that in s 24 of the ACL, Lord Bingham stated:

> The requirement of significant imbalance is met if a term is so weighted in favour of the supplier as to tilt the parties' rights and obligations under the contract significantly in his favour. This may be by the granting to the supplier of a beneficial option or discretion or power, or by the imposing on the consumer of a disadvantageous burden or risk or duty.[28]

Whether a term is not reasonably necessary to protect the legitimate interests of the party who would be advantaged by the term will also depend upon the facts of the matter. However, s 24(4) sets up a rebuttable presumption that the term is not reasonably necessary; in other words, the business must prove that the term is reasonably necessary. In its *Guide to the Unfair Contract Terms Law*,[29] the ACCC states:

> Such evidence might include material relating to the business's costs and business structure, the need for the mitigation of risks or particular industry practices to the extent that such material is relevant.[30]

The requirement of detriment will likely be quite easy to make out on the facts should a term in a standard form contract be challenged. This is a question of fact and the consumer or small business need only show that the term is unfavourable to them.

In *Australian Competition and Consumer Commission v ACN 117 372 915 Pty Ltd (in liq) (formerly Advanced Medical Institute Pty Ltd)*,[31] the Federal Court applied the unfair contract terms scheme. The following extract from the judgment of North J demonstrates the reasoning process that the courts are likely to apply in administering the scheme.

ACCC v ACN 117 372 915 Pty Ltd (in liq) (formerly Advanced Medical Institute Pty Ltd) [2015] FCA 368

North J:

A term of a consumer contract is void if two characteristics are established, namely, that the term is unfair and the contract is a standard form contract (s 23(1) of the ACL).

It is presumed that the NRM contract is a standard form contract unless NRM proves otherwise (s 27(1)). In determining whether a contract is a standard form contact, the Court is required to take into account the factors referred to in s 27(2) of the ACL. The onus was on NRM to show that those circumstances did not exist. The circumstances were whether NRM had all or most of the bargaining power relating to the transaction, whether the contract was prepared by NRM before any discussion relating to the transaction occurred with a patient, whether the patients were in effect required to accept or reject the terms of the contract, other than the term concerning the cost of treatment, in the form in which they were presented, whether the patient was given an effective opportunity to negotiate the terms of the contract other than the term concerning the cost of treatment,

27 [2002] 1 AC 481.
28 [2002] 1 AC 481, 499.
29 ACCC, *A Guide to the Unfair Contract Terms Law* (Commonwealth of Australia, Canberra, July 2010).
30 ACCC, *A Guide to the Unfair Contract Terms Law* (Commonwealth of Australia, Canberra, July 2010), 11.
31 [2015] FCA 368. See also *Ferme v Kimberley Discovery Cruises Pty Ltd* [2015] FCCA 2384.

and whether the terms of the contract took into account the particular characteristics of the patient or of the particular transaction.

NRM failed to show that these circumstances did not exist. In fact, the evidence positively established that NRM had a dominant bargaining position obtained by using high-pressure selling techniques. The pressure applied to the patients denied them the power to resist entering into the agreement. This was manifested in the NRM patients who said they felt pressured and in the case of some who tried to cancel their contracts immediately following the phone call. Patients did not have the chance to negotiate the terms of the contract apart from price. The terms were set by the parameters of the business model of NRM. The terms were set out in the instruction booklet sent to patients, often after they had entered into the contract, and were in the same form irrespective of the individual circumstances of the patient.

The next question is whether the refund term was unfair within the meaning of s 24(1) of the ACL. The section requires the Court to examine three factors.

One factor is whether the term was reasonably necessary in order to protect the legitimate interests of NRM (s 24(1)(b)). It is presumed that the term was not reasonably necessary to protect the legitimate interests of NRM unless NRM proved otherwise (s 24(4)). NRM did not so prove.

Then, the term is unfair if it would cause a significant imbalance in the parties' rights and obligations arising under the contract (s 24(1)(a)), and would cause detriment, whether financial or otherwise, to the patient if it were to be applied or relied upon (s 24(1)(c)). These two factors may be considered together and in the light of one of the examples of an unfair term provided by s 25(1)(c). That section provides that a term which has the effect of penalising one party and not the other for terminating the contract may be unfair. As to the nature of a significant imbalance in rights, in *Director General of Fair Trading v First National Bank plc* [2001] UKHL 52; [2002] 1 AC 481 at 494; [2001] UKHL 52, Lord Bingham said at [17] of a regulation in similar terms:

> The requirement of significant imbalance is met if a term is so weighted in favour of the supplier as to tilt the parties' rights and obligations under the contract significantly in his favour. This may be by the granting to the supplier of a beneficial option or discretion or power, or by the imposing on the consumer of a disadvantageous burden or risk or duty.

The NRM refund term required the patient to pay a 15 per cent administration fee, a pro-rata fee for the expired portion of the treatment, a pro-rata fee for the 30-day notice period, and the cost of medication supplied or prepared for the patient. The term operated whether the reason for the termination was a change of mind very soon after the phone consultation, a severe adverse side effect, or where the medication proved ineffective. The term thus caused detriment to the patient, if relied upon, within the meaning of s 24(1)(c). It also caused a significant imbalance in the parties' rights and obligations because it had the effect of binding patients to continue treatment in disadvantageous circumstances, or alternatively suffer a financial penalty.

In determining whether a term of consumer contract is unfair, the Court must take into account the extent to which the term is transparent and also take into account the contract as a whole (s 24(2)). A term is transparent if it is expressed in reasonably plain language, is legible, is presented clearly, and is readily available to any party affected by the term (s 24(3)).

The NRM refund term lacked transparency to a significant extent. The basis on which the administration fee was calculated was not disclosed to the patient at all. The method of calculation of the cost of the medication was not disclosed to the patient at all. At the time that the agreement was made, the patient was told about the NRM refund term in a recorded message which suffered from the deficiencies outlined at [858] of these reasons for judgment. The patient was not provided with a written copy of the refund term until after the contract was entered into, save in the case of patients who attended clinics.

When regard is had to the contract as a whole, the unfairness of the term becomes incontrovertible. The contract provided for the supply of medications which were not regarded by the medical profession as the usual forms of treatment and there was no cogent evidence that they were effective to treat ED or PE. In those circumstances it was unfair to hold the patient to the agreement on penalty of payment of fees, the method of calculation of which was unknown, imposed in order to cancel the treatment.

13.7 The ACL list of unfair terms

Section 25(1) of the ACL contains a list of examples of potential unfair terms. While s 25 does not stipulate that these terms will automatically be considered to be unfair, it appears highly likely that there will be a presumption, at least at an informal level, that the existence of such a clause will lead to a finding that a term is unfair. Note that s 25(1) does not preclude other types of terms from being found to be unfair under s 24.

Section 25(1) provides:

Examples of unfair terms

(1) Without limiting section 24, the following are examples of the kinds of terms of a consumer contract or small business contract that may be unfair:

(a) a term that permits, or has the effect of permitting, one party (but not another party) to avoid or limit performance of the contract;

(b) a term that permits, or has the effect of permitting, one party (but not another party) to terminate the contract;

(c) a term that penalises, or has the effect of penalising, one party (but not another party) for a breach or termination of the contract;

(d) a term that permits, or has the effect of permitting, one party (but not another party) to vary the terms of the contract;

(e) a term that permits, or has the effect of permitting, one party (but not another party) to renew or not renew the contract;

(f) a term that permits, or has the effect of permitting, one party to vary the upfront price payable under the contract without the right of another party to terminate the contract;

(g) a term that permits, or has the effect of permitting, one party unilaterally to vary the characteristics of the goods or services to be supplied, or the interest in land to be sold or granted, under the contract;

(h) a term that permits, or has the effect of permitting, one party unilaterally to determine whether the contract has been breached or to interpret its meaning;

(i) a term that limits, or has the effect of limiting, one party's vicarious liability for its agents;

(j) a term that permits, or has the effect of permitting, one party to assign the contract to the detriment of another party without that other party's consent;

(k) a term that limits, or has the effect of limiting, one party's right to sue another party;

(l) a term that limits, or has the effect of limiting, the evidence one party can adduce in proceedings relating to the contract;

(m) a term that imposes, or has the effect of imposing, the evidential burden on one party in proceedings relating to the contract;

(n) a term of a kind, or a term that has an effect of a kind, prescribed by the regulations.

The examples set out in s 25(1) are consistent with the small business contract cases of *JJ Richards*[32] and *Servcorp*.[33] In *J J Richards*, the Federal Court declared that eight contract terms were unfair, including an automatic renewal clause, a unilateral price variation clause, a clause requiring payment of all monies by small business clients before they could terminate the contract, and an indemnity clause.[34] Similar contractual provisions were held to be unfair in *Servcorp*. Notably, the automatic renewal clause (which allowed Servcorp to unilaterally vary the price payable under the contract) was held to be unfair despite the small business having an opportunity to terminate the contract prior to the price increase coming into effect. In ruling the provision was unfair, the court noted that Servcorp had 'no obligation ... to notify the [other party] of any price increase prior to expiry of the notice period, which is the period during which the counterparty can terminate the contract'.[35] Considering this provision within the contract as a whole, the court held that this provision created 'a significant power imbalance in the respective rights and obligations of the parties. Servcorp [is] more likely to be aware of when contracts are due for renewal than small business customers. Consequently, these small businesses may unknowingly find themselves locked into a new term at a higher price.'[36]

13.8 Remedies

Section 23(1) stipulates that an unfair contract term will be void. Under s 250 of the ACL, a party to a standard form consumer contract or small business contract or the regulator (the ACCC) might also seek a declaration from a court that a term is void. An injunction might be sought under s 232(3), and damages and compensation orders are available under ss 236 and 237, respectively. The ACCC has further orders it can seek to prevent the ongoing use of unfair contract terms. For example, in resolving the small business contract case of *Servcorp* (with the consent of Servcorp), the ACCC sought an order requiring the businesses and their staff to participate in a compliance program.[37]

32 [2017] FCA 1224.
33 [2018] FCA 1044.
34 *J J Richards* [2017] FCA 1224, [45]–[46], [51]–[52].
35 *Servcorp* [2018] FCA 1044, [39].
36 *Servcorp* [2018] FCA 1044, [40].
37 See *Servcorp* [2018] FCA 1044, [59]–[64]. The compliance order mirrored an order that could have been imposed under s 246 of the ACL were a contravention of Chapter 2, 3 or 4 of the ACL to have occurred; instead, the court used power granted under s 23 of the *Federal Court Act of Australia 1976* (Cth) to make orders it considers appropriate to impose the order.

13.9 Key points

- The ACL applies uniformly throughout Australia through the use of state and territory legislation that applies the Commonwealth Act within each respective jurisdiction.
- The unfair contract terms scheme is designed to protect consumers and small businesses from sophisticated and 'savvy' businesses who can exploit their market power when drafting contracts.
- The unfair contract terms scheme targets a regulatory gap that was not perfectly covered under the former TPA.
- The scheme is contained within ss 23–28 of the ACL.
- There are three key requirements for a contract term or terms to be unfair:
  - the contract must be a consumer or small business contract (see the respective requirements contained within ss 23(3)–(5));
  - the contract must be a standard form contract (see the rebuttable presumption contained within s 27(1)); and
  - the term or terms in question must be unfair (see s 24).

13.10 DISCUSSION QUESTIONS

1. What is the purpose of the unfair contract terms regime?
2. How do the unfair contract terms provisions interact with other forms of contractual protection?
3. How do you define a consumer contract?
4. How would you argue a cause of action in relation to unfair contract terms?
5. What kind of conduct can be regarded as marginally unfair, yet be outside the scope of the unfair contract terms provisions?

13.11 FURTHER READING

Sims, A, 'Unfair Contract Terms: A New Dawn in Australia and New Zealand?' (2013) 39(3) *Monash University Law Review* 739.

14

PRODUCT LIABILITY

14.0 Introduction

This chapter explores the topic of product liability. The Explanatory Memorandum to the Trade Practice Amendment (Australian Consumer Law) Bill (No 2) 2010 (Cth) states:

> The Australian Consumer Law (ACL) contains a statutory liability regime for manufacturers of goods with a safety defect. The manufacturer's liability in the Bill continues the operation of the current Pt VA of the TPA. However[,] the drafting of the provisions has been amended to reflect the drafting style used for other provisions of the ACL.[1]

Under the Australian Consumer Law (ACL), a manufacturer is liable for producing goods with safety defects. The ACL provides for an action to be brought against the manufacturer of the defective good where there has been loss and damage suffered because:

- injuries were sustained as a result of the safety defect;
- another good was destroyed or damaged as a result of the safety defect; or
- a building or fixture was destroyed or damaged as a result of the safety defect.

Under the *Trade Practices Act 1974* (Cth) (TPA), consumers were able to pursue actions against manufacturers unhampered by the limitations deriving from the implied terms regime at TPA, Part V, Divisions 2 and 2A. The ACL continues the form and content of the product liability regime under the TPA. Accordingly, the jurisprudence developed under the TPA is informative for the ACL.

14.1 ACL Chapter 3, Part 3-5

Under Division 1 of Chapter 3, Part 3-5 of the ACL, manufacturers of defective goods are liable if the consumer *qua* individual has suffered loss or damage,[2] if a person other than the individual consumer has suffered loss or damage,[3] if other goods have been destroyed or damaged as a result of the good's defects,[4] or if the defective goods have caused damage or destruction to land, buildings or fixtures.[5]

Division 2 sets out the parameters of the actions that may be taken against the manufacturer of defective goods. It sets out the time for commencing the defective goods action,[6] the requirements for joint and several liability,[7] the requirements for the survival of actions,[8] the relationship between the ACL and workers compensation laws,[9] what is to be done when the manufacturer cannot be identified,[10] the liability of a manufacturer who has not

1 At [12.1] and [12.2].
2 Section 138.
3 Section 139.
4 Section 140.
5 Section 141.
6 Section 143.
7 Section 144.
8 Section 145.
9 Section 146.
10 Section 147.

complied with a mandatory Commonwealth standard,[11] and the bringing of representative actions by the regulator.

The legislation under Chapter 3, Part 3-5 establishes the 'defective goods action' as a regime of strict liability, and enumerates four specific causes of action. The four defective goods actions are described at ss 138–141. Section 138 provides consumers with an action for loss or damage caused by injuries suffered by a person as a result of the defective product. Section 139 is a cause of action available to a person who has suffered loss or damage as a result of injuries suffered by another person. At s 140, a person may sue for loss or damage they have suffered as a result of damage or destruction of other goods resulting from the defective product. Section 141 provides that a person who has suffered loss or damage resulting from the damage to or destruction of land, buildings or fixtures has a cause of action against the manufacturer.

Section 142 at Part 3-5 sets out the defences available to the manufacturer against defective goods actions brought by plaintiffs alleging loss or damage resulting from defective goods. The four defences are: (1) that the safety defect alleged to have caused the loss or damage did not exist in the goods at the time the goods were supplied by the manufacturer;[12] (2) that the safety defect was caused by its compliance with a mandatory standard;[13] (3) that the safety defect could not have been discovered by the manufacturer because of the state of scientific or technical knowledge at the time of manufacture;[14] and (4) that other goods 'comprised in other goods' (ie comprised of safety defective goods) were defective only because of the design,[15] the markings on or accompanying,[16] or the instructions or warnings given by the manufacturers of[17] the other goods.

A plaintiff successful in establishing a defective goods action against a manufacturer may recover damages under s 236 of the ACL, compensation orders pursuant to s 237, and other orders specified at s 243. Further, under s 149 the Australian Competition and Consumer Commission (ACCC) is empowered to bring representative actions on behalf of a person or persons who have suffered loss or damage because of defects in manufactured goods. The success of a defective goods action will depend (1) on the claim being brought being a defective goods action; (2) the action being brought against the proper defendant being the manufacturer; (3) the supply of the goods being 'in trade or commerce'; and (4) the defect being a safety defect.

14.2 Defective goods action

The term 'defective goods action', which is used throughout the ACL, is defined at s 2(1) of the ACL to mean 'an action under section 138, 139, 140 or 141, and includes such an action because of section 138(3) or 145'. In other words, as well as the four causes of action already

11 Section 148.
12 Section 142(a).
13 Section 142(b).
14 Section 142(c).
15 Section 142(c)(i).
16 Section 142(c)(ii).
17 Section 142(c)(iii).

referred to, causes of action are found at s 138(3) and s 145. At s 138(3), a cause of action arises and the manufacturer's liability falls to be determined under state or territory laws when an individual dies because of a safety defective product. Section 145 refers to the survival of actions under state and territory laws and is thereby applicable.

14.3 Injury to persons caused by unsafe goods

Part 3-5 of the ACL provides compensation for injuries or death, or damage to property, caused by unsafe goods, whether to the consumer or any other person. Section 138 of the ACL provides:

> **Liability for loss or damage suffered by an injured individual**
>
> (1) [Manufacturer's liability for injuring individual] A manufacturer of goods is liable to compensate an individual if:
> (a) the manufacturer supplies the goods in trade or commerce; and
> (b) the goods have a safety defect; and
> (c) the individual suffers injuries because of the safety defect.
>
> (2) [Recovery action] The individual may recover, by action against the manufacturer, the amount of the loss or damage suffered by the individual.
>
> (3) [State/Territory law on liability in respect of death] If the individual dies because of the injuries, a law of a State or a Territory about liability in respect of the death of individuals applies as if:
> (a) the action were an action under the law of the State or Territory for damages in respect of the injuries; and
> (b) the safety defect were the manufacturer's wrongful act, neglect or default.

Section 138(1)(c) emphasises that the link must be between the defective good and the injury suffered by the plaintiff, not the loss or damage.[18] The test imposed by s 138 requires only proof of the defect in the good and injury to the person caused by the defect, free of any limitation of reasonable foreseeability.[19] The action for damages survives the consumer's death by the injuries sustained and is available to the estate of the deceased.[20] A person cannot recover for consequential loss due to injuries sustained by another if the loss is due to a business or professional relationship with the injured or deceased person.[21] Otherwise, consequential losses can be recovered for losses caused by injury to another person.

Only damage to or destruction of goods 'ordinarily acquired for personal, domestic or household use or consumption'[22] will be covered by the compensation regime. The type of

18 *Bright v Femcare Ltd* (2000) 175 ALR 50.
19 *Crump v Equine Nutrition Systems Pty Ltd* [2006] NSWSC 512, [264].
20 Section 145.
21 Section 146 provides that Part 3-5 of the Act will not apply where the loss is covered by workers compensation schemes.
22 Section 140(1)(c).

goods to which a manufacturer's liability relates is not restricted to consumer goods, but applies to goods of all kinds. By definition, goods includes: '(a) ships, aircraft and other vehicles; and (b) animals, including fish; and (c) minerals, trees and crops, whether on, under or attached to land or not; and (d) gas and electricity; and (e) computer software; and (f) second-hand goods; and (g) any component part of, or accessory to, goods'.[23] The manufacturer may be liable even if the goods supplied are not consumer goods as long as the manufacturer supplied the goods in trade or commerce. Goods supplied in any other way do not fall within the definition of goods for the purposes of manufacturer's liability under the Act.[24]

14.4 Manufacturer

The manufacturer is the party liable to a defective goods action. The definition of 'manufacturer' given under s 7 of the ACL, and derived from the TPA, s 74A, is as follows:

> **Meaning of manufacturer**
>
> (1) A manufacturer includes the following:
>
> (a) a person who grows, extracts, produces, processes or assembles goods;
>
> (b) a person who holds himself or herself out to the public as the manufacturer of goods;
>
> (c) a person who causes or permits the name of the person, a name by which the person carries on business or a brand or mark of the person to be applied to goods supplied by the person;
>
> (d) a person (the first person) who causes or permits another person, in connection with:
>
> (i) the supply or possible supply of goods by that person; or
>
> (ii) the promotion by that other person by any means of the supply or use of goods; to hold out the first person to the public as the manufacturer of the goods;
>
> (e) a person who imports goods into Australia if:
>
> (i) the person is not the manufacturer of the goods; and
>
> (ii) at the time of the importation, the manufacturer of the goods does not have a place of business in Australia.
>
> (2) For the purposes of subsection 1(c):
>
> (a) a name, brand or mark is taken to be applied to goods if:
>
> (i) it is woven in, impressed on, worked into, annexed or affixed to the goods; or
>
> (ii) it is applied to a covering, label, reel or thing in or with which the goods are supplied; and
>
> (b) if the name of a person, a name by which a person carries on business or a brand or mark of a person is applied to goods, it is presumed, unless the

23 Section 2(1).
24 Sections 138(1)(a), 139(1)(a), 140(1)(a).

contrary is established, that the person caused or permitted the name, brand or mark to be applied to the goods.

(3) If goods are imported into Australia on behalf of a person, the person is taken, for the purposes of paragraph (1)(e), to have imported the goods into Australia.

The definition of 'manufacturer' recognises the commercial reality that in modern complex societies consumers deal with goods bearing labels on which numerous corporate entities may be identified as being associated with the goods' importation, branding, packaging, labelling and distribution. The Explanatory Memorandum[25] observed that a manufacturer may be involved in numerous activities, including:

- growing, extracting, producing, processing, or assembling the goods which may in turn encompass a wide range of agricultural, mining, forestry, fishing and aqua-culture, manufacturing, product assembly, trade, craft and artisanal activities;
- a person holding themselves out to the public as being the manufacturer of the relevant goods including importers, agents, manufacturers' local representatives;
- causing or permitting the name of the person, a name by which the person carries on business, or a trade or mark of the person to be applied to goods supplied to the person including activities related to importing, acting as an agent for the goods, or being a local representative of the manufacturer for those goods;
- causing or permitting another person in connection with the supply or possible supply, or the promotion of the supply, of the goods, to hold out the first person to the public as the manufacturer of the goods including activities related to the acts of importers, agents, and the local representatives of manufacturers;
- importing goods into Australia if that person is not the actual manufacturer of the goods and, simultaneously, the importation of the goods where the manufacturer does not have a place of business in Australia.

For the purposes of the ACL, the term 'manufacturer' is defined broadly, and may refer to the person who actually manufactures the goods, or who holds themselves out to the public as manufacturing the goods, or causes or permits their name or brand name to be applied to the goods, or permits another person to promote the goods as being goods they manufacture, or imports the goods. A person may do any one or more of these things and, further, more than one person may, by doing any one or more of these things, be considered a manufacturer for the purposes of the ACL.

A manufacturer is therefore a person who undertakes any of a wide range of activities such as growing, extracting, producing, processing or assembling goods; identifies themselves as a manufacturer of goods to the public; brands or marks the goods with their name or business name; or, in cases where the manufacturer does not have a place of business in Australia, imports goods. Accordingly, an oyster farmer has been held to be a manufacturer of goods[26] and a corporation that applies their label to a product has been held to be a manufacturer.[27]

25 At [2.38].
26 *Ryan v Great Lakes Council* (1999) ATPR ¶46-191 under equivalent provisions of the former TPA.
27 *Australian Competition and Consumer Commission v Glendale Chemical Products Pty Ltd* (1998) ATPR ¶41-632.

If the manufacturer of certain goods is not known, a person may, by written notice to any or each supplier of the goods, request that the supplier give particulars of, or information sufficient to identify, the manufacturer or sufficient within 30 days. If, after the 30-day period has expired, the person still does not know who the manufacturer is, the supplier is deemed to be the manufacturer under the Act.[28]

In *Leeks v FXC Corporation*,[29] the issue was who the manufacturer was for the purposes of s 75AD of the TPA. Mr Leeks purchased a parachuting device, the function of which was to automatically deploy a reserve canopy. The goods were purchased from the second and third respondents – respectively, the Australian Parachuting Safety Council Inc and Mr Chapman. The device was manufactured by FXC Corporations (FXC), a company incorporated in the United States. The device deployed incorrectly when Mr Leeks was parachuting, causing the reserve chute to open when not required or intended. The opening of the reserve chute impaired the function of the main chute, and Mr Leeks suffered serious injuries as a result of the impact on landing.

Mr Leeks made claims against FXC in respect of injuries he had sustained, including for the contravention, as a manufacturer, of ss 74B, 74D, 74E and 74G of Division 2A of Part V of the TPA; and for contravention, as a manufacturer, of s 75AD of Part VA of the TPA. Section 75AD is expressed in the same terms as s 138 of the ACL. FXC sought to strike out these claims. The basis of the strike-out claim was that FXC was not the manufacturer of the product for the purposes of s 75AD of the TPA, for which s 74A(4) provided the relevant definition. Under s 74A(4) of the TPA the importer of the product, the Parachuting Safety Council, was the manufacturer. It was FXC's argument that s 74A(4) of the Act could not be invoked in order to deem the second and/or third respondents the manufacturers of the goods for the purposes of the claims, and at the same time make parallel claims against FXC as the actual manufacturer.

Finn J noted that s 74A was not expressed in such a way as to indicate that the legislature intended to relieve the actual manufacturer of liability under Division 2A only for the reason that a manufacturer could be deemed. To arrive at this construction of s 74A, in his Honour's view, was not to be done lightly. Finn J said:

> It has since been judicially accepted that, notwithstanding the deeming provisions, an actual foreign manufacturer can properly be a party as well to proceedings brought by a consumer against local deemed manufacturers. In *White v Eurocycle Pty Ltd* (1994) ATPR ¶41-330 Boehm AJ observed:
>
>> I have wondered . . . whether subsection (4) of s 74A can, or is intended to be construed so as to restrict the meaning on facts such as those before me to refer to the deemed manufacturer only. Clearly, Russell Miller, in his work *Annotated Trade Practices Act* (14th ed) would not think so (see at p 337) since he includes the actual manufacturer as a person to whom the section applies. I have adopted that approach.[30]

Finn J found that the legislation professed an approach of 'concurrent liability' rather than exclusivity of liability. His Honour could see no reason for construing the various provisions of

28 Section 147.
29 (2002) 189 ALR 288.
30 (2002) 189 ALR 288.

s 74A(3) and (4) as mutually exclusive, thereby permitting only one of the deemed manufacturers to be sued. It was not questionable that the legislature had intended that the provisions of Division 2A and of Part VA applied to actual manufacturers. The various claims were capable of being made directly against FXC as the actual manufacturer. Further, the consumer was not required under s 74A to choose which manufacturer (actual or deemed) to proceed against.

14.5 Unknown manufacturer

Where a person injured by a defective product does not know the identity of the manufacturer, s 147 provides as follows:

> **Unidentified manufacturer**
>
> (1) A person who:
>
> (a) wishes to institute a defective goods action; but
>
> (b) does not know who is the manufacturer of the goods to which the action would relate;
>
> may, by written notice given to a supplier, or each supplier, of the goods who is known to the person, request the supplier or suppliers to give the person particulars identifying the manufacturer of the goods, or the supplier of the goods to the supplier requested.
>
> (2) If, 30 days after the person made the request or requests, the person still does not know who is the manufacturer of the goods, then each supplier:
>
> (a) to whom the request was made; and
>
> (b) who did not comply with the request;
>
> is taken, for the purposes of the defective goods liability action (but not for the purposes of section 142(c)), to be the manufacturer of the goods.

Under the process outlined in s 147, the consumer requests information that would enable them to identify the actual manufacturer of the goods from the original supplier. After 30 days from the time the request is made, the supplier or suppliers, who have or have not provided the requested information, are deemed to be the manufacturer or manufacturers for the purpose of the plaintiff's defective goods claim under the Act.

14.6 Supply 'in trade or commerce'

Defective goods actions can only be pursued if loss or damage is caused by goods that have been supplied by manufacturers in trade or commerce. It follows that supplies of goods that are not in trade or commerce, even if they have caused loss or damage to a person, thing, land or building, will not give rise to a defective goods action.

In *Cook v Pasminco Ltd*,[31] the applicants brought class action proceedings in the Federal Court under Part IVA of the *Federal Court of Australia Act 1976* (Cth) against the owner of

31 (2000) 99 FCR 548.

smelters at Cockle Creek in New South Wales and Port Pirie in South Australia. The claimants' causes of action were in negligence, nuisance and contraventions of ss 75AD and 75AG of the TPA for damages for injury to their health alleged to have been caused by noxious emissions, and additionally a claim for damage to real estate.

The applicant pleaded a claim alleging that, for the purposes of Part VA of the TPA, ss 75AD and 75AG, the noxious emissions were 'goods' manufactured by Pasminco and supplied in trade or commerce in circumstances where the defects in the emissions were said to have caused injury to the applicant and group members.[32] Lindgren J dismissed the application as incompetent as it was beyond the jurisdiction of the Federal Court under Part IVA. His Honour held that the federal element of the claim sought to be relied on under the TPA was 'not genuine', 'untenable' or designed to 'fabricate' a basis for the court's jurisdiction.[33]

The emissions were not 'supplied' to the plaintiff by the defendant because they:

> did not move from the respondents to the applicants or anyone else as part of a consensual transaction or dealing. Accordingly, the applicants will not be able to prove that the respondents 'supplied' the emissions.[34]

There being no supply, neither was there a supply occurring in trade or commerce. Such a supply 'must occur as an aspect or element of activities or transactions which themselves have a trading or commercial character'.[35]

Pasminco was successful in its application to strike out the applicant's claim. The application was dismissed as incompetent[36] as a representative proceeding under Part IVA of the *Federal Court of Australia Act 1976* (Cth).

14.7 Safety defect: The consumer expectation test

Defective goods actions under ss 138–141 may be brought against manufacturers who supply 'goods that have a safety defect'. The loss or damage suffered by the applicant must have been due to a defect in the goods supplied in trade or commerce. Section 9 defines 'safety defect' as follows:

> **Meaning of safety defect in relation to goods**
>
> (1) For the purposes of this Schedule, goods have a safety defect if their safety is not such as persons generally are entitled to expect.
>
> (2) In determining the extent of the safety of goods, regard is to be given to all relevant circumstances, including:
>
> (a) the manner in which and the purposes for which they have been marketed; and

32 (2000) 99 FCR 548, [9].
33 (2000) 99 FCR 548, [16].
34 (2000) 99 FCR 548, [27].
35 (2000) 99 FCR 548, [28].
36 (2000) 99 FCR 548, [35].

(b) their packaging; and
(c) the use of any mark in relation to them; and
(d) any instructions for, or warnings with respect to, doing, or refraining from doing, anything with or in relation to them; and
(e) what might reasonably be expected to be done with or in relation to them; and
(f) the time when they were supplied by their manufacturer.

(3) An inference that goods have a safety defect is not to be made only because of the fact that, after they were supplied by their manufacturer, safer goods of the same kind were supplied.

(4) An inference that goods have a safety defect is not to be made only because:
(a) there was compliance with a Commonwealth mandatory standard for them; and
(b) that standard was not the safest possible standard having regard to the latest state of scientific or technical knowledge when they were supplied by the manufacturer.

Section 9 therefore establishes that in order for goods to be found to have a safety defect, they must fail to meet a general standard in that the goods are not as safe 'as persons generally are entitled to expect' (s 9(1)), and the failure to meet that standard may be determined by reference to the considerations provided at s 9(2). The knowledge and expectations relevant to the factors listed at s 9(2) are those of the community, and not those of an individual consumer. The standard of product safety is defined objectively, as 'what the public at large, rather than any particular individual, is entitled to expect',[37] and not subjectively.[38] The perspective from which this determination is made is that of the reasonable person, taking into account the class of people to whom the goods are marketed or directed, including 'the astute and the gullible, the intelligent and the not so intelligent, the well educated and the poorly educated',[39] rather than the particular consumer. In other words, the test is grounded in reasonable public expectations,[40] taking into consideration all relevant circumstances.

In *Cook v Pasminco* the court referred to s 75AC(1), which defined goods as having defects 'if their safety is not such as persons generally are entitled to expect'. The court stated that the test to be applied was whether 'the emissions were not as safe, because of a defect in them, as persons generally were entitled to expect them to be'.[41] Precisely what consumers are entitled to expect is easier to establish in the case of malfunctioning goods since the community's expectation is that they will perform their function as intended. However, appropriate standards of safety are more difficult to establish. The court in *Cook v Pasminco* observed that 'it is a poison that does not do its deadly work that is defective rather than one that does'.[42] It is a safe,

37 Explanatory Memorandum, [14].
38 See *Australian Competition and Consumer Commission v Glendale Chemical Products* (1998) ATPR ¶41-632.
39 *Campomar Sociedad Limitada v Nike International Ltd* (2000) 202 CLR 45.
40 *Bright v Femcare Ltd* [2000] FCA 1179, [92].
41 (2000) 99 FCR 548, [32].
42 (2000) 99 FCR 548, [32].

not an unsafe, poison that is defective. The emissions were not dangerous because of a defect, but because it was in their nature to be so.

In *Australian Competition and Consumer Commission v Glendale Chemical Products Pty Ltd*,[43] a consumer purchased 500 g of a caustic soda called 'DRANO' at a local store named Glendale Chemical Products Pty Ltd for him to use to unblock a pipe in the shower recess. Following a friend's advice, the consumer poured hot water into the drain and immediately sprinkled the caustic soda over it. The combination of hot water and caustic soda caused an explosion in the confined space of the pipe such that the liquid was propelled from the drain, causing injury to his face and eyes. Glendale was the deemed manufacturer, not the actual manufacturer, of the caustic soda. It purchased the product in bulk from Redox Chemicals and repackaged the goods with its own label. The product packaging contained some safety warning but none regarding the contents' reaction in contact with boiling water in confined spaces. There was no recommendation to wear protective gear in the case of reflux.

The general point raised by the case is whether consumers can be expected to be knowledgeable enough about a product not to have unrealistic expectations about its safety.

In *Glendale*, the lack of warning regarding the serious hazard constituted the defect in the product. The Federal Court held that Glendale was strictly liable for burns to the body of a consumer because '[t]he nature of the product and the purpose for which it was marketed entitled consumers to expect to be warned of the danger or lack of safety'. It is to be noted that the court observed in this case that goods may be defective even if they operate as intended.[44]

In *Laws v GWS Machinery Pty Ltd*,[45] the plaintiff father and son who suffered injury when a tractor tyre exploded while being inflated succeeded in an action under the TPA, Part VA (now Part 3-5 of the ACL). Rothman J held that the safety of the tyre was not such as persons generally were entitled to expect. The tyres were sold without any warning as to the dangers attendant to the fitting process, and the court held that fitting tyres to a wheel rim was a reasonable consumer expectation in the absence of a warning to the contrary. 'Instruction' under the ACL is not limited to the use of the goods, but extends to the installation of the goods.[46]

Adverse inferences regarding the defectiveness of supplied goods may not be drawn merely because, after the goods were supplied, safer goods of the same type were supplied onto the market by the manufacturer,[47] nor because they failed to comply with the highest Commonwealth mandatory standard but complied with a mandatory standard.[48] A mandatory standard is one that must be complied with at the time the goods are supplied and non-compliance with which may result in an offence or liability.[49]

43 (1998) ATPR ¶41-632.
44 (1998) ATPR ¶41-632, 619.
45 (2007) 209 FLR 53.
46 Section 9; see *Skerbic v McCormack* [2007] ACTSC 93, [41].
47 Section 9(3).
48 Section 9(4).
49 Section 2.

14.8 Defective goods actions

Part 3-5 of the ACL establishes four defective goods actions at ss 138–141:

1. If, because of a defect in a defective good, an individual suffers death or injury, s 138 imposes liability on the manufacturer of the defective good to the amount of actual loss suffered as a result of those injuries or that death.
2. If, because of a defect in a defective good, an individual suffers death or injury, causing thereby another individual to suffer loss, s 139 imposes liability on the manufacturer of the defective good to compensate the dependent of the dead or injured person, but does not extend to a person in a business, commercial or employment relationship with the dead or injured individual.
3. If, because of a defect in a defective good, goods 'of a kind ordinarily acquired for personal, household or domestic use or consumption' (s 140(1)(c)) are destroyed or damaged, resulting in loss to the person using or intending to use the goods, s 140 imposes liability on the manufacturer.
4. If, because of a defect in a defective good, land, buildings or fixtures that have been acquired for private use (s 141(1)(d)) are destroyed or damaged, resulting in loss to the person using them or intending to use them, s 141 imposes liability on the manufacturer.

14.9 Defences

The four defences to a defective goods action are outlined at s 142 of the ACL. Section 142(a) provides that a manufacturer will have an effective defence where the manufacturer is able to prove that the goods were not defective at the time they were supplied but developed a defect at a later time. A manufacturer may avail themselves of a defence under s 142(b) if they are able to prove that the defect in question was the result of compliance with a Commonwealth, state or territory mandatory standard, and the Commonwealth, state or territory government will be liable for the loss instead. The state of the art defence at s 142(c) provides that, where the state of scientific or technical knowledge at the time the goods were supplied made it impossible for the manufacturer to discover the defect in the good supplied, the manufacturer will not be liable for loss or damage caused by the defect. If loss or damage is caused by a defect in a component of an assembled good, liability extends jointly and severally to the manufacturer and assembler of the finished goods, unless the defect was caused by the product's design, or the lack of appropriate instructions, in which case a defence may be available under s 142(d).

14.9.1 Timing of defect development defence

Section 142(a) provides:

> (a) the safety defect in the goods that is alleged to have caused the loss or damage did not exist:

(i) in the case of electricity – at the time at which the electricity was generated, being a time before it was transmitted or distributed; or
(ii) in any other case – at the time when the goods were supplied by their actual manufacturer.

There is limited case law in Australia examining this defence. The Federal Court decision in *Carey-Hazell v Getz Brothers & Co (Australia) Pty Ltd*[50] considered a defence to liability under s 75AK(1)(a) of Part VA of the TPA, which provides a defence if it is established that 'the defect in the action goods that is alleged to have caused the loss did not exist at the supply time'.

A defence that the defect did not exist at the time the goods were actually supplied by the manufacturer was considered in *Effem Foods Ltd v Nicholls*.[51] The manufacturer was found liable when a consumer swallowed a safety pin that was in a Snickers chocolate bar. The manufacturer was unable to prove that, despite the processes of manufacture and detection employed, the safety pin was not in the goods supplied. In *Erwin v Iveco Trucks Australia Ltd*,[52] Erwin sought contribution or indemnity from the manufacturer for a design fault in a truck's pinch-bolt mechanism. Erwin was not able to show that the problems with the truck's steering, causing an accident, were not due to the faulty adjustment of the pinch bolt, and was liable for failing to properly maintain the supplied vehicle. In *Saint-Gobain Abrasives Pty Ltd v McPherson*,[53] McPherson's hand was injured by a grinding disc that disintegrated when the grinder was switched on. On the issue of whether the disc was defective at the time of its supply, the court held that the defect did not exist at the time of supply or that there was at best a speculative possibility that the disc had been damaged after it left the control of the appellant.

14.9.2 The regulatory compliance defence (s 142(b))

Section 142(b) provides:

> [T]he goods had that safety defect only because there was compliance with a mandatory standard for them.

Compliance with government regulations does not of itself preclude a finding of a product defect. But sub-s (b) indicates that it is defence to a finding of a safety defect when compliance is the only cause of that defect. When the manufacturer raises the defence of compliance with a safety standard, the court must determine the issue of product defectiveness in accordance with the regulatory safety standards. The regulatory compliance defence stipulates that a manufacturer's product is not unreasonably dangerous if it complies with the controlling governmental regulations or industry safety standards. A plaintiff's product liability claim should fail if the product is not unreasonably dangerous.

Will mere compliance with the standards suffice to ground the defence? If the standard is a minimum standard, where the regime was based on tort law, compliance with all applicable laws and regulations is not an absolute defence in a product liability case where a reasonable person would have taken additional precautions, and the manufacturer should have exceeded

50 (2004) ATPR ¶42-014.
51 (2000) ATPR ¶42-034.
52 (2010) 267 ALR 752.
53 [2009] NSWCA 214.

laws and regulations pertaining to safety. However, s 142(b) appears to introduce the prospect of summary judgment for a defendant who is able to demonstrate regulatory compliance.

It appears that the manufacturer is rewarded for meeting the mandatory standard, and need not verify that there are no additional or alternative technical solutions objectively possible and reasonable to further improve the safety of their product, and be relieved of liability to compensate the consumer only if they implemented these measures. It will be sufficient for the manufacturer to point to industry standards and demonstrate conformity. Compliance will probably be conclusive where there is no evidence to show that the product was not reasonably unsafe for any reason other than the standard. In other words, loss or damage, or injury to a person, will not suffice to establish the safety defectiveness of a product where the manufacturer is regulatorily compliant.

14.9.3 State of the art defence (s 142(c))

Section 142(c) provides:

> [T]he state of scientific or technical knowledge at the time when the goods were supplied by their manufacturer was not such as to enable that safety defect to be discovered.

It is a defence to a manufacturer that they can establish that their manufacturing process is in accordance with the then existing 'state of the art'. In *Ryan v Great Lakes Council*,[54] the defendant supplied contaminated oysters from which consumers contracted hepatitis A. In that case, tried under the TPA Part VA, the 'state of scientific knowledge' proved a complete defence. The defence argued successfully that because the oysters were destroyed during and by the testing process, and tests could only be carried out on samples, the detection of the defect and the supply of the oysters were completely separate and mutually exclusive processes, and the defect in the supplied oysters could not be discovered under the circumstances.

The Full Federal Court also considered information regarding testing procedures and the characteristics of the contaminating viruses. It heard that polymerise chain reaction (PCR) testing was a sophisticated technology available at the time and could have detected the presence of the contamination. However, PCR testing could only be undertaken by skilled technicians in advanced laboratories, and not by the untrained oyster farmers themselves. PCR testing was also costly at between $50 and $200 per sample, was capable of false positive results and therefore unreliable, and was not routinely applied to the detection of viruses in oysters anywhere in the world. Other, cheaper tests such as the presence of the *E. coli* bacterium in the oysters was not a guide to viral infection. Further, the contaminating virus tended to occur in clusters rather than diffusely throughout a bed of oysters such that a bed might contain only one contaminated oyster. However, the extreme virulence of the contaminant meant that a small amount of virus in a single oyster was sufficient to cause illness.

Lindgren J considered how strictly or reasonably the defence was to be interpreted:

> If the problem of 'false negatives' had not existed and if it had been appropriate to test by sample, an interesting question would have arisen as to whether the expression 'such as to enable that defect to be discovered' in s 75AK(1)(c) was to be construed as importing a

54 (1999) ATPR ¶46-191.

> modifying notion of reasonableness or practicability. Let it be assumed that extrapolation from sample to bulk was valid, but that the testing of the sample had to take place at a laboratory a considerable distance from the grower's establishment, the cost of the testing was great and the results could not be known for some days. A question would have arisen whether it could be truly said in these circumstances that the state of scientific or technical knowledge enabled the defect to be discovered.[55]

The 'state of scientific knowledge' proved a complete defence in this case. The technical knowledge did not exist, but had it been available the defendants would have been required to have used it. In the Federal Court, Lindgren J raised the issue of whether the statutory provision might be modified by reasonableness and practicability. The High Court, however, resolved the issue of any divergence between statutory and common law obligations. The reasonableness of the defendant's response was decided on the basis that no test for the detection of hepatitis A in estuarine waters existed.

To date, the only other Australian case to have considered this defence is *Peterson v Merck Sharpe & Dohme (Australia) Pty Ltd.*[56] The case concerned the Merck Sharpe & Dohme ('Merck') anti-inflammatory drug Vioxx. The plaintiff alleged that the cardiac arrest he suffered in December 2003 was caused by the manufacturer's drug, Vioxx. The action was based on s 75AD of the TPA, alleging that the drug was defective. Jessup J held that the drug was defective in the sense that its safety was not such as persons generally would expect, but upheld the first respondent's defence under s 75AK(c) (equivalent to the ACL provision) that the state of scientific or technical knowledge at the time Vioxx was supplied would not have enabled the defect to be discovered, finding for the respondent.

Peterson took Vioxx for an arthritic condition more or less continuously from May 2001 until it was withdrawn from the market in September 2004. He had a heart attack in December 2003, alleging that Vioxx was a contributing factor to its occurrence. Peterson alleged that Vioxx had a defect within the meaning of s 75AD of the TPA. The safety of Vioxx was therefore not as persons generally were entitled to expect. Peterson submitted that, well before September 2004, the respondents knew, or ought to have known, that the consumption of Vioxx increased the risk of cardiovascular disease. In the alternative, Peterson alleged that the respondents should have been aware of the realistic prospect that the consumption of Vioxx increased the risk of cardiovascular disease, at least since March 2000, in the context of uncertain scientific evidence that should have made the manufacturer apprehensive about its possibility. The defendant argued that it had acted reasonably given the state of knowledge at the relevant time.

Jessup J considered the history of findings of Vioxx's impacts on health. Specifically, his Honour took into consideration, first, that testing conducted from 2000 suggested the possibility of a relationship between the drug and cardiovascular disease – specifically, that it was linked with a suspected doubling of the risk of heart attacks, although this was not confirmed until September 2004.[57] So, for the whole of the period that Vioxx was on the market the question of the link between the drug and cardiovascular disease was not settled.[58] Second,

55 [1999] FCA 177, [549].
56 (2010) 184 FCR 1.
57 At [3].

Jessup J considered two major placebo controlled clinical trials of Vioxx conducted between 2000 and 2004. One involved patients with a history of colorectal adenomas. This trial was terminated in September 2004 when results revealed twice the rate of certain cardiovascular disease among patients being administered Vioxx compared with those on the placebo, leading the respondents to withdraw the drug from the market.[59] A second placebo trial involved administering the drug or a placebo to patients suffering arthritis but was terminated under an ethical cloud when questions about the appropriateness of involving persons suffering and having to continue to endure arthritic pain.

Jessup J held that Vioxx was defective in accordance with the definition provided by the TPA, in the sense that the safety of Vioxx was not such as persons generally were entitled to expect. His Honour upheld the allegation that Vioxx had contributed to the plaintiff's heart attack, having regard to what was known at the time of the trial about the relationship between the consumption of Vioxx and cardiovascular disease, and to the applicant's own condition at the time. However, his Honour found in favour of the first respondent, who raised the defence that the state of scientific or technical knowledge at the time when Vioxx was supplied to the applicant was not such as would enable the defect to be discovered. Jessup J upheld the defence under s 75AK(c) of the TPA, and rejected the claim under s 75AD of the TPA.

The relevant period for determining whether the defence applied was the time prior to September 2004. Prior to that time, the information available to the defendant's doctors, although sufficiently strong to raise concerns about the effects of the drug, did not amount to scientific evidence founding knowledge of its health risks.[60] While his Honour did accept that the applicant's submission that results of the trials constituted a 'worrisome and important signal of potential cardiovascular risk',[61] this in itself did not constitute 'the level of scientific knowledge required to enable a defect to be discovered during the relevant period'.[62]

Given the respondent's knowledge and the level of uncertainty surrounding the effects of the drug, Jessup J held that Merck had acted 'reasonably'[63] and that it could not have reasonably concluded before September 2004 that the drug posed a risk of causing heart attack. The defence was available because the defect could not be reasonably discovered even though there was sufficient suspicion to warrant a warning of the side effect.[64]

On appeal, the Full Federal Court affirmed the Federal Court's finding.[65] The Full Federal Court further added that a defence invoking the state of scientific knowledge must include consideration of 'not just the results of the [adverse reaction] study but the conclusions to be drawn from it'.[66] In considering the defence, the Federal Court interpreted it as being subject to a test of reasonableness, and that mitigating factors such as practicality and the nature of the industry were to be taken into account. Further, Jessup J classified defects into three types and proposed that classification was relevant to the question of when the defence applies.

58 At [6].
59 At [3].
60 (2010) 184 FCR 1, [927].
61 (2010) 184 FCR 1, [682].
62 (2010) 184 FCR 1, [926]–[927].
63 (2010) 184 FCR 1, [680]–[681].
64 (2010) 184 FCR 1, [929].
65 *Merck Sharpe & Dohme (Australia) Pty Ltd v Peterson* (2011) 196 FCR 145, [206].
66 (2010) 184 FCR 1, [207].

Having considered the nature of the defence, Jessup J discussed the nature of a defect for the purposes of the TPA:

> [O]n one view at least by the terms of s75AC a defect is a situation rather than a particular aspect of the composition of the goods in question. And it is a situation the existence of which must be determined as a matter of judgment only after consideration of all relevant circumstances. In the present case I have effectively held that persons generally were entitled to expect [that the defendants] would have given to medical practitioners a warning which would have conveyed some idea of the signal of risk ... The state of scientific knowledge was such as would have enabled such warning to be given.[67]

Applying the typology and distinction between situational and compositional defects to the product, Vioxx, Jessup J recognised that Vioxx was defective in two respects: instructional (situation) and design (composition). His Honour made further observations about how the relevant defence was to be applied to the defect:

> [The defence] contemplates the existence of a defect capable of being discovered by reference to the current state of scientific or technical knowledge. It is not concerned with the kind of contextual circumstances referred to in [determining the existence of a defect]. My conclusion that the respondents ought to have acted consistently with the cardiovascular risk signal yielded by VIGOR is in the nature of a judgment as to how persons generally were entitled to expect that MSDA would act. By all means it informed my determination that there was a defect, but the content of persons' expectations did not constitute the defect itself. The defect was something inherent in Vioxx as a matter of composition. I consider that the intent of s 75AK(1)(c) is that if that defect could not be discovered according to the state of scientific or technical knowledge, the defence should be available, notwithstanding that enough was suspected about the product to activate an implied obligation to give warnings of the kind mentioned in s 75AC(2)(d). I propose to uphold MSDA's defence under s 75AK(1).[68]

14.9.4 Defect in a component of an assembled good defence (s 142(d))

Section 142(d) deals with defects in assembled goods. Section 142(d) provides:

> [I]f the goods that had that safety defect were comprised in other goods – that safety defect is attributable only to:
>
> (i) the design of the other goods; or
> (ii) markings on the other goods; or
> (iii) the instructions or warnings by the manufacturer of the other goods.

67 *Peterson v Merck Sharpe & Dohme (Australia) Pty Ltd* (2010) 184 FCR 1, [928].
68 *Peterson v Merck Sharpe & Dohme (Australia) Pty Ltd* (2010) 184 FCR 1, [929].

It is a defence that goods that have the safety defect are comprised in other goods, and the safety defect is attributable only to the design of the other goods, markings on the other goods, or instructions or warnings by the manufacturer of the other goods. In *Skerbic v McCormack*,[69] the plaintiff was injured when a garage door she was standing under collapsed, striking her on the head and causing serious injuries. The door collapsed because one of the brackets anchoring it to a brick wall gave way. The cause of the accident was found to be that the particular plastic masonry plugs used were inadequate.

Initially, Skerbic commenced proceedings against McCormack, the owner of the unit she and her husband leased. However, Skerbic withdrew her action against her landlord and commenced an action in negligence and under s 75AD of the TPA against the manufacturers and suppliers of the roller door, Gliderol International Pty Ltd ('Gliderol'). Plaintiff and defendant then joined Sheridan, the supplier and installer of the garage door.

Skerbic argued that Gliderol's installation instructions as supplied with the garage door were inadequate. Against Sheridan, Skerbic argued was that having held himself to be an expert in the installation of garage doors Sheridan should have known and applied the correct method of fixing the brackets to the brickwork. Further, that Gliderol was in breach of s 75AD of the TPA, in that her injuries were caused by defects in the goods supplied and manufactured by Gliderol.

Examining the four-page printed installation instructions supplied by Gliderol to its installers along with the garage doors, the court noted that they appeared to be addressed to the 'consumer or individual end-purchaser, rather than to a retailer, distributor or installer', and that '[t]he instructions should have been clear and intelligible to persons without any relevant trade qualifications or experience'.

The goods supplied at 'step 2' of the instructions included support brackets with coach screws (for securing to timber) and support brackets with masonry anchor plugs (for securing to brick). The type of masonry anchor plug to be used was not specified. It was the plaintiff's and Gliderol's argument that the installer should have understood the instructions as requiring that the brackets be affixed to the brick wall using metal anchor plugs. Sheridan gave evidence that plastic anchor plugs had been used elsewhere on the same door, on other doors in the body corporate, and had been his practice of affixing brackets to brickwork in all his time as an installer without incident.

On the claim of negligence, the court found Gliderol, but not Sheridan, liable. The court also found that Gliderol had breached their statutory duty under ss 75AD and 75AC of the TPA. The court observed that s 75AC of the TPA provides that goods should be as safe as persons generally are entitled to expect. Goods that do not meet this expectation are defective. In determining whether the expectation is satisfied, the court may have regard to the purposes for which they have been marketed; and any instructions for doing anything with or in relation to them. While instructions normally refer to the consumer's use of the goods, in this case they referred to the goods' installation, and were sufficiently inadequate to fall within the definition of 'defective' as applied to s 75AC of the TPA.

69 [2007] ACTSC 93.

The case was appealed in *Gliderol International Pty Ltd v Skerbic & McCormack & Sheridan*.[70] The Court of Appeal affirmed the Master's findings with respect to Gliderol's statutory liability, but departed from them in finding Sheridan contributorily negligent (60 per cent/40 per cent) for the installation of the door.

14.9.5 Contributory negligence defence

The plaintiff's contributory actions or omissions may reduce the manufacturer's liability. The ACL at s 137A provides as follows:

> **Contributory acts or omissions to reduce compensation in defective goods actions**
>
> (1) If the loss or damage to which a defective goods action under section 138 or 139 of the Australian Consumer Law relates was caused by both:
> (a) an act or omission of:
> (i) the individual who suffers the injuries referred to in that section; or
> (ii) a person for whom that individual is responsible; and
> (b) a safety defect of the goods to which the action relates; the amount of the loss or damage is to be reduced to such extent (which may be to nil) as the court thinks fit having regard to that individual's share in the responsibility for the loss or damage.
>
> (2) If the loss or damage to which a defective goods action under section 140 or 141 of the Australian Consumer Law relates was caused by both:
> (a) an act or omission of:
> (i) the person who suffered the loss or damage; or
> (ii) another person for whom that person is responsible; and
> (b) a safety defect of the goods to which the action relates;
> the amount of the loss or damage is to be reduced to such extent (which may be to nil) as the court thinks fit having regard to the person's share in the responsibility for the loss or damage.

The provision applies 'where any damage is caused partly by the defect in the product and partly by the person suffering the damage' by an act that falls below the legal standard for protecting oneself from an unreasonable risk of harm. The voluntary assumption of risk must occur in circumstances where the product is accompanied by explicit warnings of the dangers involved in the use of the product. The consumer will then be contributorily negligent in the loss they have suffered, thereby reducing the compensation payable by a manufacturer of a defective good.

In *Norton Australia Ltd v Streets Ice Cream Pty Ltd*,[71] the appellant manufactured an adhesive – Bear Black General Purpose Adhesive BM 226. The respondent sued it for damage to the respondent's premises alleged to have been caused by the appellant's negligence in failing to give a purchaser of the adhesive adequate warning of its dangerous quality.

---

70 (2009) 170 ACTR 1.
71 (1968) 120 CLR 635.

The product contained the warning that it was 'highly flammable'. The court held that this was sufficient to deny liability in circumstances where the plaintiff exposed the product to a naked flame causing damage to their premises. The plaintiff had voluntarily assumed the risk.

14.10 Exclusion clauses (s 150)

In relation to whether the manufacturer's liability be excluded, s 150 provides:

> **Application of all or any provisions of this Part etc. not to be excluded or modified**
>
> (1) Any term of a contract (including a term that is not set out in the contract but is incorporated in the contract by another term) that purports to exclude, restrict or modify, or has the effect of excluding, restricting or modifying, any of the following is void:
> (a) the application of all or any of the provisions of this Part;
> (b) the exercise of a right conferred by any of those provisions;
> (c) any liability under any of those provisions.
>
> (2) A term of a contract is not taken to exclude, restrict or modify the application of a provision of this Part unless the term does so expressly or is inconsistent with that provision.

Therefore, any term of a contract that purports to exclude, restrict or modify, or has the effect of excluding, restricting or modifying, the provisions is void.

14.11 Limitations of actions (s 143)

Consumers have ten years from the time the manufacturer supplies the goods to them to commence an action. Further, they must commence an action within three years of discovering a defect, the loss it has caused, and the identity of the manufacturer. Section 143 of the ACL provides:

> **Time for commencing defective goods actions**
>
> (1) Subject to subsection (2), a person may commence a defective goods action at any time within 3 years after the time the person became aware, or ought reasonably to have become aware, of all of the following:
> (a) the alleged loss or damage;
> (b) the safety defect of the goods;
> (c) the identity of the person who manufactured the goods.
>
> (2) A defective goods action must be commenced within 10 years of the supply by the manufacturer of the goods to which the action relates.

Therefore, the consumer cannot commence an action more than three years after discovering a defect in a good. Moreover, the consumer cannot commence an action even if it falls within the three-year limit if the goods were supplied more than ten years prior.

14.12 Manufacturer's indemnification of suppliers

If a supplier, having supplied goods to a consumer, becomes liable to pay damages under s 259(4) that the manufacturer would have been liable to pay under s 271, the supplier has a right to be indemnified by the manufacturer. A supplier who incurs costs because goods fail to comply with the guarantee as to acceptable quality, fitness for purpose or correspondence with the description may be indemnified by the manufacturer.[72] The supplier must seek indemnification within three years. The three-year period commencement is calculated from either the time the supplier made a payment with respect to liability or the time the consumer commenced action for damages against the supplier.[73]

Section 276 provides for restriction to the manufacturer's liability under certain circumstances. The manufacturer is only liable for the lesser of the cost of replacing or repairing the goods if they are goods of a kind normally acquired for personal, domestic, or household use or consumption. The restriction does not apply if the supplier is able to demonstrate that the restriction is neither fair nor reasonable in the circumstances.[74] The factors to which the court has regard to determine whether the restriction on the manufacturer's liability is fair and reasonable in the circumstances include whether suitable alternatives or equivalent goods are available or whether the supplier ordered the goods to be specially manufactured, processed or adapted.[75] Section 276A(4) provides that a higher liability than that imposed by statute may be imposed by the agreement between supplier and manufacturer, which takes precedence over sub-s (1).

14.13 Supplier's claims against manufacturers

An affected person may recover from a manufacturer for the failure to comply with the guarantees that the goods supplied are of an acceptable quality,[76] or that the goods would match the description provided by the manufacturer.[77] Exceptions include where the failure to comply with the guarantee is due to 'an act, default or omission of, or any representation made by, any person other than the manufacturer or an employee or agent of the manufacturer; or a cause independent of human control that occurred after the goods left the control of the manufacturer'.[78]

Section 272 entitles an affected person to recover damages for reductions in the value of goods, the price the consumer paid, the average retail price at the time of supply, or loss or damage suffered by the person resulting from a failure to comply with a guarantee.[79]

72 Section 274(2).
73 Section 274(4).
74 Section 276A(2).
75 Section 276A(3).
76 Section 54.
77 Section 56.
78 Section 271.
79 Section 272.

The affected person has three years to commence an action, the time running from when they were first aware or ought to have been aware that the relevant guarantee was not complied with.[80] Section 274 of the Act provides that a supplier of goods is indemnified against the manufacturer for loss or damage caused by a breach of a guarantee at Part 3-2 of the Act that the consumer may recover under s 259(4), if the manufacturer may have been made liable under s 271.

If the seller establishes this is not fair or reasonable, then the manufacturer's liability may not be so limited.[81] Section 131C provides that the remedies available under Part 3-5 are additional to other remedies. A plaintiff pursuing alternate remedies is under an election to pursue a particular remedy, and must exercise that election before final judgment.[82] Recovery under Part 3-5, Division 1 is not permitted when recovery may or has been effected either under workers compensation laws or pursuant to an international agreement.[83]

Manufacturer's liability provisions cannot be excluded, restricted or modified,[84] except expressly by a clear contractual term, or a provision of a contract being clearly inconsistent with the operation of the manufacturer's liability.[85]

14.14 Role of the ACCC (s 149)

Section 149 of the ACL provides:

> **Representative actions by the regulator**
>
> (1) The regulator may, by application, commence a defective goods action on behalf of one or more persons identified in the application who have suffered the loss or damage in relation to which the action is commenced.
>
> (2) The regulator may only make the application if it has obtained the written consent of the person, or each of the persons, on whose behalf the application is being made.

Section 149(1) entitles a representative defective goods action to be brought by a regulator against a manufacturer for goods alleged to be unsafe on behalf of a person who has suffered loss or damage, after first obtaining written consent from the person being so represented.[86]

14.15 Key points

- Under Division 1 of Chapter 3, Part 3-5 of the ACL, manufacturers of defective goods are liable if the consumer has suffered loss or damage.
- The four defective goods actions are described at ss 138–141.

---

80 Section 273.

81 Section 276A(2).

82 *Laws v GWS Machinery Pty Ltd* (2007) 209 FLR 53, [192], citing *Graham Barclay Oysters Pty Ltd v Ryan* (2002) 211 CLR 540, 591; *Crump v Equine Nutrition Systems Pty Ltd* [2006] NSWSC 512, [266]–[267].

83 Section 146 ACL; see also *Elms v Ansell Ltd* [2007] NSWSC 618.

84 Section 150(1).

85 Section 150(2).

86 Section 149(2).

- Section 138 provides consumers with an action for loss or damage caused by injuries suffered by a person as a result of the defective product.
- Section 139 is a cause of action available to a person who has suffered loss or damage as a result of injuries suffered by another person.
- Section 140 provides that a person may sue for loss or damage they have suffered as a result of damage or destruction of other goods resulting from the defective product.
- Section 141 provides that a person who has suffered loss or damage resulting from the damage to or destruction of land, buildings or fixtures has a cause of action against the manufacturer.
- Section 142 in Part 3-5 sets out the defences available to the manufacturer against defective goods actions brought by plaintiffs alleging loss or damage resulting from defective goods.

14.16 DISCUSSION QUESTIONS

1. What is product liability as a legal concept?
2. What are the key statutory rules governing product liability?
3. What is the standard required for acceptable commercial conduct in relation to product safety?
4. What legal options does a consumer have in the event that a product is unsafe?
5. How might the product liability regime be improved?

14.17 FURTHER READING

Corbett, A, 'Australia: An Integrated Scheme for Regulating Liability for Medical Malpractice and Indemnity Insurance Markets that Does Not Include the Goal of Improving the Safety and Quality of Health Care' (2011) 4 *Drexel Law Review* 199.

Goldberg, R, 'Epidemiological Uncertainty, Causation and Drug Product Liability' (2014) 59 *McGill Law Journal* 777.

Hynes, P F, 'Doctors, Devices and Defects: Product Liability for Defective Medical Expert Systems in Australia' (2004) 15(2) *Journal of Law, Information and Science* 7.

Terry, N P, 'When the Machine That Goes "Ping" Causes Harm: Default Torts Rules and Technologically-mediated Health Care Injuries' (2002) 46 *St Louis University Law Journal* 27.

15

CONSUMER GUARANTEES

15.0 Introduction

This chapter addresses the topic of consumer guarantees. Consumer guarantees apply to any contract for the supply of goods or services to a consumer made after 1 January 2011. They replace the implied warranties and conditions in the former *Trade Practices Act 1974* (Cth) (TPA). Goods are covered by the consumer guarantees not only if they are sold in trade or commerce and bought by a *consumer*, but also if they are second-hand, leased or hired. However, some consumer guarantees apply regardless of whether the goods are sold in trade or commerce, such as the guarantees as to title, undisturbed possession and undisclosed securities. The terms 'trade' or 'commerce' relate to a supplier's or manufacturer's business or professional activities, including a non-profit business or activity. There is a degree of complexity to the consumer guarantees scheme. In *Scenic Tours Pty Ltd v Moore*,[1] Sackville AJA noted that this complexity might undercut the purpose of the scheme.

Given that the consumer guarantees are intended to provide protection to consumers in their dealings with service providers, the statutory regime is anything but straightforward. A consumer would need to be particularly well informed (or advised) to understand their rights under the regime.[2]

15.1 Consumer guarantees

The consumer guarantees provision of the Australian Consumer Law (ACL) and statutory remedies for breaching them protect only *consumers*. So, the first step in deciding whether they apply is to determine whether the person acquiring the goods is a 'consumer'. The extent of consumer protections available to business-to-business transactions has been the subject of considerable political debate. In some circumstances, even a major multinational corporation can be taken to be a consumer for the purposes of the consumer law. Federal Treasury's initial reform proposal was to narrow the definition of 'consumer' so as to exclude businesses and transaction between businesses. However, business groups mounted a successful campaign and the idea was abandoned.

The ACL adopts three definitions of the term 'consumer'. The guarantees provisions relevantly define it by reference to the kinds of goods and services purchased (the objective approach). The 'unfair terms' approach sees it defined by reference to the purpose for which goods are acquired (the subjective approach). The product safety, recall and reporting provisions adopt a hybrid approach: consumer goods are defined by reference to the intentions of the supplier (subjective) and the kinds of goods supplied (objective).

Section 3(1) adopts an objective test, and focuses on the uses to which goods or services are ordinarily put. The definition of 'consumer' at s 3 has two parts, discussed below.

15.1.1 Acquiring goods as a consumer

Section 3(1) provides that a person shall be taken to have acquired particular goods as a consumer if, and only if, the price paid was less than $40 000 or any other prescribed amount,

1 (2018) 361 ALR 456.
2 [2018] NSWCA 238, [119].

or the goods consisted of a vehicle or trailer acquired to be used principally in the transport of goods or services on public roads.

Section 3(2) contains an exception:

> However, subsection (1) does not apply if the person acquired the goods, or held himself or herself out as acquiring the goods:
>
> (a) for the purpose of re-supply; or
>
> (b) for the purpose of using them up or transforming them, in trade or commerce:
>
> (i) in the course of a process of production or manufacture; or
>
> (ii) in the course of repairing or treating other goods or fixtures on land.

The section adopts a subjective test and focuses on the purpose of a particular acquirer. If the acquirer is an 'excluded' acquirer, they are not a consumer even if the goods acquired are ordinarily acquired for personal, domestic or household use or consumption.

A consumer is a person who buys any type of goods or services costing up to $40 000 (or any other amount set by the ACL in future); or buys a vehicle or trailer used mainly to transport goods.

The section also defines a consumer in relation to the acquisition of services. Section 3(3) duplicates s 3(1) with respect to services. 'Consumer goods' is defined at s 2 of the ACL. Section 64 of the ACL provides that the consumer guarantees cannot be excluded, restricted or modified by contract. Parliament was presented with the opportunity, when considering the enactment of the ACL, to reform the definition of a consumer as it had appeared in the TPA. It did not do so. So, the term, albeit with a few exceptions, more or less retains the scope it had under the TPA.

15.1.2 Prescribed amount

Section 3 provides for the way in which the amount payable for the goods or services is calculated. Initially, it is the amount paid or payable by the person for the goods or services. A person acquires goods or services if the price does not exceed the prescribed amount: currently $40 000. If the amount payable is less than $40 000, the statutory guarantee that goods are of an acceptable quality applies to all circumstances where a person supplies, in trade or commerce, goods to another person.

Where the price is not more than $40 000, the person will be a consumer and there will be no need to enquire as to the nature of the goods. For example, in the case of *Crawford v Mayne Nickless Ltd*,[3] s 74 of the TPA still applied even though a security system costing less than $40 000 was installed on the plaintiff's commercial premises. It will also apply if the amount payable exceeds $40 000, providing the goods were of a kind ordinarily acquired for personal, domestic or household use or consumption.

Section 3(11) refers to a mixed supply of goods or services, and provides:

> A purchase or other acquisition of goods or services is made by a mixed supply if the goods or services are purchased or acquired together with other property or services, or together with both other property and other services.

3 (1992) ATPR (Digest) ¶46-091.

15.2 Ordinarily acquired for personal, domestic, or household use or consumption

The definition of a consumer is objective. Under s 3 of the ACL, a person is taken to have acquired goods or services as a consumer if the amount paid or payable for the goods or services does not exceed $40 000 (or such other greater amount as may be prescribed) or the goods or services are of a kind ordinarily acquired for personal, domestic or household use or consumption.

15.3 The non-consumer exception

The non-consumer exception is set out at s 3(2): if the person acquired goods or services, or held themselves out as acquiring the goods for the purpose of re-supply; or for the purpose of using them up or transforming them, in trade or commerce in the course of a process of production or manufacture, or in the course of repairing or treating other goods or fixtures on land, that person is not a consumer for the purposes of the ACL.

The reference to re-supply at paragraph (a), for example, means that a retailer purchasing goods for sale is not a consumer in relation to those goods. In s 2, 'supply' is defined to include re-supply by sale, exchange, lease, hire and hire-purchase. So, firms that lease cars, boats and equipment (even domestic equipment such as floor cleaners) are excluded from being consumers. Paragraph (b) distinguishes between 'using' goods and 'using goods up'. Goods acquired to be used in a manufacturing process – for example, sheet metal for producing car bodies or domestic appliances – are excluded. However, were the manufacturer to buy tools valued at less than $40 000 to use in manufacturing the product, they are a consumer in relation to those tools and the non-consumer exception does not apply.

The same item may be treated differently under the ACL, depending on the purpose for which it was purchased. A car manufacturer who purchases a tyre to affix to a car that it produces to sell will not be purchasing something to be used up or consumed. Rather, it will have been acquired for the purpose of re-supply. It is therefore not a consumer good. However, if an owner of the vehicle or the owner's agent (eg an auto repairer) were to purchase a tyre to replace a worn existing tyre, or to effect repairs on a vehicle, they will have acquired it as a consumer, and will not be exempt from the application of the consumer law.

Part V, Divisions 2 and 2A of the TPA imposed a liability on suppliers, manufacturers and importers of certain goods to consumers who have suffered loss or damage as a result of their use. This liability generally cannot be excluded (per s 74A).

In *Laws v GWS Machinery Pty Ltd*,[4] the plaintiff claimed damages for serious injuries suffered when a tyre he was fitting to his tractor exploded. GWS argued that Mr Laws was not a consumer because, although the tyre was purchased for less than the prescribed amount, they argued, the tyres were purchased for the purpose of using them up. In their submission, GWS maintained that the term 'use up' includes 'consumed the whole of or exhaust'; and,

4 (2007) 209 FLR 53.

because the tyre is perishable and may blow out and be damaged beyond repair, it is consumed in whole or exhausted.

Bonham J rejected GWS's submission in the following terms:

> The fallacy in the submission of GWS is that it omits the words 'in the course of' and reads the section as if the word 'of' did not appear before the words 'repairing or treating'. The use there of the word 'of', after the word 'or', means that the reading of the subsection requires that the alternative ('of repairing or treating other goods') is an alternative to one of: the purpose of re-supply, or the purpose of using them up; or the purpose of production or manufacture. The last-mentioned reading is the only logical result. In that way, the person 'remains a consumer even though goods are acquired for the purpose of using them up unless the goods are used up, relevantly, "in the course of repairing or treating other goods" or "in the course of the process of repairing or treating other goods"'.[5]
>
> On that construction, a manufacturer who purchases biscuits for its staff is a consumer, even if the staff members eat the biscuits while manufacturing, repairing, etc. Also, a manufacturer or owner of other goods is still a consumer if it acquires goods for the purpose of using them up but the consumption of them is not in the course of a process of production or manufacture or in the course of repair or treating other goods. For example, a tyre on a car would be acquired for the purpose of using it up but would not be used up in the course of that repair or treatment. Rather, it would be used up by the use of the tyre (or goods on which it was fitted) once it had been repaired or treated.[6]

15.4 Consumer guarantees for goods

Part 3-2, Division 1, Subdivision A of the ACL imposes nine guarantees in relation to the supply of goods:

- s 51 – guarantee that the supplier has the right to sell the goods;
- s 52 – guarantee that the consumer will have undisturbed possession;
- s 53 – guarantee that the goods are free from undisclosed security;
- s 54 – guarantee that the goods are of 'acceptable quality';
- s 55 – guarantee that the goods are fit for a particular purpose made known to the supplier by the consumer;
- s 56 – guarantee that the goods comply with description when sold by description;
- s 57 – guarantee that the goods comply with the sample or model when sold by sample or demonstration model;
- s 58 – guarantee that the manufacturer will take reasonable action to ensure that facilities for repair of the goods and parts for goods are reasonably available for a reasonable period after goods are supplied;
- s 59 – guarantee that the manufacturer or supplier will comply with express warranty where the manufacturer or supplier provides an express warranty.

5 *Lewis v GWS Machinery Pty Ltd* (2007) 209 FLR 53, 81.
6 At [142]–[143].

These guarantees have far-reaching implications and applications. The consumer guarantees regime adopts a 'single enterprise' approach under which the manufacturer assumes joint responsibility with other suppliers for the goods or services they release into the marketplace, and exist independently of the contract.

The rationale undergirding these guarantees is: (1) that it is the manufacturer who should be responsible for ensuring that the quality of the goods is acceptable, and should accept responsibility if their goods are unsuitable or defective; (2) that manufacturers are responsible for packaging and labelling and should be responsible if the goods do not comply with their description; (3) that manufacturers are responsible for any promotional material that has a natural tendency to induce the sale of their products, and they should therefore accept responsibility for any express warranties in that material; and (4) that manufacturers should ensure that consumers have the full benefit of the goods they have acquired over the expected life of the goods by ensuring an adequate supply of spare parts and repair services.

15.5 Guarantee as to title

Section 51 provides that the supplier guarantees that they have a right to sell the goods, unless a contrary intention appears in a contract or can be inferred from the circumstances of that contract. The section provides a guarantee that the supplier will have the right to dispose of the property in the goods when that property is to pass to the consumer. If the goods are specific or ascertained, property passes when the parties intend it to. Intention is determined from the terms of the contract, the conduct of the parties and the circumstances of the case. If the goods are unascertained, property cannot pass until the goods are ascertained.

When a seller undertakes that they have the right to sell the goods, they undertake that they will transfer an absolute title to the buyer. The provision obviously covers situations where the supplier has no title to the goods sold. However, because of the words 'right to dispose of the property in the goods', it is not restricted to the case where the seller owns the goods and can pass property in them, but has no right to sell the goods.

An exception is provided under s 51(2). By s 51(2), the guarantee as to title does not apply if supply is of limited title. A supply of limited title occurs when the supplier tells the prospective purchaser that they do not know whether there are any claims over particular goods and that, in the event of sale, they will be transferring only the title they have. By s 51(3), a supply will also be of 'limited title' under, for example, hire or lease agreements, or otherwise where the intention is clear from either the contract or the circumstances of the contract that the goods were not to be sold to the consumer. In these cases, the consumer acquires only a right to use goods for a certain period of time but does not acquire title to them.

15.6 Guarantee as to undisturbed possession

Section 52(1) provides that the 'consumer has the right to undisturbed possession of the goods unless there is a pre-existing security, charge or encumbrance'.

The ACL provides that in the absence of a different intention the supplier provides the buyer with a warranty that the buyer shall have and enjoy quiet possession of the goods and the goods shall be free of any charge or encumbrance in favour of any third party not declared or known to the buyer before or at the time of the contract.

Section 52(2) provides that 'if the consumer is told about securities, charges or encumbrances that relate to the goods, the guarantee of undisturbed possession does not apply' if the possessions are disturbed by a security charge or encumbrance that the consumer was told about prior to supply.

The guarantee of undisturbed possession and guarantee of title may run from different times, and the guarantee to undisturbed possession may run when the guarantee to title does not. The exception is that this guarantee does not apply to a supply of 'limited title'. This may be the period of any hire or lease agreements, or where the intention is clear that ownership in the goods is to be transferred to another person between the supplier and the consumer.

Although the very influential editors of the fifth edition of *Benjamin's Sale of Personal Property*[7] declare that 'no warranty in a sale of goods ... for quiet possession was part of the common law',[8] the *Conveyancing and Law of Property Act 1881* (Vic)[9] when applied to 'conveyances' of personality provides that a covenant for title and quiet possession is always imported unless expressly negatived.[10] The real property covenant of quiet possession, however, was and is still not a fully integrated concept.[11]

15.7 Guarantee as to undisclosed securities

Section 53(1) provides that 'the supplier will supply to a consumer goods that are free from any security, charge or encumbrance'.

This section imposes a guarantee that 'goods are free from any security, charge or encumbrance that was either not disclosed to the consumer, in writing, before the consumer agreed to the supply or that was not created by or with the consent of the consumer. The goods must remain free from undisclosed securities until property in the goods passes to the consumer.'

Section 53(3) provides that, in relation to a supply of limited title, there is 'a guarantee that all securities, charges or encumbrances known to the supplier and not known to the consumer were disclosed to the consumer before the consumer agreed to the supply'. Section 53(4) provides that the guarantee as to undisclosed securities does not apply to supply by way of hire or lease. This guarantee does not apply to a supply of 'limited title', where a supplier has disclosed to a consumer all known securities and charges on a good prior to the sale. In Australia, the only recorded case on this subsection is *Steinke v Edwards*.[12]

---

7 Sweet & Maxwell, London, 5th edn, 1906.

8 Fifth edn, 1906, 673.

9 44 & 45 Vict C 41.

10 Chalmers, *The Sale of Goods Act, 1893 Including the Factors Acts 1889 & 1890* (William Clowes & Sons Ltd, London, 1894), 26. Counsel's argument in *Niblett Ltd v Confectioners' Materials Co Ltd* [1921] 3 KB 387, 384, based on that Act, was rejected by the Court of Appeal.

11 See *Williams v Barrell* (1845) 1 CB 402; *Baynes v Lloyd* [1895] 2 QB 610; *Jones v Lavington* [1903] 1 KB 253; and *Jones v Consolidated Anthracite Collieries* [1916] 1 KB 123, 136–7.

12 Unreported, Local Court of Adelaide, SD Ronald SM, 1935, but noted in (1935) 8 ALJ 368.

15.8 Acceptable quality

Section 54 provides:

> Goods that are supplied to a consumer (except when they are supplied by auction) will be of acceptable quality.

Suppliers and manufacturers guarantee that goods sold to a consumer are of acceptable quality.[13] This guarantee also applies to goods that are leased or hired to a consumer.

Section 54(2) of the ACL provides that goods are considered to be of 'acceptable quality' if a reasonable consumer fully acquainted with the goods (including any defects) regards the goods as being of acceptable quality:

> if they are as:
>
> (a) fit for all the purposes for which goods of that kind are supplied; and
> (b) acceptable in appearance and finish; and
> (c) free from defects; and
> (d) safe; and
> (e) durable
>
> as a reasonable consumer fully acquainted with the state and condition of the goods (including any hidden defects of the goods) would regard as acceptable having regard to the matters in subsection (3).

In considering acceptability of the goods, a reasonable consumer can be expected to have regard to the following (s 54(3)):

> The matters for the purposes of subsection (2) are:
>
> (a) the nature of the goods; and
> (b) the price of the goods (if relevant); and
> (c) any statements made about the goods on any packaging or label on the goods; and
> (d) any representation made about the goods by the supplier or manufacturer of the goods; and
> (e) any other relevant circumstances relating to the supply of the goods.

Whether the goods are of an acceptable quality is a question of fact.[14]

Factors to be taken into consideration include: (1) the nature of the goods (expectations of durability); (2) the price of the goods (whether a 'premium' price had been paid for a high-quality product); (3) any statements made about the goods on any packaging or label on the goods; (4) any representation made about the goods by the supplier or manufacturer of the goods; (5) and other relevant circumstances relating to the supply of the goods (s 54(3)).

13 See *Australian Competition and Consumer Commission v LG Electronics Australia Pty Ltd* [2017] FCA 1047.

14 *Australian Competition and Consumer Commission v LG Electronics Australia Pty Ltd* [2017] FCA 1047, [167]–[168], per Middleton J. See also *Australian Competition and Consumer Commission v LG Electronics Australia Pty Ltd* [2018] FCAFC 96.

Whether goods are of acceptable quality is to be determined at the time they are supplied to the consumer.

15.9 Fitness for purpose

Section 55 provides that 'goods that are supplied to a consumer (except when the goods are supplied by auction) will be reasonably fit for any disclosed purpose, and any purpose which the supplier represents they are reasonably fit for'.

The fitness for purpose guarantee under the ACL operates in the same manner as it does under the various Sale of Goods Acts. The fitness for purpose guarantee under the ACL also supplements the acceptable quality guarantee. This guarantee will not apply 'if the circumstances show that the consumer did not rely on, or it was unreasonable for the consumer to rely on, the skill or judgment of the supplier, manufacturer or person making the representation that the goods would be fit for purpose'.[15]

15.10 Correspondence with description

Section 56 provides that goods that are supplied by description will correspond with that description (unless the goods are supplied by auction).

In substance, the guarantee as to description mirrors the implied term as to correspondence with description under the various Sale of Goods Acts. If the consumer has previously inspected the goods before purchase, this guarantee may also apply. The guarantees in s 57 will also apply to any goods supplied in this manner.

15.11 Supply of goods by sample

Section 57 provides that goods that are supplied (unless supplied by auction) with reference to a sample or demonstration model must correspond with the sample or demonstration model in quality, state or condition. The consumer should have a reasonable opportunity to compare the goods with the sample. The goods should be free from any defect that would not be apparent on reasonable examination of the sample or demonstration model. Section 57 provides:

> (1) If:
>
> (a) a person supplies, in trade or commerce, goods to a consumer by reference to a sample or demonstration model; and
>
> (b) the supply does not occur by way of sale by auction;
>
> there is a guarantee that:
>
> (c) the goods correspond with the sample or demonstration model in quality, state or condition; and
>
> (d) if the goods are supplied by reference to a sample – the consumer will have a reasonable opportunity to compare the goods with the sample; and

15 Section 55(3).

(e) the goods are free from any defect that:

(i) would not be apparent on reasonable examination of the sample or demonstration model; and

(ii) would cause the goods not to be of acceptable quality.

(2) If goods are supplied by reference to a sample or demonstration model as well as by description, the guarantees in section 56 and in this section both apply.

The guarantee contained in s 56 will also apply to any supply of goods in this manner if the supply was also by description (s 57(2)).

15.12 Guarantee as to repairs and spare parts

Section 58 provides that there is a guarantee the manufacturer of the goods will take reasonable action to ensure that facilities for the repair of the goods, and parts for the goods, are reasonably available for a reasonable period after the goods are supplied. Reasonableness under s 58 is contextual to the matter at hand.

15.13 Guarantee as to express warranties

Section 59 of the ACL provides as follows:

(1) **[Express warranty: manufacturer]** If:

(a) a person supplies, in trade or commerce, goods to a consumer; and

(b) the supply does not occur by way of sale by auction;

there is a guarantee that the manufacturer of the goods will comply with any express warranty given or made by the manufacturer in relation to the goods.

(2) **[Express warranty: supplier]** If:

(a) a person supplies, in trade or commerce, goods to a consumer; and

(b) the supply does not occur by way of sale by auction;

there is a guarantee that the supplier will comply with any express warranty given or made by the supplier in relation to the goods.

Under the provision, the manufacturer and supplier of the goods will comply with any express warranty given or made by the manufacturer or the supplier in relation to the goods (unless the goods were supplied by auction). Furthermore, the manufacturer and supplier guarantee that the goods will comply with any express warranty given by the manufacturer or supplier. An express warranty can include a 'warranty against defects' provided by a manufacturer.[16]

Section 2 defines 'express warranty' to mean:

16 There are further requirements that apply from 1 January 2012 for the form and content of a 'warranty against defects'. These are found in the *Competition and Consumer Regulations 2010* (Cth).

an undertaking, assertion or representation:

(a) that relates to:
  (i) the quality, state, condition, performance or characteristics of the goods; or
  (ii) the provision of services that are or may at any time be required for the goods; or
  (iii) the supply of parts that are or may at any time be required for the goods; or
  (iv) the future availability of identical goods, or of goods constituting or forming part of a set of which the goods, in relation to which the undertaking, assertion or representation is given or made, form part; and
(b) that is given or made in connection with the supply of the goods, or in connection with the promotion by any means of the supply or use of the goods; and
(c) the natural tendency of which is to induce persons to acquire the goods.

Express warranty is therefore defined very widely, and is broad enough to capture representations made by suppliers and manufacturers in negotiations preceding and preparatory to the supply of goods, including those made in and through advertisements. If a representation is covered by the statutory guarantee, consumers are able to seek remedies for the inducement to enter a contract by means of that false representation. If the representation related to the condition, quality, use or description of the goods, it may be contractually binding.

15.14 Guarantees as to due care and skill

Section 60 of the ACL provides a guarantee that where services are supplied in a consumer transaction the supplier will use due care and skill. Likewise, in s 61 of the ACL there is a guarantee that the service will be fit for purpose. Sections 60 and 61(1) provide as follows:

60 Guarantee as to due care and skill

If a person supplies, in trade or commerce, services to a consumer, there is a guarantee that the services will be rendered with due care and skill.

61 Guarantees as to fitness for a particular purpose etc.

(1) If: (a) a person (the supplier) supplies, in trade or commerce, services to a consumer; and
  (b) the consumer, expressly or by implication, makes known to the supplier any particular purpose for which the services are being acquired by the consumer;

there is a guarantee that the services, and any product resulting from the services, will be reasonably fit for that purpose.

Section 61(1) does not actually require that the consumer relies upon the skill and judgment of the supplier. Instead, the consumer must simply make known *any* purpose for which the service is required and the guarantee will arise.[17]

17 *Scenic Tours Pty Ltd v Moore* (2018) 361 ALR 456, [219], per Sackville AJA.

The guarantee provided under s 60 cannot be ousted by contract. Nor does a contract between the supplier and consumer necessarily condition the application of the guarantee. In *Scenic Tours Pty Ltd v Moore*, Sackville AJA stated:

> Despite the awkwardness of the statutory construct, the evident intention to be derived from the text of s 60 is that a person who, in trade or commerce, is to provide rights, benefits, privileges or facilities to a consumer is required to render them with due care and skill. The use of the future tense in the closing words of s 60 reinforces the conclusion that the Care Guarantee applies to services that are to be supplied to the consumer at some time in the future. The Care Guarantee may be enlivened by the supplier and consumer entering into a contract, as where the consumer pays a deposit and signs a standard form contract. But the Care Guarantee may also be enlivened without any enforceable contract coming into existence. For example, a consumer may have a contract with one person but the services may be supplied by a third person with whom the consumer has no contractual relationship.
>
> The text of s 60 does not imply and certainly does not compel the conclusion that if there is a contract in place between the supplier and the consumer the obligations imposed on the supplier by the Care Guarantee are co-extensive with the supplier's contractual obligations. Unless there is some contextual reason to construe the Care Guarantee in s 60 of the ACL as applying only to 'services' that are co-extensive with the supplier's contractual obligations, there is no basis for doing so. The same can be said for the Purpose and Result Guarantees.
>
> In my view there is no contextual reason to construe any of the Consumer Guarantees in this way. To construe the Care Guarantee as applying only to services that are co-extensive with the supplier's contractual obligations would not achieve the object and purpose of the legislation ascertained from the text and structure of the statute. The Care Guarantee is plainly designed to protect consumers by ensuring that the benefits, facilities or other services with which they are to be provided will be rendered with due care and skill. Parliament has expressly stated that a term of a contract which purports to exclude, restrict or modify the application of any of the Consumer Guarantees or any liability of a person for a failure to comply with any of the Consumer Guarantees, is void.
>
> It can hardly be intended that a person who is to provide benefits or facilities to a consumer can avoid the statutory obligation to exercise due care and skill simply by entering into a skilfully worded standard form contract with the consumer which defines the services to be provided in a manner that effectively avoids any obligation to exercise due care and skill.[18]

15.15 Remedies for non-compliance with consumer guarantees

The explicit listing of consumers' rights under the ACL, and who has the right to select the appropriate remedy, is a significant development in the consumer law. The remedies available

18 [2018] NSWCA 238, [173]–[175]. See also *Australian Competition and Consumer Commission v MSY Technology Pty Ltd* [2017] FCA 1251.

for a breach of a consumer guarantee vary with the severity of the breach.[19] In *Director of Consumer Affairs Victoria v The Good Guys Discount Warehouses (Australia) Pty Ltd*,[20] Moshinsky J stated of the consumer guarantees scheme:

> It is apparent from the sections of the Australian Consumer Law ... that there is some complexity to these provisions and that the ability of a customer to rely on the consumer rights and related remedies will depend on a range of variables such as the nature of the goods, the price of the goods, any statements made about the goods on any packaging or label on the goods, any representations made about the goods by the supplier or manufacturer, and other relevant circumstances. In the context of a television that breaks down or is faulty more than 12 months after purchase, the price of the television, the time since purchase, and the nature of the problem are likely to be material factors in determining whether the rights are applicable and a remedy is available.[21]

The breach of a consumer guarantee may be 'major' or 'minor'. The ACL requires a failure of compliance to constitute a 'major failure', as defined at s 260. Section 260 provides that, except for breaches of ss 58 and 59(1), a major failure of a guarantee provision occurs when:

> (a) the goods would not have been acquired by a reasonable consumer fully acquainted with the nature and extent of the failure; or
> (b) the goods depart in one or more significant respects:
> (i) if supplied by description – from that description; or
> (ii) if supplied by reference to a sample or demonstration model – from that sample or model; or
> (c) the goods are substantially unfit for a purpose for which goods of the same kind are commonly supplied and they cannot, easily and within a reasonable time, be remedied to make them fit for such a purpose; or
> (d) the goods are unfit for a disclosed purpose that was made known to:
> (i) the supplier of the goods; or
> (ii) a person by whom any prior negotiations or arrangements in relation to the acquisition of the goods were conducted or made; and they cannot, easily and within a reasonable time, be remedied to make them fit for that purpose; or
> (e) the goods are not of acceptable quality because the goods are unsafe.

Section 259(3) provides that a consumer may either reject goods or seek compensation for the difference between the price paid for the goods and their actual value. Any reasonably foreseeable loss or damage suffered by the consumer as a result of the failure of the goods may be recovered.[22]

Consumers can require the supplier to remedy a failure that is not a major failure within a reasonable period of time.[23] If the supplier refuses or fails to do so, the consumer may have the

19 See *Director of Consumer Affairs Victoria v The Good Guys Discount Warehouses (Australia) Pty Ltd* (2016) 245 FCR 529.
20 (2016) 245 FCR 529.
21 [2016] 245 FCR 529, [31].
22 Section 259(4).
23 Section 259(2)(a).

item repaired and seek to recover the expense of doing so from the supplier, or reject the goods and obtain a refund of the payment price.[24] The consumer may also recover damages in the case of goods that suffer from non-major failure causing foreseeable damage or loss.[25]

The right to reject goods is subject to certain limits. Section 262 provides that the consumer may not reject the goods when they have not acted within their rights within a reasonable time; the consumer has disposed of the goods, or they have been lost or destroyed; the goods were damaged after being delivered but the damage was unrelated to their state or condition at the time the goods were supplied; or the goods have become part of real or personal property by attachment and incorporation, and detachment would damage them.

If the consumer, by reason of the nature of the goods,[26] is unable to return them, the supplier must collect the goods[27] and replace them or return the purchase price of the goods.[28]

15.15.1 Actions against manufacturer

Goods that fail to comply with the guarantees as to acceptable quality, correspondence with description, spare parts and repair facilities, and express warranties give rise to a right to recover damages. In each case, limitations are imposed on the right of recovery. Restrictions will apply in the following instances. First, recovery will be restricted if it is sought only because the guarantee of acceptable quality was not complied with on the grounds that someone other than the manufacturer or the manufacturer's agent acted, or omitted to act, in a particular way. Second, it may be restricted if the goods' quality became unacceptable after the goods left the manufacturer due to actions over which no person had control. And, third, goods are not of unacceptable quality merely because the supplier charged a higher-than-average price for them.[29]

Recovery for the reason that the goods fail to correspond with their description is restricted if the goods fail to so correspond because of actions other than those of the manufacturer or the manufacturer's agent, or because, after leaving the manufacturer, an intervening cause beyond human control caused the goods to fail to correspond with their description.[30]

If a manufacturer fails to make spare parts available for a reasonable period after the purchase of the goods, or breaches the guarantee as to express warranties, the consumer can seek compensation for the reduction in the value of the goods and for other reasonably foreseeable losses. The reduction in the value of the goods is the difference between their current worth and whichever is lower of the price paid for the goods or their average price on the market.[31]

24 Section 259(2)(b).
25 Section 259(4), (6).
26 Section 263(3)(b).
27 Section 263(3).
28 Section 264.
29 Section 271(2).
30 Section 271(4).
31 Section 272.

15.15.2 Manufacturer's indemnification of supplier

If a supplier, having supplied goods to a consumer, becomes liable to pay damages under s 259(4) which the manufacturer would have been liable to pay under s 271, the supplier has a right to be indemnified by the manufacturer. A supplier who incurs costs because goods fail to comply with the guarantee as to acceptable quality, fitness for purpose, or correspondence with the description, may be indemnified by the manufacturer.[32] The supplier must seek indemnification within three years. The three-year period commencement is calculated from either the time the supplier made a payment with respect to liability or the time the consumer commenced action for damages against the supplier.[33]

Section 276 provides for restrictions to the manufacturer's liability under certain circumstances. The manufacturer is liable for the lesser of the cost of replacing or repairing the goods only if they are goods of a kind normally acquired for personal, domestic or household use or consumption. The restriction does not apply if the supplier is able to demonstrate that the restriction is neither fair nor reasonable in the circumstances.[34] The factors to which the court has regard to determine whether the restriction on the manufacturer's liability is fair and reasonable in the circumstances include whether suitable alternatives or equivalent goods are available, or whether the supplier ordered the goods to be specially manufactured, processed or adapted.[35]

Section 276A(4) provides that where a higher liability than that provided by statute is imposed by the agreement between supplier and manufacturer, the agreement takes precedence.

15.16 Key points

- Consumer guarantees apply to any contract for the supply of goods or services to a consumer made after 1 January 2011.
- They replace the implied warranties and conditions in the former *Trade Practices Act 1974* (Cth).
- Goods are covered by the consumer guarantees as long as they are sold in trade or commerce and bought by a consumer.
- Part 3-2, Division 1, Subdivision A of the ACL imposes nine guarantees in relation to the supply of goods:
  s 51 – guarantee that the supplier has the right to sell the goods;
  s 52 – guarantee that the consumer will have undisturbed possession;
  s 53 – guarantee that the goods are free from undisclosed security;
  s 54 – guarantee that the goods are of 'acceptable quality';
  s 55 – guarantee that the goods are fit for a particular purpose made known to the supplier by the consumer;
  s 56 – guarantee that the goods comply with description when sold by description;

32 Section 274(2).
33 Section 274(4).
34 Section 276A(2).
35 Section 276A(3).

s 57 – guarantee that the goods comply with the sample or model when sold by sample or demonstration model;

s 58 – guarantee that the manufacturer will take reasonable action to ensure that facilities for repair of the goods and parts for goods are reasonably available for a reasonable period after goods are supplied; and

s 59 – guarantee that the manufacturer or supplier will comply with express warranty where the manufacturer or supplier provides an express warranty.

15.17 DISCUSSION QUESTIONS

1. What are the key consumer guarantees?
2. What relationship do these guarantees have with the implied terms under the Goods and Sale of Goods Acts?
3. What does 'fit for purpose' mean as a legal concept?
4. How does s 53 of the ACL interact with the *Personal Property Securities Act* 2009 (Cth)?
5. Are there any deficiencies in the consumer guarantees regime?

15.18 FURTHER READING

Paterson, J M, 'The New Consumer Guarantee Law and the Reasons for Replacing the Regime of Statutory Implied Terms in Consumer Transactions' (2011) 35 *Melbourne University Law Review* 252.

16

UNCONSCIONABLE CONDUCT

16.0 Introduction

This chapter deals with unconscionable conduct in the context of commercial law. There are a number of statutory schemes that regulate unconscionable conduct in the commercial sphere. The Australian Consumer Law (ACL), contained in Schedule 2 to the *Competition and Consumer Act 2010* (Cth) (CCA), provides a broad-ranging scheme that covers most commercial dealings within which unconscionable conduct may occur. The unconscionable conduct scheme under the ACL (Schedule 2 to the CCA) does not apply 'to the supply, or possible supply, of services that are financial services, or of financial products'.[1] Financial services and financial products are regulated under the *Australian Securities and Investments Commission Act 2001* (Cth) ('ASIC Act'). The ASIC Act provided a statutory scheme regulating unconscionable conduct concerning financial services in trade or commerce.[2] Similarly, the *Corporations Act 2001* (Cth) contains a provision to prohibit unconscionable conduct of a financial services licensee.[3] This chapter deals primarily with the unconscionable conduct regime set out by the ACL. That scheme has arguably the most direct application to commercial law, as it governs the interactions between corporations and consumers and small businesses. The chapter first examines the equitable doctrine of unconscionable conduct, from which all the statutory regimes are derived, before considering ss 20–22 of the ACL.[4]

16.1 Unconscionable conduct

The doctrine of unconscionable conduct developed in the 18th century as the English courts of equity sought to protect expectant heirs from the capricious dealings of those who preyed upon their youth and naivety.[5] The plight of the expectant heirs was such that, although they anticipated future wealth, they were often without the immediate means to fund their lifestyles.[6] In *Aylesford v Morris*, Lord Selborne summarised the disparity of experience and power between the expectant heirs and those seeking to 'catch bargains' by stating: '[P]ower and influence are generally possessed, in every transaction of this kind, by those who trade upon the follies and vices of unprotected youth, inexperience, and moral imbecility.'[7] The underlying problem that required a remedy clearly had an application beyond the narrow interests of expectant heirs.[8] Consequently, doctrine soon expanded to protect all those who suffered from some serious disadvantage and who had been unconscientiously taken advantage of by another party in a superior bargaining position. For example, in *Baker v Monk*,[9] the court

1 Section 131A of the CCA.
2 See also A Coorey, *Australian Consumer Law* (LexisNexis Butterworths Australia, Sydney, 2015), 284 (where it is stated: 'The current unconscionable conduct provisions in Ch2 Pt 2-2 ss 20–22 of the ACL are mirrored respectively in Pt 2 Div 2 Sub-Div C ss 12CA, 12CB and 12CC of the ASIC Act').
3 Section 991A of the *Corporations Act 2001* (Cth).
4 Unconscionable conduct provisions can be found in 'Part 2-2 Unconscionable conduct' of the ACL, which only contains four provisions – ss 20, 21, 22 and 22A.
5 See *Earl of Chesterfield v Janssen* (1751) 28 ER 32.
6 *Earl of Potmore v Taylor* (1831) 4 Sim 182.
7 (1873) 8 Ch App 484, 491 (CA).
8 J Dawson, 'Economic Duress' (1947) 45 *Michigan Law Review* 253, 268.
9 (1864) 55 ER 430.

held that the sale of two cottages by an elderly and illiterate woman to the mayor of Faversham had been procured in a manner that was undeniably unconscionable. In cases such as *Baker v Monk*, transactions were set aside where the circumstances were such that one party was clearly disadvantaged by some constitutional disadvantage of which the other party was well aware and who had subsequently taken advantage of the situation.

16.1.1 The elements of unconscionability

The doctrine of unconscionable conduct is well established in Australian law. There are three main elements of unconscionability.

1. One party must be at a special disadvantage.[10]
2. The other party must know that the special disadvantage exists.[11]
3. The other party must have taken an unconscientious advantage of the party with the special disability.[12]

The primary defence to a claim of unconscionability is to show that the transaction was fair, just and reasonable.[13]

The notion of a special disadvantage was purposefully explored by the High Court in the case of *Blomley v Ryan*.[14] In *Blomley*, the High Court held that a sale of land procured from a drunken landowner was unconscionable. The purchaser was aware that the landowner, Ryan, had a drinking habit. During one of his bouts of drinking, the purchaser had Ryan sign a contract of sale. Ryan later sought to withdraw from the agreement. In finding in favour of the landowner, Fullagar J set out in *Blomley* a series of categories that give rise to a special disadvantage. Fullagar J stated:

> The circumstances adversely affecting a party, which may induce a court of equity either to refuse its aid or to set a transaction aside, are of great variety and can hardly be satisfactorily classified. Among them are poverty or need of any kind, sickness, age, sex, infirmity of body or mind, drunkenness, illiteracy or lack of education, lack of assistance or explanation where assistance or explanation is necessary. The common characteristic seems to be that they have the effect of placing one party at a serious disadvantage vis-a-vis the other.[15]

The formulation provided by Fullagar J has been cited with approval in a number of cases. However, it must be slightly qualified. Later courts have not recognised sex as a basis for

10 See *Commercial Bank of Australia Ltd v Amadio* (1983) 151 CLR 447; *Louth v Diprose* (1992) 175 CLR 621; *Bridgewater v Leahy* (1998) 194 CLR 457. See also *Aboody v Ryan* (2012) 17 BPR 32,359; *Virginia Nemeth (by her Tutor) v Australian Litigation Funders Pty Ltd* [2013] NSWSC 529; *Gel Custodians Pty Ltd v Dyer* [2014] WASC 177.

11 See *Garcia v National Australia Bank Ltd* (1998) 194 CLR 395; *Commercial Bank of Australia Ltd v Amadio* (1983) 151 CLR 447; *Louth v Diprose* (1992) 175 CLR 621.

12 *Commercial Bank of Australia Ltd v Amadio* (1983) 151 CLR 447; *Louth v Diprose* (1992) 175 CLR 621; *Bridgewater v Leahy* (1998) 194 CLR 457.

13 *Commercial Bank of Australia Ltd v Amadio* (1983) 151 CLR 447, 474.

14 (1956) 99 CLR 362.

15 (1956) 99 CLR 362, 405.

creating a special disadvantage.[16] Similarly, in *Permanent Mortgages Pty Ltd v Vandenbergh*,[17] Murphy JA suggested that 'advanced age of itself does not constitute a special disadvantage but may, in combination with other factors, contribute to the condition of being under a special disadvantage'.[18] Corones has noted that where the special disadvantage is constitutional in nature, 'it must lead to an inability to make a rational judgment'.[19] The existence of indicia that might otherwise suggest special disadvantage will not be sufficient if the surrounding facts suggest that no real disadvantage existed.[20] In *Luong v Du*,[21] the fact that the plaintiffs had difficulties with the English language did not give rise to a special disadvantage where they understood the transaction and were aware of the need to obtain legal advice. In *Luong*, Emerton J stated that 'the suggested disability or disadvantage arising from their limited command of English did not affect the ability of the plaintiffs to make a judgement as to their best interests in the circumstances of this case'.[22]

The level of special disadvantage must be such that the degree of inequality between the parties is more than equity can tolerate. Nonetheless, the existence of a special disadvantage alone is not sufficient to trigger the intervention of equity. The stronger party must be aware of the weakness and must knowingly choose to exploit it for their own advantage.[23] In the case of *Johnson v Smith*,[24] Allsop P stated:

> [W]hat lies at the heart of the doctrine is that advantage is taken of the special disadvantage. This may occur because of the unconscientious use of power arising or existing in the circumstances or (as here) the unconscientious attempt to retain the benefit obtained from the person with the special disadvantage.[25]

In this sense, the doctrine of unconscionable conduct is concerned with the conduct of the stronger party rather than the quality of the consent of the weaker party. As Deane J noted in *Louth v Diprose*, the special disadvantage must be 'sufficiently evident to the other party to make it prima facie unfair or "unconscionable" that that other party procure, accept or retain the benefit of, the disadvantaged party's assent to the impugned transaction in the circumstances in which he or she procured or accepted it'.[26]

The stronger party must be aware of the existence of the special disadvantage.[27] Prior to the High Court's decision in *Kakavas v Crown Melbourne Ltd*,[28] there was some doubt as to

16 For a discussion of gender inequality, see D Otto, 'A Barren Future? Equity's Conscience and Women's Inequality' (1992) 18 *Melbourne University Law Review* 808.
17 (2010) 41 WAR 353.
18 [2010] WASC 10, [234]. See also *Australia & New Zealand Banking Group Ltd v Dzienciol* [2001] WASC 305.
19 S Corones, *The Australian Consumer Law* (Thomson Reuters Australia, Sydney, 2nd edn, 2013), 182.
20 *Luong v Du* [2013] VSC 723.
21 [2013] VSC 723.
22 [2013] VSC 723, [126].
23 *Johnson v Smith* [2010] NSWCA 306.
24 [2010] NSWCA 306.
25 [2010] NSWCA 306, [5].
26 (1992) 175 CLR 621, 637.
27 *Permanent Mortgages Pty Ltd v Vandenbergh* (2010) 41 WAR 353.
28 (2013) 250 CLR 392.

whether constructive knowledge might satisfy the knowledge requirement. In *Commercial Bank of Australia Ltd v Amadio*,[29] Mason J stated, with regard to the stronger party's knowledge of the special disadvantage, that 'if, instead of having actual knowledge of that situation, A is aware of the possibility that that situation may exist or is aware of facts that would raise that possibility in the mind of any reasonable person, the result will be the same'.[30] This proposition was subsequently applied in *Lopwell Pty Ltd v Clarke*[31] and *Kenneth Charles Ward v Brian Charles*.[32] In *Lopwell*, MacFarlan JA raised the obiter remarks of Mason J in *Amadio*, but decided that it was in any case sufficiently evident to the stronger party in that case that the special disadvantage existed. In *Ward v Ward*, Brereton J stated: '[A]ctual knowledge of any specific diagnosis or condition is not required, and it suffices that the Defendant knew, or ought reasonably have known that the Plaintiff was not in a position to look after his or her own interests.'[33] However, in *Kakavas* the High Court stated that Mason J, as his Honour then was in *Amadio*, could not be taken to have been supporting importing constructive knowledge into the doctrine of unconscionable conduct. In *Kakavas*, the High Court stated:

> It is apparent from what Mason J said in relation to the transaction under consideration in *Amadio* that his Honour was speaking of wilful ignorance, which, for the purposes of relieving against equitable fraud, is not different from actual knowledge. In this regard, Mason J observed that it must have been obvious to the appellant bank's officer that the transaction was an improvident one from the respondents' point of view.[34]

It must be said, then, that the level of knowledge required needs to be actual knowledge, but that the former now extends to situations of what might be considered 'wilful blindness'.[35] This precludes the possibility of a stronger party purposefully closing its eyes to any special disadvantage.[36] In *Permanent Mortgages Pty Ltd v Vandenbergh*, Murphy JA stated: '[T]he special disadvantage will be sufficiently evident to the other party if the other party knows facts which would raise the possibility of the special disadvantage in the mind of a reasonable person.'[37] Where the stronger party has no reason to know of the existence of a special disadvantage and is unaware of it, no unconscionable conduct will exist.[38]

Some cases that illustrate the principles of unconscionable conduct are considered in the following sections.[39]

29 (1983) 151 CLR 447.
30 *Commercial Bank of Australia Ltd v Amadio* (1983) 151 CLR 447, 467.
31 [2009] NSWCA 165.
32 [2011] NSWSC 107.
33 [2011] NSWSC 107, [33]. This must now be qualified in light of the High Court's decision in *Kakavas*.
34 (2013) 250 CLR 392, [156].
35 *Commercial Bank of Australia Ltd v Amadio* (1983) 151 CLR 447; *Permanent Mortgages Pty Ltd v Vandenbergh* (2010) 41 WAR 353.
36 *Lee v Ah Gee* [1920] VLR 278.
37 (2010) 41 WAR 353, [221].
38 *Australian Competition and Consumer Commission v Radio Rentals Ltd* (2005) 146 FCR 292.
39 See Sections 16.1.2 (one case) and 16.2 (three cases) of this chapter.

16.1.2 Three-element test in *Commercial Bank of Australia Ltd v Amadio*

The case of *Commercial Bank of Australia Ltd v Amadio*[40] is often regarded as the leading Australian decision on unconscionable conduct. This case quite neatly demonstrates the application of the three elements of unconscionability. Vincenzo Amadio was a builder. His company had encountered serious financial difficulties. As Vincenzo was a close friend of his banker, Mr Virgo, the latter would help out by propping up his business by increasing the overdraft and getting Vincenzo to selectively dishonour cheques. Vincenzo's overdraft had been selectively increased from $80 000 to $125 000. By March 1977, Vincenzo owed $193 000. Furthermore, the primary asset that Vincenzo had provided as security was not correctly valued. Vincenzo had valued an office property that he owned at $200 000, but the bank had correctly valued it at $153 000 in the event of a forced sale. The bank subsequently reduced this valuation to $120 000. With his company's overdraft in a perilous position, Vincenzo spoke to his parents to see whether they would provide security for $50 000 for up to six months.

Vincenzo's parents were not fluent in English. They were also elderly and inexperienced in commercial matters. Vincenzo told the bank that his parents would provide a guarantee and mortgage over an investment property. This property was the only asset of Mr and Mrs Amadio apart from their home. Mr Virgo visited the Amadios, believing that Vincenzo had explained the true nature of the guarantee and the mortgage. Mr and Mrs Amadio signed the prepared documents without properly reading them. During the meeting, Mr Amadio said that he understood that the guarantee would be operative for only six months. Mr Virgo corrected him, but the Amadios did not appear to comprehend Mr Virgo's statement.

Vincenzo's business deteriorated and went into liquidation. The bank sought to enforce the guarantee. In the High Court, a majority of judges found that Mr and Mrs Amadio could not be bound by the mortgage and the guarantee.

Deane J stated in *Amadio*:

> The jurisdiction of courts of equity to relieve against unconscionable dealing developed from the jurisdiction which the Court of Chancery assumed, at a very early period, to set aside transactions in which expectant heirs had dealt with their expectations without being adequately protected against the pressure put upon them by their poverty (see *O'Rorke v. Bolingbroke* (1877) 2 App Cas 814, at p 822). The jurisdiction is long established as extending generally to circumstances in which (i) a party to a transaction was under a special disability in dealing with the other party with the consequence that there was an absence of any reasonable degree of equality between them and (ii) that disability was sufficiently evident to the stronger party to make it prima facie unfair or 'unconscientious' that he procure, or accept, the weaker party's assent to the impugned transaction in the circumstances in which he procured or accepted it. Where such circumstances are shown to have existed, an onus is cast upon the stronger party to show that the transaction was fair, just and reasonable: 'the burthen of shewing the fairness of the transaction is thrown on the person who seeks to obtain the benefit of the contract'.[41]

40 (1983) 151 CLR 447.
41 (1983) 151 CLR 447, 474.

In *Amadio* all the majority of the applicable elements of unconscionability were available. The Amadios had a unique inability by virture of their poor English, advanced age, absence of business experience and elevated level of dependence on their son. The bank officer, Virgo, knew their circumstance; yet, regardless, he proceeded with the transaction. Further, under these circumstances, there was no defence of reasonableness that the bank could make out.

16.2 Section 20 of the Australian Consumer Law

Prior to the enactment of the CCA and the ACL, unconscionable dealings were regulated under the *Trade Practices Act 1974* (Cth) (TPA). Unconscionable conduct was dealt with under ss 51AA, 51AB and 51AC of the TPA. Section 51AA dealt with unconscionable conduct under the unwritten law.[42] Section 51AB dealt with unconscionable conduct in relation to a corporation providing goods or services to consumers.[43] Section 51AC dealt with unconscionable conduct in relation to a corporation receiving goods or services from an individual or small business. When the CCA was first enacted ss 51AA, 51AB and 51AC of the TPA were replaced by ss 20, 21 and 22 of the ACL. In effect, ss 20, 21 and 22 almost perfectly replicated the statutory language of ss 51AA, 51AB and 51AC of the TPA, respectively. After the commencement of the ACL, ss 21 and 22 were amended so that s 21 sets out one cause of action for unconscionable conduct in the course of supply or receiving goods and services, whereas s 22 sets out a set of statutory factors to be considered in evaluating s 21.

Section 20 of the ACL provides:

> (1) A person must not, in trade or commerce, engage in conduct that is unconscionable, within the meaning of the unwritten law from time to time.
> Note: A pecuniary penalty may be imposed for a contravention of this subsection.
>
> (2) This section does not apply to conduct that is prohibited by section 21.

Section 20 of the ACL is tied to the concept of unconscionable conduct as developed by the courts of equity and the common law. In contrast, s 21 has a broader field of application due to the enumerated factors in s 22.[44] The relationship of the new ss 21 and 22 of the ACL and the defunct ss 51AB and 51AC of the TPA is considered in more depth in Section 16.3 below.

Given the relative infancy of the ACL, the relevant case law for assessing s 20 must be those cases that were decided under s 51AA of the TPA. There are three leading cases that have explored the meaning of unconscionable conduct under the unwritten law: *Australian Competition and Consumer Commission v CG Berbatis Holdings Pty Ltd*,[45] *Australian Competition*

42 See *Australian Competition and Consumer Commission v CG Berbatis Holdings Pty Ltd* (2003) 214 CLR 51.

43 See *Alievski v Cross Country Realty Victoria Pty Ltd* [2010] VSC 316.

44 A Bruce, *Consumer Protection in Australia* (LexisNexis Butterworths Australia, Sydney, 2014), 151. Also, *Australian Competition and Consumer Commission v Radio Rentals Ltd* (2005) 146 FCR 292.

45 (2003) 214 CLR 51.

and Consumer Commission v Samton Holdings[46] and *Australian Competition and Consumer Commission v Zanok Technologies Pty Ltd.*[47]

16.2.1 *Australian Competition and Consumer Commission v CG Berbatis* (2003)

In *Australian Competition and Consumer Commission v C G Berbatis*,[48] a majority of the High Court found that harsh dealings of a landlord with respect to small tenants in a shopping mall did not amount to unconscionability. The Roberts family ran a fish-and-chips shop in a shopping centre. Their landlords were the owners of the shopping centre. Along with some other tenants, the Roberts family had sought to sue their landlords over some charges levied under the terms of their respective leases. The Roberts were suing their landlords for the sum of $50 000. This figure represented the overpayments that they had made. The Roberts family encountered some difficulties and became keen to sell their business. The daughter of the Roberts family was very sick, which placed a strain on the family. With their lease expiring, the Roberts found a potential purchaser, who told them he would buy the business provided they had a lease in place. The Roberts family communicated this to their landlords, who suggested that they would be agreeable on the basis that the tenants sign a new lease with a clause 14, which stipulated that any claim in relation to the overpayments be dropped.

The Australian Competition and Consumer Commission (ACCC) agreed to act on behalf of the Roberts family and to sue Berbatis Holdings and other defendants in the Federal Court. The first case, before French J in the Federal Court, was decided in favour of the ACCC. On appeal, the Full Court of the Federal Court found in favour of the defendants. This finding was affirmed on appeal to the High Court. The majority of the High Court found that although the Roberts were under a disadvantage, it was not a *special* disadvantage as required under the *Amadio* test. Nor was a majority of the High Court of the view that the landlords had taken advantage. Instead, the majority found that it was commercially prudent for the landlords to want the litigation to be resolved prior to agreeing to a new lease. Justice Kirby dissented, but on the narrower grounds that there had been no actual error of law in the original decision of French J.

16.2.2 *Australian Competition and Consumer Commission v Samton Holdings* (2002)

In *Australian Competition and Consumer Commission v Samton Holdings*,[49] a landlord required his lessee to pay $70 000 in order to renew a commercial lease. The lessee had an option in his favour to renew the lease, but had failed to do so within the requisite time. The landlord then required the payment of $70 000 in order to renew the lease. The lessee subsequently argued that the landlord's conduct was unconscionable under s 51AA of the

46 (2002) 117 FCR 301.
47 [2009] FCA 1124.
48 (2003) 214 CLR 51. For a detailed discussion of *ACCC v CG Berbatis*, see N Dean, 'ACCC v Berbatis Holdings' (2004) 26(2) *Sydney Law Review* 255.
49 (2002) 117 FCR 301.

TPA. However, the Full Court of the Federal Court found that the mere existence of unequal bargaining power did not amount to a special disadvantage. As such, the claim of unconscionable conduct could not be successfully made out. The court stated:

> Characterisation of disadvantage as 'special' involves the recognition that it would be unconscionable knowingly to deal with the person so affected without regard to his or her disability, be it constitutional, in the sense of inherent, or situational, in the sense of arising from a particular set of circumstances. In effect this may require some special conduct or care which is not necessary in the absence of such disadvantage. If, for example, the disability relates to language, illiteracy or lack of education, conscientious dealing may ensure the bargaining deficit is compensated for by the provision of special assistance such as independent advice which will either enable a proper understanding of the transaction or overcome the disadvantage arising from want of a proper understanding.
>
> In this case it is difficult to see how the respondents might have catered for the disadvantage suffered by the Ranaldis and Executive Bloodstock other than by granting them a new lease on the same terms as would have applied had the option been exercised in accordance with the first lease. Yet it was accepted on all sides that the respondents were not obliged to offer the lessee a further term. The Ranaldis' situation could not be characterised as one of special disadvantage only because the respondents failed to make an offer that they had no obligation to make. It cannot be the case that any tenant whose careless failure to exercise an option to renew a lease results in economic disadvantage would be entitled to a renewal of the term. A fortiori it cannot be the case that a tenant in that situation and absent other circumstances, is in a situation of special disadvantage.[50]

The court did acknowledge that the facts may have supported an argument for economic duress. As such, had s 51AC of the TPA or its equivalent in s 21 of the ACL been in operation, the outcome may have been different. Both *Samton Holdings* and *Berbatis* demonstrate the increasing unwillingness of the courts to regard inequality of bargaining power as akin to a special disadvantage. The pursuit of rational commercial objectives, unaccompanied by any morally questionable conduct, will not give rise to a finding of unconscionable conduct even where there is some significant disadvantage to the weaker party.[51]

16.2.3 *Australian Competition and Consumer Commission v Zanok Technologies* (2009)

In *Australian Competition and Consumer Commission v Zanok Technologies*[52] a company provided IT training for a fee to jobseekers on the understanding that it would employ them afterwards. The company was aware that many of the jobseekers were individuals who were in Australia on temporary visas. As such, they required employment to remain in the country. When the jobseekers had completed their training and subsequently sought employment with

50 (2002) 117 FCR 301.

51 See *PSAL Ltd v Kellas Sharpe* [2012] QSC 31. See also *Chilcott v Homesec Finance Express Pty Ltd* [2011] FCA 729.

52 [2009] FCA 1124.

the company, the latter reneged on the representations it had made. In the Federal Court, Edmonds J stated:

> Unconscionability is a concept which requires a high level of moral obloquy. It is not necessary for the party who has benefited from a transaction challenged as unconscionable to itself have created the special advantage which forms the basis of the unconscionability claim. It is sufficient if that party knows, or ought to have known, of the other party's situation of special disadvantage and takes unfair advantage of the opportunity presented . . .
>
> In the present circumstances, the unconscionable conduct on the part of Zanok was the promise that, in return for a fee, the applicant would receive training and thereafter guaranteed skilled employment in circumstances where Zanok knew or ought to have known that many of the applicants were temporary residents and anxious to find skilled employment to assist with their applications for permanent resident status. This conduct constituted more than simply taking advantage of a superior bargaining position but involved an unconscientious exploitation of another's inability or diminished ability to conserve his or her own interests. Dangling the 'employment carrot' in return for a fee in circumstances in which the applicant faces having to leave Australia constitutes a high level of moral obloquy especially where the promised employment does not exist.[53]

16.3 Sections 21 and 22 of the Australian Consumer Law before 2019

Both ss 21 and 22 of the ACL have been amended by the *Competition and Consumer Legislation Amendment Act 2011* (Cth) (CCLAA). The CCLAA came into effect on 1 January 2012. Previously, ss 21 and 22 included a separate list of factors to which a court could have regard in determining whether conduct is unconscionable. The CCLAA redrafted these sections to draw together the factors in both sections into a single provision in s 22. The aim of the new s 22 is so that there is no risk of the courts according different meanings to unconscionable conduct. The new ss 21 and 22 have removed the reference to 'consumer' and have substituted it with 'customer'. However, this excludes listed public companies, as these companies do not require the protection of the unconscionable conduct provisions of the ACL. Nevertheless, ss 21 and 22 have been further amended in 2019, and have removed the exclusion for 'listed public companies'. In other words, the ACL has now extended unconscionable conduct protections to publicly listed companies.[54] (More details about the rationale behind the 2019 amendment will be introduced in Section 16.7.)

Prior to the CCLAA amendments, the original s 21 of the ACL regulated unconscionable conduct in business to consumer transactions, whereas s 22 regulated unconscionable conduct

53 [2009] FCA 1124, [16]–[17].

54 See ss 21–22 of the CCA 2010 (Cth), Schedule 2: https://www.legislation.gov.au/Details/C2019C00149/Html/Volume_3, at 98.

by business against small business. The forerunner to the original s 21 of the ACL was s 51AB of the TPA. Likewise, the forerunner to the original s 22 of the ACL was s 51AC of the TPA.

To discern the meaning of the new s 21 of the ACL, some consideration must be given to the structure and content of the now defunct ss 51AB and 51AC of the TPA. Section 51AB introduced, in effect, a general duty to trade fairly in relation to consumers by proscribing conduct that is unconscionable. Section 51AB(1) established a norm of conduct by prohibiting unconscionable conduct in connection with the supply of goods or services. Section 51AB(2) set out a series of considerations to which a court could have regard for the purpose of determining whether a corporation has engaged in unconscionable conduct. Section 51AC involves the sale of goods or services to a corporation or the purchase of goods or services from a corporation. As with s 51AB, s 51AC set a base line for commercial dealings with small businesses. In *Body Bronze International Pty Ltd v Fehcorp Pty Ltd*,[55] Macaulay AJA observed that s 51AC 'prescribes a standard rather than a rule wherein the boundaries of its application are normative rather than logical'.[56]

In assessing the meaning of unconscionable conduct under both ss 51AB and 51AC of the TPA, the Federal Court often drew upon equitable notions of unconscionability. For example, in *Hurley v McDonalds Australia Ltd*,[57] the Full Court of the Federal Court stated:

> For conduct to be regarded as unconscionable, serious misconduct or something clearly unfair or unreasonable, must be demonstrated – *Cameron v Qantas Airways Ltd* . . . [1995] FCA 1304; (1994) 55 FCR 147 at 179. Whatever 'unconscionable' means in sections 51AB and 51AC, the term carries the meaning given by the Shorter Oxford English Dictionary, namely, actions showing no regard for conscience, or that are irreconcilable with what is right or reasonable – *Qantas Airways Ltd v Cameron* . . . [1996] FCA 1483; (1996) 66 FCR 246 at 262. The various synonyms used in relation to the term 'unconscionable' import a pejorative moral judgment.[58]

Similarly, in *Australian Competition and Consumer Commission v Lux Pty Ltd*,[59] Nicholson J stated:

> The word unconscionable is not a term of art . . . It bears its ordinary meaning of 'showing no regard for conscience, irreconcilable with what is right or reasonable'. What is required is 'serious misconduct or something clearly unfair or unreasonable'. It will be relevant whether advantage is taken of an innocent party who, though not deprived of an independent and voluntary will, is unable to make a worthwhile judgment as to what is in his or her best interests.[60]

The notion that unconscionable conduct contained some significant moral wrongdoing featured heavily in the jurisprudence under both s 51AB and s 51AC. In *Australian Competition*

55 (2011) 34 VR 536.
56 (2011) 34 VR 536, [88].
57 [1999] FCA 1728.
58 [1999] FCA 1728, [22]. See also *Attorney-General (NSW) v World Best Holdings Ltd* (2005) 63 NSWLR 557, 583; *Director of Consumer Affairs Victoria v Scully [No 3]* [2012] VSC 444. See also *W & K Holdings (NSW) Pty Ltd v Mayo* [2013] NSWSC 1063; *Allianz Australia Insurance Ltd v Vitale* [2014] NSWSC 364.
59 [2004] FCA 926.
60 [2004] FCA 926, [98].

and Consumer Commission v 4WD Systems Pty Ltd,[61] Selway J noted that 'mere unreasonableness or unfairness may not be sufficient, at least in the absence of some moral fault'.[62] As such, some deliberate or reckless wrongdoing was required to enliven the parameters of unconscionability.[63] However, not all deliberate acts gave rise to a sufficient level of moral obloquy required to reach unconscionable conduct. In *Body Bronze International*, Macaulay AJA stated that 'it should be recognised that not every breach of contract, even a deliberate breach, necessarily involves the moral obloquy that the authorities suggest needs be present for unconscionable conduct in breach of s 51AC to be made out'.[64] Further, a superior bargaining position and knowledge of the other side's weaker position is not sufficient on its own to create unconscionable conduct.[65] In *Allianz Australia Insurance Ltd v Vitale*,[66] Sackar J stated that 'merely because one party to contractual negotiations may be in a stronger commercial position, or because in a bargaining process a party may feel compelled to agree to a term because it may feel unable to resist, does not automatically lead to a finding of unconscionability'.[67]

It was generally agreed that the parameters of ss 51AB and 51AC of the TPA were wider than that of s 51AA.[68] In *Australian Competition and Consumer Commission v Allphones Retail Pty Ltd [No 2]*,[69] Foster J stated: '[T]he scope of s 51AC is wider than that of s 51AA. The meaning of unconscionable for the purposes of s 51AC is not limited to the meaning of the word according to established principles of common law and equity.'[70] In *Dai v Telstra Corporation Ltd*,[71] the Full Court of the Federal Court observed that the enumerated factors in s 51AB(2) 'are expressly stated to be non-exhaustive and may arguably take the s 51AB concept of unconscionability beyond that developed by courts of equity'. Similarly, in *Australian Competition and Consumer Commission v Simply No-Knead (Franchising) Pty Ltd*,[72] Sundberg J stated: '[U]nconscionable in s 51AC is not limited to the cases of equitable or unwritten law unconscionability the subject of s 51AA.' In *Simply No-Knead*, Sundberg J supported his contention that the concept of 'unconscionability' in s 51AC of the TPA went beyond that of unconscionability in s 51AA because of the existence of the factors in s 51AC(3). Within these factors in s 51AC(3), which were similar to but somewhat more extensive than those contained in s 51AB(2), were items that went beyond the equitable concept of unconscionability. Consequently, the range of acts that might give rise to unconscionable conduct is

61 (2003) 200 ALR 491.
62 (2003) 200 ALR 491, [185].
63 *Australian Competition and Consumer Commission v Allphones Retail Pty Ltd [No 2]* (2009) 253 ALR 324, [113]; *ACCC v Dukemaster Pty Ltd* [2009] FCA 682, [17]; *Australian Competition and Consumer Commission v Seal-a-Fridge Pty Ltd* (2010) 268 ALR 321, [16].
64 (2011) 34 VR 536, [91]. See also *Nitschke v Foraco Australia Pty Ltd* (2014) 120 SASR 162, [86].
65 *Allianz Australia Insurance Ltd v Vitale* [2014] NSWSC 364.
66 [2014] NSWSC 364.
67 [2014] NSWSC 364, [112].
68 *Sundararajah v Teachers Federation Health Ltd* (2011) 283 ALR 720; *Australian Competition and Consumer Commission v CG Berbatis Holdings Pty Ltd [No 2]* (2000) 169 ALR 324; *Perfection Fresh Australia Pty Ltd v Melbourne Market Authority* [2013] VSC 287.
69 (2009) ATPR ¶42-274.
70 (2009) ATPR ¶42-274, [113].
71 (2000) 171 ALR 348.
72 (2000) 104 FCR 253.

potentially quite extensive. In *Tonto Home Loans Australia Pty Ltd v Tavares*,[73] in relation to s 12CC of the *Australian Securities Investments Commission Act 2001* (Cth), which contains a list of factors similar to that in s 22 of the ACL, the NSW Supreme Court stated:

> The concept of unconscionable in this context is wider than the general law and the provisions are intended to build on and not be constrained by cases at general law and equity. The statutory provisions focus on the conduct of the person said to have acted unconscionably. It is neither possible nor desirable to provide a comprehensive definition. The range of conduct is wide and can include bullying and thuggish behaviour, undue pressure and unfair tactics, taking advantage of vulnerability or lack of understanding, trickery or misleading conduct. A finding requires an examination of all the circumstances.[74]

The effect of the amalgamation of ss 21 and 22 of the ACL poses some interpretive difficulty. The original s 21(2) of the ACL, which contained a list of factors equivalent to those in s 51AB(2) of the TPA, was less extensive than that contained in the original s 21(2) of the ACL. After the CCLAA's amendments, s 21 applies equally to consumer and small business transactions. More to the point, the extensive list that is now contained in s 22, and reproduced below, applies to both consumer and small business transactions. It seems beyond doubt that the effect of the s 22 factors is that the concept of 'unconscionable' under s 21 of the ACL will be broader than that of 'unconscionable' in s 20.

Section 21(1) of the ACL provides:

> **Unconscionable conduct in connection with goods or services**
>
> (1) A person must not, in trade or commerce, in connection with:
> (a) the supply or possible supply of goods or services to a person; or
> (b) the acquisition or possible acquisition of goods or services from a person;
> engage in conduct that is, in all the circumstances, unconscionable.

Section 21(4) explicitly states that the conduct considered unconscionable under s 21 is broader than that under s 20 of the ACL. The notion of unconscionability under s 21 may be evaluated with regard to the set of factors set out in s 22.

Section 22 provides as follows:

> **Matters the court may have regard to for the purposes of section 21**
>
> (1) Without limiting the matters to which the court may have regard for the purpose of determining whether a person (the supplier) has contravened section 21 in connection with the supply or possible supply of goods or services to a person (the customer), the court may have regard to: (a) the relative strengths of the bargaining positions of the supplier and the customer; and (b) whether, as a result of conduct engaged in by the supplier, the customer was required to comply with conditions that were not reasonably necessary for the protection of the legitimate interests of

73 [2011] NSWCA 389.
74 [2011] NSWCA 389, [291].

the supplier; and (c) whether the customer was able to understand any documents relating to the supply or possible supply of the goods or services; and (d) whether any undue influence or pressure was exerted on, or any unfair tactics were used against, the customer or a person acting on behalf of the customer by the supplier or a person acting on behalf of the supplier in relation to the supply or possible supply of the goods or services; and (e) the amount for which, and the circumstances under which, the customer could have acquired identical or equivalent goods or services from a person other than the supplier; and (f) the extent to which the supplier's conduct towards the customer was consistent with the supplier's conduct in similar transactions between the supplier and other like customers; and (g) the requirements of any applicable industry code; and (h) the requirements of any other industry code, if the customer acted on the reasonable belief that the supplier would comply with that code; and (i) the extent to which the supplier unreasonably failed to disclose to the customer: (i) any intended conduct of the supplier that might affect the interests of the customer; and (ii) any risks to the customer arising from the supplier's intended conduct (being risks that the supplier should have foreseen would not be apparent to the customer); and (j) if there is a contract between the supplier and the customer for the supply of the goods or services: (i) the extent to which the supplier was willing to negotiate the terms and conditions of the contract with the customer; and (ii) the terms and conditions of the contract; and (iii) the conduct of the supplier and the customer in complying with the terms and conditions of the contract; and (iv) any conduct that the supplier or the customer engaged in, in connection with their commercial relationship, after they entered into the contract; and (k) without limiting paragraph (j), whether the supplier has a contractual right to vary unilaterally a term or condition of a contract between the supplier and the customer for the supply of the goods or services; and (l) the extent to which the supplier and the customer acted in good faith.

(2) Without limiting the matters to which the court may have regard for the purpose of determining whether a person (the acquirer) has contravened section 21 in connection with the acquisition or possible acquisition of goods or services from a person (the supplier), the court may have regard to: (a) the relative strengths of the bargaining positions of the acquirer and the supplier; and (b) whether, as a result of conduct engaged in by the acquirer, the supplier was required to comply with conditions that were not reasonably necessary for the protection of the legitimate interests of the acquirer; and (c) whether the supplier was able to understand any documents relating to the acquisition or possible acquisition of the goods or services; and (d) whether any undue influence or pressure was exerted on, or any unfair tactics were used against, the supplier or a person acting on behalf of the supplier by the acquirer or a person acting on behalf of the acquirer in relation to the acquisition or possible acquisition of the goods or services; and (e) the amount for which, and the circumstances in which, the supplier could have supplied identical or equivalent goods or services to a person other than the acquirer; and (f) the extent to which the acquirer's conduct towards the supplier was consistent with the acquirer's conduct in similar transactions between the acquirer and other like suppliers; and (g) the requirements of any applicable industry code; and (h) the requirements of any other industry code, if

> the supplier acted on the reasonable belief that the acquirer would comply with that code; and (i) the extent to which the acquirer unreasonably failed to disclose to the supplier: (i) any intended conduct of the acquirer that might affect the interests of the supplier; and (ii) any risks to the supplier arising from the acquirer's intended conduct (being risks that the acquirer should have foreseen would not be apparent to the supplier); and (j) if there is a contract between the acquirer and the supplier for the acquisition of the goods or services: (i) the extent to which the acquirer was willing to negotiate the terms and conditions of the contract with the supplier; and (ii) the terms and conditions of the contract; and (iii) the conduct of the acquirer and the supplier in complying with the terms and conditions of the contract; and (iv) any conduct that the acquirer or the supplier engaged in, in connection with their commercial relationship, after they entered into the contract; and (k) without limiting paragraph (j), whether the acquirer has a contractual right to vary unilaterally a term or condition of a contract between the acquirer and the supplier for the acquisition of the goods or services; and (l) the extent to which the acquirer and the supplier acted in good faith.

There exists some case law from the old TPA regime, under ss 51AB and 51AC, which may provide some useful guidance for the interpretation and application of ss 21 and 22 of the ACL.

16.4 The s 22 factors

Section 22 sets out a list of factors that a court may take into account in determining whether the relevant conduct is unconscionable under s 21 of the ACL. Section 22 has been modelled on s 51(3) of the TPA and replicates many of the components of the latter provision. Not every factor that is contained in s 22 will be relevant in every dispute, but the applicable factors should be exchanged and weighed as a whole. The factors are not exhaustive.[75] The s 22 factors are clearly quite broad and reach into both the substantive unfairness of the contract itself and the unconscionable manner in which the deal was made.

Subsections 22(1)(a) and 22(2)(a) both refer to the relative strengths of the bargaining positions of the parties. As such, where one party has a substantially stronger bargaining position and unconscionably takes advantage of this, then they may fall foul of s 21. On this basis, s 21 is plainly applicable to situations where s 20 cannot apply. It is certainly quite possible that were a case such as *Australian Competition and Consumer Commission v CG Berbatis* (2003) (introduced in Section 16.2.1) to be argued under s 21, rather than the s 20 equivalent of s 51AA of the TPA, that the outcome might be rather different. In *Hoy Mobile Pty Ltd v Allphones Retail Pty Ltd [No 2]*,[76] the actions of a franchisor in using its superior bargaining position to extract concessions from its franchisee were found to be unconscionable.[77]

75 *Commonwealth Bank of Australia v Thompson* [2013] NSWSC 149.
76 (2008) ATPR ¶42-240.
77 Also, as introduced above in Section 16.3, Foster J stated: '[T]he scope of s 51AC is wider than that of s 51AA. The meaning of unconscionable for the purposes of s 51AC is not limited to the meaning of the word according to established principles of common law and equity.'

Sections 22(1)(b) and 22(2)(b) refer to the consideration of whether one party was required to comply with conditions that were not reasonably necessary for the protection of the legitimate interests of the other party. It is open to a party to still act in their best interests. However, conduct that demonstrates an absence of good faith and reasonableness will attract the operation of ss 22(1)(b) and 22(2)(b).

Sections 22(1)(c) and 22(2)(c) are concerned, respectively, with whether one party was able to understand the relevant documents relating to the supply or acquisition of goods or services. These subsections would plainly cover *Amadio*-type situations[78] and other instances where the true meaning of a particular bargain is obscured for some reason.

Sections 22(1)(d) and 22(2)(d) refer to undue influence, pressure or unfair tactics. In the case of *Australian Competition and Consumer Commission v Simply No-Knead*, the actions of a franchisor in making unreasonable requests on the franchisees, and making them pay for services that were not required, were held to be unconscionable conduct. In *Simply No-Knead*, the franchisor refused to deliver franchised products, deleted the franchisees' telephone numbers from directories and excluded them from advertising.

Sections 22(1)(e) and 22(2)(e) refer to the amount for which, and the circumstances in which, the identical or equivalent goods or services could have been supplied or acquired. In effect, this is concerned with whether one party attempts to engage in price gouging against the other.

Sections 22(1)(f) and 22(2)(f) are concerned with inconsistent treatment. This would have most direct application in a franchisor–franchisee relationship if the franchisor treated some franchisees very favourably but was unfair to other franchisees.

Sections 22(1)(g) and 22(2)(g) permit the court to have regard to applicable industry codes.

Sections 22(1)(h) and 22(2)(h) permit reference to other industry codes that may be relevant.

Sections 22(1)(i) and 22(2)(i) refer to a failure to disclose intended conduct or risk. If one party enters into a contract with another party, but then engages in subsequent pre-planned conduct that renders the bargain nugatory, the failure to disclose the intended conduct may be unconscionable. As such, ss 22(1)(i) and (ii), and 22(2)(i) and (ii), recognise that types of misrepresentations may give rise to unconscionable conduct.

Sections 22(1)(j) and 22(2)(j) refer to the circumstances where there is a contract for the acquisition of the goods or service. Sections 22(1)(j)(i) and 22(2)(j)(i) refer to the extent to which one party was willing to negotiate the terms and conditions of the contract with the other party. There is no obligation to agree or to negotiate. However, a refusal to negotiate may be unreasonable under some circumstances. Sections 22(1)(j)(ii) and 22(2)(j)(ii) refer to the terms and conditions of the contract. These sections are concerned with the existence of substantive unconscionability. Sections 22(1)(j)(iii) and 22(2)(j)(iii) refer to the conduct of the acquirer and the supplier in complying with the terms and conditions of the contract. A course of dealing that is capricious and unreasonable, and intentionally so, will most likely attract a finding of unconscionable conduct under this subsection.[79] Sections 22(1)(j)(iv) and 22(2)(j)(iv) refer to conduct in connection with a commercial relationship. As noted above, in

78 See Section 16.1.2 of this chapter.

79 *Automasters Australia Pty Ltd v Bruness Pty Ltd* [2002] WASC 286.

Body Bronze International, Macaulay AJA stated: '[I]t should be recognised that not every breach of contract, even a deliberate breach, necessarily involves the moral obloquy that the authorities suggest needs be present for unconscionable conduct in breach of s 51AC to be made out.'[80] In assessing ss 22(1)(j)(iv) and 22(2)(j)(iv), a court would have to have regard to all the surrounding circumstances so as to assess whether the relevant actions were reasonable and non-malicious. Some actions of deliberate breach may be so capricious and unreasonable as to give rise to unconscionable conduct.

Sections 22(1)(l) and 22(2)(l) are concerned with a lack of good faith. Although good faith has been a controversial concept within the common law, there is some strong support for regarding the duty of good faith as being one of reasonableness and fidelity to the bargain. Actions that are plainly unreasonable and that show a surreptitious intent to violate the bargain are likely to constitute bad faith conduct.

16.5 Leading statutory unconscionability cases

In this section, we will consider three leading cases on statutory unconscionability.

16.5.1 *Australian Competition and Consumer Commission v Lux Pty Ltd* (2004)

The case of *Australian Competition and Consumer Commission v Lux Pty Ltd*[81] concerned the circumstances surrounding the sale of a vacuum cleaner by the first respondent (Lux) acting through its agent, the second respondent, Mr Podger, to Mrs Janis Standing. Mr Podger had met Mr Standing, the husband of Mrs Standing, at a McDonald's restaurant. They had a brief conversation during which Mr Standing informed Mr Podger that the Standings had an Electrolux vacuum cleaner that was playing up. As Mr Podger worked for Electrolux as a sales representative, he agreed to visit the Standings.

Mr Podger visited the house when Mrs Standing was home alone. Both Mr and Mrs Standing were illiterate and intellectually disabled. Although the court found that this issue was not determinative, it did note that Mrs Standing had 'the reasonable appearance of intellectual disability'. During his time at the Standing house, Mr Podger pressured Mrs Standing to buy a new vacuum cleaner. Mrs Standing was not able to assess her financial ability to purchase a new vacuum cleaner and did not comprehend the terms of the credit agreement. Nicholson J stated:

> It was in my view 'irreconcilable with what is right or reasonable'. Mr Podger came close to realising this when he thought of the question whether Mrs Standing should receive independent advice. He veered away from that course because he considered she had told him that she could read (evidence I have not accepted) ... While it is clear she was not deprived of an independent and voluntary will, it must have been apparent to him that

80 *Body Bronze International Pty Ltd v Fehcorp Pty Ltd* (2011) 34 VR 536, [91].

81 [2004] FCA 926. See also *Australian Competition and Consumer Commission v Lux Distributors Pty Ltd* (2013) ATPR ¶42-429.

> she was not able to make a worthwhile judgement as to what was in her best interests in the circumstances.[82]

In *Australian Competition and Consumer Commission v Lux*, the court paid particular attention to the relative strengths of the parties, the ability of the weaker party to understand any relevant documents and the existence of any unfair pressure. The court found that it was quite significant that although Mr Podger considered that Mrs Standing should obtain independent advice, he deliberately refrained from pursuing this matter. The fact that Mrs Standing was not able to fully comprehend the significance of the transaction, combined with Mr Podger's knowledge of this fact and his indifference to it, amounted to unconscionable conduct.

16.5.2 *Australian Competition and Consumer Commission v Keshow* (2005)

Australian Competition and Consumer Commission v Keshow[83] concerned the sale of books to illiterate and disadvantaged Indigenous women in the Northern Territory. The ACCC alleged that in the period between September 1998 and May 2003 the respondent, in his dealings with eight residents of Indigenous communities in Central Australia, engaged in conduct that was unconscionable and misleading. The eight Indigenous residents with whom the respondent dealt were financially inexperienced and had poor literacy. Nonetheless, the respondent signed them up to open-ended payment agreements; he failed to deliver all the promised goods, and the books that were sold were of dubious value to the residents. The court found:

> They were each, to differing degrees, vulnerable by reason of their personal circumstances to succumb to the unsolicited proposal of someone such as the respondent to sign an open-ended periodical payment form ... They were each indigenous female persons living in relatively poor circumstances, dependent primarily upon government welfare payments, and who had limited commercial experience ... a number of those traits would have been apparent to the respondent at the time.[84]

In some instances, the direct debit payments continued even after the full value of the goods had been received. The respondent was aware of the financial situation of the residents. He was also aware of their poor levels of literacy and their lack of financial sophistication. The court held that the procurement of further payments, even after he had already been overpaid, was clearly unconscionable. His conduct in enticing the residents into individual agreements that they did not fully understand was unconscionable.

16.5.3 *Australian Competition and Consumer Commission v Simply No-Knead* (2000)[85]

Simply No-Knead (SNK) was at all relevant times the owner of a business trading under the name 'Simply No-Knead'. SNK supplied training and materials for making bread and related

82 [2004] FCA 926, [112].
83 [2005] FCA 558.
84 [2005] FCA 558, [108].
85 [2000] FCA 1365. See also *Video Ezy International Pty Ltd v Sedema Pty Ltd* [2014] NSWSC 143.

products in the home. It had several franchisees. The relationship between SNK and the franchisees was highly problematic. In particular, SNK decided that it would embark on a course of conduct that would undermine the businesses of certain franchisees and result in the eventual termination of their franchises. This set the basis for the resulting dispute. The offending conduct was neatly described by the ACCC as falling within six categories of conduct which, it alleged, contravened s 51AC(1):

- refusing to deliver franchised products to franchises;
- deleting the telephone numbers of franchises from Telstra's 013 Telephone Directory Assistance Service without the consent or knowledge of the franchisees;
- unreasonably refusing requests from the franchisees to negotiate matters in dispute with SNK and to discuss matters of concern to the franchisees;
- producing and distributing advertising and promotional material which omitted the names of the franchisees and their franchised businesses;
- selling and offering to sell its products in the territories of the franchisees;
- refusing to provide current disclosure.

There was little, if any, commercial justification for the conduct of SNK. It aggressively undermined the business of its franchisees and it sought payments for work that was neither requested nor required. The Federal Court stated:

> Having had regard to the ... circumstances of the case, I have concluded that the accumulation of incidents ... discloses an overwhelming case of unreasonable, unfair, bullying and thuggish behaviour in relation to each franchisee that amounts to unconscionable conduct by SNK for the purposes of s 51AC(1) ... SNK devised a plan intended to cause the franchisees to terminate or not renew their franchise agreements. SNK's conduct achieved its aim.[86]

Accordingly, SNK's plan and its implementation constitute unconscionable conduct for the purposes of s 51AC(1). The clear lack of good faith and the deliberate plan to ruin the franchisees rendered the conduct indefensible.

16.5.4 *Ipstar Australia Pty Ltd v APS Satellite Pty Ltd* (2018)

In *Ipstar Australia Pty Ltd v APS Satellite Pty Ltd*,[87] the NSW Court of Appeal (NSWCA) has clarified the meaning of unconscionable conduct under the ACL, especially as it applies to relations between 'experienced commercial parties'. The appellant, Ipstar Australia Pty Ltd ('Ipstar'), is a wholesaler of satellite broadband services, and the respondent, APS Satellite Pty Ltd (APS) (once known as SkyMesh Pty Ltd), was a licensed telecommunications carrier.

86 [2000] FCA 1365, [51].
87 (2018) 356 ALR 440.

In 2007, Ipstar and APS reached a supply contract under which Ipstar provided bandwidth to APS at a value for each megabyte every second of the month. At the conclusion of that contract, APS received numerous complaints from its clients about defective hardware equipment and unreliable internet connections. APS incurred significant expenses in making the necessary service calls and in replacing defective hardware equipment with new (and often equally faulty) Ipstar equipment, without any reimbursement from Ipstar. APS advised Ipstar of these problems and of its intention to look for indemnification for such costs outlaid through either a contractual warranty or statutory warranty in accordance with the ACL. Ipstar dismissed all of APS's statutory warranty claims and rejected reimbursement or indemnification.

While the warranty issue remained in dispute, the supply contract between the parties was due for renewal. Without explanation, Ipstar proposed to raise the cost of its bandwidth services to APS by 20 per cent. Unknown and undisclosed to APS, Ipstar had determined the full cost of fulfilling its hardware statutory warranty commitments, and was endeavouring to pass on that cost of 'doing business' to APS by simply increasing the price of its bandwidth services.

Due to the extortionate cost of changing suppliers, APS had little choice but to accept Ipstar's revised charges, which were significantly higher than those Ipstar charged APS's competitors.

In the initial hearing, Rein J held that Ipstar had acted unconscionably in raising its cost for the future supply of broadband services to recover losses it anticipated in satisfying its past statutory warranty obligations. The Court of Appeal held that while in isolation the way APS operated its business and the fact that it had no contractual right to bandwidth did not make it unconscionable for Ipstar to utilise its better bargaining position to accomplish its legitimate commercial interests, the conduct of rising the price should be considered in all of the circumstances of the case.[88] Therefore, it held that Ipstar had acted unconscionably on the ground that it set out to impose a price increment on APS that had been determined by reference to its exposure to statutory warranty claims in conditions where it had dismissed claims it knew were substantial and was declining to consider claims it was obliged to evaluate.[89]

16.6 Remedies for contravention

Civil remedies are available for contravention of the unconscionable conduct provisions (ss 20 or 21), such as injunction (s 232), damages for the loss suffered (s 236), adverse publicity order (s 237), disqualification order (s 248), and declarations (s 163A).

Contravention of the unconscionable conduct provisions does not give rise to a criminal offence. However, a pecuniary penalty (s 224) may be imposed.

88 See S Black and K Silvers, 'Unconscionable Conduct Bringing Experienced Commercial Parties Back Down to Earth in *Ipstar Australia Pty Ltd v APS Satellite Ptd Ltd* [2018] NSWCA 15' (Carroll & O'Dea, 22 March 2018): https://www.codea.com.au/.

89 L Gehrig and R Norton, 'NSW Court of Appeal Clarifies Unconscionable Conduct' (Thomson Geer Lawyers, 20 February 2018): www.tglaw.com.au/.

A person contravening s 20 or s 21 of the ACL may be liable to pay a pecuniary penalty of up to $1.1 million for a body corporate and $222 000 for other persons.[90]

16.7 Recent developments

In 2005, the Consumer Affairs Australia and New Zealand (CAANZ) commenced a scheduled review of the ACL. In April 2017, the CAANZ released its final report, and recommended 19 different amendments (Final Report).[91] In relation to unconscionability legislation, the Final Report recommended extending unconscionable conduct provisions to publicly listed companies.

Traditionally, the unconscionable conduct provisions under the ACL (and related provisions under the ASIC Act) do not extend to publicly listed companies.[92] Accordingly, some listed companies that ought to be protected are not currently protected (eg small companies that come up short on the bargaining power to defend their own interests).[93]

The unconscionable conduct provisions are intended to keep people from taking part in practices that go against good conscience as judged against the norms of society.[94] The prohibition against unconscionable conduct was initially accessible to consumers only. It was later extended to business transactions, excluding publicly listed companies, where the transaction value was under $1 million. This was expanded up to $3 million (in 2001), $10 million (in 2007) and then removed entirely (in 2011). In any case, the exclusion of publicly listed companies remained in place.[95]

Historically, public listing was seen as a 'reasonable indication of a trader's size and ability to protect its own interests'.[96] The CAANZ believed that this view of publicly listed companies as being capable of protecting their own interests, and therefore as not being deserving of protection from unconscionable conduct, was outdated. It stated in the Final Report: '[P]ublic listing is not necessarily a reflection of a trader's size, level of resourcing or its ability to withstand unconscionable conduct.'[97]

90 See also A Coorey, *Australian Consumer Law* (LexisNexis Butterworths Australia, Sydney, 2015), 322.

91 Consumer Affairs Australia and New Zealand (CAANZ), *Australian Consumer Law Review Final Report* (March 2017): https://cdn.tspace.gov.au/

92 Consumer Affairs Australia and New Zealand (CAANZ), *Australian Consumer Law Review Final Report* (March 2017), 50.

93 Consumer Affairs Australia and New Zealand (CAANZ), *Australian Consumer Law Review Final Report* (March 2017), 50.

94 Consumer Affairs Australia and New Zealand (CAANZ), *Australian Consumer Law Review Final Report* (March 2017), 50.

95 Consumer Affairs Australia and New Zealand (CAANZ), *Australian Consumer Law Review Final Report* (March 2017), 50.

96 Consumer Affairs Australia and New Zealand (CAANZ), *Australian Consumer Law Review Final Report* (March 2017), 50.

97 Consumer Affairs Australia and New Zealand (CAANZ), *Australian Consumer Law Review Final Report* (March 2017), 50.

Further, the current unconscionable conduct provisions provide 'inconsistent levels of protection for traders of comparable size and resources',[98] since some privately owned companies may be larger or better resourced than some listed companies.

Parliament has responded to the Final Report by releasing an exposure draft amendment bill, the Treasury Laws Amendment (Australian Consumer Law Review) Bill 2018 ('Draft Bill'),[99] and an amendment bill on penalties, the Treasury Laws Amendment (2018 Measures No 3) Bill 2018 ('Penalties Bill').[100] The Draft Bill removes the exemption for listed public companies under the relevant provisions of both the ACL and the *Australian Securities and Investments Commission Act* 2001 (Cth). The Draft Bill has been passed by both houses,[101] and the Amendment was enacted in April 2019.[102] These changes will prevent any business from engaging in unconscionable conduct towards a publicly listed business. In other words, these changes will enable publicly listed companies to bring an unconscionable conduct claim under the ACL.

16.8 Key points

- The doctrine of unconscionable conduct is well established in Australian law.
- There are three main elements of unconscionability: (1) one party must be at a special disadvantage; (2) the other party must know that the special disadvantage exists; and (3) the other party must have taken an unconscientious advantage of the party with the special disability.
- Section 20 of the ACL provides that a person must not, in trade or commerce, engage in conduct that is unconscionable, within the meaning of the unwritten law from time to time.
- Section 20(2) provides that the section does not apply to conduct that is prohibited by s 21.
- Section 20 of the ACL is tied to the concept of unconscionable conduct as developed by the courts of equity and the common law. In contrast, s 21 has a broader field of application due to the enumerated factors in s 22.
- Section 21 sets out one cause of action for unconscionable conduct in the course of supply or receiving goods and services, whereas s 22 sets out a set of statutory factors to be considered in evaluating s 21.

98 Consumer Affairs Australia and New Zealand (CAANZ), *Australian Consumer Law Review Final Report* (March 2017), 50.

99 Treasury Laws Amendment (Australian Consumer Law Review) Bill 2018, Schedule 2, 'Listed public companies': http://parlinfo.aph.gov.au/.

100 See the Treasury Laws Amendment (2018 Measures No 3) Bill 2018 (Cth).

101 The Treasury Laws Amendment (Australian Consumer Law Review) Bill 2018 was finally passed by both Houses on 18 October 2018. See Parliament of Australia, Treasury Laws Amendment (Australian Consumer Law Review) Bill 2018: https://www.aph.gov.au/.

102 See *Treasury Laws Amendment (Australian Consumer Law Review) Act 2018*. See also s 296 of Chapter 5, Schedule 2, vol 3 of the CCA 2010:

296 Application – listed public companies

The amendments made by items 4 and 5 of Schedule 2 to the Treasury Laws Amendment (Australian Consumer Law Review) Act 2018 apply in relation to acts or omissions on or after the day that Schedule commences.

16.9 DISCUSSION QUESTIONS

1. Section 20 of the Australian Consumer Law defines unconscionable conduct in terms of the 'unwritten law from time to time'. What does this mean?
2. What are the three requisite elements of unconscionable conduct under s 20 of the ACL?
3. Is constructive knowledge sufficient to satisfy the third requisite element of unconscionable conduct under s 20 of the ACL?
4. Are the matters listed under s 22 of the ACL an exhaustive list of indicative factors of unconscionable conduct?
5. Does unconscionable conduct protection under s 21 apply to publicly listed companies?
6. The cases that have granted relief on the basis of unconscionable conduct have often referred to a plaintiff as being under a 'special disability'. What does this mean? Give some examples.

16.10 PROBLEM QUESTION

Smart Call Ltd is a mobile phone company incorporated in Sydney. It provides mobile phone services to customers across Australia. Smart Call promoted its services through telephone marketing (telemarketing) calls by representatives of SkyVoice India and other call centres in India, Singapore and the Philippines.

Smart Call provided representatives of SkyVoice India and other call centres with the scripts to be used in the telemarketing calls and directed the telemarketers to follow the scripts.

Potential customers were contacted by telemarketers who offered the customer an enticement to contract, namely the 'gift' of a phone and holiday vouchers. The mobile contracts offered were on a 24-month plan, and contained a 'day cap' clause. The plans consisted of a minimum monthly fee, for which customers would receive a set daily allowance for calls and text messages, depending upon the plan they chose. The most commonly selected contract was the A$30 per month plan, for which customers received a daily allowance for calls and text messages capped at A$2. Any costs incurred outside the cap would be added to the monthly bill.

However, the scripted explanation of the cap set out above was not included in any recorded phone conversations between telemarketers and customers. Instead, the telemarketers simply said words to the effect of: '[F]or only $30, you get $60 worth of calls.'

The application of the 'day cap' clause in its mobile contact in some cases allowed a customer to make only one call of approximately two minutes per day before being charged fees in excess of the monthly contract charge. The structure of the contracts meant that customers were very likely to incur high excess usage charges, as the operation of this term was not adequately disclosed. A large number of consumers across all parts of Australia were affected by Smart Call's conduct.

In addition to the 'day cap' clause, the mobile contracts contained a A$75 'cool off' fee that customers were required to pay, as well as a A$195 charge imposed for returning a damaged phone, even if only the box was damaged.

1. Do customers who entered into mobile contracts with Smart Call have a remedy under the unconscionable conduct provisions of the Australian Consumer Law?
2. Would your answer be different if Smart Call was a listed public company?

16.11 FURTHER READING

Bigwood, R, '*Kakavas v Crown Melbourne Ltd* – Still Curbing Unconscionability: *Kakavas* in the High Court of Australia' (2013) 37(2) *Melbourne University Law Review* 463.

Consumer Affairs Australia and New Zealand (CAANZ), *Australian Consumer Law Review Final Report* (March 2017): https://cdn.tspace.gov.au/.

Flitcroft, R, Cameron, J, and Kuhne, M, 'What You Need to Know about Proposed Changes to the Australian Consumer Law' (Corrs, 23 February 2018): www.corrs.com.au/.

Treasury Laws Amendment (Australian Consumer Law Review) Bill 2018: http://parlinfo.aph.gov.au/.

17

MISLEADING OR DECEPTIVE CONDUCT

17.0 Introduction

This chapter engages with the substantive law pertaining to misleading or deceptive conduct. The statutory prohibition on misleading or deceptive conduct first appeared in the now defunct *Trade Practices Act 1974* (Cth) (TPA). Section 52 of the TPA provided that a corporation shall not, in trade or commerce, engage in conduct that is misleading or deceptive or is likely to mislead or deceive. The TPA has now been repealed. In its place has emerged the Australian Consumer Law (ACL), which contains the same prohibition on misleading or deceptive conduct. The ACL is contained in Schedule 2 to the *Competition and Consumer Act 2010* (Cth). The TPA s 52 equivalent is s 18 of the ACL. Section 18 provides that a *person* shall not, in trade or commerce, engage in conduct that is misleading or deceptive or is likely to mislead or deceive. This chapter looks solely at misleading or deceptive conduct under s 18 of the ACL.

The key difference between s 52 of the TPA and s 18 of the ACL is that the latter applies to persons, which includes corporations and individuals. Accordingly, the scope of s 18 of the ACL is somewhat wider than that of its statutory predecessor. Nonetheless, the vast body of jurisprudence that has developed under s 52 of the TPA is now applicable to s 18 of the ACL. This chapter refers to s 18 of the ACL, even though the case law that is discussed refers to s 52 of the TPA as these cases were decided under that provision.

There are two substantive parts to s 18. The first is determining whether the conduct is in trade or commerce. The second concerns whether the conduct is misleading or deceptive or likely to mislead or deceive.

17.1 The purpose of s 18

The purpose of s 18 of the ACL is to render unlawful a particular type of commercial conduct. In effect, s 18 sets a base-line standard for commercial behaviour.[1] In *Brown v Jam Factory Pty Ltd*, the Federal Court stated that '[s]ection 52 does not purport to create liability at all; rather it establishes a norm of conduct'.[2] The remedies that are available under s 18 are set out elsewhere in the ACL.

Section 2(2) of the ACL defines 'engaging in conduct' as 'doing or refusing to do any act'. Misleading or deceptive conduct can be seen as the statutory form of the common law doctrine of misrepresentation.[3] However, the conduct that is prohibited under s 18 is not limited to representations, and a wide range of activities are covered by the provision.[4] In the case of *Henjo Investments Pty Ltd v Collins Marrickville Pty Ltd*,[5] Lockhart J stated:

> Misleading or deceptive conduct generally consists of representations, whether express or by silence; but it is erroneous to approach section 52 on the assumption that its application is confined exclusively to circumstances which constitute some form of representation.[6]

1 *Brown v Jam Factory Pty Ltd* (1981) 53 FLR 340, 348.
2 *Brown v Jam Factory Pty Ltd* (1981) 53 FLR 340, 348.
3 See *Taco Co of Australia Inc v Taco Bell Pty Ltd* (1982) ATPR ¶40-303, 43,751.
4 *Butcher v Lachlan Elder Realty Pty Ltd* (2002) 55 NSWLR 558.
5 (1988) 79 ALR 83.
6 (1988) 79 ALR 83, 93.

The central inquiry under s 18 is whether the conduct of the person or corporation, whether by representation or otherwise, has 'the tendency to lead members of the public into error'.[7] That is, if the conduct is such that it causes members of the public to reach erroneous conclusions, which then influence or may potentially influence their conduct, then the person or corporation responsible will have infringed the limits set out by s 18.[8] There is no requirement that the person or corporation must have deliberately set out to lead others into error.[9] It is quite possible that a person may be acting honestly, but might still inadvertently engage in misleading or deceptive conduct.[10] Liability under s 18 will be imposed on the maker of the relevant representation, not on the intermediary who facilitates the advertisement.[11] The liability imposed by s 18 focuses on whether the conduct is likely to mislead or deceive or whether it has done so. Fault in the form of a failure to take reasonable care is relevant, but is not crucial in finding a contravention of s 18.

17.2 Conduct in trade or commerce

In any putative case of misleading or deceptive conduct, the threshold question that must first be addressed is whether the conduct took place in trade or commerce. This issue must be addressed before any attention can be paid to the substantive matter of whether the conduct complained of is in fact misleading or deceptive, or likely to be so.

17.2.1 Jurisdictional requirement

The jurisdictional requirement must be satisfied in that the trade or commerce must take place in Australia, or be between entities in Australia and places outside of Australia.[12] The Explanatory Memorandum to the ACL Bill states:

> Section 18 of the ACL applies to conduct 'in trade or commerce'. 'Trade or commerce' is defined as meaning 'trade or commerce within Australia, or between Australia and places outside Australia, and includes any business or professional activity (whether or not carried on for profit)'. The ACL applies to conduct engaged in outside of Australia, provided that at least some aspect of the trading relationship between two or more parties has taken place in Australia.[13]

The definition suggests that the ACL takes a rather expansive view of the phrase in 'trade or commerce' but that the conduct must have an ostensibly trading character.

---

7 (1991) ATPR ¶41-110, 52,711.

8 *Australian Competition and Consumer Commission v TPG Internet Pty Ltd* (2013) 250 CLR 640.

9 *CI JI Family Pty Ltd v National Australian Nappies (NAN) Pty Ltd* [2014] FCA 79; *Yorke v Lucas* (1985) 158 CLR 661; *Google Inc v Australian Competition and Consumer Commission* (2013) 249 CLR 435.

10 *Select Personnel Pty Ltd v Morgan & Banks Pty Ltd* (1988) 12 IPR 167; *Macquarie Bank Ltd v Seagle* (2008) 79 IPR 72.

11 *Google Inc v Australian Competition and Consumer Commission* (2013) 249 CLR 435.

12 ACL, s 2.

13 Explanatory Memorandum, Trade Practices Amendment (Australian Consumer Law) Bill (No 2), paragraph 3.12.

17.2.2 Broad versus narrow views

Whether an expansive interpretation of 'trade or commerce' should be adopted is important, as not all the functions of a corporation can be defined as being trading in nature. For example, in *Bevanere Pty Ltd v Lubidineuse*,[14] it was held that the one-off sale of a company's principal asset took place in trade or commerce. In *Bevanere*, the court based its decision on the fact that the sale of the asset took place as a part of the overall process of trade or commerce.

The early jurisprudence under the TPA suggested that an expansive interpretation of 'trade or commerce' would prevail.[15] In *Re Ku-ring-gai Cooperative Building Society (No 12) Ltd*,[16] Deane J stated that the terms 'trade or commerce' were 'clearly of the widest import'.[17] However, the clear danger in such an expansive approach is that it would cast the net too wide and would thereby capture activity that was not of a trading nature.[18]

In *Concrete Constructions (NSW) Pty Ltd v Nelson*[19] the High Court recognised the dangers posed by the expansive approach and established the limitations on whether conduct was in trade or commerce under s 52 of the TPA. This limitation will most likely continue to apply to s 18 of the ACL. In *Concrete Constructions*, Mason CJ, Deane, Dawson and Gaudron JJ stated:

> Nonetheless, when the section is read in the context provided by other features of the Act, which is 'An Act relating to certain Trade Practices', the narrower (i.e. the second) of the alternative constructions of the requirement 'in trade or commerce' is the preferable one. Indeed, in the context of Pt V of the Act with its heading 'Consumer Protection', it is plain that s.52 was not intended to extend to all conduct, regardless of its nature, in which a corporation might engage in the course of, or for the purposes of, its overall trading or commercial business. Put differently, the section was not intended to impose, by a side-wind, an overlay of Commonwealth law upon every field of legislative control into which a corporation might stray for the purposes of, or in connection with, carrying on its trading or commercial activities. What the section is concerned with is the conduct of a corporation towards persons, be they consumers or not, with whom it (or those whose interests it represents or is seeking to promote) has or may have dealings in the course of those activities or transactions which, of their nature, bear a trading or commercial character.[20]

In *Concrete Constructions*, a construction worker was working on metal grates that covered air-conditioning shafts when one of the grates gave way. He fell and sustained serious injuries. He had been advised by the foreman, an employee of Concrete Constructions, that the grates were secured. As it turned out, they were not secure and caused his accident. Mr Nelson, the injured construction worker, argued that this conduct was misleading or deceptive. At first instance in the Federal Court, Einfeld J held that the matter in dispute could be decided under s 52. On appeal to the High Court, a majority held that the conduct did not occur within trade

14 (1985) 7 FCR 325.
15 *Larmer v Power Machinery Pty Ltd* (1977) 14 ALR 243.
16 (1978) 22 ALR 621.
17 (1978) 22 ALR 621, 648–9.
18 *Barto v GPR Management Services Pty Ltd* (1992) ATPR ¶41-162, 40,210.
19 (1990) 169 CLR 594.
20 (1990) 169 CLR 594, 604.

or commerce under s 52 of the TPA. The majority noted that there were arguments in favour of a wide or narrow interpretation of the phrase 'in trade or commerce', but decided in favour of a narrow interpretation. In *Concrete Constructions*, the High Court stated:

> The phrase 'in trade or commerce' in s.52 has a restrictive operation ... So construed, to borrow and adapt words used by Dixon J. in a different context in Bank of N.S.W. v. The Commonwealth [1948] HCA 7; (1948) 76 CLR 1, at p 381, the words 'in trade or commerce' refer to 'the central conception' of trade or commerce and not to the 'immense field of activities' in which corporations may engage in the course of, or for the purposes of, carrying on some overall trading or commercial business.[21]

The restrictive operation of 'trade or commerce' in s 52 has been applied in a number of cases.[22] The effect of this restrictive operation is to place activities that are incidental to trade or commerce outside of the reach of s 18 of the ACL. As the Full Court of the Federal Court noted in *Village Building Co Ltd v Canberra International Airport Pty Ltd*,[23] the activities must 'of their nature, bear a trading or commercial character'. In *Village Building*, French, Sackville and Conti JJ stated in relation to the High Court's decision in *Concrete Constructions*:

> The phrase 'in trade or commerce' in s 52 has a restrictive operation (at 602) ... Two competing constructions of the phrase are available. The broader view would encompass (at 602–603): 'conduct in the course of the myriad of activities which are not, of their nature, of a trading or commercial character but which are undertaken in the course of, or as incidental to, the carrying on of an overall trading or commercial business'. This would extend, for example, to a case where one employee gives inaccurate information to another in the course of carrying on the building activities of a commercial builder. The narrower view is that the phrase 'in trade or commerce' refers only (at 603): 'to conduct which is itself an aspect or element of activities or transactions which, of their nature, bear a trading or commercial character. So construed ... the words "in trade or commerce" refer to "the central conception" of trade or commerce and not to the "immense field of activities" in which corporations may engage in the course of, or for the purposes of, carrying on some overall trading or commercial business'. The narrower view is the correct construction of s 52.[24]

The dichotomy appears to centre primarily around activities that are essentially trading in character and from which a misrepresentation may arise and those that are not primarily trading-related in nature. This does not necessarily mean that intermediaries, who themselves are not engaged in trade or commerce, cannot make representations in trade or commerce.

Despite the seemingly clear divide between the *broad* and the *narrow* interpretations of 'trade or commerce', the application of the dicta in *Concrete Constructions* is not always a simple matter. For example, in *Shahid v Australasian College of Dermatologists*,[25] the appellant, a dermatologist, sought to become a Fellow of the Australasian College of Dermatologists. Over a period of five years, the appellant sought to undertake supervised training. Between

21 (1990) 169 CLR 594, 602–3.
22 See, for example, *Village Building Co Ltd v Canberra International Airport Pty Ltd* (2004) 139 FCR 330.
23 (2004) 139 FCR 330.
24 (2004) 139 FCR 330, [44].
25 (2008) 168 FCR 46.

2000 and 2004, the appellant applied for the one trainee post that was available at the Royal Perth Hospital. The college controlled every aspect of the application process. Shahid was unsuccessful on each occasion on which she applied. When she sought to appeal the decisions, her appeals were not heard by the college. Eventually, she sued the college, claiming that representations they had made to her were misleading. On appeal, the Full Court of the Federal Court disagreed on the question of whether the activities of the college took place in trade or commerce. Jessup J stated:

> Considering all of the appellant's propositions, neither individually nor together do they lead to the conclusion that the particular aspects of the College's training program with which we are here concerned consisted of activities or transactions which, of their nature, bore a trading or commercial character. Training for professional qualifications is not an inherently commercial activity. Whether it is commercial in any particular case will depend upon the nature of the transactions by which it is provided to trainees. In the present case, looked at broadly, the College did not sell training services to the applicant or other trainees. It required them to meet certain standards, and it did so rigorously and systematically. At various points along the way, the College and the trainees engaged in transactions which, in themselves, were of a trading or commercial character (such as the sale of some books and the attendance at some conferences). But those instances did not have the effect of impressing such a character on the program as a whole, even the clearly non-commercial aspects of it such as those in the course of which the representations impugned in the present case were made.[26]

In addressing whether the conduct occurred in trade or commerce, Jessup J considered *each aspect* of the college's activities before forming his view. However, Branson and Stone JJ supported a *global view*, one that considered the significant sums the college sought from applicants. Branson and Stone JJ stated:

> In our view, in reaching a judgment on whether the College published its Handbooks 'in trade or commerce', it is important to consider the cumulative significance of the above evidence rather than to consider each aspect of the evidence as though it stood alone. Additionally, it must be borne in mind that the words 'trade' and 'commerce' in s 52, and other relevant provisions of the Trade Practices Act, carry their ordinary meanings. In Concrete Constructions at 602 the majority described them as 'terms of common knowledge of the widest import'. In Re Ku-ring-gai Co-operative Building Society (No 12) Ltd [1978] FCA 50; (1978) 36 FLR 134 at 167 Deane J said of these terms:
>
>> They are not restricted to dealings or communications which can properly be described as being at arm's length in the sense that they are within open markets or between strangers or have a dominant objective of profit-making. They are apt to include commercial or business dealings in finance between a company and its members which are not within the mainstream of ordinary commercial activities and which, while being commercial in character, are marked by a degree of altruism which is not compatible with a dominant objective of profit-making.

26 (2008) 168 FCR 46, [160].

> In our view, the evidence outlined above supports the conclusion that the College had a commercial relationship with practitioners, such as the appellant, who intended to apply for a position as a trainee registrar and with those who obtained such positions. It charged them significant examination fees. It generated further revenue from them from the sale of prescribed texts and the conduct of seminars and courses relevant to their examinations and training – some of which it required trainee registrars to attend. It subjected them, initially upon passing the Part I Examination and in later years upon their commencing training as a registrar, to an annual levy. If they chose to challenge decisions of the College affecting their admission to training or their acceptance as Fellows of the College they were required to pay substantial fees.[27]

The *global view* considers all of the conduct of the person taken as a whole. Provided that the transaction fits in with other relevant activities that are of a trading nature, then the conduct will most likely be within trade or commerce. This would suggest that transactions such as one-off sales by private individuals are very likely to be outside trade or commerce.[28] In the case of *O'Brien v Smolonogov*,[29] the Full Federal Court stated:

> But, in our view, the mere use, by a person not acting in the course of carrying on a business, of facilities commonly employed in commercial transactions, cannot transform a dealing which lacks any business character into something done in trade or commerce. Of course, the facilities mentioned have applications which are not commercial in any sense: advertisements in newspapers and the telephone are used by persons for purposes which are not commercial at all. With all respect to the learned Judge, we are not persuaded that resort to them can create the business context required by the reference to 'trade or commerce' in s.53A. The conduct complained of was not something done by the appellants in the course of carrying on a business and it lacked trading or commercial character as a transaction.[30]

17.2.3 Statements in public education campaigns without commercial purpose

In contrast, one-off sales by commercial enterprises may well be in trade or commerce. However, statements made in public debate or public education campaigns are not likely to fall within the parameters of trade or commerce.[31] In *Plimer v Roberts*, Dr Roberts delivered a series of talks on biblical matters and geology. The discussion of geology was used to give credence to Dr Roberts's suggestion that certain biblical events had actually occurred. Dr Plimer believed that the biblical stories were untrue and that the statements that Dr Roberts had made were misleading. Dr Plimer sued under s 52 of the TPA. The lectures were organised by the Noah's Ark Research Fund (NARF). Even though NARF had charged fees for admission and sold tapes of the lectures, the Federal Court held that Dr Roberts's conduct was not a

27 (2008) 168 FCR 46, [26]–[27].
28 *O'Brien v Smolonogov* (1983) 53 ALR 107; *Argy v Blunts & Lane Cove Real Estate Pty Ltd* (1990) 26 FCR 112.
29 *O'Brien v Smolonogov* (1983) 53 ALR 107.
30 (1983) 53 ALR 107.
31 *Plimer v Roberts* (1997) 80 FCR 303.

commercial activity. The court held that while NARF's actions in charging for admission and selling tapes might have been in trade or commerce, there was nothing misleading about this conduct. In contrast, the conduct of Dr Roberts might have been misleading, but it was not in trade or commerce. Lindgren J stated:

> The delivery of the lectures was not inherently a trading or commercial activity. The misrepresentations, made in the course of the giving of them, were not in the nature of a promotion of NARF's selling of door tickets or videotapes or audio cassettes. The misrepresentations were no different, in the present respect, from misrepresentations made in the course of the giving of lectures or addresses in many familiar factual settings. A professor delivers a lecture to university students; an academic or other person presents a paper at a conference or seminar held for the practitioners of a profession; a public figure addresses a crowd in a hall. Assume that in each case the speaker is not paid but understands that the institution or organisation which has arranged the event is making an admission charge or will sell various recorded forms of the lecture or address, or both. In such cases, what is said in the course of the delivery of the lecture or address will not ordinarily be 'in' trade or commerce, even if the charging and selling by the institution or organisation is. Dr Roberts' misrepresentations were not placed 'in trade or commerce' by the fact that, to his knowledge, an admission charge was being imposed and audio and video recordings were being made and were to be sold.[32]

17.2.4 Statements in public debate with commercial purpose

However, statements that are made, ostensibly to engage in public debate, but which clearly have a commercial purpose, will be deemed to be in trade or commerce. In *Tobacco Institute of Australia Ltd v Australian Federation of Consumer Organisations Inc*,[33] an advertisement made by the Tobacco Institute suggesting that environmental smoke was not generally harmful was found to be in trade or commerce. While the advertisement itself did not promote a particular brand of cigarettes, it certainly promoted a message that was broadly supportive of an industry that was actively engaged in trade and commerce. Sheppard J stated:

> [T]he message conveyed by the advertisement was that environmental tobacco smoke was not harmful to the health of non-smokers. It might be annoying and might cause discomfort but nothing more was involved. Those problems were to be overcome by tolerance, understanding and mutual respect. So the message was one of reassurance.
>
> . . . I suppose that it is possible that it was published on behalf of sporting and other bodies which tobacco companies frequently sponsor. And, it may indeed have been published for commercial reasons i.e. to promote or maintain the sales of the commercial commodity, cigarettes, which were the subject of it. I find it difficult to think of other possibilities.
>
> One problem I have about possibilities other than that associated with trade or commerce is the extent of the publication. The evidence does not appear to disclose

32 (1997) 80 FCR 303.
33 (1992) 38 FCR 1.

how many newspapers were involved altogether. In those that are referred to, the advertisement occupied half of one whole page, not in the classified advertisement section, but on pages of the various papers devoted to general items of news, or, in the case of the *Australian Financial Review*, business affairs. There is no evidence, I think, of the cost of inserting the advertisement, but one's common knowledge of affairs tells one that the total cost of the exercise must have amounted to some tens of thousands of dollars. One asks oneself the question why would any person or body spend such a substantial sum of money unless it saw in the publication some commercial advantage. This may reflect a cynical attitude on my part but I think the question is realistic.[34]

17.2.5 Public statements about a competitor

Public statements made about a competitor, even within a forum that might usually be regarded as private, may still occur in trade or commerce.

MADDEN *v* SEAFOLLY PTY LTD (2014) 313 ALR 1

Fact: The appellant, Madden, made a series of false claims on her Facebook page to the effect that Seafolly had infringed copyright in her dress designs. Seafolly sued for misleading or deceptive conduct. On appeal, Madden pleaded that the Facebook comments were made privately and not in trade or commerce.

Issue: Whether the Facebook comments were made privately or in trade or commerce.

Decision: Rares and Robertson JJ stated:

> [A] substantial number of those who made comments on the personal Facebook page were in the fashion industry. Ms Madden posted comments on her personal site using both her own name and the name 'White Sands Swimwear Australia' responding to the postings of her Facebook 'friends' or, perhaps more accurately, correspondents. For example, she wrote on her personal page under the White Sands name: 'Lucy and Holly!!! These are the rip offs Seafolly did! Jeeze, you girls. We have them in Black, in store now:)'. Taking these matters in combination it should not be concluded, in our opinion, that any of the Facebook statements were of a private character and in our opinion there was no error in the conclusion of the primary judge that the statements had a trading or commercial character.[35]

17.3 Intermediary liability

It is possible for an intermediary to be found liable for misleading or deceptive conduct. That is, an intermediary will face liability where they pass on or provide a message originating from

34 (1992) 38 FCR 1, [45]–[47].
35 (2014) 313 ALR 1, [98].

some other party that is misleading or deceptive, if it appears that they themselves are the source of the message or if they endorse its contents.[36] However, caution should be exercised in attempting to apply any general principles, as the entirety of the intermediary's conduct should be assessed.[37] Indeed, it will be 'a question of fact' as to whether liability should apply: *Google Inc v Australian Competition and Consumer Commission*.[38]

BUTCHER *v* LACHLAN ELDER REALTY PTY LTD (2004) 218 CLR 592

Fact: A real estate agent provided a purchaser with a brochure that reproduced an inaccurate diagram. The brochure contained a disclaimer about the reliability of the materials and noted that it had been put together from different sources.

Issue: Whether an agent should be found liable for the misleading or deceptive conduct of a principal.

Decision: In the High Court, Gleeson CJ, Hayne and Heydon JJ stated:

> [T]he agent did not engage in conduct towards the purchasers which was misleading. Whatever representation the vendor made to the purchasers by authorising the agent to issue the brochure, it was not made by the agent to the purchasers. The agent did no more than communicate what the vendor was representing, without adopting it or endorsing it. That conclusion flows from the nature of the parties, the character of the transaction contemplated, and the contents of the brochure itself.[39]

YORKE *v* LUCAS (1985) 158 CLR 661

Fact: A vendor sold a business through an agent. The vendor made misleading statements about the company's turnover, which the vendor dutifully passed on to the purchaser. The purchaser later sued the agent.

36 *Butcher v Lachlan Elder Realty Pty Ltd* (2004) 218 CLR 592; *Gardam v George Wills & Co Ltd* (1988) 82 ALR 415.

37 *Butcher v Lachlan Elder Realty Pty Ltd* (2004) 218 CLR 592.

38 (2013) 249 CLR 435, [15]. French CJ, Crennan and Kiefel JJ stated: 'It has been established in relation to intermediaries or agents that the question whether a corporation which publishes, communicates or passes on the misleading representation of another has itself engaged in misleading or deceptive conduct will depend on whether it would appear to ordinary and reasonable members of the relevant class that the corporation has adopted or endorsed that representation. It has also been established that, if that question arises, it will be a question of fact to be decided by reference to all the circumstances of a particular case.'

39 (2004) 218 CLR 592, 605.

***Issue**:* Whether the agent should be liable for the misleading statement of the vendor.

***Decision**:* At trial, it was held that the agent company had unwittingly made misleading or deceptive statements. However, ultimately on appeal in the High Court, Mason ACJ, Wilson, Deane and Dawson JJ stated:

> [E]ven though a corporation acts honestly and reasonably, it may nonetheless engage in conduct that is misleading or deceptive or is likely to mislead or deceive ... That does not, however, mean that a corporation which purports to do no more than pass on information supplied by another must nevertheless be engaging in misleading or deceptive conduct if the information turns out to be false. If the circumstances are such as to make it apparent that the corporation is not the source of the information and that it expressly or impliedly disclaims any belief in its truth or falsity, merely passing it on for what it is worth, we very much doubt that the corporation can properly be said to be itself engaging in conduct that is misleading or deceptive.[40]

GOOGLE INC *v* AUSTRALIAN COMPETITION AND CONSUMER COMMISSION (2013) 249 CLR 435

***Fact**:* The ACCC claimed that Google had engaged in misleading or deceptive conduct by publishing sponsored links, a form of online advertising attached to Google's search engine, which occasionally contained misleading or deceptive claims made by others. Google did have a system in place to capture and remove misleading advertisements, but this was not always effective particularly where Google had received no notification as to a specific advertisement. Moreover, Google never endorsed any of the misleading content.

***Issue**:* Whether Google should be liable for misleading or deceptive claims made by its clients.

***Decision**:* The High Court found that Google had not contravened s 52 of the TPA.

17.4 Methodology for establishing misleading or deceptive conduct

As noted, a variety of situations might give rise to claims of misleading or deceptive conduct. Given the need to maintain coherency within the jurisprudence, it is essential that a basic process of evaluation is followed to assess these claims. The leading case with regard to the question of a s 18 methodology is the Federal Court's decision in *Taco Co of Australia Inc v*

40 (1985) 158 CLR 661, 666.

Taco Bell Pty Ltd,[41] which set up the *Taco Bell* steps that have frequently been employed by subsequent courts to evaluate s 52 matters.[42]

17.4.1 Four-part methodology in *Taco Bell*

In effect, the Federal Court in *Taco Bell* set out a four-part methodology for dealing with claims of misleading or deceptive conduct.

First, the relevant segment of the population that might be affected by the misleading or deceptive conduct must be identified.[43] It is imperative that a class of consumers who may have been misled or deceived, or who are susceptible to being misled or deceived, is identified.[44] The relevant person within this class is the ordinary and reasonable person. The identity of the ordinary and reasonable person will vary depending upon the context in which the conduct was made and the class of persons at whom it was aimed.

Second, the question of misleading or deceptive conduct must be considered while taking into account the full breadth and depth of the relevant segment of the population. In *Taco Bell*, Deane and Fitzgerald JJ stated:

> [O]nce the relevant section of the public is established, the matter is to be considered by reference to all who come within it, 'including the astute and the gullible, the intelligent and the not so intelligent, the well-educated as well as the poorly educated, men and women of various ages pursuing a variety of vocations'.[45]

Even though the target audience may have some knowledge of the relevant product or industry, an advertisement may still be misleading if its dominant message creates an impression that is untrue.[46]

AUSTRALIAN COMPETITION AND CONSUMER COMMISSION *v* TPG INTERNET PTY LTD (2013) 250 CLR 640

Fact: An advertisement by the defendant gave the impression that an internet service would be available at $29.99 per month. The advertisement did not clearly spell out that this price was dependent on the purchase and bundling of other products.

---

41 (1982) 42 ALR 177.

42 See, for example, *Apotex Pty Ltd v Les Laboratoires Servier [No 2]* (2008) ATPR ¶42-235; *Cassidy v Saatchi & Saatchi Australia Pty Ltd* (2004) 134 FCR 585; *Domain Names Australia Pty Ltd v .au Domain Administration Ltd* (2004) 139 FCR 215.

43 *Australian Competition and Consumer Commission v Breast Check Pty Ltd* [2014] FCA 190. See also *Butcher v Lachlan Elder Realty Pty Ltd* (2002) 55 NSWLR 558; *Parkdale Custom Built Furniture Pty Ltd v Puxu Pty Ltd* (1982) 149 CLR 191; *Campomar Sociedad Limitada v Nike International Ltd* (2000) 202 CLR 45.

44 (1982) 42 ALR 177. In Taco Bell, Deane and Fitzgerald JJ stated: 'It is necessary to identify the relevant section (or sections) of the public (which may be the public at large) by reference to whom the question of whether conduct is, or is likely to be, misleading or deceptive falls to be tested.'

45 (1982) 42 ALR 177.

46 *Australian Competition and Consumer Commission v TPG Internet Pty Ltd* (2013) 250 CLR 640.

Issue: Whether the TPG's advertisement constitutes misleading or deceptive conduct.

Decision: The majority, French CJ, Crennan, Keifel and Keane JJ, stated that 'where a representation is made in terms apt to create a particular mental impression in the representee, and is intended to do so, it may properly be inferred that it has had that effect'.[47]

Third, actual evidence that some individual has been misled is useful, but not essential.[48] The test for establishing misleading or deceptive conduct is objective and must be assessed by the court. It is sufficient that the conduct is likely to mislead or deceive.[49] However, there is some value in leading evidence that consumers have been misled. In *ACCC v Coles Supermarkets Australia*,[50] Allsop CJ stated:

> Evidence that someone was actually misled or deceived may be given weight. The presence or absence of such evidence is relevant to an evaluation of all the circumstances relating to the impugned conduct. Where the conduct and representations are to the public generally and concern a body of simple direct advertising, the absence of individuals saying they were misled may not be of great significance.[51]

AUSTRALIAN COMPETITION AND CONSUMER COMMISSION *v* COLES SUPERMARKETS AUSTRALIA (2014) 317 ALR 73

Fact: Coles invariably marketed bakery products as 'Freshly Baked', 'Baked Today, Sold Today' and 'Freshly Baked In-Store'. In truth, the products had been pre-baked and frozen and then thawed and re-baked for sale. The ACCC did not advance any evidence that consumers had been misled. Coles Supermarkets sought to suggest that this was a weakness in the ACCC's case.

Issue: Whether Coles Supermarkets had engaged in misleading or deceptive conduct in the way in which it had marketed its bread products.

Decision: The court found that Coles had indeed contravened s 18 of the ACL. Allsop CJ stated:

> The objective assessment of advertising using ordinary English words in an attempt to persuade can be undertaken without the lengthening of a trial by the bringing of witnesses of indeterminate numbers. Language, especially advertising,

47 (2013) 250 CLR 640, [55].

48 *Parkdale Custom Built Furniture Pty Ltd v Puxu Pty Ltd* (1982) 149 CLR 191, 198; *CPA Australia Ltd v Dunn* (2007) 74 IPR 495, 500–1.

49 *Australian Competition and Consumer Commission v Turi Foods Pty Ltd [No 4]* [2013] FCA 665.

50 (2014) 317 ALR 73.

51 (2014) 317 ALR 73, [45].

> seeking to raise intuitive senses and associations, can have its ambiguities and subtleties. The task of evaluating the objective character and meaning of the language in the minds of reasonable members of the public is not necessarily one that will be assisted in any cost-effective manner by calling members of the public. The question is one for the court.[52]

Fourth, there must be a causal link between the impugned actions and the relevant misconceptions.[53] In *Nextra Australia Pty Ltd v Fletcher*, Collier J stated that 'there must be a sufficient causal link between the conduct and the error on the part of persons exposed to it'.[54] The entirety of the defendant's conduct must be considered. That is, the conduct must be considered as a whole and in context.[55] It is inappropriate to view particular acts or words in isolation when their wider context would demonstrate that they are not misleading. It is also quite possible that conduct might cause confusion, but not fall afoul of s 18 of the ACL. The conduct must be misleading or deceptive within the parameters of the statutory concept.

The *Taco Bell* methodology has been endorsed by the Federal Court in a number of cases. For example, in *Domain Names Australia Pty Ltd v .au Domain Administration Ltd*,[56] the Full Court of the Federal Court stated as follows:

> It has long been established that:
>
> - When the question is whether conduct has been likely to mislead or deceive it is unnecessary to prove anyone was actually misled or deceived: *Parkdale Custom Built Furniture Pty Ltd v Puxu Pty Ltd* (1982) 49 CLR 191 at 198.
> - Evidence of actual misleading or deception is admissible, and may be persuasive, but is not essential: *Global Sportsman Pty Ltd v Mirror Newspapers Pty Ltd* [1984] FCA 180; (1984) 2 FCR 82 at 87.
> - The test is objective and the court must determine the question for itself: *Taco Company Australia Inc v Taco Bell Pty Ltd* [1982] FCA 136; (1982) 42 ALR 177 at 202.
> - Conduct is likely to mislead or deceive if that is a real or not remote possibility, regardless of whether it is less or more than fifty per cent.[57]

There has been no challenge within the jurisprudence to the *Taco Bell* methodology. The basic principles that have emerged from *Taco Bell* and which have been affirmed in subsequent cases will continue to be relevant under s 18 of the ACL.

52 (2014) 317 ALR 73, [45].
53 *Nextra Australia Pty Ltd v Fletcher* [2014] FCA 399, [68]; *Australian Competition and Consumer Commission v TPG Internet Pty Ltd* (2013) 250 CLR 640, [39].
54 [2014] FCA 399, [68].
55 *Australian Competition and Consumer Commission v Coles Supermarkets Australia* (2014) 317 ALR 73, [38]; *Google Inc v Australian Competition and Consumer Commission* (2013) 294 ALR 404, 423–4, [89].
56 (2004) 139 FCR 215.
57 (2004) 139 FCR 215, [17].

17.4.2 A framework for determining the relevant class of consumers

The case of *Campomar Sociedad Limitada v Nike International Ltd*[58] provides a framework for determining the relevant class of consumers under s 18.

CAMPOMAR SOCIEDAD LIMITADA *v* NIKE INTERNATIONAL LTD (2000) 202 CLR 45

Fact: The defendant sold a fragrance known as 'Nike Sports Fragrance'. Nike alleged that this conduct was misleading or deceptive.

Issue: Whether Campomar's conduct was misleading or deceptive, and how to determine the relevant class of consumers that had been affected.

Decision: The High Court held that, in the context of representations that are made to the public at large, the central issue is how the ordinary and reasonable member of that class would be affected. Some limitations do apply, as these members are expected to take basic precautions to protect their own interests.[59] However, in *Campomar*, the fact that consumers did not see that the small print on the packaging disavowed any actual connection to Nike did not amount to a failure to take care. The High Court stated:

> In their joint judgment in Taco Company of Australia Inc v Taco Bell Pty Ltd, Deane and Fitzgerald JJ observed that whether or not conduct amounted to a representation was 'a question of fact to be decided by considering what [was] said and done against the background of all surrounding circumstances'. Their Honours continued:
>
>> In some cases, such as an express untrue representation made only to identified individuals, the process of deciding that question of fact may be direct and uncomplicated. In other cases, the process will be more complicated and call for the assistance of certain guidelines upon the path to decision.
>>
>> ...
>
> It is in these cases of representations to the public, of which the first appeal is one, that there enter the 'ordinary' or 'reasonable' members of the class of prospective purchasers. Although a class of consumers may be expected to include a wide range of persons, in isolating the 'ordinary' or 'reasonable' members of that class, there is an objective attribution of certain characteristics.[60]

There is a *crucial difference* between a representation made direct to *identified individuals* and that made to the *broader public*. In the former case, the misleading conduct will be easier to identify. In the latter case, the relevant class of people must be identified. Within the

58 (2000) 202 CLR 45.
59 See *Parkdale Custom Built Furniture Pty Ltd v Puxu Pty Ltd* (1982) 149 CLR 191.
60 (2000) 202 CLR 45, 84–5.

parameters of that group, a hypothetical ordinary reasonable person must then be constructed.[61] This group may contain people who are gullible or ill disposed to attend to their own best interests. In constructing the ordinary reasonable person, those who are extremely careless or inclined to extreme beliefs and ideas must be disregarded. The ordinary reasonable member must be found to have been misled or deceived because of the actual conduct of the defendant. The personal misconceptions of the ordinary reasonable member must play no role in assessing the conduct.

17.5 Examples of misleading or deceptive cases

As the jurisprudence on s 52 of the TPA developed, a number of categories of misleading or deceptive conduct developed. This section of the chapter examines the categories of (1) comparative advertising; (2) puffery; (3) silence; (4) promises; (5) character merchandising; and (6) misleading or deceptive conduct on the internet.

17.5.1 Comparative advertising

Comparative advertising takes place when a manufacturer or service provider directly compares their product or service with that of a competitor in an advertisement. Inevitably, the advertiser portrays their product as being superior to that of the competitor's product. For their part, the competitor is quite likely to complain that the portrayal of their product is misleading. From a consumer welfare standpoint, comparative advertising may be useful in terms of providing information to consumers. Nevertheless, every claim made in a comparative advertisement must be verifiable lest the advertisement misleads the public.[62]

TELSTRA CORPORATION LTD v SINGTEL OPTUS PTY LTD [2014] VSC 35

Fact: Optus claimed in an advertisement that it had a geographic coverage in Australia that differed from Telstra's by less than 1 per cent.

Issue: Whether Optus's comparative advertisement was misleading.

Decision: The advertisement was found to be misleading.

Implication: In assessing whether an advertisement contravenes s 18 of the ACL, the advertisement must be *assessed as a whole*. It is insufficient to focus on specific parts of the advertisement in isolation from its context and true meaning.

61 *Lego Australia Pty Ltd v Paul's (Merchants) Pty Ltd* (1982) 42 ALR 344.
62 *Telstra Corporation Ltd v Singtel Optus Pty Ltd* [2014] VSC 35.

GILLETTE AUSTRALIA PTY LTD v ENERGIZER AUSTRALIA PTY LTD (2002) 193 ALR 629

Fact: A claim of misleading or deceptive conduct arose out of an advertisement that compared Energizer and Duracell batteries. The two batteries were different in their composition. The Duracell batteries were alkaline and the Energizer batteries were carbon–zinc. Alkaline batteries last longer than carbon–zinc batteries.

Issue: Energizer's claim was that as Duracell was not comparing like with like, nor mentioning the higher cost of alkaline batteries, the advertisement was misleading.

Decision: The Full Court of the Federal Court held that the advertisements were not misleading or deceptive, as favourably comparing one aspect of a manufacturer's product with the same aspect of a competitor's product did not entail any untrue statements or misleading half-truths. The fact that Duracell made no mention of cost in its advertisement was not misleading. Heerey J held that 'Duracell is entitled, in my opinion, to point out truthfully to consumers a feature of its product which is superior to that of a rival product'.

In *Gillette*, Heerey J stated:

> The characterisation of advertising as comparative does not of itself have legal significance, or create any kind of presumption in favour of a party alleging a breach of Pt V of the TPA. There is no basis in the TPA for regarding comparative advertising as an inherently disreputable form of commercial conduct, to be viewed with suspicion by the courts. On the contrary, to the extent that comparative advertising provides consumers with accurate hard facts about competing products, it assists in the making of better informed consumer choices and thereby results in more effective competition. Of course, the more actual comparisons that are used, the more potential there is for error (and half-truth). So advertisers have to be careful.[63]

Comparative advertising does assist consumers by providing information about competing products. Yet there is a clear potential for serious error in this form of advertising. That said, the courts have demonstrated a clear willingness to offer a degree of latitude to advertisers in comparative advertising cases. In order for a claim to be successful, there must be a real chance that the public would be misled.[64]

In *Reckitt Benckiser (Australia) Pty Ltd v S C Johnson & Son Pty Ltd*,[65] the Federal Court set out a detailed list of principles that are relevant to comparative advertising claims for the purposes of s 18 of the ACL. In *Reckitt Benckiser*, Conti J stated:

> Because of the nature of, as well as context to, the misleading or deceptive claims framed by Reckitt, and S C Johnson's responses, it is appropriate to reproduce below, at this early stage of my reasons for judgment, the carefully framed digest of potentially relevant

63 (2002) 193 ALR 629.
64 *Global Sportsman Pty Ltd v Mirror Newspapers Ltd* (1984) 2 FCR 82.
65 (2004) ATPR ¶42-026.

Australian judicial precedent undertaken by the parties as to the principles of operation of ss 52 and 53 of the TP Act, particularly upon product competitive advertising:

(i) in identifying what may constitute relevant conduct, the packaging and advertising of the product must be viewed as a whole, rather than by endeavouring to ascertain in isolation the meaning of the critical words: *Sterling Winthrop Pty Ltd v R & C Products Pty Ltd* [1994] FCA 1000; (1994) ATPR 41–308 at 42,126 (Lockhart J); *Telstra Corporation Ltd v Optus Communications Pty Ltd* (1996) 36 IPR 515 at 523 (Merkel J); and *Bristol-Myers Squib Australia Pty Ltd v Astra Pharmaceuticals Pty Ltd* [1999] FCA 256; (1999) 45 IPR 144 at 164 (Weinberg J);

(ii) it is the first impression conveyed by the packaging or other advertising which creates the impact on a reader or viewer, rather than an analysis of the constituent parts of the advertised message: *Sterling Winthrop* at 42,126 (also 42,133 per Sheppard and Burchett JJ); *Telstra* at 523; and *Bristol-Myers* at 16;

(iii) the whole of the message the subject of a controversial promotion etc should be considered in context; thus where a false dominant impression is conveyed, its message will not be ameliorated by the accuracy which may be derived from a careful analysis of all the constituent parts of the whole; most readers or viewers would not make a close study for instance of the subject packaging or television advertisement, but would absorb the general thrust thereof: *Stirling Winthrop* at 42,126 and 42,133; *Telstra* at 523; *Bristol-Myers* at 164; . . .

(iv) particular care must be taken by a person who engages in comparative advertising to ensure the comparison made is correct; thus in *Stuart Alexander & Co (Interstate) Pty Ltd v Blenders Pty Ltd* [1981] FCA 152; (1981) 37 ALR 161 at 163, Lockhart J said:

> When a person produces a television commercial that not only boosts his own product but, as in this case, compares it critically with the product of another so that the other is shown up in an unfavourable light by the comparison, in my view he ought to take particular care to ensure that the statements are correct . . .

(v) moreover any inaccuracy, half-truth, ambiguity or omission, made in the context of comparative advertising, may have greater potential to mislead consumers than in other spheres of advertising . . .

(vi) that is not to postulate that there are different legal principles to be applied in respect of comparative advertising; the preceding statements of principle in relation to comparative advertising merely recognise the fact that inaccurate or unfair comparisons are inherently likely to mislead consumers . . .

(vii) intention may be relevant to, albeit not a requirement for, establishing contravention of ss 52 and 53 of the TP Act; where however a person engaging in advertising or promotion intends to convey a particular impression so as to influence consumers in a particular way, the Court may more readily infer that the attempt has succeeded, and that consumers were so influenced.[66]

66 [2004] FCA 1237, [38].

17.5.2 Puffery: Statement of opinion versus statement of fact

Puffery will generally not be sufficient to sustain a claim of misleading or deceptive conduct. In *Nextra Australia Pty Ltd v Fletcher*, Collier J stated that 'whether "puffery" is misleading or deceptive for the purposes of s 18 of the ACL will depend on the facts and circumstances'.[67] Advertisers frequently make exaggerated claims that knowing audiences disregard as mere statements of opinion. As such, the courts have tended to take the view that the public is well accustomed to puffs and are able to distinguish them from statements of fact.[68]

In *Stuart Alexander & Co (Interstate) Pty Ltd v Blenders Pty Ltd* ,[69] Lockhart J called for a 'robust approach' in deciding whether television commercials were misleading or deceptive.[70] The difficulty arises when advertising claims move beyond the realm of harmless statements of opinion and are instead presented as statements of fact.

If a claim is capable of misleading or deceiving consumers, it will be an actionable misrepresentation.[71] Where a statement is clearly false in light of its context, it will not be mere puffery. For example, a claim of 'bigger and better' in relation to an action movie is not likely to be misleading or deceptive, but it would be in the context of apartments where size is a very relevant and pertinent concern.[72] Where the words are very specific and invite the audience to take action on the basis that what is being said is true, an actionable misrepresentation may arise. For example, in *Eveready Australia Pty Ltd v Gillette Australia Pty Ltd*,[73] Lindgren J stated:

> [T]he words 'lasts up to four times longer' hold out to the viewer that Duracell batteries do offer a meaningful advantage over competing brands. The specificity of those words is inconsistent with the nature of advertising puff. To my mind it is misleading and deceptive to appear to a reasonable television viewer to be saying something meaningful on which the viewer is invited to rely as a basis for action, when only a degree of analysis foreign to the realities of the market place would show the viewer that what was said is meaningless.[74]

17.5.3 Silence where disclosure is expected

It has been established that silence can constitute conduct for the purposes of s 52 of the TPA and, as such, this will satisfy s 18 of the ACL.[75] In essence, refusing to provide information or refraining from doing so when such information is clearly pertinent will fall within the parameters of s 2(2) of the ACL.

Notwithstanding the fact that silence may constitute conduct, the silence must be sufficient to meet the threshold for misleading or deceptive conduct. Generally, there is no duty in trade

67 [2014] FCA 399, [68].
68 *Byers v Dorotea Pty Ltd* (1986) 69 ALR 715.
69 (1981) ATPR ¶40-244.
70 (1981) ATPR ¶40-244, 43,204.
71 *Sabre Corporation Pty Ltd v Laboratories Pharma-A-Care Pty Ltd* (1995) ATPR ¶41-396.
72 *Byers v Dorotea Pty Ltd* (1986) 69 ALR 715.
73 [1999] FCA 1824.
74 [1999] FCA 1824, [59].
75 *Miller & Associates Insurance Broking Pty Ltd v BMW Australia Finance Ltd* (2010) 241 CLR 357.

or commerce to disclose every matter known to a business, particularly in the context of a commercial negotiation. However, circumstances may arise where there is *a reasonable expectation of disclosure*.[76]

The *reasonable expectation test* is now well established.[77] The test is 'whether in the light of all the circumstances constituted by acts, omissions, statements or silence, there has been conduct which is misleading or deceptive'.[78]

- The defendant must have actual knowledge of the information that they choose not to disclose.[79]
- The defendant need not have intended to mislead the other party by failing to disclose the information.[80]

The reasonable expectations test emphasises the effect upon the party that is disadvantaged by the silence. In *Demagogue Pty Ltd v Ramensky*,[81] Black CJ stated:

> Silence is to be assessed as a circumstance like any other. To say this is certainly not to impose any general duty of disclosure; the question is simply whether, having regard to all the relevant circumstances, there has been conduct that is misleading or deceptive or that is likely to mislead or deceive. To speak of 'mere silence' or of a duty of disclosure can divert attention from that primary question. Although 'mere silence' is a convenient way of describing some fact situations, there is in truth no such thing as 'mere silence' because the significance of silence always falls to be considered in the context in which it occurs. That context may or may not include facts giving rise to a reasonable expectation, in the circumstances of the case, that if particular matters exist they will be disclosed.[82]

In *Henjo Investments Pty Ltd v Collins Marrickville Pty Ltd*,[83] a statement that a restaurant could seat 128 people, coupled with the non-disclosure that the local authority only permitted the restaurant to seat 84 people, was held to amount to misleading or deceptive conduct.

In *Nagy v Masters Dairy Ltd*,[84] the non-disclosure by Masters Dairy that it had entered a distribution relationship with another business was held to constitute misleading or deceptive conduct in the context of negotiations between itself and Nagy that were undertaken with a view to the two companies entering a distribution relationship.

The key issue in these cases was that the *circumstances* were such that it was reasonable to expect that certain information would be disclosed.

In *Miller & Associates Insurance Broking Pty Ltd v BMW Australia Finance Ltd*,[85] the High Court stated:

76 *Miller & Associates Insurance Broking Pty Ltd v BMW Australia Finance Ltd* (2010) 241 CLR 357; *Demagogue Pty Ltd v Ramensky* (1992) 110 ALR 608.
77 *Miller & Associates Insurance Broking Pty Ltd v BMW Australia Finance Ltd* (2010) 241 CLR 357.
78 *Demagogue Pty Ltd v Ramensky* (1992) 110 ALR 608, 618.
79 *Semrani v Manoun* [2001] NSWCA 337.
80 *Johnson Tiles Pty Ltd v Esso Australia* (2001) ATPR ¶41-794.
81 (1992) 110 ALR 608.
82 (1992) 110 ALR 608, 609.
83 (1988) 39 FCR 546.
84 (1996) 150 ALR 273.
85 (2010) 241 CLR 357.

> The language of reasonable expectation is not statutory. It indicates an approach which can be taken to the [*sic*] characterisation, for the purposes of s 52, of conduct consisting of, or including, non-disclosure of information. That approach may differ in its application according to whether the conduct is said to be misleading or deceptive to members of the public, or whether it arises between entities in commercial negotiations.[86]

MILLER & ASSOCIATES INSURANCE BROKING PTY LTD *v* BMW AUSTRALIA FINANCE LTD (2010) 241 CLR 357

Fact: Miller had provided BMW with the relevant policy document, but had failed to draw BMW's attention to the fact that it could not be assigned or cancelled.

Issue: Whether the failure to disclose that an insurance policy was not assignable or cancellable was misleading or deceptive.

Analysis: This failure was an inadvertent act and there was no intent to mislead. Notwithstanding Miller's omission, BMW did not read the policy document. If BMW had read the policy document, it would have seen that it could not be assigned or cancelled.

Decision: The High Court held that the failure to disclose that an insurance policy was not assignable or cancellable was not misleading or deceptive because the parties were commercially sophisticated.

Half-truths can also amount to misleading or deceptive conduct. Where a half-truth is concerned, a statement is made that is literally true, but the failure to add qualifying information makes the statement as a whole misleading or deceptive. In this sense, cases of half-truths necessarily involve partial silence. In *Coles Supermarkets*, the use of language that suggested that the bread had been freshly baked when this was only partly true was found to be misleading. In relation to half-truths generally, Allsop CJ stated that 'half-truths may be misleading by the insufficiency of information that permits a reasonably open but erroneous conclusion to be drawn'.[87]

17.5.4 Promises and statements of future actions

Promises of a contractual nature may give rise to claims of misleading or deceptive conduct if they are not fulfilled. Section 18 might be utilised in this context where the party who is disadvantaged is a third party who would otherwise be excluded from contractual remedies by the doctrine of privity. Promises about future conduct may bring about liability under s 18 of the ACL for pre-contractual statements.[88] Where pre-contractual statements are concerned, some caution should be exercised in ensuring that conversations are accurately recalled. As McLelland CJ in Eq stated in *Watson v Foxman*:[89]

86 (2010) 241 CLR 357, 369.
87 (2014) 317 ALR 73, [46]. See also *Fraser v NRMA Holdings Ltd* (1994) 124 ALR 548, 563; *Tobacco Institute of Australia Ltd v Australian Federation of Consumer Organisations Inc* (1992) 38 FCR 1.
88 *Nescor Industries Group Pty Ltd v Miba Pty Ltd* (1998) 150 ALR 633.
89 (1995) 49 NSWLR 315.

> Where, in civil proceedings, a party alleges that the conduct of another was misleading or deceptive, or likely to mislead or deceive ... within the meaning of s 52 of the *Trade Practices Act 1974* (Cth) ... it is ordinarily necessary for that party to prove to the reasonable satisfaction of the court: (1) what the alleged conduct was; and (2) circumstances which rendered the conduct misleading. Where the conduct is the speaking of words in the course of a conversation, it is necessary that the words spoken be proved with a degree of precision sufficient to enable the court to be reasonably satisfied that they were in fact misleading in the proved circumstances. In many cases (but not all) the question whether spoken words were misleading may depend upon what, if examined at the time, may have been seen to be relatively subtle nuances flowing from the use of one word, phrase or grammatical construction rather than another, or the presence or absence of some qualifying word or phrase, or condition. Furthermore, human memory of what was said in a conversation is fallible for a variety of reasons, and ordinarily the degree of fallibility increases with the passage of time, particularly where disputes or litigation intervene, and the processes of memory are overlaid, often subconsciously, by perceptions or self-interest as well as conscious consideration of what should have been said or could have been said. All too often what is actually remembered is little more than an impression from which plausible details are then, again often subconsciously, constructed. All this is a matter of ordinary human experience.[90]

Promises about future conduct may also support claims for misleading or deceptive conduct. However, the mere fact that a statement about future conduct is not subsequently fulfilled does not render the statement misleading or deceptive.[91] In *Phoenix Court Pty Ltd v Melbourne Central Pty Ltd*, the Federal Court provided sound guidance:[92]

> Although the mere fact that a representation as to future conduct or the happening of a future event does not occur does not make the representation misleading or deceptive, such a representation can ripen into misleading or deceptive conduct for the purposes of s 52 in a number of circumstances; namely, if there is an implied statement in the representation as to a present or past fact; if the representation represents impliedly that the representor has a present intention to make good the promise or has the means or ability to do so; if the representation involves a representation that the representor has a present state of mind; or if a representation is made, which having regard to relevant circumstances at the time, requires a qualification because of the possibility of its non-fulfilment ... In any of these circumstances it is necessary to plead more than simply the fact of the representation as to the future matter and the fact that it does not occur. One has to plead material facts in relation to the implication in the statement of the present or past fact, the present intention and the means to carry it out, the relevant state of mind and the fact that there was no basis for it, and the relevant circumstance giving rise to the qualification. Without pleading such matters all the material facts necessary to complete the cause of action have not been stated and the respondent does not know what case it has to meet.[93]

90 (1995) 49 NSWLR 315, 318–19.
91 *James v Australia and New Zealand Banking Group Ltd* (1986) 64 ALR 347.
92 (1997) ATPR (Digest) ¶46-179.
93 (1997) ATPR (Digest) ¶46-179, 54,431–2.

Further, s 4(1) of the ACL provides that a representation as to a future matter that is made without reasonable grounds will be deemed to be misleading. Section 4(1) replaces s 51A of the TPA. Section 4(2) provides that unless the party who makes the representation adduces evidence to the contrary, the representation will be regarded as having been unreasonable. Effectively, where the plaintiff claims that the defendant did not have reasonable grounds for making a representation as to future matters, the latter may attempt to refute that claim.[94]

17.5.5 Character merchandising and passing off

A business will often seek to bolster the status of its product in the market by claiming a relationship to a famous person or even a fictitious character. It is the implication that such a relationship exists that is misleading or deceptive.[95] Character merchandising can be extremely effective and there is very often no logical reason for associating a particular person or character with a product. Moreover, while Australian law does not recognise the intellectual property right of rights in personality, which is well developed in the United States, the manner in which these cases have developed under s 52 of the TPA basically provides for a similar level of protection, albeit in a non-intellectual property context. In *Pacific Dunlop Ltd v Hogan*, Burchett J stated:

> Character merchandising through television advertisements should not be seen as setting off a logical train of thought in the minds of television viewers. Its appeal is nothing like the insistence of a logical argument on behalf of a product, which may persuade ... An association of some desirable character with the product proceeds more subtly to foster favourable inclination towards it, a good feeling about it, an emotional attachment to it . . .[96]

PACIFIC DUNLOP *v* HOGAN (1989) 23 FCR 553

Fact: An advertisement for shoes involved a scene that was very similar to a scene in the film *Crocodile Dundee*, which starred the actor Paul Hogan. In particular, the distinctive clothing of Hogan's character was mirrored in the advertisement. Hogan sued Pacific Dunlop under s 52 of the TPA on the basis of character merchandising.

Issue: Whether the advertisement suggested an association between the manufacturer and Paul Hogan.

Decision: A misrepresentation was found to exist.

Those character-merchandising claims that were made under s 52 of the TPA, and those that will now be made under s 18 of the ACL, can also be regarded as *passing off*. The tort of passing off applies where one business feigns an association with another in order to capture some of the goodwill that the market associates with the other business.[97] Passing off might be

94 *Re Colorado Products Pty Ltd (in prov liq)* (2014) 101 ACSR 233, [88].
95 *Buttrose v The Senior's Choice (Australia) Pty Ltd* [2013] FCCA 2050.
96 (1989) 23 FCR 553.
97 *MDI International Pty Ltd v Trio Brothers* [2010] FCA 486; *Red Bull Australia Pty Ltd v Sydneywide Distributors Pty Ltd* (2001) 53 IPR 481.

manifested by using deceptively similar product names.[98] Passing off can also be constituted by suggesting that a particular person is associated with a product or business.[99] Where this occurs, an actionable claim under s 18 of the ACL will also arise.

17.5.6 Misleading or deceptive conduct on the internet: Online review cases

Since 2017, the ACCC has taken enforcement action in a number of matters involving new or developing areas of the ACL – in particular, misleading or deceptive conduct on the internet.

AUSTRALIAN COMPETITION AND CONSUMER COMMISSION *v* MERITON PROPERTY SERVICES PTY LTD (2017) 350 ALR 494

Fact: Meriton's management directed staff to engage in 'masking' to stop potentially negative reviews from appearing on TripAdvisor. This gave the impression that Meriton accommodation was of a higher standard than otherwise may have been the case.

Issue: Whether Meriton breached s 18 of the ACL by manipulating TripAdvisor reviews.

Decision: The Federal Court held that Meriton engaged in misleading conduct by taking steps to prevent guests it suspected would give unfavourable reviews from receiving email prompts from review websites. Further, on 31 July 2018, the Federal Court ordered Meriton to pay penalties of $3 million for manipulating TripAdvisor reviews, in breach of the ACL.[100]

AUSTRALIAN COMPETITION AND CONSUMER COMMISSION *v* AVELING HOMES PTY LTD [2017] FCA 1470

Fact: Aveling is a Perth-based home building company that operates and controls the review website <www.avelinghomesproductreviews.com.au> and until 3 February 2017 also operated and controlled the review website <www.firsthomeownerscentreproductreviews.com.au>. During periods in 2016, Aveling represented that each of its review websites were independent of Aveling and were affiliated with the website <www.productreview.com.au> when that was not the case. Aveling held back bad reviews from its review website to give a more favourable impression of its services.[101]

---

98 *Prospero Publishing Pty Ltd v Rumcoast Holdings Pty Ltd* (2000) ATPR ¶41-762.

99 *Shoshana Pty Ltd v 10th Cantanae Pty Ltd* (1987) 18 FCR 285; *Newton-John v Scholl-Plough (Australia) Ltd* (1986) ATPR ¶40-697.

100 See also ACCC, 'Meriton to pay $3 million for misleading consumers on TripAdvisor', media release, 31 July 2018: https://www.accc.gov.au/.

101 See also ACCC, 'Aveling Homes ordered to pay penalties of $380,000 for misleading review websites', media release, 30 November 2017: https://www.accc.gov.au/.

Issue: Whether Aveling's conduct constituted a breach of s 18 of the ACL.

Decision: The court ordered penalties totalling $380 000 against Aveling Homes Pty Ltd for engaging in conduct liable to mislead the public in connection with these two online review websites on 30 November 2017.

17.6 Recent developments

The misleading or deceptive conduct scheme under the ACL (Schedule 2 to the CCA) does not apply 'to the supply, or possible supply, of services that are financial services, or of financial products'.[102] Financial services and financial products are regulated under the *Australian Securities and Investments Commission Act 2001* (Cth). The ASIC Act provided a statutory scheme regulating misleading or deceptive conduct concerning financial services in trade or commerce.[103]

Section 12DA of the ASIC Act states:

Misleading or deceptive conduct

(1) A person must not, in trade or commerce, engage in conduct in relation to financial services that is misleading or deceptive or is likely to mislead or deceive.

(1A) Conduct:

(a) that contravenes:

(i) section 670A of the Corporations Act (misleading or deceptive takeover document); or

(ii) section 728 of the Corporations Act (misleading or deceptive fundraising document); or

(iii) section 738Y of the Corporations Act (other liabilities relating to CSF [crowd-sourced funding] offer documents); or

(b) in relation to a disclosure document or statement within the meaning of section 953A of the Corporations Act; or

(c) in relation to a disclosure document or statement within the meaning of section 1022A of the Corporations Act;

does not contravene subsection (1). For this purpose, conduct contravenes the provision even if the conduct does not constitute an offence, or does not lead to any liability, because of the availability of a defence.

(2) Nothing in sections 12DB to 12DN limits by implication the generality of subsection (1).

---

102 *Competition and Consumer Act 2010* (Cth), s 131A.

103 See also A Coorey, *Australian Consumer Law* (LexisNexis Butterworths Australia, Sydney, 2015), 272, where it is stated: 'Section 12DA of the ASIC Act prohibits misleading or deceptive conduct, in trade or commerce, in relation to financial services and financial products.' Nevertheless, 'conduct which relates to both financial services and non-financial services may be be actionable under both the ASIC Act and ACL' [at 273]. Thus, it may be necessary to plead under both legislative schemes. See also S G Corones, *Australian Consumer Law* (Thomson Reuters Australia, Sydney, 3rd edn, 2016), 156.

It is clear that s 12DA of the ASIC Act is mirrored in s 18 of the ACL. To the extent that the wording of each provision is the same, they should be interpreted in the same way: *GPG (Australia Trading) Pty Ltd v GIO Australia Holdings Ltd.*[104]

On 4 February 2019, the Commonwealth government released the landmark *Final Report of the Royal Commission into Misconduct in the Banking, Superannuation and Financial Services Industry*. The report contains a total of 76 recommendations, including 17 recommendations relating to consumer credit.[105] The government has also committed to take action on all recommendations in the final report.[106] The report highlights the significance of industry culture and governance, and provided some specific recommendations in relation to restoring and establishing a proper culture and governance for financial service entities,[107] including recommendations in relation to developing a more effective approach to the conflict of interest between the duty to customers and the self-interest of financial service entities.

Some important recommendations in the report may have significant implications for preventing misleading or deceptive conduct by financial service entities and their employees.

As an important part of reshaping industry culture, the report requires mortgage brokers to act in the best interests of borrowers.[108] It recommends reforming the existing mortgage broker remuneration scheme, removing upfront commissions, and moving to a borrower pays remuneration structure. This means that borrowers should pay mortgage brokers a fee for helping with the home lending process, and lenders should not pay any commission to mortgage brokers. As a response, the government has committed to remove conflicts of interest between brokers and consumers by banning trail commissions and other inappropriate forms of lender-paid commissions on new loans from 1 July 2020, and to conduct a further review in three years on the implications of the borrower pays remuneration structure. This would arguably create a strong economic incentive for mortgage brokers to act in the best interest of borrowers, and not to mislead or deceive them, since they will be paid by the borrower rather than by the lender.

The report also treats mortgage brokers as financial advisers. It recommends that mortgage brokers should be subject to and regulated by the law that applies to entities providing financial product advice to retail clients.[109] In other words, mortgage brokers are now subject to laws regulating financial advisers. The report further recommended extending the

104 (2001) 117 FCR 23, [100], per Giles J. See also A Coorey, *Australian Consumer Law* (LexisNexis Butterworths Australia, Sydney, 2015), 273.

105 See R Cheung's fine summary in *Consumer Credit – Banking Royal Commission Final Report*, 6 February 2019: https://www.wolterskluwercentral.com.au/.

106 See R Cheung's fine summary in *Consumer Credit – Banking Royal Commission Final Report*, 6 February 2019. See also Australian Government, *Restoring Trust in Australia's Financial System: The Government Response to the Royal Commission into Misconduct in the Banking, Superannuation and Financial Services Industry*, February 2019. https://static.treasury.gov.au/.

107 See Recommendations 5.6: 'Changing culture and governance' and 5.7: 'Supervision of culture and governance', *Final Report of the Royal Commission into Misconduct in the Banking, Superannuation and Financial Services Industry* (2019). See also Australian Government, *Restoring Trust in Australia's Financial System: The Government Response to the Royal Commission into Misconduct in the Banking, Superannuation and Financial Services Industry* (February 2019), 30.

108 Recommendation 1.2: 'Best interests duty', *Final Report of the Royal Commission into Misconduct in the Banking, Superannuation and Financial Services Industry* (2019).

109 Recommendation 1.5: 'Mortgage brokers as financial advisers', *Final Report of the Royal Commission into Misconduct in the Banking, Superannuation and Financial Services Industry* (2019).

information-sharing and reporting obligations for Australian Credit Licence (ACL) holders to misconduct by mortgage brokers.[110] The government has agreed to this recommendation, and requires ACL holders to make all reasonably necessary inquiries to determine the misconduct, and to inform and remediate affected borrowers promptly.[111] This requirement may arguably make mortgage brokers more cautious when providing advice to retail clients, and may indirectly decrease the chances of their conduct misleading or deceiving their customers.

The report further contains some specific recommendations protecting vulnerable consumers from unsolicited selling (anti-hawking), including a prohibition on hawking for superannuation[112] and insurance products.[113] The definition of 'hawking' will be clarified to include 'selling of a financial product during a meeting, call or other contact initiated to discuss an unrelated financial product'.[114] This may arguably lower the bar for the determination of misleading or deceptive conduct in the process of selling superannuation and insurance products.

It is also noteworthy that the report included a recommendation to establish enforceable code provisions[115] that would empower ASIC to approve codes of conduct, including codes relating to all APRA-regulated institutions and ACL holders.[116] These codes may include provisions that permit contraventions to be seen as breaches of the law, and permit ASIC to take the inclusion of such provisions into account when determining whether to approve a code. Remedies for breaching the enforceable code provisions could be similar to those set out in Part VI of the *Competition and Consumer Act 2010* (Cth). In other words, under this regime, a breach of an enforceable code provision will be seen as a breach of the law.[117] The government has agreed to amend the law to set up such a regime.[118] This may arguably significantly increase the enforceability of financial services industry codes.[119]

110 Recommendation 1.6: 'Misconduct by mortgage brokers', *Final Report of the Royal Commission into Misconduct in the Banking, Superannuation and Financial Services Industry* (2019).

111 Australian Government, *Restoring Trust in Australia's Financial System: The Government Response to the Royal Commission into Misconduct in the Banking, Superannuation and Financial Services Industry*, February 2019, 8: https://static.treasury.gov.au/.

112 Recommendation 3.4: 'No hawking', *Final Report of the Royal Commission into Misconduct in the Banking, Superannuation and Financial Services Industry* (2019).

113 Recommendation 4.1: 'No hawking of insurance', *Final Report of the Royal Commission into Misconduct in the Banking, Superannuation and Financial Services Industry* (2019).

114 See responses to Recommendations 3.4 and 4.1, Australian Government, *Restoring Trust in Australia's Financial System: The Government Response to the Royal Commission into Misconduct in the Banking, Superannuation and Financial Services Industry*, February 2019, 19 and 21.

115 Recommendation 1.15: 'Enforceable code provisions', *Final Report of the Royal Commission into Misconduct in the Banking, Superannuation and Financial Services Industry* (2019).

116 ASIC is the regulator that administers the laws in relation to consumer protection and the conduct of licensed businesses in the financial services sector The Australian Prudential Regulation Authority (APRA) is 'an independent statutory authority that supervises institutions across banking, insurance and superannuation and promotes financial system stability in Australia'. See APRA at https://www.apra.gov.au/.

117 See Australian Government, *Restoring Trust in Australia's Financial System: The Government Response to the Royal Commission into Misconduct in the Banking, Superannuation and Financial Services Industry*, February 2019, 11.

118 See Australian Government, *Restoring Trust in Australia's Financial System: The Government Response to the Royal Commission into Misconduct in the Banking, Superannuation and Financial Services Industry*, February 2019, 11.

119 For example, under the new requirement, brokers may arguably have more obligations to disclose potential risks of financial products and services to their retail clients, and may no longer keep silent about those risks. See also Section 17.5.3 of this chapter.

While this chapter has focused mainly on general misleading or deceptive conduct under the Australian Consumer Law, rather than in relation to financial products and services under the ASIC Act, it is necessary to pay attention to some important recommendations in the government's final report. These recommendations may not only help to prevent misleading or deceptive conduct in the financial services industry, but may also inspire future enforcement by the ACL of provisions aimed at preventing misleading or deceptive conduct in other industries, particularly those recommendations in relation to improving the industry culture and governance, as well as the enforceability of industry codes.

17.7 Key points

- The purpose of s 18 of the ACL is to render unlawful a particular type of commercial conduct.
- The central inquiry under s 18 is whether the conduct of the person or corporation, whether by representation or otherwise, has 'the tendency to lead members of the public into error'.
- In any putative case of misleading or deceptive conduct, the threshold question that must first be addressed is whether the conduct took place in trade or commerce.
- The leading case with regard to the question of a s 18 methodology is the Federal Court's decision in *Taco Co of Australia Inc v Taco Bell Pty Ltd*,[120] which set up the *Taco Bell* steps that have frequently been employed by subsequent courts to evaluate s 52 matters.
- As the jurisprudence on s 52 of the TPA developed, a number of categories of misleading or deceptive conduct developed. The chapter examined the categories of (1) comparative advertising; (2) puffery; (3) silence; (4) promises; (5) character merchandising; and misleading or deceptive conduct on the internet.

17.8 Discussion questions

1. What does 'in trade or commerce' under s 18 of the ACL mean?
2. Can comparative advertising constitute a breach of the misleading or deceptive conduct provision under s 18 of the ACL? If yes, provide an example.
3. Can puffery constitute a breach of the misleading or deceptive conduct provision under s 18 of the ACL? If yes, provide an example.
4. Can silence constitute a breach of the misleading or deceptive conduct provision under s 18 of the ACL? If yes, provide an example.
5. Could the liability for breaching s 18 of the ACL be 'contracted out'?
6. Could an honest mistake breach s 18 of the ACL?
7. What are jurisdictional requirements for implementing s 18 of the ACL?

120 (1982) 42 ALR 177.

17.9 PROBLEM QUESTION

Easybuy Ltd is a Sydney-based online shopping company, founded in 2012, that provides an online sales service for retail clients through its website <easybuy.com.au>. Coolbuy Ltd is a new (founded in 2019) Sydney-based online shopping company that provides an online sales service, through its website <coolbuy.com.au>, that is in direct competition with Easybuy. By providing good-quality service and frequent online discounts, Coolbuy has attracted many clients, including many former clients of Easybuy.

Easybuy Ltd operates and controls a review website <www.cybershopreview.com> (CSR), which represents that each of its reviewed websites is independent of CSR. Under instruction from Easybuy, CSR has removed from its site some bad reviews of <easybuy.com> and some good reviews of <coolbuy.com>. By doing so, it is attempting to give online readers the impression that Easybuy Ltd is a superior business to Coolbuy Ltd.

Has CSR's conduct constituted a breach of s 18 of the ACL?

17.10 FURTHER READING

Corones, S, '*Australian Competition and Consumer Commission v. TPG Internet Pty Ltd., Forrest v. Australian Securities and Investments Commission*: Misleading Conduct Arising from Public Statements: Establishing the Knowledge Base of the Target Audience' (2014) 38 *Melbourne University Law Review* 281.

Lockhart, C, *The Law of Misleading or Deceptive Conduct* (LexisNexis Butterworths Australia, Sydney, 5th edn, 2018).

Pengilley, W, 'Misleading or Deceptive Conduct Considered by the High Court. Does *Butcher's* case Indicate a New Judicial Conservatism?' (2005) 12 *Competition & Consumer Law Journal* 314.

INTERNATIONAL COMMERCIAL LAW

18

INTERNATIONAL COMMERCIAL LAW

18.0 Introduction

This chapter engages with international aspects of commercial law. It first provides a background introduction to private international law, and an overview of recent developments in the main treaties on international trade. The US–China trade conflicts and Brexit are referred to. The chapter then focuses on two specific topics in relation to international sales contracts. The first of these is the Australian rules on private international law in relation to contracts with a foreign element. The chapter examines the theory of private international law, the main treaties on international trade (including Brexit and the Australia–UK Free Trade Agreement), and the key principles for determinating the proper law of contract under private international law. The second topic is the international sale of goods. The chapter focuses, in particular, on the *Convention on Contracts for the International Sale of Goods 1980* (CISG, or Vienna Convention) and the *Incoterms* of the International Chamber of Commerce (ICC). The CISG frequently applies to contracts for the sale of goods between parties in countries that are CISG member countries. It contains provisions regulating the application of the CISG to an international sale of goods contract, formation of the contract, the seller's conformity obligations under the contract, performance of the contract, and the remedies for breaches of contract. *Incoterms*, developed by the ICC, are international rules for the interpretation of trade terms. These standard trade definitions are most commonly used in international contracts. They may significantly facilitate cross-border transactions of goods and help traders in different countries to understand one another.[1]

18.1 Relevance of private international law to commercial law

18.1.1 What is private international law?

Private international law, also known as 'conflict of laws',[2] is the body of principles, rules and, at time, policies that indicate how a foreign element in a legal problem of dispute should be dealt with.[3] In comparison with 'public international law' or the law dealing with relations between sovereign states (eg laws of war, territory, diplomatic relations), private international law focuses on the relations of private parties to each other in an international context.

1 See Australian Trade and Investment Commission, 'What are Incoterms?'.

2 'Private international law', as the subject of this chapter is generally called in civil law countries and often also in the United Kingdom, is really a misnomer. The same is true for 'conflict of laws', as the subject is called in the United States and in most common law countries. '"Conflict of Laws" (or "Conflicts" for short, in American usage) suggests competition, a quest for dominance. Yet in many (if not most) cases, the question is rather which of different potentially applicable laws is the most appropriate for the problem at hand': P Hay, *Advanced Introduction to Private International Law and Procedure* (Edward Elgar, Cheltenham, UK and Northampton, MA, 2018) 1.

3 R Mortensen, R Garnett and M Keyes, *Private International Law in Australia* (LexisNexis Butterworths Australia, Sydney, 2nd edn, 2011), Part 1.

18.1.1.1 The substance of private international law

Private international law primarily focuses on legal problems that arise when a court deliberates on a case involving a contract with both a domestic and a foreign law element and determines which system of law will apply.

In the classic and narrowest view, private international law is the rules applied by local courts to determine which laws apply to cases that involve individual or business entities in different countries, or cross-border transactions ('choice of laws').[4] Most texts adopt a broader approach, in which the definition expands to cover issues about the exercise of domestic jurisdiction, and the recognition and enforcement of foreign judgement.[5]

In the other words, private international law commonly covers three main areas:

- *Jurisdiction (choice of forum):* Does a local court have power to hear and determine a case, or is another 'forum' – either interstate of overseas – more appropriate?
- *Choice of law:* Even if a court claims jurisdiction, should it apply the law of the forum or of the interstate or foreign law?
- *Recognition* and *enforcement* of foreign judgments.

18.1.1.2 Sources of international laws

The main sources of international law include treaties between states, international customary law, general principles of law as recognised by civilised nations, judicial decisions and scholarly writings.[6]

The sources of laws in private international law include national law, international treaties and case law, as discussed below.

(A) NATIONAL LAW

National law contains both international civil procedure and private international law (choice of law). Unlike public international law (the law applicable to state-to-state relations), it is not 'international' in its origin or application.

Even when a court follows the 'conflicts' rules of another country about what substantive law ultimately applies, it does so because its own conflicts law directs it to do so, and not because of some outside mandate.

(B) INTERNATIONAL TREATIES

Many conflicts rules originate from international conventions, such as those sponsored by The Hague Conference on Private International Law. However, they apply only in contracting countries that have adopted them as their domestic law, not because of any external mandate.

---

4 See D P Stewart, 'Private International Law: A Dynamic and Developing Field Anniversary Contributions – Private International Law' (2009) 30(4) *University of Pennsylvania Journal of International Law* 1121.

5 D P Stewart, 'Private International Law: A Dynamic and Developing Field Anniversary Contributions – Private International Law' (2009) 30(4) *University of Pennsylvania Journal of International Law* 1121.

6 See Statute of the International Court of Justice, art 38. See also C Greenwood, *Sources of International Law: An Introduction* (Office of Legal Affairs, United Nations, 2008).

Nevertheless, private international law (conflicts rules) of the European Union (EU) may be an exception. The EU Regulations on jurisdiction and on applicable law have a binding legal effect on the courts of the EU member countries, as they are directly applicable EU law, subject to limited recourse to the EU Court of Justice.

(C) CASE LAW

Most countries in the world have cast their law of international procedure and private international law into domestic legislation. The United States, as well as many other common law countries (other than the EU countries, which are subject to the EU conflicts rules – as stated above), follow the case law (common law) approach. In other words, precedents of the relevant highest court will have a binding legal effect on lower courts in future cases that involve similar issues.

18.2 Treaties on international trade

18.2.1 Multinationalism: World Trade Organization

The World Trade Organization (WTO) was established on 1 January 1995 in Geneva, Switzerland, and has been regarded as the most important development in the history of international trade.[7] Its primary concern is the rules of trade between nations or independent customs territories at the multinational level, and is the only international organisation to do so.[8] Despite achieving international status, the WTO is not a special agency of the United Nations. The WTO currently has 164 members representing over 98 per cent of world trade.[9] Its main function is to 'ensure that trade flows as smoothly, predictably and freely as possible'.[10] More specifically, the WTO operates a global system of trade rules, acts as a forum for negotiating trade agreements, settles trade disputes between its member states, and supports the needs of developing countries, among fulfilling many other roles.[11]

The WTO is often described as a 'rules-based' system.[12] The rules are agreements that have been negotiated by the governments of member countries.[13] WTO agreements have six main parts:

- 'umbrella agreement', or the Agreement Establishing the WTO;
- General Agreement on Tariffs and Trade (GATT) (the agreement for the trade of goods);
- General Agreement on Trade in Services (GATS);

7 J Mo, *International Commercial Law* (LexisNexis, Butterworths Australia, Sydney, 4th edn, 2009), Chapter 9, 704.

8 J Mo, *International Commercial Law* (LexisNexis Butterworths Australia, Sydney, 4th edn, 2009), Chapter 9, 704. See also WTO, *WTO in Brief*, at https://www.wto.org/.

9 See WTO, *Fact Profile*, at https://www.wto.org/.

10 See WTO, *WTO in Brief*, at https://www.wto.org/.

11 See WTO, *What is WTO?*, at https://www.wto.org/.

12 WTO, *Understanding the WTO: The Agreement – Overview: A Navigational Guide*, at https://www.wto.org/.

13 'The table of contents of "The Results of the Uruguay Round of Multilateral Trade Negotiations: The Legal Texts" is a daunting list of about 60 agreements, annexes, decisions and understandings': WTO, *Understanding the WTO: The Agreement – Overview: A Navigational Guide*, at https://www.wto.org/.

- Trade-Related Aspects of Intellectual Property Rights (TRIPS) (agreements for the protection and trade of intellectual property);
- dispute settlement; and
- reviews of governments' trade policies.

These agreements are summarised in Table 18.1.

Table 18.1 How do the six main areas of WTO agreements fit together?[14]

Umbrella agreement	Agreement establishing the WTO		
	Goods	Services	Intellectual property
Basic principles	GATT	GATS	TRIPS
Additional principles	Other goods agreements/annexes	Services annexes	
Market access	Schedules of commitments by country	Schedules of commitments by country, including MFN exemptions	
Dispute settlement	Dispute settlement		
Public accountability and transparency	Trade policy reviews		

The WTO agreements are both complex legal texts covering a wide range of commercial transactions (ie agriculture, textiles, banking, sanitation regulations, intellectual property) and documents that contain a number of simple, fundamental principles that constitute the foundation of the multilateral trading system.[15] The five main principles are as follows:

1. Non-discrimination. This principle has two major components. The first is the 'most favoured nation (MFN)' rule, in which a WTO member must apply the same conditions to all trade with other WTO members. The second component is the national treatment policy, which requires that imported goods should be treated no less favourably than domestically produced goods.
2. Freer trade through negotiation.
3. Predictability, by promoting binding and transparency.
4. Promotion of fair competition.
5. Encouragement of development and economic reform.

One of the key developments of the WTO is the adoption of a dispute settlement mechanism that is capable of solving disputes, thereby producing a credible system that effectively

14 Adapted from WTO, *Understanding the WTO: The Agreement – Overview: A Navigational Guide*, at https://www.wto.org/.

15 WTO, *Understanding the WTO: The Agreement – Overview: A Navigational Guide*, at https://www.wto.org/; WTO, *Understanding the WTO: Basics – Principles of the Trading System*, at https://www.wto.org/.

implements the treaty obligations of WTO members.[16] Settlement of trade disputes is one of the core activities of the WTO. A dispute arises when a WTO member government believes another WTO member government has violated an agreement or a commitment under the WTO. As one of the most active international dispute settlement mechanisms in the world, the WTO has processed over 500 disputes between member governments, and issued over 350 rulings since it was established in 1995.[17] It is noteworthy that, as a governmental body, the WTO only deals with disputes between member governments. It does not handle any disputes brought by private enterprises in member countries. If a private enterprise in one member country believes any trade policies or laws in another member country have breached the WTO rules, the enterprise must lobby the government of its residential country to initiate a dispute to the WTO.

Through the TRIPS Agreement, for the first time, the WTO set up a formal connection between intellectual property (IP) and trade. Since the TRIPS Agreement is under the WTO framework, the dispute settlement mechanism naturally also applies to any breach of the TRIPS Agreement. This has arguably significantly enhanced the enforceability of IP rights at the international level.

18.2.2 Protectionism versus free trade

18.2.2.1 Trade conflicts between the US and China

Trade tensions escalated between the US and China, the world's two largest economies, in 2018 and 2019, mostly via bilateral trade restrictions. On 10 May 2019, the US increased tariffs on US$200 billion worth of Chinese goods from 10 per cent to 25 per cent. Three days later, China responded by raising tariffs on US$60 billion worth of US goods to 25 per cent from 1 June 2019, extending a bilateral trade war.[18] Under the globalisation environment, the US–China trade war may affect the economic development of other countries also.[19] The World Economic Forum estimates that 'a full-blown US–China tariff war could reduce global GDP growth by 0.7 percentage points (pp) to 2.8 percent in 2019'.[20] It was estimated that the US–China trade war could cost Australia's economy at least A$36 billion.[21] The tensions between the US and China will affect Australian exporters and consumers, with fears that 'a trade-induced economic shock would crimp global demand, hitting farmers, miners and manufacturing suppliers'.[22]

16 See G Moens and P Gillies, *International Trade and Business: Law, Policy and Ethics* (Routledge Cavendish, Abingdon, UK, 2nd edn, 2006), 361.

17 See WTO, *Dispute Settlement*, at https://www.wto.org/.

18 'A Timeline of the U.S.–China Trade War', *Bloomberg News*, 14 May 2019.

19 M Mesquita, 'How a Trade War Would Impact Global Growth', blog update, *World Economic Forum*, 18 January 2019: https://weforum.org. (This article is part of the World Economic Forum Annual Meeting.)

20 M Mesquita, 'How a Trade War Would Impact Global Growth', blog update, *World Economic Forum*, 18 January 2019: https://weforum.org.

21 See E Bagshaw, 'Donald Trump's Trade War Will Cost Australia's Economy at Least $36 billion', *Sydney Morning Herald*, 7 September 2018.

22 See E Bagshaw, 'Donald Trump's Trade War Will Cost Australia's Economy at Least $36 billion', *Sydney Morning Herald*, 7 September 2018.

18.2.2.2 Free trade agreements

The escalation in trade tensions was partly compensated by the advances in regional economic integration, such as the African Continental Free Trade Area (AfCFTA), the Regional Comprehensive Economic Partnership (RCEP) agreement, and the Comprehensive and Progressive Agreement for Trans-Pacific Partnership (CPTPP). Over the past decade, Australia has been pursuing free trade agreements (FTAs) with all its major trading partners, such as the United States, China, Japan and South Korea. It is in the process of concluding FTAs with both the EU and a post-Brexit UK.[23] Regional trade agreements are 'becoming the main neutralizing factor for protectionist pressures in the global economy'.[24]

(A) REGIONAL AGREEMENTS: TPP AND CPTPP

After more than five years of negotiation, the Trans-Pacific Partnership Agreement (TPP) was finally concluded on 6 October 2015.[25] The TPP was negotiated among 12 Pacific countries, including Australia, Brunei, Canada, Chile, Japan, Malaysia, Mexico, Peru, New Zealand, Singapore, the United States and Vietnam,[26] covering 40 per cent of the global economy.[27] However, on 30 January 2017, only days after his inauguration as US President, Trump withdrew the United States from the TPP.[28] Nevertheless, the withdrawal of the US has not affected the decisions of the other 11 countries.

The Comprehensive and Progressive Agreement for Trans-Pacific Partnership, which incorporates the former TPP,[29] was signed by the 11 countries on 8 March 2018.[30] The CPTPP entered into force on 30 December 2018 for Australia, Canada, Japan, Mexico, New Zealand and Singapore, and on 14 January 2019 for Vietnam. The CPTPP will come into force for Brunei Darussalam, Chile, Malaysia and Peru 60 days after they complete their ratification processes.[31]

Like the TPP, the CPTPP contains not only chapters in relation to the removal of trade barriers and the promotion of market access and investment, but also a special chapter on

23 The Department of Foreign Affairs and Trade (DFAT) provides a list of FTAs in which Australia is a party, including 'FTAs in force', 'FTAs concluded but not yet in force', 'FTAs under negotiation', and 'Prospective FTA negotiations': https://dfat.gov.au/.

24 Y Lissovolik, *Regionalism vs Protectionism: Looking Ahead to 2019* (Valdai Club, 28 December 2018): http://valdaiclub.com/.

25 DFAT, 'Summary of the Trans-Pacific Partnership Agreement': https://dfat.gov.au/.

26 DFAT, 'Summary of the Trans-Pacific Partnership Agreement': https://dfat.gov.au/.

27 See J McBride and A Chatzky, 'What is the Trans-Pacific Partnership (TPP)?', Council on Foreign Affair Relations, 4 January 2019: https://www.cfr.org/. See also Y Tian, 'Current Issues of Cross-Border Personal Data Protection in the Context of Cloud Computing and Trans-Pacific Partnership Agreement: Join or Withdraw' (2016) 34 *Wisconsin International Law Journal* 367, 372.

28 On 30 January 2017, the Office of the US Trade Representative (USTR) issued a letter to signatories of the TPP that the United States had formally withdrawn from the agreement, per guidance from the President of the United States. See Office of the USTR, 'The United States Officially Withdraws from the Trans-Pacific Partnership': https://ustr.gov/.

29 DFAT, *Comprehensive and Progressive Agreement for Trans-Pacific Partnership (CPTPP)*: https://dfat.gov.au/.

30 The full text of the CPTPP is at https://dfat.gov.au/.

31 DFAT, *Comprehensive and Progressive Agreement for Trans-Pacific Partnership (CPTPP)*: https://dfat.gov.au/. The website will be updated to reflect the dates of entry into force for each country.

e-commerce for electronic trade transactions between member countries.[32] It explicitly requires all member countries to protect personal data, freedom of cross-border data, and information flows for the first time.[33]

There are dual dispute settlement mechanisms under the TPP. One is an investor–state dispute settlement (ISDS) mechanism under Chapter 9, 'Investment'. Unlike the government-versus-government mechanism under the WTO, it enables private companies in one member country to bring a dispute against the government in the other member country. More specifically, the ISDS mechanism is potentially available for any company (investor) in one member country so long as it has an investment in the territory of the other member country.[34] If an investor believes a TPP member government has breached its investment obligations, and its attempts at resolution have failed, the investor can take the matter directly to arbitration against the member government.[35] The TTP further requires the arbitration proceedings to be open and transparent,[36] and to be conducted under rules administered by a respected international arbitration body selected by the parties in the dispute.[37]

The second dispute settlement mechanism is under Chapter 28 of the TPP, 'Dispute Settlement'. Like the scheme under the WTO, the dispute settlement chapter of the TPP governs disputes between governments of TPP members, and does not apply to disputes between private parties and governments.[38] Chapter 28 allows all TPP members to have disputes in relation to breach of TPP obligations to be resolved by arbitration.

These two dispute settlement mechanisms have different scopes of application. The ISDS mechanism applies exclusively to any potential breach of commitments under the investment chapter (Chapter 9) and applies only to disputes between private parties and governments (not to disputes between member governments).[39] The scope of the dispute settlement mechanism under Chapter 28 is much broader, and generally applies across the whole TPP Agreement;[40]

32 Y Tian, 'Current Issues of Cross-Border Personal Data Protection in the Context of Cloud Computing and Trans-Pacific Partnership Agreement: Join or Withdraw' (2016) 34 *Wisconsin International Law Journal* 367, 386.

33 Y Tian, 'Current Issues of Cross-Border Personal Data Protection in the Context of Cloud Computing and Trans-Pacific Partnership Agreement: Join or Withdraw' (2016) 34 *Wisconsin International Law Journal* 367, 386.

34 Y Tian, 'Current Issues of Cross-Border Personal Data Protection in the Context of Cloud Computing and Trans-Pacific Partnership Agreement: Join or Withdraw' (2016) 34 *Wisconsin International Law Journal* 367, 390. See also TPP, art 9.19.

35 Y Tian, 'Current Issues of Cross-Border Personal Data Protection in the Context of Cloud Computing and Trans-Pacific Partnership Agreement: Join or Withdraw' (2016) 34 *Wisconsin International Law Journal* 367, 390. See also TPP, art 9.1.

36 TPP, art 9.24.

37 See Y Tian, 'Current Issues of Cross-Border Personal Data Protection in the Context of Cloud Computing and Trans-Pacific Partnership Agreement: Join or Withdraw' (2016) 34 *Wisconsin International Law Journal* 367, 390–1. See also TPP, art 19.19.5.

38 TPP, Chapter 28: Dispute Settlement.

39 TPP, art 9.6.3 explicitly provides: 'A determination that there has been a breach of another provision of this Agreement, or of a separate international agreement, does not establish that there has been a breach of this Article.'

40 TPP, arts 28.7–28.9. If a TPP member considers that another member's 'actual or proposed measure' does not comply with any obligations under the TPP, the TPP member can directly rely on the dispute settlement scheme under Chapter 28 to resolve the dispute. See Y Tian, 'Current Issues of Cross-Border Personal Data Protection in the Context of Cloud Computing and Trans-Pacific Partnership Agreement: Join or Withdraw' (2016) 34 *Wisconsin International Law Journal* 367, 391.

however, it applies only to disputes between member governments (not to disputes between private parties).

(B) BILATERAL FREE TRADE AGREEMENTS

It is also noteworthy that both the US and China are important trade partners of Australia, and have FTAs with Australia. The Australia–US Free Trade Agreement (AUSFTA) was concluded in 2005, while the China–Australia FTA (ChAFTA) was entered into force on 20 December 2015.[41] Both have a significant impact on the Australian economy. For example, based on a statement made by the DFAT, the ChAFTA provides Australia with significant opportunities in China, which is Australia's largest export market for goods and services and a growing source of foreign investment, accounting for nearly a third of total Australian exports.[42]

Like the TRIPS Agreement under the WTO, in addition to promoting exports of Australian goods and services to China, the ChAFTA contains chapters on e-commerce and intellectual property.[43] Like the TPP, the ChAFTA also contains a dual dispute settlement system. Chapter 9 contains an ISDS mechanism by which Australian and Chinese investors can directly enforce obligations under the 'Investment' chapter.[44] The ISDS scheme 'only applies to a breach of either Party's obligation to provide non-discriminatory ("national") treatment to established investments of the other Party'.[45] It does not apply to a breach of commitments in another chapter.[46] Chapter 15 contains a dispute settlement mechanism that generally applies across the whole ChAFTA Agreement. The chapter applies to the settlement of disputes between the parties in relation to the implementation, interpretation and application of the ChAFTA, and wherever a party considers that the other party has breached its obligations under the ChAFTA.[47]

18.2.2.3 Other recent developments

(A) BREXIT

'Brexit' refers to the expected withdrawal of the United Kingdom from the European Union. In a referendum held on 23 June 2016, the majority (51.9 per cent) of British citizens voted to leave the EU.

In order to explore the possible implications of 'Brexit' for Australia's trade with the UK and the EU, the Australian Parliament issued in October 2017 an interim report entitled *Inquiry into Australia's Trade and Investment Relationship with the United Kingdom*.[48] On the one hand, it

---

41 See DFAT, *China–Australia Free Trade Agreement*: https://dfat.gov.au/.

42 See DFAT, *China–Australia Free Trade Agreement*: https://dfat.gov.au/. (See the statement made by DFAT at https://dfat.gov.au/trade/agreements/in-force/chafta/pages/australia-china-fta.aspx.)

43 See DFAT, *ChAFTA fact sheet: Electronic commerce, IP, competition policy and government procurement*: https://dfat.gov.au/.

44 See DFAT, *ChAFTA fact sheet: Investment and investor–state dispute settlement (ISDS)*: https://dfat.gov.au/.

45 See DFAT, *ChAFTA fact sheet: Investment and investor–state dispute settlement (ISDS)*: https://dfat.gov.au/.

46 Neither does ISDS apply to decisions made concerning investments that are subject to review under Australia's Foreign Investment Framework, such as decisions of the Foreign Investment Review Board (FIRB). See DFAT, *ChAFTA fact sheet: Investment and investor–state dispute settlement (ISDS)*: https://dfat.gov.au/. For more on FTAs signed by Australia that contain ISDS provisions, see https://dfat.gov.au/.

47 See ChAFTA, art 15.2, 'Scope of Application', in Chapter 15, 'Dispute Settlement'.

48 See Parliament of Australia, *Inquiry into Australia's Trade and Investment Relationship with the United Kingdom*, October 2017, [4.120]: https://www.aph.gov.au/.

found that the UK's decision to depart from the EU had brought great uncertainty and challenges, and may result in 'serious [and] complex consequences for the European region'.[49] On the other hand, it cautioned, these challenges should not be overstated. As the DFAT observed, the effect of Brexit on the Australian economy and its financial sector had been 'limited' so far, because Australia's trade links are focused mainly on Asia, and Australian banks have 'limited direct exposure to the UK and Europe'.[50] Moreover, Brexit will provide the UK with new trading opportunities, such as negotiating new FTAs with other countries, including Australia.[51]

(B) AUSTRALIA–UK FREE TRADE AGREEMENT

The UK is Australia's seventh-largest trading partner. In 2017/18, two-way trade between Australia and the UK was valued at A$27.8 billion. The UK is also the second-largest source of total foreign investment in Australia, valued at A$481.4 billion in 2017.[52]

Australia and the UK have been negotiating to establish a comprehensive FTA since September 2016. That negotiation process has been temporarily affected by Brexit. According to the EU rules, the UK shall not conduct FTA negotiations with any third-country parties until it formally exits the EU.[53] Nevertheless, both the UK and Australia have committed to ensure an expeditious start to FTA negotiations once the UK has left the EU.[54] It is believed that a new Australia–UK FTA may help to modernise the bilateral rules in relation to trade in goods, services and investment between the two countries, and in particular may promote the digital economy and innovation more effectively.[55]

18.2.3 Trade agreements and cross-border trade disputes

Multinational, regional and bilateral trade agreements would arguably increase the volumes of cross-border commercial transactions among member countries. With the increase in cross-border transactions, the potential for trade disputes would also arguably increase. These cross-border transactions and disputes all have 'foreign elements', and thus fit into the category of private international law. In order to effectively settle cross-border disputes, it is important to

49 See Parliament of Australia, *Inquiry into Australia's Trade and Investment Relationship with the United Kingdom*, October 2017, [4.120]: https://www.aph.gov.au/. (Chapter 4 of the report, on the possible implications of Brexit for Australia's trade with the UK and the EU, concludes with concerns by Australian governments and businesses that more restrictive conditions may apply for Australian workers and visa holders wishing to work in the UK.) See also Council of Financial Regulation, *Report on the Implications of Brexit*, https://treasury.gov.au/, where it is stated: 'The Australian economy may also be affected if the UK transition out of the EU is not orderly and uncertainty remains heightened for a significant period.'

50 See Parliament of Australia, *Inquiry into Australia's Trade and Investment Relationship with the United Kingdom*, October 2017: https://www.aph.gov.au/. (The inquiry lapsed when the Joint Standing Committee on Foreign Affairs, Defence and Trade ceased to exist at the dissolution of the House of Representatives on 11 April 2019.)

51 See Parliament of Australia, *Inquiry into Australia's Trade and Investment Relationship with the United Kingdom*, October 2017, [4.120]: https://www.aph.gov.au/.

52 See DFAT, *Prospective Australia–United Kingdom Free Trade Agreement*,: https://dfat.gov.au/.

53 See DFAT, *Prospective Australia–United Kingdom Free Trade Agreement*: https://dfat.gov.au/

54 See DFAT, *Prospective Australia–United Kingdom Free Trade Agreement*: https://dfat.gov.au/.

55 See DFAT, *Prospective Australia–United Kingdom Free Trade Agreement*: at https://dfat.gov.au/.

understand the basic private international law principles in relation to the choice of law, the choice of forum, and the applicability of relevant international treaties and customs.

18.3 Proper law of contract in commercial transactions

18.3.1 General principles

In relation to the determination of the proper law of contract, the general rule is that an Australian court has jurisdiction in actions on contract when the defendant:

- has been served in the jurisdiction; or
- being out of the jurisdiction, has been served in accordance with the rules of the court and the legislative provisions relating to service out of the jurisdiction; or
- has submitted to the jurisdiction.[56]

18.3.1.1 Rule 1: The place of forming the contract

An international contract of sale is usually governed by the law of the country where the contract is made. In *Bonython v Commonwealth*,[57] Lord Simonds defined the proper law governing a contract as 'the system of law by reference to which the contract was made or that with which the transaction has its closest and most real connection'.

18.3.1.2 Rule 2: Parties' intention (party autonomy)

A 'choice of law' clause (or governing law clause) is used to indicate the parties' intention (party autonomy[58]) in relation to which law they wish to apply to a dispute arising from their contract.[59] It permits the parties to designate the specific law, whether a country law or a state law, that will apply to the conclusion and interpretation of their contract, including the parties' rights and obligations under the contract.[60]

Courts usually respect a 'choice of law' clause in the contract so long as contracting parties have 'genuinely and validly (expressly or impliedly) selected a law to govern their contract'.[61]

56 C Turner and J Trone, 'International Sales Contracts', *Australian Commercial Law* (Thomson Reuters Australia, Sydney, 31st edn, 2016), 311.

57 [1951] AC 201, 219.

58 See also M R Baniassadi, 'Do Mandatory Rules of Public Law Limit Choice of Law in International Commercial Arbitration?' (1992) 10 *International Tax & Business Law* 59: 'The general principle of "party autonomy" allows contracting parties to choose the substantive law that will govern their contract.'

59 See 'Choice of Law (Governing Law) Boilerplate Clause' (Gibert + Tobin), 2: https://smartcounsel.gtlaw.com.au/.

60 See 'Choice of Law (Governing Law) Boilerplate Clause' (Gibert + Tobin), 2: https://smartcounsel.gtlaw.com.au/. Generally speaking, when interpreting a contract concluded in a foreign country, the law applicable is deemed to be the law that the parties intend should apply. This is termed the 'proper law' of the contract.

61 See 'Choice of Law (Governing Law) Boilerplate Clause' (Gibert + Tobin), 2: https://smartcounsel.gtlaw.com.au/.

In case no law has been chosen in a contract, or if that clause is invalid, a 'two-stage test' is often adopted by Australian courts to determine the governing law for the contract.[62]

First, the court will examine the parties' intentions on governing law, and examine 'whether the parties have expressly or impliedly intended that a certain law should apply to govern the contract'.[63] Parties do not have to explicitly select governing law; 'in the absence of an express choice of law, a court may infer a choice of law': *Akai*.[64]

Second, if the court cannot determine the parties' intention in relation to governing law, it will 'ascribe a "proper law of the contract" through an objective process', and determine 'the system of law with which the transaction has its closest and most real connection'.[65]

In the normal case, it is presumed that such law is the law of the place where the contract was concluded (as introduced above – Rule 1). However, circumstances may alter this. For example, where the contract is to be performed in a different country from that in which it is made, there is a presumption that the parties intend the law of the place of performance to apply. This was confirmed in *Merwin Pastoral Co Pty Ltd v Moolpa Pastoral Co Pty Ltd*.[66] The court held that the 'intention of the parties' will be judged on 'considerations such as the place of the making of the contract, the place of its fulfilment, and the place with which the transaction has the most real and *substantial connection*'.[67]

18.3.2 Apart from general principles

As has been discussed above, the concept of party autonomy means that parties to a contract are free to determine the governing law. However, there are certain important principles of international law that limit the freedom of the parties to select the governing law. Those principles are discussed below.

18.3.2.1 Rule 1: Application of the mandatory provision: Overriding forum statutes

A 'choice of law' clause (governing law clause) under a contract will not be enforceable if a statutory law expressly or impliedly applies.[68]

Some Australian laws are 'mandatory', and apply irrespective of anything to the contrary in a contract. In other words, the jurisdiction clause in a contract can be overridden by statute – for example, s 8 of *the Insurance Contracts Act 1984* (Cth) in *Akai Pty Ltd v The People's Insurance Co Ltd*.

62 See 'Choice of Law (Governing Law) Boilerplate Clause' (Gibert + Tobin), 2–3: https://smartcounsel.gtlaw.com.au/.

63 See 'Choice of Law (Governing Law) Boilerplate Clause' (Gibert + Tobin), 2–3: https://smartcounsel.gtlaw.com.au/.

64 See M Douglas and N Loadsman, 'The Impact of The Hague Principles on Choice of Law on Choice of Law in International Commercial Contracts' (2018) 19(1) *Melbourne Journal of International Law* 4. See also *Akai* (1996) 188 CLR 418, 441, per Toohey, Gaudron and Gummow JJ.

65 See M Douglas and N Loadsman, 'The Impact of The Hague Principles on Choice of Law on Choice of Law in International Commercial Contracts' (2018) 19(1) *Melbourne Journal of International Law* 4. See also *Marshall v Fleming* [2017] NSWSC 1107 [96].

66 (1933) 48 CLR 565.

67 (1933) 48 CLR 565, 580.

68 See 'Choice of Law (Governing Law) Boilerplate Clause' (Gibert + Tobin), 2: https://smartcounsel.gtlaw.com.au/.

AKAI PTY LTD *v* THE PEOPLE'S INSURANCE CO LTD (1996) 188 CLR 418

Fact: The People's insurance Company Ltd (PIC) is an insurer incorporated in Singapore. Akai is a company incorporated in NSW (but also a subsidiary of a Japanese company). Under a policy of insurance, PIC agreed to indemnify Akai for contain losses. Norman Ross Homeworks Pty Ltd owed money to Akai but went into liquidation. Clause 9 of the insurance policy provided: 'This policy shall be governed by the Laws of England. Any dispute arising from the policy shall be referred to the Courts of England.' This provision was a compromise agreed after negotiations. PIC wanted Singapore law to apply and disputes to be dealt with by Singapore courts. Akai wanted Australian law to apply and Australian courts to have jurisdiction.

Akai contended that the *Insurance Contracts Act 1984* (Cth) applied to the insurance contract. Section 8 of the Act provides that:

> (1) Subject to section 9, the application of this Act extends to contracts of insurance and proposed contracts of insurance the proper law of which is or would be the law of a State or the law of a Territory in which this Act applies or to which this Act extends.
>
> (2) For the purposes of subsection (1), where the *proper law of a contract* or proposed contract would, but for an express provision to the contrary included or to be included in the contract or in some other contract, *be the law of a State or of a Territory in which this Act applies* or to which this Act extends, then, notwithstanding that provision, *the proper law of the contract is the law of that State or Territory.*

Section 52 of the Act further states:

> Where a provision of a contract of insurance . . . purports to exclude, restrict or modify, or would, but for this subsection, have the effect of excluding, restricting or modifying, to the prejudice of a person other than the insurer, the operation of this Act, the provision is void.

Held: Section 8 of the Act should be read with s 52, which prohibits contracting out of the operation of the Act.

> . . . Taken together, ss 52 and 8 manifest a legislative intent not only that there should be no power to contract out of the provisions of the Act, but also that the regime established by the Act should be respected as regards contracts the proper law of which is, or but for selection of another law would be, that of a State or Territory. This defeats evasion of the legislative regime by the choice of some other body of law as the governing law of the contract . . . [at 433]
>
> . . . the State of New South Wales contained the system of law with which the contract of insurance comprised in the Policy had the closest and most real connection. Accordingly, s 8 of the Act operated to render it applicable to the Policy. [at 437]

Therefore, the applicable law was that of New South Wales, not that of England.

In addition to s 8 of the *Insurance Contracts Act 1984* (Cth) considered in the *Akai case,* the Australian Consumer Law (ACL) contains similar provisions, such as ss 64 and 67.

Section 64: Guarantees not to be excluded etc. by contract

(1) A term of a contract (including a term that is not set out in the contract but is incorporated in the contract by another term of the contract) is void to the extent that the term purports to exclude, restrict or modify, or has the effect of excluding, restricting or modifying:
  (a) the application of all or any of the provisions of this Division; or
  (b) the exercise of a right conferred by such a provision; or
  (c) any liability of a person for a failure to comply with a guarantee that applies under this Division to a supply of goods or services.

(2) A term of a contract is not taken, for the purposes of this section, to exclude, restrict or modify the application of a provision of this Division unless the term does so expressly or is inconsistent with the provision.

Section 67: Conflict of laws

If:

(a) the proper law of a contract for the supply of goods or services to a consumer would be the law of any part of Australia but for a term of the contract that provides otherwise; or

(b) a contract for the supply of goods or services to a consumer contains a term that purports to substitute, or has the effect of substituting, the following provisions for all or any of the provisions of this Division:
  (i) the provisions of the law of a country other than Australia;
  (ii) the provisions of the law of a State or a Territory;

the provisions of this Division apply in relation to the supply under the contract despite that term.

Put simply, according to s 67(b) of the ACL, in the event that a contract for the supply of goods or services to a consumer contains a term that implies to, or has the impact of, substituting the provisions of the foreign law for the ACL consumer guarantees, those provisions apply in spite of that term.[69]

The application of the mandatory provision was recently examined in *Australian Competition and Consumer Commission v Valve Corporation [No 3].*

AUSTRALIAN COMPETITION AND CONSUMER COMMISSION *v* VALVE CORPORATION [NO 3] (2016) 337 ALR 647

Fact: The Australian Competition and Consumer Commission (ACCC) sued Valve Corporation, a US software company, in the Australian Federal Court, alleging that Valve's refund policies and subscriber agreements for its Steam platform (cloud platform) had breached relevant provisions under the Australian Consumer Law.

69 J Saunders, 'Game Over', *InCompetition*, 8 April 2016: https://incompetition.com.au/.

Valve admitted that 'it has made available to Australian consumers online access to use video games through Steam Client pursuant to the terms of a Steam Subscriber Agreement (SSA)', but it denied that it carried on business in Australia.[70] Valve further claimed that the law of the SSA was the law of the State of Washington, and therefore 'the SSA is not a contract to which the ACL applies'.[71]

Valve's contract contained a provision on 'choice of law', and specified that the consumer acknowledged that 'this Agreement shall be deemed to have been made and executed in the State of Washington, and any dispute arising hereunder shall be resolved in accordance with the law of Washington'.[72]

Key issue: If the law which has the 'closest and most real connection' to the contract is the law of another country (in this case, the law of Washington State in the US), could the ACL still apply?

Held: The court held that Washington State law in the US was the proper law of the contract, rather than Australian law. But this did not affect the application to Valve of the provisions on consumer guarantees under the ACL.

The court found that s 67 did not limit the ACL consumer guarantees by limiting their application to situations where the Australian law was the closest and most real connection to the contract.[73] Under the Valve contract, the 'choice of law' clause was found to be, in the words of s 67(b), 'a term that purports to substitute, or has the effect of substituting' the consumer guarantees of the ACL.[74] Subsequently, the provisions of the ACL's consumer guarantees continued to apply.

The Full Court of the Federal Court of Australia dismissed an appeal by Valve Corporation.[75] In April 2018, the High Court of Australia also dismissed Valve's special leave to appeal application.[76]

Implications: The court's finding in relation to the jurisdiction issue arguably would have strong implications for all overseas-based suppliers providing goods and services to consumers in Australia, particularly for those engaged in e-commerce.

The court's decision indicated that s 67(b) includes not just a discrete substitute of Australian law provisions for discrete foreign law provisions, but where all the applicable law alleged to cover the contract was the law of a foreign country.[77] In other words, this case

70 Y Tian, 'Current Issues of Cross-Border Personal Data Protection in the Context of Cloud Computing and Trans-Pacific Partnership Agreement: Join or Withdraw' (2016) 34 *Wisconsin International Law Journal* 367, 382.

71 Y Tian, 'Current Issues of Cross-Border Personal Data Protection in the Context of Cloud Computing and Trans-Pacific Partnership Agreement: Join or Withdraw' (2016) 34 *Wisconsin International Law Journal* 367, 382.

72 *Australian Competition and Consumer Commission v Valve Corporation [No 3]* (2016) 337 ALR 647, [72].

73 J Saunders, 'Game Over', *InCompetition*, 8 April 2016: https://incompetition.com.au.

74 J Saunders, 'Game Over', *InCompetition*, 8 April 2016: https://incompetition.com.au/

75 *Valve Corporation v Australian Competition and Consumer Commission* (2017) 351 ALR 584.

76 *Valve Corporation v Australian Competition and Consumer Commission* [2018] HCASL 99.

77 J Saunders, 'Game Over', *InCompetition*, 8 April 2016: https://incompetition.com.au/.

clarified that the court's finding that the proper law of the contract as a whole was a foreign law alone would not be adequate to exclude the application of the provisions on consumer guarantees in the ACL.[78]

18.3.2.2 Rule 2: Contrary to public policy

A 'choice of law' clause will be invalid if it is conflict with public policy. Generally speaking, public policy may override the validity of a 'choice of law' clause in the following circumstances:

(a) where the clause is contrary to an express or implied prohibition under statutory law, such as consumer guarantees provisions under the ACL (as introduced in Rule 1 above);

(b) where the clause is not directly contrary to such a prohibition, but it is contrary to the 'policy of the law', which will be 'discerned from the scope and purpose of the particular statute or of the Constitution'.[79] For example, in *Akai* (at 447) it was held that the policy of the law and of the Constitution 'militated against enforcing the 'choice of law' clause';[80]

(c) where the clause would apply a foreign law that is in conflict with the court's notions of public policy. For example, in *Vita Food Products Inc v Unus Shipping Co Ltd*,[81] the court found that 'delivering the judgment of the Privy Council referred to there being no "reason for avoiding the choice on the ground of public policy"'.[82]

18.3.2.3 Rule 3: Lack of bona fides: *Golden Acres v Queensland Estates*

A 'choice of law' clause may also be invalid if the selection of the foreign law is not bona fide. In *Golden Acres Ltd v Queensland Estate Pty Ltd*,[83] for the first time the Australian court refused to accept the parties' express choice of the governing law of their contract.

GOLDEN ACRES LTD *v* QUEENSLAND ESTATES PTY LTD [1969] QD R 378

Fact: A contract for sale of real estate relating to sale on commission was made between a Queensland company and a company based in Hong Kong. The contract contains a 'choice

78 J Saunders, 'Game Over', *InCompetition*, 8 April 2016, n 10: https://incompetition.com.au/.

79 See 'Choice of Law (Governing Law) Boilerplate Clause' (Gibert + Tobin), 1: https://smartcounsel.gtlaw.com.au/.

80 See 'Choice of Law (Governing Law) Boilerplate Clause' (Gibert + Tobin), 1, n 5: https://smartcounsel.gtlaw.com.au/.

81 [1939] AC 277.

82 See also 'Choice of Law (Governing Law) Boilerplate Clause' (Gibert + Tobin), 1, n 6: https://smartcounsel.gtlaw.com.au/.

83 [1969] Qd R 378.

of law' clause, stating: 'For all purposes arising under this agreement, the same shall be deemed to be entered into in the colony of Hong Kong.'

Richardson summarised the case as follows: '[T]he latter was doing business in Queensland as a real estate agent, and the contract involved the sale of some Queensland land to, amongst others, persons from Hong Kong. Queensland statute law required that real estate agents be licensed and provided for maximum rates of commission chargeable by real estate agents. The Hong Kong Company had charged excessive commission and was unlicensed. It was considered that in order to circumvent the Queensland law the parties had made Hong Kong law the proper law of the contract.'[84] In other words, the arrangement made in the contract is specifically prohibited by the *Auctioneers, Real Estate Agents, Debt Collectors and Motor Dealers Act 1922* (Qld).

Held: The court held that their choice was not bona fide and that the law of Queensland was the proper law of the contract. 'I am satisfied that the attempted selection of this (Hong Kong) law was for no other purpose than to avoid the operation of the Queensland law. Under all the circumstances, I conclude that the purported selection of the Hong Kong law was not a bona fide selection' (Hoare J, at 385).

18.3.2.4 Rule 4: Other practical considerations: Choice of jurisdiction clause

'Choice of jurisdiction' clause refers to the clause that nominates the forum in which disputes arising in the contract should be litigated. A 'choice of law' clause should always be read together with a 'choice of jurisdiction' clause.[85] As Douglas and Loadsman noted, 'although choice of jurisdiction clauses are distinguishable from choice of law clauses, "policy" bases for refusing to give effect to each run in parallel, and are often dealt with together'.[86]

In the absence of a clear 'choice of law' clause, a 'choice of jurisdiction' clause alone may not be sufficicent to indicate an inferred choice of law, but it may be 'one of the factors' that the court will take into account when determining 'whether the parties intended the contract to be governed by the law of that forum'.[87]

Moreover, it is possible for the court to infer a choice of the law of the chosen court by referring to an exclusive foreign jurisdiction clause.[88] For example, in *Lewis Construction Co*

84 S M Richardson, 'International Contracts and the Choice of Law' (PhD Thesis), University of Canterbury (1988), 38: https://core.ac.uk/.

85 See 'Choice of Law (Governing Law) Boilerplate Clause' (Gibert + Tobin), 2: https://smartcounsel.gtlaw.com.au/.

86 See M Douglas and N Loadsman, 'The Impact of The Hague Principles on Choice of Law on Choice of Law in International Commercial Contracts' (2018) 19(1) *Melbourne Journal of International Law* 20, where it was stated: '[A] jurisdiction or arbitration agreement is not 'itself equivalent' to a choice of law. At a surface level, this is consistent with the principle emphasised by the High Court in *John Pfeiffer Pty Ltd v Rogerson* ("Pfeiffer"), that the issue of whether a court has jurisdiction is distinct from the issue of the applicable law.'

87 M Douglas and N Loadsman, 'The Impact of The Hague Principles on Choice of Law on Choice of Law in International Commercial Contracts' (2018) 19(1) *Melbourne Journal of International Law* 11.

88 Hague Conference on Private International Law, 'Commentary on the Principles on Choice of Law in International Commercial Contracts', in 'Principles on Choice of Law in International Commercial Contracts' (The Hague Conference on Private International Law Permanent Bureau, 2015), 45, [4.11]:

Pty Ltd v M Tichauer Société Anonyme, the agreement between contracting parties contains a provision as follows: '[I]n case of litigation the Commercial Court of Lyons is the only competent Court; even in the case of recourse on the guarantee or in case of multiple defendants.'[89] The court held that this clause was the 'determining factor' that indicated 'an implied selection of the law of France as the proper law of the contract'.[90]

18.4 International sale of goods

18.4.1 United Nations Convention on Contracts for the International Sale of Goods

18.4.1.1 What is CISG?

The *United Nations Convention on Contracts for the International Sale of Goods* (CISG, or 'Vienna Convention') is regarded as the 'most successful attempt to unify a broad area of commercial law at the international level'.[91] The Convention aims to reduce obstacles to international trade (but particularly those associated with 'choice of law' issues) by creating 'substantive rules governing the rights and obligations of parties to international sales contracts'.[92] As stated in the Preamble to CISG:[93]

> **Preamble**
>
> Being of the opinion that the adoption of uniform rules which govern contracts for the international sale of goods and take into account the different social, economic and legal systems would contribute to the removal of legal barriers in international trade and promote the development of international trade.

The CISG has attracted 89 contracting countries as of February 2019.[94] It covers more than two-thirds of international trade in goods, representing exceptional economic, geographic and cultural diversity.[95] It is noteworthy that some major economies, such as the UK and India, are not contracting countries of the CISG.[96]

https://assets.hcch.net/ ('Hague Principles Commentary'), cited by M Douglas and N Loadsman, 'The Impact of The Hague Principles on Choice of Law on Choice of Law in International Commercial Contracts', (2018) 19(1) *Melbourne Journal of International Law* 11.

89 *Lewis Construction Co Pty Ltd v M Tichauer Société Anonyme* [1966] VR 341, 346.

90 Hague Conference on Private International Law, 'Commentary on the Principles on Choice of Law in International Commercial Contracts', in 'Principles on Choice of Law in International Commercial Contracts' (The Hague Conference on Private International Law Permanent Bureau, 2015), 45, [4.11]: https://assets.hcch.net/ ('Hague Principles Commentary').

91 See H M Flechtner, 'Introductory Note – *United Nations Convention on Contracts for the International Sale of Goods* (United Nations Audiovisual Library of International Law).

92 See H M Flechtner, 'Introductory Note – *United Nations Convention on Contracts for the International Sale of Goods* (United Nations Audiovisual Library of International Law).

93 *United Nations Convention on Contracts for the International Sale of Goods.*

94 See *United Nations Treaty Collection*, Chapter X, 'International Trade and Development', 2019.

95 See H M Flechtner, 'Introductory Note', *United Nations Convention on Contracts for the International Sale of Goods* (United Nations Audiovisual Library of International Law).

96 For a list of existing members, see *United Nations Treaty Collection*, Chapter X, International Trade and Development, 2019.

18.4.1.2 Application of CISG

(A) APPLICABILITY

The CISG is given force of law in Australia through domestic legislation such as the *Sale of Goods (Vienna Convention) Act 1986* (NSW).

The CISG applies to international sales contracts between individuals or corporations if:

(a) both parties are located in Contracting States; or

(b) private international law leads to the application of the law of a Contracting State: art 1(1)(a) and (b).

Nevertheless, as permitted by the CISG (art 95), several contracting states have declared that they are not bound by the latter ground.

(B) MATTERS COVERED AND NOT COVERED

The CISG does not govern every issue that can arise from an international sales contract. The CISG governs only (a) the formation of the contract of sale, and (b) the rights and obligations of the seller and the buyer arising from such contract (art 4).

Article 2 of CISG explicitly states that the CISG does not apply to: goods bought for personal, family or household use; auction sales; sales by authority of law; sales of stocks, shares, investment securities, negotiable instruments or money; sales of ships, vessels, hovercraft or aircraft; and sales of electricity.

Moreover, it does not deal with 'the validity of the contract' or 'the effect which the contract may have on the property in the goods sold' (art 4). Neither does the CISG extend to the seller's liability for death or personal injury induced by the products (art 5).

(C) AUTONOMY OF THE PARTIES AND OPT-OUT CLAUSE

The autonomy of the contract parties to international sales contracts has been 'a fundamental theme of the CISG'.[97] According to arts 6 and 12 of the CISG, the eligible parties can, 'by agreement, derogate from virtually any CISG rule, or can exclude the applicability of the CISG entirely in favour of other law'.[98]

In order to exclude the application of the CISG, the opt-out provision in the contract must be explicit, and standard governing law provision is not enough. A sample opt-out clause can be: 'The United Nations Convention on the International Sale of Goods, and any local implementing legislation shall not apply to the Agreement.'

18.4.1.3 Formation of the contract

Articles 14–24 of the CISG concern formation of the contract. The elements of a contract under the CISG are different from those at common law. Agreement (offer and acceptance) and intention to be bound are elements of a contract under the CISG, but the consideration element is not (art 23).

97 See H M Flechtner, Introductory Note', *United Nations Convention on Contracts for the International Sale of Goods* (United Nations Audiovisual Library of International Law).

98 Article 6 explicitly stated that parties may exclude the application of the CISG or, subject to art 12, derogate from or vary the effect of any of its provisions.

(A) OFFER

In relation to criteria for an offer, an offer must be sufficiently definite and indicate an intention to be bound. That is, it must indicate the goods and expressly or implicitly fix or make provision for determining the quantity and the price (art 14). An offer becomes effective when it reaches the offeree.[99] The offer can be revoked before the offeree has dispatched an acceptance.[100] However, an offer cannot be revoked 'if it indicates, whether by stating a fixed time for acceptance or otherwise, that it is irrevocable' (art 16(2)(a)).

(B) ACCEPTANCE

Acceptance is a statement or other conduct by the offeree indicating assent to an offer (art 18(1)). The acceptance becomes effective when the indication of assent reaches the offeror. It is not effective if the assent does not reach the offeror within the time the offer has fixed, or within a reasonable time if no time is fixed (art 18(2)).

Silence or inactivity do not constitute acceptance (art 18(1)); however, in combination with other circumstances, silence may constitute acceptance (art 18(1)); for example, where a party voluntarily assumes the duty to respond, silence will constitute acceptance.

(C) REQUIREMENT AS TO FORM – WRITING

The CISG also includes a provision eliminating written-form requirements for international sales contracts within its scope. Contract does not need to be in 'writing'[101] and is not subject to any other requirement as to form (art 11).

However, the CISG authorises contracting states to reserve out of this provision, and a number have done so. In accordance with art 12, CISG provisions in relation to the formation of a contract of sale of goods will not apply whenever a party of the contract has its place of business in a state which has declared that these provisions are not to apply.[102]

18.4.1.4 General obligations of seller and buyer

Chapter II of the CISG contains detailed provisions on the seller's obligations (arts 31–52). Section III of Chapter II of the CISG contains detailed provisions on the buyer's remedies in relation to the delivery of conforming goods on time (arts 45–52). [103]

(A) SELLER'S CONFORMITY OBLIGATIONS UNDER THE CONTRACT (ARTS 35–36)

Article 35 of the CISG obligates the seller to ensure that the goods conform to the quantity, quality and description under contract, and are packaged appropriately (art 35(1)):

---

99 CISG, art 15(1). 'An offer . . . may be withdrawn if [it] reaches the offeree before or at the same time as the offer' (art 15(2)).

100 CISG, art 16(1).

101 Under the Convention, the term 'writing' includes a telegram or telex (art 13).

102 CISG, art 12 states: 'Any provision of article 11, article 29 or Part II of this Convention that allows a contract of sale or its modification or termination by agreement or any offer, acceptance or other indication of intention to be made in any form other than in writing does not apply where any party has his place of business in a Contracting State which has made a declaration under article 96 of this Convention. The parties may not derogate from or vary the effect of this article.'

103 B Stone, 'Contracts for the International Sale of Goods: The Convention and the Code' (2015) 23(3) *Michigan State International Law Review* 753.

Article 35

(1) The seller must deliver goods which are of the quantity, quality and description required by the contract and which are contained or packaged in the manner required by the contract.

(2) Except where the parties have agreed otherwise, the goods do not conform with the contract unless they:

 (a) are fit for purposes for which goods of the same description would ordinarily be used;

 (b) are fit for any particular purpose expressly or impliedly made known to the seller at the time of the conclusion of the contract, except where the circumstances show that the buyer did not rely, or it was unreasonable for him to rely, on the seller's skill and judgement;

 (c) possess the qualities of goods which the seller has held out to the buyer as a sample or model;

 (d) are contained or packaged in the manner usual for such goods or, where there is no such manner, in a manner adequate to preserve and protect the goods.

(3) The seller is not liable under subparagraphs (a) to (d) of the preceding paragraph for any lack of conformity of the goods if, at the time of the conclusion of the contract, the buyer knew or could not have been unaware of such lack of conformity.

The goods will not conform with the contract:

- if they fail to fit the purpose for which goods of the same description are ordinarily used;
- if they fail to fit the buyer's particular purpose, which was made known to the seller (either impliedly or expressly) when the contract was concluded;
- if their qualities are not the same as those of the samples or models which the seller has shown to buyers; or
- if they are packaged inappropriately (art 35(2)).[104]

However, the seller will not be liable if the buyer knew or should have known that the goods did not conform to the contract when the contact was concluded (art 35(3)).

Article 36

(1) The seller is liable in accordance with the contract and this Convention for any lack of conformity which exists at the time when the risk passes to the buyer, even though the lack of conformity becomes *apparent* only after that time.

(2) The seller is also liable for any lack of conformity which occurs after the time indicated in the preceding paragraph and which is due to a *breach* of any of his obligations, including a breach of any guarantee that for a period of time the goods will remain fit for their ordinary purpose or for some particular purpose or will retain specified qualities or characteristics.

104 See *Contracts for International Sale of Goods* (Law Teacher – The Law Essay Professionals, 2 February 2018): https://www.lawteacher.net/.

Article 36 (1) further obligates the seller to be liable for any non-conformity existing at the time when the risk passes to the buyer, even though the non-conformity becomes apparent at a later time. Article 36(2) obligates the seller to be liable for any non-conformity after the risk has passed to the buyer, and which is due to a breach of any of the seller's obligations, such as a breach of any guarantee.

(B) EXAMINATION OF GOODS (ART 38)

Article 38 (1) of the CISG obligates the buyer to examine the goods for non-conformity within the shortest period practicable in the circumstances. It is for the buyer to prove that they examined the goods within the shortest practicable time.

If the buyer fails to notify the seller of the nature of non-conformity within a reasonable time after discovery or within a reasonable period from the time when the non-conformity ought to have been discovered, the buyer will lose the right to rely on any non-conformity (art 39(1)).

If the buyer has a reasonable excuse for their failure to notify, the buyer may reduce the price or claim damages other than for loss of profit (art 44).

Nevertheless, unless a contractual guarantee provides otherwise, the buyer will lose the rights to rely on any non-conformity if they fail to notify the seller within two years of the date when the goods were delivered to the buyer.

(C) THIRD PARTY CLAIMS (ARTS 41–42)

Article 41

The seller must deliver goods which are free from any right or claim of a third party, unless the buyer agreed to take the goods subject to that right or claim. However, if such right or claim is based on industrial property or other intellectual property, the seller's obligation is governed by article 42.

Article 42

(1) The seller must deliver goods which are free from any right or claim of a third party based on industrial property or other intellectual property, of which at the time of the conclusion of the contract the seller knew or could not have been unaware, provided that the right or claim is based on industrial property or other intellectual property:
  (a) under the law of the State where the goods will be resold or otherwise used, if it was contemplated by the parties at the time of the conclusion of the contract that the goods would be resold or otherwise used in that State; or
  (b) in any other case, under the law of the State where the buyer has his place of business.

(2) The obligation of the seller under the preceding paragraph does not extend to cases where:
  (a) at the time of the conclusion of the contract the buyer knew or could not have been unaware of the right or claim; or
  (b) the right or claim results from the seller's compliance with technical drawings, designs, formulae or other such specifications furnished by the buyer.

It is clear that, unless the buyer agreed to take the goods subject to that right or claim, the seller must deliver goods that are free from any right or claim of a third party (art 41). The seller must ensure that the goods delivered are free from any right or claim of a third party based on industrial property or other intellectual property (IP) (art 42(1)). The CISG also provides exemptions for the third party claim obligation of the seller. The obligation to deliver goods free from third party IP claims does not apply if the buyer knew or could not have been unaware of the right or claim at the time the contract was concluded (art 42(2)(a)).[105]

The obligation will also not apply if the claim results from the seller's compliance with technical drawings, designs, formulae or other such specifications furnished by the buyer (art 42(2)(b)).

18.4.1.5 Performance of the contract

(A) PAYMENT OF THE PRICE

The buyer is obligated to pay the price for the goods, and to take delivery of them as required by the contract and the CISG (art 53).

The buyer's obligation to pay the price includes taking any steps required under the contract or by any law to enable payment to be made (art 54).

DOWNS INVESTMENTS PTY LTD *v* PERWAJA STEEL SDN BHD [2000] QSC 421

Fact: The contract provided that the buyer would pay for the goods by letter of credit. The buyer did not obtain the letter of credit.

Held: The Queensland Supreme Court held that the obligation to pay for the goods included the taking of steps required to enable payment to be made. Therefore, the failure to obtain the letter of credit constituted a breach of art 54.

(B) DELIVERY

The seller must deliver the goods, hand over any documents relating to them and transfer the property in the goods, as required by the contract and the CISG (art 30).

In relation to the place for delivery, where the buyer has not specified any other particular place, the delivery is usually accomplished by 'handing the goods over to the first carrier for transmission to the buyer' (art 31(a)).

In relation to the time for delivery, art 33 obligates the seller to deliver the goods:

(a) on the date fixed by the contract; or
(b) within any period of time specified by the contract, unless the circumstances indicate that the buyer is to choose the date; or
(c) within a reasonable time after the conclusion of the contract.

Article 34 further provides that if the seller is bound to hand over documents relating to the goods, they must hand them over at the time and place and in the form required by the contract.

105 Further, the CISG provides that the buyer will lose the right under art 41 or art 42 if they have not notified the seller of the specific nature of the right or claim of the third party within a reasonable time after they have become aware, or ought to have become aware, of the right or claim (art 43).

(C) PASSING OF RISK

As introduced above, art 36(1) provides: 'The seller is liable in accordance with the contract and this Convention for any lack of conformity which exists at the time when the risk passes to the buyer.'

Article 66 further provides that loss or damage to the goods after the risk has passed to the buyer does not discharge the buyer's obligation to pay for the goods, unless the loss or damage is caused by the seller's act or omission.

The CISG also provides detailed provisions (arts 67–70) for determining when the risk of loss or damage will pass to the buyer:

Risk when the contract involves carriage

Under the CISG, if the contract of sale involves carriage of the goods, the risk will pass to the buyer 'when the goods are handed over to the first carrier for transmission to the buyer' (art 67(1)). Nevertheless, the risk will not pass to the buyer until the goods are clearly identified to the contract, 'whether by markings on the goods, by shipping documents, by notice given to the buyer or otherwise' (art 67(2)).

Sale of goods during transit

Article 68 of the CISG governs contracts in which goods are sold while in the possession of a 'carrier'. As a general rule under the CISG, the risk in relation to goods sold in transit passes to the buyer *from the time* that the contract was made (art 68). Exceptionally, if the circumstances so indicate, the risk passes to the buyer from the time the goods were handed over to the carrier who issued the documents embodying the carriage contract.

General residual rules on risk

Article 69 of the CISG governs cases not within (i) art 67 (cases where seller hands goods over to a 'carrier' for transmission to the buyer, and (ii) art 68 (cases where goods are sold while in possession of a 'carrier').

In cases not within arts 67 and 68, the risk passes to the buyer when the buyer takes over the goods. If the buyer does not take over the goods in due time, the risk passes to the buyer from the time when the goods are placed at their disposal, and the buyer commits a breach of contract by failing to take delivery (art 69(1)).

Risk when seller is in breach

Article 70 of CISG deals with the question whether a fundamental breach of contract conducted by the seller will prevent the risk from passing to the buyer.[106] Article 70 explicitly provides that '[i]f the seller has committed a fundamental breach of contract, articles 67, 68 and 69 do not impair the remedies available to the buyer on account of the breach'.

For example, art 67(1) provides that the risk of loss will pass to the buyer once the goods have been passed to 'the first carrier for transmission to the buyer'. We assume that the goods delivered to the carrier by the seller are seriously defective and constitute a fundamental breach of the contract. The buyer will then obtain the right to reject the

106 See B Stone, 'Contracts for the International Sale of Goods: The Convention and the Code' (2015) 23(3) *Michigan State International Law Review* 753, 805.

goods (the right to avoid the contract). While in transit, the goods are damaged. Article 70 will ensure that the buyer will not lose such a right of rejection 'because of damage to the goods during transit'.[107]

(D) PRESERVATION OF THE GOODS

The CISG imposes on both parties the duty to preserve any goods in their possession belonging to the other party.

If the buyer delays in taking delivery of the goods, or if they fail to pay the price, the seller must take reasonable steps to preserve the goods. The seller is entitled to retain the goods until the seller is reimbursed by the buyer for reasonable expenses (art 85). For example, if the buyer delays in taking delivery of a quantity of ice cream, the seller must take reasonable steps to preserve the ice cream, such as by storing it in an ice-cream warehouse. The buyer needs to reimburse the seller's reasonable preservation expenses for renting or using the ice-cream warehouse.

If the buyer has received the goods and intends to exercise a right to reject them, the buyer must take reasonable steps to preserve them. Again, the buyer is entitled to retain the goods until they are reimbursed by the seller for reasonable expenses (art 86(1)). For example, a buyer who ordered green tea-flavoured ice cream, but received coffee-flavoured ice cream and intends to exercise a right to reject the goods, must take reasonable steps to preserve the ice cream.

(E) ADDITIONAL TIME TO PERFORM (NACHFRIST NOTICE)

In civil law systems, the concept of a *nachfrist* notice allows a buyer or seller to establish *a further period for performance* after the performance time established by the contract has expired. A similar concept is also applied by the CISG in several provisions (arts 47, 48, 63).[108]

On the one hand, the CISG provides that the buyer may fix an 'additional period of time' of reasonable length for performance by the seller of their obligations (art 47(1)). Unless the buyer has obtained a notice from the seller that the seller will not execute within such a set period, the buyer may not resort to any remedy for violation of contract during that period. However, the buyer still retains the right to claim damages for performance delay by the seller (art 47(2)).

Even if the delivery date has passed, the seller may, at their own expense, remedy any failure to fulfil their obligations if they can do so without undue delay and without unreasonable inconvenience to the buyer. Again, the buyer still retains the right to claim damages (art 48(1)).

If the seller requests the buyer to indicate whether performance will be accepted, but the buyer fails to do so within a reasonable time, the seller may perform within the time indicated in the request. The buyer may not resort to any remedy that is inconsistent with performance by the seller during that period of time (art 48(2)).

On the other hand, the CISG also allows the seller to fix an additional period of time of reasonable length for performance by the buyer of their obligations (art 63(1)). Unless the

107 See B Stone, 'Contracts for the International Sale of Goods: The Convention and the Code' (2015) 23(3) *Michigan State International Law Review* 753, 805.

108 C Turner and J Trone, 'International Sales Contracts', *Australian Commercial Law* (Thomson Reuters Australia, Sydney, 31st edn, 2016), 304.

seller has obtained a notice from the buyer that the buyer will not act within such a set period, the seller may not have recourse during that period to any remedy for breaching contract. Once again, the seller *retains the rights* to claim damages for performance delay of the buyer (art 63(2)).

(F) EXEMPTION FROM PERFORMANCE

A party shall not be liable for a failure to fulfil any of its obligations if the party demonstrated that (i) the failure was due to an impediment beyond its control, and that (ii) at the moment of the conclusion of the contract, the party could not reasonably be assumed to have taken the impediment into account or to have avoided or overcome it, or its consequences (art 79(1)).

If the party's failure to perform obligations is due to the failure by a third party engaged to perform the contract, that party is exempt from liability only if both of the parties fulfil the conditions for exemption under art 79(1) (introduced above) (art 79(2)). The exemption has effect so long as the impediment exists (art 79(3)).

The party that fails to perform (the defaulting party) must notify the other party of the impediment, and of its impact on its capacity to perform. If the notice is not obtained by the other party within a reasonable time after the defaulting party has known or ought to have known of the impediment, the defaulting party shall be responsible for damages arising from the failure to receive the notification (art 79(4)).

(G) ANTICIPATORY BREACH

The CISG contains special clauses for the scenario where it becomes apparent, before the date on which performance is due, that one party will not perform a substantial part of the obligations of the party or commit a fundamental breach of the contract.

Under the CISG, a party to a contract may *suspend* the performance of their obligations if, after the conclusion of the contract, it becomes apparent that the other party will not perform a substantial part of their obligations due to (a) a serious deficiency in their ability to perform, or in their creditworthiness; or (b) their conduct in preparing to perform or in performing the contract (art 71(1)).

A party that suspends performance is obliged to notify the other party instantly of the suspension, and to continue performing if the other party gives sufficient assurance in relation to performance (art 71(3)).

It is notable that a distinction is drawn between (1) those cases where the other party may *suspend* its own performance of the contract, but the contract remains in existence for future events; and (2) those cases where the other party is entitled to declare the contract *avoided*.[109]

(H) FUNDAMENTAL BREACH

The meaning of a 'fundamental breach' of contract has been set out in an Explanatory Note by the UNCITRAL Secretariat on the *United Nations Convention on Contracts for the International Sale of Goods*, as follows:

109 See also D Saidov, *The Law of Damages in International Sales: The CISG and other International Instruments* (Hart Publishing, Oxford and Portland, OR, 2008).

> For a breach of contract to be fundamental, it must result in such detriment to the other party as substantially to deprive him of what he is entitled to expect under the contract, unless the result was neither foreseen by the party in breach nor foreseeable by a reasonable person of the same kind in the same circumstances.[110]

However, a breach of contract committed by a party will not constitute a fundamental breach if the party in breach 'did not foresee, and a reasonable person of the same kind in the same circumstances would not have foreseen such a result' (art 25). Non-payment is a common form of fundamental breach.

DOWNS INVESTMENTS PTY LTD (IN LIQ) v PERWAJA STEEL SDN BHD [2002] 2 QD R 464

Fact: The contract provided that the buyer would pay for the goods by letter of credit. The buyer did not obtain the letter of credit.

Held: The Queensland Court of Appeal held that the failure to obtain the letter of credit amounted to a fundamental breach. This failure deprived the seller of the benefit of the contract, entitling them to rescind. The buyers had no intention of meeting their obligations under the contract, which was itself a fundamental breach.

18.4.1.6 Remedies for breach

Generally speaking, under the CISG the provisions on a buyer's remedies for a seller's breach are listed in with the provisions on a seller's obligations, while the provisions on a seller's remedies for a buyer's breach are listed in connection with the provisions on a buyer's obligations.[111] This structure makes it easier for traders to use and understand the operation of the CISG.[112]

The general pattern of remedies for the buyer and the seller is the same. If all the listed conditions are met, the aggrieved party may '(a) require performance of the other party's obligations, (b) claim damages, or (c) avoid the contract'.[113]

(A) BUYER'S REMEDIES FOR BREACH BY THE SELLER

If the seller fails to perform an obligation, the buyer may exercise their rights provided by arts 46–52 of the CISG, claim damages as provided in arts 74–77, and make a declaration of avoidance of the contract (arts 81–83), by:

110 'II. Explanatory Note by the UNCITRAL Secretariat', *United Nations Convention on Contracts for the International Sale of Goods*, 39: https://www.uncitral.org/.

111 'II. Explanatory Note by the UNCITRAL Secretariat', *United Nations Convention on Contracts for the International Sale of Goods*, 39: https://www.uncitral.org/.

112 'II. Explanatory Note by the UNCITRAL Secretariat', *United Nations Convention on Contracts for the International Sale of Goods*, 39: https://www.uncitral.org/.

113 'II. Explanatory Note by the UNCITRAL Secretariat', *United Nations Convention on Contracts for the International Sale of Goods*, 39: https://www.uncitral.org/.

- requiring performance of the seller's obligations (unless other remedies are sought): art 46(1);
- requesting substitute goods: art 46(2);
- repairing the non-conformity: art 46(3);
- giving a *nachfrist* extension: art 47;
- declaring the contract avoided: arts 49 and 81; or
- reducing the price: art 50; and
- claiming damages: arts 45 and 74–76.

(B) SELLER'S REMEDIES FOR BREACH BY BUYER

By virtue of art 61 of the CISG, the failure to perform any obligation under the contract of sale may 'justify claim for damages, independent of the existence of a fault of the buyer'.[114] More specifically, if the buyer fails to perform an obligation, the seller may exercise the rights provided by arts 62–65, claim damages as provided in arts 74–77, and make a declaration of avoidance of contract (arts 81–83) by:[115]

- requiring performance: art 62;[116]
- giving a *nachfrist* extension: art 63;
- declaring the contract avoided: arts 64 and 81(1); or
- making a necessary specification for the buyer: art 65(1); and
- claiming damages: art 61(1).

In relation to avoidance of the contract, the CISG does not provide for automatic avoidance. Therefore, a contract is avoided only after a party makes a declaration to that effect. The direct legal consequence of avoidance is to release both parties from their contractual obligations, subject to the payment of damages.[117] However, avoidance has no effect upon contractual provisions regarding dispute settlement or regarding rights and obligations upon avoidance (art 81(1)).

In relation to claiming damages, damages for breach of contract by one party under the CISG are the amount of the loss suffered by the other party as a result of the breach, which includes lost profits. But such damages may not exceed the loss that the party in breach foresaw or ought to have foreseen at the time the contract was entered into as a possible consequence of the breach (art 74).

114 F Bortolotti, 'Remedies Available to the Seller and Seller's Right to Require Specific Performance (Articles 61, 62 and 28)' (2005–06) 25 *Journal of Law and Commerce* 335.

115 F Bortolotti, 'Remedies Available to the Seller and Seller's Right to Require Specific Performance (Articles 61, 62 and 28)' (2005–06) 25 *Journal of Law and Commerce* 335.

116 Article 62 of the CISG expressly recognises the seller's right to require the buyer to pay the price, take delivery or perform other obligations, unless the seller has resorted to a remedy that is inconsistent with this requirement. See also F Bortolotti, 'Remedies Available to the Seller and Seller's Right to Require Specific Performance (Articles 61, 62 and 28)' (2005–06) 25 *Journal of Law and Commerce* 335, 337.

117 C Turner and J Trone, 'International Sales Contracts', *Australian Commercial Law* (Thomson Reuters Australia, Sydney, 31st edn, 2016), 304, 307.

18.4.2 Incoterms

Incoterms rules are the world's essential terms of trade for the sale of goods, first created by the International Chamber of Commerce (ICC) in 1936. They provide specific guidance to individuals that participate in international trade on a daily basis.[118] They are uniform trade terms that define the responsibilities of sellers and buyers for the delivery of goods under sales contracts for domestic and international trade.

Incoterms rules cover a range of issues, including: when delivery takes place; when risk passes; who is obliged to arrange and pay for insurance; responsibility for customs clearance on import and export; and responsibility for arranging and paying for transport. Incoterms do not cover: determination of ownership or transfer title to the goods; payment terms; service contracts; contractual rights or obligations (except for delivery) or breach of contract remedies; protection of parties from their own risk or loss; and details of the transfer, transport and delivery of the goods.[119]

Incoterms help traders in different countries to understand one another because they have standard agreed meanings that apply to all transactions where they are used. Unlike the CISG, Incoterms rules do not have statutory force since the rules are developed by the ICC, and there is no governing treaty on them. They have binding legal force only when parties expressly refer to them in their contract.

Incoterms are subject to periodic revision – every ten years. The second set of Incoterms was published in 2010 to replace Incoterms® 2000, and came into effect from 1 January 2011. The latest set of Incoterms was published in late 2019, and entered into force on 1 January 2020. Since Incoterms® 2020 came into effect only recently, most ongoing agreements are still under Incoterms® 2010 and it is therefore important to understand the operations of Incoterms® 2010.

More specifically, ICC provides a summary of the 11 rules from the Incoterms® 2010 edition,[120] divided into two groups. One group contains seven rules for any mode or modes of transport. The definitions of these are as follows:[121]

1. EXW (Ex Works) means that the seller delivers when they place the goods at the disposal of the buyer at the seller's premises or at another named place (ie works, factory, warehouse, etc). The seller does not need to load the goods on any collecting vehicle, nor do they need to clear the goods for export where such clearance is applicable.
2. FCA (Free Carrier) means that the seller delivers the goods to the carrier or another person nominated by the buyer at the seller's premises or another named place. The parties are well advised to specify as clearly as possible the point within the named place of delivery, as the risk passes to the buyer at that point. The seller may be responsible for clearing the

118 ICC, Incoterms® Rules 2020: *ICC Official Rules for the Interpretation of Trade Terms*: https://iccwbo.org/.

119 See ICC, Incoterms® Rules 2010, *ICC Official Rules for the Interpretation of Trade Terms*: https://iccwbo.org/.

120 See ICC, Incoterms® Rules 2010, *ICC Official Rules for the Interpretation of Trade Terms*, where it is stated: 'These should be read in the context of the full official text of the rules, which can be obtained from the ICC Store': https://iccwbo.org/.

121 https://iccwbo.org/.

goods for export (filing the electronic export information, or EEI). FCA is more realistic than EXW, because it includes loading at pick-up, which is commonly expected, and sellers are more concerned about export violations.[122]

3. CPT (Carriage Paid to) means that the seller delivers the goods to the carrier or another person nominated by the seller at an agreed place (if any such place is agreed between the parties), and that the seller must contract for and pay the costs of carriage necessary to bring the goods to the named place of destination.
4. CIP (Carriage and Insurance Paid to) means that the seller delivers the goods to the carrier, or another person nominated by the seller, at an agreed place (if any such place is agreed between the parties) and that the seller must contract for and pay the costs of carriage necessary to bring the goods to the named place of destination. The seller also contracts for insurance cover against the buyer's risk of loss of or damage to the goods during the carriage. The buyer should note that under CIP the seller is required to obtain insurance only on minimum cover. Should the buyer wish to have more insurance protection, they will need either to agree as much expressly with the seller or to make their own extra insurance arrangements.
5. DAT (Delivered at Terminal) means that the seller delivers when the goods, once unloaded from the arriving means of transport, are placed at the disposal of the buyer at a named terminal at the named port or place of destination. 'Terminal' includes a place, whether covered or not, such as a quay, warehouse, container yard or road, rail or air cargo terminal. The seller bears all risks involved in bringing the goods to and unloading them at the terminal at the named port or place of destination. DAT replaced DES (Delivered Ex Ship) and DEQ (Delivered Ex Quay) under Incoterms® 2000.
6. DAP (Delivered at Place) means that the seller delivers when the goods are placed at the disposal of the buyer on the arriving means of transport ready for unloading at the named place of destination. The seller bears all risks involved in bringing the goods to the named place. DAP replaced DAF (Delivered At Frontier) and DDU (Delivered Duty Unpaid) under Incoterms® 2000.[123]
7. DDP (Delivered Duty Paid) means that the seller delivers the goods when the goods are placed at the disposal of the buyer, cleared for import on the arriving means of transport ready for unloading at the named place of destination. The seller bears all the costs and risks involved in bringing the goods to the place of destination. They have an obligation to clear the goods not only for export but also for import, to pay any duty for both export and import, and to carry out all customs formalities.

The second group contains four rules for sea and inland waterway transport.[124]

122 See ICC, Incoterms® Rules 2010, *ICC Official Rules for the Interpretation of Trade Terms*: https://iccwbo.org/.

123 See ICC, Incoterms® Rules 2010, *ICC Official Rules for the Interpretation of Trade Terms*: https://iccwbo.org/.

124 See ICC, Incoterms® Rules 2010, *ICC Official Rules for the Interpretation of Trade Terms*: https://iccwbo.org/.

1. FAS (Free Alongside Ship) means that the seller delivers when the goods are placed alongside the vessel (eg on a quay or a barge) nominated by the buyer at the named port of shipment. The risk of loss of or damage to the goods passes when the goods are alongside the ship, and the buyer bears all costs from that moment onwards.
2. FOB (Free on Board) means that the seller delivers the goods on board the vessel nominated by the buyer at the named port of shipment or procures the goods already so delivered. The risk of loss of or damage to the goods passes when the goods are on board the vessel, and the buyer bears all costs from that moment onwards.
3. CFR (Cost and Freight) means that the seller delivers the goods on board the vessel or procures the goods already so delivered. The risk of loss of or damage to the goods passes when the goods are on board the vessel. The seller must contract for and pay the costs and freight necessary to bring the goods to the named port of destination.
4. CIF (Cost, Insurance and Freight) means that the seller delivers the goods on board the vessel or procures the goods already so delivered. The risk of loss of or damage to the goods passes when the goods are on board the vessel. The seller must contract for and pay the costs and freight necessary to bring the goods to the named port of destination. The seller also contracts for insurance cover against the buyer's risk of loss of or damage to the goods during the carriage. The buyer should note that under CIF the seller is required to obtain insurance only on minimum cover. Should the buyer wish to have more insurance protection, they will need either to agree as much expressly with the seller or to make their own extra insurance arrangements.

18.4.2.1 Comparison of Incoterms® 2000 and Incoterms® 2010

As introduced above, Incoterms® 2000 are an older version of the rules and have been superseded by Incoterms® 2010. Incoterms® 2010 were introduced in response to concerns surrounding global terrorism. They reflect changes in international shipping practices, especially increased security measures.

One of main concerns in relation to the application of Incoterms is that the parties may select the wrong term.[125] In order to facilitate the application of Incoterms® 2010, the ICC provides detailed *Guidance Notes* (including diagrams) on use of the rules.

The principal changes to the 2000 version are outlined below.

(A) RECLASSIFICATION OF RULES

The Incoterms® 2000 rules were divided into four groups:

- Group E: Departure terms, including EXW;
- Group F: Main carriage unpaid (buyer pays), including FCA, FAS and FOB;
- Group C: Main carriage paid (seller pays), including DFR, CIF and CPT; and
- Group D: Arrival terms, including DAF, DES, DEQ, DDU and DDP.

The Incoterms® 2010 rules have been divided into two groups:

125 See S Shepherd and T Graham, 'New Incoterms 2010: A Summary of the Principal Changes to Incoterms 2000': www.mondaq.com/uk/.

- seven rules associated with any mode or modes of transport, including no maritime transport and partial maritime transport; and
- four rules for sea and inland waterway transport only.[126]

(B) 'SHIP'S RAIL' VERSUS 'ON BOARD'

In relation to FOB, CFR and CIF, all reference to 'over the ship's rail' (under Incoterms® 2000) as the delivery point has been omitted, and replaced with the goods being delivered when they are 'on board the vessel'.[127]

(C) SCOPE OF APPLICATIONS

The Incoterms® 2010 rules are suitable for both international and domestic transactions. This represents a fundamental change from the Incoterms® 2000 rules. The Incoterms have traditionally been used for international sales contracts only. The Incoterms® 2010 rules now formally recognise that they can be used for both domestic and international sales contracts.[128]

(D) REPLACEMENT OF RULES

Incoterms® 2000's 13 rules have been reduced to 11 rules in Incoterms® 2010. As mentioned above, this has been achieved by replacing DEQ, DAF, DES and DDU with two new rules: DAT (Delivered at Terminal) and DAP (Delivered at Place).[129] As the ICC has summarised, under both new rules, delivery of goods occurs at a named distinction: 'in DAT, at the buyer's disposal unloaded from the arriving vehicle (as under the former DEQ rule); in DAP, likewise at the buyer's disposal, but ready for unloading (as under the former DAF, DES and DDU rules)'.[130] The new rules make DES and DEQ under the Incoterms® 2000 rules unnecessary. Under DAT, the named terminal in DAT could be in a port, and DAT can therefore safely be used to replace the Incoterms® 2000 rule's DEQ. Likewise, under DAP, the arriving 'vehicle' could be a ship and the named place of destination could be a port; DAP can therefore be safely used to replace DES (Delivered Ex Ship) under the Incoterms® 2000 rule.[131] These changes would arguably make Incoterm rules more concise and user-friendly.

(E) INSURANCE COVER AND SECURITY-RELATED CLEARANCES

The Incoterms® 2010 rules take into account the revision of the Institute Cargo Clauses, and expressly include information duties relating to insurance.[132] They also allocate obligations

126 Seven rules associated with all modes of transport: EXW, FCA, CPT, CIP, DAT, DAP and DDP; four rules for maritime transport and inland waterway transport: FAS, FOB, CFR and CIF. See ICC, Incoterms® Rules 2010, *ICC Official Rules for the Interpretation of Trade Terms*: https://iccwbo.org/.

127 See ICC, Incoterms® Rules 2010, *ICC Official Rules for the Interpretation of Trade Terms*: https://iccwbo.org/.

128 See ICC, Incoterms® Rules 2010, *ICC Official Rules for the Interpretation of Trade Terms*: https://iccwbo.org/.

129 See ICC, Incoterms® Rules 2010, *ICC Official Rules for the Interpretation of Trade Terms*: https://iccwbo.org/.

130 See ICC, Incoterms® Rules 2010, *ICC Official Rules for the Interpretation of Trade Terms*: https://iccwbo.org/.

131 See ICC, Incoterms® Rules 2010, *ICC Official Rules for the Interpretation of Trade Terms*: https://iccwbo.org/.

132 See ICC, Incoterms® Rules 2010, *ICC Official Rules for the Interpretation of Trade Terms*, [6]: https://iccwbo.org/. See also arts A3/B3 of the Incoterms® 2010 rules, which deal with contracts of carriage and insurance.

between the buyer and seller to obtain, or assist in obtaining, security-related clearances in relation to the goods in question, such as 'chain-if-custody information'.[133]

(F) TERMINAL HANDLING CHARGES

Under certain Incoterms 2000® rules (eg CIF/CFR), the buyer may potentially have to pay for the same service twice: 'once to the seller as part of the total selling price and once independently to the carrier or the terminal operator'.[134] In order to avoid confusion in relation to which party shall pay for the terminal handling charges under CPT, CIP, CFR, CIF, DAT, DAP and DDP, A6/B6 of these terms explicitly state the seller's and buyer's obligations to pay at different stages of the transaction.[135]

(G) STRING SALES

Unlike the sale of manufactured goods, in the sale of commodities, cargoes are often sold many times during transit through a string of sale contracts (string sales).[136] Although many sellers are involved in string sales, only the first seller is responsible for shipping the goods. Any seller in the middle of the string sales (except the first seller) will not have responsibility to 'ship' the goods, since the goods have already been shipped by the first seller in the string.[137] Therefore, any seller in the middle of the string sales has an obligation towards its buyer not to 'ship' the goods, but only to 'procure' goods that have been shipped.[138] The Incoterms® 2010 rules have been amended in order to reflect this. As an alternative to the obligation to 'ship goods', the obligation to 'procure goods shipped' has been incorporated into the relevant terms, FAS or FOB, which are suitable for a string sale.[139]

(H) DOCUMENTATION: HARD COPIES AND ELECTRONIC VERSIONS

The Incoterm 2000 rules have specified those documents that can be replaced by electronic data interchange (EDI) messages. The Incoterms® 2010 rules have extended the scope of application of electronic communication by 'giv[ing] electronic means of communication the same effect as paper communication, as long as the parties so agree or where customary'.[140]

---

133 See ICC, Incoterms® Rules 2010, *ICC Official Rules for the Interpretation of Trade Terms*, [7]: https://iccwbo.org/. See also arts A2/B2 and A10/B10 of the Incoterms® 2010 rules.

134 See ICC, Incoterms® Rules 2010, *ICC Official Rules for the Interpretation of Trade Terms*, [8]: https://iccwbo.org/.

135 J Mo, *International Commercial Law* (LexisNexis Butterworths Australia, Sydney, 3rd edn, 2013), 11.

136 See ICC, Incoterms® Rules 2010, *ICC Official Rules for the Interpretation of Trade Terms* [9]: https://iccwbo.org/.

137 See ICC, Incoterms® Rules 2010, *ICC Official Rules for the Interpretation of Trade Terms* [9]: https://iccwbo.org/.

138 See ICC, Incoterms® Rules 2010, *ICC Official Rules for the Interpretation of Trade Terms* [9]: https://iccwbo.org/.

139 See ICC, Incoterms® Rules 2010, *ICC Official Rules for the Interpretation of Trade Terms* [9]: https://iccwbo.org/. See also J Mo, *International Commercial Law* (LexisNexis Butterworths Australia, Sydney, 3rd edn, 2013), 11.

140 See ICC, Incoterms® Rules 2010, *ICC Official Rules for the Interpretation of Trade Terms* [5], where it is stated: 'This formulation facilitates the evolution of new electronic procedures throughout the lifetime of the Incoterms® 2010 rules': https://iccwbo.org/. See also arts A1/B1 of the Incoterms® 2010 rules.

(I) APPLICATION OF INCOTERMS® 2010

If parties wish to adopt the Incoterms® 2010 rules in their sale contracts, they must explicitly state this in the contract. In order to differentiate the use of Incoterms® 2010 from the use of Incoterms® 2000, it is recommended that the expression 'Incoterms® 2010' is used as postfix when any of the 11 terms are incorporated into a sale contract.[141] If the parties wish to incorporate a specific rule from Incoterms® 2000 (rather than Incoterms® 2010), again they must make specific reference to this in their contractual documents.[142]

18.4.2.2 Recent development: Incoterms® 2020

Late in its centenary year, ICC officially released Incoterms® 2020, which entered into force on 1 January 2020.

The Incoterms® 2020 Drafting Group was formed by the ICC in 2016. It consists of nine experts from different countries, including three ICC Trade and Investment Directors from Asia, two from the US, and four from Europe.[143] Since it was established, the Drafting Group has met to analyse, discuss and consider more than 3000 comments from ICC national committees. The ICC's international editorial board met 12 times between July 2016 and September 2018 in order to examine the proposed changes and recommendations made by the ICC national committees.[144] In drafting the Incoterms® 2020 rules, the ICC has reflected on the emergence of new technologies, government policies and environmental regulations, and has attempted to use the updated Incoterms to 'provide a common framework for the future of trade'.[145]

In order to make the Incoterms more accessible and easier to use, Incoterms® 2020 includes more detailed explanatory notes and enhanced graphics to explain the responsibilities of importers and exporters. It also includes a more detailed explanation in relation to 'how to choose the most appropriate Incoterms® rule for a given transaction', and 'how a sales contract interacts with ancillary contracts'.[146]

ICC highlights some of the main improvements of Incoterms® 2020:

- Incoterms® 2020 provides for demonstrated market need in relation to bills of lading (BL) with an on-board notation and the Free Carrier (FCA) Incoterms® rule.
- Incoterms® 2020 aligns different levels of insurance coverage in Cost, Insurance and Freight (CIF) and Carriage and Insurance Paid to (CIP).
- Incoterms® 2020 includes arrangements for carriage with own means of transport in FCA, Delivered at Place (DAP), Delivered at Place Unloaded (DPU), and Delivered Duty Paid (DDP).

141 J Mo, *International Commercial Law* (LexisNexis Butterworths Australia, Sydney, 3rd edn, 2013), 11.
142 See S Shepherd and T Graham, 'New Incoterms 2010: A Summary of the Principal Changes to Incoterms 2000' (21 October 2010): http://www.mondaq.com/uk/. A contract that refers to Incoterms® 2000 is still valid. For example, if a contract was concluded in 2009, and it contains a clause providing that the contract will be automatically renewed every 10 years unless parties suggest otherwise, the contract will be still valid after 2010. ICC last updated the Incoterms® rules in 2019. While Incoterms® 2020 is the most current version of the trade terms, Incoterms® 2010 is still in effect today.
143 See ICC, 'ICC prepares to launch Incoterms® 2020', media release, 1 April 2019: https://iccwbo.org/.
144 See ICC, 'ICC prepares to launch Incoterms® 2020', media release, 1 April 2019: https://iccwbo.org/.
145 See ICC, 'ICC prepares to launch Incoterms® 2020', media release, 1 April 2019: https://iccwbo.org/.
146 https://iccwbo.org/media-wall/news-speeches/icc-releases-incoterms-2020/.

- There is a change in the three-letter name for Delivered at Terminal (DAT) to DPU.
- Incoterms® 2020 includes security-related requirements within carriage obligations and costs.

Since Incoterms® 2020 was recently taken into effect, it may be too soon to assess its effectiveness in practice. As stated earlier, while Incoterms® 2020 is the most current version of the trade terms, Incoterms® 2010 remains in effect.

18.5 DISCUSSION QUESTIONS

1. What is private international law?
2. What does 'conflict of laws' mean?
3. How is the proper law of a contract determined?
4. How are jurisdictional clauses interpreted by the courts following the decision in *Akai*?
5. What are the main differences between Incoterms® 2000, Incoterms® 2010 and Incoterms® 2020?

18.6 PROBLEM QUESTION

Trish is a third-year undergraduate student at the University of Freeland Business School in Sydney. She has booked herself and her best friend into the Palace Hotel Bangkok, part of a leading worldwide chain of hotels, for a one-week stay during the summer holidays.

On 23 November 2019, Trish received an email from the Palace Hotel Bangkok confirming her booking, which was guaranteed by her Visa credit card issued by the Central Australian Bank. On 2 December 2019, Trish and her friend arrived at the hotel, where Trish filled out and signed a guest registration form that included the following statement:

> In consideration of accepting my reservation and providing me with accommodation and/or hotel services, I agree that any dispute or claim that arises out of or is related to such accommodation and/or services shall be subject to the law of Thailand and the exclusive jurisdiction of the courts of Thailand.

The next day, Trish and her friend went to an exercise class at the gym on the grounds of the hotel. Trish fell and seriously injured her right leg. She alleged that the hotel was negligent in maintaining the floor of the gym, which was in a dangerous and excessively slippery condition, thereby causing her accident.

Trish commenced proceedings in the NSW Supreme Court against the owner company of the Palace Hotel Bangkok ('the defendant'). The defendant is now seeking a stay of proceedings on the basis that the NSW Supreme Court is an inappropriate forum for the trial, and contends that the proceedings should 'be subject to the law of Thailand and the exclusive jurisdiction of the courts of Thailand'.

Advise Trish on whether the NSW Supreme Court is an appropriate forum to determine her claim.

18.7 FURTHER READING

Bortolotti, F, 'Remedies Available to the Seller and Seller's Right to Require Specific Performance (Articles 61, 62 and 28)' (2005–06) 25 *Journal of Law and Commerce* 335.

Garnett, R, 'Jurisdiction Clauses Since *Akai*' (2013) 87 *Australian Law Journal* 134.

Gunning, P, 'All Steamed up about Consumer Guarantees' (2014) *InCompetition*, September, 9.

Incoterms 2010: https://iccwbo.org/; Quick Reference Chart: https://www.wcl-shipping.com/wcl-17/wcl/images/pdf/incoterms_2010_chart.pdf.

Lin, T Y, 'Good Faith Choice of a Law to Govern a Contract' (2014) *Singapore Journal of Legal Studies* 307–27.

Schwenzer, I, 'Avoidance of the Contract in Case of Non-Conforming Goods (Article 49(1)(A) CISG)' (2006) 25 *Journal of Law and Commerce* 437.

Stone, B, 'Contracts for the International Sale of Goods: The Convention and the Code', (2015) 23(3) *Michigan State International Law Review* 753.

United Nations, 'Explanatory Note' by the UNCITRAL Secretariat on the *United Nations Convention on Contracts for the International Sale of Goods*, 2010, 33–42: https://www.uncitral.org/.

United Nations, *United Nations Convention on Contracts for the International Sale of Goods* 2010, 1–32: https://www.uncitral.org/.

Whincop, M and Keyes, M, 'Putting the "Private" Back into Private International Law: Default Rules and the Proper Law of the Contract' (1997) 21 *Melbourne University Law Review* 516–43.

INDEX

For EU product safety concerns, contact us at Calle de José Abascal, 56–1°, 28003 Madrid, Spain or eugpsr@cambridge.org.

www.ingramcontent.com/pod-product-compliance
Ingram Content Group UK Ltd.
Pitfield, Milton Keynes, MK11 3LW, UK
UKHW061102161026
15824UKWH00015B/636

* 9 7 8 1 1 0 8 7 2 8 4 9 2 *